Snow Leopard™ Server

Daniel Eran Dilger

Wiley Publishing, Inc.

Snow Leopard™ Server

Published by
Wiley Publishing, Inc.
10475 Crosspoint Blvd.
Indianapolis, IN 46256
www.wiley.com

ISBN: 978-0-470-52131-1

Manufactured in the United States of America

10 9 8 7 6 5 4 3 2 1

For general information on our other products and services or to obtain technical support, please contact our Customer Care Department within the U.S. at (877) 762-2974, outside the U.S. at (317) 572-3993 or fax (317) 572-4002.

Library of Congress Control Number: 2009936561

For Arfy, who doggedly kept me going with a wagging tail, and my mom Betty and dad Carl, who booted me up, installed a powerful operating system, and imposed some difficult quotas that demanded that I think creatively, ask difficult questions, and stay curious. Thanks.

Credits

Acquisitions Editor
Aaron Black

Project Editor
Christopher Stolle

Technical Editor
Dennis Cohen

Copy Editor
Scott Tullis

Editorial Director
Robyn Siesky

Editorial Manager
Cricket Krengel

Business Manager
Amy Knies

Senior Marketing Manager
Sandy Smith

Vice President and Executive Group Publisher
Richard Swadley

Vice President and Executive Publisher
Barry Pruett

Project Coordinator
Katie Crocker

Graphics and Production Specialists
Jennifer Mayberry
Andrea Hornberger

Quality Control Technician
Jessica Kramer

Media Development Project Manager
Laura Moss

Media Development Assistant Project Manager
Jenny Swisher

Media Development Associate Producer
Josh Frank or Shawn Patrick

Proofreading and Indexing
Laura L. Bowman
Broccoli Information Management

About the Author

Daniel Eran Dilger started in computing with an Apple II+ and spent the 1980s banging away on 8-bit systems: the Atari ST, an Apple IIGS, and a series of Macs, starting with the 512Ke. By 1989, he was engrossed in the NeXT Bible while tapping into FidoNet and finding ways to access the Internet from the backwoods of Montana. He started writing about technology in high school and began self-publishing a monthly newsletter mailed to an international audience of Apple IIGS users.

Since moving to San Francisco, he has kept a close watch on Apple, as the company teetered precariously close to failure in the mid-1990s before acquiring NeXT and embarking on the monumental task of reinventing itself as well as rethinking the desktop operating system with what resulted in Mac OS X. He served as the network administrator and IT director for moderately large operations at San Francisco General Hospital and then rode out the dotcom era by managing IT operations for a rapidly growing South of Market startup. Over the last decade, he's supported a variety of large and small clients as a technology consultant and has written extensively on the history and future of the technology landscape at roughlydrafted.com while serving as a contributing editor to a variety of technology-related websites.

Despite a variety of emergency room visits, a few broken bones, and a couple smashed laptops, he continues to enjoy riding motorcycles around San Francisco and has a passion for traveling.

Acknowledgments

Special thanks to all the people who supported and encouraged me to complete this project, starting with Aaron Black at Wiley, who initially invited me to get started; Christopher Stolle, who served as my patient project editor; and Dennis Cohen, my detail-oriented technical editor.

I also appreciate the efforts of all the other people who worked on this book behind the scenes at Wiley. I have additional gratitude for Apple employees — who answered my questions, provided documentation, and helped line up hardware for testing — as well as the community of people outside of Apple who also contributed additional information and assistance.

Contents

Foreword

OS X Server has certainly made its way through a good number of the big cats out there. Much to a few people's chagrin, the Tabby cat version is as still yet to rear its head, but today, we're tossing a ball of yarn for the Snow Leopard. When we all first heard about Snow Leopard, the general idea was that it was going to be like Leopard (10.5) but with a lot more work under the hood for optimization, speed, and stability, and this has certainly not been missed from the released product. What we also got was some new unexpected bells and whistles that really make Snow Leopard Server the strongest server solution provided by Apple thus far (not that anyone would really expect anything new to go in a backward direction, would we?).

When you look at statistics like Mail Server performance being 1.7 times faster than the Sun Java Messaging Server, previously one of the best-performing mail server products available, Snow Leopard Server is now in the class of server that the enterprise should be interested in. While we're talking enterprise, the new Mobile Access Server should be a welcome addition to anyone who's previously had sleepless nights after opening ports on the firewall or had equally frustrating moments teaching users how to use VPN on a machine or iPhone.

What I would like to touch on is the subject of the Mac community. More frequently than not, I come across Mac system administrators who feel like they're living on their own little island — they may be the only Mac administrator in their organization, surrounded by a sea of Windows or Linux folks, or they may be someone who's been tasked with being the Mac administrator in their small business while also continuing on with their main job. If you're one of these folks, you're on the right track for more information by buying this book, but what about when you've finished this book?

This is where I've seen the higher education administrators shine. Educational institutions tend to have a built-in idea of sharing what they've learned and what works for them and then want to help others succeed. There are a number of websites that can help you grow as an administrator as well as give you the chance to ask questions, compare notes, and allow you to contribute back to the community. As well as the Apple mailing lists you can find at lists.apple.com, there's also MacEnterprise.org, which posts articles on its website, hosts webcasts, and provides a valuable mailing list; AFP548.com, which posts in-depth articles and has an active forum page; and technology-specific websites such as Xsanity.com for Xsan and Final Cut Server related topics.

I think getting involved in these communities helps the individual Mac system administrator — I know this is where I started out learning from others, posting questions, and eventually answering questions for others — and can also help maintain and hopefully grow the Mac community. With more support out there in the community for the new administrators as well as for the seasoned veterans, OS X Server can only become stronger and more widespread in its usage — and that's good news for all of us.

In short, learn from this book, kick the tires on your Snow Leopard Server, and then ask questions — get involved. The Mac community may be a small world at the moment, but it's a great world to get into with a lot of knowledgeable and helpful folks in it.

Andrina Kelly
Magpies Consulting
adrina@magpies.ca

Introduction

A pple's Mac OS X Server celebrates its ten-year anniversary in 2009 with the new release of Snow Leopard Server. Whether you're experienced with Apple's server product or new to the platform, this book has been designed to help you stitch together the powerful, proven legacy behind Unix, the rapidly advancing technology available from open-source software, and the ease of use and rich integration Apple builds into its products.

This book covers lots of ground quickly but is designed to guide you through practical, in-depth server administration tasks while providing a helpful background in how things work in Apple's server operating system.

What's Inside This Book

Part I begins with an overview of the advanced planning required to successfully deploy servers, the administration tools you'll use, the configurations Apple has designated to serve the needs of both basic and advanced users, and an introduction to the layers within Mac OS X, which starts at the kernel, moves up through Unix and its open-source software components, into Apple's specialized server applications, and finally moves beyond the server itself into managing users and client computers on the network.

Successive sections delve deeper into each of these subject areas, providing additional details on how to get the most from Mac OS X Server from the planning stages through installation and configuration and how to effectively monitor and optimize for performance.

Origins of Mac OS X Server

Apple's release of Mac OS X Snow Leopard Server represents the company's eighth major reference release, dating back to the first product to be given the name in 1999. The origins of Mac OS X Server date back even further to the NeXTSTEP operating system, which was released between 1988 and Apple's acquisition of NeXT, Inc. in 1996.

However, that lineage isn't just worth mentioning for nostalgic purposes. The design of today's Mac OS X Server shares much of the same foundational software and the same strategic intent as the Unix-based NeXTSTEP did.

NeXTSTEP was originally envisioned in the mid-1980s by a group of engineers, many of whom had come from Apple to join Steve Jobs in delivering the next great thing after the Mac.

Instead of building an entirely new operating system from scratch — as IBM started with Microsoft in their OS/2 partnership, as Microsoft later did in creating Windows NT, or as Be, Inc. would later attempt with its BeOS — the software architects at NeXT realized that much of the underlying software they needed to deliver their vision for a next-generation computing system already existed.

By building on software components that were already complete and tested, NeXT was able to quickly release a new product that added advanced new capabilities and usability on top of a rock-solid foundation that was already familiar to users in the academic market NeXT was targeting.

The underlying foundation of Unix and the strategic use of open-source software pioneered by NeXT Inc.'s NeXTSTEP operating system continues 20 years later in Apple's Mac OS X Server.

Leveraging open-source software before Linux

The Unix foundation NeXT selected was BSD Unix, a free and open-source implementation of AT&T's commercial Unix offered by the University of California at Berkeley beginning in the mid-1970s. Known as the Berkeley Standard Distribution, the software predated the development of Linux, which didn't get started until 1991. Linux later eclipsed BSD in popularity after the latter project became entangled in an infringement lawsuit filed by AT&T in the early 1990s, which wasn't resolved until 1994.

However, BSD's pioneering decision to liberally offer its code without strings to commercial users helped engender compatibility and performance in the emerging Internet because many companies took advantage of the high-quality work its contributors had already completed. BSD served as the foundation of Sun's original SunOS and provided the core networking features of many embedded routers and stand-alone operating systems, including Microsoft's Windows.

The premise of building original value on a solid foundation of existing software technology also remains a basic design principle in Mac OS X Server today. Apple even markets its server product as "open source made easy," a reference to not just its BSD foundation but also the many other open-source components Apple integrates together in the package.

From NeXT to Mac OS X Server

When Apple acquired NeXT in the final days of 1996, it inherited a legacy of reliance on open-source foundations. Apple itself had already begun experimenting with open-source software in its MkLinux project, a distribution of Linux designed specifically to run on the company's Mac hardware.

Just as NeXT had been able to ship its new NeXTSTEP operating system within a few years of development in the late 1980s, Apple was similarly able to ship a modernized version of NeXTSTEP as the foundation of its future operating system strategy in record time, under the code name Rhapsody. However, Apple still needed to convince its installed base of Mac users to migrate to the new operating system — a task that proved to be more difficult than the company originally expected.

So much work was required to migrate the existing classic Mac OS platform to run on the Unix foundation of NeXTSTEP that the company was forced to delay its original plans to rapidly deploy Rhapsody as its next Mac OS for consumers. Instead, Apple first released its new operating system under the name Mac OS X Server 1.0.

Mac OS X Server 1.0

The new server offering was positioned both as a superior replacement for the company's existing Apple Workgroup Server product based on the classic Mac OS running AppleShare as well as a suitable stand-in for its Apple Network Servers, which ran IBM's AIX variant of Unix. Apple had also managed its own distribution of Unix under the name A/UX starting in 1988, but that software had been left behind in the move to PowerPC.

Aimed specifically at education markets, Mac OS X Server 1.0 provided Apple File Services for file sharing and the Apache 1.3 web server and debuted NetBoot, a new service designed to boot iMacs directly from a disk image on the server over the network.

The release also included QuickTime Streaming Server and the WebObjects web application deployment software Apple acquired from NeXT. It also carried forward the classic Mac OS AppleShare's Macintosh Manager, a tool for administering user and group access from networked Macs.

The initial release of Mac OS X Server 1.0 served as a proof of concept for the future of Mac OS X. It painted the classic Mac OS appearance on top of NeXTSTEP, making it appear more familiar to Apple's core Mac server audience in education while still providing advanced operating system features unique to Unix.

The release validated Apple's new strategy of leveraging open-source software to build an attractive commercial product greater than the sum of its parts. That strategy has continued in the company's Safari browser, which was based on the open-source Web Kit.

The company doesn't just contribute to existing open-source projects it borrows from either; for Leopard Server, it created a new open-source Calendar Server project as the basis for its commercial iCal Server.

Mac OS X Server 10.0 and 10.1

In 2001, Apple finally shipped the initial release of Mac OS X for its desktop computers, although the new system was initially offered only as a secondary boot option for early adopters. Macs continued to start in the classic Mac OS by default. On the server side, however, Mac OS X Server had already acted as Apple's default operating system for two years.

This discrepancy highlighted the strength of Unix in server applications, where reliability and performance were far more critical factors than compatibility with existing desktop applications. In large part, Apple provided most of the server applications that its server users neededUsers could supply additional server functions on their own by using Mac OS X Server's ability to compile and run existing Unix open-source server software packages with only minor tweaks.

The fact that Mac OS X Server shared the same code base as Apple's desktop Mac OS X would eventually help to make its use more familiar to the Mac audience, but it more immediately gave it unique desktop-oriented features missing from other operating systems targeted primarily at servers, such as Linux or Windows NT.

For example, the new Mac OS X Server 10.0 inherited the work Apple undertook to move its Rhapsody code base to its consumer desktop. This included a radical replacement of the Display PostScript windowing engine from NeXTSTEP with a new advanced graphics compositing engine developed by Apple called Quartz, using Adobe's open and free PDF specification as its core imaging model. That directly gave Mac OS X Server new and arguably superfluous graphics savvy.

At the same time, however, the change also allowed Apple to avoid Display PostScript licensing issues with Adobe that were standing in the way of releasing the core foundation of Apple's new operating system as an open-source project of its own, named Darwin, which happened in 2000.

Although Apple's efforts were focused on delivering Mac OS X for its consumer desktops, upgrading Mac OS X Server was relatively easy because the company could leverage advances developed by the open-source community, such as including PHP and WebDAV support for Apache.

Mac OS X Jaguar Server 10.2

Following a largely consumer-oriented 10.1 release in 2001, Apple launched Mac OS X Server 10.2 in 2002 with a series of new features aimed directly at the server market.

These included the new Open Directory, which upgraded security for NeXT's NetInfo directory domain system by using an external Authentication Manager for storing passwords independently from the directory.

The release also initiated support for Kerberos authentication, allowing the new operating system to better fit into the existing security infrastructure in use at many universities.

The release also added early support for IPsec and IPv6 networking protocols as well as new multicast DNS support (originally branded by Apple as Rendezvous and later Bonjour), which provided the innovative discovery services of the old AppleTalk protocol over standard IP networks.

On the open-source front, Apple incorporated support for CUPS printing, SAMBA software for serving up Windows file sharing, and a variety of other enhancements taken from FreeBSD. Apple also added file system journaling to its native HFS+, an update that first appeared in Mac OS X Server before reaching the Mac desktop.

Mac OS X Panther Server 10.3

In 2003, Apple deprecated the NetInfo directory service it had inherited from NeXT and moved Open Directory 2 to the more familiar and standard LDAPv3, again using open-source software: OpenLDAP and the directory-optimized Berkeley DB.

Apple also replaced the former Authentication Manager with a new Password Server and enhanced Open Directory's ability to integrate with an external Kerberos key distribution server, again increasing its value among larger education users.

Apple also incorporated enhancements from FreeBSD 4.8 and FreeBSD 5 into Mac OS X Server 10.3, updated MySQL and PHP for web services, and added familiar open-source mail services: Postfix as its new SMTP mail server, Cyrus for POP and IMAP services, the Mailman list server, and an enhanced SquirrelMail for webmail services.

To enhance its credentials as a general-purpose server, the new release also incorporated the latest SAMBA 3, enabling it to act as a Primary Domain Controller for Windows clients and subsequently serve as a drop-in replacement for the aging Windows NT 4 systems that were then approaching the end of their support cycle from Microsoft.

Mac OS X Tiger Server 10.4

In 2005, the next reference release of Mac OS X Server added support for running 64-bit processes and allocating 64-bit userland address spaces on the PowerPC G5, giving Apple new credibility in the high-performance computing market by matching Microsoft's own 64-bit releases for desktop workstations and servers using AMD's new 64-bit CPUs.

The new Tiger Server also incorporated support for Windows-compatible access control lists (ACLs) for advanced file permissions and released Open Directory 3 with support for participating in Microsoft's Active Directory installations as a Domain Member.

On top of its open-source foundation synced to FreeBSD 5, Apple added a series of advanced new services, many also derived from an open-source core. For example, the new iChat Server was built on Jabber for secure instant messaging, new weblogs services were based on Blojsom, and mail services were enhanced by using adaptive junk mail filtering services from SpamAssassin and virus detection by using ClamAV.

Apple also added new tools, including the Gateway Setup Assistant for quickly setting up basic DNS, DHCP, and NAT services in small business settings; Software Update Server for managing and distributing locally cached update downloads; and the company's original Xgrid-distributed computing technology for harnessing available machines on the network to participate in the shared processing of tasks queued up for applications in scientific computing or graphics and animation rendering.

On the hardware front, Mac OS X Server 10.4 also enabled support for Network Interface Failover and IEEE 802.3ad Ethernet Link Aggregation, which bonds multiple network ports into a single interface to support higher link speeds and improved redundancy. Tiger Server was also subsequently ported to the new Intel x86 platform to support a new generation of Intel-based Mac servers.

Mac OS X Leopard Server 10.5

Released in 2007, Mac OS X Server 10.5 was the first version registered with Open Brand Unix 03 as compliant with the SUSv3 and POSIX 1003.1 specifications, finally making it officially Unix and certified as capable of compiling and running any software compliant with Unix 03.The release also extended 64-bit support to graphical applications, and many bundled server applications were delivered with 64-bit binaries, including Apache 2, MySQL 5, Postfix, Podcast Producer, and QuickTime Streaming Server.

Apple also began bundling Ruby on Rails by default and added a variety of enhanced security features, including an Application Layer Firewall, code signing for verifying that applications hadn't been tampered with, and kernel support for role-based access control for application sandboxing.

Leopard Server also added read-only support for volumes by using Sun's ZFS and added cross-domain authorization support to Open Directory and built-in RADIUS support for authorizing wireless users.

New services unique to Apple were also added, including Podcast Producer for automating video production workflows from capture to processing to optimized publishing in formats from HD to mobile devices; a new Wiki Server that incorporated a web-based calendar, blogging, and mailing lists; an original iCal Server based on the CalDAV standard (also opened up by Apple as a open-source project); and a Spotlight Server for indexing file shares for rapid search of network volumes.

Apple also worked to further simplify administration, with new configuration tiers ranging from simplified administration tools for basic server users to more advanced tools for customers with unconstrained needs for complex and customized configurations.

Leopard Server introduced Server Preferences as a highly simplified administration tool targeted toward users with basic needs while continuing to use Server Admin to provide advanced users with expanded configuration options.

Mac OS X Snow Leopard Server 10.6

New features in Snow Leopard Server are presented in greater detail in Chapter 1, but Apple's latest release covers familiar territory, incrementally advancing existing features while adding new services and streamlined tools that advance further Apple's plans for expanding its server product's utility and reach.

Snow Leopard's new 64-bit kernel allows for access to vast new amounts of RAM and enhances security features. It also adds full ZFS support for advanced volume handling. New mail services based on the open-source Dovecot enhance performance and scalability, while Apple also adds new push messaging support and remote access services for mobile devices.

Snow Leopard Server continues the tradition of adding unique value built on top of an open-source Unix foundation, resulting in a powerful server product that's also easy to set up and administer.

On the Web

For some configuration files for Snow Leopard Server, more information about this book, and more on other books in the Developer Reference series, please visit `wileydevreference.com`.

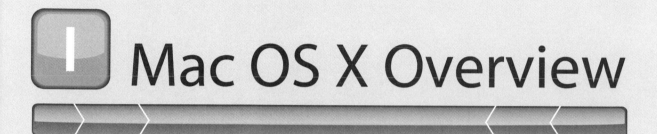

Mac OS X Overview

Introducing
Mac OS X Server

M ac OS X 10.6 Snow Leopard Server builds on a decade of development at Apple to create an operating system and server applications that pair the security, stability, scalability, and performance of a Unix core and open-source software with the company's hallmark ability to design approachable, attractive, and easy-to-use tools as its administrative interface.

This chapter presents an overview of the following:

- The advanced planning required to successfully deploy Snow Leopard Server
- The administration tools used to configure and manage the server
- The configuration options available to serve the needs of both basic and advanced users
- An introduction to the layers within Mac OS X, starting at the kernel, moving up through Unix and its open-source software components, and then into the specialized server applications from Apple
- Moving beyond the server itself into managing users and client computers on the network
- The features and improvements new to Snow Leopard Server

Planning Mac OS X Server Deployments

A critical aspect of deploying any server product is adequate planning performed well in advance of any procurement decisions. Although Mac OS X Server represents a refined, powerful software tool well-suited for many tasks, it's not necessarily the right choice in every circumstance.

CROSS-REF
For more on installing and deploying Mac OS X Server, see Chapters 3–6.

In This Chapter

Planning Mac OS X
Server deployments

Administration tools

Basic versus advanced
management roles

Kernel, Unix, and
open-source services

Specialized server
applications

Managing network
client resources

What's new in
Snow Leopard Server

Planning for ongoing maintenance

Before any deployment planning takes place, users should evaluate both the strengths and limitations of Mac OS X Server as a product. One of the first attractions of Apple's server software is its ease of use and interface familiarity to current Mac users.

That familiarity may allow small businesses to administer their own servers with only minimal outside assistance instead of requiring them to hire full-time network administrators with expertise in Windows Server or Linux system administration.

For organizations that lack any familiarity with Mac OS X, the opposite may be true, requiring them to employ professionals with expertise in managing an Apple server. Evaluating the existing skill set of available administrative resources against the costs involved in training to support Mac OS X Server is one initial consideration among many that's important to make early.

Planning for software expenses

A less obvious but very significant factor favoring the selection of Mac OS X Server is cost. Apple bundles its server software on new Xserves at no additional cost as a way to add value to its hardware sales. This makes Mac OS X Server competitive — even with free operating systems, such as Linux — when bundled on name-brand server hardware.

It also makes Mac OS X Server far less expensive than comparable Windows Server deployments, which involve a significant investment not only in the core server operating system software but also in separately sold server applications (such as two Microsoft products: Exchange Server for mail services and SharePoint for serving wikis, blogs, and RSS feeds) as well as the cost of the client access licenses (CALs) that Microsoft requires per user to access each of those services as a client.

Even a small business deployment of Windows Server can easily balloon into tens of thousands of dollars in software expenses on top of the hardware needed, as shown in Table 1.1. CAL fees aren't incurred with Mac OS X Server because Apple licenses only the use of the operating system itself.

At the same time, Apple does charge for server software upgrades when delivering a new reference release. Those optional upgrades are the same cost as buying Mac OS X Server at retail: $500 per server for an unlimited user license. Potential users should evaluate those costs as well as the labor expenses related to upgrades when making long-term plans.

As with new server purchases, Windows Server upgrades also incur additional server application costs as well as new CAL upgrades and are subsequently always far more expensive than the upgrade fees charged by Apple for Mac OS X Server.

Some users may find that free software such as Linux may be more cost-effective to address specific needs, either when used on existing or new hardware in do-it-yourself projects or in embedded server appliance products, such as stand-alone file servers providing network-attached storage (NAS).

Table 1.1 Software Costs Related to Server Deployment

Entity	Windows Server	Mac OS X Server
Dual Quad Core 2.26 GHz Xeon 5500, 6 GB RAM, 160 SATA, IU	Dell PowerEdge 1950 = $3,215	Xserve = $3,749
64-bit server operating system software	Windows Server 2008 (5 CALs included) = $799; $4,014 total	Mac OS X Server (unlimited users included) = $0; $3,749 total
Mail and collaborative software	Exchange Server 2007 (Standard) = $700	Included
	SharePoint Server 2007 (Standard) = $4,424	
For 10 users	+5 Windows CALs = $199	No extra cost
	+10 Exchange CALs = $670	
	+10 SharePoint CALs = $940	
For 25 users	+20 Windows CALs = $800	No extra cost
	+20 Exchange CALs = $1,340	
	+20 SharePoint CALs = $1,880	
For 100 users	5 × +20 Windows CALs = $4,000	No extra cost
	+100 Exchange CALs = $6,700	
	+100 SharePoint CALs = $9,400	
Total cost for 100 users	$23,315	$3,749

Similarly, many basic workgroup services, such as web and file sharing, can also be run from the desktop version of Mac OS X at no extra cost. Mac OS X Server primarily becomes worth buying when users reach the point of needing Open Directory for sophisticated management of users and groups and to take full advantage of the more advanced features Apple bundles in its server product.

Planning for hardware expenses

One restriction unique to Apple in Mac OS X Server is that it can be legally run only on the server hardware from Apple. That factors into long-term hardware-buying decisions. Mitigating that situation is the fact that with the move to the Intel platform, Apple servers can now be re-purposed as Windows servers if a buyer's needs and circumstances change, and they're also easier to set up to run as Linux servers compared to the company's previous generations of PowerPC Macs.

Additionally, it's now also feasible to run multiple, heterogeneous virtual servers on Mac hardware by using a product like VMWare Fusion or Parallels Server for Mac, enabling administrators to host multiple instances of Windows Server, Linux, and Mac OS X Server at once, as shown in Figure 1.1.

Figure 1.1

Virtualization software, such as Parallels Server for Mac, enables administrators to streamline server provisioning by combining multiple server software instances on the same server hardware.

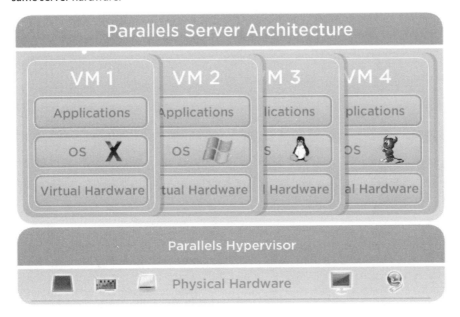

Using virtualization, server administrators can maximize the value of buying Apple server hardware because individual servers that would normally leave most of their underlying machine's hardware idle can now be hosted together on a single machine. However, Apple doesn't allow users to virtualize instances of Mac OS X Server on non-Apple hardware.

Planning for practical use

Along with cost, another area for consideration in early planning is having a realistic view of the needs to be addressed. For small-business users planning to set up basic web and file-sharing services, a dedicated Mac OS X Server is probably a somewhat expensive alternative to a simple network appliance or re-purposed workstation running shared services via Linux or Mac OS X, although it may also serve as a good option for users with simple needs because it can be administered by an advanced user without much specialized training.

Mac OS X Server is ideally suited to more advanced business or education environments with needs for high-performance mail services, shared calendar and contact services, shared wikis and blogs, custom web application development using Ruby on Rails or PHP, secure remote access, distributed computing grids, managed client control, and podcast production workflows. That sweet spot is exactly what Apple targets in its server software development.

On the other hand, it's less realistic to attempt to make Mac OS X Server a drop-in replacement for large-scale server deployments that attempt to replicate use cases that exist outside of Apple's core markets. For example, while Mac OS X Server can suitably replace Microsoft Exchange Server in many small-business scenarios, it would be a harrowing undertaking to attempt to deploy it as a drop-in replacement for the kind of large corporate messaging infrastructure that Microsoft targets Exchange at.

Administration Tools

Properly introducing Mac OS X Server requires matching a name and job description to its primary interfaces: the Mac OS X Server administration tools. Although they come bundled for use on the server itself, they're also intended for installation on any number of administrator Macs for the remote management of multiple servers at once.

Basic administration tools

Starting with Leopard Server, Apple introduced two configuration tiers of administration tools. The first — for entry-level users who want a server as easy to manage as the Mac desktop — presents very basic configuration settings within Server Preferences, an app similar to System Preferences on the Mac desktop.

The streamlined Server Preferences, shown in Figure 1.2, enables entry-level users to manage their own services without becoming experts in all the details related to configuring network services, from file sharing to mail to collaboration servers.

For basic monitoring, Apple provides a Server Status Widget for quick access to vital statistics from the Mac OS X Dashboard.

CROSS-REF
For more on basic administration tools, see Chapters 7–8.

Figure 1.2

Server Preferences makes basic administration simple.

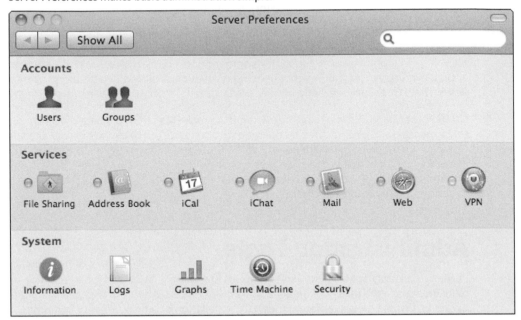

Advanced administration tools

For more advanced users, Apple continues to provide Server Admin, shown in Figure 1.3, for configuring and monitoring advanced services and system settings, viewing system logs and performance graphs, and managing security certificates.

CROSS-REF

For more on Server Admin, see Chapter 9.

Apple also supplies Workgroup Manager, shown in Figure 1.4, for creating, configuring, and managing users, groups, computers, and groups of computers within the directory domain.

CROSS-REF

For more on Workgroup Manager, see Chapter 10.

Figure 1.3

Server Admin allows system administrators to manage and configure services, file shares, and server updates as well as view console logs and performance graphs of multiple servers.

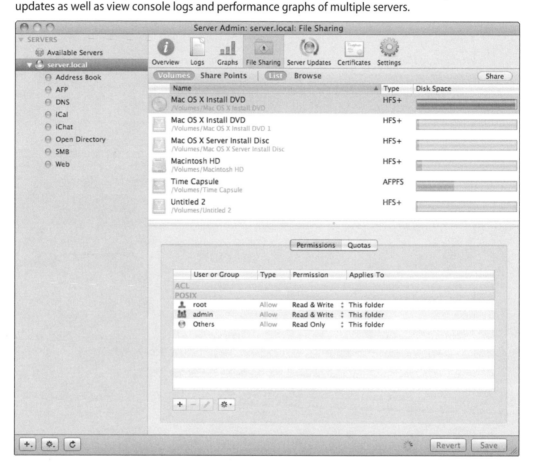

In addition to a variety of command-line utilities, other administration tools that ship with Mac OS X Server include:

- **Server Monitor.** This is used for remote monitoring of Xserve hardware features, such as processor, network, and disk use, fan speed, and intrusion detection.
- **RAID Admin.** This is used for managing Xserve RAID hardware.
- **System Image Utility.** This is used for creating NetBoot and NetInstall images.
- **Xgrid Admin.** This is used for managing distributed computing tasks and workflows.

CROSS-REF

For more on command-line utilities and other administration tools, see Chapter 11.

Figure 1.4

Workgroup Manager manages access and privileges for users and computers on the network.

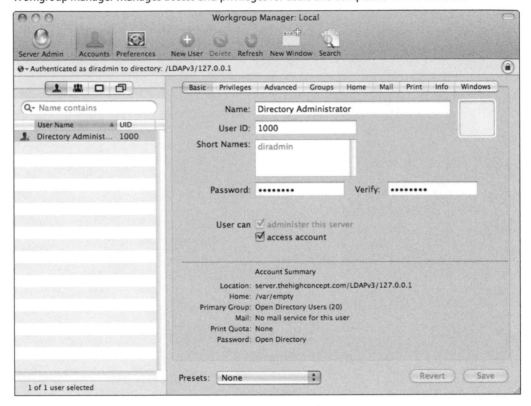

Basic versus Advanced Management Roles

Which set of administration tools a user works with depends on how the server is originally configured. Apple defines three configuration modes:

- **Standard configuration.** Sets up its services automatically, is managed with basic administration tools, operates as its own self-contained directory server, and has no requirements for existing network services

- **Workgroup configuration.** Can set up some services automatically, is managed with basic administration tools, plugs into an existing directory server infrastructure, and requires existing DNS to be configured and operational on the network
- **Advanced configuration.** Requires an administrator to set up all services manually, is managed with advanced administration tools, may act as its own directory server or may plug into an existing directory server infrastructure, and requires existing DNS to be configured and operational on the network

The configuration mode selected during installation has an impact on what advanced services are available on the server and how the system can interact with outside directory infrastructures.

A server originally configured in standard or workgroup configuration can also be moved between the two configurations and can also be upgraded to advanced configuration, but you can't downgrade an advanced server to standard or workgroup without reinstalling the server software or reverting to a backup.

Basic management in standard and workgroup configurations

Standard and workgroup configurations are designed to use the basic administration tool: Server Preferences. This greatly simplifies both the complexity and sophistication of the server's configuration but also limits what tasks the server can provide.

Standard configuration is designed for scenarios where Mac OS X Server acts as the only server in a small organization and is administered by users with little or no server experience.

Workgroup configuration is similarly streamlined and limited but allows the server to participate in existing network infrastructure already in place, such as serving the needs of a workgroup or a department within a larger organization that already maintains DNS, DHCP, Open Directory, and mail services.

The similarities between these two configurations allow a server originally set up in standard configuration to change to workgroup configuration simply by joining an existing, external directory server. Similarly, a server in the workgroup configuration can disconnect from its directory server to enter standard configuration.

Advanced management in advanced configurations

In the advanced configuration, there's no automated setup of services, and administrators instead need to use the advanced administration tools, which include Server Admin for configuring services and machine settings and Workgroup Manager for controlling the permissions and preferences of users, groups, and computers. When upgrading an existing Mac OS X Server installation, advanced configuration is the only available option.

Although the advanced administration tools are more complex to use, they also provide full access to a variety of services that aren't available when working within the other basic configurations, including advanced user and workgroup management as well as:

- FTP and NFS file sharing
- A dedicated print server rather than simple printer sharing
- RADIUS authorization of wireless users
- NetBoot and NetInstall system imaging
- Podcast Producer
- Software Update Server
- QuickTime Streaming Server
- Xgrid distributed processing

A server originally installed with a standard or workgroup configuration can be converted to advanced mode simply by beginning to use the advanced administration tools. Once an advanced configuration is made, however, it's no longer possible to go back to operating exclusively within the protected, simpler world of Server Preferences without reinstalling or reverting to a backup.

CROSS-REF

For more on Mac OS X Server configurations, see Chapter 3.

Moving beyond advanced management

Along similar lines, it's also possible to operate outside the Apple administration tools entirely, installing additional server software, updating the versions of installed open-source components, and making super-advanced modifications to the system by using command-line utilities and manually editing the scripts and configuration files intended to be managed only by the provided administration tools.

However, after significantly modifying how the system works, Mac OS X Server can no longer be expected to behave as it was originally designed, converting it instead into something more like a Linux installation where the system administrator is in full control but also fully responsible for managing all the complex security and compatibility implications involved in a do-it-yourself server.

Kernel, Unix, and Open-Source Services

Apple has designed Mac OS X Server to operate by using conventions that strive to offer as few limitations as possible while also greatly reducing the complexity that administrators need to manage.

For example, instead of leaving system administrators to choose from a variety of different services to install, configure, and manage themselves, Apple bundles a select group of preconfigured services, optimizes them to work together, and provides simplified graphical tools for customizing how they operate.

Apart from Apple's pre-arranged administrative conventions, the system shares many architectural similarities with other Unix or Linux distributions — at least underneath its graphical interface. However, there are still many significant differences between Mac OS X Server and the typical Unix or Linux server.

The Mac OS X kernel

One of the more significant differences is the operating system's kernel, which acts as an executive control program for every process running on the system. Mac OS X's kernel, called XNU (for XNU's Not Unix, one of those recursive acronyms that computer science nerds find humorous), is derived from work done at NeXT to make use of a hybrid Mach and BSD kernel originally developed at Carnegie Mellon University.

NOTE

There's a long history of creating playfully recursive acronyms and invented backronyms to create product names, particularly in the open-source world. XNU is a direct play off the GNU kernel, derived from GNU Not Unix. Another example is PHP, which originally stood for Personal Home Page but was later changed to stand for PHP Hypertext Preprocessor.

The origins of Mac OS X's Mach/BSD kernel

In the late 1980s, academia began researching alternatives to the conventional monolithic Unix kernel typified by AT&T and BSD Unix. Many researchers began experimenting with microkernel designs, which attempted to remove large portions of what had long been considered core parts of the kernel (such as device drivers, file system, and networking support) into an external user mode server that interacted with a highly efficient, streamlined microkernel by using inter-process communication. This intended to improve security, performance, and maintainability of the kernel.

In the early to mid-1990s, IBM's OS/2 and AIX, OSF's Unix, GNU's HURD, Apple's Copland, Taligent, and MkLinux, and Microsoft's Windows NT all experimented with microkernel designs, but the new architecture didn't result in the efficiencies originally expected of it. As a result, most microkernel designs were compromised into becoming hybrid kernels with few significant differences over the previous generation's monolithic designs.

When Linux was developed during the early 1990s, it expressly avoided the prevailing trend toward microkernels and chose to stick to a conventional monolithic design, preferring to err on the conservative side rather than get bogged down in experimental and unproven technology.

Conversely, the CMU Mach microkernel project selected as the kernel for NeXTSTEP was not yet a microkernel design at the point that NeXT began using it in the late 1980s. Mach intended to eventually grow into a true microkernel by weaning itself from the conventional BSD kernel it had been grafted onto during early development.

At NeXT, however, Mach only ever served as a low-level enhancement to the conventional BSD kernel, resulting in a hybrid Unix-like kernel with modern Mach plumbing handling its virtual memory management, multi-threading model, and other low-level functions. To users, the Mach/BSD hybrid kernel in NeXTSTEP behaved very similarly to a standard BSD Unix kernel.

Apple modifications to the Mach/BSD kernel

After acquiring NeXT, Apple compared NeXT's Mach/BSD kernel with its own Copland NuKernel and the MkLinux kernel it had in development. The company decided to pursue a strategy centered on Mach/BSD, incorporating technology (and the Nu name) from Apple's in-house work. Although neither NeXT's original kernel nor Apple's XNU have ever been real microkernels, Apple's marketing frequently refers to the Mach microkernel in Mac OS X.

Apple also incorporated a half-decade of advancements made to BSD over the years since NeXT had halted the active development of its Mach/BSD kernel. Among those advancements was work to remove any licensing of AT&T Unix code; a lawsuit filed against BSD had claimed copyright infringement of code owned by AT&T. That suit was resolved in 1994, giving Apple the ability to use new, non-infringing BSD code to avoid the licensing fees that had been required in NeXTSTEP.

The Darwin open-source project

That new independence from outside proprietary licensing also allowed Apple to release its unique Mach/BSD kernel as an open-source project, which it did in 2000 under the name Darwin, a year before Mac OS X was first released to desktop users commercially.

Unlike Linux and the FreeBSD, OpenBSD, and NetBSD open-source projects, the Darwin project isn't primarily intended to benefit from contributions from the open-source community. Instead, it gives third-party developers greater insight into how Apple's unique kernel software works, making it easier for them to debug their own software.

Apple regularly incorporates new kernel technology from a variety of open-source projects, primarily keeping in sync with FreeBSD. It also borrows from the other BSDs and Sun's OpenSolaris.

The kernel's I/O Kit

While bringing the BSD components of its kernel up to date, Apple also enhanced the XNU kernel with an improved implementation of NeXT's Driver Kit, now called the I/O Kit. This modern, object-oriented device driver architecture supplies sophisticated support for power management, plug-and-play and hot pluggable devices, and inheritance and driver stacking, which makes it easier for developers to deliver drivers for new or customized devices by building on existing generic drivers.

The modularity of the XNU kernel into its machine-level Mach, its driver-level I/O Kit, and its process-level BSD portions gives the various layers well-defined interfaces that simplify Apple's ability to make changes and improvements.

Unique features of the XNU kernel

Unlike Linux, XNU offers a stable ABI for kernel extensions (or kexts), allowing software extensions developed for Mac OS X to continue to work across many versions of the system.

The kernel also uses the unique Mach-O binary format, which supports the use of multiple CPU binaries in the same executable. That makes cross-platform support of Intel and PowerPC — as well as 32- and 64-bit code — simple and transparent to end users. Most platforms require the specific installation of a binary matched to the host computer's processor.

Starting with Leopard, Apple also made enough changes to its kernel to allow it to be certified as compatible with the Unix 03 specification and subsequently to be marketed as Unix. Beginning with Snow Leopard, the Mac OS X kernel is also now fully 64 bit, enabling it to handle vast amounts of RAM and providing it with new security enhancements.

The Mac OS X Unix userland of open-source services

Above its XNU kernel, Mac OS X provides a typical userland of utility programs common to BSD and Linux distributions. Because Linux is technically only a kernel itself, its userland is supplied by software written by GNU, resulting in a package sometimes referred to as GNU/Linux.

Mac OS X distributes a similar (and often overlapping) variety of Unix utilities and programs derived from BSD distributions, which Apple refers to as Mac OS X's BSD subsystem during installation. This package includes many of the GNU programs distributed with Linux, along with versions of some Unix utilities modified for compatibility with Apple's other software, including support for features unique to the Mac, such as the HFS+ file system and resource forks.

These lower-level software tools handle the core services of Mac OS X Server, including:

- DNS for hostname resolution
- DHCP for dynamic IP address assignment
- NAT for gateway IP address translation
- NTP for clock synchronization
- IP firewall services
- RADIUS network authorization services
- VPN for secure remote access
- Portions of Apple's Open Directory architecture supplied by OpenLDAP and Berkeley DB

Apple also includes open-source code of its own, including multicast DNS software commercially branded as Bonjour, its implementation of HFS+, and the `launchd` service management framework first introduced in Mac OS X Tiger 10.4.

Apple also distributes common Unix developer tools (including gcc and gdb, the C language compiler and debugger, respectively, developed by GNU) for Mac OS X separately as an optional install, paired with the company's own Xcode IDE, its Cocoa and Carbon frameworks, and other proprietary development tools unique to Apple.

Together with the XNU kernel and portions of the developer tools, the BSD subsystem of userland programs make up most of the Darwin open-source core. The similarities between the userland environments of Mac OS X and Linux also make adapting most other open-source software targeted at Linux fairly straightforward to get running on Mac OS X, although certain types of software, such as Linux device drivers and kernel extensions, aren't useable because of the significant differences between the two operating systems' kernels and how they implement device drivers and kernel extensions.

CROSS-REF
For more on the core services of Mac OS X, see Chapters 12–19. For more on security and Open Directory, see Chapters 20 and 21, respectively.

Specialized Server Applications

Above the core services supplied by Unix tools living in the userland BSD subsystem, Apple also ships a series of higher-level, advanced services, many of which are also based on open-source projects, including:

- Windows domain and file services, based on the open-source SAMBA project
- An FTP server
- Web services, based on the open-source Apache
- IMAP and POP mail services, based on Dovecot
- Print services, using the open-source CUPS project, which is run by Apple
- Apple's Darwin Streaming Server, bundled commercially as QuickTime Streaming Server
- Apple's new open-source Calendar Server, packaged in Mac OS X Server as iCal Server
- iChat Server, based on the open-source Jabber instant messaging server

Mac OS X Snow Leopard Server also supplies a variety of advanced server applications proprietary to Apple, including:

- The AFP file server for native Mac file sharing
- Podcast Producer, which first appeared in Leopard Server
- Address Book Server, new to Snow Leopard Server
- Wikis, blogs, and RSS collaboration features designed by Apple

- Xgrid distributed processing
- Software Update Server
- Time Machine Server for client machine backups
- Spotlight network search services

Apple ties together all these services with a streamlined administration interface in Server Admin and provides Workgroup Manager with the ability to set account permissions, access, and preferences.

CROSS-REF
For more on advanced services, see Chapters 22–31.

Managing Network Client Resources

In addition to the core and advanced network services that Mac OS X Server provides, three primary tasks are related to managing network client computers: NetBoot, NetInstall, and the Managed Clients features of Open Directory.

NetBoot

NetBoot is a service for starting client computers on the network from a server-hosted disk image. Apple developed this for the first release of Mac OS X Server in 1999 at a time when NC (network computer) — a diskless computer that booted over the network — was a popular buzzword.

With NetBoot, shown in Figure 1.5, system administrators create a NetBoot image that contains the applications and configurations they want to use for their networked Macs and then designate that as a bootable image.

Client computers configured to NetBoot obtain a network address, discover the image on the server, and begin booting directly over the network. This simplifies network administration of client computers in that the system administrator only needs to update the image on the server rather than touch each machine on the network to roll out security patches, install new software, or clean up files that users left behind.

CROSS-REF
For more on NetBoot, see Chapter 34.

Figure 1.5

The NetBoot service is administered from within Server Admin.

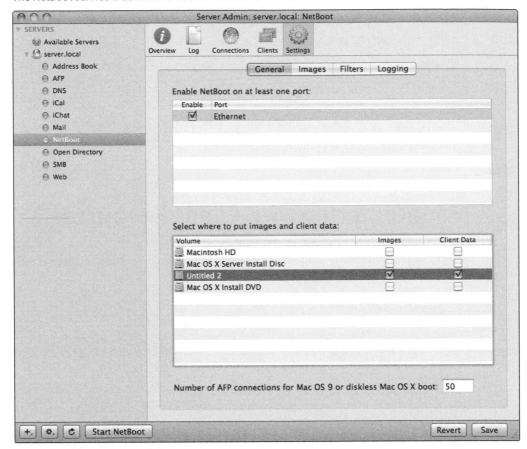

NetInstall and NetRestore

Similar to NetBoot, the NetInstall service, shown in Figure 1.6, allows administrators to define a disk image that contains the applications and configurations they want to use for their networked Macs and designate that as a bootable image. With NetInstall, however, the disk image is booted just long enough to install or update the software on the local drives of those machines.

This similarly simplifies network administration of client computers in that the system administrator can update machines on the network remotely to roll out security patches, install new software, or clean up files that users left behind.

The advantage of NetInstall over NetBoot is that it doesn't impact the network in surges as classrooms of computers all booting up at the same time might. Apple could use NetInstall to refresh the computers on display at its retail stores every day, ensuring that any files or changes that visitors make are cleaned off and the systems are kept up to date with the latest software and settings.

NetRestore similarly centralizes software installation and disk management by allowing administrators to create disk images that can be applied to fleets of computers at once, even at the same time, by using multicast imaging.

Figure 1.6

NetInstall allows a central administrator to manage multiple disk images for client computers.

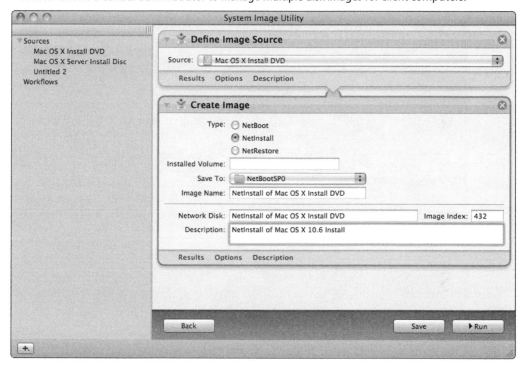

CROSS-REF

For more on NetInstall and NetRestore, see Chapter 35.

Managed Clients

The third mechanism for managing network resources is performed through Open Directory by using Workgroup Manager, shown in Figure 1.7. Network administrators can set policy for Managed Clients, customizing the experience of network users in a centralized fashion and limiting their access and control.

Managed Clients can be assigned access to network printers and personal network home folders or shared group folders. Computer settings can also be managed on an individual or group level, designating computer preferences for users or groups of users or assigning settings for individual computers or groups of computers.

Figure 1.7

Workgroup Manager enables administrators to set preferences per user, per group, per computer, and per groups of computers.

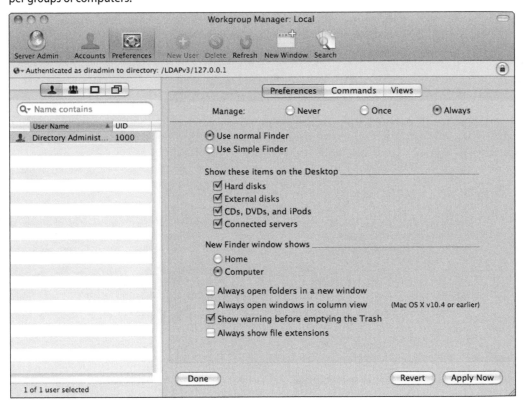

For example, a network administrator could give an individual access to his or her own home folder on the network as well as access to a group share related to that user's department. The user may also be assigned a specific set of preferences that presents a standard corporate desktop at first login. Those settings can be designed as a starting place for the user to customize or as a set standard that limits what changes the user can make, such as not allowing the user to modify the Dock or install programs.

Preferences can also be managed on a computer level so machines in a specific department could be set up with specific preferences regardless of which user logs in to use it. Settings made per user, per user group, per computer, and per groups of computers are given a specific order of precedence so that the permissions granted in complex management cases are predictable.

CROSS-REF
For more on managed network client resources, see Chapter 36.

What's New in Snow Leopard Server

With every release of Mac OS X Server, Apple has bolstered the underlying core of the operating system, updated its open-source components to maintain the pace of external server developments, and added to and enhanced on the advanced services unique to the system. Snow Leopard Server adds:

- A new Address Book Server for shared contacts
- An enhanced iCal Server 2
- New mail services based on Devcot
- A new Push Notification Server
- An enhanced Podcast Producer 2
- A new 64-bit kernel
- Mobile Access

There are also a few components intentionally missing from Snow Leopard Server:

- Compatibility with PowerPC Macs
- Support for AppleTalk printing
- Apache Axis and WebObjects deployment tools

Address Book Server

Entirely new in Snow Leopard Server, Address Book Server follows in the footsteps of the iCal Server that debuted with Leopard Server. The new service allows network users to access their personal and group contacts across multiple computers, just as iCal Server shares calendar events.

Both services are also similar in that they rely on open specifications for the data they share: Address Book Server uses the new CardDAV, whereas iCal Server uses CalDAV. Both are based on WebDAV, which uses open web standards to support a two-way information exchange.

Address Book Server's CardDAV specification updates and modifies contact records as vCards by using the underlying WebDAV protocol.

Moving contacts out of LDAP

Prior to Snow Leopard Server, Apple supplied Directory.app for adding expanded contact information to the domain's directory, which is stored by using LDAP (Lightweight Directory Access Protocol). This melded contact records — used for tracking information, such as phone numbers and user photos — with directory records, which include users' network GUID (globally unique identifier) and the location of their home directories.

There are various problems with simply adding all this contact data into the LDAP directory. Although LDAP was designed as a lightweight version of the original DAP specification, it still involves a large amount of overhead, which raises performance problems when using it to store and share contact records.

Schema issues are also involved with expanding the directory database to accommodate contact information, particularly where Open Directory needs to synchronize its records with an outside directory, such as when a department's Mac OS X Server integrates into a larger corporate directory.

Additionally, security issues are involved with exposing directory records to share contact information. To resolve these problems, Apple has moved contact information from the Open Directory LDAP database and now stores it separately, managed by the new Address Book Server.

Exchange-style contacts

This change also expands the Mac OS X Server capacity from simply working primarily with contact records pertaining to company or institutional users already in the directory to a wider role of managing the full address book of each user.

In the realm of managing contact records, this makes Snow Leopard Server closer in practice to a messaging server, such as the Microsoft Exchange Server, rather than just a server operating system, such as Windows Server.

Microsoft originally developed its user contact management within Exchange Server separately from that software's internal user directory, which was later migrated into Windows 2000 to become Active Directory. Apple is essentially developing similar services in the opposite direction, first expanding its operating system's directory records into a contact directory with the release of Leopard Server and then splitting off a distinct contact service with Address Book Server to manage the private contact records of each user along with shared group contacts and lists of available, bookable resources.

Address Book Server also differs from Exchange in that it uses vCards to represent contact records and communicates between the server and the client by using WebDAV. Exchange stores users' contact records as specialized emails and talks to clients either by using Microsoft's MAPI or Exchange ActiveSync protocols.

CROSS-REF
For more on Address Book Server, see Chapter 28.

iCal Server 2

Following up on the debut release of iCal Server with Leopard Server, Snow Leopard Server increments calendar services to version 2.0, implementing group calendars, shared calendaring, push notification for mobile devices, a mechanism for sending meeting invitations to users who aren't iCal Server users, and a web application calendar interface for remote users.

As with the new Address Book Server, iCal Server is based on CalDAV, an emerging specification for interoperable calendaring services. iCal Server was the first commercial release of a CalDAV-compliant calendar server product.

Prior to the commercial delivery of iCal Server in Leopard Server, Apple released the server as an open-source project under the name Darwin Calendar Server. Both iCal Server and its Darwin Calendar Server sibling are written in the Python programming language by using the Twisted framework.

In large part, the release of Darwin Calendar Server was to popularize CalDAV by giving FreeBSD and Linux server administrators a ready-to-install alternative to selecting an Exchange Server clone for their calendaring services.

CROSS-REF
For more on iCal Server, see Chapter 26.

New mail services

Apple is dramatically increasing the performance and scalability of Mac OS X Server mail services with a new open-source engine designed to handle thousands of simultaneous connections. Mail service has been enhanced with server-side email rules and vacation messages and includes integrated support for junk mail and virus filtering by using SpamAssassin and ClamAV, respectively, as shown in Figure 1.8.

Figure 1.8

Mail configuration in Server Admin

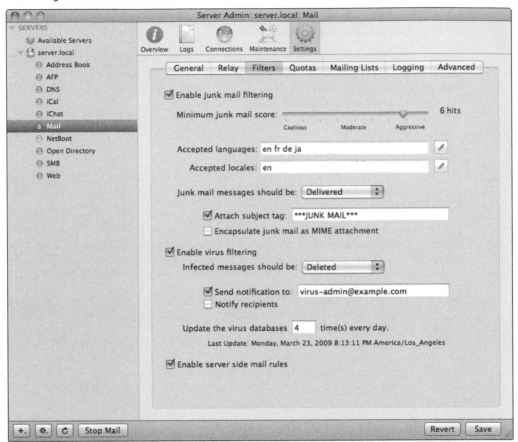

Since the release of Panther Server 10.3 in 2003, Apple has used the open-source Cyrus for incoming email services. Starting with Snow Leopard Server, Apple is now using Dovecot for its POP and IMAP email services.

The move was made to benefit from Dovecot's enhanced scalability in handling more uses, its improved data reliability, and new features the package offers, including automatic self-healing for data corruption detection and repair.

The Dovecot open-source project is also known for its focus on security as well as full compliance with the IMAP specification. The latest version of Dovecot fully passed a battery of over 440 IMAP tests, whereas Cyrus, the popular IMAP software Apple had been using, failed at least a couple dozen of those tests.

Strict adherence to the IMAP specification is as important in email software as web standards compliance is in a web server or browser. In many cases, it's even more critical because poor implementation of standards on the web usually only results in improperly formatted pages or flaws in using web applications, whereas errors in IMAP can result in email data loss for users.

Dovecot's website notes that the software is also "among the highest performing IMAP servers," using self-optimizing, transparent indexing of mail folders that support modification by multiple concurrent users. The software also supports IMAP extensions, including IDLE push notifications, and provides plug-ins for handling access control list (ACL) support and quota limitations.

CROSS-REF
For more on mail services, see Chapter 23.

Push Notification Server

In conjunction with its new and improved calendar and mail services, Snow Leopard Server also focuses its attention on push notifications. In the realm of messaging services, push notifications solve two major problems. The first relates to the performance of mobile devices, and the second relates to keeping data in sync between mobile and desktop clients.

Push messaging works by sending a notification alert from the server to clients, indicating that new messages are available or noting the change of existing contact records or calendar events. The actual update of that information is performed by using standard pull requests initiated by the client.

The Apple Push Notification Server (PNS) in Mac OS X Snow Leopard Server is part of a broader strategy that involves its own cloud services in MobileMe, client push support in its desktop and mobile products, the company's unique push notification relay service for mobile applications, and corporate support for push services that use Exchange ActiveSync.

All these services are based on WebDAV technology, an open-specification extension to the HTTP protocol for serving web pages. The Apple PNS is based on PubSub, part of the XMPP (eXtensible Messaging and Presence Protocol), a similarly open specification used in Jabber instant messaging services. Essentially, Mac OS X Server sends IM alerts to mail or calendaring clients whenever new or updated data is ready for download.

Unlike the Microsoft Exchange Server, which has to talk to an external RIM BlackBerry Enterprise Server or Microsoft's own external Exchange ActiveSync service to notify remote mobile clients of changes made within the Exchange messaging database, Apple is assembling a best-of breed collection of open, standards-based Internet services and supplying a Push Notification Server that interacts with each by using familiar web standards.

The new Apple Push Notification Server, combined with the Mac OS X Server standards-based Dovcot IMAP mail service, CalDAV-compliant iCal Server, and the new CardDAV-compliant Address Book Server, offers a credible alternative to Exchange Server and RIM BES or Microsoft EAS add-ons for push.

Apple's biggest advantage, apart from tight iPhone integration, is the fact that the company doesn't charge expensive CAL fees for every user, as Microsoft does with Exchange and as RIM does with BES.

CROSS-REF
For more on Push Notification Server, see Chapter 33.

Podcast Producer 2

Apple positions Snow Leopard's Podcast Producer 2 as a complete workflow solution for capturing, encoding, publishing, and distributing high-production-quality video podcasts. The update includes an intuitive new workflow editor that steps users through the process of creating a successful podcast.

Users can enhance podcast video with titles, transitions, and effects, such as adding watermarks or overlays, and then specify encoding formats to target the desired destinations, including distribution by using the Mac OS X Server wiki and blog, by using iTunes U, or as a public podcast feed.

The new revision also adds support for dual-video source capture to enable users to record both a presenter and a presentation screen, providing picture-in-picture slides for podcasting lectures.

Podcast Producer also includes Podcast Library, which lets users host syndicated feeds of their podcasts for subscription by category by using automatically generated Atom RSS feeds.

CROSS-REF
For more on Podcast Producer, see Chapter 30.

64-bit kernel

Snow Leopard Server adds a new 64-bit kernel to support huge amounts of RAM, up to a theoretical 16 TB, shattering the 32 GB limit of current hardware. That enables server applications to run faster and dramatically increases the number of simultaneous network connections possible.

The previous 32-bit kernel of Leopard Server could run 64-bit applications, and many of the advanced services included with it, including Apache, Podcast Producer, mail, and others, were provided 64-bit binaries to take advantage of this feature. However, with the new 64-bit kernel, all the applications in the system work as 64-bit processes, providing a system-wide performance boost related to 64-bit hardware enhancements made in the underlying Intel x86 architecture.

The new 64-bit kernel also requires updated device drivers, an issue that may affect users upgrading from previous versions of Mac OS X Server who use specialized hardware devices.

The new kernel also adds new features for maximizing the efficiency of hardware by using multiple processors and multiple cores. Referred to as Grand Central Dispatch, the new technology works to optimize processor utilization by allocating tasks across multiple cores and processors.

The new architecture also makes it easier for developers to optimize their applications to take full advantage of the multiple processors and cores available in high-end server hardware without requiring them to have special expertise in multiprocessing.

Snow Leopard also adds support for OpenCL, an open specification for developing code optimized for General Purpose Graphics Processor Unit (GPGPU) computing. GPGPU is a new trend toward making full use of the powerful graphics processing units that can now rival or exceed the primary processor in raw data processing capacity.

Mobile Access

Mobile Access is a new feature of Snow Leopard Server designed to enable companies to expose email and web-based services, including access to the CalDAV iCal Server and CardDAV Address Book Server, to outside mobile users securely and with minimal client configuration.

In contrast to setting up a general purpose VPN connection, Mobile Access enables email and web services to use standard TLS (Transport Layer Security, also referred to as SSL) encryption to access internal servers with the same level of security that banks use to secure their online transactions.

This results in mobile devices being able to access private data without making any security compromises in the name of convenience.

CROSS-REF
For more on Mobile Access, see Chapter 32.

Other new Snow Leopard features

Conversely, there are also new features of Mac OS X Snow Leopard that will make their way into the server version but apply more directly to Apple's desktop users. Major new consumer features touted for Snow Leopard include Exchange Server integration, which may directly impact users who deploy Mac OS X Server but don't factor into the server product itself.

A variety of other improvements included in Snow Leopard may also enhance the general desktop environment of Mac OS X Server but aren't as relevant in discussing server features. These include:

- Security enhancements to the Common Unix Printing System (CUPS)
- Data detectors and advanced text handling, including auto-correction features
- Auto-activation of fonts
- Advances to Safari web browsing and JavaScript execution
- New multi-touch trackpad gestures
- Greatly reduced file sizes of system applications and utilities
- A refined system interface with enhanced support for resolution independence

Summary

- Snow Leopard Server expands on Mac OS X Server with a series of improvements and new features designed to make it easier for new users to manage while also building on its sophistication for more advanced administrators.
- Apple's licensing model offers a major cost advantage over the CAL fees associated with Windows Server and Exchange.
- Mac OS X Server presents multiple configuration options with administration tools customized to the differing needs of users.
- Snow Leopard Server builds on a solid foundation of Unix software and incorporates features from a variety of open-source projects that supply the engines behind Apple's graphical user interface (GUI).
- Mac OS X Server provides tools for managing client machines and users on the network, including disk imaging and network boot features.
- Snow Leopard Server's new Address Book Server enhances contact management and sharing, whereas iCal Server 2 gains new group calendaring features.
- Mail and directory services are improved in Snow Leopard Server to support more connections from more users, and the new Push Notification Server supports mobile calendar and email users.
- Podcast Producer 2 makes sophisticated video production workflows easier to manage in Snow Leopard Server.

Mac OS X Server for Windows Users

Mac OS X Snow Leopard Server is designed to work seamlessly with Mac clients. However, it's also designed for interoperability with other platforms, including Microsoft Windows.

Mac OS X Server incorporates a range of features that makes it an appealing alternative to Windows Server and its expensive requirements for CALs. Mac OS X Server delivers:

- Exceptional ease of use for delegating server management roles to workgroup users, with appropriate security for managing administrative permissions by using service access control lists (SACLs)

- Unlimited user licensing for access to standards-based instant messaging, push email and calendaring, contact sharing, print and file sharing, and web application development

- Support for hosting shared Mac and Windows home folders so users working across platforms can easily access their documents no matter what system they're using

- Cross-platform web collaboration tools for hosting shared version-controlled wikis, blogs, webmail, and web-based calendar access

- Integration with existing Active Directory domains for user authentication and support for hosting Windows domain logins, roaming profiles, and user folders

- Rich media support for video streaming, client video capture, and podcast production workflows

- Advanced user and computer management by using centralized group policy to shape users' environments and enforce security measures

This chapter introduces how Mac OS X Server is designed to integrate with existing Windows Server installations, how it can be used to replace more expensive alternatives, and what's involved in making the move.

In This Chapter

Integrating with Active Directory

Hosting services for Windows clients

Migrating from Windows Server

Integrating with Active Directory

If your organization already operates a significantly sized Windows Server environment, you're likely using Active Directory to provide domain user authentication.

Apple's Open Directory architecture in Mac OS X Server enables it to integrate with a variety of different directory services, including Active Directory, by using directory service plug-ins.

Multiple directory domains can be defined with a search policy that determines the order in which those directories are consulted when performing user authentication or searching for other directory information, such as group membership or managed client policy.

Mac OS X Server and Mac OS X clients can both add Active Directory to their search policy for authentication information by using Apple's supplied Active Directory plug-in for Open Directory. This is configured from Directory Utility, shown in Figure 2.1.

Figure 2.1

Directory Utility

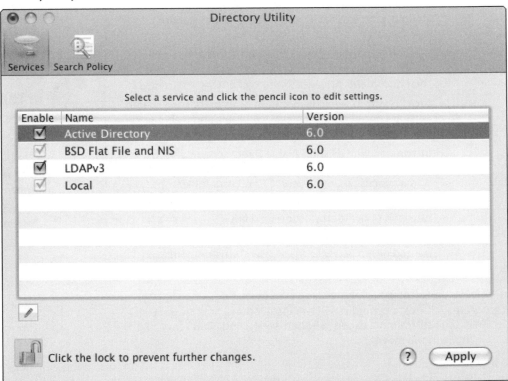

Just like Windows clients, Mac systems bind to your existing Active Directory domain in order to access domain user accounts for authenticating client login. The Active Directory bind sheet is shown in Figure 2.2. Instructions on advanced binding configuration with Active Directory are detailed shortly.

Figure 2.2

Active Directory binding in Directory Utility

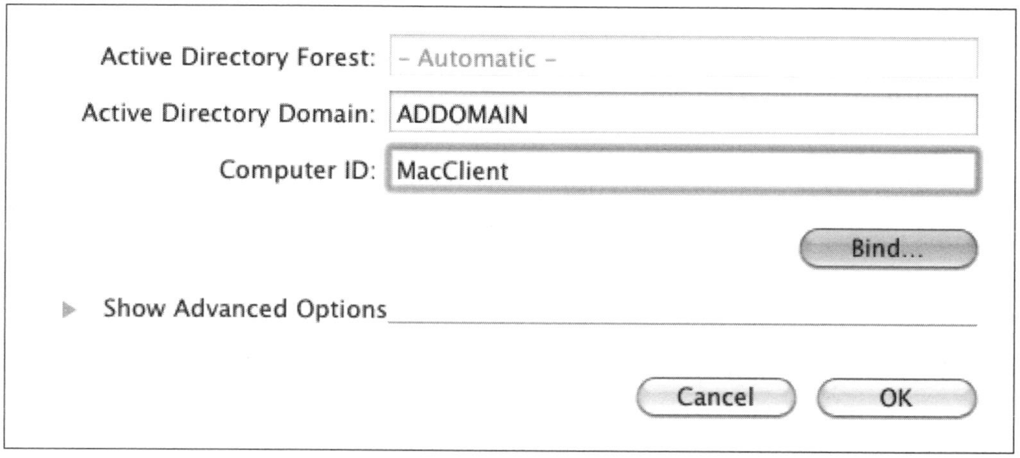

Using the Active Directory plug-in to bind Macs to the directory domain also enables:

- Domain admin groups to be granted local administrator access on Macs bound to the Active Directory domain
- Enforcement of Active Directory's defined password policy
- Single sign-on (SSO) access to the Active Directory domain via Kerberos
- Network home directories for Mac users based on the home shares defined in Active Directory
- Offline Portable Home Directories for mobile Mac users, which mirror network home directories and users' settings locally for cached login similar to roaming profiles on Windows

Mac OS X Server similarly supports integration with Active Directory to enable:

- Windows users to access file sharing, web-based collaboration tools, and other services hosted by Mac OS X Server by using their Active Directory account information for authentication
- SSO access by both Mac and Windows clients to secure network services hosted on Mac OS X Server or, alternatively, client Kerberos authentication to Active Directory, which can be used to supply authentication tickets to services on Mac OS X Server

- Network home directories for Mac users based on the home shares defined in Active Directory
- A Magic Triangle of directory services that supports Active Directory for user authentication and Open Directory for managed preferences
- Offline Portable Home Directories for mobile Mac users, which mirror network home directories and users' settings locally for cached login similar to roaming profiles on Windows

Understanding Active Directory and Open Directory

Interoperability between Active Directory and Open Directory is based on the shared use of both LDAP, originally developed at the University of Michigan, and Kerberos, an SSO authentication protocol developed by MIT; Open Directory doesn't use Microsoft's proprietary Active Directory Services Interface (ADSI) for directory browsing or authentication.

Introducing Open Directory

Mac OS X's Open Directory architecture integrates a variety of proven components, many of which leverage the use of open-source software to:

- Maximize interoperability with other systems via close adherence to standards
- Incorporate regular improvements made by the larger community to enhance security and performance

Open Directory uses:

- OpenLDAP to provide directory services
- Berkeley DB to store directory records
- Kerberos for SSO authentication
- Apple Password Server to store authentication credentials for alternative authentication methods, including Microsoft's NTLMv2 and MS-CHAPv2

Open Directory as an architecture is designed to abstract away the differences in various implementations of directory services so local processes only need to know how to talk to Mac OS X's Directory Services itself, which can then obtain information from Active Directory, multiple tiers of Apple's own Open Directory domains, Sun's NIS, Novell eDirectory, and any other standard LDAPv3 directory services the system is configured to use.

CROSS-REF
For more on Open Directory, see Chapter 21.

Managed preferences

Mac OS X supports a fully managed environment for controlling policy for users, groups, and computers via managed preferences, also known as Managed Clients for Mac OS X (MCX).

Configured within Workgroup Manager, shown in Figure 2.3, managed preferences enable administrators to either set or force specific configurations for network users, groups of users, or computers or across groups of computers.

Figure 2.3

Assigning managed preferences in Workgroup Manager

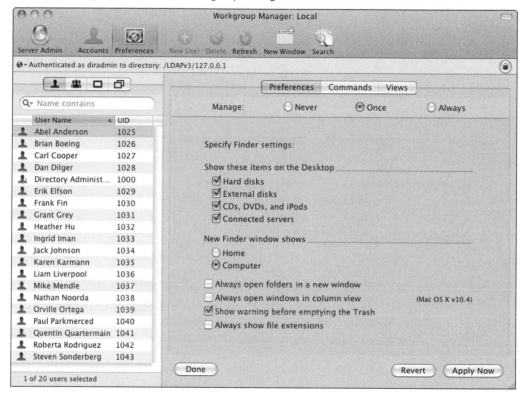

Active Directory stores Group Policy Objects (GPOs) to perform a similar task for managing group policy for Windows users and machines. Mac OS X's mechanism for storing preferences is different than the Registry that Windows clients use, so GPOs can't be applied to Macs.

Instead, there are several different options, depending on your organization's circumstances, for managing Mac settings using policy defined within directory services:

- **Use basic policy supported by Apple's Open Directory plug-in.** This includes Active Directory authentication, including full support of password policies, as well as the use of directory-defined network homes for Mac users.

- **Extend the schema used by Active Directory to handle advanced management.** You can add 36 attributes and 10 classes to your Active Directory schema to enable support for all Mac OS X management policies. Once Active Directory is configured with extended schema, you can use Workgroup Manager to directly add MCX managed preferences to users, groups, computers, and groups of computers in the Active Directory domain.

- **Use a Magic Triangle of Active Directory and Mac OS X Server.** By configuring Mac clients to use both Active Directory and an Open Directory domain hosted by Mac OS X Server, Active Directory users and groups can be included within groups defined in Open Directory. Those groups can then have MCX managed preferences applied to them.

- **Use the augmented records feature supported in modern Mac OS X clients.** Directory accounts are imported from Active Directory and appended with MCX managed preferences in Open Directory. This avoids any need to change Active Directory schema but still requires a Magic Triangle of directory servers.

CROSS-REF

For more on Workgroup Manager, see Chapter 10. For more on managed preferences, see Chapter 36.

Home directories

Mac OS X can be configured to store a user's home folder of user documents and system configuration files, analogous to a unified Windows home directory and roaming profile, by using settings defined in Active Directory independent from managed preferences:

- **Local home folders, a bind configuration option when using the Active Directory plug-in, leaves users' homes on their client system.** If a network home is defined in Active Directory, that share automatically mounts on the user's desktop.

- **Network home folders for Mac users can be defined in Active Directory, just as they are for Windows users, by using Microsoft's backward slash convention of** `\\server\share\user`. The Open Directory plug-in uses the specified path to create a standard URL: `smb://server.example.com/share/user`. It expands the name of the server to a fully qualified domain name by using your Active Directory's domain name. If you support AFP home directories, you can alternatively configure your Macs to automatically assume use of that protocol instead of SMB.

- **Portable Home Directories can be configured to allow mobile users to locally cache their network home folders and any associated managed preference settings.** This enables notebook users to work offline by using their Active Directory account and then synchronize with their network home when they reconnect, similar to roaming profiles on a Windows system.

Using Mac OS X Server with Active Directory

To create a Magic Triangle configuration for your Mac clients to support authentication from Active Directory and managed preferences defined in Open Directory, you need to be familiar with the customized configuration of your Active Directory domain, and you need domain administrator access to bind clients to Active Directory (specifically, write access to the computer OU) because it doesn't allow anonymous binding by default.

When configuring your Mac clients and Open Directory server, order is important:

● **Bind your Mac OS X Server to Active Directory.** The soon-to-be Open Directory server must initially be configured as a Standalone Server in the Open Directory pane of Server Admin, shown in Figure 2.4.

Figure 2.4

Server Admin's Open Directory pane

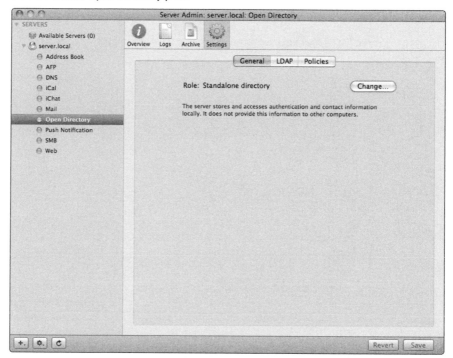

● **Promote your Mac OS X Server to an Open Directory master.** As Mac OS X Server assumes the role of hosting a new Open Directory domain, it automatically configures itself as subordinate to Active Directory because of the previous binding.

● **Within Workgroup Manager, add Active Directory users and groups to Open Directory groups.** You can also add Active Directory computers to Open Directory computer groups. This enables you to apply managed preferences to the user and computer groups.

● **Bind your Mac client systems to Open Directory by using Mac OS X Snow Leopard's Directory Utility.** You can simply add the address of the Open Directory server as a Network Account Server from the Accounts pane of System Preferences within Login Options.

● **Bind your Mac client systems to Active Directory by using Mac OS X Snow Leopard's Directory Utility.** Instructions on performing an Active Directory bind are described shortly; the process is identical between Mac OS X Server and Mac clients.

To configure directory services in Directory Utility, follow these steps:

1. **Launch System Preferences and then click the Accounts tab.**

2. **Authenticate as a local user and then click Login Options.**

3. **Click Edit Network Account Server.** You can bind a client system to an Open Directory domain by supplying the DNS name of your Mac OS X Server here. The simple list of Network Account Servers is shown in Figure 2.5.

Figure 2.5

Adding Network Account Servers from the Accounts pane of System Preferences

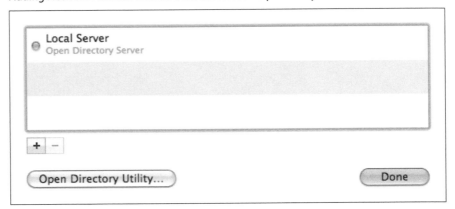

4. **Click the Open Directory Utility button.**

5. **From the Services page of Directory Utility, click the lock icon to authenticate as a local administrator.**

6. **Enable and configure the Active Directory plug-in as described in the next set of steps and then click Apply.**

To enable support for Active Directory in Directory Utility, follow these steps:

1. **From the Services page in Directory Utility, click the Active Directory check box.**

2. **Double-click the Active Directory listing to open the configuration dialog box.** A sheet drops down.

3. **Optionally, type the name of the Active Directory Forest.** By default, this is set automatically (as evidenced by the - Automatic -).

4. **Type the name of the Active Directory domain.**

5. **Type a name for the local system as Computer ID.** This becomes a computer record in Active Directory.

6. **Click the Show Advanced Options triangle and then click the User Experience tab, shown in Figure 2.6.**

Figure 2.6

Active Directory advanced configuration in Directory Utility

7. **Click the Create mobile account at login check box.** A mobile account uses a local home folder on the system's startup volume to mirror the user's network home folder as defined in Active Directory, creating a Portable Home Directory. A mobile account also locally caches the user's Active Directory authentication credentials, enabling the user to log in by using the Active Directory account even when the directory server is unavailable.

8. **Click the Use UNC path from Active Directory to derive network home location check box to enable a path stored in Microsoft's** `\\server\share\user` **notation to be translated to the standard** `afp://server/share/user` **for mounting by Mac OS X.**

9. **From the pop-up menu, choose the network protocol to be used for network home folders.** The default is SMB, but if the network home file server supports AFP, you can choose that instead for the Mac's home folder.

10. **Configure a default user shell if desired.**

11. **From the Mappings pane, you can remap the default settings for user ID numbers to Active Directory attributes that you specify.** If left alone, the Active Directory plug-in dynamically generates a unique user ID and a primary group ID from the account's Globally Unique ID (GUID) in Active Directory. The generated user ID and primary group ID are the same for each user account, even if the account is used to log in to different systems.

12. **From the Administrative pane, you can set a preferred domain server and assign local administration privileges to Active Directory groups.** By default, the domain admins and enterprise admins groups are granted local administrative access. You can also allow authentication from any domain in the forest by clicking the check box.

13. **Click Bind and then authenticate as a local administrator.** The system configures the computer account for the system in Active Directory and begins allowing authentication and local login by Active Directory accounts.

14. **Click OK to save the settings for Active Directory.**

After binding your Mac clients to Open Directory and then Active Directory, they can log in by using their Active Directory user account, and the membership of that account in an Open Directory group enforces the managed preferences assigned to the group.

Mac OS X client software and network services also support SSO by using Active Directory's support for Kerberos authentication, which prevents passwords from being sent over the network and provides other security enhancements, including mutual authentication of the server to the client as well as from the client to the server.

Active Directory accounts can also be specified in SACLs in Server Admin to limit access to services Mac OS X Server provides to specific users.

CROSS-REF

For more on using Server Admin, see Chapter 9. For more on security and SACLs, see Chapter 20.

Hosting Services for Windows Clients

Through integrated support of the Samba 3 open-source package, Mac OS X Server can host an NT domain for Windows users and provide them with domain login and authentication services, including Windows file and print services, hosted user profiles, and home directories.

Samba configuration is managed in the SMB pane of Server Admin, shown in Figure 2.7.

Figure 2.7

Samba configuration in Server Admin

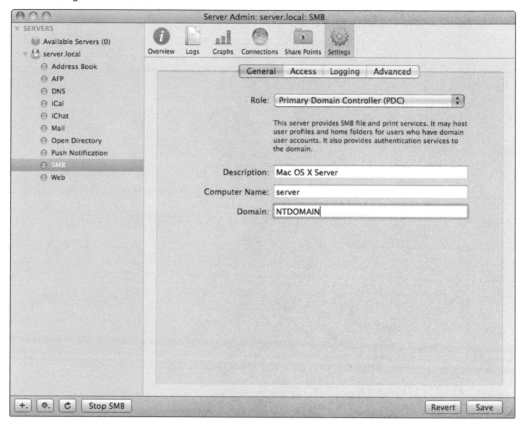

Mac OS X Server uses the same network-visible Open Directory domain to support Windows users as it does to support its own Mac-native directory services, so accounts created in Workgroup Manager can be used for logging in to both Macs and Windows.

Open Directory domain configuration is managed in the Open Directory pane of Server Admin.

By default, users' home folders are set up to be the same location on both platforms, making it easier for users who work across platforms to work with the same documents.

From Workgroup Manager's Windows pane, shown in Figure 2.8, a user may also be configured to use a custom home directory and user profile location.

Figure 2.8

Windows user configuration in Workgroup Manager

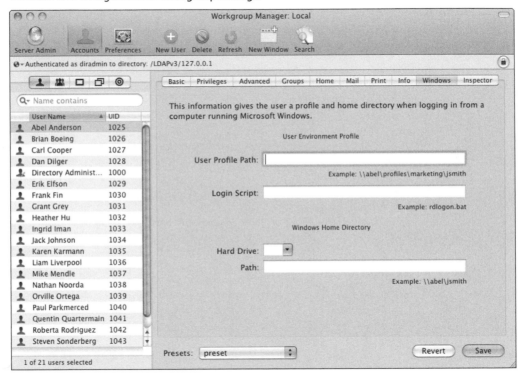

In preparation to being configured to serve Windows clients as a domain controller, Mac OS X Server may be configured as:

- **An Open Directory Standalone Directory Server configured as a Standalone Server in the SMB service.** This doesn't provide a network-visible directory domain or an NT domain; it only maintains local accounts for use on the server. This enables Windows users to access file and print services on the server, but they can't authenticate to log in to a Windows domain. The server can't host user profiles or home folders either. Promoting a Standalone Directory Server to an Open Directory master enables you to promote the server from a Standalone Server to a Primary Domain Controller within the SMB service.

- **An Open Directory Standalone Directory Server configured as a Domain Member in the SMB service.** This doesn't provide a network-visible directory domain or NT domain; it only maintains local accounts for use on the server. However, as a Domain Member, the server is connected to another server acting as a Primary Domain Controller, enabling Mac OS X Server to host user profiles and home folders for users authenticated by the Primary Domain Controller, in addition to providing basic Windows file and print services. Promoting a Standalone Directory Server to an Open Directory master enables you to also promote the server from a Domain Member to a Primary Domain Controller within the SMB service. However, an NT domain can have only one Primary Domain Controller, so the server also needs to create a new NT domain.

- **An existing Open Directory master configured as a Standalone Server in the SMB service.** This can be upgraded to a Primary Domain Controller.

- **An existing Open Directory master configured as a Domain Member in the SMB service.** This can be upgraded to a Primary Domain Controller. However, an NT domain can have only one Primary Domain Controller, so the server also needs to create a new NT domain.

- **An existing Open Directory replica configured as a Standalone Server or Domain Member in the SMB service.** This can't be upgraded to a Primary Domain Controller but can be designated as a Backup Domain Controller.

Acting as a Primary Domain Controller

To act as a Primary Domain Controller, Mac OS X Server must be configured as an Open Directory master.

To determine the configured role of a server in Server Admin, follow these steps:

1. **Launch Server Admin and then connect to the desired server.**

2. **Click Open Directory and then click Settings on the toolbar.**

3. **Click the General tab.**

4. **View the designated Role:**

- If the server is currently a Standalone Directory Server, you must promote it to an Open Directory master prior to configuring it as a Primary Domain Controller.

- If the server is currently an Open Directory master, you can set it up to serve as a Primary Domain Controller from the SMB service.

- If the server is currently an Open Directory replica or relay, it can't act as a Primary Domain Controller but can be configured as a Backup Domain Controller.

To promote a server to a Primary Domain Controller in Server Admin, follow these steps:

1. **Launch Server Admin and then connect to the desired server.**

2. **Click SMB and then click Settings on the toolbar.**

3. **Click the General tab.**

4. **Click Change next to the designated Role:**

- A Standalone Server can be promoted to a Primary Domain Controller, creating a new NT domain.

- A Domain Member can be promoted to a Primary Domain Controller, creating a new NT domain.

5. **Choose Primary Domain Controller.**

6. **Type the domain information for the new Primary Domain Controller:**

- **Description.** This is visible to Windows clients.

- **Computer Name.** This is the NetBIOS name of the server. It can't contain spaces or more than 15 characters, and most punctuation or special characters are illegal.

- **Domain.** This is the new NT domain you're creating. It can't contain more than 15 characters, can't be WORKGROUP, and can't be the same as any existing NT domain on the network.

7. **Click Save.** You're prompted to type a directory administrator account. You can't use a regular local administrator account to set up a Primary Domain Controller.

CROSS-REF

For more on configuring the SMB service, see Chapter 22.

Acting as a Backup Domain Controller

A Backup Domain Controller acts as a read-only backup of NT domain directory records to support the job of the Primary Domain Controller in providing authentication and directory information to Windows clients.

If the Primary Domain Controller fails, Windows clients using it can switch to using an available Backup Domain Controller. When functioning normally, the Backup Domain Controllers receive regular updates via the replication of the Open Directory master to an Open Directory replica.

This also means that to act as a Backup Domain Controller, a server must be configured as an Open Directory replica.

Prior to becoming a Backup Domain Controller, Mac OS X Server may be configured as:

- **An Open Directory Standalone Directory Server configured as a Standalone Server in the SMB service.** Promoting a Standalone Directory Server to an Open Directory replica enables you to promote the server from a Standalone Server to a Backup Domain Controller within the SMB service.

- **An Open Directory Standalone Directory Server configured as a Domain Member in the SMB service.** Promoting a Standalone Directory Server to an Open Directory replica enables you to also promote the server from a Domain Member to a Backup Domain Controller within the SMB service. The Backup Domain Controller can join the NT domain it was formerly only a member of, now in a controller role.

- **An existing Open Directory master configured as a Standalone Server or Domain Member in the SMB service.** This can't be upgraded to a Backup Domain Controller but can be promoted to act as a Primary Domain Controller. This also creates a new NT domain.

- **An existing Open Directory replica configured as a Standalone Server or Domain Member in the SMB service.** This can be upgraded to serve as a Backup Domain Controller.

To determine the configured role of a server in Server Admin, follow these steps:

1. **Launch Server Admin and then connect to the desired server.**

2. **Click Open Directory and then click Settings on the toolbar.**

3. **Click the General tab.**

4. **View the designated Role:**

- If the server is currently a Standalone Directory Server, you must promote it to an Open Directory replica prior to configuring it as a Backup Domain Controller in the SMB service. A Primary Domain Controller for the NT domain must also already exist.

- If the server is currently an Open Directory master, you can't set it up to serve as a Backup Domain Controller.

- If the server is currently an Open Directory replica or relay, it can be configured as a Backup Domain Controller from the SMB service.

To promote a server to a Backup Domain Controller in Server Admin, follow these steps:

1. **Launch Server Admin and then connect to the desired server.**

2. **Click SMB and then click Settings on the toolbar.**

3. **Click the General tab.**

4. **Click Change next to the designated Role:**

- A Standalone Server can be promoted to a Backup Domain Controller if a Primary Domain Controller is already in place.

- A Domain Member can be promoted to a Backup Domain Controller to serve the NT domain it was formerly only a member of.

5. **Choose Backup Domain Controller.**

6. **Type the domain information for the new Backup Domain Controller:**

- **Description.** This is visible to Windows clients.
- **Computer Name.** This is the NetBIOS name of the server. It can't contain spaces or more than 15 characters, and most punctuation or special characters are illegal.
- **Domain** is the NT domain of the existing Primary Domain Controller.

7. **Click Save.** You're prompted to type a directory administrator account. You can't use a regular local administrator account to set up a Backup Domain Controller.

Migrating from Windows Server

Mac OS X Server can expand on or replace services offered by Windows Server to provide:

- Substantial cost savings from the elimination of any need to buy CALs
- Standard VPN and RADIUS authentication services as well as other core network services, including DNS, DHCP, firewall, and NAT
- Cross-platform, standards-based support for Mac, Windows, and Unix clients for file- and print-sharing, mail, instant messaging, calendar, and contact-sharing services
- Support for open, interoperable, standards-based web development
- Secure remote Mobile Access and push messaging features for mobile devices
- Easy-to-use wiki and blog collaboration features, including rich support for next-generation mobile web clients, such as the iPhone and iPod touch, shown in Figure 2.9

CROSS-REF
For more on core network services provided by Mac OS X Server, see Chapters 12–19. For more on advanced services, including email, web, instant messaging, calendar, and contact sharing, see Chapters 22–28. For more on Mobile Access and push notification, see Chapters 32–33, respectively.

Windows shops have in the past incorporated Mac users into their operations by using solutions such as the now-obsolete and discontinued Services for Macintosh package that Microsoft formerly shipped with Windows Server.

Mac OS X Server can be added to existing Windows shops to provide missing support for Mac clients and can even replace Windows Server in acting as a domain controller for Windows clients for organizations that don't use or require investing in deploying an Active Directory infrastructure.

Existing records managed by a Windows domain can be migrated to Mac OS X Server acting as an Open Directory master, thanks to the integrated support for acting as a Primary Domain Controller for Windows clients. This allows administrators to continue to use their existing:

- User and group accounts
- Computer account records for machines that are members of the Windows domain
- Windows users' existing login scripts

- Windows users' existing home directory folders and documents
- Windows users' existing roaming profiles

Figure 2.9

Snow Leopard Server makes it easy to deploy collaboration services for mobile devices.

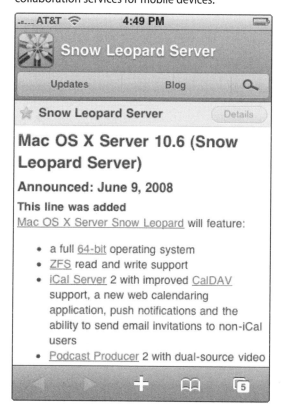

Once migrated to Mac OS X Server, the same accounts can be used to log in to Macs, creating a seamless experience for users who move back and forth between Macs and Windows PCs.

Apart from additional features and simplified management, migration to Mac OS X Server results in substantial cost savings. Apple sells Mac OS X Server for use by an unlimited number of users for $499, and it ships free with new Mac Xserve systems.

PC server systems don't bundle Windows Server for free, yet they cost about the same as Apple's Mac server offerings:

- **Windows Server.** Around $799 for five users
- **Exchange Server.** For messaging, at around $700
- **Sharepoint Server.** For web collaboration, at around $4,424

Once you add in these costs, you end up with a bill for Microsoft software that in itself costs around twice as much as the hardware for a server in the class of Apple's Xserve, but then you have to add CALs for all your users. Just to serve 100 users in a moderately sized workgroup, you face an additional bill that includes:

- 100 Windows Server CALs for around $4,000
- 100 Exchange Server CALs for around $6,700
- 100 Sharepoint Server CALs for around $9,400

Your combined hardware and software expenses are now nearly $30,000 for a single server, compared to around $3,750 for a comparable Xserve with Mac OS X Server with unlimited access to messaging and collaboration services in addition to a host of other services.

Add up the Windows premium across the servers in your organization, and the high costs of running a Microsoft shop begin to dwarf other expenses, from personnel to hardware.

Every time you upgrade your operating system, you face similar sticker shock in buying upgrades for server and client software and all new CALs, compared to the nominal $499 upgrade price Apple has set for reference releases of Mac OS X Server.

CROSS-REF
For more on migrating to Mac OS X Server, see Chapter 5.

Summary

- Mac OS X Server can integrate into an organization's existing Active Directory domain to obtain centralized authentication information for the domain users it provides services to.

- Configured in a Magic Triangle, Mac OS X Server can provide managed preferences to set and enforce group policy for Mac users on the domain.

- Mac OS X Server can also host Windows users' home directories and roaming profiles, acting as a Primary Domain Controller for Windows clients by using the same accounts it uses to authenticate Mac users.

- Using Mac OS X Server to replace Windows Server in workgroups or across the organization results in substantial software savings because Apple licenses its services for unlimited users, eliminating the need to buy expensive CALs.

Installing
Mac OS X Server

Planning Deployment Complexity

M ac OS X Server attempts to cover a wide range of uses:

- The relatively basic needs of small business users for email and file sharing
- The more advanced needs of higher education and corporate groups using Podcast Producer, iChat Server, and wikis, blogs, and web calendars
- The very customized needs of large organizations and enterprise groups who need to integrate their servers into an existing corporate directory and install their own server applications

Creating one product with the ability to cover such a broad range of needs is challenging. On one end, there are users who want everything to be as simple and intuitive as their Mac OS X desktops; at the opposite pole, there are users who need to get down and dirty with advanced customizations.

In Mac OS X Leopard Server, Apple defined three configurations to allow users with different needs to either limit the complexity they have to deal with or, alternatively, to expose the complexity they need to deploy customized, advanced services:

- Standard configuration
- Workgroup configuration
- Advanced configuration

The first two configurations were designed to use the simple Server Preferences application for most of their initial configurations and ongoing administration. This application is designed to mimic the Mac's System Preferences, reducing administration down to a series of approachable panes of options.

In This Chapter

Standard configuration

Workgroup configuration

Advanced configuration

CROSS-REF

For more on Server Preferences, see Chapter 7.

Leopard Server's advanced configuration continued to use the standard Server Admin and Workgroup Manager applications for setting up and configuring services and working with domain users, groups, file shares, and computer settings. These advanced tools also scale up to manage large numbers of servers at once.

CROSS-REF

For more on Server Admin, see Chapter 9. For more on Workgroup Manager, see Chapter 10.

The most advanced administrators still frequently need to use command-line tools or manually edit text configuration files within the Unix environment to use features and options not exposed in the Apple graphical administration tools.

With each release, Mac OS X Server has incrementally improved in the range and depth of the features that can be managed by using its graphical tools. Apple has also increasingly taken steps to allow administrators to add their own manual customizations to core settings in ways that remain compatible with the configuration performed by using the supplied administration tools.

CAUTION

There's still the possibility of error in the overwriting of custom settings when moving back and forth between the manual editing of configuration files and the automated file editing of Apple's supplied administration tools. Users with advanced needs should proceed with caution when making changes and take steps to allow either a clean rollback of any changes or a recovery of their custom settings from appropriate backups. Every plan of attack needs an exit strategy!

The three configurations of Leopard Server largely revolved around how the server's directory services were being managed. When installing Snow Leopard Server, Apple asks a series of questions to determine how best to configure the server. This starts with Users and Groups, which presents three options:

- **Manage Users and Groups.** This uses Open Directory to locally manage the user and group accounts, resulting in a standard configuration.
- **Import Users and Groups.** This imports users and group account information from an existing directory server on the network, resulting in a workgroup configuration.
- **Configure Manually.** This presents more complex options for customized directory service deployments, resulting in an advanced configuration.

CROSS-REF

For more on installing Snow Leopard Server, see Chapter 6.

Standard Configuration

The Mac OS X Server standard configuration limits the complexity users have to manage. It's intended for use as the first or only server within a small organization. Although this configuration is easier to manage, it's also limited to a subset of features available in the advanced configuration.

Standard configuration sets up all services automatically, leaving the administrator to add users and change simple settings within Server Preferences, as shown in Figure 3.1.

Figure 3.1

Server Preferences exposes simple settings for users working within the standard configuration.

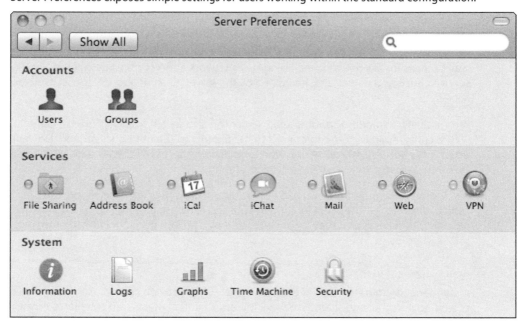

Evaluating the capabilities of standard configuration

The main defining characteristic of a standard configuration server is that it maintains its own stand-alone directory server instead of importing users and groups from an external directory server as part of a larger organization.

Using the Server Preferences Users and Groups panes, administrators can add user and group records, assign users contact information, and individually allow or deny a user access to services provided by the server, such as file sharing, calendar, address book, instant messaging, mail, VPN, or Time Machine backups.

Users can also be assigned to groups, and groups can be given attributes, such as access to a shared folder, a group wiki page, or an instant messaging auto-buddy list that populates the group's membership into users' iChat buddy lists.

For more complex user and workgroup management, an upgrade to an advanced configuration server is required, which is detailed later in this chapter.

DNS and DHCP services

In standard configuration, core network services such as DNS and DHCP are likely to be supplied by an appliance router, such as an AirPort wireless base station, with DNS records being managed by the outside ISP.

There's no provision for managing DNS records or DHCP leases from within Server Preferences.

Network firewall, NAT, RADIUS, and VPN services

An AirPort base station can also be configured within Server Preferences to supply gateway firewall services for the network, including NAT (network address translation) for mapping inside services, such as a public website hosted by the server, to an IP address that outside users can access.

Alternatively, a standard configuration server can also switch from AirPort management to firewall security, enabling the server itself to handle NAT as the network's firewall. However, it doesn't support RADIUS authentication for managing access to the wireless network, which is a task that requires working in the advanced configuration.

A standard configuration server can also act as the network's VPN (virtual private network) server, allowing remote users to authenticate and establish a secure connection to access internal network services as if they were connected by a private network link rather than over the public Internet.

Advanced services

A standard configuration server is set up by default to provide shared user and group accounts, providing personal and shared network folders, shared contacts and calendars, email, instant messaging, and web services supporting wikis and blogs.

However, standard configuration only supports a subset of the file services available in the advanced configuration. It automatically serves up shared files to both Macs (by using Apple Filing Protocol [AFP]) and Windows PCs (by using Server Message Block [SMB]) but can't be configured to set up FTP or NFS file shares by using the File Sharing pane in Server Preferences. It does support users being able to target the server as a repository for their Time Machine backups.

The Address Book, iCal, and iChat panes in Server Preferences supply simple one-button activation and just one or two configurable settings for each service. To customize these services further, the server needs to be upgraded to an advanced configuration.

Mail service is similarly streamlined in Server Preferences, with just three options for relaying outgoing email through the ISP, enabling virus and junk mail filtering with a sliding scale of aggressiveness, and activating a spam blacklist server.

Web services are also presented in Server Preferences with a single check box for activating wikis, web calendars, blogs, and webmail. It also allows administrators to set up additional custom websites, each with its own domain name.

QuickTime Streaming Server, Podcast Producer, and print services

In standard configuration, Mac OS X Server offers neither support for managing QuickTime Streaming Server or Podcast Producer nor Xgrid services for distributed processing (which is primarily used in conjunction with Podcast Producer) within Server Preferences.

Standard configuration also provides no support for printer queues and quotas, but the system can host a simple shared printer attached via USB or FireWire, just as the desktop version of Mac OS X can, which is similar to the USB printer sharing available from an AirPort base station.

Client computer management

A server in standard configuration is also not intended for use in managing and serving NetBoot and NetInstall disk images, and it can't serve as a local Software Update Server. Managed client options are also unavailable without an upgrade to advanced configuration.

Moving beyond standard configuration

Although the standard configuration offers a server that's easy to set up and configure, it doesn't allow administrators to touch any of the more advanced settings or even access many of the advertised features of Mac OS X. It also offers no support for working with outside directory services.

Moving to workgroup configuration

To access outside directory services, a standard configuration can be turned into a workgroup configuration by simply connecting the server to another directory server in the organization. This change can be undone later by simply disconnecting from the outside directory service.

To connect a standard configuration server to another directory server within the organization, follow these steps:

1. **Open Server Preferences and then click Accounts.**

2. **If the Accounts pane is locked, click the lock icon in the lower left and then authenticate by typing the local administrator account name and password.**

3. **Click Login Options and then click the Edit button next to Server Connection.**

4. **Click the Add (+) button and then type the DNS name or IP address of the directory server to connect to.**

5. **Type a user account name and password to authenticate with the remote directory server.** This can be a standard user account and doesn't need to be the directory administrator account. Once connected, you can add remote users defined on that directory server as external members of your local groups and grant any of the remote directory's users permission to access the local server's private collaboration websites.

CROSS-REF

For more on importing remote users in Server Preferences, see Chapter 7.

Upgrading to advanced configuration

A standard configuration server can also be upgraded to the advanced configuration by simply connecting to the system remotely from System Admin. The application warns that the server is currently in standard configuration and provides the option to make a permanent change to advanced configuration.

CAUTION

This step ends the innocence of the standard configuration and simple administration by using Server Preferences! There's no way to return the server back to standard configuration without reinstalling the operating system or reverting to a server backup.

After moving to the advanced configuration, administrators need to continue to use the Server Admin and Workgroup Manager tools to manage the server; attempting to revert to the simpler Server Preferences application may result in unintended consequences because it doesn't provide access to the more advanced settings made in the advanced administration tools.

Workgroup Configuration

The Mac OS X Server workgroup configuration is identical to standard configuration apart from being connected to an outside directory server. Just as with standard configuration, workgroup configuration limits the complexity users have to manage, using the same simple Server Preferences for managing the server.

Workgroup configuration is intended for use as a department server within a larger organization. Although this configuration pairs easier management with expanded directory services integration, it's limited to a subset of features available in the advanced configuration.

Evaluating the capabilities of workgroup configuration

Using the Server Preferences Users and Groups panes, administrators can add user and group records to the local directory or import users from an external directory. New local users are assigned contact information and can be individually allowed or denied access to services provided by the local server, such as file sharing, calendar, address book, instant messaging, mail, VPN, or Time Machine backups.

Users can also be assigned to groups, and groups can be given attributes, such as access to a shared folder, a group wiki page, or an instant messaging auto-buddy list that populates the group's membership into users' iChat buddy lists.

Because a workgroup configuration server connects to a larger directory server infrastructure, it can also import users and groups from an external directory server, add remote users defined on another directory server as external members of local groups, and grant any of the remote directory's users permission to access the local server's private collaboration websites.

Imported users are given a mail and iChat address and a personal calendar, access to the local server's file shares and private websites, and VPN access to connect to the server remotely. Just as with local accounts, each of these services can be granted or denied access individually.

NOTE

Mac OS X Server in workgroup configuration can connect to an external Mac OS X Server Open Directory or a Microsoft Windows Server Active Directory Domain to import users or reference external accounts.

To import user accounts to a workgroup configuration server from another directory server within the organization, follow these steps:

1. **Open Server Preferences and then click the Users pane.**

2. **Click the Action button marked with a gear icon and then choose Import User From Directory from the pop-up menu.** If there's no pop-up menu displayed, the server is in standard configuration and needs to be connected to another directory server, which is mentioned earlier in this chapter.

3. **Select the user to be imported from a connected directory server and then click Import.**

4. **When finished importing users, click Done.** Imported users are marked as imported in the Users pane of Server Preferences.

NOTE

Groups of users can also be identically imported from the Groups pane. When a group is imported, all its members' users are also imported. The local server also monitors the external directory service and synchronizes membership of imported groups by adding or removing users as needed. Imported groups are therefore marked as automatic in the group listing.

For more complex user and workgroup management, an upgrade to an advanced configuration server is required, which is detailed later in this chapter.

DNS and DHCP services

In workgroup configuration, core network services such as DNS and DHCP are likely to be supplied by the organization's IT group.

There's no provision for managing DNS records or DHCP leases from within Server Preferences.

Network firewall, NAT, RADIUS, and VPN services

Similarly, a workgroup server will likely have firewall, NAT, RADIUS, and VPN services handled by the organization. Just as in standard configuration, it's also possible for an AirPort base station to be configured within Server Preferences to supply gateway firewall services for the local network or to maintain its own firewall security.

Server Preferences can also act as a VPN server for the local network, but it doesn't support RADIUS authentication for managing access to the wireless network.

Advanced services

A workgroup configuration server is set up by default to host its own shared user and group accounts and to import user and group accounts from external directory servers, allowing it to provide personal and shared network folders, shared contacts and calendars, email, instant messaging, and web services supporting wikis and blogs for users created locally as well as for imported users and automatic groups.

However, workgroup configuration supports only a subset of the file services available in the advanced configuration. It automatically serves up shared files to both Macs (by using AFP) and Windows PCs (by using SMB) but can't be configured to set up FTP or NFS file shares by using the File Sharing pane in Server Preferences. It does support users being able to target the server as a repository for their Time Machine backups.

The Address Book, iCal, and iChat panes in Server Preferences supply simple one-button activation and just one or two configurable settings for each service. To customize these services further, the server needs to be upgraded to an advanced configuration.

Mail service is similarly streamlined in Server Preferences, with just three options for relaying outgoing email through the ISP, enabling virus and junk mail filtering with a sliding scale of aggressiveness, and activating a spam blacklist server.

Web services are also presented in Server Preferences with a single check box for activating wikis, web calendars, blogs, and webmail. The software also allows administrators to set up additional custom websites, each with its own domain name.

NOTE
The workgroup configuration is also aimed at providing web services, file sharing, and Jabber instant messaging services to Windows clients, although setting up non-Mac clients typically requires more manual configuration. Apple automates much of the client configuration for Mac OS X Snow Leopard users.

QuickTime Streaming Server, Podcast Producer, and print services

In workgroup configuration, Mac OS X Server offers neither support for managing QuickTime Streaming Server or Podcast Producer nor Xgrid services for distributed processing (which is primarily used in conjunction with Podcast Producer) within Server Preferences.

Workgroup configuration also provides no support for printer queues and quotas, but the system can host a simple shared printer attached via USB or FireWire, just as the desktop version of Mac OS X can and similar to the USB printer sharing available from an AirPort base station. In a typical workgroup scenario, the organization may also manage printer queues.

Client computer management

A server in workgroup configuration is also neither intended for use in managing and serving NetBoot and NetInstall disk images nor can it serve as a local Software Update Server. Managed client options are also unavailable without an upgrade to advanced configuration.

Moving away from a workgroup configuration

Although the workgroup configuration offers a server that's easy to set up and configure for departments that act as part of a larger organization, it doesn't allow administrators to touch any of the more advanced settings or even access many of the advertised features of Mac OS X.

Moving to standard configuration

If access to outside directory services isn't required, a workgroup configuration can be turned into a standard configuration by simply disconnecting the server from any external directory servers in the organization. This change can be undone later by simply reconnecting to a directory service.

To disconnect a workgroup configuration server from another directory server within the organization, follow these steps:

1. **Open Server Preferences and then click Accounts.**

2. **If the Accounts pane is locked, click the lock icon in the lower left and then authenticate by typing the local administrator account name and password.**

3. **Click Login Options and then click the Edit button next to Server Connection.**

4. **Select the directory to disconnect from and then click the Delete (–) button.** Once disconnected, automatic groups are no longer kept in sync with the external directory, and users may no longer be imported.

Upgrading to advanced configuration

A workgroup configuration server can also be upgraded to the advanced configuration by simply connecting to the system remotely from System Admin. The application warns that the server is making a permanent change to advanced configuration.

CAUTION
This step ends the innocence of the workgroup configuration and simple administration by using Server Preferences! There's no way to return the server back to the workgroup configuration without reinstalling the operating system or reverting to a previous backup.

After moving to the advanced configuration, administrators need to continue to use the Server Admin and Workgroup Manager tools to manage the server; attempting to revert to the simpler Server Preferences application may result in unintended consequences because it doesn't provide access to the more advanced settings made in the advanced administration tools.

Advanced Configuration

The Mac OS X Server advanced configuration does nothing to artificially limit the complexity administrators have to manage; instead, it trades the simplicity of Server Preferences for the sophistication of Server Admin. It's intended for anyone with needs outside of those addressed by the standard or workgroup configurations, whether a large organization or simply an individual user with specialized needs.

Although this configuration is more complex to manage, it also supports all the advanced features available in Mac OS X Server.

Advanced configuration gives the administrator full control over which services to activate and configure and allows multiple servers to be managed from a single console by using Server Admin, as shown in Figure 3.2.

Evaluating the capabilities of advanced configuration

Not surprisingly, an advanced configuration server offers the most flexibility in setting up directory services. It can maintain its own stand-alone directory server, serve as an Open Directory master, or be configured as an Open Directory replica.

An Open Directory master maintains the authoritative directory records for the domain, whereas a replica serves as a synchronized copy of those records. Other servers in an advanced or workgroup configuration can import users and groups from an advanced configuration server acting as the master or replica directory server for a larger organization. An advanced configuration server can also participate in an Active Directory Domain.

Administrators of an advanced configuration server create and manage user and group accounts within Workgroup Manager, as shown in Figure 3.3, instead of using the Server Preferences Users and Groups panes, which are used in the standard and workgroup configurations.

DNS and DHCP services

In an advanced configuration, core network services such as DNS and DHCP are managed by using Server Admin, which provides graphical tools for creating DNS zone and machine records as well as for creating and managing DHCP pools and leases. These features are available only to administrators working in the advanced configuration.

Figure 3.2

Server Admin exposes more complex options to users working within the advanced configuration.

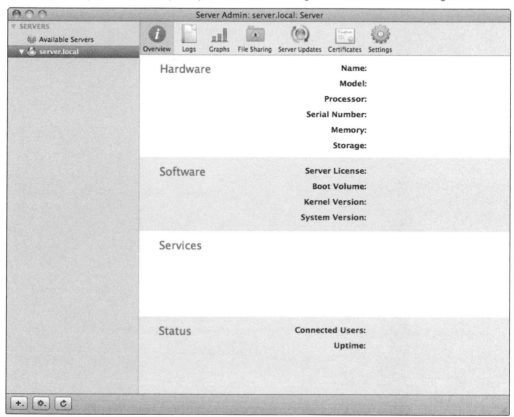

Network firewall, NAT, RADIUS, and VPN services

The advanced configuration also supplies management tools for managing more complex firewall configurations in Server Preferences, allowing the server to act as a dedicated network gateway. It also provides a more advanced graphical interface for configuring NAT used to map inside services, such as a public website hosted by the server, to an IP address that can be accessed by outside users.

Server Admin also supports configuring RADIUS authentication for managing access to a wireless network as well as more involved and customizable settings for configuring a VPN server to allow remote users to authenticate and establish a secure connection to access internal network services as if they were connected by a private network link rather than over the public Internet.

Figure 3.3

Workgroup Manager allows sophisticated management of users and groups and related settings within the advanced configuration.

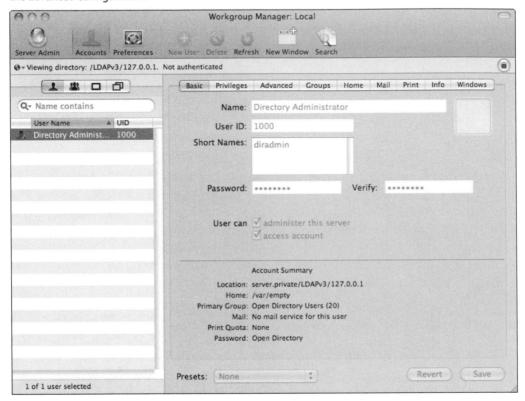

Advanced services

The advanced configuration also exposes more complexity in setting up shared user and group network folders as share points, with support for FTP or NFS file shares as well as the AFP (the Mac native file-sharing protocol) and SMB (used by Windows file sharing) protocols supported in standard and workgroup configurations.

An advanced configuration server can also support IP failover to enable a backup server to take over the IP address if the master server goes offline, ensuring high availability of network services, such as file sharing.

It can also be configured to support a shared RAID (redundant array of independent [or inexpensive] disks) unit providing an Xsan storage area network (SAN), which supplies a networked storage device (such as an Xserve RAID) as a locally attached volume but manages access to it so that multiple servers can access its file system concurrently without causing file corruption.

Although it can support users being able to target the server as a repository for their Time Machine backups, the advanced configuration doesn't set this service up automatically, as the standard and workgroup configurations do.

With the advanced configuration, administrators also have much more sophisticated control over how shared contacts and calendars, email, instant messaging, and web services supporting wikis and blogs are configured and customized to fit the needs of a given organization.

Web service configuration in Server Admin makes it straightforward to activate collaborative wikis, web calendars, blogs, and webmail and to set up additional custom websites — each with its own domain name — WebDAV realms, and CGI, SSI, and SSL configurations.

Users with needs for web application development and deployment will work in the advanced configuration, which supplies access to the nuts and bolts of Tomcat Java servlets and JSP, MySQL, PHP, and Ruby on Rails.

QuickTime Streaming Server, Podcast Producer, and print services

In advanced configuration, Mac OS X Server offers complete support for managing QuickTime Streaming Server for authenticated content delivery; Podcast Producer for managing the capture, production, and distribution of podcasts; and Xgrid services for distributed processing (which is primarily used in conjunction with Podcast Producer) within Server Admin and related server tools.

Advanced configuration also provides support for printer queues and quotas. An advanced configuration server isn't designed to host a simple shared printer attached via USB or FireWire, however, as the other configurations of Mac OS X Server, the desktop version of Mac OS X, and the USB printer sharing feature available on most AirPort base stations can.

Client computer management

A server in advanced configuration can also manage and serve NetBoot and NetInstall disk images for controlling the software used to boot client machines on the network. Other managed client options are also available in advanced configuration.

An advanced configuration server can also serve as a local Software Update Server, enabling the server to download and cache Apple software updates for efficient, managed distribution to network clients.

CROSS-REF

For more on NetBoot, see Chapter 34. For more on NetInstall, see Chapter 35. For more on Software Update Server, see Chapter 37.

Upgrading from standard and workgroup configurations

A standard or workgroup configuration server can be upgraded to the advanced configuration by simply connecting to the system remotely from System Admin. The application warns that the server is making a permanent change to advanced configuration.

CAUTION

This step ends the innocence of the standard or workgroup configuration and simple administration by using Server Preferences! There's no way to return the server back to the standard or workgroup configuration without reinstalling the operating system or reverting to a previous backup.

After moving to the advanced configuration, administrators need to continue to use the Server Admin and Workgroup Manager tools to manage the server; attempting to revert to the simpler Server Preferences application may result in unintended consequences because it doesn't provide access to the more advanced settings made in the advanced administration tools.

Summary

- Mac OS X Server defines three configurations designed to fit the needs of typical users: standard, workgroup, and advanced.

- Standard configuration offers simple configuration tools and a largely automated setup that doesn't require any existing network services to be operational on the network.

- Workgroup configuration allows groups within a department to integrate with existing services in their organization while retaining simple configuration tools for easy management of local services.

- Advanced configuration allows administrators full access to all features in Mac OS X Server but also requires more experience and advanced planning to manage that additional complexity.

- Configurations can be upgraded with little effort. However, moving to the advanced configuration is a permanent decision that can't be undone later to return to a simplified standard or workgroup configuration without complete reinstallation or reverting to a previous backup.

Evaluating Hardware Requirements

The decision to use Mac OS X Snow Leopard Server is also a decision to use Apple's hardware. The requirements for Snow Leopard Server also limit it to running on modern machines.

That limits certain applications of Mac OS X Snow Leopard Server, as it's not designed or licensed to run on do-it-yourself hobby servers or any of the older Apple servers or generic PC equipment you may already have on hand.

However, if you're interested in Apple's server operating system, tight hardware and software integration is probably a primary consideration. You're also less likely to be looking for an Erector Set solution that requires lots of your own resources to finish the missing integration links.

That makes evaluating hardware needs a lot easier; you're simply unable to get Snow Leopard Server running on outdated server equipment that isn't capable of working properly. The flip side: The hardware you buy to run it is modern and reliable.

Snow Leopard Server's new 64-bit kernel enables you to run your services on top of a system that can take full advantage of existing hardware capable of using up to 32 GB of RAM today and accommodate even more RAM in the future.

It's also possible to run Snow Leopard Server on consumer machines such as the iMac and Mac mini, although you probably want to reserve those efforts for testing purposes rather than use them for full deployment in a production environment because the hardware you use to deploy your servers has a big impact on the performance and reliability of the services you can provide your users.

With Mac OS X Server, you save so much in server software licensing fees in comparison to Windows Server, particularly with regard to CALs for all your clients, that you effectively have a fantastically higher hardware budget to use in delivering top performance for your clients.

This chapter introduces a series of hardware-related considerations you need to make in drafting plans to run Snow Leopard Server, explains what's involved in planning for the number of servers you need, and presents subjects to consider when planning your storage strategy and in building out your servers' network.

In This Chapter

Evaluating server hardware needs

Planning server and network data storage

Network performance requirements

Evaluating Server Hardware Needs

The process of evaluating your server needs is a classic example of the project triangle in engineering: a balance between fast, good, and cheap — where you can pick any two:

- **Fast.** Planning and building out your server deployment in a short time period
- **Good.** Developing a high-quality plan that's ideally executed
- **Cheap.** Rolling out a project on an efficient budget

On the software side, Apple has already invested lots of time and money into Mac OS X Server to deliver a high-quality product. That makes your hardware plans a bit easier because you won't need to be coordinating your hardware deployment decisions to work with a package of software that isn't ready for prime time, isn't engineered to be of very good quality, or is so expensive that it blows your budget.

However, your hardware plans are constrained by the fact that Apple licenses Mac OS X Server to run only on its own hardware. Additionally, Snow Leopard Server runs only on modern Intel-based Macs, which narrows the scope of hardware to Macs introduced since 2006.

In the server realm, that includes:

- Xserve systems with Intel Xeon Woodcrest CPUs sold since August 2006
- Mac Pro systems with Intel Xeon Woodcrest CPUs sold since August 2006
- Xserve systems with Intel Xeon Harpertown CPUs sold since January 2008
- Mac Pro systems with Intel Xeon Harpertown CPUs sold since January 2008
- Xserve systems with Intel Xeon Nehalem CPUs sold since April 2009
- Mac Pro systems with Intel Xeon Nehalem CPUs sold since April 2009

Other Mac hardware is also capable of running Mac OS X Server, although Apple doesn't bundle its server operating system on its consumer hardware offerings. The retail version of Mac OS X Snow Leopard can be purchased to run on modern Intel desktops, including:

- 32-bit iMac systems with Intel Core Duo CPUs sold since January 2006
- 32-bit Mac mini systems with Intel Core Solo or Duo CPUs sold since February 2006
- 64-bit iMac systems with Intel Core 2 Duo CPUs sold since September 2006
- 64-bit Mac mini systems with Intel Core 2 Duo CPUs sold since August 2007

Although it's technically possible to install Mac OS X Server on Intel-based Mac notebooks, such as the MacBook and MacBook Pro lines, it doesn't make sense to do so apart from testing purposes. Mobile machines are designed for portability, with a thermal envelope and light-duty components that aren't intended to be used for always-on server duties.

This effectively leaves a few different options for Mac OS X Server users:

- **Xserve rack-mounted systems scale from a single department or small-office server installed alongside network and telephone equipment to large installations of systems in a data center.** Xserve comes bundled with Mac OS X Server, a $500 value. Xserves currently offer two quad core processors, up to 32 GB of installed RAM, and three full-sized drive bays for up to 3 TB of internal data storage.

- **Mac Pro stand-alone systems offer installation-free server applications for small and medium-sized businesses that lack the need for compact mounting of their server equipment in racks.** Using Mac Pro as a server requires a separate purchase of Mac OS X Server, although the software is now just $500 for an unlimited client license. Mac Pros currently offer two quad core processors, up to 32 GB of installed RAM, and four full-sized drive bays for up to 4 TB of internal data storage.

- **iMac systems could be used as a simple department server but offer poor value in a server because of the large, high-quality screen that's unnecessary for a server.** Current iMacs are also limited to 8 GB of installed RAM and have only a single internal drive.

- **Mac mini systems may make sense for compact home or small department uses and can be installed in tight spaces or even stacked in a small array.** However, the Mac mini is limited to 4 GB of installed RAM and uses a light-duty, notebook-sized hard drive, making it more appropriate for testing purposes than always-on production server roles.

Apple's minimum requirements for running Snow Leopard Server are quite low, specifying only an Intel processor and 2 GB of RAM. In general, you should install as much RAM as you can afford to install.

Buying high-quality aftermarket RAM from a reputable vendor is much cheaper than buying it directly from Apple. However, you should stick to top name brands and research the recommendations of other users before buying because faulty or problematic RAM can result in difficult-to-isolate problems down the road.

CROSS-REF
For more on integrating Mac OS X Server with an existing infrastructure, see Chapter 5.

Planning for essential hardware requirements

With the line in the sand drawn at Intel Macs, your plans to move to Snow Leopard Server might likely require a hardware purchase because existing PowerPC servers can't be upgraded. However, instead of orienting your plans around Snow Leopard Server, you should consider your existing server resources and then determine how well they meet your current needs:

- Are your existing servers performing existing tasks adequately?
- Do users and network services have access to adequate storage?
- Is your current network fast enough to support your existing needs?

If your current systems aren't adequate, you might base your plans around a wholesale replacement. If they are meeting your existing needs, you might instead consider simply augmenting your current systems with a new server to handle new features.

Next, consider what maintenance improvements you need to make simply to continue to deliver the same level of services to your users with your existing infrastructure:

- To accommodate user growth, what new server hardware, RAM, or storage resources are required to maintain existing services?
- To meet basic security requirements, what updates and upgrades are needed?
- To maintain vendor support, what updates and changes do you need to make?

Although your existing servers may meet your current needs, they may also require so much extra investment over the next few years that a new overall plan using modern equipment might be more efficient and less expensive over the long haul.

For example, you may currently be doing fine operating software that has been deprecated by its vendor, such as:

- A Microsoft shop running Services for Macintosh to support Mac users
- A Microsoft shop operating NT domains to authenticate its Windows users
- An AppleShare IP server to support Mac users
- Macintosh Manager to support client machines
- A Mac OS X Server directory domain by using NetInfo

Each of those scenarios could spend significant resources maintaining support for obsolete server configurations, which lack any remaining avenues of support from the original vendors. Mac OS X Snow Leopard Server can be used to replace all those systems at a fixed cost and to support all their features with modern equivalents that are all fully supported by the vendor.

CROSS-REF

For more on providing services for Windows users, see Chapter 2. For more on Open Directory domain services, see Chapter 21.

Now, consider what new services you want to offer your users:

- Do you need to support interoperability for users on different platforms?
- Do you have mobile users who need support for push messaging, collaboration tools, and secure remote access features?
- Do you need better management options for your client systems?
- Do you want to provide diskless network booting to manage classrooms?
- Do you need to integrate with external directory servers?

- Do you want to provide centralized 802.1x authentication for wireless access points?
- Do you need to offer SSO authentication services?

Depending on your answers, your circumstances might lead you to Snow Leopard Server to provide a solution by:

- Replacing your entire system with a new, centralized directory service and integrated support for advanced services to support a cross-platform user base of Mac, Unix, and Windows users
- Adding of a single server to handle manageable localized services for a workgroup
- Using a single server deployment to make a specific service available to a large number of users in your organization, such as support for push messaging and Mobile Access for iPhone mobile users or serving new web collaboration features for wikis, blogs, and group calendaring

Your plans can begin small by using a single server to fit into your organization's existing services and to potentially take advantage of such existing services as:

- Existing core network services, such as DNS, DHCP, and LDAP or Active Directory for authentication and directory services
- Other existing services already supplied by your company or ISP, such as local mail delivery or SMTP service, wireless authentication, VPN access, and proxy services
- Existing NFS, SMB, or AFP file-sharing services to host your new server's home directories for Mac or Windows users

This strategy can be used to leverage the services your organization already handles, enabling a new workgroup server to focus its resources on adding unique value.

Used only for file sharing, print, email, calendar, contact-sharing, and web collaboration services, a new workgroup server using Snow Leopard Server costs a fraction of the price of a comparable server running Windows Server, particularly because CALs add up past a few users.

Building to scale for future needs

Although you can get started, for less than $3,000, with a single server that's equipped to handle the basic initial needs of a small company, you want to operate with a plan that accounts for growth and future needs.

As your needs scale up, a single server can be upgraded with more storage and RAM to handle more tasks concurrently. Adding RAM is a particularly easy way to make your server operate more efficiently. However, there are more effective and successful ways to plan for growth than simply throwing all your resources at a central server.

Growing upward using a central server results in a single point of failure. In many cases, you can accomplish more with less by planning to build out an integrated network of servers that spreads services around to provide resilience to outages and that maximizes response times for clients.

An analysis of the current load of the services running on your server, users' demands on your server, and a look at where and how users access your services can assist you in making plans that:

- Isolate high-demand services on high-performance servers, such as running directory services, mail services, and file-sharing services on separate servers to balance the load on each

- Move services closer to your users, such as setting up Open Directory Replicas to provide high availability and rapid access to directory services for users working at different sites in your organization

- Configure services to support failover, allowing services to survive a significant hardware problem by promoting a hot spare server to take the place of the server that stopped working

- Accommodate growth by making plans, for example, to host user folders by using a storage strategy that can handle projected needs for some time in order to prevent having to rethink how to handle user data and be forced to update lots of user records and share point settings because of inadequate initial plans

- Virtualize services by running multiple instances of different operating systems on the same hardware to pool secondary services and conserve hardware deployment

Additionally, your future plans should include:

- How to scale up intelligently as users' needs for storage and networking capacity increase

- How to manage and shape growth by using quotas and managed preferences to prevent having to accommodate unnecessary demands for storage and network use

The next two sections focus on planning for growth in storage and in network capacity, but first, consider the variety of ways Snow Leopard Server can help to prevent demands for data storage and network capacity from growing out of hand:

- Quotas can be imposed on users' home folders and mailboxes to force users to manage their documents and messages on a regular basis before they can grow into unmanageable messes that require hours of work to resolve. Once storage gets out of hand, the easiest solution is to pay for more storage, which only encourages slack management of your existing resources. In turn, that results in either needing more storage sooner than originally anticipated or simply having to shovel around lots of garbage data that slows down your backups and complicates disaster recovery.

- Virtual share points enable users who work on both Mac and Windows systems to use the same network home folder.

- Portable Home Directories can be used to minimize mobile users' demands on the network by providing them with a locally cached copy of their network home folder. Contents are efficiently kept in sync with the network on the schedule you define.

- Managed preferences can be imposed on Mac OS X users, groups, and computers to shape how systems behave, automate cleanup, such as configuring the deletion of unused home directories on client machines, and enforce policy related to operations, such as backups.

CROSS-REF

For more on working with quotas, share points, and home directories, see Chapter 9. For more on managed preferences, see Chapter 36.

Planning Server and Network Data Storage

Your server itself will have several data stores that each requires a storage strategy, a growth strategy, and regular management and assessment, including:

- **Mail data stores for user mailboxes.** The original data store is created by default on the server's boot volume, but you eventually need to define appropriate additional stores as users' mailboxes fill up and as the server's use pattern changes and new services are initiated. If you deploy clustered email services, you need a shared storage solution for your cluster servers to use.

- **Wiki collaboration data stores for version-controlled wiki sites and blogs.** The original data store is created by default on the server's boot volume, but you eventually need to define appropriate additional stores as users create new wikis and upload documents.

- **Address Book Server and iCal Server data stores for contact and calendar server content.** The original data stores are created by default on the server's boot volume, but you eventually need to define appropriate additional stores, particularly for calendar services that allow file uploads of users' documents.

- **LDAP data stores for directory service records.** The original data store is created by default on the server's boot volume. Although you can't customize the location of the LDAP store in Server Admin, growth in the use of directory services may require that other services be moved to different servers.

- **Websites and file service share points are all created by default on the server's boot volume.** But you eventually need to define appropriate additional stores as users' needs for publishing and sharing data increase.

- **Time Machine Server can gobble up huge amounts of disk storage as users copy the contents of their local hard drives to the server for easy-to-recover backups.** Deciding where to put all this requires advanced planning.

- **NetBoot and NetInstall images served to client machines over the network can quickly eat up the internal storage available on a server.**
- **Streaming video and content captured with Podcast Producer can quickly add up and overwhelm the internal storage of a basic server.**

CROSS-REF

For more on configuring advanced services and managing client machines, see Chapters 22–38.

Evaluating storage needs

For a workgroup server, the 3 to 4 TB of internal disk space available in today's Xserve and Mac Pro systems might seem like a lot of storage. In fact, it might sound like overkill. If you're serving 100 users with basic workgroup services, that's nearly 40 GB of space per user.

If you're providing only 2 GB for mail, 10 GB for file sharing, and basic calendaring and web collaboration, you could easily serve 100 users with half that. However, if you're venturing into heavier data uses, such as allowing Time Machine Server backups, storing projects that compound daily with new revisions, or serving up video, your initial server will run out of space quickly.

Other aspects of storage needs to consider are backups and redundancy. If your users are taking up 1 TB of data, you should plan to have a hot spare of that data as well as an offsite backup. You might also need to keep incremental backups of their data to cover for losses that occurred weeks ago but were discovered only just recently. By themselves, those three types of backups more than triple your effective storage needs.

Additionally, you may want to apply redundancy to make your drives more resilient to errors or to speed performance. RAID storage, as noted shortly, can again more than double your storage needs.

When buying internal storage for your server, consider opting for the largest drives you can afford rather than filling up your bays with lower-capacity disks. This provides you with the most bang for your buy and reduces the number of times you need to wastefully throw out hardware or look for opportunities to recycle it as you upgrade.

When buying external storage, consider RAID appliances that provide for growth, both in terms of storage as well as the throughput of their internal drive interface and their local interface with the server.

Determining the most appropriate storage technology

When planning for capacity, it's important to ensure that the amount and type of storage you select serves not only your immediate needs but also your near-term growth requirements. It also needs to be able to scale with your long-term requirements.

If your chosen storage solution can't keep up with your needs for growth, you may likely find yourself needing to replace it, at considerable expense, rather than being able to grow along with it. The need to start over and develop a new storage plan after implementing your file-sharing system will likely end up costing more than if you had slightly overbuilt your system but ended up with a foundation that supported future growth.

Using RAID storage

One aspect of storage planning related to a disk-intensive activity, such as file sharing, involves RAID, a technology that allows administrators to configure specialized volumes that do one of the following:

- Span multiple drives to deliver cost-effective storage by avoiding the need to use the most expensive, largest-capacity drives currently in production
- Stripe data across multiple drives to deliver top disk performance while avoiding the need to use the most expensive, fastest drives currently in production
- Duplicate redundant data across multiple disks to deliver more reliability than the most expensive drives can promise
- Combine these aspects of storage size, performance, and high availability as needed

Snow Leopard enables you to create software RAID volumes by using Disk Utility. However, a software RAID offers limitations both in performance and in reliability through redundancy because the operating system is forced to handle the work of managing RAID disks.

For more serious needs in storage performance and resiliency, investigate the use of freestanding RAID arrays that operate as a direct-attached storage (DAS) or as a storage area network (SAN). These hardware RAIDs can provide far better performance and much more sophisticated protection from disk errors or drive failure than a software-based solution can.

Storage types

Another aspect of storage planning relates to the technologies used to connect the server to the storage device. The names of these technologies are often used incorrectly, even in Apple's server documentation, but the terminology used is less important than understanding how each works and recognizing what advantages and drawbacks each has:

- **Direct-attached storage (DAS).** This refers to volumes connected as local devices via direct local interfaces, such as internal SATA or Serial Attached SCSI (SAS) drives or external SCSI, USB, or FireWire devices. A DAS volume may be either a freestanding drive or a JBOD (just a bunch of disks) or a RAID unit exposing itself as a DAS volume with a SCSI, FireWire, or USB interface.
- **Network-attached storage (NAS).** This refers to a network volume served by a freestanding appliance server, often containing a RAID array or simply a collection of drives. A NAS unit serves its volumes to network clients by using a network file system such as NFS or SMB (CIFS), although some also support AFP. Regardless of the network file system used, a NAS device always appears to be a network share to client computers (such as your server).

- **Storage area network (SAN).** This refers to a storage device, typically a RAID array, that connects to servers or workstations by using a specialized network interface, often Fibre Channel or iSCSI. However, instead of appearing as a network share, the device appears to be a locally attached disk volume. In other words, SAN clients have block-level access to the SAN device rather than file-level access, as they would with a NAS. Multiple clients can connect to a single SAN over the same storage network, but because each system connects as if it were a locally attached drive, the SAN needs special management software to prevent the connected systems from overwriting each other's data. Apple markets its Xsan clustered file system for use with SAN devices.

To configure Mac OS X's mail service in a cluster configuration, you need to provision a SAN so that all your node servers can access the same mail store. Podcast Producer can also take advantage of the scalable, high-availability, high-performance storage a SAN provides.

Service availability

In addition to planning adequate disk capacity, your storage strategy also needs to accommodate service availability.

Many of the services you provide to network users are dependent on access to core network services, such as DNS, file shares, and directory services; if any of those services fall offline because of storage failure, users lose the ability to successfully log in, connect to their home folders, or find other services on the network.

This makes high availability a particularly critical part of your storage plans. Planning for high availability involves:

- Spreading out the server workload so an unanticipated hardware failure has an impact only on a limited number of users or a specific service. This avoids inadvertently setting up a single point of failure that can bring down your entire network.

- Incorporating fail-resistant redundancy measures by using RAID to accommodate drive failure, a UPS (Uninterruptible Power Supply) and backup power source to accommodate power failures, and redundant cooling systems and power supplies to enable systems to continue working even after a component stops.

- Maintaining an appropriate server environment where server components are less likely to fail or to be destroyed by accident. This includes enforcing secured access and keeping the area clean and dry with adequate climate control for both temperature and humidity levels and appropriate cable management.

- Planning for IP failover so a replacement server is available and ready to take over a failed system's roles, helping to mitigate any hardware failures that do occur.

Network Performance Requirements

Although the server's processing specifications, RAM, and storage speed and capacity are primary aspects of the performance that users experience, those factors simply don't matter if your network can't adequately deliver data fast enough.

The resources you allocate to servers should be balanced with the resources you invest in your network capacity and reliability.

Macs have sported Gigabit Ethernet ports since the turn of the decade. If you don't yet provide Gigabit Ethernet to your clients, there's little remaining reason to hold out.

Upgrading your network benefits every service you provide. Conversely, trying to roll out new services running on fast servers while operating a 100 Mb Fast Ethernet network is a poor use of funds.

Planning network needs for basic services

A variety of services unique to Apple are designed to take full advantage of fast networks. Among them are:

- **Podcast Producer.** This is designed to capture and deliver video streams that may be as large as 26 GB for a 2-hour video. Over Gigabit Ethernet, delivering that content in ideal circumstances takes about 3.5 minutes. Over 100 Mb Ethernet, that same video takes at least 35 minutes in ideal conditions.

- **NetBoot.** This starts clients using a boot image over the network. The number of clients that can start over a network falls dramatically if the network isn't operating at top speed.

- **NetInstall.** This is used to push updated disk images to clients' machines over the network. The number of clients that can be updated over a network falls dramatically if the network isn't operating at top speed.

- **Time Machine Server.** This works adequately over Gigabit Ethernet but isn't so useful if the network is only one-tenth as fast.

- **Network home folders.** These are fine over Gigabit Ethernet but can be unusable over slower networks.

- **File sharing and web collaboration services.** These go from basically functional to dramatically more productive when the network is operating fast enough to support instant results.

Ironically, Apple has also pioneered the use of Wi-Fi wireless networking, which, although convenient, is dramatically slower than even the most basic wired networking that was being rolled out ten years ago.

Wireless networking enables mobile users so much more freedom that you've probably already incorporated support for it. By incorporating support for the latest, fastest protocols, you can give users the best experience while still supporting mobility.

Dual-band wireless networks can supply 802.11b/g support to slower devices, such as iPhones and older equipment, while providing 802.11n support to modern notebook users. Using the 5 GHz band, you can support wide channel support that ups the theoretical maximum speed to 350 Mbps.

Security for wireless networks is also critical because it effectively gives anyone the ability to physically plug into your network. Using the RADIUS authentication service in Snow Leopard Server, you can provide industry standard 802.1x authentication and securely authorize wireless network access to your directory domain users.

Building to scale for future needs

Modern Mac server hardware supports link aggregation in software on Mac OS X Server. This allows you to connect multiple Ethernet interfaces to a switch advertised as supporting 802.3ad or LACP (Link Aggregate Control Protocol).

The individual connections are aggregated to provide twice the theoretical bandwidth. This means the switch sends requests addressed to the server over any of the aggregated links, enabling the server to establish two or even four times the connections it could with only one link. It doesn't make the pipe bigger but rather gives the server multiple links for accepting requests from concurrent clients at full speed.

Link aggregation also allows for resiliency from network interface card or port failure or cabling issues because the loss of one interrupted link can be survived by the alternative link to maintain availability of the server on the network.

Although typically thought of as a storage solution, SAN can link together client systems with fast access to shared data or link servers together for high performance and high availability in clustered mail or calendar services or for distributing encoding tasks among many users with Podcast Producer.

If standard file sharing over Gigabit Ethernet doesn't deliver the results your users need, consider setting up a Fibre Channel switch to allow them direct access to SAN storage at 4 GB/s speeds.

At under $1,000, Apple's Xsan cluster file system delivers a much less expensive SAN solution than is available elsewhere.

Summary

- Mac OS X Snow Leopard Server works exclusively on Intel Macs, dramatically narrowing your hardware deployment options to modern hardware built since 2006.
- When planning Snow Leopard Server deployments, consider the features you need and whether your existing server resources can be used to support those features or whether it makes more sense to entirely replace your existing services.
- In planning for growth, consider that multiple servers can be used to deliver services that will provide greater scalability and availability than one massively overbuilt server.

- In evaluating storage needs, don't forget to consider your needs for hot spare backups and/or the benefits of using RAID for data resiliency and performance.

- You can plan for future growth by keeping your network up to speed with your server resources.

- Link aggregation can be used to increase the number of concurrent client connections your server can support.

- With a storage area network, you can set up clustering in mail or calendar servers or support fast access to shared data among clients with high-performance needs.

Integrating with the Existing Server Infrastructure

M ac OS X Snow Leopard Server incrementally builds on Leopard Server, adding some entirely new services while refining existing ones and bolstering its core operating system foundation.

This makes upgrading from Leopard Server relatively simple and straightforward. However, there are some changes that have an impact on migration, including the move to the new Dovecot mail service for POP and IMAP and the new 64-bit kernel, which requires 64-bit drivers for printers and any specialized hardware.

Any application plug-ins you use, including third-party panes in System Preferences, also need to be upgraded to support the 64-bit version of System Preferences that ships with Snow Leopard Server.

If you're planning to migrate from earlier versions of Mac OS X Server, there are more significant changes you need to accommodate depending on the version of Mac OS X Server you're currently using.

You may also be migrating services from Windows Server or moving your entire domain controller infrastructure from the now-obsolete Windows NT to be handled by Mac OS X Server's Open Directory support for hosting Windows domains.

This enables Windows clients to log in locally by using a network domain account as well as to access a network home directory and roaming profile.

Windows clients as well as Unix and Linux users can also benefit from Snow Leopard Server's easy-to-use web collaboration tools, including version-controlled wikis, blogs, and web calendaring.

This chapter outlines what's involved in moving from your existing server to the new Mac OS X Snow Leopard Server, what's involved in planning for your transition, and the steps required to move to your new server.

In This Chapter

Upgrading from Mac OS X Leopard Server

Migrating from previous versions of Mac OS X Server

Migrating from Windows Server

Integrating with existing network services

Upgrading from Mac OS X Leopard Server

If you currently use Leopard Server, upgrading to Snow Leopard is designed to be painless and easy. However, you need to meet the minimum requirements for Snow Leopard Server, which demands an Intel-based Mac.

If you currently operate PowerPC servers, you need to decide whether to continue to use a mix of servers running different versions or to move to new, Intel-based server hardware, which conveniently also includes a free upgrade to Snow Leopard Server.

In addition to the new hardware requirement on the server side, Snow Leopard Server also requires the use of new Server Admin tools that run only on Snow Leopard.

Like Snow Leopard itself, the new server tools are Intel only, which requires an upgrade to any administrative workstations you use that are still running on PowerPC Macs. If you're already running Intel hardware, the upgrade to Snow Leopard on the desktop end is only $29.

Mac OS X Snow Leopard Server's 64-bit kernel

As with Leopard Server, services in Snow Leopard Server run as 64-bit processes. New in Snow Leopard Server is support for running a 64-bit kernel. On supported hardware, you can boot your server into the 64-bit kernel by:

- Pressing and holding the 6 and 4 keys while starting up
- Setting `arch=x86_64` in the server's NVRAM boot-args by using the `nvram` command

When running with a 64-bit kernel, the `uname -v` command reports `RELEASE_X86_64`.

For compatibility reasons related to 32-bit kernel extensions, such as the ability to use existing drivers for various peripherals, including printers, you may want to boot Snow Leopard Server using the 32-bit kernel by:

- Pressing and holding 3 and 2 keys while starting up
- Setting `arch=i386` in the server's NVRAM boot-args by using the `nvram` command

When running with a 32-bit kernel, the `uname -v` command reports `RELEASE_I386`.

Changes in Mac OS X Snow Leopard Server software

Apart from the hardware-related changes, Table 5.1 shows a variety of software changes in Snow Leopard Server that will have an impact on your upgrade process.

Table 5.1 Software Changes in Snow Leopard Server

New Software Services	Deprecated Services
A new Address Book Server for shared contacts	Apache Axis and WebObjects no longer included for web application deployment
An enhanced iCal Server 2	Apache 1.4 and PHP 4 no longer supported
New mail services based on Dovecot	AppleTalk Printer Access Protocol no longer supported for sharing printers
A new Push Notification Server	
New Mobile Access services	
Improved web collaboration services with support for the iPhone	
An enhanced Podcast Producer 2	

Planning server upgrades

During the upgrade process, Snow Leopard Server should directly import data and service configuration used in Leopard Server.

Prior to updating, however, you should:

- Make a bootable full backup of your server in case you discover a reason to back out of the upgrade process.
- Back up your current service configuration settings by using Server Admin. From the Server menu, choose Export ➪ Service Settings.
- Archive your Open Directory master by using the archive page of the Open Directory pane of Server Admin.
- Make note of your existing CUPS printer queue names and IDs, and back up a copy of your print settings by using the command `serveradmin settings print`.

CROSS-REF
For more on Server Admin, see Chapter 9. For more on print services, see Chapter 31.

The Snow Leopard Server updater is designed to migrate your existing server settings and data for you, including the migration of mail from Cyrus, used in Leopard Server, to the new Dovecot.

Existing websites configured to use Apache 1.4 and/or PHP 4 must be upgraded to use Apache 2.2 and PHP 5. New sites configured under Leopard Server should use Apache 2.2 by default. When you upgrade, verify that any special Apache modules you use are available in a version compatible with Apache 2.

When upgrading Open Directory domain servers:

- **Upgrade your Open Directory master first.** During the upgrade, you can direct users to your replicas by specifying their locations as LDAP servers in DHCP.
- **Upgrade your Open Directory replicas.**
- **Reconnect your replicas to your master.**

CROSS-REF
For more on configuring Open Directory servers, see Chapter 21.

After an upgrade installation, the Server Assistant takes you through the server's current configuration, allowing you to make any changes as needed.

CROSS-REF
For more on the installation process, see Chapter 6.

Migrating from Previous Versions of Mac OS X Server

Data and service configuration used in versions of Mac OS X earlier than Leopard Server, including Tiger Server 10.4 and Panther Server 10.3, won't upgrade in place for any PowerPC Macs because of the lack of support for Snow Leopard's hardware requirements.

You can import data by using the Migration Assistant in Snow Leopard Server during the upgrade process or you can set up your new server manually and then import users and groups and service configuration data as needed after the initial clean install.

Mac OS X Jaguar Server 10.2 also requires manual migration of data. NetBoot and NetInstall images created in Jaguar Server 10.2 can't be used in Snow Leopard.

During migration, you should:

- Retain your server as a bootable full backup in case you discover a reason to back out of the migration process and reinstate your previous services.
- Archive your LDAP Open Directory master by using the archive page of the Open Directory pane of Server Admin for import.
- Make note of your existing CUPS printer queue names and IDs, and back up a copy of your print settings by using the command `serveradmin settings print`.

Earlier versions of Mac OS X Server may be configured to use one or more services that have been removed from Snow Leopard Server:

- **A variety of process management services have been replaced by** `launchd` **starting with Leopard Server, including** `watchdog` **and** `hwmond`**.** Use the Energy Saver pane in System Preferences to re-enable automatic hardware restart after a power failure. And settings services you've added to `/etc/watchdog.conf` must be replaced with a `launchd plist` file. Install it into `/System/Library/LaunchDaemons/` instead. Use of `launchd` is documented on its man page.

- **NetInfo directory services must be converted to LDAP for use in Snow Leopard Server.** You can export users for manual import or use Server Admin in Tiger Server 10.4 to perform NetInfo Migration from the Protocols pane of the Open Directory pane's Settings page.

- **Nested user groups and computer groups are new since Leopard Server.** Previous versions used basic groups and computer lists that couldn't accommodate other groups within them. These can be upgraded after import by using Workgroup Manager.

- **Macintosh Manager hasn't been supported since Tiger Server.**

- **QuickTime Streaming Server Publisher hasn't been supported since Tiger Server.**

Migrating from Windows Server

There are several compelling reasons to migrate from Windows Server to Mac OS X Snow Leopard Server, but none are quite as compelling as the huge savings in software fees that can amount to tens of thousands of dollars per server once you count the costs of buying the required CALs needed for as few as a hundred different users.

Migration from Windows Server is easy given Snow Leopard Server's ability to speak the same protocols Windows servers and clients use and its ability to import information from Windows Servers, including:

- User and group accounts
- Computer account records for machines that are members of the Windows domain
- Windows users' existing login scripts
- Windows users' existing home directory folders and documents
- Windows users' existing roaming profiles

Planning to migrate services to Snow Leopard Server

If you currently operate a legacy network of Windows PCs using an NT-style domain, you can migrate to a Snow Leopard Server acting as an Open Directory master. Migrated users can:

- Authenticate and log in to the new domain by using their existing usernames, passwords, and computer accounts
- Use roaming profiles hosted by the new server or any Domain Member
- Use network home directories hosted by the new server or any Domain Member
- Retain existing group memberships
- Access shared network folders hosted by Mac OS X Server by using native SMB Windows file sharing
- Use print queues configured on Mac OS X Server
- Use WINS (Windows Internet Naming Service) browsing and Bonjour to discover network resources, such as file shares and printers
- Connect to the network remotely by using PPTP or L2TP VPN access
- Use standard WPA2 802.1x authentication for Wi-Fi networks
- Access mail, instant messaging, calendar and contact-sharing services, and web collaboration features hosted by Mac OS X Server

Steps involved include:

- Configuring your Mac OS X Server to act as a Primary Domain Controller
- Migrating users, groups, and computers to the new server
- Provisioning home directories and roaming user profiles for users
- Migrating Windows file service documents
- Configuring Windows access to print services

Windows domain migration to Snow Leopard Server

Through integrated support of the Samba 3 open-source package, Mac OS X Server can host an NT domain for Windows users and provide them with domain login and authentication services, including Windows file and print services, hosted user profiles, and home directories.

Mac OS X Server uses the same network-visible Open Directory domain to support Windows users as it does to support its own Mac-native directory services, so accounts created in Workgroup Manager can be used for logging in to both Macs and Windows PCs.

By default, users' home folders are set up to be the same location on both platforms, making it easier for users who work across platforms to work with the same documents.

Acting as a Primary Domain Controller

In preparation to being configured to serve Windows clients as a domain controller, Mac OS X Server may be configured as:

- **An Open Directory Standalone Directory Server configured as a Standalone Server in the SMB service.** This doesn't provide a network-visible directory domain or an NT domain; it only maintains local accounts for use on the server. This enables Windows users to access file and print services on the server, but they can't authenticate to log in to a Windows domain. The server can't host user profiles or home folders either. Promoting a Standalone Directory Server to an Open Directory master enables you to promote the server from a Standalone Server to a Primary Domain Controller within the SMB service.

- **An Open Directory Standalone Directory Server configured as a Domain Member in the SMB service.** This doesn't provide a network-visible directory domain or NT domain; it only maintains local accounts for use on the server. However, as a Domain Member, the server is connected to another server acting as a Primary Domain Controller, enabling Mac OS X Server to host user profiles and home folders for users authenticated by the Primary Domain Controller, in addition to providing basic Windows file and print services. Promoting a Standalone Directory Server to an Open Directory master enables you to also promote the server from a Domain Member to a Primary Domain Controller within the SMB service. However, an NT domain can have only one Primary Domain Controller, so the server also needs to create a new NT domain.

- **An existing Open Directory master configured as a Standalone Server in the SMB service.** This can be upgraded to a Primary Domain Controller.

- **An existing Open Directory master configured as a Domain Member in the SMB service.** This can be upgraded to a Primary Domain Controller. However, an NT domain can have only one Primary Domain Controller, so the server also needs to create a new NT domain.

- **An existing Open Directory replica configured as a Standalone Server or Domain Member in the SMB service.** This can't be upgraded to a Primary Domain Controller but can be designated as a Backup Domain Controller.

To act as a Primary Domain Controller, Mac OS X Server must be configured as an Open Directory master.

To determine the configured role of a server in Server Admin, follow these steps:

1. Launch Server Admin and then connect to the desired server.

2. Click Open Directory and then click Settings on the toolbar.

3. Click the General tab, shown in Figure 5.1.

Figure 5.1

Open Directory configuration in Server Admin

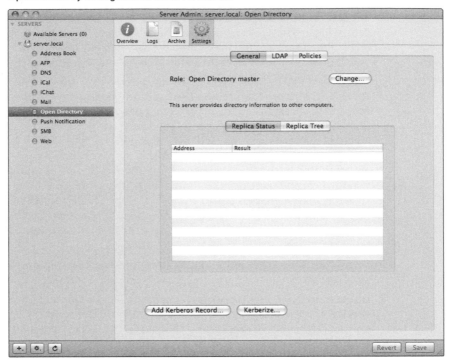

4. **View the designated Role:**

- If the server is currently a Standalone Directory Server, you must promote it to an Open Directory master prior to configuring it as a Primary Domain Controller.

- If the server is currently an Open Directory master, you can set it up to serve as a Primary Domain Controller from the SMB service.

- If the server is currently an Open Directory replica or relay, it can't act as a Primary Domain Controller but can be configured as a Backup Domain Controller.

To promote a server to a Primary Domain Controller in Server Admin, follow these steps:

1. **Launch Server Admin and then connect to the desired server.**

2. **Click SMB and then click Settings on the toolbar.**

3. **Click the General tab, shown in Figure 5.2.**

Figure 5.2

SMB configuration in Server Admin

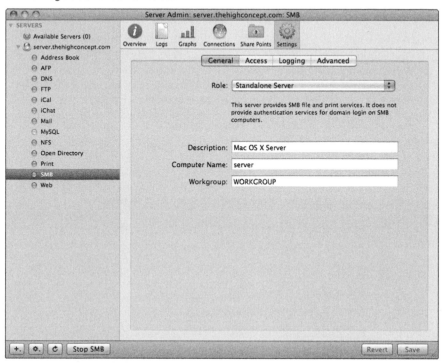

4. **Choose the designated server Role by using the pop-up menu:**

   - A Standalone Server can be promoted to a Primary Domain Controller, creating a new NT domain.
   - A Domain Member can be promoted to a Primary Domain Controller, creating a new NT domain.

5. **Choose Primary Domain Controller.**

6. **Type the domain information for the new Primary Domain Controller:**

   - **Description.** This is visible to Windows clients.
   - **Computer Name.** This is the NetBIOS name of the server. It can't contain more than 15 characters or any special characters or punctuation.
   - **Workgroup.** This is the new NT domain you're creating. It can't contain more than 15 characters, can't be WORKGROUP, and can't be the same as any existing NT domain on the network.

7. **Click Save.** You're prompted to type a directory administrator account. You can't use a regular local administrator account to set up a Primary Domain Controller.

CROSS-REF

For more on working with Open Directory, see Chapter 21. For more on configuring the SMB service, see Chapter 22.

Migrating users, groups, and computers to the new server

Once configured as a Primary Domain Controller, Mac OS X Server can be configured to begin WINS naming services for Windows clients, and Windows users need to copy their home directory files local to their computers in preparation for the switchover from the existing Windows Primary Domain Controller to the new service that will be set up on the Open Directory master.

Mac OS X Server can then obtain a list of accounts from the existing domain controller for import into its local LDAP directory.

To initiate WINS services on Mac OS X Server, follow these steps:

1. **Launch Server Admin and then connect to the desired server.**

2. **Click SMB and then click Settings on the toolbar.**

3. **Click the Advanced tab, shown in Figure 5.3.**

Figure 5.3

The Advanced pane of the Settings page

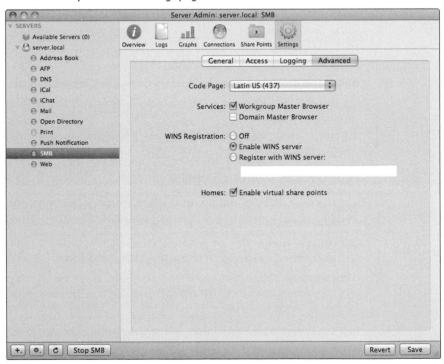

4. Configure WINS registration:

- Select Register with WINS server if another server is currently providing WINS services on the network. Type that server's IP address or DNS name.
- Select Enable WINS server if there's not currently a designated WINS server on the network.

5. Click Save.

6. Instruct users to copy their home directory files local to their computers to their desktops, for example.

7. Stop the SMB service on Mac OS X. This enables a proper import of user, group, and computer accounts in the next set of steps.

To migrate accounts to Mac OS X Server, follow these steps:

1. Launch Terminal.

2. Type sudo /usr/sbin/ntdomainmigration.sh *<ntdomain> <ntserver> <ntadmin> <diradmin>* **and then replace these placeholders with values:**

- `<ntdomain>` is the name of the Primary Domain Controller's domain.
- `<ntserver>` is the name of the current Primary Domain Controller.
- `<ntadmin>` is an admin account for the current domain controller.
- `<diradmin>` is a directory admin account for the Open Directory domain.

3. Authenticate as a local admin to sudo.

4. When prompted, type passwords for the `<ntadmin>` **and** `<diradmin>` **accounts.** The script begins migration, adding any encountered errors to the system log at `/var/log/system.log`. When finished, the script reports Successfully Migrated Domain.

5. Select imported accounts in Workgroup Manager and then set a password policy to force users to reset their passwords at next login by clicking the Options button under the Advanced tab. Until users reset their passwords, their accounts will only have hashes for the authentication methods Windows uses. Resetting passwords stores new encrypted password versions for other authentication methods in Open Directory's Apple Password Server.

6. Add the new user accounts to existing groups, as desired, from the Groups pane, shown in Figure 5.4.

Figure 5.4

Groups configuration in Workgroup Manager

7. **Select user accounts and configure mail service settings from the Mail pane of Workgroup Manager.**

8. **Start the SMB service in Server Admin.**

9. **Remove the former Primary Domain Controller from service.**

Provisioning home directories and roaming user profiles for users

Once users have been imported, you can host home directories and user profiles for them on the same server or another server configured as a Domain Member and hosting SMB services.

The default location for Windows home directories is the same as the home folder defined for the user on the Home tab in Workgroup Manager. This share point must support both AFP and SMB protocols to be used for both Mac and Windows home folders, respectively. Follow these steps:

1. **In the SMB service, click the Advanced tab and then click the Enable virtual share points check box.**

2. **In the Share Point configuration, under Protocol Options, the SMB tab must be set with:**
   - Enable strict locking on to prevent problems while being shared as AFP
   - Enable oplocks off to prevent problems while being shared as AFP

3. **To use Windows login scripts, copy the scripts to** `/etc/netlogon/` **on the Open Directory master server and then type the path relative to that folder in the login script location field in Workgroup Manager's Windows pane.**

4. **Instruct users to copy their local copy of their home directory to their new home, available from the Open Directory master or the Domain Member system you configured to act as the home directory share point.**

5. **Instruct users to log out.** This copies their locally cached roaming profile to the new server acting as the Primary Domain Controller. When users log back in, their roaming profile is synced back again. The next time they log in to another system using that account, their roaming profile is also synced to that system.

You can now set up additional share points on the server for your Windows users and copy files previously available on the old server to the new server.

CROSS-REF
For more on working with share points and file-sharing services, see Chapter 22.

Configure Windows access to print service

Configure printer queues in the Print pane of Server Admin. Enable the SMB protocol from the Queues page, shown in Figure 5.5, to allow Windows users access.

You can also enforce quotas for this queue if you've established print quotas in Workgroup Manager under the Print tab, shown in Figure 5.6.

CROSS-REF

For more on print services, see Chapter 31.

Figure 5.5

Printer queue configuration in Server Admin

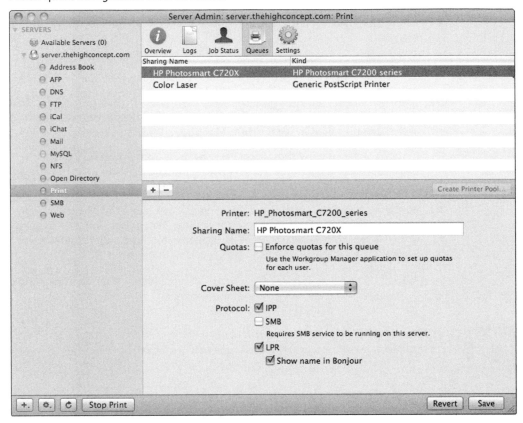

Figure 5.6

Printer quota configuration in Workgroup Manager

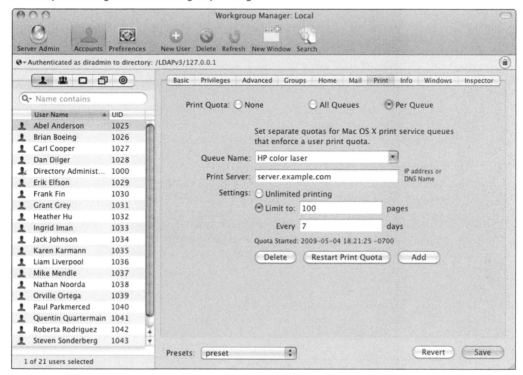

Integrating with Existing Network Services

Apple has designed Mac OS X Server to fit into a variety of existing network and software environments, from Unix to Windows and from Java to IETF-standard (Internet Engineering Task Force) networking.

Mac OS X Snow Leopard is certified as Unix and conforming to the SUSv3 and POSIX 1003.1 specifications under the Open Brand Unix 03 Registered Product program. That makes it easy to port existing software to the platform.

It also makes the platform easy to integrate into standard TCP/IP networks, with support for standard DNS, DHCP, PPTP, and L2PV/IPsec VPN access and RADIUS authentication protocols.

Operating in heterogeneous server environments

Mac OS X server also supports existing network directory services, including:

- Active Directory domain membership for directory services and SSO Kerberos authentication services
- Network Information Service (NIS) domains for directory services
- Novell eDirectory, LDAPv2, and LDAPv3 domains for directory services

Mac OS X Server uses Open Directory as its directory services architecture to abstract away the differences in various implementations of directory services so local processes only need to know how to talk to Mac OS X's Directory Services itself.

The system can then obtain information from Active Directory, multiple tiers of Apple's own Open Directory domains, Sun's NIS, Novell's eDirectory, and any other standard LDAPv3 directory services the system is configured to use.

Open Directory domains can also be used in conjunction with Active Directory to create a Magic Triangle that uses existing Active Directory servers to authenticate users and applies managed preferences to groups of users and computers by using the Open Directory domain.

CROSS-REF
For more on integrating with Active Directory, see Chapter 2.

To configure directory services in Directory Utility, follow these steps:

1. **Launch System Preferences and then click Accounts on the toolbar.**

2. **Authenticate as a local user and then click Login Options.**

3. **Click Edit Network Account Server.** You can bind a client system to an Open Directory domain by typing the DNS name of your Mac OS X Server here.

4. **Click the Open Directory Utility button.**

5. **From the Services page of Directory Utility, shown in Figure 5.7, click the lock icon to authenticate as a local administrator.**

6. **Enable and configure other directory services as described in the next set of steps and then click Apply.**

Figure 5.7

Configuring directory services in Directory Utility

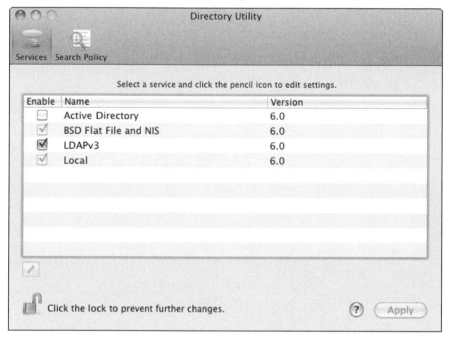

To enable support for Active Directory in Directory Utility, follow these steps:

1. **From the Services page in Directory Utility, click the Active Directory check box.**

2. **Double-click the Active Directory listing to open the configuration dialog box.** A sheet drops down.

3. **Optionally, type the Active Directory Forest name.** By default, this is set automatically.

4. **Type the name of the Active Directory domain.**

5. **Type a name for the local system as Computer ID.** This becomes a computer record in Active Directory.

6. **Click the Show Advanced Options triangle and then click the User Experience tab, shown in Figure 5.8.**

Figure 5.8

Active Directory advanced configuration in Directory Utility

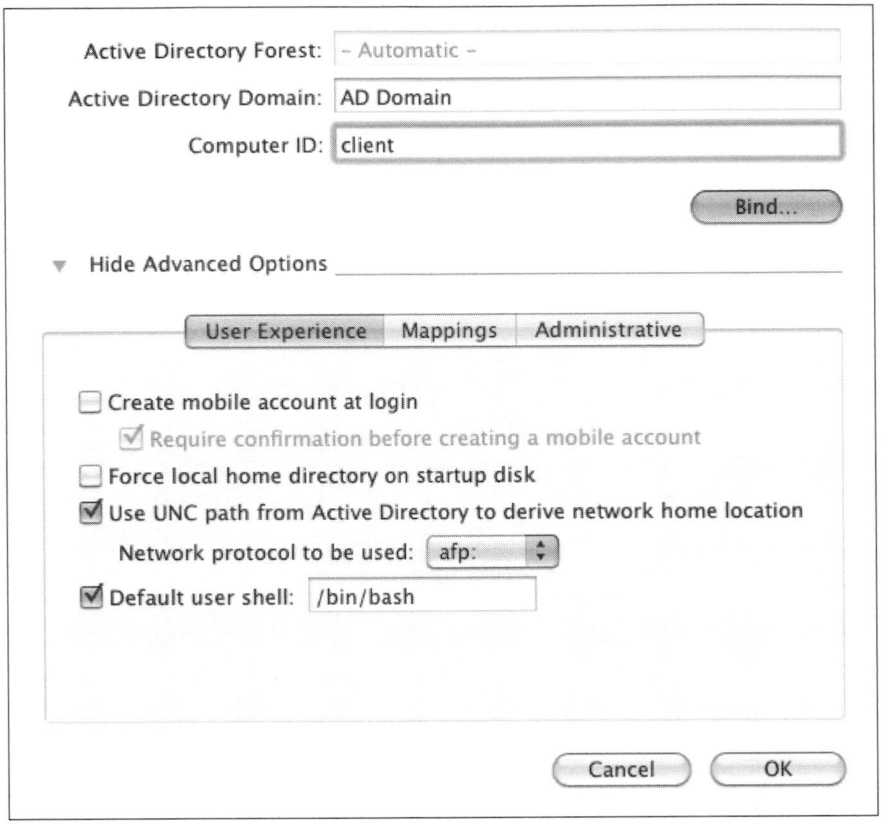

Active Directory Forest: – Automatic –

Active Directory Domain: AD Domain

Computer ID: client

Bind…

▼ Hide Advanced Options

User Experience | Mappings | Administrative

☐ Create mobile account at login

    ☑ Require confirmation before creating a mobile account

☐ Force local home directory on startup disk

☑ Use UNC path from Active Directory to derive network home location

    Network protocol to be used: afp: ⬍

☑ Default user shell: /bin/bash

Cancel | OK

7. **Click the Create mobile account at login check box.** A mobile account uses a local home folder on the system's startup volume to mirror the user's network home folder as defined in Active Directory, creating a Portable Home Directory. A mobile account also locally caches the user's Active Directory authentication credentials, enabling the user to log in by using the Active Directory account even when the directory server is unavailable.

8. **Click the Use UNC path from Active Directory to derive network home location check box to enable a path stored in Microsoft's** \\server\share\user **notation to be translated to the standard** afp://server/share/user **notation for mounting by Mac OS X.**

9. **From the pop-up menu, choose the network protocol to be used for network home folders.** The default is SMB, but if the network home file server supports AFP, you can choose that instead for the Mac's home folder.

10. **If desired, designate a default user shell.**

11. **From the Mappings tab, you can remap the default settings for user ID numbers to Active Directory attributes that you specify.** If left alone, the Active Directory plug-in dynamically generates a unique user ID and a primary group ID from the account's Globally Unique ID (GUID) in Active Directory. The generated user ID and primary group ID are the same for each user account, even if the account is used to log in to different systems.

12. **From the Administrative tab, you can set a preferred domain server and assign local administration privileges to Active Directory groups.** By default, the domain admins and enterprise admins groups are granted local administrative access. You can also allow authentication from any domain in the forest by clicking the check box.

13. **Click Bind and then authenticate as a local administrator.** The system configures the computer account for the system in Active Directory and then begins allowing authentication and local login by Active Directory accounts.

14. **Click OK to save the settings for Active Directory.**

To enable support for Unix-style flat files and NIS in Directory Utility, follow these steps:

1. **From the Services page in Directory Utility, click the BSD Flat File and NIS check box.**

2. **Double-click the listing to open the configuration dialog box, shown in Figure 5.9.**

3. **Click the Use User and Group records in BSD local node check box.** This allows the system to access any account and resource information defined in Unix-style text files. The information can't be edited in Workgroup Manager but can be modified by using command-line tools. BSD flat files include:

- /etc/master.passwd for usernames, passwords, IDs, and primary group IDs
- /etc/group for group names, IDs, and members
- /etc/fstab for NFS mounts
- /etc/hosts for computer names and addresses
- /etc/networks for network names and addresses
- /etc/services for service names, ports, and protocols
- /etc/protocols for IP protocol names and numbers
- /etc/rpcs for Open Network Computing RPC servers
- /etc/printcap for printer names and capabilities
- /etc/bootparams for bootparam settings
- /etc/bootp for bootp settings
- /etc/aliases for mail aliases and distribution lists
- /etc/netgroup for network-wide group names and members

Figure 5.9

BSD flat file and NIS configuration in Directory Utility

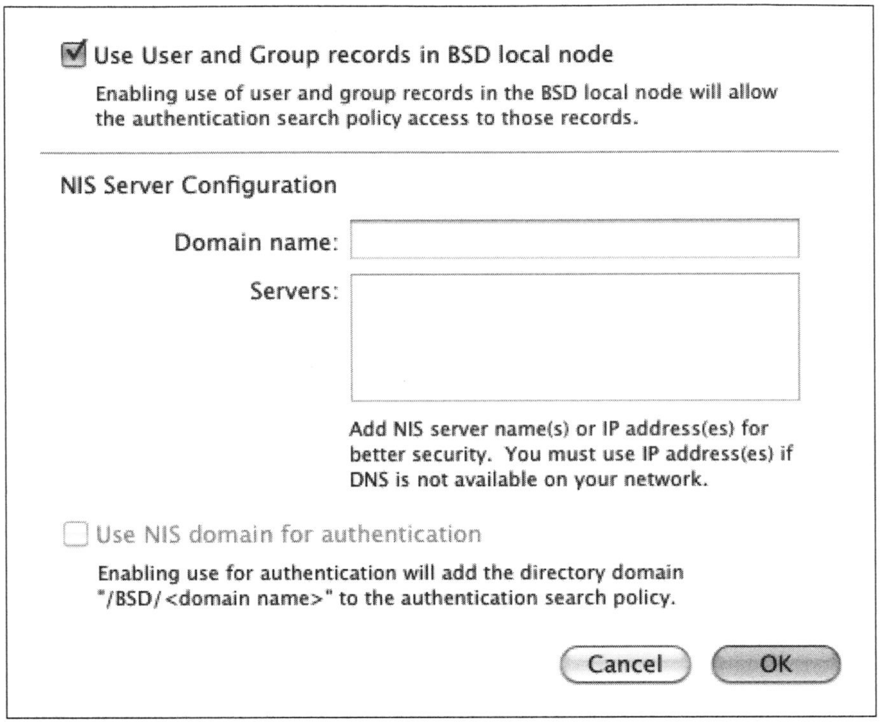

☑ **Use User and Group records in BSD local node**

> Enabling use of user and group records in the BSD local node will allow the authentication search policy access to those records.

NIS Server Configuration

Domain name: _____

Servers: _____

> Add NIS server name(s) or IP address(es) for better security. You must use IP address(es) if DNS is not available on your network.

☐ Use NIS domain for authentication

> Enabling use for authentication will add the directory domain "/BSD/<domain name>" to the authentication search policy.

(Cancel) (OK)

4. Type NIS domain and server names or IP addresses.

5. Click the Use NIS domain for authentication check box.

6. Click OK to save the settings for NIS.

To configure support for LDAP in Directory Utility, follow these steps:

1. From the Services page of Directory Utility, double-click LDAPv3 to open the configuration dialog box, shown in Figure 5.10.

2. Click the check boxes for the defined LDAP servers you want to enable.

3. Add another LDAP directory by using the New or Duplicate button.

4. Click the check box for SSL for LDAP servers that support encryption.

5. **Use the pop-up menu to choose the schema mappings for the LDAP directory:**

- As supplied by the server
- Using Active Directory schema mappings
- Using Open Directory schema mappings
- Using schema mappings typical for Linux directory servers (RFC 2307). Type the search base for the LDAP server when prompted.

Figure 5.10

LDAP configuration in Directory Utility

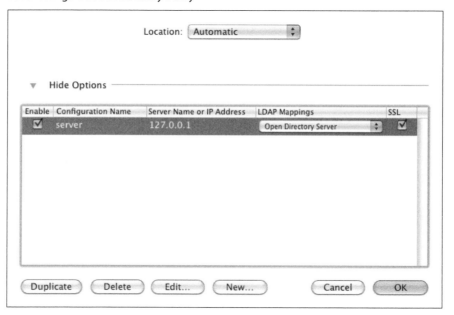

6. **Click Edit to set advanced LDAP settings:**

- The use of a custom TCP port
- Customized attribute mappings
- User authentication settings
- Security policy, such as disabling cleartext passwords, digitally signing packets, encrypting packets, and blocking man-in-the-middle attacks

7. **Click OK to leave the advanced editing window.**

8. **Click OK to save the settings for LDAP servers.**

Serving heterogeneous clients

Apple has also integrated support in Mac OS X Snow Leopard Server for a variety of services designed to support users on multiple platforms:

- Windows and Linux users with SMB file and print sharing
- Linux and Unix users with NFS file exports
- Domain login for Windows users with network hosted roaming profiles and home directories
- Industry-standard SSL security for email, web, and other services, including Mobile Access services for remote users
- Web standards-based collaboration tools for wikis, blogs, and group calendaring that work in any modern browser
- Standards-based mail, instant messaging, calendar, and contact-sharing services

CROSS-REF

For more on SMB and NFS file sharing, mail services, instant messaging, calendar, contact, and web collaboration services, see Chapters 22–28.

Summary

- You can upgrade to Mac OS X Snow Leopard from recent versions of Mac OS X Server or perform a move from older hardware by using Migration Assistant.
- Snow Leopard Server and its Server Administration Software both require Intel Macs to install.
- You can migrate from legacy Windows domains to Mac OS X Server by using Open Directory and the SMB service to provide the same Windows PC login authentication, roaming profiles, login scripts, and file and print services, in addition to centralizing on a central directory service for your Windows and Mac users and extending new services to your Windows users — all with no extra per-client licensing fees.
- Mac OS X Server is designed to integrate into existing directory services by using Open Directory plug-ins to bridge the differences in each.
- Snow Leopard Server is designed to provide cross-platform services to clients by using standards-based protocols.

Software Installation and Initial Configuration

M ac OS X Server uses the same installer process as its desktop operating system sibling. In fact, Mac OS X Server is the desktop Mac OS X with some additional server software installation packages and a few minor configuration changes.

However, some very significant installation differences do exist. One involves Open Directory, the directory services infrastructure that Mac OS X Server uses to manage account records for users, groups, and computers.

A Mac OS X desktop machine manages local user accounts, which are used to log in or authenticate when remotely accessing the machine, such as for personal file sharing. However, desktop systems don't export these user records to other systems, and they don't provide external authentication for other systems; for example, you can't log in to a desktop Mac with an account created on a Mac notebook. The closest you can come to that is setting up identical accounts on both machines.

Every Mac maintains its own sense of authority in terms of user accounts unless it's bound to a directory service domain, which it then trusts to provide authorization. User accounts created on Mac OS X Server can not only provide access to file shares and local login to the server but may also be used to log in to machines bound to the domain.

Managing client login and network authentication services is a key feature of Mac OS X Server, requiring special installation choices that aren't necessary when installing Mac OS X on the desktop.

In addition to Open Directory, Mac OS X Server also hosts a series of advanced network services — from calendar, contacts, email, and instant messaging to serving collaborative wikis, blogs, and group file shares.

The initial installation of files is followed by a configuration step using Server Assistant to set these services up as desired. It also manages the task of setting up Open Directory, as needed, to either manage the entire directory domain as a master or to act as a domain helper by joining an existing directory structure and syncing its directory records as a replica.

In This Chapter

Installing Mac OS X Server

Remote interactive installation

Automatic installation

The two-phase installation process of Mac OS X Server also figures into how administrators set up multiple servers at once or commission individual new servers remotely without needing to attach a keyboard and monitor. This chapter details the installation process and the different options that may apply according to an administrator's needs when deploying Mac OS X Server.

Installing Mac OS X Server

A few prerequisites must be checked off before getting started with installing Mac OS X Server. The software is licensed to run only on Apple-branded hardware, and Snow Leopard Server supports only Intel-based Macs.

Because that limits supported machines to Mac models from 2006 to today, there's no additional specific demand on the minimum speed of the processor needed because any Intel processor is sufficient. The Snow Leopard Server 64-bit kernel takes the fullest advantage of 64-bit Macs, including those with a Core 2 Duo or Xeon (used in the Mac Pro and Xserve) processor and 64-bit EFI firmware (most models sold after 2008); of course, faster clock speeds are always better.

Unlike the desktop version of Mac OS X, Apple Server products require a license key, which must also be unique to the machine on the network. Administrators can't set up a series of servers all using the same license key, and Snow Leopard Server won't work with keys for Leopard Server or earlier versions. The other minimum hardware requirements are:

- **At least 2 GB of RAM.** As with any computer, you should try to install as much RAM as you can afford. For some Macs, that means 4 GB or less. However, late-model Xserve and Mac Pro hardware can support up to 32 GB, although installing more than 16 GB of RAM is currently fairly expensive.

- **At least 20 GB of available disk space.** You also need disk space for all the files you and any network users plan to share, the email users will accumulate, their calendars with file attachments, and any Time Machine backups that users push to the server from their client machines. While 20 GB is the minimum of required disk space needed to run the server, you need to carefully plan for the additional needs your users might have, which may range from a couple GB per user for email and light file sharing to large, high-performance storage requirements demanded by services such as Podcast Producer.

- **A secure Ethernet network connection.** It's also important to make sure that the new server is being installed on a secured network and in a secure location because during the install process, SSH remote login and VNC screen sharing are enabled with the server's serial number as their passwords. This is done to allow remote, unattended installation.

- **A DVD optical media drive.** If it isn't built in, it's possible to use an external FireWire or USB drive or another DVD-equipped Mac in FireWire target mode as the installer's boot drive. Alternatively, the DVD media can be imaged to a hard drive by using Disk Utility, and that hard drive disk clone can be used to install the software on the server. If you're installing on lots of new servers, using NetInstall with the NetBoot service may make commissioning those new servers easier and faster.

- **To install locally, you also need a display.** If this isn't convenient, a remote installation can be performed by using another Mac running the server administration tools, a process outlined later in this chapter.
- **The most important prerequisite, however, is a complete installation plan.** Prior to setting up Mac OS X Server, you need to outline and provision your hardware requirements, and in many cases, you need to make sure that supporting core network services (in particular, DNS and directory services) are in place because you need to provide those network configuration details during the installation.

Compiling installation details

Apple has an installation checklist to follow in collecting installation details, but the primary details to have available relate to DNS, directory services, and IP addressing details for the subnet.

If you're planning to run Mac OS X Server as a stand-alone server in the standard configuration, it's possible to install the system without pre-existing DNS or directory services in place on the network; the new server is set up to provide those services itself.

If you're working as part of a larger organization in the workgroup configuration, the organization should provide the necessary information on existing DNS and directory services and IP subnet numbering conventions.

Administrators working in the advanced configuration need to plan and arrange for these details in advance because outside of standard configuration and the relatively simple world of Server Preferences, Mac OS X Server can't properly work without fully functional and correctly configured DNS already in place on the network.

CROSS-REF
For more on standard, workgroup, and advanced configurations, see Chapter 3.

Preparing the server environment

Your new server needs a hostname, and unless you're building a new stand-alone server in the standard configuration, that means it needs a machine record and a PTR reverse lookup entry created for the chosen hostname within the organization's DNS.

The server attempts to look up its own name and IP address in DNS, and if it fails, so do a variety of services on the machine that depend on correctly configured DNS records.

The server also needs a secured network in place during installation, which requires an appropriate firewall barrier between the local network and the public Internet, something that an AirPort base station or another appliance router might provide for small installations or that a dedicated firewall unit might provide in a larger organization.

In addition to protection from outside security threats, the network must also be secured from casual access to local network jacks. For example, in a corporate or education environment, Ethernet ports on the server's local network can't be left active for anyone to connect to, and wireless networks can't be given unauthenticated access to the private network.

CROSS-REF
For more on securing the server, see Chapter 20.

Gather details on how the server integrates into the existing directory domain (if applicable) and how the IP network subnet is set up (including the server's assigned IP address, gateway router, DNS server, and subnet mask). All these outside elements must be in place prior to installation.

Before installing Mac OS X Snow Leopard Server on the server, administrators should install the latest Snow Leopard Server administration tools on a local Mac for remote management. Previous versions of the software designed for Leopard Server or earlier versions shouldn't be used with the new server software, although the new software should work with previous server versions. These tools are included on the installer DVD.

Choosing an installation startup method

Once all the planning and preparations are complete, the procedures required to actually install Snow Leopard Server depend on your specific circumstances.

Standard DVD installation

If you're going to do a conventional, interactive local installation to a blank target drive by using the Snow Leopard Server DVDs from a retail package, continue reading this section. You install the DVDs while sitting at the server console.

Remote interactive installation

If you're going to perform an interactive remote installation by using the DVDs from a retail package, continue reading this section. However, you can complete the installation from the comfort of a remote machine on the network by using VNC screen sharing. Remote interactive installation is detailed toward the end of this chapter.

Preinstalled server

If Mac OS X Snow Leopard Server shipped preinstalled on the server you're going to use, you can skip ahead to the section on using Server Assistant to perform the initial configuration. This can also be performed remotely; remote interactive installation is detailed toward the end of this chapter.

However, you may want to use a different boot volume configuration than the default provided from the factory. For example, you might want the new server to boot from a new drive partition or from a newly created RAID volume to supply disk mirroring redundancy or disk striping performance or a combination of both features together.

CROSS-REF
For more on evaluating hardware requirements, including disk storage, see Chapter 4.

Any of those alternative boot disk options require reformatting the existing boot volume and installing Snow Leopard Server software from scratch by using the supplied DVDs, effectively reverting to a standard DVD installation.

Upgrade an existing server
If you're upgrading an existing Mac OS X Server to Snow Leopard Server, you should start by backing up your existing server, performing an upgrade install from the DVDs, and then continuing to use the same Server Assistant steps as other installation types, either from the console or remotely — unless, for any reason, you want to back up the existing boot disk, wipe or replace the drive, and then install from scratch.

Using a different boot volume configuration is one reason for doing this or you may want to simply upgrade to a larger or faster drive at the same time as the software upgrade. This would again effectively turn the upgrade into a standard DVD installation.

CROSS-REF
For more on upgrading an existing server to Snow Leopard Server, see Chapter 5.

Upgrade an existing Mac OS X machine to Server
If you're upgrading an existing desktop machine running Mac OS X Snow Leopard to Snow Leopard Server, you can skip the step of reinstalling the operating system and instead install only the server-related components required.

Instead of booting from the install DVD, simply mount the disk from the Snow Leopard desktop and then run the `MacOSXServerInstall.mpkg` installer from the DVD's Other Installs folder. The final step of running Server Assistant can again be performed locally or remotely.

If you're planning to upgrade an earlier version of Mac OS X, you must first upgrade to Snow Leopard and then install the Snow Leopard Server components. You might also consider to instead perform a clean install, particularly if you don't have much existing data to migrate.

Upgrading to Snow Leopard in place requires Mac OS X Tiger or later, but because it also requires an Intel Mac, the options for upgrading older models are already limited.

NetBoot and automatic installation

If you have a NetBoot infrastructure in place for imaging client computers, you can use it to deploy large numbers of servers too. After booting the new machines from a NetInstall image of the installer DVDs, administrators can run through the file installation initial configuration process via one of the following methods:

- Interactively by using the graphical installer tools locally at the server console (although this would be impractical given the alternatives)
- Interactively by using the graphical installer tools remotely via VNC screen sharing
- Manually by using the command-line `installer` tool over SSH remote login
- Automatically by using server-setup data files that supply a listing of desired configuration options the installer uses to set up the server

Remote interactive and automatic installations are detailed near the end of this chapter.

Preparing the boot volume

If the existing boot volume for the server needs to be reformatted or partitioned, this can be done by using Disk Utility, shown in Figure 6.1. The server can boot from the installer DVD and then run Disk Utility directly from the disc prior to installation or the server can be put into FireWire target mode and then the target volume can be set up from another Mac.

To install Snow Leopard Server, the boot disk must be formatted by using GPT (GUID Partition Table). Any drive that originally shipped with an Intel Mac already has this, and any new blank drives freshly partitioned by Disk Utility on an Intel Mac should also work. However, if you're installing to a RAID volume or another disk that was originally used to boot a PowerPC Mac or server, it may use APM (Apple Partition Map) and therefore require a fresh partitioning. This destroys any existing data on the drive, so it must be backed up first.

To create a fresh partition on a boot drive by using Disk Utility, follow these steps:

1. **Make sure any data on a disk you partition is safely backed up.**

2. **Boot the server by using the Snow Leopard Server DVD.** This launches the Mac OS X Installer.

3. **Launch Disk Utility by selecting it from Utilities on the top menu bar.**

4. **Select the disk to be partitioned and then click the Partition tab in the right pane.**

5. **Select 1 Partition as the volume scheme or choose multiple partitions if desired.** The target installation partition must be at least 20 GB.

6. **Choose a Format for each partition created.** The default option is Mac OS Extended (Journaled), also known as HFS+J. This format supports *file system journaling*, which can reduce the need for a lengthy file system check following a crash or power failure event. Another option some server administrators may prefer is Mac OS Extended

(Case-sensitive, Journaled), also known as HFSX. This additionally supports case-sensitive file and directory names, allowing the system to recognize multiple files in the same directory, all spelled identically and only differing by case, such as `Index.html`, `index.html`, and `InDeX.html`. Identically named files aren't possible when using the standard HFS+J, but case-sensitivity is customary in much of the Unix world.

7. **Click Apply.** The Partition Map Scheme in the lower right should now indicate GUID Partition Table.

Figure 6.1

Disk Utility makes full preparation of the boot drive possible right from the DVD installer disc.

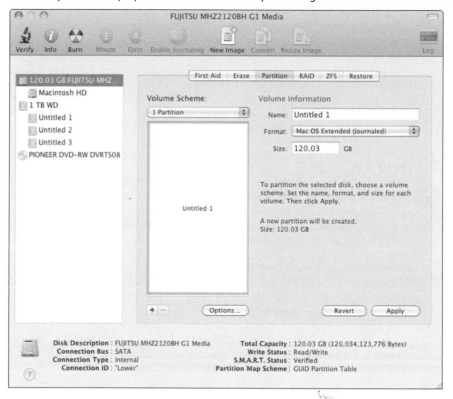

In addition to targeting a partition on a single disk, an administrator might choose to use Disk Utility to set up a software RAID or ZFS pool as the target boot volume. Both options offer to mirror or stripe multiple drives together to create a faster, larger, or more redundant logical volume. For the boot volume, however, a dedicated hardware RAID probably makes more sense.

The Xserve and Mac Pro support high performance PCI-Express RAID interface cards that can offer faster striping performance and more resilient redundancy protection than the software RAID set up within Disk Utility, which relies on the server's processor to do the heavy lifting.

The same caveat applies to using Snow Leopard's new software implementation of ZFS zpools. Because of the newness of ZFS, most administrators working in a production environment probably wouldn't want to experiment with ZFS as their server boot volume format.

A hardware RAID unit can be targeted for installation just as a regular drive can be by following the previous instructions to create and format a new partition on a normal disk.

Installing Mac OS X Server files

Copying over the server install files targets the prepared boot volume, offers to customize some options regarding the files copied to the disk, and then reboots the server to start the next step under Server Assistant.

For users performing a conventional installation from DVD on new hardware, this involves booting the system with the C key held down or holding down Option to select the disc in the optical drive as the boot disk. Once booted, the Installer DVD presents some installation options in a series of screens detailed shortly.

NOTE

From this point, the installation can continue locally on the server or a remote installation can begin. To initiate a remote installation, see the section on remote interactive installation near the end of this chapter. It's also possible to set up new servers by using automatic server setup, which uses setup files stored on the network to automate the configuration of one or many new servers all at once without any interactive involvement from an administrator. This option is detailed in the section on automatic installation near the end of this chapter.

The initial screen sets the language to be used during installation as well as the localization of the server. This can be changed after installation by using the International pane of System Preferences. From the Install Mac OS X Server screen, shown in Figure 6.2, choose the desired target volume prepared earlier.

Prior to beginning the actual file installation, click Customize and then deselect the packages you don't need from the customize sheet, shown in Figure 6.3. This can save up to 2 GB of unnecessary disk space and the time needed to copy those files.

With all the optional packages deselected, the minimum installation footprint for Snow Leopard Server is just slightly larger than 8 GB. The packages installed in a complete install are:

- **Essential System Software.** This is Mac OS X Snow Leopard.
- **Essential Server Software.** These are additional server software packages.
- **Server Administration Software.** These are the required administration tools.
- **Application Server Software.** These are required additional server applications.
- **Language Translations.** These optional localization files can be deselected.

- **Printer Support.** These optional printer drivers can be deselected.
- **X11.** This optional support for graphical X Window Unix applications can be deselected.
- **Rosetta.** This optional support for running PowerPC applications can be deselected if you plan to only ever run Universal Binary applications. If you discover later that you need support for older PowerPC-only software, you can install this package later.

After customizing the desired install files, the installer then prompts you to accept the licensing terms of the software. Once you accept the licensing terms, the installer begins to copy over files, which can take nearly an hour. The installer then sets the server to restart from the newly installed disk and then automatically restarts, booting up to run Server Assistant for the final basic configuration.

To delay the configuration process, an administrator can quit Server Assistant and shut the machine down; after the next restart, Server Assistant starts up to complete its initial configuration.

Figure 6.2

The initial installation screen presents a list of available target drives.

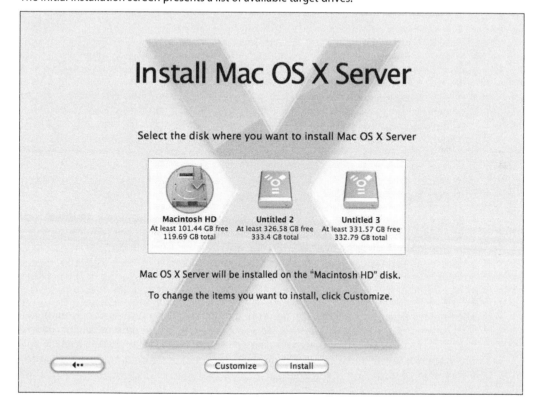

Figure 6.3

The customize sheet allows administrators to deselect lots of unnecessary files during the installation.

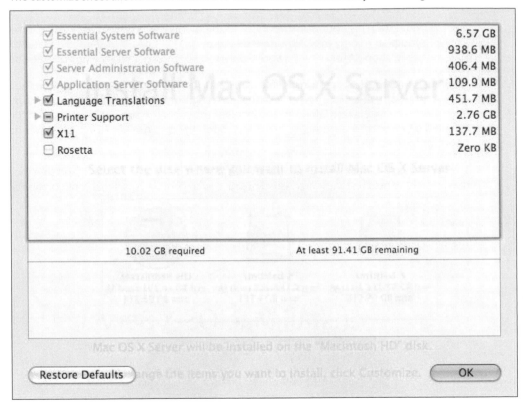

☑ Essential System Software	6.57 GB
☑ Essential Server Software	938.6 MB
☑ Server Administration Software	406.4 MB
☑ Application Server Software	109.9 MB
▶ ☑ Language Translations	451.7 MB
▶ ☐ Printer Support	2.76 GB
☑ X11	137.7 MB
☐ Rosetta	Zero KB

10.02 GB required	At least 91.41 GB remaining

Restore Defaults   OK

Using Server Assistant

At first reboot, a new installation of Mac OS X Server launches the Server Assistant application to complete the initial configuration of the system. At any point prior to finishing the configuration, the Server Assistant application can be quit by using ⌘+Q, and the server shuts down with a blank configuration, ready to boot up at a later point and configure.

Local or remote

The final configuration step can be performed interactively from the server itself or, alternatively, interactively by using a remote Mac running a VNC screen-sharing client or by using the Server Assistant application, which is included in the server administration tools supplied on the Mac OS X Server install DVDs. This option is outlined in the section on remote interactive installation near the end of this chapter.

Automatic

It's also possible to set up new servers by using automatic server setup, which uses setup files stored on a mounted disk or the network directory to automate the configuration of one or many new servers all at once without any interactive involvement from an administrator.

During installation, Server Assistant looks for saved setup data files. If none are found, Server Assistant continues with the regular configuration; however, if it discovers a saved setup file locally or in the network directory specified by DHCP, it uses the settings in that file to complete the remaining setup. This process is detailed under the section on automatic installation near the end of this chapter.

CAUTION

When performing a server upgrade, take care to ensure that one of these saved setup data files isn't inadvertently detected and used by the server to finish its configuration. If that were to occur, the preference file would wipe out the existing configuration of the server being upgraded.

The following Server Assistant screens appear in subsequent order:

- **Welcome.** The first screen presented by Server Assistant is a welcome screen that asks the user to select the local country or region.

- **Keyboard.** The next page prompts the user to set keyboard location preferences.

- **Serial Number.** Unlike the desktop version of Mac OS X, Apple Server products require a license key, which must also be unique to the machine on the network. Administrators can't set up a series of servers that all use the same license key, and the new version of Snow Leopard Server won't work with keys for Leopard Server or earlier versions.

- **Transfer an Existing Server?** The next page offers to import the server configuration settings from a previous machine by specifying either a volume or a Time Machine backup, as shown in Figure 6.4. This works similar to Migration Assistant on the desktop.

- **Product Registration.** This page can be skipped; it asks for the administrator's contact information to register the new system.

- **A Few More Questions.** This page asks about the server's use and the type and size of your organization and what services you plan to use on the new machine. If you want to provide Apple with input on how you use Mac OS X Server to influence how the company supports the product going forward, this would be how to do it.

- **Time Zone.** This page sets the clock and location.

- **Administrator Account.** This page, shown in Figure 6.5, prompts you to type a display name and short name for the administrator account on the server. This account password is also used for the directory administrator account created later. Two other options are presented here:

- **Enable administrators to log in remotely using SSH check box.** This turns on SSH (Secure Shell), which allows the administrator account to remotely connect to the server and issue additional manual or scripted configuration commands.

- **Enable administrators to share this server's screen check box.** This turns on the VNC service, which allows the administrator account to remotely connect to the server and view the screen from a VNC client, such as the Screen Sharing application in Mac OS X Leopard or later or the Apple Remote Administration console.

- **Network.** This page, shown in Figure 6.6, configures settings for installed network adapters. It sets up:

  - **An IPv4 address.** This is set to use DHCP by default to obtain an automatic number, but administrators should use a permanent IP address for the server. A regular DHCP address is subject to change, and the server's IP address can't change without running through additional configuration steps afterward. A permanent IP can be assigned by using either a static DHCP reservation configured by the DHCP administrator or a manually typed IP number with the appropriate gateway router, DNS server, and subnet mask settings for the local network.

  - **An IPv6 address.** This is set to automatic by default. Changes can be made by clicking the IPv6 button.

Figure 6.4

The Transfer an Existing Server? screen allows for the simple import of previous server settings during installation.

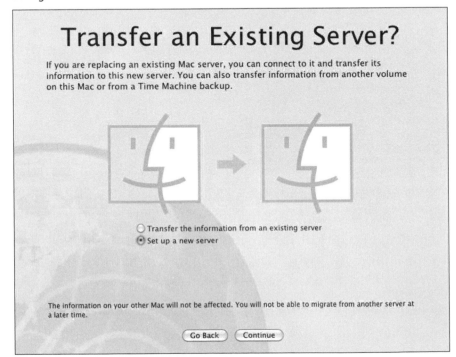

Figure 6.5

The new administrator account is used to secure remote login and screen sharing.

NOTE
If you're performing a remote install and change the IP address here, the screen-sharing session dies and you have to re-establish the connection by using the new IP address you used. However, the same serial number password continues to be used; the administrator account isn't yet active.

- **Ethernet port settings.** This is set to automatic configuration by default, but administrators with special needs can set speed, duplex settings, and MTU packet size by clicking the Ethernet button.

NOTE
Changes to network settings can be made after installation from the Network pane of System Preferences. When changing the IP address, the system runs a `changeip` command to update the Open Directory domain, the local directory domain, and various other service configuration files on the server. This command can also be run manually if there's a discrepancy in settings among the various services on the system.

Figure 6.6

The Network screen

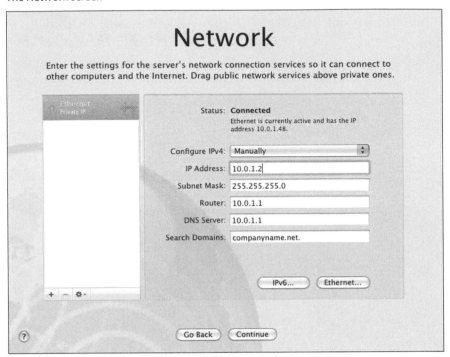

- **Network Names.** The server obtains its fully qualified DNS domain name automatically by looking itself up on the network. This makes correctly functioning DNS an important prerequisite for the server. This page of the configuration, shown in Figure 6.7, also allows the system to be assigned a network name that appears as a friendly name when network users browse for file shares, printers, or other services. The server's network hostname is resolved by running through a series of lookups based on the primary IP address assigned to the server and then choosing the first name that the queries provide:

  - The name provided by the network's DHCP server for the server's primary IP address

  - The first name returned by a reverse DNS lookup on the server's primary IP address

  - The assigned local hostname

  - The name `localhost`

NOTE

Because the system discovers its name automatically, changes to network settings shouldn't be made after installation from the Sharing pane of System Preferences. When changing the hostname, the administrator needs to issue a `changeip` command to update the Open Directory domain, the local directory domain, and various other service configuration files on the server. This command can also be run manually if there's a discrepancy in settings among the various services on the system.

- **Users and Groups.** This page presents the directory services configuration options that result in the server being set up in a standard, workgroup, or advanced configuration. The three options presented in Figure 6.8 and described here are presented in a more detailed overview shortly:

  - **Manage Users and Groups.** Standard configuration — can be upgraded later to workgroup or advanced configuration

  - **Import Users and Groups.** Workgroup configuration — can be upgraded later to advanced configuration or changed to standard configuration

  - **Configure Manually.** Advanced configuration — can't be changed to another configuration later without reinstalling the server or using a backup

Figure 6.7

The Network Names screen

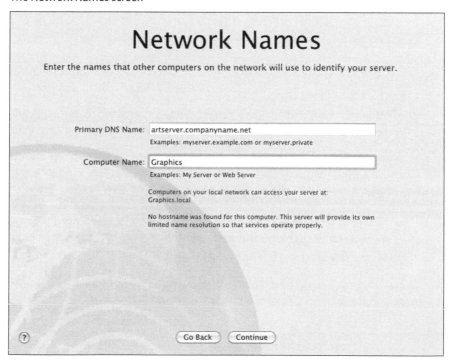

Figure 6.8

Options presented by Users and Groups

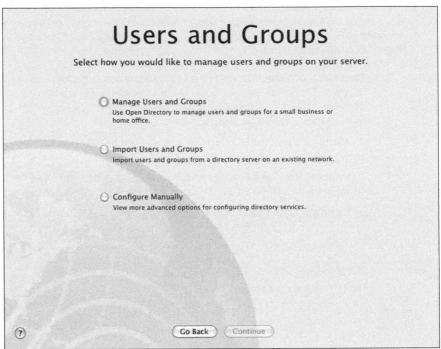

Manage Users and Groups

When Manage Users and Groups is selected, the server offers to automatically set up the following services by default, unless deselected from the Services page, shown in Figure 6.9:

- File Sharing for shared folders and Time Machine backup repositories
- Address Book for synchronized, shared contacts
- Calendar for scheduling and shared calendars
- Instant Messaging for text chat, voice, and video conferencing
- Web for wikis, blogs, and static websites
- Mail for local and Internet mail services

These services can also be enabled or disabled later within Server Preferences, both system-wide and for each specific user account created on the system.

Figure 6.9

The Services screen

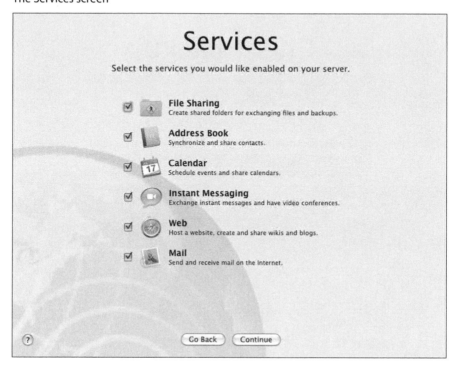

The administrator next configures a disk to be used for Client Backup, shown in Figure 6.10, allowing Time Machine Server to accept and store network users' machine backups on that selected disk as a specialized file server. This setting can be changed later by using the Time Machine pane of Server Preferences.

Mail Options presents options to forward mail through a relay server (required by some ISPs) and to send a welcome message to new mail users. These settings can also be changed later by using the Mail pane of Server Preferences.

Server Assistant is now ready to configure the server settings entered previously (including the desired localization, time zone, administrator account, and network IP address and name) and to set up the server as an Open Directory master with a diradmin user account assigned the same password supplied for the admin account previously entered. It also enables specific services based on the choices made on previous screens.

Figure 6.10

The Client Backup screen

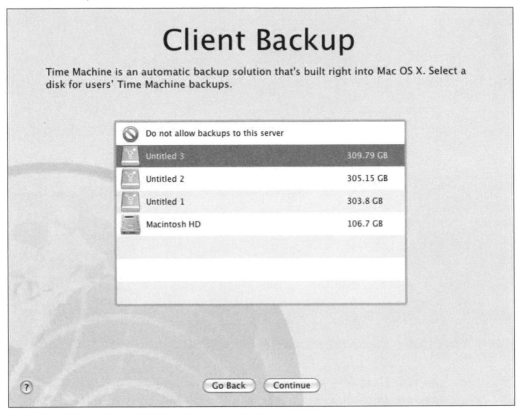

These settings can be reviewed by clicking the Details button of the Summary page, which drops down a sheet of the settings to be applied, shown in Figure 6.11. This sheet also allows the record to be saved as a summary file or an optionally encrypted preferences file that can be used to apply the same settings to another server or to a specific range of servers based on their whole or partial:

- Hardware serial number
- Network MAC address
- IP address
- Hostname

Figure 6.11

The Server Assistant summary details

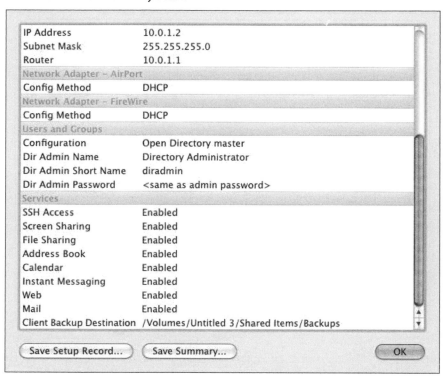

IP Address	10.0.1.2
Subnet Mask	255.255.255.0
Router	10.0.1.1
Network Adapter – AirPort	
Config Method	DHCP
Network Adapter – FireWire	
Config Method	DHCP
Users and Groups	
Configuration	Open Directory master
Dir Admin Name	Directory Administrator
Dir Admin Short Name	diradmin
Dir Admin Password	<same as admin password>
Services	
SSH Access	Enabled
Screen Sharing	Enabled
File Sharing	Enabled
Address Book	Enabled
Calendar	Enabled
Instant Messaging	Enabled
Web	Enabled
Mail	Enabled
Client Backup Destination	/Volumes/Untitled 3/Shared Items/Backups

Save Setup Record...   Save Summary...   OK

This file can subsequently be used for automatic installation of large numbers of servers, a process described later in this chapter.

Import Users and Groups

When Import Users and Groups is selected, Server Assistant asks for the address of an existing directory server it can connect with to import domain user records, as shown in Figure 6.12.

The server then offers to set up the following services:

- File Sharing for shared folders and Time Machine backup repositories
- Address Book for synchronized, shared contacts
- Calendar for scheduling and shared calendars
- Instant Messaging for text chat, voice, and video conferencing
- Web for wikis, blogs, and static websites
- Mail for local and Internet mail services

Figure 6.12

The workgroup configuration needs an address of another directory server to import users and groups.

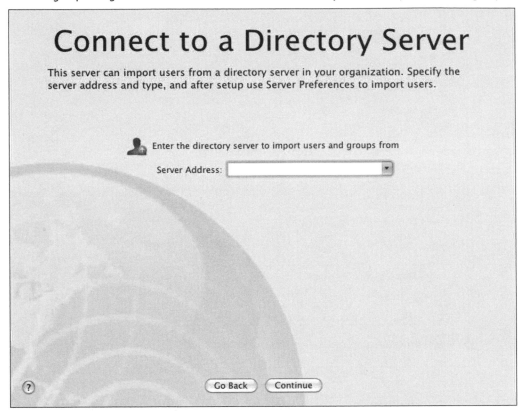

These services can also be enabled or disabled later within Server Preferences, both system-wide and for each specific user account created on the system.

The administrator next configures a disk to be used for Client Backup, allowing Time Machine Server to accept and store network users' machine backups on that selected disk as a specialized file server. This setting can be changed later by using the Time Machine pane of Server Preferences.

Mail Options presents options to forward mail through a relay server (required by some ISPs) and to send a welcome message to new mail users. These settings can also be changed later by using the Mail pane of Server Preferences.

Server Assistant is now ready to configure the server settings previously entered (including the desired localization, time zone, administrator account, and network IP address and name) and to set up the server as an Open Directory replica with a diradmin user account assigned the same password supplied for the admin account previously entered. It also enables specific services based on the choices made on previous screens.

Configure Manually

When Configure Manually is selected, an existing Open Directory or Active Directory server can be specified from the beginning or the step can be initially skipped and directory services can be set up later.

If skipped, the user is prompted to set up an Open Directory master and supply a name for the directory administrator, as shown in Figure 6.13.

Figure 6.13

With manual configuration, additional customized directory service options are available.

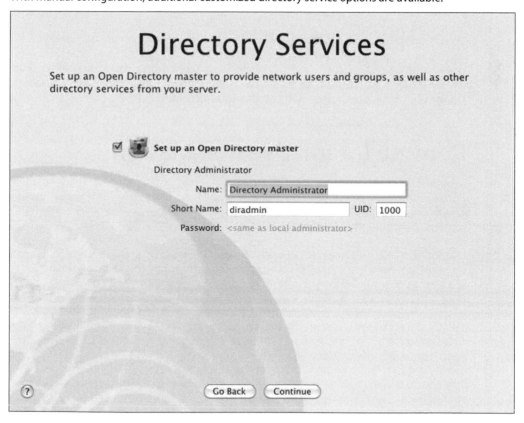

This account is automatically assigned the same password as the previously created admin account. This diradmin user can also be given a custom UID, but the default is 1000 and shouldn't be changed unless there's good reason to do this.

The server then offers to set up the following services:

- File Sharing for shared folders
- Address Book for synchronized, shared contacts
- Calendar for scheduling and shared calendars
- Instant Messaging for text chat, voice, and video conferencing
- Web for wikis, blogs, and static websites
- Mail for local and Internet mail services

Mail Options present options to forward mail through a relay server (required by some ISPs) and to send a welcome message to new mail users.

Server Assistant configures the server settings previously entered (including the desired localization, time zone, administrator account, and network IP address and name) and sets up the server as an Open Directory master or replica, as desired, with a diradmin user account assigned the same password supplied for the admin account previously entered. It also enables specific services based on the choices made on previous screens.

Remote Interactive Installation

After booting the server from the Snow Leopard Server installation DVD (or from a NetBoot disk image of the DVD), the installer automatically opens up VNC (Virtual Network Computing) screen sharing and SSH remote login, enabling administrators to complete the installation without attaching a monitor, mouse, or keyboard to the server.

The server needs only a secure network connection and access to a DHCP server, and the administrator needs to know only the server's serial number, the first eight characters of which are used as the password for accessing remote login or screen sharing on the server. This eight-digit password is case-sensitive, but all letters in Mac serial numbers are capitals.

The IP address of the installation server can be found by looking at DHCP leases for the network or by using the sa_srchr command-line tool, included in the Mac OS X Server administration tools, to identify available servers on the local subnet.

Typing this command returns an IP address and Ethernet ID for any servers on the local subnet that have booted the installer DVD and are waiting for remote connection:

```
/System/Library/Serversetup/sa_srchr 224.0.0.1
```

Remote installation by using Server Assistant

After installing the server administration tools on a separate administrative Mac running Snow Leopard (the latest tools require Mac OS X 10.6, and earlier versions of the tools don't work with Snow Leopard Server), the Server Assistant application installed within the `/Applications/Server/` directory can be used to remotely walk through the same installation steps previously outlined.

Server Assistant can also be used to set up multiple servers in parallel — if their configurations will all be identical — by using the Set up a remote server option.

During the installation process, if the IP address is changed, the Server Assistant connection fails and needs to be reinitiated by using the new IP address.

Remote installation by using VNC screen sharing

To connect to the server remotely without installing the server tools, open a screen-sharing connection by using the standard VNC client on any platform. The built-in VNC client in Mac OS X Leopard or later at `/Library/CoreServices/Screen Sharing` works, and Apple Remote Administration can also be used if you already use that to manage clients on the network.

During the installation process, if the IP address is changed, the VNC screen-sharing connection fails and needs to be reinitiated by using the new IP address.

Remote configuration by using the command line

A variety of configuration functions can also be run remotely from the command line by using the server setup tool at `/System/Library/ServerSetup/serversetup`, which is installed as part of the server administration tools.

Server setup can be used to set the server language; set date, time, and time zone; get or set the server's license key; turn software update on or off; set the server's DNS hostname; and perform a variety of other functions.

CROSS-REF
For more on using the command-line tools, see Chapter 11.

Automatic Installation

Administrators deploying large numbers of servers can automate the process of interactively stepping through the install process by using automatic installation. This process uses preference files created by Server Assistant, which boils down the options compiled in an installation and initial configuration session and saves them as a preferences file that can subsequently be applied to other servers.

When a server is booted from the install DVD, it searches for this preferences file within any of the attached drives. This enables administrators to save a preset configuration file to a copy of the install DVD or to an external USB or FireWire drive (including a flash drive or a mountable iPod) or even to make it available from the organization's directory so that any servers booted from the Mac OS X Server installer that find the appropriate file can set themselves up as specified in the file.

To make the automatic installation configuration file available from an attached drive, copy it to the drive within a folder named `Auto Server Setup`, creating a path that looks like this:

```
/Volumes/Drive name/Auto Server Setup/configuration file name.
plist
```

The drive name is the name of the mounted volume to be used, whereas the configuration file name needs to be one of the following:

- The network MAC address (including any leading zeros but omitting colons) of the server that should use the file; for example, `0016cbc1b826.plist`
- The IP address of the server; for example, `10.0.1.2.plist`
- A partial IP address of the server; for example, `10.0.plist`, which would match both `10.0.1.2` and `10.0.0.254`
- The partial DNS name of the server; for example, `servername.plist`
- The server's fully qualified DNS name; for example, `servername.company.net.plist`
- The first eight characters of the server's serial number; for example, `YM3209FQ.plist`
- `generic.plist`, a file that will be used by any server without needing a matching MAC or IP address or DNS name in the title of the configuration file

The server only uses the file if its MAC address, IP address, DNS name, or serial number matches the name of the preferences file or if the file is named `generic.plist`. If it can't find a file on locally attached volumes, it also searches the company directory if it's configured to bind to a directory in DHCP.

The file can also be optionally encrypted. If it is, the password either needs to be supplied interactively at installation or supplied in a text file copied into the same `Auto Server Setup` directory on the drive. The password file is given the same rule-matching name as the `.plist` configuration file but uses the file extension `.pass`, such as `generic.pass` or `10.0.1.2.pass`.

CAUTION

When performing a server upgrade, take care to ensure that one of these saved setup data files isn't inadvertently detected and used by the server to finish its configuration. If that were to occur, the preferences file would wipe out the existing configuration of the server being upgraded.

Summary

- The time and attention spent planning an installation can make the actual installation faster and more successful.
- When booted from the installation DVD, a new server is exposed to remote login and screen sharing. Make sure to secure network and physical access to the server.
- Install the server admin tools on another Mac to perform a remote installation.
- Automatic installation can enable administrators to roll out many servers in parallel.

Basic
Mac OS X Server
Management

Server Preferences

Basic Mac OS X Server management is tied to the standard and workgroup configurations, both of which primarily depend on the Server Preferences application to activate and configure services.

Servers in advanced configuration don't use Server Preferences and don't allow a remote connection from a computer using the application.

CAUTION

Administrators shouldn't attempt to use Server Preferences to modify server settings on an advanced configuration server because it may result in unintended consequences related to overwriting the more advanced settings made in Server Admin with the simpler subset of configuration settings managed by Server Preferences.

Before getting started with Server Preferences, administrators should review the installation steps for Mac OS X Snow Leopard Server, including the planning stages of selecting the appropriate configuration for the server.

CROSS-REF

For more on configuration planning, see Chapter 3.

The Server Preferences application is designed to mimic the Mac's desktop System Preferences, reducing administration to a series of approachable panes with just a few options each.

What Server Preferences offers in simplicity is also balanced with certain limitations. Administrators may eventually need to upgrade their standard or workgroup configuration to the advanced configuration as they grow beyond the capabilities offered within Server Preferences and need to take on the advanced complexity and deeper feature set available within Server Admin.

CROSS-REF

For more on Server Admin, see Chapter 9.

In This Chapter

Managing users and groups

Managing services

Managing system information

Performing basic server administration

However, Server Preferences offers an approachable starting point for new or less experienced server administrators, and it's possible (and easy) for users to upgrade their server to the advanced configuration without losing the existing work invested in starting out with the Server Preferences application.

Because it's not possible to begin with an advanced configuration and then later decide to scale down to the simpler standard or workgroup configurations, it's better to underestimate the server's needs and grow into them rather than take on an advanced configuration and then be unable to move back to using the simpler Server Preferences application.

This may particularly be the case for administrators who want to delegate management of a workgroup server to a local department with streamlined server needs. Server Preferences not only needs little training to use, but it also offers less room for error in server configuration compared to Server Admin.

The option of using the simpler Server Preferences or the more complex Server Admin is made when installing Snow Leopard Server. The installer asks a series of questions to determine how best to configure the server. This starts with the pane titled Users and Groups, which presents three options:

- **Manage Users and Groups.** This uses Open Directory to locally manage the user and group accounts, resulting in a standard configuration.
- **Import Users and Groups.** This imports users and group account information from an existing directory server on the network, resulting in a workgroup configuration.
- **Configure Manually.** This presents more complex options for customized directory service deployments, resulting in an advanced configuration.

If Configure Manually is chosen, there's no option to use the Server Preferences application to manage the server.

CROSS-REF

For more on installing Snow Leopard Server, see Chapter 6.

Server Preferences looks similar to System Preferences, the modular desktop application of preference panes that presents Mac OS X users with local machine settings for options such as file sharing and local user accounts.

Had Apple not changed Mac OS X Leopard's System Preferences icon (to match the new icon created for the iPhone's setting application), both applications' icons would also appear similar, with a light switch control representing preference settings rather than the iPhone's newfangled gears.

Mac OS X Server includes the same System Preferences application for managing these local machine settings, but the included version doesn't supply some of the personal sharing features available to desktop users. These are instead managed by Server Preferences, which offers additional features and settings. These differences between desktop and server include the following personal sharing options:

- **File sharing.** Managed by Server Preferences, Snow Leopard Server's file sharing is integrated with user and group accounts to provide centralized access control.

- **Web sharing.** Server Preferences presents additional options for serving wikis, web calendars, blogs, and webmail as well as arbitrary web shares (the desktop Mac OS X shares websites located only in specific machine and user folders).

- **Xgrid sharing.** Xgrid is Apple's computational grid system for distributing tasks to available, idle systems on the network. This sharing feature is included on the desktop to enable users to offer their machines to an Xgrid controller and accept Xgrid tasks from it. The server is configured to act as both a controller and an agent within the Xgrid pane of Server Admin, thus no option to volunteer for Xgrid tasks is provided or needed.

CROSS-REF
For more on Xgrid, see Chapter 18.

- **Internet sharing.** On the desktop, this option automatically configures the machine to act as an ad hoc gateway for sharing its Internet connection with other machines connected on a separate network interface. In a server environment, this is likely to be set up by using the server or a network router as a permanent Internet gateway instead.

Outside of Sharing, two other features within the desktop System Preferences are superseded in Mac OS X Server by Server Preferences:

- **Parental Controls.** On the desktop, these settings are used to allow parents to limit the applications a child's account can access and when he or she is allowed to log in. In a server environment, these settings are referred to as *managed users*. There are some per-user service access limitations exposed in Server Preferences, but to make full use of managed users, administrators need to upgrade to an advanced configuration and use Workgroup Manager to set up user, group, and machine restrictions and configurations as desired to fit the organization's user and group policy.

- **Accounts.** Whereas System Preferences creates user and group accounts for the local machine, in a server environment, the network needs an authority to share a centralized listing of user and group records. This is known as *directory services*. User and group records can be managed on a standard or workgroup server within Server Preferences.

CROSS-REF
For more on directory services, see Chapter 21. For more on managed users, see Chapter 36.

Managing Users and Groups

Mac OS X Server presents users and group settings on two separate panes within Server Preferences. Both panes present Apple's familiar user interface listing items on the left and a pane of settings on the right. Figure 7.1 presents a fresh Users pane prior to the addition of any accounts.

Figure 7.1

The Server Preferences Users pane offers options for creating accounts, assigning contact information, selectively allowing access to services, and assigning users memberships to groups.

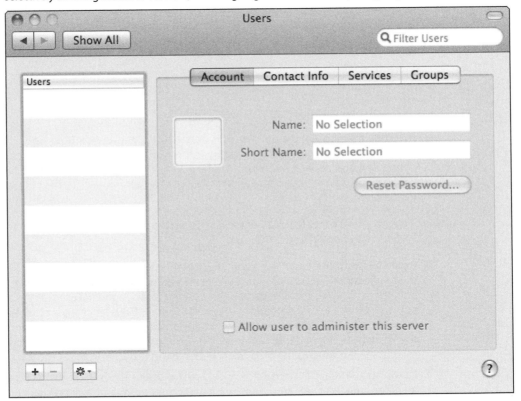

Creating new accounts

To provide services, such as file sharing, a personal calendar, and mail service, to network users, each user first needs an individual account set up within Server Preferences.

Unlike new local accounts created within System Preferences, accounts created in Server Preferences exist in a separate directory. These new accounts also don't get a user home folder created in the typical /Users/ directory, although they do gain login rights to the server itself. However, they don't get administrative rights on the server unless they're expressly granted this.

Conversely, local accounts created on the server by using System Preferences have only local login access and can't be given access to services such as mail or wikis, and they can't be added to server group memberships or exported to another server. This is because they exist in a private, local directory node that's not exposed to the network.

NOTE

The `admin` administrator account created during installation is a local account and appears in System Preferences but not Server Preferences. That's why a second diradmin directory administrator account is also created during installation and given the same password. Although it doesn't appear in the listing of server accounts within Server Preferences, diradmin is a member of that separate directory of accounts, referred to as the `/LDAPv3/` `127.0.0.1` directory. This means it's stored in LDAP by the local host — or, in other words, the local server's OpenDirectory listings. These accounts are available to the network.

To create a new network user account with Server Preferences, follow these steps:

1. **Open Server Preferences and then click the Users pane.**

2. **Click the Add (+) button.** This drops down a sheet asking for the following information, as shown in Figure 7.2:

   - **Name.** This is the display name for the account, which appears in all listings.

   - **Short Name.** This is the internal username, which is used for the user's email address, for example. The user can supply either name when logging in or authenticating.

   - **Password.** This is the account's password, which the user can change. The key icon opens the standard Mac OS X Password Assistant for suggesting secure passwords to use.

   - **Verify.** The password must be retyped to help ensure that the administrator typed the intended password correctly.

   - **Allow user to administer this server.** This check box grants the given user account administrative privileges to directly and remotely manage the server.

3. **When finished, click Create Account.** This creates a listing for the new user. If the user's password is forgotten, it can be reset by clicking the Reset Password button. There's also a familiar Mac OS X picture well for dropping a photo of the user.

4. **If the account is incorrectly created, select it in the Users list and then click the Delete (–) button to delete the account.** If the display name is typed incorrectly, it can be changed, as depicted by the editable Name field in Figure 7.3. However, you can't change the short name once the account is created; if the short name is wrong, delete the account and then create the user again.

CAUTION

Deleting an active user's account results in the immediate deletion of the user's data, including the mailbox, shared calendar, and any contacts hosted on the server.

Figure 7.2

The add user sheet drops down from the Users pane of Server Preferences.

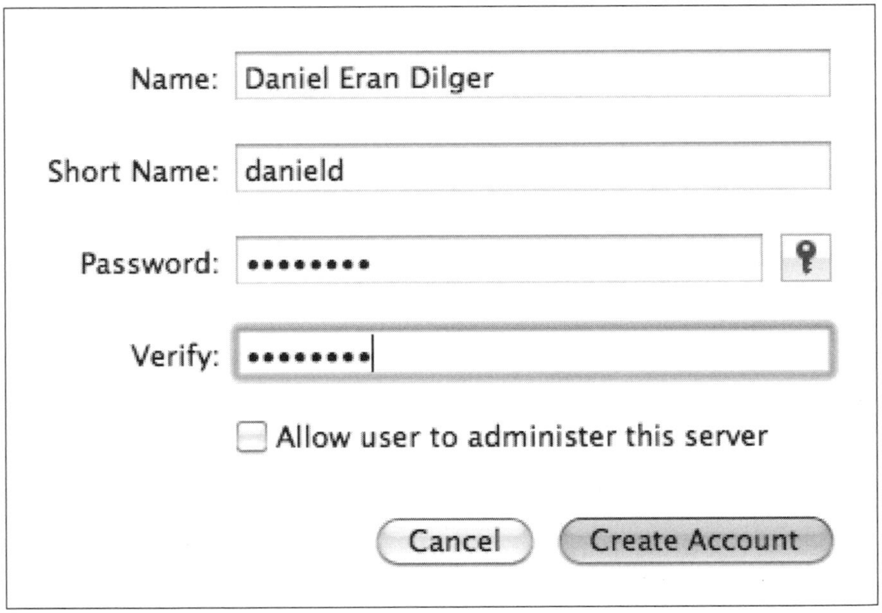

Name:	Daniel Eran Dilger
Short Name:	danield
Password:	••••••••
Verify:	••••••••

☐ Allow user to administer this server

Cancel   Create Account

Figure 7.3

The Server Preferences Users pane can put a face on the user account and allows administrators to reset users' passwords.

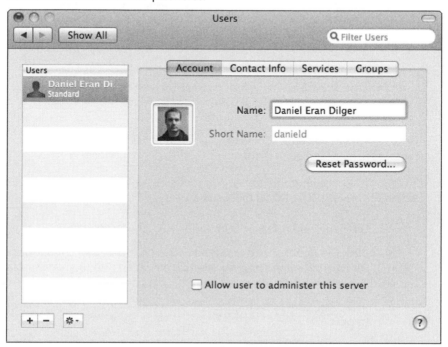

Importing user accounts from another directory

If user accounts have already been defined on an external directory server, System Preferences can import these accounts instead of creating parallel accounts on the local server. This requires that the local server establish a connection to the remote directory server, a reversible step that promotes a standard configuration server into a workgroup configuration.

To connect a server to another directory server within the organization, follow these steps:

1. **Open System Preferences and then click Accounts.**

2. **If the Accounts pane is locked, click the lock icon in the lower left and then authenticate by typing the local administrator account name and password.**

3. **Click Login Options and then click the Edit button next to Server Connection.**

4. **Click the Add (+) button and then type the DNS name or IP address of the directory server to connect to.**

5. **Type a user account name and password to authenticate with the remote directory server.** This can be a standard user account and doesn't need to be the directory administrator account.

N O T E

Mac OS X Server in workgroup configuration can connect to either a Mac OS X Server Open Directory or a Microsoft Windows Server Active Directory Domain to import users or reference external accounts.

Once connected to a remote directory, the local server can then import user accounts from the remote directory and grant them membership to local groups and access to local services.

To import user accounts to a workgroup configuration server from another directory server within the organization, follow these steps:

1. **Open Server Preferences and then click the Users pane.**

2. **Click the Action button marked with a gear icon and choose Import User From Directory from the pop-up menu.** If there's no pop-up menu displayed, the server is in standard configuration and needs to be connected to another directory server.

3. **Select the user to be imported from a connected directory server and then click Import.**

4. **When finished importing users, click Done.** Imported users are marked as imported in the Users pane of Server Preferences.

Assigning contact information to an account

After creating an account, an administrator can fill in the user's contact information, providing a mailing address, multiple email accounts and phone numbers, instant messenger accounts for Jabber, AIM, MSN, ICQ, and Yahoo IM, and a personal website and weblog address, as shown in Figure 7.4.

Imported users may have contact information that can't be edited on the local server because the information is maintained by the remote directory service.

An account's locally created contact information is stored within the local Open Directory. Users can edit their contact information directly by using Directory.app in Leopard; however, in Snow Leopard, this program has been replaced by iCal Server Utility, which doesn't allow direct access to the directory by end users. A directory administrator needs to maintain directory records by using Workgroup Manager.

In Snow Leopard, users can now share their own listings of contacts via the new Address Book Server for retrieval and editing from Address Book.

Figure 7.4

The Contact Info pane of the Server Preferences Users pane provides contact details for an account.

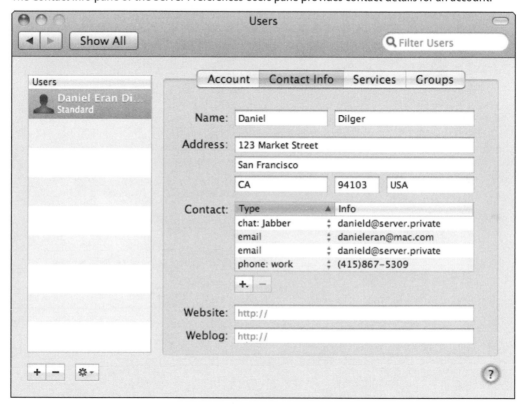

Allowing or denying an account's access to services

Access to specific services can be controlled from the Services tab of the Users pane. Each service listed provides a check box for enabling the account with access, as shown in Figure 7.5.

CAUTION

Removing access to a service may result in the immediate deletion of the user's related information, including the mailbox, the shared calendar, and any contacts hosted on the server.

Figure 7.5

The Services pane of the Server Preferences Users pane enables the administrator to selectively allow or deny an account's access to local services.

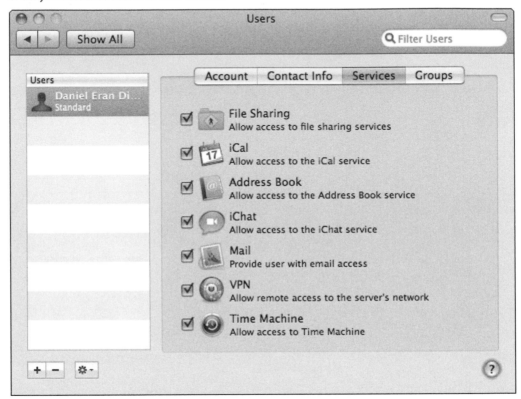

Sending a welcome message to new accounts

Server Preferences also provides a way for administrators to send an initial email welcome message to new and imported users. The message includes the network administrator's name, email address, and a personal introduction — supplied by the administrator — that prefaces the standard welcome email.

The remainder of the message outlines basic network details for the new user, including his or her email address, the network's DNS address, and a listing of services available on the local server, with links to available file shares and web services.

Prior to setting up accounts, the administrator needs to configure this welcome message, which is subsequently sent out automatically whenever a new account is created locally or imported from another directory server. Mail service must be turned on for welcome messages to be sent out.

To configure and send out welcome messages, follow these steps:

1. **Open Server Preferences and then click the Users pane.**

2. **Click the Action button marked with a gear icon and then choose Email Message Settings from the pop-up menu.**

3. **On the sheet that appears, type the following information, as shown in Figure 7.6:**
   - **Administrator Full Name.** This is only the display name, so it can be anything.
   - **Administrator Email.** This is the administrator's sending address on the local server.
   - **Custom Email Introduction Welcome.** This can be any text the administrator wants to add to the beginning of the welcome message to new users.

4. **When finished, click Save.** Subsequent new accounts are automatically sent the message.

5. **To manually resend a welcome message, select the desired account, click the Action button, and then choose Send invitation to *User* from the pop-up menu.**

Figure 7.6

The add user sheet drops down from the Users pane of Server Preferences.

Email Message Settings (required)	
Administrator Full Name:	John Admin
Administrator Email:	john@server.com
Custom Email Introduction (optional)	
Welcome:	Welcome to Server, Inc. Please feel free to contact your IT department for help in getting set up with our network. This welcome letter

(?)   Cancel   Save

Editing group membership for an account

Administrators can add or remove an account from any of the defined groups from the Groups tab of the Server Preferences Users pane, as shown in Figure 7.7. To edit the user's group membership, click the Edit Membership button and then click or deselect the check boxes for each defined group as desired.

Figure 7.7

The Groups pane of the Server Preferences Users pane is used to edit an account's group memberships.

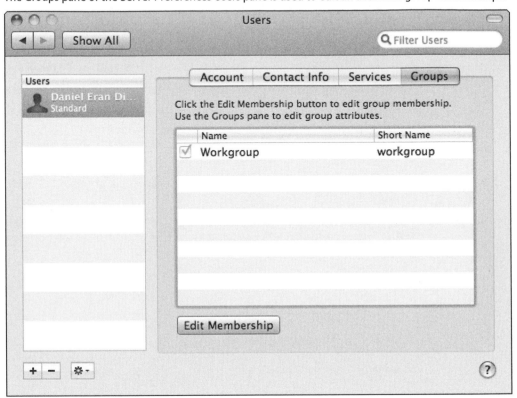

Creating new groups

In addition to setting up user accounts individually, administrators can also create groups of users and assign attributes to those groups, such as shared access to a network file share, a shared contacts list, shared calendar, shared wikis, and a group iChat auto-buddy list.

To create a new group, follow these steps:

1. **Open Server Preferences and then click the Groups pane.**

2. **Click the Add (+) button, and on the sheet that appears, complete the following fields:**

- **Group Name.** This is only the display name, so it can be anything, and it can be changed.

- **Short Name.** This is the internal name and can't be edited later.

3. **Click the Create group wiki button.** This launches the wiki interface for group editing.

4. **When finished, click Create Group.** With the group selected from the Groups listing, additional services can be activated, including a file-sharing folder limited to the group membership and an iChat auto-buddy list, which makes group members buddies within iChat. Figure 7.8 shows the Group tab for a new installation, with the default Workgroup highlighted.

Figure 7.8

The Group pane of the Server Preferences Groups pane is used to create new groups and assign them attributes, such as shared group services.

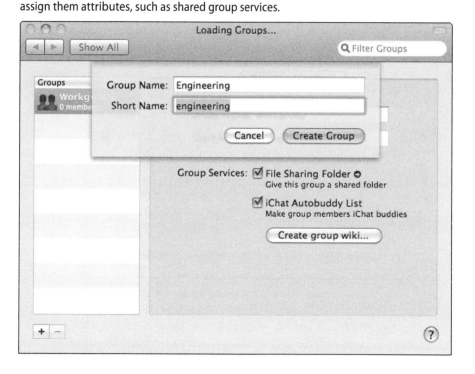

Importing group accounts from another directory

Server Preferences can import group accounts that have already been defined on an external directory server instead of creating parallel group accounts on the local server. Imported groups are marked as automatic, and their membership of users is kept synchronized with changes made to that group on the directory server it's imported from.

Importing groups requires that the local server establish a connection to a remote directory server, a reversible step that promotes a standard configuration server into a workgroup configuration.

To connect a server to another directory server within the organization, follow these steps:

1. **Open Server Preferences and then click Accounts.**

2. **If the Accounts pane is locked, click the lock icon in the lower left and then authenticate by typing the local administrator account name and password.**

3. **Click Login Options and then click the Edit button next to Server Connection.**

4. **Click the Add (+) button and then type the DNS name or IP address of the directory server to connect to.**

5. **Type a user account name and password to authenticate with the remote directory server.** This can be a standard user account and doesn't need to be the directory administrator account.

NOTE
Mac OS X Server in workgroup configuration can connect to either a Mac OS X Server Open Directory or a Microsoft Windows Server Active Directory Domain to import the member users of automatic groups.

Once connected to a remote directory, you can now add remote groups defined on that directory server as automatic groups on the local server. This also imports all the users within the group and periodically updates the group's membership by adding or deleting users to reflect any membership changes made on the remote directory.

To import group accounts from another directory server within the organization, follow these steps:

1. **Open Server Preferences and then click the Users pane.**

2. **Click the Action button marked with a gear icon and then choose Import Users From Groups from the pop-up menu.** If there's no pop-up menu displayed, the server is in standard configuration and needs to be connected to another directory server.

3. **Select the group to be imported from a connected directory server and then click Import.**

4. **When finished importing users, click Done.** Imported groups are marked as automatic in the Groups pane of Server Preferences.

Managing group memberships

Although users can be assigned to and removed from local group memberships within the Groups tab of the Users pane, administrators can also selectively add and remove members from a group by using the Members tab of the Groups pane.

To edit a local group's membership, follow these steps:

1. **Open Server Preferences, click the Groups pane, and then click the Members tab.**

2. **Click the Edit Membership button.** The existing list of members is replaced by a listing of all users, with members checked and nonmembers unchecked, as shown in Figure 7.9.

Figure 7.9

The Members pane of the Server Preferences Groups pane is used to edit the membership of a local group.

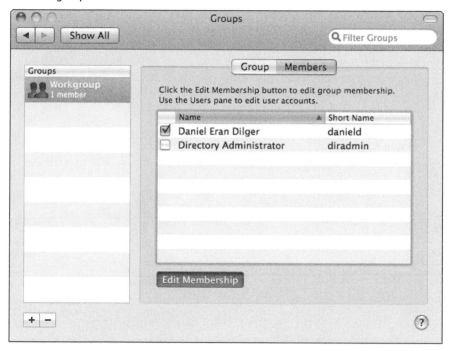

3. **Select the usernames for membership in the group.**

4. **When finished, click Edit Membership.** The Members tab now reverts to displaying only the group's actual members.

Managing Services

Once user and group accounts are either created locally or imported from another directory, Server Preferences can be used to activate services and perform some basic configuration.

After the initial configuration, users with advanced needs may find that they need to leave Server Preferences behind and take on the more complex but full-featured configuration options available in Server Admin.

CROSS-REF
For more on Server Admin, see Chapter 9.

For many users, however, Server Preferences may effectively reduce the effort of managing a department's server down to a simple task that can even be delegated away to users who have little or no experience in server management, outweighing any missing features.

File Sharing

One of the first services users should have access to is file shares. Server Preferences provides file-sharing services that are turned on with a giant switch that looks borrowed from the iPhone. Nearly all services in Server Preferences are laid out identically, with a single switch opposite a list of a few sparse configuration options, as shown in Figure 7.10.

Figure 7.10

The sparse File Sharing pane in Server Preferences

Default file shares

With Time Machine Server activated, Mac OS X Snow Leopard Server sets up four default file shares:

- **Backups.** This is where the Time Machine backups of network clients are copied. It's located at `/Shared Items/Backups/` and is accessible to all users who have the Time Machine service activated for their user account. File permissions can't be edited within Server Preferences.

- **Groups.** This share is located at `/Groups/` and is accessible to all registered users. Additional group shares are created within this folder, making them viewable to other users. Files within this share have read and write access to all users by default.

- **Public.** This share is located at `/Shared Items/Public/` and is accessible to all registered users. Users can read and copy items from this folder but can't add anything new; only an administrator can copy files here. This makes it a good place to put common documents, software installers, and other openly shared files.

- **Users.** This share is located at `/Users/` and is accessible to all registered users. Additional individual user shares can be created within this folder, making them viewable to other users. Files within this share have read and write access to all users by default.

Adding a new file share is as simple as the Mac OS X desktop's personal file sharing: Simply click the Add (+) button and then select the folder to be shared. Once a share is defined, click the Edit Permissions button to customize permissions.

As shown in Figure 7.11, the permissions editing sheet is even simpler than the personal file-sharing options available to Mac OS X desktop systems, which allow for read-only, read and write, or write-only (drop box) permissions per user.

In Server Preferences, the default option is to allow read and write to all registered users, and the only configurable option is to limit read and write access to specific users or groups. There's no way to allow read-only or write-only permissions per user or per group, only read-only access to guest users.

Share permissions versus file permissions

Creating a shared folder sets up share permissions that limit which users can access the share from the network. Files and folders placed within that share also have file permissions, so just because a user has access to the share doesn't mean he or she has read and write access to those items.

When new groups are created and given a shared folder, that folder is assigned file permissions restricted to the group membership, so although all registered users have read and write permission to the Groups folder, they can actually access files and folders only for the groups they belong to.

Figure 7.11

The limited options for editing file permissions for shares within the File Sharing pane

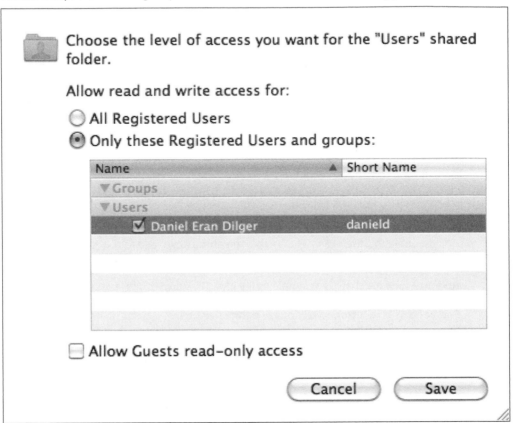

The same is true with individual user folders created within the Users folder. Administrators can create folders accessible to individual users, although Server Preferences doesn't accommodate creating user folders itself.

Moving beyond simple file-sharing options

Although administrators can manually set up their own complex file permissions on manually created files and folders, Apple's simple share permissions were designed in response to feedback from department users with simple needs who want default security settings that are sensible and easy to understand.

Server Preferences delivers that core simplicity; users who need more options will want to move to Workgroup Manager, which allows for more complex configurations that enable share points on different servers, more complex access permissions, network and Portable Home Directories with mobile file sync, quotas, and other more advanced features.

File sharing can be disabled on a per-user basis from the Services tab of the Users pane.

CROSS-REF
For more on Workgroup Manager, see Chapter 10.

Address Book service

New to Mac OS X Snow Leopard Server, Address Book Server allows users on the network to connect to the server via the desktop Address Book application to access a searchable directory of shared contacts, add their own user records to the shared contacts for a group, and copy their own private contacts to the server for access from multiple computers or mobile devices.

Address Book Server works as a specialized web server by using the WebDAV protocol to enable both writing to and reading from the server. It extends WebDAV with the new CardDAV specification, which exchanges contact records as standard vCards.

In Server Preferences, there are only two settings, as shown in Figure 7.12: an on/off switch for the service and the option to set a quota to limit the size of each user's address book, which by default is set to 100 MB. Contact data is saved to /Library/AddressBookServer/ Documents.

Address Book Server can be disabled on a per-user basis from the Services tab of the Users pane. Outside System Preferences, there isn't much additional configuration possible, although Server Admin can enable SSL certificate-based encryption for the service.

Figure 7.12

The limited options for managing Address Book Server in Server Preferences

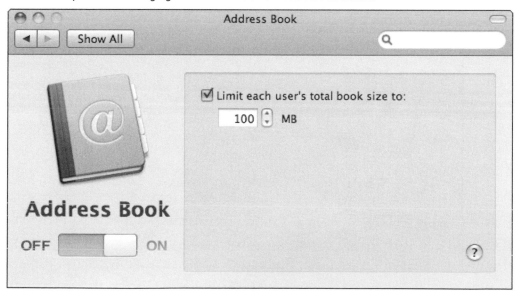

iCal service

The 2.0 release of iCal Server in Snow Leopard Server supports shared calendars, meeting invitations, user and resource availability, and the ability to reserve conference rooms and equipment, such as a video projector. Meeting invitations can also now be sent to external users, who can respond via email to update their meeting attendance plans.

Just like Address Book Server, iCal Server is based on WebDAV and uses the CalDAV specification for exchanging events, invitations, availability, meeting attendance, and resource booking as iCalendar messages. This enables iCal Server to be used with other client applications that support the CalDAV standard, in addition to iCal on the Mac desktop and the Calendar app on the iPhone. Support for the CalDAV standard is just beginning to gain traction, so outside Apple's calendaring applications, the options are currently limited. For example, Microsoft Outlook doesn't provide native CalDAV support, although a third-party open-source plug-in is currently in beta.

Server Preferences turns the service on or off and supplies two options, shown in Figure 7.13:

- **A quota limiting the size of each calendar event's size.** This is primarily a limitation on the amount of file space that can be attached to a calendar event, set by default to 1 MB.

- **A quota limit on each user's total calendar size.** This applies to all the events, to-do items, and other calendar data stored on the server, including all files attached to calendar events. This is set to 100 MB by default.

Figure 7.13

The limited options for managing iCal Server in Server Preferences

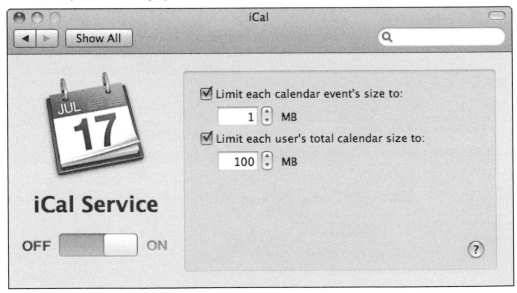

Calendar data is stored on the server at `/Library/CalendarServer/Documents/`. iCal Server can be disabled on a per-user basis from the Services tab of the Users pane. To activate web calendars, use the Web Server pane of Server Preferences.

Server Preferences doesn't offer to set up push notifications, so administrators supporting iPhone users might want to consider upgrading to Server Admin for push calendar updates as well as SSL certificate-based encryption for the service.

iChat service

The Mac OS X Server iChat service is based on XMPP (also branded as Jabber), which iChat uses to support buddy availability discovery for instant messaging and to initiate audio chats and video conferencing.

The server also supports standard Jabber instant messaging clients on the Mac or other platforms, including Google Talk, and can optionally be federated with other outside Jabber services to relay instant messages across servers.

Server Preferences turns the service on or off and supplies two options, shown in Figure 7.14:

- **Log and archive all chats check box.** This allows you to automatically save chat transcripts and archive these weekly into a compressed file at `/var/jabberd/message_archives/`.
- **Enable server-to-server communication check box.** This enables local iChat users to share their availability presence information to other Jabber XMPP instant messaging systems, such as Google Talk, so that outside users can see buddies online and chat with them.

Figure 7.14

The limited options for managing the iChat service in Server Preferences

NOTE

Other proprietary instant messenger systems, including AIM, MSN, and Yahoo IM, don't directly support XMPP federation. Apple's MobileMe accounts are linked to AIM rather than an XMPP server. An iChat client can connect to both the iChat server and AIM at the same time, but this doesn't allow buddies on both systems to see each other; it only allows the user to chat with users on either system.

iChat Server can be disabled on a per-user basis from the Services tab of the Users pane. There are a few other options available to advanced administration working with Server Admin, including multiple host domains, selective federation with either multiple or specifically selected domains, SSL certificate-based encryption of messages, and customized chat logging and archive options.

Mail service

The Mac OS X Snow Leopard Server mail service is now based on Dovecot, which supplies high-performance POP and IMAP outgoing mail service. It also employs SpamAssassin for junk mail spam filtering and ClamAV for virus scanning.

Server Preferences offers extremely basic (and therefore simple) configuration of mail service, with only controls to turn it on or off and three options, as shown in Figure 7.15:

- **Relay outgoing mail through ISP check box.** This is necessary only when the ISP requires that all outgoing mail be sent through a specific server or if the organization passes all email through the company firewall by using a relay server. The address of the relay server is specified after clicking the Edit button by using either the DNS name or its IP address. If required, this option also supports turning on SMTP relay authentication for outgoing mail sent through the relay server.

- **Enable junk mail and virus filtering check box.** A slider adjusts the minimum point score that defines how aggressive the junk mail filtering should be. The server doesn't delete mail it thinks is junk; it just adds a Junk Mail tag to the subject line, allowing the email client to filter it out easier. Mail containing a suspected virus is deleted, and the server sends an alert to the administrator. Virus definitions are updated daily.

- **Use spam blacklist server (Domain Name Service Black Lists [DNSBLs]) check box.** This enables access to the free Spamhaus blacklist for blocking emails from known spam domains. Use of these servers is limited to noncommercial sites with fewer than 100,000 SMTP connections and 300,000 DNSBL queries per day. Another blacklist server can also be specified.

To activate webmail service, use the Web Server pane of Server Preferences. Mail service can be disabled on a per-user basis from the Services tab of the Users pane.

Advanced users can find a variety of additional configuration options in Server Admin, including support for push notifications, selective SMTP relay acceptance, an option to enable server-side mail rules, mailbox quota limits, support for mailing lists, additional logging options,

SSL certificate-based IMAP, POP, and SMTP mail connections, virtual email hosts for supporting mail from multiple domain names, mail store options, and server clustering support.

Server Admin also supplies account maintenance features for rebuilding the mail database and retrying or deleting messages stuck in the mail delivery queue.

Figure 7.15

The simple options for managing mail in Server Preferences

Web Server

Mac OS X Server provides a number of features that depend on web services, which are useable from any standards-based browser, including mobile users on the iPhone or iPod touch. These include:

- **Conventional web hosting.** You can use static HTML pages or dynamic web content with interactivity built by using JavaScript, Adobe Flash, or a full web application authored with tools such as WebObjects or Ruby on Rails. By default, Mac OS X Server sets up a server home page at `http://www.server.com/` (where `server.com` is the server's DNS hostname), sharing any files located at `/Library/WebServer/ Documents`. This default server home page can also be changed to point to one of the wikis defined on the server instead by using the Home Page pop-up menu on the Wiki tab of the Web pane in Server Preferences. Additional websites can be defined for alternative DNS names from any folder location on the server by using the Custom Sites tab, as described later in this chapter.

- **User editable wikis.** These are built by using Apple's supplied tools directly within a browser window. Users can be given permission to update information and add or delete pages from personal wikis or collaboration wikis created for a group. Individuals with a user account on the server can create new wikis after logging in to their own wiki. To create a group collaboration wiki, click the Create a wiki for this group check box when creating the new group in the Groups pane of Server Preferences. Group wikis appear at `http://www.server.com/groups/groupname`. Wikis can be turned on or off system-wide from the Wiki tab of the Web pane in Server Preferences, which also supplies a hyperlink to a listing of available wikis.

- **Web calendars.** These are integrated with wiki pages and are created for users with local accounts and iCal Server calendars. The web interface for calendars is built by the same software that manages wikis. It gets its data from the same underlying iCal Server process that supplies calendar data to iCal or other CalDAV desktop clients (including the iPhone), ensuring that calendar information is kept in sync across web, desktop, and mobile clients. Web calendars can be turned on or off system-wide from the Wiki tab of the Web pane in Server Preferences, which also supplies a hyperlink to a listing of available calendars.

- **Blogs.** These are also tied into wiki and web calendar pages and allow users with accounts on the server to maintain a dynamic site with regularly updated articles, RSS syndication feeds, user comments, file uploads, and other features exposed directly from the web interface. Individual blogs appear at `http://www.server.com/users/username` and can be turned on or off system-wide from the Wiki tab of the Web pane in Server Preferences.

- **Webmail.** This allows users with accounts on the server to log in and check their messages directly from a web browser. It requires the mail server to be active, and individual users need to have mail service enabled for their account on the Services tab of the Users pane in Server Preferences. Webmail can be turned on or off system-wide from the Wiki tab of the Web pane in Server Preferences, which also supplies a hyperlink to the webmail site.

These individual services can't be activated or de-activated on a per-user basis from within Server Preferences; individual features are only turned on or off system-wide, as shown in Figure 7.16.

To create additional websites that serve files from any arbitrary folder location on the server under any designated DNS name, click the Custom Sites tab, shown in Figure 7.17, and then define the site.

Figure 7.16

The simple options for managing web and collaboration services in Server Preferences

Figure 7.17

Creating custom websites in Server Preferences

To define a custom website, follow these steps:

1. **Click the Add (+) button.** The sheet shown in Figure 7.18 drops down.

Figure 7.18

The add sheet drops down from the Custom Sites pane of the Web pane.

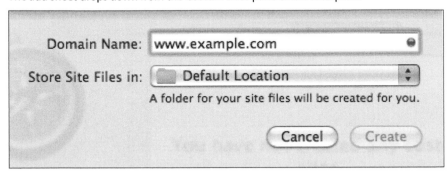

2. **On the sheet, type the desired domain name for the site.** The provided domain name must point to the server in DNS; local administrators need to coordinate with their ISP or their organization's DNS manager to set up a CNAME record for the chosen domain that resolves to the hostname of the local server or set up a new record that maps a domain name to an IP address configured on the local server.

3. **Accept the default location to store site files in.** This creates a folder for your new site at the location /Library/WebServer/Sites/selected domain name/site; alternatively, you can specify a folder location for the custom site manually by using the pop-up menu.

4. **Click Create to begin sharing the folder at the specified domain name.**

5. **Specify group access permissions on the custom site by clicking the Edit button marked with a pencil logo, and then choose the desired group from the Who can view this site pop-up menu.**

A variety of advanced web service configuration options are available only from Server Admin, including finer-grained access permissions by using realms, customizable logging options to enable more sophisticated analytics of web traffic, the capacity to create independent sites (each with its own wiki, blogs, calendar, and webmail options), and support for SSL certificate-based security.

For small groups or departments with basic needs, however, the simple web service settings in Server Preferences, along with the configuration options available within the web-based collaboration site, may be entirely sufficient to set up very useful, cross-platform group collaboration services at low cost that are very easy to administer.

VPN service

Virtual private networking (VPN) enables Mac OS X Server to allow secure access to local network services from remote clients across the open Internet. It works by setting up an encrypted tunnel for all traffic between the remote client and the server by using L2TP (Layer 2 Tunneling Protocol) over the IPsec specification.

Remote clients can connect through the VPN as if dialing up the server to obtain an Internet connection to the server's resources; without establishing an encrypted VPN link, access to many of those services would likely be blocked by the firewall (on the server itself or an external network gateway, such as an AirPort base station or another router) to prevent unauthorized access by the general public to any private services within the local network.

A VPN connection can route all traffic from the remote client to the private network inside the firewall or, alternatively, only send traffic bound to that private domain through the VPN link and continue to communicate with other domains outside its VPN connection, an option that reduces the load on the VPN server for traffic that doesn't need to be sent through it.

Establishing a VPN link requires the remote user to supply user authentication, typically by using his or her standard account name and password. Additionally, the VPN may be configured to also require machine authentication by using a shared secret password used by multiple users.

The VPN configuration also specifies an IP address range for remote users, which designates a pool of addresses on the local network that remote users can be temporarily assigned while connected. This pool is part of the local subnet and can't be shared by the pool of addresses used by DHCP to assign addresses to local machines.

For example, if an AirPort base station is creating the server's local network, its default settings are to set up a DHCP pool of addresses starting at 10.0.1.3 and continuing through 10.0.1.60, providing nearly 60 IP addresses for local machines to use. Additional IP addresses can be manually assigned to devices above that pool in the range between 10.0.1.61 and 10.0.1.254.

By default, the VPN service sets up a separate range of IP addresses from 10.0.1.200 through 10.0.1.220, allowing remote users to obtain an address that doesn't conflict with the addresses dynamically assigned by the DHCP server. Any manually assigned IP addresses would also need to avoid this range because each machine on the network must have a unique IP address.

Remote users connecting to the local network via VPN are given an address from this pool in addition to the IP address they already have from their local DHCP server, which may also be an AirPort device (and therefore default to the same 10.0.1.x subnet). If both their local address and their remote VPN address are in the same subnet, there can be problems correctly forwarding traffic between the two networks.

Administrators should advise remote users to configure their local network outside the subnet used by the VPN server or, alternatively, set up the local server's network on a unique subnet, such as `10.0.5.x` or `192.168.10.x` or another private address subnet that remote users are less likely to already be using.

CROSS-REF
For more on VPN services, see Chapter 16.

Server Preferences provides the same simple on and off switch for the VPN service, along with the option to set a shared secret and configure a customized IP address range, as shown in Figure 7.19.

Figure 7.19

VPN settings in Server Preferences

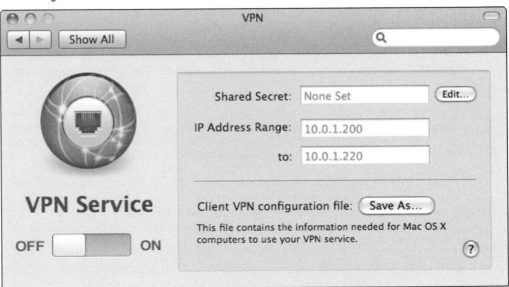

Once configured, the pane also enables administrators to generate a configuration file that Mac OS X users can simply double-click to configure VPN settings on their client computer. The file is saved by default to the Groups file share for users to easily access.

After opening the VPN configuration file, users only need to type their network account name and password, both of which can be saved in their VPN configuration under the Network pane of System Preferences, under VPN (L2TP) settings.

The name of the server and any configured shared secret is already typed as part of the saved configuration file. The user's name can be typed as the Account Name, and the password can optionally be saved under Authentication Settings. Without saving this information, the user is simply prompted to type it at every connection.

A VPN connection is established by clicking Connect in the Network pane of System Preferences, as shown in Figure 7.20, or, alternatively, by selecting the name of the server from the VPN status menu in the menu bar, a feature that's activated from the Network pane by default.

Figure 7.20

Client VPN settings in the Network pane in System Preferences

To allow outside users to connect to the VPN, any network firewalls must be configured to allow traffic on UDP ports 500, 1701, and 4500; on TCP port 1723; and on IP protocol 50. This is automated in the Security pane of Server Preferences by simply allowing the VPN service on the local firewall or for a remotely configured AirPort base station, as detailed shortly.

Additional advanced VPN configuration options for setting up PPTP (Point-to-Point Tunneling Protocol) VPNs common to the Windows environment, using RADIUS authentication, configuring network routing definitions, load balancing, connection monitoring, and other features are available in Server Admin.

Firewall

The Mac OS X Server standard configuration limits the complexity users have to manage the firewall. It's intended for use as the first or only server within a small organization. Although this configuration is easier to manage, it's also limited to a subset of features available in the advanced configuration. Standard configuration sets up all services automatically, leaving the administrator to add users and change simple settings within Server Preferences.

Managing System Information

In addition to configuring basic services, Server Preferences also presents some simple options for managing the server's general settings, reviewing error and user access logs to assist in troubleshooting, and viewing graphs of processor use, network traffic loads, and disk availability as well as traffic trends for file sharing and web services.

Information

The Information pane of Server Preferences provides a simple overview of machine settings, as shown in Figure 7.21, including:

- The version of Mac OS X Server installed, along with the server's processor and RAM
- The server's IP address, DNS name, and local machine name, which appears when browsing the server's file and printer shares on the network
- The server's license status, along with an Edit button for typing a license number
- A way to set up email alerts triggered by selectable factors, such as:
  - Low disk space
  - The availability of new software updates
  - Warnings of expiring certificates
  - A virus being detected in incoming email
- A way to designate an SSL certificate for securing services on the server

Figure 7.21

The Information pane in Server Preferences presents a simple overview of settings.

The SSL certificate options include links to create a self-signed certificate by using Certificate Assistant or to import an existing public certificate, private key, or other non-identity certificates obtained from an external certificate signing authority.

Additional details on the server's installed hardware and software are available from the System Profiler application located in /Applications/Utilities. The Information pane in Server Preferences is a simplified version of that presented in Server Admin by selecting the server name and then clicking Overview, Certificates, or Settings on the toolbar.

Server Admin also presents additional options for enabling additional server network protocols, sending alert notifications to multiple email addresses, restricting services to specific users and groups, and other settings.

Logs

The Logs pane of Server Preferences, as shown in Figure 7.22, provides a simple view for checking a variety of log files generated by different processes, including:

- The System log at /var/log/system.log
- Address Book error and access logs within /var/log/cardavd/
- File Sharing error and access logs for AFP, stored at /Library/Logs/ AppleFileService

- File Sharing logs for Windows SMB, stored at `/var/log/samba/log.smbd`
- iCal Server error and access logs within `/var/log/caldavd/`
- iChat Server logs within `/var/log/jabberd/`
- Mail logs at `/var/log/mailaccess.log` and `/var/log/mail.log`
- Web Server error and access logs within `/var/log/apache2/`
- Wiki error and access logs at `/Library/Logs/wikid/`
- VPN Server logs within `/var/log/ppp/`
- Open Directory error logs for directory services, the password authentication server, and LDAP configuration within `/Library/Logs`

Figure 7.22

The Logs pane in Server Preferences presents a way to review error and access logs.

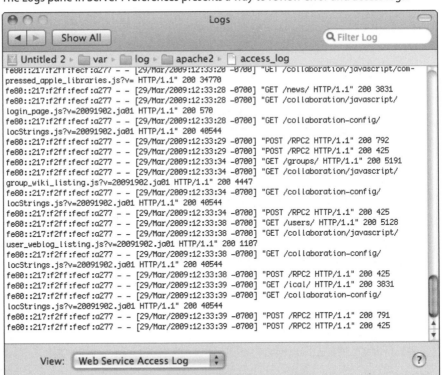

Additional system logs are viewable by using the Console and System Profiler applications located in `/Applications/Utilities`. Server Admin also provides access from the tool-bar to logs for each of the configured services it manages.

Graphs

Visualizing the overall performance of the server and the use of its underlying hardware is easy to do with the basic graphing features within the Graphs pane of Server Preferences. As shown in Figure 7.23, graphs present statistics over time — from a one-hour period to the default four-hour window to several hours or several days, up to a weeklong period. The metrics available are:

- Processor usage as a percentage of CPU capacity
- Inbound and outbound network traffic in megabytes per second
- Currently available disk space across all mounted volumes
- File-sharing traffic in megabytes per second
- Web traffic in megabytes per second

Figure 7.23

The Graphs pane in Server Preferences charts CPU, disk, and network use.

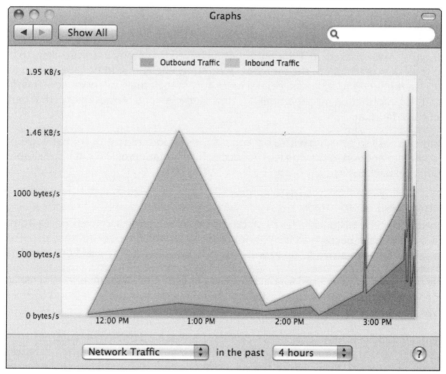

The graphs available within Server Preferences are actually an expansion on what's available within Server Admin. For Xserve hardware, additional remote logging and data visualization features are available in Server Monitor, which can track memory, disk, power, network, temperature, and fan speed statistics reported by the hardware.

Performing Basic Server Administration

Three of the most important ongoing server administration tasks related to Mac OS X Server are:

- Maintaining appropriate server backups
- Keeping the server's software up to date
- Managing a firewall of protection from security threats from outside the local network

This section discusses each, relating how each task on Mac OS X Server compares to the parallel needs for backups, updates, and firewall protection on local client machines.

Planning for backup and restoration

Keeping the server backed up is doubly important given that many users are likely to be backing up their own machines to the server by using Time Machine. Additionally, network users' reliance on the server to act as the central repository of their mail, calendar, contacts, files, and other critical information makes proper backups of the server a serious matter that demands careful consideration.

Although it's easy to come up with a backup plan, it's important to ensure that backups are both complete enough to provide for the successful restoration of lost data and simple enough to ensure the backups actually occur.

Selecting backup media

Administrators have historically relied on tape drives to store the archives of data from a server, but hard drives have become an increasingly popular alternative because they're more flexible to use, relatively inexpensive, faster to write to, and much faster to recover from in an emergency.

Optical media may also be used for backups, but conventional hard drives are increasingly becoming more cost-effective and faster than burning data to optical disc, and the steady improvements in hard disk capacity and speed are widening this gulf.

The remaining advantage in tape or optical media is that hard drive mechanisms can be damaged by mechanical shock, mechanism failure (something that's less likely to occur with tape cassettes), or magnetic fields (which optical disc media aren't affected by). However, tape and optical disc are both fragile in their own ways.

Tape is prone to wearing out, de-magnetizing, or experiencing other physical problems, including not working properly in a drive other than the one that was used to originally write the tape. Optical discs are easy to scratch or break and may degrade (a particular problem with rewritable discs) to the point of being unreadable.

Selecting storage device types

Installed internally as standard SATA or SAS (Serial Attached SCSI, a high-performance drive interface option available in the Mac Pro and Xserve) drives, magnetic (or, at some point in the future, solid state) hard disks can serve as a high-performance, online backup device for rapid or near-instantaneous recovery of missing data.

Attached via Fibre Channel, a SAN unit such as Apple's now-discontinued Xserve RAID can supply large amounts of redundant data storage to multiple network servers as if they were all attached to it directly as a local data store. Concurrent access is managed by using Apple's Xsan file system.

A NAS device is simply an appliance file server hosting a drive or RAID unit. It may offer a cost-effective way to create a backup of files that can be rapidly restored.

Directly connected via FireWire, SCSI, eSATA, or even USB, external hard drives can serve as offline or even offsite backup options, keeping options open to restore data availability even if the server and the rest of the network are destroyed in a fire or flood.

Removable media devices, such as tape or optical drives, may also serve as low-cost ways to archive data for offline storage, but both involve lengthy recovery sessions when restoring lots of data.

CROSS-REF
For more on planning for hardware server needs, see Chapter 4.

Selecting backup strategies

Using multiple layers of different types of backups, administrators can prepare to successfully weather different types of data loss scenarios and emerge as heroes for the users who depend on them. Here are several strategies that can be combined to limit the risk of data loss and recover missing data rapidly:

- **Online, full backup data redundancy.** At a low level, administrators can use techniques such as RAID mirroring for resiliency from drive failure, periodic disk cloning for bootable backups, and high-availability IP failover server deployments to keep network services working even if a server dies completely. All these options duplicate data and the hardware that stores it so the server can be rapidly — perhaps even instantly — returned to operation even after a significant hardware failure. This is also the most expensive avenue for limiting data loss.

- **Incremental backups.** To limit the time required to perform backups, an incremental system completes a full backup at first run and then subsequently backs up only changes and new files. Incrementals are more efficient to process and store during the backup but can require more time to stitch back together when performing a data restoration. Backups can also become more fragile if the system needs incremental data stored on a variety of disks or tapes to perform a full recovery; the failure of one media might complicate recovery. For that reason, the incremental cycle is often regularly started over from scratch, retaining copies of earlier generations of backups to allow both the recovery of recently lost data and the restoration of old data from months or even years ago.

- **Offsite storage.** In addition to planning for data loss, offsite copies of backups stored on either removable tape or optical media or external, portable hard drives can accommodate disaster recovery scenarios where the server itself may need to be rebuilt from scratch.

Having a backup strategy that can only restore the server to where it was before today's drive failure won't help if data is needed from last year and all the historical archives have been tossed out to focus exclusively on more recent data loss events. Having perfect archives that burn down along with the server room in a fire are similarly useless.

Combining the previously discussed strategies to create as many safety nets as possible results in the most flexibility when it comes down to crunch time. However, all these options also cost money and consume storage media that could otherwise be used for other purposes.

Therefore, a backup plan needs to strike a balance between the resources it consumes — both in time and equipment — and the security it can offer. It also needs to be understood that the value of a backup system won't be apparent until something bad happens — particularly something unexpected.

Time Machine Server

For Mac OS X Leopard, Apple took a look at how backups could be simplified to make them easier to do (and therefore more likely to get done) and to restore. Mac OS X Server offers Time Machine Server as a marketing feature, but this is really just a fancy way of saying the server's file server can accept Time Machine backups, which are simply disk image files.

Administrators who want to use Time Machine Server to back up client computers need to make sure they provide enough space to store client computers' data so those backups don't eat up all the available disk space on the server. Backups are saved to a share at `/Shared Items/Backups/` on the drive selected by the administrator from the Time Machine pane of Server Preferences.

To enable client backups by using Time Machine Server, follow these steps:

1. **Open the Time Machine pane of Server Preferences, shown in Figure 7.24.**

Figure 7.24

The Time Machine pane in Server Preferences

2. **Click the Select Disk button to choose a drive and then turn the service on by moving the switch.**

In addition to disk space, Time Machine also demands fast networking. Although Apple markets the technology as suitable for the personal backups for home users with 802.11n wireless networking, it really demands at least a gigabit Ethernet connection to a fast network file share and optimally wants to use a local SATA, FireWire, or USB drive.

In scenarios that involve more than several users on a small network, using Time Machine Server to manage central backups of all client machines on the network might not make as much sense as giving users the ability to back up their own casual data, either to a secondary internal drive or to an external portable drive they manage themselves.

This isn't a problem with Time Machine Server so much as it's an intrinsic problem with trying to back up everything users might have on their local machines without regard for how valuable that data might be. In many cases, the data users store on their local machines is often mostly music or installer disk images and other files that have little value for the organization to manage.

Backing up the server: local Time Machine

Data on the server, however, is critically important to back up, even if it may include lots of low-value music and media files, email attachments, and other space-consuming files that users generate. In this case, Time Machine makes a lot of sense because it allows the server to back itself up in a way that maintains a long-term trail of archives while balancing the need for efficient use of the backup archives repository, whether that's a locally connected drive, SAN, or NAS.

Time Machine uses file system *hard links*, a special type of directory reference that enables a single file on disk to effectively be in more than one folder on the drive without actually consuming more space on disk than a single copy of the file needs.

This means Time Machine can act as an incremental backup system without the fragility that affects incremental systems that span multiple tapes or discs or the redundancy that occurs when the incremental backups are started over from scratch and a previous generation of backups are archived.

Time Machine strikes a good balance between making older versions of files available without consuming as much storage media as a typical backup system would. However, Time Machine isn't intended to be an archival system; it's just a very convenient backup program.

Administrators who need to maintain archives of email and other documents can't rely on Time Machine to do this for them because the system is designed to selectively weed out old archives as needed to keep space available for more recent backups.

At the same time, Time Machine makes it so easy to restore data — particularly elements of data within a database, such as contact records within Address Book or any other application designed with Time Machine in mind — that it can serve as a very useful element in an overall backup strategy.

To set up server backups to a drive by using Time Machine, follow these steps:

1. **Open the Time Machine pane of System Preferences.**

2. **Click the Select Disk button to choose a drive and then turn the service on by moving the switch.**

Just as on the Mac desktop, Time Machine makes a full backup of all the drives on the server and then makes subsequent hourly backups of incremental changes, which are thrown out after 24 hours outside of a daily archive. The dailies are kept for a month and then weeded back to weekly archives, which are retained until disk space on the backup drive hits the point where old weeklies are thrown out to make space for new backups.

This creates a great balance between the backups kept and the space needed on the drive. Administrators can optimize the process by making sure the Time Machine disk is fast enough to not slow down the server during backups and by excluding anything on the server that doesn't need to be backed up. As with the identical Time Machine feature on the Mac desktop, this is done by clicking the Options button and then adding volumes or folders that don't need to be backed up.

Realistically, because so many smaller departmental systems aren't properly backed up, Time Machine may likely serve as the entire backup plan for many small server users. This is certainly better than nothing and is also better than a sophisticated backup system that isn't backed up regularly enough to be useful. However, it really needs to be augmented at a bare minimum with a secondary safety net that provides both a bootable backup and provisions for offsite backups.

Bootable backups

An easy way to provide a bootable backup on the cheap is to dedicate a drive to serve as a hot spare for the server's boot drive and then use a *block copy* disk utility, such as SuperDuper, to periodically clone the drive at night. A block copy makes an exact replica of the data on disk to another disk rather than reading each individual file and writing them all back out to another volume, which is a much more time-intensive process.

A RAID 0 mirroring configuration does something similar but doesn't protect the system from configuration errors or corruption that might render both identical drives unbootable at once.

The goal of a bootable backup is to enable the server to be restored back to operation by simply rebooting the system from the spare drive. Without a bootable backup, the server may need to be reinstalled from scratch by using the Snow Leopard Server DVDs. Although this process can also import the backups made by Time Machine during the install process, this entire cycle may take many hours to complete.

With a bootable backup, the server can immediately be returned to operation and then just the last day's changes can be restored by using Time Machine afterward at a bit more leisured pace.

Offsite backups

Although a bootable hot spare will save the day when the server's own boot drive fails, it won't be useful if it ends up lost along with the server in a fire, flood, hurricane, earthquake, theft, or other disaster scenario. For that reason, it's critically important that an additional copy of backups be taken to a safe alternative location.

Taking backups offsite isn't just a critically important element of a backup plan but also a potential security risk. The private data stored on backups is likely carefully secured on the server, but once taken offsite, the hard drives or other storage media are much easier to steal or modify. For this reason, adequate security measures must be taken to make sure that backups are treated as carefully as server equipment and access to resources on the network itself.

CROSS-REF

For more on securing your Mac, see the *Mac Security Bible* by Joe Kissell (Wiley, 2010).

Managing software updates

In addition to making sure the server's data can be restored to a given point in the past, it's also very important to ensure that the server's software is kept up to date with the latest updates and security patches. Apple makes this easy to do with Software Update, but administrators need to also be aware of best practices in this area.

Updating network machines: Software Update Server

Apple provides a centralized update service in Mac OS X Server designed to act as a proxy for obtaining updates issued by Apple and then selectively serving only approved updates to client computers on the network, which use the local Software Update Server instead of getting their updates from Apple's servers directly.

This saves on network bandwidth because large updates are obtained from Apple's outside servers only once and also gives administrators control over when updates are rolled out to client machines.

This feature doesn't really offer much benefit to smaller sites running in standard configuration, which are unlikely to see any real impact from users all downloading and installing their updates directly, whereas independent departments running in workgroup configuration may benefit from the Software Update Server maintained by the larger organization. Therefore, there's no provision to set up Software Update Server from Server Preferences. Users who need to run this need to use Server Admin and upgrade to the advanced configuration.

Updating the server: local Software Update

Keeping the server up to date isn't any different than updating the Mac desktop. Snow Leopard Server uses the same Software Update pane in System Preferences, with the same options to periodically check for updates and download available software as it becomes available.

As with updates released for the desktop, administrators should delay installing the updates until any potential problems with the new version of the software can be discovered and addressed. This is even more important in a server environment, where interruptions caused by unintended problems will have more significant impact on users, and installed software updates may be more difficult to roll back than on a desktop system.

A server may also have customized settings or other unique circumstances that may combine with an update flaw or simply an unanticipated change to result in complex problems for administrators to address. This makes it even more important for server administrators to watch for any problems that other server users are reporting before installing any new updates.

Ideally, an isolated test environment can be used to provide administrators with the ability to install server updates and see if there are any problems before rolling the new software out on their production servers. Users who lack the resources to set this up should wait for those who do to report their experiences.

Fortunately, even the most critical software security updates are rarely necessary to install immediately, thanks to the current lack of attention that crackers and malware producers give to the Mac OS X platform. At the same time, however, administrators need to keep themselves up to date on the current state of security threats and existing software problems and carefully weigh those against the potential for interruption or compatibility problems that new updates might introduce.

Firewall

Software updates can provide hardened security for the server, but a firewall hedges all bets by limiting the traffic and, therefore, the vectors for malicious assault that can even reach it.

Mac OS X Snow Leopard Server provides an easy-to-configure IP firewall interface within the Security pane of Server Preferences. This interface can be used to expose specific services based on presets defined for common services or by supplying defining allowed services and the port numbers they use.

Outside of the services that are expressly given access, other incoming traffic is blocked at the firewall. This limits incoming, unsolicited connection attempts from touching the server anywhere apart from the designated ports related to those services. IP port numbers identify different kinds of network traffic directed to an IP address to enable applications to selectively listen only to specific ports. By filtering which ports are allowed through the firewall, the system's applications can be protected from unsolicited, potentially malicious communication attempts.

The result is that even if the server provides an insecure service to the local network, such as SMB Windows file sharing, outside attackers can't talk to the SMB server and exploit its vulnerabilities because the firewall doesn't allow incoming traffic on the ports SMB uses.

The flip side of this is that administrators must be selective in what traffic they allow through their firewall because a firewall that allows all traffic is more dangerous than not having any firewall, if only because it offers a false sense of security.

Services commonly exposed to the open Internet, such as web hosting at port 80 or SSH remote login at port 22, are designed to incorporate security practices, either by carefully limiting what contact remote hosts can initiate, as web servers do, or by requiring authenticated access, as SSH does.

Services that do incorporate adequate security measures to stand up to public assault on the open Internet (such as FTP) need to be exposed to remote users with external security wrapping by using SSH port forwarding, a secured L2TP VPN connection, or similar protection.

Two application firewalls

The firewall interface presented by Server Preferences can be used to configure the local firewall on the server, called Firewall security on the Security pane, or, alternatively, to set up the firewall of an AirPort base station, called AirPort management.

If an AirPort is already acting as the network's firewall, being able to configure its firewall settings from Server Preferences is handy. The AirPort's firewall (or any other appliance router and firewall in place on the network) may also be configured to route all incoming traffic to the server's IP address, requiring the server to provide its own layer of firewall protection. Setting up public access to local services through the firewall is identical in either case.

To expose services though the firewall, follow these steps:

1. **Open the Security pane of Server Preferences, shown in Figure 7.25.**

2. **Turn the service on by moving the switch.**

Figure 7.25

The Security pane in Server Preferences

3. **Click the Add (+) button.** From the sheet that appears, select a predefined service or select Other and then type a service name and port number to allow.

4. **Click Add.** The service appears in the list allowed through the firewall.

Advanced IP firewall

In addition to the simple firewall service presented by Server Preferences, Mac OS X Server also provides an advanced IP firewall interface in Server Admin that provides more sophisticated and complex management options for accepting or denying traffic based on additional criteria, such as where the traffic originates. The firewall service can also be configured from the command line or by using third-party tools, without requiring the server to enter the advanced configuration.

CROSS-REF

For more on advanced firewall configuration, see Chapter 14.

Summary

- Server Preferences makes it easy to administer Mac OS X Server by greatly reducing the complexity of the options available, but this also limits what administrators can do.

- The basic configuration possible in Server Preferences can act as a stepping-stone toward a more sophisticated setup in the advanced configuration with Server Admin, but once this step is taken, there's no easy way to return to the simpler past.

- Server Preferences simplifies the management of users and groups, which can be created locally or imported from another directory server in the organization.

- A variety of powerful collaboration and network services are possible to set up and maintain in Server Preferences without much experience in server administration.

- Careful planning is needed to ensure that backups are being made and that those backups are actually useful when a crisis occurs.

- Software updates should be managed to prevent unanticipated changes from interrupting availability of the server.

- Server Preferences simplifies the task of securing a network firewall by either setting up a firewall in the server or delegating that task to an AirPort base station.

Additional Basic Admin Tools

I n addition to using Server Preferences to activate and configure basic services, Mac OS X Server in the standard and workgroup configurations also presents a Server Status widget for remote monitoring of server statistics from Dashboard.

This widget can be installed on any computer running Mac OS X Snow Leopard as part of the Mac OS X Server Admin tools package. Multiple servers can each be monitored with separate instances of the widget.

Apart from presenting a simple overview of the network, CPU, and disk resources in use on a given server, the widget also presents the status of services running on the server and provides links to the appropriate panes in Server Preferences for each.

Although the Server Status widget can be used with servers running in advanced configuration, those servers don't use the basic Server Preferences and don't even allow a remote connection from computers running the application. Therefore, the direct links to Server Preferences presented within the Server Status widget won't work.

That makes the rather limited utility of the Server Status widget of much use only to server administrators with the basic needs of a standard or workgroup configuration.

Outside of the Server Status widget, a variety of other graphical and command-line tools exist that can be used in Mac OS X Server under the standard or workgroup configurations, but caution should be taken to avoid inadvertently crossing the complexity boundary and entering the world of the advanced configuration because there's no way to go back once that Pandora's box has been opened.

Administrators may eventually need to upgrade their standard or workgroup configuration to the advanced configuration as they grow beyond the capabilities offered within Server Preferences and need to take on the advanced complexity and deeper feature set available within Server Admin.

CROSS-REF
For more on Server Admin, see Chapter 9.

Monitoring Server Statistics from Dashboard with the Server Status Widget

The Server Status widget can be installed on any Mac OS X Server or Mac OS X desktop system, although the version of the widget, as with Apple's other Mac OS X Server administration tools, must match the reference release version of the server being remotely managed or monitored.

Organizations with both Leopard Server and Snow Leopard Server deployed should be able to use the latest version of the administration tools with older versions of Mac OS X Server but will run into problems trying to use previous versions of the administration tools with the latest release of the Mac OS X Server operating system.

Additionally, the latest Snow Leopard Server administration tools require and can run only on Mac OS X Snow Leopard, so administrators using a PowerPC Mac or other hardware running Leopard or earlier can't use that system to manage Snow Leopard Server.

NOTE
Even the simple Server Status widget makes enough use of Snow Leopard features that it won't work on Leopard, even when manually installed as a widget itself.

To install the Server Status widget on an administrator's desktop, follow these steps:

1. **Insert the Mac OS X Server install DVD.** From the Other Installs folder, open `ServerAdministrationSoftware.mpkg` to install the tools.

2. **Open Dashboard by using the Dock icon or by pressing either the F4 or F12 key (depending on which is set as the Dock hotkey in System Preferences).** If the Server Status widget isn't visible, click the plus (+) icon in the lower left to reveal the Dashboard widget bar and then drag Server Status onto the Dashboard desktop.

3. **Type the Server name and an administrator account's username and password to log in to the server, as shown in Figure 8.1.** Additional instances of the widget can be opened to monitor multiple servers. The server name can be either the DNS name or its IP address.

4. **Click Done.**

NOTE
Full installation of the Server administration tools is approximately 350 MB. There's no way to selectively install just the Server Status widget or other specific tools from within the installer, although unneeded tools can be deleted from the `/Applications/Server` folder after they're installed.

Figure 8.1

Server login from the Server Status widget

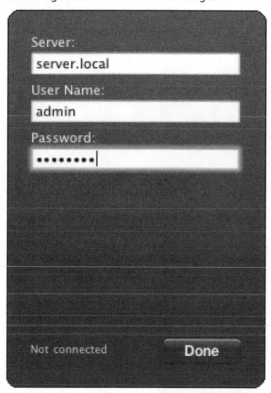

Server Status resource charts

The Server Status widget presents three statistics modes:

- **CPU Utilization.** This is represented by a graph icon with two peaks, as shown in Figure 8.2, and shows the per-processor load as a percentage over time. Mousing over the text of the label above the graph offers three time options for the data being presented: one hour, one day, or one week.

Figure 8.2

CPU Utilization in the Server Status widget

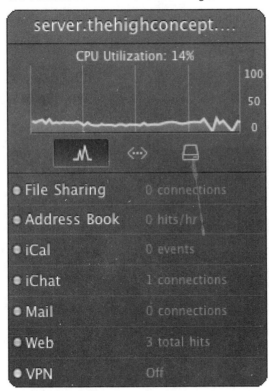

● **Network Load.** This is represented by an Ethernet icon, as shown in Figure 8.3, and shows network use as a graph up and down from a center line, representing inbound and outbound traffic, respectively. As with CPU Utilization, mousing over the text of the label above the graph offers three time options for the data being presented: one hour, one day, or one week.

Figure 8.3

Network Load in the Server Status widget

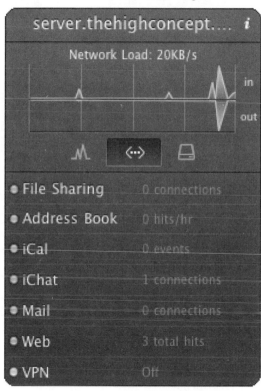

● **Disk Usage.** This is represented by a hard drive icon, as shown in Figure 8.4, and shows proportional free disk availability as a pie chart. The display defaults to the boot volume, but clicking the chart cycles through the attached drives on the system.

Figure 8.4

Disk Usage in the Server Status widget

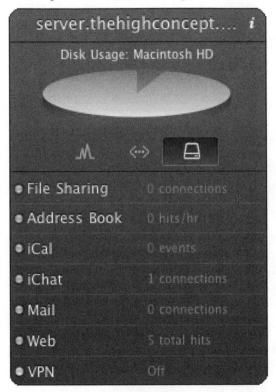

Server Status service monitoring

Under the chart area, the Server Status widget presents a status bar for the following services:

● File Sharing
● Address Book
● iCal
● iChat
● Mail
● Web
● VPN

Each indicates if the service is running and presents a hyperlink to the related pane within Server Preferences when the bar is moused over.

Upgrading to Advanced Tools

Moving outside of Apple's limited standard configuration or workgroup configuration is required to access the more advanced features in Mac OS X Server, but that move also requires taking on more complexity. When running Snow Leopard Server on an Xserve, the more sophisticated Server Monitor application, shown in Figure 8.5, can be used to remotely view a wider variety of system attributes, from fan speeds and system temperatures to detailed disk and network use. It can even obtain a System Profiler report remotely.

Figure 8.5

Server Monitor

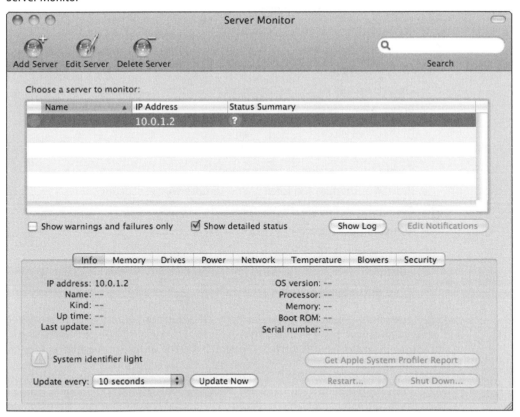

CROSS-REF
For more on Server Monitor, see Chapter 11.

One-way migration risks with Server Admin

Server Admin presents an administration interface for working with a wider range of services and more depth in the management features of each service. Among the services presented in Server Admin that aren't available in Server Preferences are:

- DHCP subnets with static reservations
- Configurable DNS zones
- Advanced IP firewall configuration
- FTP
- Mobile Access for secure remote access for iPhone users
- MySQL database management
- Configurable NAT and IP forwarding
- NetBoot management
- NFS file sharing
- Open Directory policy management and database archiving
- Podcast Producer
- Print queue services
- Push notification services for mobile users
- QuickTime Streaming Server management
- RADIUS authentication for WPA2-Enterprise wireless security
- Configurable SMB file sharing for Windows users
- Software Update Server
- Configurable PPTP VPN services
- Advanced web sharing services, including WebDAV realms and SSL encryption
- Xgrid distributed computing

In some cases, users working in a standard or workgroup configuration can open Server Admin and activate advanced services that don't impact how Server Preferences works, allowing the use of some advanced services while still maintaining the simple configuration available within Server Preferences.

However, moving back and forth between these two tools prompts an initial warning because settings made in the two tools may overwrite each other or create other unanticipated problems. That's because Server Preferences assumes it's in full control of the server.

Once a server has been upgraded to become an advanced configuration, opening Server Preferences to make additional changes can wipe out portions of the advanced configuration, creating problems that may be difficult to solve.

Apple works around this potential issue by limiting a remote user from connecting to an advanced configuration server from Server Preferences. Realistically, once users find the need to move beyond the simple Server Preferences, there's little reason to want to move back.

Unless a group wants to operate a limited duty server or delegate administration to a less experienced user, the limitations of Server Preferences can quickly become rather strangling. Server Admin itself presents a fairly easy to use interface, shown in Figure 8.6, that users who have outgrown Server Preferences should be able to pick up quickly.

Figure 8.6

Server Admin

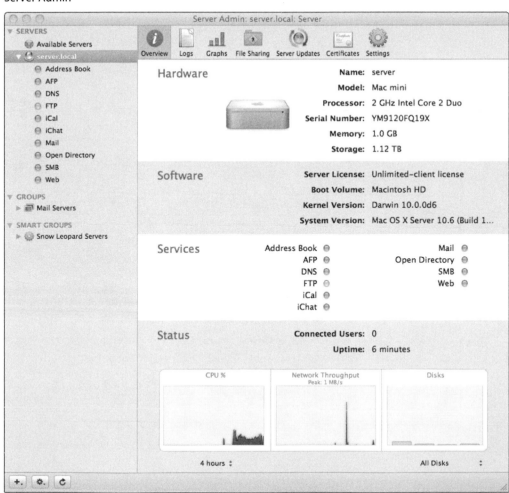

CROSS-REF
For more on Server Admin, see Chapter 9.

One-way migration risks with Workgroup Manager

Workgroup Manager similarly presents a more advanced interface for working with users, groups, and computer accounts. Server Preferences enables administrators to create or import users and groups from outside directory servers, but Workgroup Manager presents full access to Open Directory account information and settings, as shown in Figure 8.7. That includes managed user preferences for users and computers bound to the Open Directory domain as well as advanced control of users' home directories, mail quotas, and print queue access.

Figure 8.7

Workgroup Manager

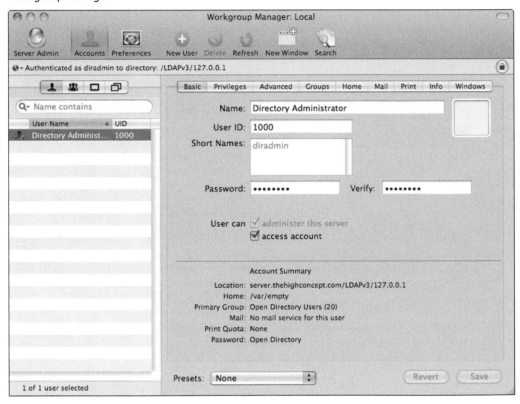

Once users are associated with advanced settings in Workgroup Manager, the same potential issue of inadvertently overwriting settings occurs if users attempt to manage user account settings from Server Preferences.

CROSS-REF
For more on Workgroup Manager, see Chapter 10.

Command-line utilities in standard configuration

Just as Server Admin and Workgroup Manager offer the potential for conflict with the settings made in Server Preferences, command-line utilities may also be used to edit records or customize the system in ways that aren't compatible with Server Preferences.

This also applies to administrators working in the advanced configuration by using Server Admin and Workgroup Manager; customizations to services such as DNS can result in either the loss of those customizations when subsequently returning to work in Apple's administration tools or difficulty in troubleshooting problems where the full configuration of the server simply isn't visible within the graphical tools.

Apple has taken efforts to make its graphical tools as compatible as possible with manual customizations made from the command line, but administrators who take on additional complexity outside the tools Apple provides must keep in mind that they're working without a net and must exercise caution. That includes fully documenting every manual configuration made.

Summary

- The Server Status widget presents a simple overview of resources in use on the server.
- The widget is installable on any server or desktop Mac system running at least Mac OS X Snow Leopard.
- The widget is linked to Server Preferences, making it most useful to administrators working with a standard or workgroup configuration server.

Advanced Mac OS X Server Management

Server Admin

9

A lthough Apple presents Server Preferences and the Server Status widget as entry-level tools for managing Snow Leopard Server, advanced users should instead use Server Admin for configuring services and Workgroup Manager for managing network users, groups, and computers.

CROSS-REF
For more on Workgroup Manager, see Chapter 10.

Administrators working with a standard or workgroup configuration may likely want to upgrade to the advanced configuration as they grow beyond the capabilities offered within Server Preferences and need to take on the advanced complexity and deeper feature set available within Server Admin.

Starting with Mac OS X 10.3 Panther Server, Apple combined the previous Server Status and Server Settings applications into one unified tool for activating, configuring, and monitoring everything from core network services, such as DNS and firewall, to basic file and print services to the specialized services Apple adds, including QuickTime Streaming Server, NetBoot, and Xgrid.

Server Admin is also used to create and manage SSL certificates to secure services; manage file-sharing features, such as quotas; and limit which users have access to specific services running on the server.

The application can be used to monitor a single server or a fleet of servers, including machines at remote locations, provided that the appropriate ports are open on the firewall to allow traffic between the server and the management system running Server Admin.

It can be installed on any administrative Mac desktop or laptop as part of the Server Administration Software package, which is included on the Snow Leopard Server installer DVD, inside the Other Installs folder, appearing as `ServerAdministrationSoftware.mpkg`.

As with other apps installed by the Server Administration Software package, it does require Mac OS X Snow Leopard, which runs only on Intel Macs; therefore, Server Admin can't be installed on PowerPC Macs or other hardware running Leopard or earlier versions of Mac OS X.

In This Chapter

Authenticating with a server to be administered

Exploring the interface

Managing and configuring services

Reviewing logs

Monitoring performance

Configuring file share points, permissions, and quotas

Updating server software

Managing certificates

Configuring settings

Working with multiple servers in groups and smart groups

This chapter describes how Server Admin is used to manage either one or a series of servers, either locally or from an administrator system, and presents an overview of its graphical user interface.

Authenticating with a Server

After installing the Server Administration Software package, Server Admin can be launched from `/Applications/Server`. On the server itself, it can be launched from the Server Stack installed by default on the Snow Leopard Server Dock.

Once launched, the application prompts for a server to connect to; administrators can connect by the server's DNS name or the IP address of the server by using an account name and password with administrator access.

Server Admin supports administration of any number of servers in different locations and can group servers into arbitrary collections or create dynamic Smart Groups of servers that create collections based on criteria, including the use of the server, current resources in use, IP addresses, or other factors. In order to remotely log in to a machine with Server Admin over a secure SSL connection, TCP port 311 must be allowed through the firewall.

Once a variety of servers are configured, Server Admin settings can be exported to a file with password encryption to allow administrators to set up additional administrative workstations with the same configuration, including any server passwords.

The specific settings of a particular server and all its configured services can also be exported to a file by using Export Server Settings and then imported to allow a new server to be set up with an identical configuration. The export process allows the user to select any or all of the currently configured services as part of the settings to be exported.

Exploring the Interface

Server Admin presents a consistent interface across all the services it manages, showing a list of available servers in a source listing on the left, a toolbar across the top, a pane of controls and monitoring displays below the toolbar, and an action bar along the bottom of the Server Admin window, as shown in Figure 9.1.

Server list and action bar

The server list presents all the currently defined servers. At the top of the list is an Available Servers browser listing, which uses Bonjour to discover any servers visible on the local network.

Figure 9.1

The Server Admin interface

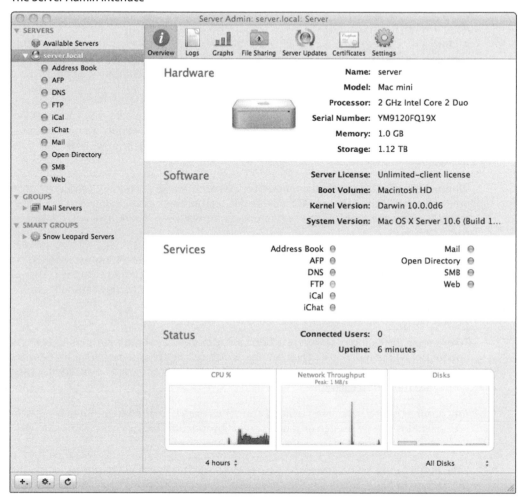

Below each server's listing is a sublisting of the defined services activated on that server; each service may be actively running (indicated by a green dot) or stopped (indicated by a gray dot).

Below the server list is the action bar, which stretches across the length of the window. At the left end of the action bar, there are three buttons: an Add button, an Action button, and a Refresh button. If a service is selected, a fourth button appears, offering to start or stop that service on the selected server.

The Add (+) button displays a pop-up menu offering to add a new server to the list, create a new group, create a new Smart Group, or add a service to a server.

Add Server

Adding a new server requires specifying a DNS name or IP address of the server and logging in with an administrative username and password. If added by IP address, Server Admin attempts to resolve the DNS name for the listing but displays its shorter computer name. These behaviors can be changed in the Server Admin preferences.

Another preference that can be disabled is the warning that appears when attempting to connect to a server running in standard configuration from Server Admin. It's not recommended to make configuration changes in Server Admin on any server that you want to administer by using Server Preferences.

When you log in to a standard configuration server from Server Admin remotely, Server Admin offers to convert the system to the advanced configuration; once changed, it's not possible to revert to using the simpler Server Preferences afterward without reinstalling the software or using a backup.

If a server in the list becomes unresponsive or is no longer available, the server's entry in the list is grayed-out; a connection icon appears that can be used to reconnect to the server. Server Admin may also offer to remove the server's listing if it's unreachable at launch.

Add Group

To organize the listing of servers, a group can be defined to act as a containing folder. Groups appear below the individual server listings, which can be collapsed entirely to present groups as the main interface. Servers can be arbitrarily added to a group simply by dragging the server name into the group listing.

Any number of groups can be defined, and servers can be added to multiple groups. Individual group listings can be used to organize servers by function, location, hardware configuration, or whatever arrangement makes sense for an organization.

Selecting a group listing presents an overview of all the servers in the group, listing their name, the version of Mac OS X Server they're running, a CPU utilization status bar, a numerical network throughput status, a status bar showing the available disk space for local drives, an uptime listing, and the number of connected users, as shown in Figure 9.2.

Add Smart Group

Similar to Smart Folders in the Finder or Smart Playlists in iTunes, the Server Admin Smart Group presents a dynamic grouping of configured servers that match any or all of the specified criteria, including:

- **Visible services matching a specific service.** For example, group all servers configured to handle mail
- **Running services matching a specific service.** For example, group all active web servers

- **Network throughput that's less than or greater than a specified number.** For example, group machines by active load or by idle servers

- **CPU utilization that's less than or greater than a specified percentage.** For example, all servers currently running above an 80% processor utilization threshold

- **IP address that contains, starts with, or ends with a specified number.** For example, group machines by their assigned addresses

- **Version of the operating system.** For example, group machines that are greater than, greater than or equal to, less than, or less than or equal to a specified release of Mac OS X Server

Figure 9.2

A Group listing in Server Admin

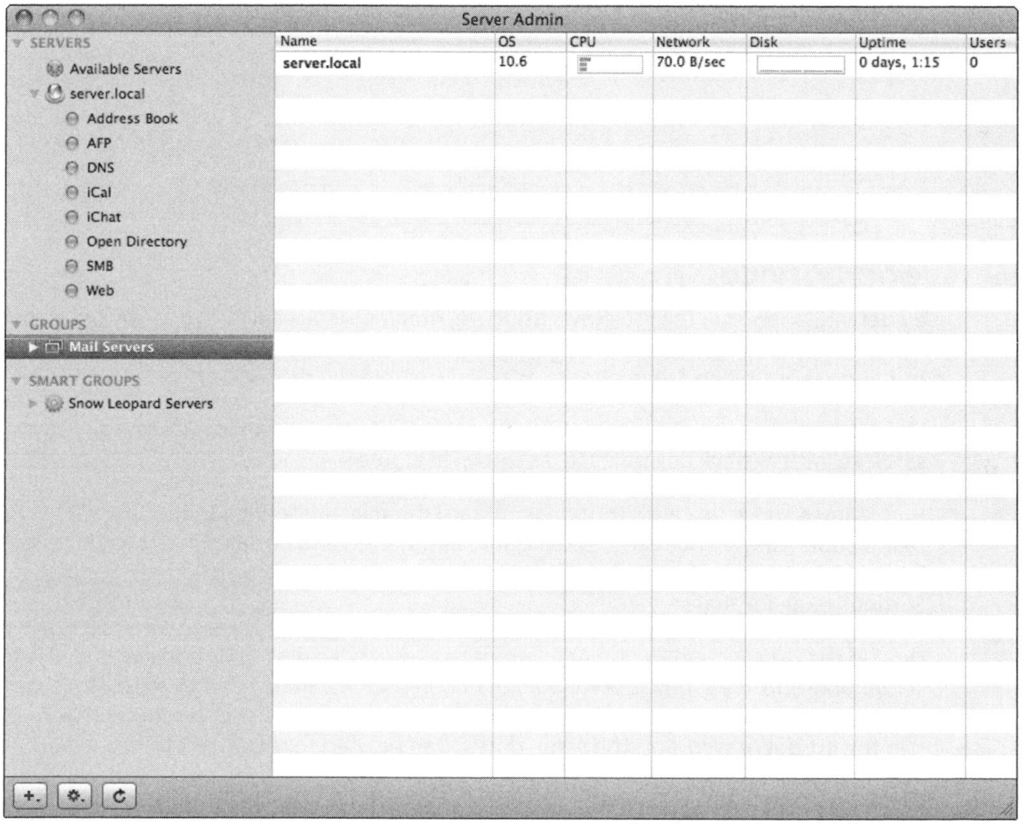

Name	OS	CPU	Network	Disk	Uptime	Users
server.local	10.6		70.0 B/sec		0 days, 1:15	0

SERVERS
- Available Servers
- server.local
  - Address Book
  - AFP
  - DNS
  - iCal
  - iChat
  - Open Directory
  - SMB
  - Web

GROUPS
- Mail Servers

SMART GROUPS
- Snow Leopard Servers

All defined servers fitting the specific definition of a Smart Group, as shown in the drop-down sheet in Figure 9.3 that appears when creating a new Smart Group, are displayed within it and updated dynamically as those factors change. Clicking a Smart Group listing presents the same streamlined status overview for the servers matched to that grouping, just like a manual Group.

Figure 9.3

The Smart Group definition sheet in Server Admin

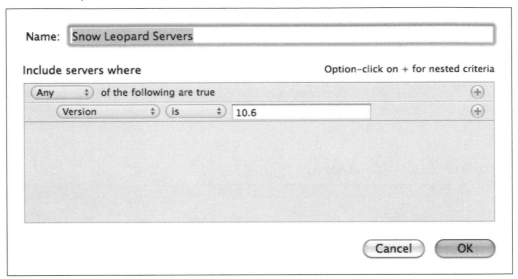

Add Service

By default, a server in the list shows its active, running services within a list below it that may be collapsed by clicking its disclosure triangle. To add additional services to a server's listing, click the Add (+) button and then choose Add Service from the drop-down menu.

This jumps to the Services tab of the Settings page for that server, which lists all the available services, with a check box for each, as shown in Figure 9.4.

Activating a check box adds (but doesn't start) the selected service to the server's listing. After being added, the service can be configured and started and remains in the listing even if it becomes inactive until it's manually removed from the check box list on the Services tab of the Settings page for that server.

Next to the Add (+) button, the Action button presents a series of options for the selected server or group. If a group is selected, the Action button can be used to delete it. If a server is selected, the Action button can be used to remove it from the list or disconnect from it, leaving it in the list but grayed-out. The same button can be used to reconnect to the server.

These actions are easier to perform directly, however, because a selected server or group can be removed from the list simply by pressing the Delete key, which pops up a window offering to remove the selected item. Press Option+Delete to remove the item without confirmation.

Figure 9.4

The Services list in Server Admin

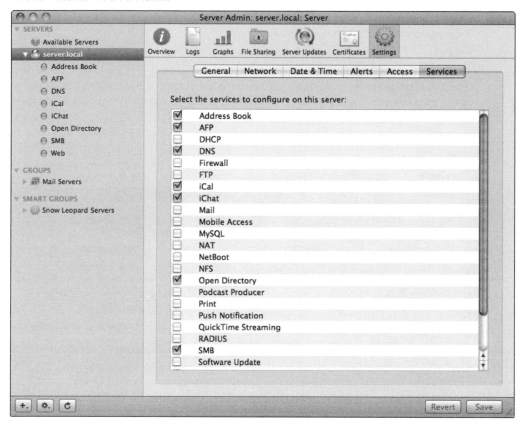

Similarly, connecting to a disconnected server is easiest to do simply by clicking the Connect button next to the server's listing, which works identically to the Reconnect button presented in Mac OS X Mail for offline accounts.

The Action button can also be used to initiate an SSH command-line session with a selected server or to initiate a VNC screen-sharing session.

Additional action bar buttons

Next to the Action button is a Refresh button, which updates the display. Server Admin auto-refreshes every 60 seconds by default, a setting that can be modified in preferences.

The fourth button starts or stops the selected service. At the right end of the action bar, specific panes or pages may present Save or Revert buttons for initiating or backing out from the con-figurations entered in the pane.

Toolbar

The Server Admin toolbar changes contextually with the selection of a server or a service running on the server. When a server is selected, the toolbar presents icons for seven pages of information related to the server itself.

Overview

The first page presents an overview of what's happening on that server in a listing of its hardware, software, configured services, and overall status, as shown in Figure 9.5. The status area presents the same information as the Server Status widget.

Figure 9.5

The Overview page in Server Admin

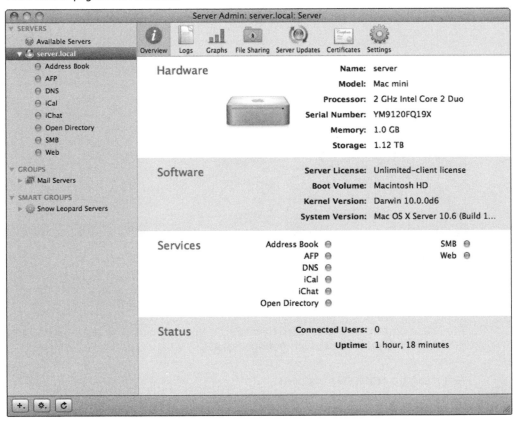

Logs

The Logs page, shown in Figure 9.6, presents an interface for reviewing the general system events recorded in `/var/log/system.log`, those events related to authentication attempts in `/var/log/secure.log`, and the Software Update log.

Figure 9.6

The Logs page in Server Admin

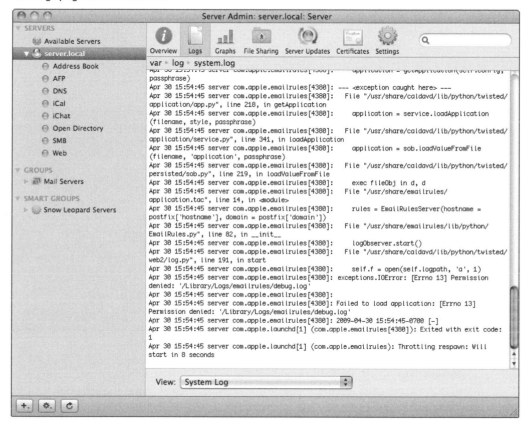

Graphs

The Graphs page tracks either CPU use or network traffic over the past 2, 4, 6, 12, or 24 hours or the last 2, 3, 5, or 7 days. Interestingly, the simpler Server Preferences also offers to graph web or file-sharing traffic, something Server Admin doesn't do.

The Graphs page, shown in Figure 9.7, offers more detailed reporting in a larger display than the Overview page but essentially tracks the same information.

Figure 9.7

The Graphs page in Server Admin

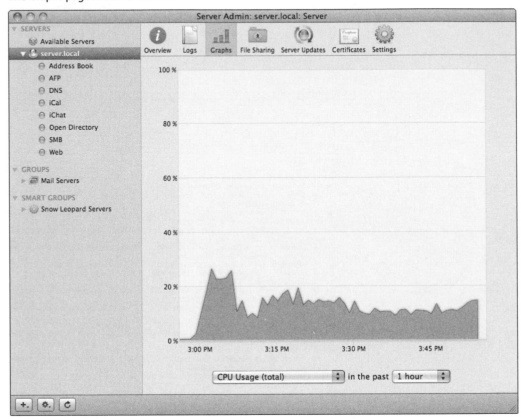

File Sharing

The File Sharing page, shown in Figure 9.8, presents a list of either the attached local volumes or the defined share points, which represent each of the folders being actively shared. Prior to Leopard Server, share points were managed from Workgroup Manager. The File Sharing page also presents an interface for managing:

- **Share point features.** These include Automount, Spotlight search, Time Machine backups, and protocol options.

- **Access permissions for shares and folders.** These use both standard Unix and ACLs.

- **Enabling quotas for volumes.** This can be used to limit the storage resources individual users consume.

Figure 9.8

The File Sharing page in Server Admin

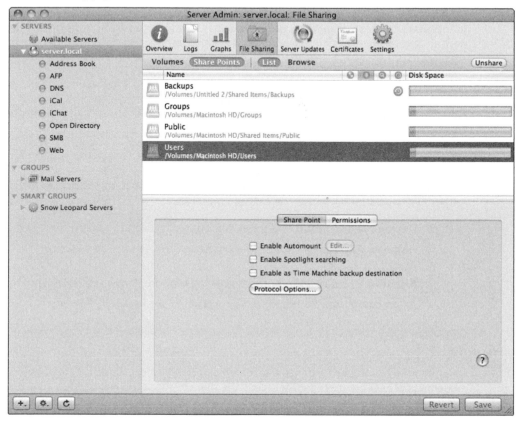

With Volumes selected, the local disks can be presented either as a simple list, which shows the format type and a bar chart representing available disk space on each, or in browse mode, which presents a column browser for navigating the contents of the volume.

From the volume browser, a new folder can be created on the drive, and any selected directory can be shared by using the buttons at the top right, creating a new share point. When a volume is selected, an additional tab appears that enables quota support on the volume, a feature that allows administrators to limit the disk resources consumed by a given user. The actual limits are defined in Workgroup Manager.

CROSS-REF

For more on configuring a user's disk quota, see Chapter 10.

When Share Points is selected, Server Admin shows only actively shared folders, again either as a list or in a browser view. A share point can be removed from file sharing by using the Unshare button.

In the Share Point list view, shares are indicated as having Automount, Spotlight searching, and/or Time Machine backup support either enabled or not on the shared folder, via the use of small icons.

Below the listing, a second lower pane displays Share Point and Permissions tabs used to configure additional settings related to the directories being shared, including Automount settings, share feature support (including activation of Spotlight searching and Time Machine backups), share protocol settings, and share access control permissions.

The Share Point tab allows administrators to selectively enable Automount support for a share, which lets directory server users automatically mount the server share point at login. When first enabled, a sheet drops down to specify the directory, the file-sharing protocol to be used (either AFP or NFS), and whether the Automount serves as:

- **User home and group folders.** Automounted by users in `/Network/Servers`
- **A shared Applications folder.** Automounted by users in `/Network/Applications`
- **A shared Library folder.** Automounted by users in `/Network/Library`
- **A custom mount.** Automounted by users at a specified path

Once defined, Automount share points can be assigned to users and groups in Workgroup Manager.

In addition to Automount settings, the Share Point tab presents the option to enable Spotlight searching for network users and/or enable the share to support being used as a destination for network users' Time Machine backups.

A Protocol Options button allows administrators to choose how to share the selected folder by using:

- **AFP (Apple Filing Protocol).** The native Mac file-sharing protocol, shown in Figure 9.9. AFP is on by default for new shares. The sheet displayed for AFP selectively enables AFP guest access and also allows administrators to choose a custom AFP name, which acts as the display name of the share for network users and may be different than the actual name of the folder or volume being shared.

- **SMB (Server Message Block).** The native Windows file-sharing protocol, also commonly supported by Linux clients, shown in Figure 9.10. The sheet displayed for SMB selectively enables SMB sharing and guest access and allows administrators to choose a custom SMB share name, which similarly serves as the display name of the share for network users and may be different than the actual name of the folder or volume being shared. Additional SMB options include enabling *oplocks* (opportunistic locks), which allow the SMB server to tell a client if it's the only user accessing a particular shared file, allowing him or her to cache the file and work on it locally without fear of other systems changing it behind the scenes, and *strict locking*, which denies additional users from accessing a file already in use. Oplocks should only be enabled if a folder is being shared via SMB; if it's also being shared as AFP or NFS, oplocks can't be safely enabled, as the SMB server has no way to be aware of clients accessing the file by using other protocols. Strict locking can be safely enabled in any circumstances. The SMB sharing sheet can also set default permissions for new files and folders. By default, this is set to create new items that are read- and write-enabled for the owner but read-only for his or her group and everyone else. Optionally, newly created items can be set to inherit the permissions of their parent folder.

Figure 9.9

The AFP configuration sheet for the File Sharing page of Server Admin

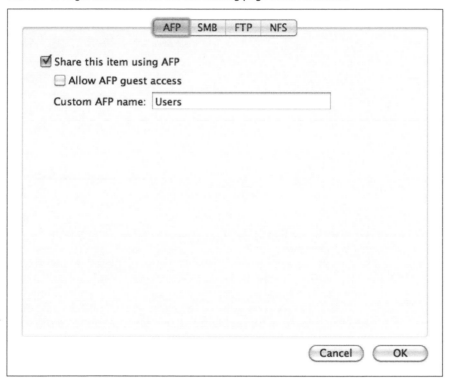

● **FTP (File Transfer Protocol).** The basic Internet file-sharing protocol, shown in Figure 9.11. The sheet displayed for FTP selectively enables FTP sharing and guest access and also allows administrators to choose a custom FTP share name.

Figure 9.10

The SMB configuration sheet for the File Sharing page of Server Admin

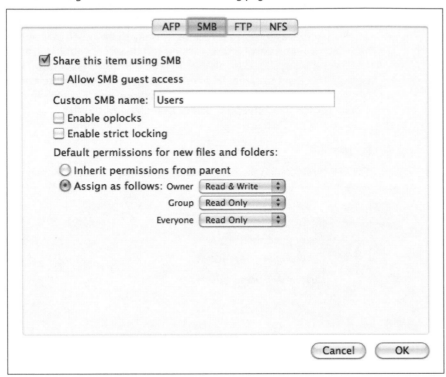

NFS (Network File System). A Unix-centric file-sharing protocol developed by Sun,
shown in Figure 9.12. The sheet displayed for NFS selectively enables NFS sharing as
an export available to World, allowing unauthenticated access to the share. A drop-
down menu can selectively export the share instead to specified hosts by their IP
address or DNS name or restrict access to a given subnet, defined by a subnet address
and subnet mask, such as 10.0.1.0 or 255.255.255.0. Additional options for
NFS shares include support for read-only mounts and subdirectory mounting by
clients.

CROSS-REF

For more on configuring file-sharing services, see Chapter 22.

Figure 9.11

The FTP configuration sheet for the File Sharing page of Server Admin

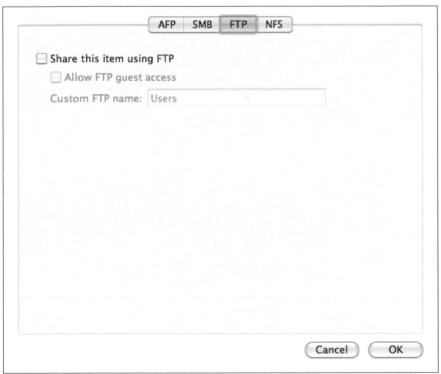

The lower pane of the File Sharing page can be used to set POSIX (standard Unix) or ACL file permissions for the aforementioned folders.

POSIX permissions set access control for files and folders based on three categories of users: the owner, members of the owner's group, and everyone else. These are the standard Unix-style permissions that grant or deny these three categories of users' read, write, and execute permissions.

This style of permissions lacks much flexibility and granularity in determining who can access particular files or folders and what kind of access they can have. Mac OS X also supports ACL permissions compatible with Microsoft's Windows Server and Windows XP/Vista.

ACL support can be enabled for a volume by using the Permissions tab, shown in Figure 9.13. This requires the use of an HFS+ file system on the volume. Once ACLs are enabled, both ACLs and standard POSIX permissions can be used together to manage access control to files on the drive.

Figure 9.12

The NFS configuration sheet for the File Sharing page of Server Admin

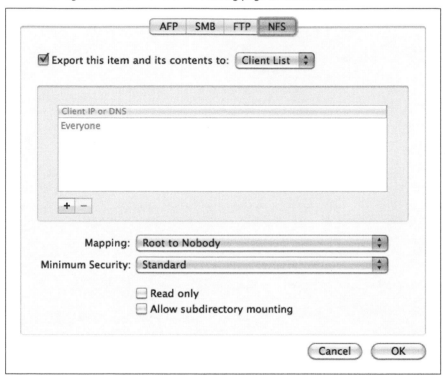

ACL-style permissions provide an extended set of controls for files or folders, enabling administrators to define individual ACEs to allow multiple users or groups very specific individual permissions. An ACE (access control entry) can selectively allow or deny a given user or group:

- **Administrative access.** To change an item's permissions or take ownership
- **Read access.** To change the item's attributes (such as name, date, and size), extended attributes (other additional metadata, such as Spotlight information), file data or folder listings, permissions, or the ability to execute the file or open a folder
- **Write access.** To change the item's attributes or extended attributes, the ability to create new files or change existing ones, the ability to append to a file or create a new folder, the ability to delete an item, and the ability to delete subfolders and their files

Figure 9.13

Permissions configuration in the Server Admin File Sharing page

An ACE can also specify if the permissions granted or denied apply to that folder, to child folders or files within it, or to all descendant items within it. Apple's ACL model orients ACEs to folders and applies permissions to files within them by using inheritance rules. When a file is created, the kernel determines the inherited ACL permissions from its parent folder.

This convention prevents applications from having to keep track of ACE metadata and write the appropriate permissions on every file. Using inheritance, files within a folder simply inherit the ACL permissions of their folder.

NOTE

ACL support for a volume requires the HFS+ file system. Additionally, only the AFP and SMB protocols provide network file system support for ACLs to client users. SMB supports users running Windows XP or newer by using Windows-compatible ACLs.

The Action button of the Permissions pane allows inheritance rules to be modified. It can:

- **Sort ACLs canonically to present the ACE records in the order they'll be evaluated.** Deny rules are always given precedence over allow rules, so if an ACE denies access to a user and then allows access to that user's group, the user is denied permission.

- **Make inherited permissions explicit to copy the inherited ACL permissions to the selected folder.** Once made explicit, they can be edited so they serve as an exception to the inherited permissions.

- **Remove inherited entries to get rid of these permissions.**

- **Propagate permissions across the files and folders within the folder you're defining permissions for.**

It's recommended to keep permissions simple and manageable by using groups to assign permissions by function rather than trying to assign every user his or her own individual permissions. Start at the root of the share and then propagate permissions to the items inside the root folder. Afterward, you can create exception ACEs for subfolders that need their own unique permissions.

CROSS-REF
For more on using file permissions, see Chapter 22.

Server Updates

The Server Updates page, shown in Figure 9.14, is largely identical to the local Software Update application in Mac OS X, although in Server Admin, you can update servers remotely.

Certificates

The Certificates page, shown in Figure 9.15, lists installed certificate identities. Under the listings, an Add (+) button opens a pop-up menu that offers to import an existing certificate identity obtained from a Certificate Authority or to create a new certificate identity, a process that involves creating a self-signed certificate by using the Mac OS X Certificate Assistant.

An Action button offers to replace a self-signed certificate with a Certificate Authority–signed one or to renew an expiring certificate. This enables administrators to start off with their own self-signed certificate and then replace it with a Certificate Authority–signed identity in the future.

Figure 9.14

The Server Updates page in Server Admin

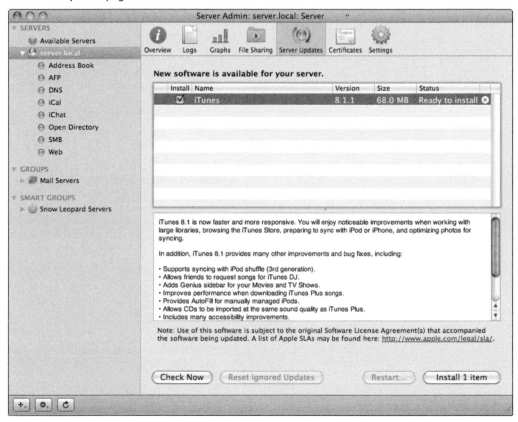

To request a Certificate Authority–signed version of your own certificate, the Action button also offers to generate a CSR (Certificate Signing Request), which can be submitted to a Certificate Authority in order to obtain a signed version of the locally generated certificate. Essentially, the Certificate Authority encrypts your certificate with its own private key, enabling third parties who trust the Certificate Authority to also trust your Certificate Authority–signed certificate.

CROSS-REF

For more on securing certificates, see Chapter 20.

Figure 9.15

The Certificates page in Server Admin

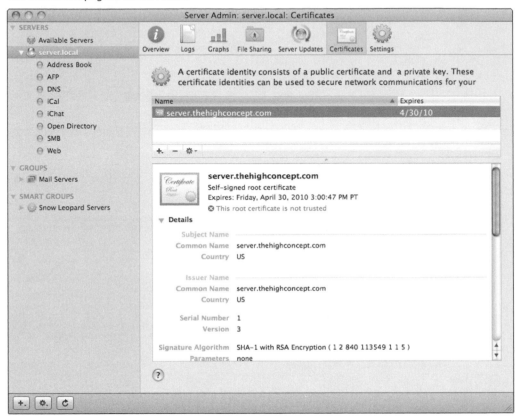

Settings

The final Settings page presents a variety of settings organized into six tabs:

- **General.** This tab, shown in Figure 9.16, presents the server's serial number and registration information, along with settings to enable a variety of supporting services:
  - **NTP (Network Time Protocol).** This is enabled by default.
  - **SNMP (Simple Network Management Protocol).** This is disabled by default but can be turned on to support sending event data to an external monitoring application. In addition to enabling the service here, it must first be manually configured within `/etc/snmpd.conf`. There's no graphical configuration interface in Server Admin. Snow Leopard Server's SNMP support uses the open-source Net-SNMP package.

- **SSH (Secure Shell).** Remote login is enabled by default unless the service is turned off during installation. SSH allows administrators to remotely connect over a command-line interface and is also required when setting up an Open Directory replica.

- **Remote Management.** This is turned off by default but can be enabled to support the use of ARD (Apple Remote Desktop) for centralized management. ARD can be used to restart a server that's not responding, obtain or modify system settings — such as the network configuration or software update status — turn services on or off, and perform screen-sharing and auditing tasks for network servers and workstations.

- **Server Side File Tracking for Mobile Home Sync.** This is off by default but can enable the server to cache file changes prior to synchronizing home directories. Client computers configured to use Portable Home Directories can sync their local home folders with their home folders on the server. Server-side file tracking accelerates this sync procedure.

- **Client Binding Discovery With Bonjour.** This is enabled by default and allows clients to discover their external IP address via Wide Area Bonjour for NAT transversal.

Figure 9.16

The General pane of the Settings page

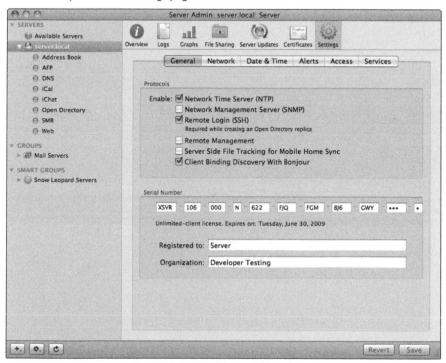

● **Network.** This tab, shown in Figure 9.17, presents the computer name and local host-name as well as a listing of configured network interfaces and the IPv4 and IPv6 addresses and DNS names associated with each. Configuring the network interface addresses or DNS names requires using System Preferences locally on the server or using command-line utilities, which may be run remotely.

Figure 9.17

The Network pane of the Settings page

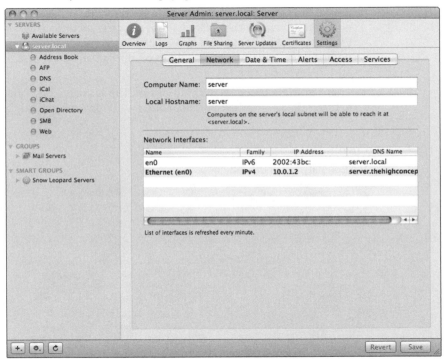

● **Date & Time.** This tab, shown in Figure 9.18, presents settings for updating the system clock and calendar and time zone. By default, the time and date are set to update automatically over the network by using Apple's time server.

Figure 9.18

The Date & Time pane of the Settings page

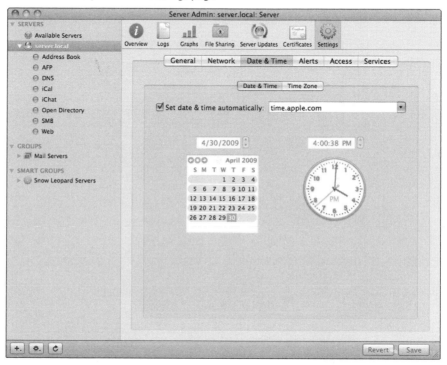

● **Alerts.** This tab, shown in Figure 9.19, enables administrators to receive email notification when a local disk reaches a given percentage threshold of free available space, when new software updates become available, and/or when a certificate is about to expire. The page presents an Add (+) button for defining the email addresses that should be notified of those events.

Figure 9.19

The Alerts pane of the Settings page

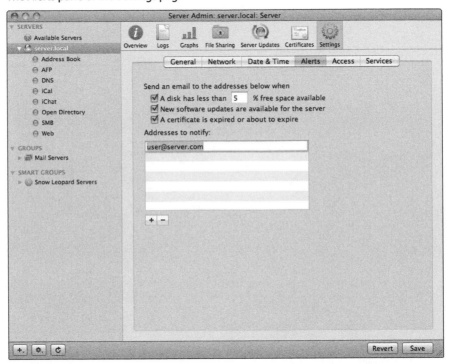

● **Access.** This tab sets SACLs for services running on the server, enabling a layer of access control that Open Directory uses to determine if an authenticated user is authorized to access a given service. The Access tab offers two tabs for settings:

   ● **Services.** This tab, shown in Figure 9.20, allows you to grant all users and groups access to all services running on the server or you can individually configure selected services to allow only specific users or groups to access them.

Figure 9.20

The Services pane of the Settings/Access page

- **Administrators.** This tab, shown in Figure 9.21, allows SACLs to be used to similarly limit which services all members of the Admin group can manage or monitor or grants specific access to only a subset of administrative users, granting the user either access to monitor, to administer, or both. With only monitor access, a Server Admin user can only view settings in the application for those services; administer access is required to make any changes that involve saving settings. These server-side SACLs are enforced by the system, so they also apply to command-line tools. That means administrators can't bypass the access controls defined here via the command line by using tools such as `serveradmin`.

Figure 9.21

The Administrators pane of the Settings/Access page

● **Services.** This tab, shown in Figure 9.22, presents a listing of all services available for configuration within Server Admin and presents check boxes for adding or removing the services from view for that server.

Figure 9.22

The Services pane of the Settings page

Managing and Configuring Services

To manage or configure a given service within Server Admin, an administrator must activate the service for configuration and have SACL permission to administer it.

To enable a service for configuration in Server Admin, follow these steps:

1. Launch Server Admin, select the desired server from the server listing, and then click Settings on the toolbar.

2. Click the Services tab.

3. Click the check box for the desired service.

4. **Click Save.** The selected service should now appear in the list of configurable services for the selected server.

To allow a user administrative access to administer a service in Server Admin, follow these steps:

1. **Launch Server Admin, select the desired server from the server listing, and then click Settings on the toolbar.**

2. **Click the Access tab and then click the Administrators tab on the Access page.**

3. **Select the desired service from the listing on the left.** If the service is currently limited to specific administrative users, then add the user or his or her group, as appropriate, to the right-side listing to allow a user to administer or monitor. Use the Add (+) button to open a Users & Groups sheet and then drag the desired user or group into the right-side listing.

4. **Once the user is added, select the desired level of permission for that user from the pop-up menu.** The default value is Monitor, which provides only view access to the service settings. Changing this to Administer allows that user or group to change and save settings.

5. **Click Save.** The selected user or group should now be able to administer the service.

Once the desired services are added to Server Admin and assigned the appropriate SACL permissions for administration or monitoring, users can simply click a service and access its overview page, logs, and other configuration pages unique to the service. Chapters throughout the rest of this book describe how to configure specific services by using Server Admin.

Reviewing Logs

Server Admin presents a Logs page for the server and each service, showing the contents of the most relevant log files. The main Logs page for a server is shown in Figure 9.6. The Logs page for a specific service is very similar, such as the AFP Logs page shown in Figure 9.23.

In some cases, logging isn't turned on by default. For example, the AFP service activates error logging only when it's turned on, but access logging is off by default. To troubleshoot access attempts, logging can be activated from the Settings page of the AFP pane in Server Admin.

Other services offer configuration of the detail of events to be logged. The more verbose the logging, the greater resources the service requires to accommodate that extra event-logging overhead and the larger the files the service generates. Many services offer to archive their event log files every few days, which compresses old logs and periodically generates a new log file that contains only recent events.

A variety of logs aren't exposed in the Server Admin interface. These can be accessed via the Console app in `/Applications/Utilities` or from the command line.

Most Unix-based or open-source software logs events to files within the directory `/var/log`, whereas Apple's own software and certain other higher-level packages bundled with Mac OS X Server, such as MySQL, save their logs to `/Library/Logs`.

Figure 9.23

The AFP Logs page in Server Admin

Monitoring Performance

Each server and several of the services running on it also present a Graphs page for monitoring their performance over time, either over a few hours or over several days.

Server Admin reports CPU use and network throughput for the server, and services — including AFP, SMB, and FTP file sharing; QuickTime Streaming Server; and the web service — all present similar metrics for tracking connected users and network load.

To monitor the performance of a number of similar servers, such as a collection of email or web servers, administrators can create a Group or Smart Group and then use Server Admin to view the servers' CPU use, network throughput, and disk use in a composite listing.

To create a Smart Group in Server Admin, follow these steps:

1. Use Server Admin's lower-right Add (+) button to choose Add Smart Group from its pop-up menu.

2. From the configuration sheet that drops down, provide a name and then define the attributes you want to define for the Smart Group. For example, you could create a collection of mail servers by defining a rule that specified `Running Services` contains `Mail`.

3. Click OK to create the Smart Group.

4. Select the Smart Group in the server list. The servers matching the rules you create now appear in a listing showing their OS version, CPU use, network throughput, disk use, uptime, and number of connected users.

File Share Points, Permissions, and Quotas

A server's File Sharing page in Server Admin presents a composite overview of all share points across the various file-sharing protocols available, from AFP and FTP to SMB and NFS. From this page, new shares can be created, share point features can be defined, protocol settings can be customized, and access permissions can be administered.

The identical Share Points pages displayed within the AFP, FTP, NFS, and SMB panes in Server Admin all expose the same features as the main File Sharing page presented for the server.

Creating share points

The File Sharing page is used to share a folder or entire volume as a share point, which can also be assigned any number of file-sharing protocols along with other share point features, including Automount support, Spotlight search indexing, or designated use for Time Machine backups. To create a new share point in Server Admin, follow these steps:

1. Launch Server Admin, select the desired server, and then click File Sharing on the toolbar.

2. Click Volumes to view local disks and then click Browse to navigate to the folder you want to share with network users.

3. With the desired folder selected, click the Share button in the upper right.

4. The lower half of the window now displays Share Point settings.

5. Enable features for the new share point, as desired, by checking the box next to Automount, Spotlight search, or Time Machine backups.

6. To change the default protocol settings, click the Protocol Options button. From the sheet that drops down, use the four tabs to configure sharing settings. By default, the new share point is exposed under AFP and SMB, guest access is off by default, and the name of the share is the same as the name of the folder.

7. Click OK after making your changes.

8. Click Save. The new share point should now be available to network users. Remember that the actual file-sharing services for the defined protocols must also be configured and running before users can see the new share points.

Defining access permissions

From the File Sharing page, access permissions can be set to allow or deny use by specific users or groups by using either POSIX-style permissions or more finely grained ACL entries.

To define access permissions for a share point in Server Admin, follow these steps:

1. Launch Server Admin, select the desired server, and then click File Sharing on the toolbar.

2. Select Share Points and then click Browse to view the existing shares on the server.

3. Select the share you want to define access permissions for and then select the Permissions tab from the lower half of the File Sharing pane.

4. To set POSIX permissions for the share point, use the pop-up menus under the Permissions column to choose Read & Write, Read Only, Write Only, or No Access for the defined owning user, their group, and Others. However, because Mac OS X defines share point POSIX permissions as being shared by the root user in the admin group and because POSIX conventions specify only one owner and one group for a share and its files, there's limited utility in editing the POSIX permissions for a share. Instead, you want to use ACL permissions.

5. **To set ACL permissions for the share point, activate ACL support for the volume, save the change, and then click the Add (+) button.** An inspector pane showing user and group accounts appears. Drag the user or group you want to define access for to the ACL area of the Permissions tab. Define the ACE as desired by using the pop-up menu under the Type column to allow or deny and the Permission column pop-up to choose Full Control, Read & Write, Read Only, Write Only, or Custom access. With Custom, a sheet drops down to allow you to create a specialized permissions entry. The Applies to column indicates your ACE will apply to items in this folder and all items within it in the folder hierarchy.

6. **Click Save.** The ACE is applied to allow or deny access as defined.

If you're changing permissions for a folder that inherits ACL permissions from a containing folder, you can use the pop-up menu of the Action button to:

- **Make Inherited Permissions Explicit.** This copies the inherited ACL permissions to the selected folder. Once made explicit, they can be edited so they serve as an exception to the inherited permissions.

- **Remove Inherited Entries.** This eliminates these permissions.

- **Propagate Permissions.** This cascades the permissions you define for this folder or volume across all the files and folders within it.

Enabling quota support on a volume

The File Sharing page can also be used to activate quota support for a selected volume, which enables Snow Leopard Server to limit the disk resources consumed by an individual user. Actual quota restrictions are managed within Workgroup Manager on a per-user basis.

To activate quota support for a volume in Server Admin, follow these steps:

1. **Launch Server Admin, select the desired server, and then click File Sharing on the toolbar.**

2. **Select Volumes and then select the desired disk you want to enable quota support for.**

3. **Click the Quotas tab in the lower half of the File Sharing pane, shown in Figure 9.24.**

4. **Click the check box to enable quotas on the volume.**

5. **Click Save.** The quota listing populates with all the accounts accessing the volume, including many background services. You can now define a quota to limit the disk resources a user can use within Workgroup Manager on this volume.

Figure 9.24

The Quotas pane of the File Sharing page

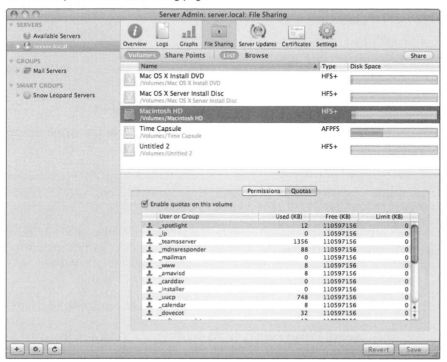

Updating Server Software

The Server Updates page can be used to update server software by using Apple's Software Update system. Notification of newly available updates can be configured from the Alerts tab of the Settings page.

To remotely run Software Update for a server by using Server Admin, follow these steps:

1. **Launch Server Admin, select the desired server, and then click Server Updates on the toolbar.**

2. **Click the Check Now button to list the software updates available.**

3. **Select the desired updates to install and then click Install.**

4. **If the updates require a server restart, click the Restart button.**

To receive an email notification when a new software update is available, follow these steps:

1. **Launch Server Admin, select the desired server, and then click Settings on the toolbar.**

2. **Click the Alerts tab.**

3. **Click the check box to enable notification when new software updates are available for this server.**

4. **Click the Add (+) button to type your email address.**

5. **Click Save.** When new updates become available, the system sends you an email notification.

Managing Certificates

The Certificates page is used to create new self-signed certificate identities, to generate the Certificate Signing Request (CSR) needed to obtain a third-party signature for your certificate from a Certificate Authority, or to import signed certificates you already own or have recently obtained.

To create a new self-signed certificate identity by using Server Admin, follow these steps:

1. **Launch Server Admin, select the desired server, and then click Certificates on the toolbar.**

2. **Click the Add (+) button and then choose Create Certificate Identity from the pop-up menu.** This launches Certificate Assistant, as shown in Figure 9.25.

3. **Certificate Assistant asks for a server name, an Identity Type, and a Certificate Type.** The Identity Type is Self Signed Root by default, which enables immediate use without requiring any outside signature. The alternative is a leaf identity, which requires external signing before use. The Certificate type is SSL Server by default, which can be used to sign most Snow Leopard Server services that support SSL. Alternative types include S/MIME for encrypting email and VPN Server.

4. **Click Continue.** The Certificate Assistant creates and installs a private key and a public certificate and then lists the new identity on the Certificates page of Server Admin. It should also become available for selection in Server Admin for services that can be secured by using a certificate. This step also creates a Certificate Signing Request (CSR), which is written to `/etc/certificates/cert.`common.name.tld.csr.

Figure 9.25

Certificate Assistant

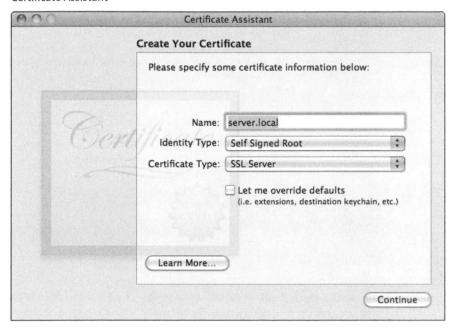

To obtain a signed certificate identity from a Certificate Authority to replace a self-signed identity, follow these steps:

1. **Launch Server Admin, select the desired server, and then click Certificates on the toolbar.**

2. **Select the desired self-signed identity from your list.**

3. **Click the Action button marked with a gear icon and then select Generate Certificate Signing Request (CSR).** This drops down a sheet containing a CSR based on the private key of the selected identity, as shown in Figure 9.26.

4. **Click Save to generate a** `.csr` **file containing the text and then submit it to the Certificate Authority.** The Certificate Authority generates a signed identity and sends it back to you.

5. **Select the self-signed identity in your list, click the Action button, and then select Replace certificate with signed or renewed certificate.** A sheet drops down.

Figure 9.26

Generating a CSR in Certificate Assistant

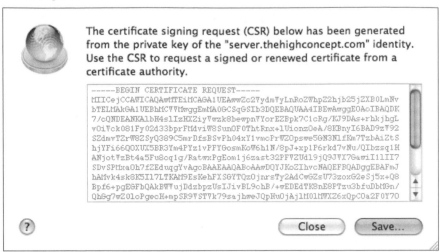

6. **Drag the signed public certificate supplied by your Certificate Authority into the sheet and then click Replace Certificate.** The self-signed public certificate is replaced with the version signed by the Certificate Authority, allowing users to automatically trust the certificate.

Certificate Manager in Server Admin doesn't support signing CSRs or issuing signed certificates as a root authority or Certificate Authority, but you can use Keychain Access in `/Applications/Utilities/` to launch the Certificate Assistant to perform these functions.

Configuring Settings

The Settings page of Server Admin manages a variety of general server configuration details, from the system serial number to administrative alerts, SACLs, and the services presented in the Server Admin interface for the given server.

Serial number upgrades or changes

You may need to upgrade or change the serial number assigned to a particular server; this is done from the General tab of the Settings page.

To upgrade or change a Mac OS X Server serial number, follow these steps:

1. **Launch Server Admin, select the desired server, and then click Settings on the toolbar.** The General tab is shown by default.

2. **Type the serial number, along with the Registered to and Organization information, that appears on your license key.**

3. **Click Save.** The server now operates under the new serial number.

Hostname or network configuration settings

You may need to modify the system's computer name — which appears when browsing in the Finder, for example — or its DNS hostname; this is done from the Network tab of the Settings page but must be followed up with the use of a command-line tool.

To change a server's hostname or network configuration, follow these steps:

1. **Launch Server Admin, select the desired server, and then click Settings on the toolbar.**

2. **Click the Network tab.**

3. **Type the computer name and local hostname.** To propagate the changes throughout the system properly, you must also use the `changeip` command-line tool. Don't simply change the server name in Server Admin or in the Sharing pane of System Preferences. Network settings may be changed in the Network pane of System Preferences, but any IP address changes on the primary interface must similarly also be followed up with the `changeip` command, as outlined shortly.

4. **Click Save and then open Terminal to complete the name change by using the** `changeip` **command.**

Use `changeip -checkhostname` to verify the server's current IP address and hostname.

Use `changeip <previous IP address> <desired IP address> <previous hostname> <desired hostname>` to update the IP address and hostname settings across the variety of internal services that need to be updated to use the proper information. This command must be run as the root user or by using the sudo command from an account with administrative privileges:

```
sudo changeip 10.0.1.2 10.0.10.10 old.example.com new.example.com
```

Use `changeip -checkhostname` to verify that the server's IP address and hostname are reported back correctly afterward. Appropriate changes must also be made in DNS because the server regularly looks up its hostname in DNS, and the information it finds must match its own settings.

Time and date settings

To update a server's time settings, use the Date & Time tab of the Settings page. This is where you set the system's time server, although the date and time can also be set manually if you don't have access to a network time server. Keeping an accurate time setting across all network systems is important for many services, including Kerberos authentication, and this is very difficult to maintain when setting clocks manually.

To update a server's time and date settings, follow these steps:

1. **Launch Server Admin, select the desired server, and then click Settings on the toolbar.**

2. **Click the Time & Date tab.** By default, the time and date are set automatically. You can use your own higher authority time server by specifying its DNS name or IP address. Apple supplies a Stratum 2 time server at `time.apple.com`, which is entered by default. Maintaining a highly accurate system clock is important for server operations, so the time shouldn't be entered manually. In order to correctly update its clock, the server's firewall must allow incoming and outgoing traffic on UTP port 123. Snow Leopard Server can also serve as an NTP server for systems on your local network and must be set up to sync with an Internet time server if it'll be used as a local NTP server. Clients may be configured in System Preferences to obtain their date by using the local server.

3. **Click Save.**

CROSS-REF
For more on NTP, see Chapter 19.

Alert notification settings

Notifications can be sent out via email to alert administrative users when certain conditions are met, such as the server running out of available disk storage, the availability of new software updates, or the expiration of the server's identity certificates. Use the Alerts tab of the Settings page to configure these settings.

To configure alert notifications on the server, follow these steps:

1. **Launch Server Admin, select the desired server, and then click Settings on the toolbar.**

2. **Click the Alerts tab.**

3. **Click the desired check boxes for alert notifications:**
   - A local disk has less than X% of free space available
   - New software updates are available for the server
   - A certificate is expired or about to expire

4. Click the Add (+) button and then type the email addresses that should be notified for any of the selected events.

5. Click Save. Snow Leopard Server activates SMTP and sends email alerts as needed. Make sure your firewall allows SMTP traffic from the server.

SACL settings

Access to the server's services on a per-user or group basis is configured by using SACLs configured within the Access tab of the Settings page.

To configure SACL-limiting services to specific users, follow these steps:

1. Launch Server Admin, select the desired server, and then click Settings on the toolbar.

2. Click the Access tab.

3. Above the left-hand column, click the For selected services below radio button.

4. Select the service you want to limit to specific users.

5. Above the right-hand column, click the Allow only users and groups below radio button and then click the Add (+) button to open a Users & Groups sheet.

6. Drag users or groups to the right-hand column to grant them access to the selected service. Repeat these steps for other services you want to restrict.

7. Click Save. Snow Leopard Server now serves only the designated users for any services with defined SACLs. Selecting the service and then clicking the Allow all users and groups radio button above the right-hand column removes the restrictions.

Limited administrative access settings

The level of administrative access granted to each service's configuration can be set on a per-user or group basis by using SACLs configured within the Access tab of the Settings page. To configure limited administrative access to specific services, follow these steps:

1. Launch Server Admin, select the desired server, and then click Settings on the toolbar.

2. Click the Access tab and then click the Administrators tab.

3. Above the left-hand column, click the For selected services below radio button.

4. Select the service you want to limit to specific administrative users.

5. Below the right-hand column labeled Allow to administer or monitor, click the Add (+) button to open a Users & Groups sheet.

6. Drag administrative users or groups to the right-hand column to grant them administrative access to the selected service.

7. From the permissions column, choose Administer from the pop-up menu for any users or groups you want to grant full administrative access to the selected service to save their configuration changes in Server Admin or by using any command-line tools. By default, selected users or groups have only monitor permissions, which allows them to view but neither change any settings in Server Admin nor make any configuration changes to the selected service using other tools. Repeat these steps for other services you want to restrict.

8. Click Save. Snow Leopard Server now enforces the defined configuration rights to allow users with administer privileges to freely configure services and to give users with monitor privileges the ability to view configurations only but accords no rights to other administrators for any services with defined SACLs. Selecting the service and then removing any defined users and groups by using the Delete button removes the restrictions.

Adding a new service for configuration

Apart from the default services set up during installation, other services require an initial activation in Server Admin before they're visible in a server's list of available services to configure and enable. This is done by using the Services tab of the Settings page. To enable a service for configuration in Server Admin, follow these steps:

1. Launch Server Admin, select the desired server from the server listing, and then click Settings on the toolbar.

2. Click the Services tab.

3. Click the check box for the desired service.

4. Click Save. The selected service should now appear in the list of configurable services for the selected server.

Working with Multiple Servers

To work with multiple servers at once within the Server Admin interface, add them by IP address or DNS name, authenticating with credentials valid on that server.

To add additional servers to Server Admin for configuration, follow these steps:

1. Launch Server Admin.

2. If the servers to be added are on the local subnet, select Available Servers from the server list and then double-click a local server in the list to add it to the server list.

3. **To connect to a remote server, click the Add (+) button and then choose Add Server from the pop-up menu.** A sheet appears, asking for an IP address or DNS name and an administrative username and password.

Using groups and Smart Groups

Smart Groups and simple arbitrary grouping of the servers being monitored within Server Admin can help organize the administration of similarly configured servers.

To group servers in Server Admin, follow these steps:

1. **Launch Server Admin.**

2. **Click the Add (+) button, choose Add Group from the pop-up menu, and then type a name for the new group.**

3. **Drag existing servers into the group.** The group's server listing can be collapsed by using its disclosure triangle. The Groups section can also be featured by collapsing the Servers section. Clicking the group name presents an overview of the servers in the group, including their name, the version of Mac OS X Server they're running, a CPU utilization status bar, a numerical network throughput status, a status bar showing the available disk space for local drives, an uptime listing, and the number of connected users.

To create a Smart Group of servers in Server Admin, follow these steps:

1. **Launch Server Admin.**

2. **Click the Add (+) button and then choose Add Smart Group from the pop-up menu.**

3. **Type a name for the Smart Group and then define the matching criteria for servers you want to dynamically appear within the Smart Group by using the drop-down sheet.**

4. **Select the Smart Group in the server list.** Connected servers fitting the definition of the Smart Group are displayed within it and updated dynamically. The Smart Group's server listing can be collapsed by using its disclosure triangle. The Servers, Groups, and Smart Groups sections can all be collapsed or expanded as desired. Clicking the Smart Group name presents the same streamlined status overview for the servers matched to that grouping, just like a manual group.

Importing and exporting server settings

The specific settings of a particular server and all its configured services can also be exported to a file by using Export Server Settings and then imported to allow a new server to be set up with an identical configuration. The export process allows the user to select any or all of the currently configured services as part of the settings to be exported.

To export server settings in Server Admin, follow these steps:

1. **Launch Server Admin and then select the desired server for configuration export.**

2. **Click Server/Export/Service Settings on the menu bar.**

3. **Select the service settings to export to a file by using the check boxes that appear next to each setting, as shown in Figure 9.27.**

Figure 9.27

Exporting server settings in Server Admin

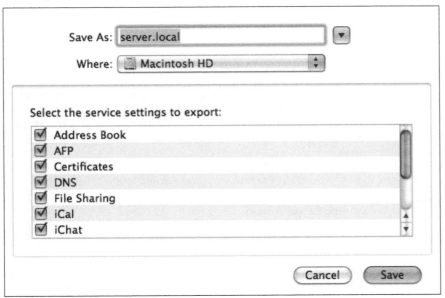

4. **Choose a name and location for the file and then click Save.** An XML property list file is created containing all the service configuration details for the selected services on that server.

To import server settings in Server Admin, follow these steps:

1. **Launch Server Admin and then select the desired server to import the configuration.**

2. **Click Server/Import/Service Settings on the menu bar.**

3. **Browse for the export file and then click Open.** The service settings contained in the XML property list are applied to the selected server.

Importing and exporting server preferences

Server Admin's server setup and preferences can be exported to a file with password encryption to allow administrators to set up additional administrative workstations with the same configuration, including any server passwords.

To export server preferences in Server Admin, follow these steps:

1. Launch Server Admin.

2. Click Server/Export/Server Admin Preferences on the menu bar.

3. Provide an encryption password for the file and then repeat the key to verify, as shown in Figure 9.28. Secure the password because the resulting file contains sensitive information, allowing anyone who has access to decrypt the file the ability to connect to and administer those servers.

Figure 9.28

Exporting Server Admin Preferences

4. Choose a name and location for the file and then click Save. An encrypted settings file is created that contains all of Server Admin's current configuration details.

To import server preferences in Server Admin, follow these steps:

1. **Launch Server Admin on a new administrative system.**

2. **Click Server/Import/Server Admin Preferences on the menu bar.**

3. **Browse for the preferences file and then click Open.** The new system's Server Admin configuration now includes all the configured servers, groups, and other preferences.

Summary

- Server Admin provides the main control interface for configuring basic server settings, security certificates, and all running services and also defines share points, activates volume quotas, and sets file permissions.

- Part of the Server Administration Software package, Server Admin is installable on any server or desktop Mac system but requires Mac OS X Snow Leopard.

- Using Server Admin converts the server into the advanced configuration, making it no longer possible to use the simpler Server Preferences to manage the server.

- Server Admin presents pages providing an overview, logs, and graphs for the server in general and for defined services. It also presents customized interface pages for each service activated on a server, including a settings page and other pages relevant to the service, such as a Share Points page for file-sharing services, such as AFP, FTP, SMB, and NFS.

- The application is designed to manage multiple servers at once, allowing administrators to organize servers into arbitrary groups or dynamic Smart Groups. Grouped servers can be monitored in a listing that presents their current status and available resources.

- Overall settings or specific service configurations can be exported to files and imported to configure a new server identically or to set up a secondary management system with the same setup of servers.

10

Workgroup Manager

Whereas Server Admin monitors services and their configuration in Snow Leopard Server, Workgroup Manager acts as the administrative interface for working with users, groups, and computers.

Specifically, Workgroup Manager is used to configure the following:

- Accounts
- Password policy
- User, workgroup, and machine preferences
- Home directories
- Group memberships
- User quotas on his or her disk
- Mail and print queues
- Related account attributes

The application manages a domain's directory service, which allows network clients to log in to domain computers with a central account that can provide them with the same desktop settings and access to the same network resources across any system.

Support for Portable Home Directories can even enable users to sync their local files between a desktop workstation and a notebook via their server home directory, allowing users to go mobile and automatically take their working files with them.

User, group, and computer accounts can be assigned managed preferences, which are used both to create a consistent environment for network users and to control and secure machines by limiting access to specific applications, dictating how features — such as the Dock, Dashboard, or Time Machine — work or disabling hardware features, such as disc burning or Bluetooth.

Managed preferences are imposed by the network directory administrator in Workgroup Manager and function similar to how Parental Controls enable a machine administrator to limit the environment allowed to other users.

Workgroup Manager can be installed on any administrative Mac desktop or laptop as part of the Server Administration Software package, which is included on the Snow Leopard Server installer DVD, inside the Other Installs folder, appearing as `ServerAdministrationSoftware.mpkg`.

As with the other applications installed by the Server Administration Software package, Workgroup Manager requires Mac OS X Snow Leopard, which runs only on Intel Macs. Therefore, Workgroup Manager can't be installed on PowerPC Macs or other hardware running Leopard or earlier versions of Mac OS X.

This chapter describes how Workgroup Manager is used to create and manage user, group, and computer accounts — either locally or from an administrator system — and presents an overview of its graphical user interface.

Authenticating with a Server

After installing the Server Administration Software package, Workgroup Manager can be launched from `/Applications/Server`. On the Server itself, it can be launched from the Server Stack placed by default in the Snow Leopard Server Dock.

Once launched, the application prompts for a server to connect with; administrators can connect by the server's DNS name or the IP address of the server by using an account name and password with administrator access.

After connecting with the server as a local administrator, the admin user is still limited to making changes to the local account directory. These accounts are useable only on the server itself, just as local workstation accounts can be used only to log in to that client computer.

User accounts in the local directory

By default, the local administrator account created during server installation is given UID (User ID) 501, and additional local accounts are assigned successively numbered accounts. On Mac client computers, local user accounts are created by employing the same numbering convention. UIDs below 500 are typically reserved for use by internal system accounts, starting with the root account with UID 0.

Various services run under their own account as a safety precaution to grant limited, specialized access to a background process. For example, the www account is UID 70; if a malicious user were to gain access to the www user via an exploit, the limited privileges of that account would help prevent the breech from resulting in complete control of the server.

System accounts are usually invisible to the user, and UIDs are rarely presented in the Mac OS X interface. Instead, the username associated with a UID in the local directory node is used. For example, file permissions are written to disk identified by UIDs, but the operating system identifies the user by name when presenting a file's permissions. The Users pane of System Preferences doesn't even show an account's UID.

If two users are ever identified by the same UID, the operating system assumes they're the same account. For example, if the first user created on a Mac writes files to an external hard drive, those files are assigned to owner 501, the conventional UID for the first user created on a system. However, the operating system presents the file's owner by username; for example, robert.

If that drive is attached to another Mac, the operating system presents the file's owner not as robert but as the user corresponding to UID 501 on that system, which may be caroline. Because the two systems use overlapping UIDs in their local account directories and don't share any information about their user account directories with other systems, there's no way for two machines on the network to respect each other's user account conventions.

The only way a set of machines could come close is if an identical set of user accounts is created on each machine so they all agree that, for example, 501 is robert, but 502 is caroline. A directory server solves this issue by acting as a centralized directory of accounts that all machines on the network trust to manage users.

User accounts in the network directory

Accounts maintained by Snow Leopard Server that are visible to network users are stored within a directory domain described as being `/LDAPv3/127.0.0.1` because Apple's Open Directory uses LDAP, and a master directory service maintains the directory locally; `127.0.0.1` is the loopback address, which refers to the server itself.

Accounts in this directory domain are separated from local accounts in the local directory node, which is referred to as `/Local/Default`. Creating and modifying accounts in the network-visible directory require authenticating with an administrative account having privileges to administer it; the local admin account doesn't have this capability. It has read-only access to the network-visible directory domain.

During initial installation, however, diradmin — a Directory Administrator account — is created by using the same password as the local admin account. That account is used to administer accounts and policy in the network-visible directory domain.

The original diradmin account is UID 1000, and all network directory accounts it creates are numbered sequentially higher, starting at 1025, making an account's UID an obvious sign of whether an account is local or visible to the network.

Network accounts have their passwords stored outside the directory in the Apple Password Server, which uses SASL (Simple Authentication and Security Layer) as its authentication mechanism. Optionally, the directory can also use the MIT Kerberos protocol for authentication.

This modular architecture allows Snow Leopard Server to scale up from a simple, self-contained standard configuration server that manages its Open Directory network users almost invisibly, up to advanced configuration servers that can integrate with existing LDAP infrastructure, including Linux-based organizations using OpenLDAP, Novell's eDirectory, or Microsoft's Active Directory implementations of LDAP, relying on those directories to store the network's accounts.

Open Directory is also integrated with Samba, an open-source package that supports compatibility with Windows file and print sharing. This enables Mac OS X Server to act as a workgroup directory server, or *domain controller*, for Windows machines that use a Windows domain.

In addition to managing user and group accounts, Open Directory also manages computer records and groups of computers. This supports managed client features, which configure network machines bound to the directory domain to act according to set policy.

This may include anything from starting up with a given set of desktop preferences or forcing a set System Update server, restrictions on hardware features, such as optical disc burning, or limitations on when a computer can be used or which approved applications or System Preferences are accessible.

Exploring the Interface

Working with this directory information is kept straightforward in Workgroup Manager. The application can be used to browse accounts in both the local directory domain and the network-visible directory domain (which is typically set up during installation during Open Directory configuration) as well as additional directory domains that may be defined on the server.

The selected directory domain's accounts are presented in Workgroup Manager with an accounts list on the left and an Account Record pane on the right, as shown in Figure 10.1.

The toolbar

Workgroup Manager presents a standard, customizable toolbar that supports display of small icons, text-only labels, icon-only buttons, or the standard large icons with text labels. By default, a Server Admin icon appears on the toolbar to launch that application; a Server Monitor icon can also be added by customizing the toolbar.

Figure 10.1

The Workgroup Manager Accounts interface

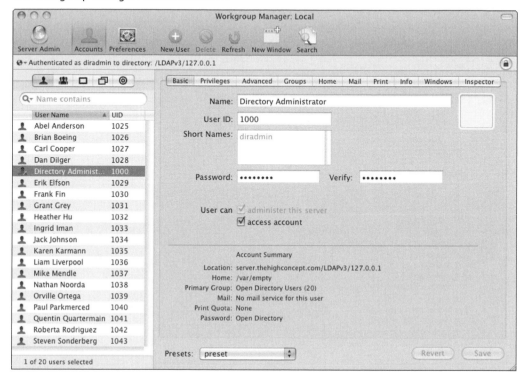

Accounts and Preferences modes

The next two buttons on the toolbar toggle between viewing Accounts and presenting Preferences associated with a user, group, computer, or group of computers, as shown in Figure 10.2. Additional details on these two modes are presented later in this chapter.

Other toolbar buttons

Additional toolbar icons offer to add a new account, delete an item, refresh the display, open a new Workgroup Manager window, or set up a search query for finding account records and optionally making batch changes to the matching range of accounts.

Figure 10.2

The Workgroup Manager Preferences interface

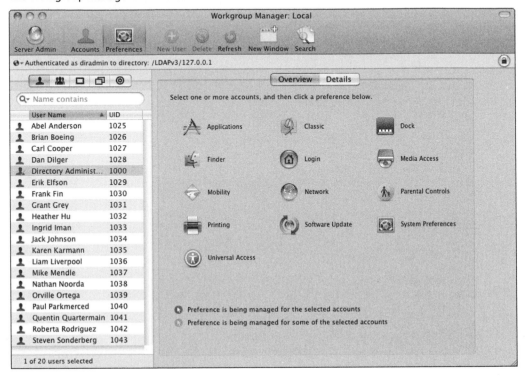

Using Search to filter accounts

After you click the Search icon, a query search sheet, shown in Figure 10.3, drops down to allow filtering of directory records based on any number of the following criteria:

- **A Record Name that is, contains, starts with, or ends with a given text string.** A Record Name is the internal or short name of an account commonly used at the command line, such as admin.

- **A Real Name that is, contains, starts with, or ends with a given text string.** A Real Name is the display name of an account used in Mac OS X, such as Administrator. Real or record names can generally be used interchangeably in the graphical interface.

- **A User ID that is, contains, is greater than, or is less than a given number.** This is the UID that uniquely identifies each account.

- **A Comment that is, contains, starts with, or ends with a given text string.** Comment is a free text field associated with account records in Workgroup Manager.

- **A Keyword that is, contains, starts with, or ends with a given text string.** Keywords can be defined and applied to account records in Workgroup Manager.

- **A Group ID that is, contains, is greater than, or is less than a given number.** A user account record has a Primary Group ID it's associated with, and each group has a Group ID that identifies its members.

Figure 10.3

The Workgroup Manager Search query sheet

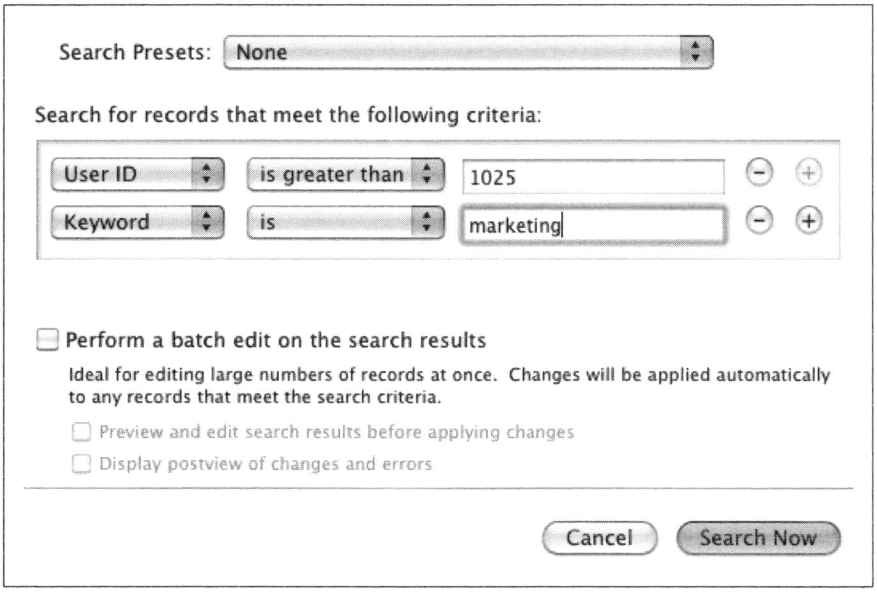

In a simple search, Workgroup Manager divides the accounts list to indicate that a query has been applied to filter the listing of accounts. The search results can be cleared or the query can be edited by using the two buttons in the query pane, as shown in Figure 10.4.

A search preset based on the criteria selected can also be saved for later use by using the pop-up menu at the top of the Search sheet. Once saved, search presets appear in the same pop-up menu.

Figure 10.4

Workgroup Manager with a search query applied to the accounts list

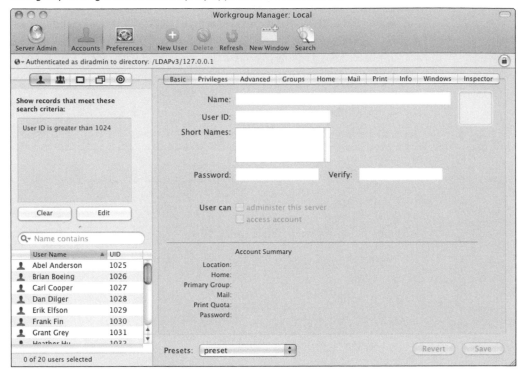

Using Search to batch-edit accounts

The Search button can also be used to perform a batch-edit of account records matching the search results by clicking the designated check box in the Search sheet. By default, changes are applied to all the records matching the search query. Two additional options provide:

- **The ability to preview and edit search results before applying changes.** Selected accounts may be removed from the preview list of pending batch edits before applying the changes.

- **A summary display of changes and errors.** This report can be saved to document the changes made and which accounts were affected.

These batch-editing features enable administrators to apply comments, keywords, company information, group assignments, preferences, and other account record details across a range of accounts at once. Workgroup Manager also allows changes to be made across a selection of records at once when the user manually selects multiple accounts from the accounts list.

The directory domain authentication strip

Between the toolbar and the Accounts pane lays a strip marked by a globe icon on the left end that shows the directory domain currently being viewed, as shown in Figure 10.5. At the right end of this strip is a lock icon that allows a Workgroup Manager user to authenticate into that domain. The two directory domains available by default are:

- The local directory node designated as `/Local/Default`
- The network directory domain node designated as `/LDAPv3/127.0.0.1`

Figure 10.5

The Workgroup Manager directory domain strip

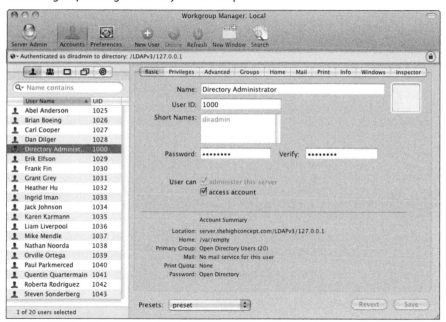

When switching to the local directory node, which is performed by clicking the currently selected directory domain and selecting the new node from the pop-up menu that appears, Workgroup Manager warns that these local accounts aren't visible from the network.

This means that local accounts can only authenticate to services running on the local server; they can't be used to log in to directory-bound Mac OS X client computers, to log in to a Windows domain from a PC, or to authenticate with other servers associated with the domain.

BSD local node accounts

In addition to the local domain, Workgroup Manager may also be configured to access the account records maintained in Unix flat files. These are designated as `/BSD/local` and aren't stored in an LDAP-accessible directory database but rather in the conventional text files typical to a Unix environment, including the accounts list maintained in `/etc/passwd`. The `/BSD/` node is also used by Sun's NIS (Network Information System) directory service.

Active Directory and LDAPv3 directory servers

Workgroup Manager can also access directory domains served by external OpenLDAP servers or Microsoft's Active Directory. To work with outside LDAPv3 directories, user account record attributes must be mapped between the conventions used by Apple's Open Directory and the configuration of the LDAP server.

The external domain also needs to be configured as a Network Account Server by using the Accounts pane of System Preferences. To provide customized configuration details about the Network Account Server, use Directory Utility, which in Snow Leopard is launched from the same Accounts pane of System Preferences.

Workgroup Manager can't create user, group, or computer accounts for a standard Active Directory domain because Active Directory doesn't support the required database schema in its default configuration. Changing schema requires full administrative access to the Active Directory domain.

External LDAP directories are designated as either `/LDAPv3/server.example.com` or, in the case of a Microsoft Windows Server directory, `/Active Directory/All Domains`.

Multiple directory domains can be used together to manage network users. For example, an organization with an Active Directory domain may bind its Mac users to that domain for authentication purposes but could also bind network Macs to an Open Directory domain to provide managed client features configured on a Mac OS X Snow Leopard Server.

CROSS-REF
For more on Open Directory, see Chapter 21.

The accounts list

For the selected directory domain, Workgroup Manager presents a column of accounts underneath a series of tabs that toggle between listings of user, group, computer, and groups of computer accounts, as shown in Figure 10.6:

- **User accounts.** Depicted in the record selection tab by an icon of a single user, this list displays the real or display usernames of all domain user accounts, along with the user's UID and a user icon. Administrative users are distinguished by an added pencil on their user icon.

- **Group accounts.** Depicted in the record selection tab by an icon of a group of users, this list displays the real or display name of the group and its GID (group ID), along with a group icon that similarly indicates administrative privilege by adding a pencil to admin groups.

- **Computer accounts.** Depicted in the record selection tab by a square, this list presents the display name of the system.

- **Computer groups.** Depicted in the record selection tab by two squares, this list presents the display name of the computer group.

- **All records listing.** Optionally revealed by enabling the feature in Workgroup Manager's preferences, this list is depicted in the record selection tab by a target icon. It presents a pop-up menu for every account record type in the directory, including Automounts, resources, and Certificate Authorities. This also exposes normally hidden accounts, such as root, and presents the normally hidden directory records in an Inspector pane that allows for detailed record attribute editing.

Figure 10.6

The Workgroup Manager accounts list

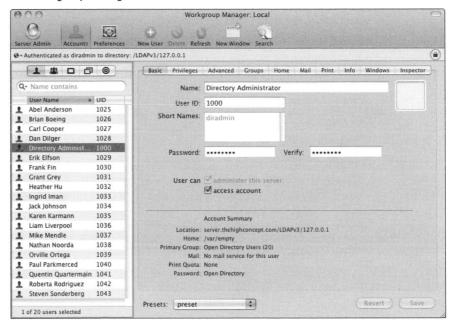

System accounts can also be exposed by choosing View ⇨ Show System Records from the menu bar.

The Account Record pane

With an account selected from the accounts list, the right-side pane displays a series of tabs that present the information connected to that account. This account information is stored in the directory, which serves as a specialized database for rapidly accessing the account information for authentication purposes as needed by applications and services.

At the bottom of the Account Record pane is a pop-up menu that offers to save an account preset. Presets are used like a template to fill out the common settings for a new account. Presets are associated with a specific directory domain and can't be applied to create accounts in another domain outside of their own.

Multiple presets can be saved for users, groups, and computers as well as for different types of accounts; for example, a preset could be created for different departments' users, each containing the basic settings related to that type of user.

A preset can be created from an existing account or a new account can be created, filled out with the common attributes, and then saved as a preset. The preset can then be used as a starting point when creating new accounts. Presets can contain the following account attribute settings:

- Simultaneous login on managed computers
- Selected default shell
- Comments
- Primary group ID
- Group membership list
- Home folder settings
- Disk quotas
- Mail settings
- Print queue settings

The Account Preferences pane

Managed preferences for user, group, computer, and computer group accounts are set by using the Preferences icon on the toolbar, which toggles Workgroup Manager's primary display from account records to preferences details.

CROSS-REF

For more on managed preferences, see Chapter 34.

Working with User Accounts

After selecting the User tab in the accounts list, you can create a new user account record or select one or multiple existing user account records and modify record settings by using the account detail pane on the right, which presents a series of tabs for configuring related settings.

The User Basic tab

With a user account selected, the User Basic tab in Workgroup Manager presents the account's display name (also called the real name or full name), UID, and any short names associated with the account.

It also provides a password setting, a picture well for adding a user photo, check boxes to provide administrator rights and make the account accessible, and a summary overview of the account's settings.

User account name

All account names should be unique to their account record type; a user and group can share the same name (such as admin user and the admin group), but users must all have unique names, and users should be unique across directory domains.

Workgroup Manager doesn't allow multiple user accounts in a domain to use the same name, but it doesn't stop users from using the same name across different domains because it works with only one domain at a time.

The display username can be up to 255 bytes, which means 255 Roman characters or fewer when using character sets that use double-byte or four-byte characters. This name can include spaces and uppercase characters, such as Steve Jobs. It can be changed at any point after the user record is created.

Account short names

The first short name assigned in a user record is used internally for several purposes, including the home folder name and email address. Once created, the first short name assigned to an account can't be changed.

The initial short name is usually eight characters or fewer (but can be as long as 255 characters) in lowercase (although uppercase and numbers are allowed), with no spaces and with only the underscore and dash allowed as special characters, such as s_jobs.

It's possible to create up to 16 additional short names. Having multiple short names enables a user to receive email at different aliases, for example. Additional short names can be edited after creation or deleted.

User ID

The UID assigned to an account uniquely identifies the account and is used internally to manage file and folder permissions. If two accounts are given the same UID, the system assumes they have the same file permissions.

For this reason, Workgroup Manager begins assigning network accounts at UID 1025. This prevents overlap with local accounts that may be created on the server or on the local client's computer.

Workgroup Manager and the Accounts pane of System Preferences create local accounts starting with UID 501. Unix typically reserves UIDs 0 to 100 for internal use, and Apple's internal processes use UIDs between 200 and 300. These accounts shouldn't be edited within Workgroup Manager.

Changing users' UIDs causes problems for users who've already started creating files with their original UIDs; once a user's UID is changed, ownership of his or her files must be changed to the new account's identity by using `chown` from the command line.

If users migrate from a local account to a network account, for example, they may shift from UID 501 to UID 1060, and their local home folder files need to be adjusted so that their new network account has permission to access them.

Password

An administrator setting up a new user record assigns an initial password by typing it twice. The password can also be changed if the user loses it, but there's no way for the administrator to discover the user's set password and remind him or her what it was; it can be reset only to something new.

Photo

A user account photo can be added to the record by dragging in a 64-pixel × 64-pixel graphic. This photo appears in the directory and is used by iChat as the user's buddy icon and within web services.

User account access and server administration

Two check boxes offer to give a user account the ability to administer the local server (off by default in new accounts) and basic access to his or her account (on by default). Deselecting account access disables the account without changing any other settings, making it easy to reinstate.

Users in both the local domain and the network Open Directory domain can be assigned the ability to administer the local server, which provides access to log in to the server locally or remotely by using Server administration tools, including Workgroup Manager or Server Admin.

The User Privileges tab

The Privileges tab appears only for users within the network Open Directory domain. Privileges assigned here allow a user account full or limited access to manage accounts in the directory domain.

Full access means the administrator can manage all records in the directory. If the account is assigned limited access, the Privileges tab presents an editable listing that can define which users and groups that account can manage, as shown in Figure 10.7, along with a series of check boxes that manage what rights the account has for each selected user or group in the list:

- Manage user passwords
- Edit managed preferences
- Edit user information
- Edit group membership

Figure 10.7

Defining a limited user's privileges

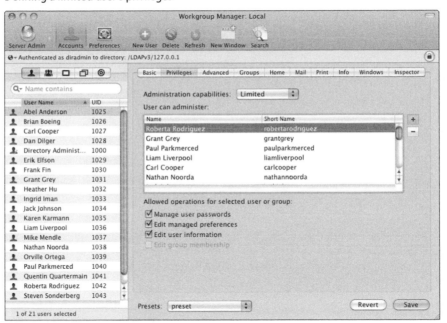

The User Advanced tab

The User Advanced tab presents options to allow simultaneous login, set the default shell, indicate the password type for the user, and set password and login policy, and it offers an interface for adding comments and keywords, as shown in Figure 10.8.

Simultaneous login

This option allows a user to log in to more than one managed computer at once. Simultaneous login can be disabled only for users with AFP home folders.

Figure 10.8

The Advanced pane

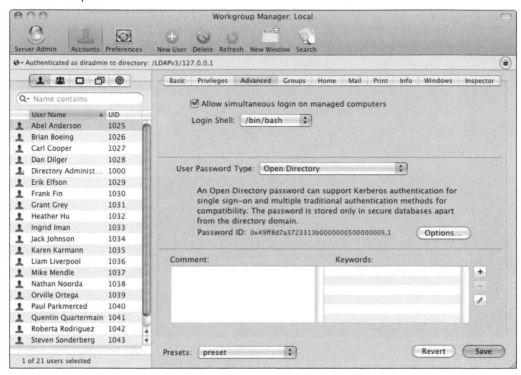

You may want to disable simultaneous login for most users. That's because users with a net-work home folder may end up overwriting their documents, preferences, or other Library items because many applications aren't aware that they could be sharing their home directory folders with another machine.

Default shell

This option sets the default command-line shell used by Terminal and when logging in remotely via SSH. Terminal allows users to set their own shell preferences.

The default shell in Mac OS X is /bin/bash, which is the same as most Linux systems. However, users may have a preference for using a different shell environment.

Password type and policy

A pop-up menu displays the default password type for accounts created in the domain, which for local accounts is Shadow Password and for network directory domain accounts is Open Directory. The alternative option is Crypt Password, which is provided for legacy reasons; it saves the password directly in the user record with encryption.

An Open Directory password is saved outside the directory domain by using the Apple Password Server and is required to support Kerberos authentication and for accounts that will log in to a Windows domain.

With an Open Directory password selected, the Options button opens a sheet, shown in Figure 10.9, that sets policy restrictions on the user's login:

- Disabling the account on a specific date
- Disabling the account after being inactive for a set number of days
- Disabling the account after a set number of failed login attempts

Figure 10.9

Defining login and password policy

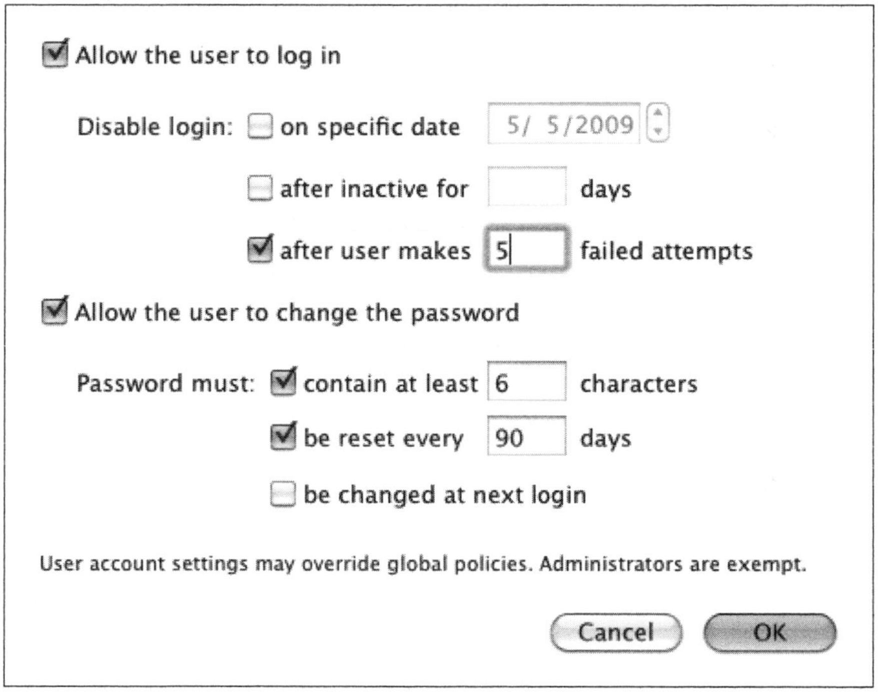

The sheet can also set password policy, forcing the user's set password to:

- Contain a minimum number of characters
- Be reset by the user after a set number of days
- Be reset after the next login, forcing the user to immediately set a new password for the new account

Comments and keywords

The comment area of the Advanced tab enables administrators to add descriptive text to the account's record, up to 32,767 bytes, which is as many characters as in a Roman character set or fewer in a language that uses multi-byte characters.

The keywords list requires setting up a master list of available keywords, which is tied to a specific directory domain. Once keywords are defined, they can be applied to individual accounts to enable quick searching and sorting of account records. The master list can be edited, added to, or deleted from at any time.

The User Groups tab

New user accounts are by default assigned to the staff group with GID 20. This primary group can be changed to any group, and a user can be assigned any number of additional group memberships. Figure 10.10 shows the Groups tab for a new user.

Figure 10.10

Setting user group membership

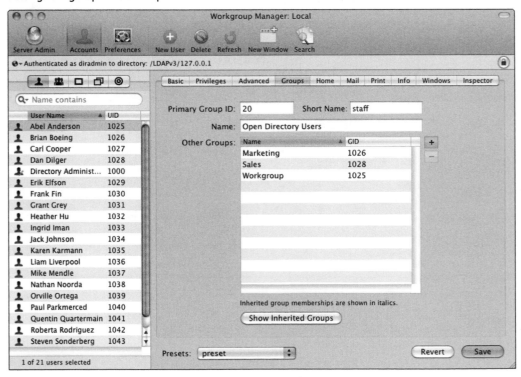

A user account's primary group determines standard POSIX permissions for files that the user doesn't own. If the primary group matches the file's group, the user inherits group access permissions.

Users who belong to multiple groups can select which group's managed preferences they want to acquire when they log in to a domain-bound machine. The selection is presented to the user as a list of workgroup options.

The User Home tab

Home folder settings for a user are configured on the Home tab, shown in Figure 10.11. Configuring a home folder requires an existing share point designated to serve home folders, which is created by using Server Admin.

Figure 10.11

User home folders and quotas

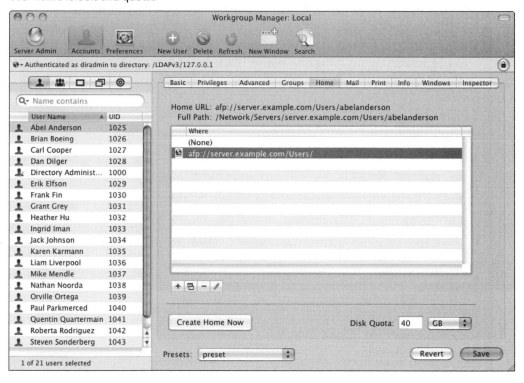

The share point configuration in Server Admin can also enable quotas on volumes, which are subsequently set on a per-user basis in Workgroup Manager within this tab.

Home folders

Mac OS X clients save user documents, preferences, and other Library data to a local directory at `/Users/username/`. When logging in to a network account, however, a network home folder allows the user to save his or her personal documents, application preferences, and related files to a network share instead.

Network home folders enable centralized, efficient backup of the user's data and allow the user to access the same set of files and settings from any machine he or she logs in to on the network.

The share point designated for network home folders may be accessed via AFP for Mac clients, NFS for Macs or Unix clients, or SMB for Windows clients. These share points don't need to be served from the directory server but can be made available across a variety of file servers to split the workload.

The share point used for network home directories must be automountable, which means that the directory server has a mount record for the share, allowing network clients to find it, and the file server needs to allow guest access. This also makes the share at `/Network/Servers` available to client systems bound to the directory domain.

By default, no home directory is set up for new accounts. From the Home tab, a network home can be created by specifying a file system URL pointing to the home directory as well as a full path that follows the network share, following this pattern:

```
/Network/Server/[server hostname]/Volumes/[drive name]/[share
    name]/[home directory path]
```

For share points using AFP or SMB, the user's network home folder is created when the user first logs in to his or her network account. For NFS home folders, the administrator needs to manually create the home folder by clicking the Create Home Now button.

Quotas

Quotas limit users from consuming more disk space than they're given. Quota support for a volume is enabled in Server Admin and requires an HFS+ formatted disk. Once enabled, users can be limited to a set number of MBs or GBs of disk use in Workgroup Manager from the Home tab.

The User Mail tab

To enable mail service for a new user account, the Mail tab's Enabled radio button exposes options, as shown in Figure 10.12, for:

- The designated mail server
- A mail quota in MB
- The delivery protocols supported for that user: POP, IMAP, or both
- The use of an alternative partition defined on the mail server

A user can also be assigned forward support, which directs any mail addressed to the user to an alternative email address.

Figure 10.12

Enabling mail support for a user account

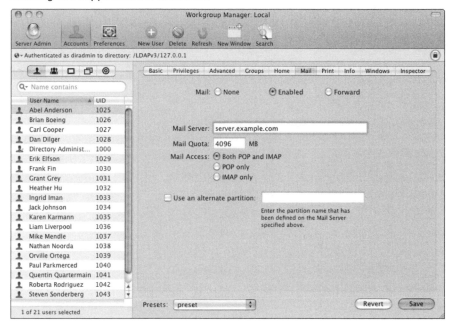

The User Print tab

Quotas limiting how many pages users can print to network print queues per day, per printer, can be set by using the Print tab, shown in Figure 10.13. By default, user records have no print quota. By clicking the All Queues radio button, administrators can limit the number of pages that can be printed within a set number of days across all printers on the server. A button restarts the print quota period.

Clicking the Per Queue radio button allows individual quotas to be set for specific printer queues on a given print server, allowing unlimited printing for specific printers and imposing a quota on others. Each printer queue is defined by using the pop-up menu, and queues can be added or deleted by using the appropriate buttons.

A time stamp shows when the quota was started, and the Restart Print Quota button can be used to reset the quota's start time.

Figure 10.13

Enabling print quotas for a user account

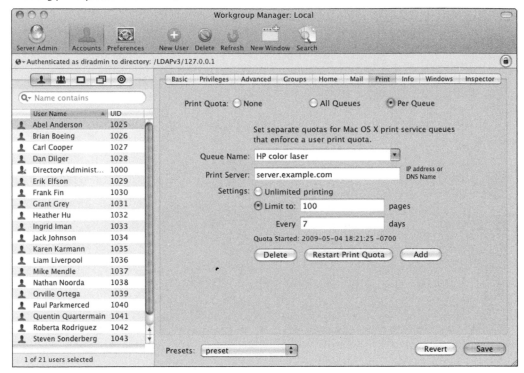

The User Info tab

A variety of contact information, as shown in Figure 10.14, can be stored in the user's directory record to support the Directory App used by Leopard clients or to be viewed or searched from Address Book:

- Name, with prefix, suffix, first, middle, and last entries
- Address fields for street, city, state, ZIP, and country
- Company, job title, and department
- Multiple phone numbers
- Multiple email addresses
- Multiple chat names for different IM protocols
- A web home page URL
- A weblog URL

Figure 10.14

Contact data for a user account

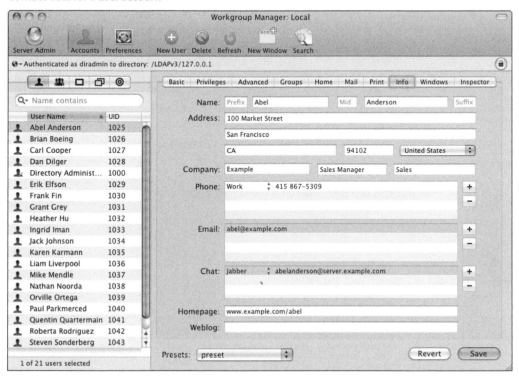

Snow Leopard Server now delegates the task of managing contact information to the independent Address Book Server, which offers a higher performance method of serving this data than the LDAP directory service.

Address Book Server also supports simplified, secured access of contact information to mobile users via Mobile Access Server.

Instead of maintaining contact records in the directory domain database, Address Book Server keeps its own data stored inside /Library/AddressBookServer/Documents.

CROSS-REF

For more on Address Book Server, see Chapter 28.

The User Windows tab

Snow Leopard Server can support Windows clients by using the SMB service, acting as one of the following:

- **Standalone SMB file server.** This simply serves Windows file and print shares. Windows users can't log in to the server as part of a domain.

- **Windows Domain Member.** This acts as part of an existing Windows domain, Microsoft's proprietary domain system associated with Windows NT prior to the delivery of the LDAP-based Active Directory. Domain members serve file and print shares and may also host user profiles and home folders for Windows domain clients.

- **Primary Domain Controller (PDC).** This manages a Windows domain and authenticates access to clients on the Windows domain, either hosting their user profiles and home folders itself or authenticating access to a Domain Member's services.

- **Backup Domain Controller (BDC).** This acts as a read-only replica for a Primary Domain Controller.

CROSS-REF

For more on Windows services in Mac OS X Server, see Chapter 2. For more on SMB file sharing, see Chapter 22.

The Windows tab of Workgroup Manager, shown in Figure 10.15, provides a user profile path and login script that can be used to support Windows roaming profiles as well as a hard drive letter-mapping and path for the Windows home directory.

Windows roaming profiles are analogous to the Library folder within Portable Home Directories in Mac OS X. A Snow Leopard Server acting as a PDC can host an SMB share point that serves as a roaming profile location for Windows clients that log in to the Windows domain.

At login, the Windows PC can connect to its server-hosted user profile as specified here or can be directed to use a local home directory on its own system. The profile path can be left blank to use the default SMB share point for user profiles, which is /Users/Profiles on the PDC.

Alternatively, another share on a different SMB file server can be specified by using Microsoft's backward slash path syntax, following this convention: \\[servername]\[share name]\[path to profile]\[username].

In either case, this creates a roaming profile that the Windows client uses to sync its application preference files. With a roaming profile, a user may log in to different Windows PCs and maintain the same user environment, syncing back any changes to the profile at logout.

Windows users may also be directed to store their profile locally on their own computer by specifying the drive letter C: to target the primary local hard disk and by specifying the customary path for a local profile, which for Windows XP is Documents and Settings\username, resulting in the user profile path: C:\Documents and Settings\bgates.

Figure 10.15

Windows login and profile settings

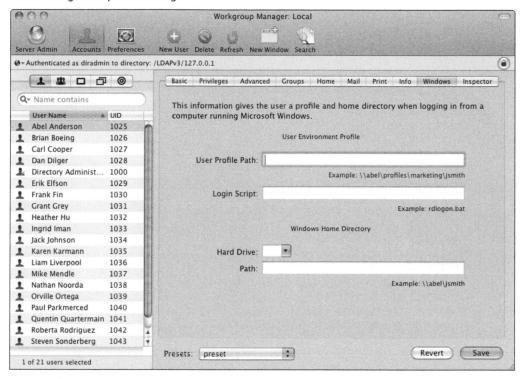

In Windows Vista or Windows 7, this same path is hard-linked for backward-compatibility reasons to the more Unix-like user path: `C:\Users\bgates`.

If you're supporting both XP and newer Windows clients, specifying the former `Documents and Settings` path works on any version.

In addition to the profile path, Windows users can also be assigned a network home directory, which is analogous to a Mac home folder without its `Library` folder. By default, the same home folder location used for Mac clients is also used as the home directory for Windows users, allowing the same user to log in from either operating system and access the same documents.

The default home directory is specified on the Home tab. To use a different home directory for Windows users, select the conventional `H:` drive letter and then specify a path by using Microsoft's backward slash notation: `\\[servername]\[share name]\[path to profile]\[username]`.

The specified path is mapped as the `H:` drive for Windows users when they log in to the Windows domain.

Windows users can also be optionally assigned a login script batch file that automatically executes at login, allowing administrators to set up various environment features on the user's PC. The script specified — for example, `login.bat` — is saved within `/etc/netlogon` on the PDC. Different scripts can be assigned to different users by using batch file names or paths to different files relative to the `/etc/netlogon` folder without a leading slash, such as `teachers/login.bat`.

The User Inspector tab

The last tab presented for user account records is visible only if the option Show "All Records" tab and inspector is enabled in Workgroup Manager's preferences.

The Inspector tab, shown in Figure 10.16, presents a raw listing of all attributes stored in the selected user's account record. This listing allows administrators to edit attributes, add new values, or add new attributes to the record.

Figure 10.16

The Inspector pane

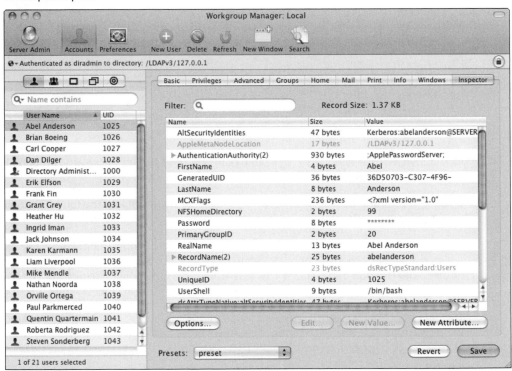

NOTE

Editing the raw attributes of a directory domain user record is an advanced feature that should be done only by users fully aware of what they're doing.

Working with Group Accounts

After selecting the Group tab in the Accounts List, you can create a new group account record or select one or multiple existing group account records and modify record settings by using the account detail pane on the right, which presents a series of tabs for configuring related settings.

The Group Basic tab

With a group account selected, the first tab in Workgroup Manager presents the group account's display name (also called the real name or full name), GID, and the short name associated with the account.

It also provides a picture path and a picture well for adding a group photo as well as a comment field, as shown in Figure 10.17.

Figure 10.17

The Basic pane

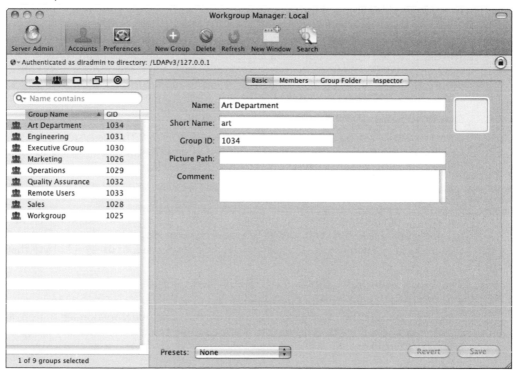

Group account name

All account names should be unique to their account record type; a user and group can share the same name (such as admin user and admin group), but groups must all have unique names, and groups should be unique across directory domains.

Workgroup Manager doesn't allow multiple group accounts in a domain to use the same name, but it doesn't stop users from using the same group name across different domains because it works with only one domain at a time.

A group's display username can be up to 255 bytes, which means 255 Roman characters or fewer when using character sets that use double-byte or four-byte characters. This name can include spaces and uppercase characters, such as Marketing Department. It can be changed at any point after the group record is created.

Group short names

The short name assigned to a group record is used internally for several purposes, including the group file share and a group email address if mailing lists are enabled. Once created, the short name assigned to an account can't be changed.

The initial short name is usually eight characters or fewer (but can be as long as 255 characters) in lowercase (although uppercase and numbers are allowed), with no spaces and with only the underscore allowed as a special character, such as marketing_1.

Group ID

The GID assigned to an account uniquely identifies the group account and is used internally to manage group file and folder permissions. If accounts in the same primary group are given the same GID, the system gives them the same group file permissions.

Photo and Photo Path

A group graphic can be assigned using a 64-x-64-pixel image. The file is stored as a path and must be available on a public share to be visible to users. Dragging an image into the well defines the path automatically; the path may also be specified manually.

Comment

The comment area enables administrators to add descriptive text to the group account's record to enable quick searching and sorting of account records, up to 32,767 bytes. That's as many characters as in a Roman character set or fewer in a language that uses multi-byte characters.

The Group Members tab

A group's membership is managed from the Members tab, shown in Figure 10.18. Groups can contain both users and other groups, either from the same directory domain or from another directory domain. For example, you can add local users or an Active Directory group to an Open Directory domain group.

Figure 10.18

The Members pane

Adding a group to another group is a feature called *hierarchical groups* and was new to Mac OS X 10.5 Leopard Server. Groups created by using an earlier version of Mac OS X Server must be upgraded by checking a box that appears on the Group Members tab when viewing a legacy folder.

Hierarchical folders are used to assign groups of users managed preferences. For example, groups could be created and assigned managed preferences that allow each group access to a specific printer. Individual users and groups of users can then be assigned membership within those groups. Each member of a group with defined managed preferences inherits those preference settings cumulatively.

A user account that's a member of several groups that are each organized into other groups with managed preferences inherits a complex combination of managed preferences. This makes it important to ensure that a group isn't assigned membership within a group it also contains because this loop would result in unpredictable behavior.

CROSS-REF

For more on using managed preferences in Open Directory, see Chapter 21. For more on managed preferences, see Chapter 34.

Group Folder tab

A shared folder for a group can be assigned by using the Group Folder tab, shown in Figure 10.19. This requires a pre-existing share point definition in Server Admin. By default, Snow Leopard Server creates a Groups share; folders or subfolders within this share can be designated as the Group Folder for a given group.

Figure 10.19

The Group Folder pane

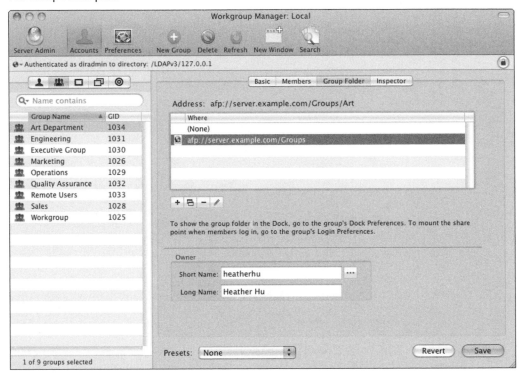

To create a Group Folder for a group, the share point URL and the path to the specific folder required for use as the Group Folder within that share point must be typed in, such as:

- **URL:** `afp://server.example.com/Groups`
- **Path:** `Marketing/Art`

This would designate the folder `/Groups/Marketing/Art` as the Group Folder if the server's `Groups` share point is in the default location at the root of the server's file system.

An owner for the Group Folder is designated under the Owner field in the Group Folder tab. This owner acts as the administrator for files within the folder.

Once defined, a Group Folder doesn't automatically mount when a user logs in, as his or her home folder does. Users must manually connect to the share, just like with any other file share. However, using managed preferences, an administrator can set login preferences for Mac OS X members of the group so the share is mounted at login. Dock preferences may also be managed to add the Group Folder to the Dock of that group's members.

Windows users who are members of the group aren't impacted by managed preferences but can connect to the share manually using the Network Neighborhood browser if the share point is being served as an SMB share.

The Group Inspector tab

The last tab presented for group account records is visible only if the option Show "All Records" tab and inspector is enabled in Workgroup Manager's preferences.

The Group Inspector tab, shown in Figure 10.20, presents a raw listing of all attributes stored in the selected group's account record. This listing allows administrators to edit attributes, add new values, or add new attributes to the record.

Figure 10.20

The Inspector pane

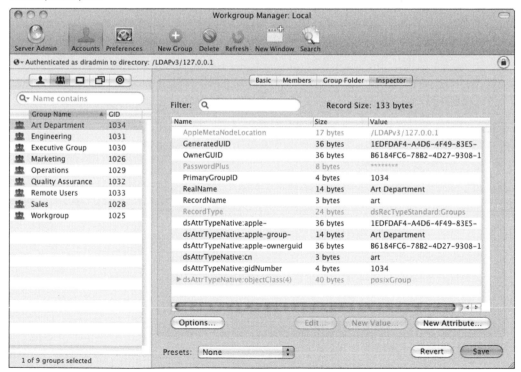

NOTE

Editing the raw attributes of a directory domain user record is an advanced feature that should be done only by users fully aware of what they're doing.

Working with Computer Accounts

Computer accounts are created to manage individual systems' preferences, which include options such as:

- Power management features
- Mobile accounts and Portable Home Directory sync rules
- Hardware features, such as external hard drive use or optical disc reading or burning
- Access to network printers
- Time Machine backup and Software Update settings
- Parental Control restrictions, including content filtering and time limits

To create computer accounts, you need the Ethernet ID (also called the MAC address) of the system you want to manage. It's not necessary or recommended to add Windows 2000, XP, Vista, or 7 clients as computer accounts in Workgroup Manager because they don't use managed preferences defined by Snow Leopard Server. Instead, add them to the PDC by joining its Windows domain.

A guest computer account can be created to apply managed preferences to systems that don't have a computer account. To create a guest computer account, use `Server/Create Guest Computer` from the main menu bar of Workgroup Manager.

The Computer General tab

On the General tab, shown in Figure 10.21, administrators create a computer account by using a display name (which can be the computer's actual name or simply a convenient label) and short name and then optionally adding a comment and keywords, just as with user account records.

Snow Leopard Server also now identifies computers by their Hardware UUID (Universally Unique ID), which is computed by combining a time and date with the Ethernet ID to create a 128-bit number guaranteed to be unique.

Figure 10.21

The General pane

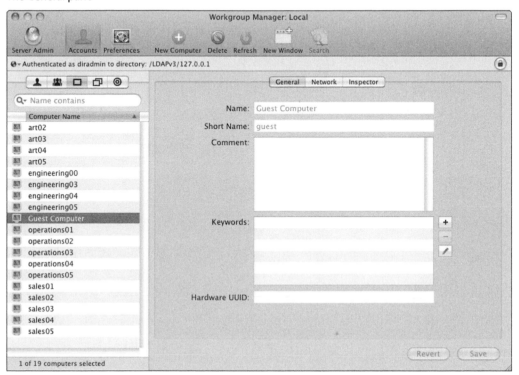

The Computer Network tab

From the Computer Network tab, shown in Figure 10.22, supply the computer's Ethernet ID and IP address if the system has a static address. URLs can be optionally supplied for managing network browsing.

The guest computer account can't have network information supplied for it because it represents any computer that doesn't match the existing computer account records.

Figure 10.22

The Network pane

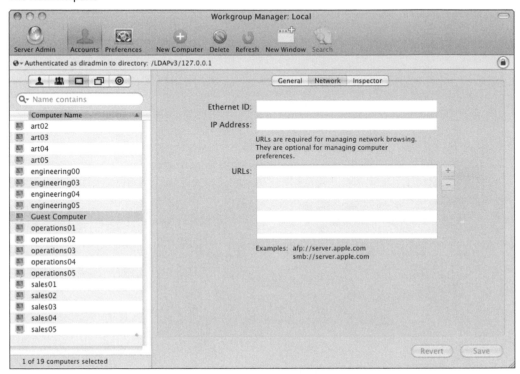

The Computer Inspector tab

The last tab presented for computer account records is visible only if the option Show "All Records" tab and inspector is enabled in Workgroup Manager's preferences.

The Computer Inspector tab, shown in Figure 10.23, presents a raw listing of all attributes stored in the selected computer account's directory record. This listing allows administrators to edit attributes, add new values, or add new attributes to the record.

NOTE

Editing the raw attributes of a directory domain user record is an advanced feature that should be done only by users fully aware of what they're doing.

Figure 10.23

The Inspector pane

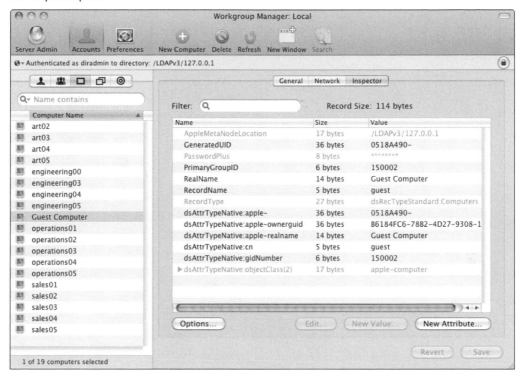

Working with Computer Group Accounts

Computer group accounts organize computer accounts to assign them managed preferences. Computer groups were new to Leopard Server and replaced the former computer lists.

Unlike a list, a computer group can contain both individual computer records and other computer groups, creating the same hierarchical groupings available in user groups to create more sophisticated ways to manage groups of computers efficiently by using inherited managed preferences.

A computer account can also belong to multiple computer groups; previously, a computer account could belong to only one computer list.

Computers running Mac OS X prior to 10.5 Leopard don't inherit managed permissions from computer groups, and Windows PCs don't use managed permissions at all.

The Computer Group Basic tab

For each computer group, the Basic tab, shown in Figure 10.24, is used to supply a display name, a short name, a Group ID, and a comment.

Figure 10.24

The Basic pane

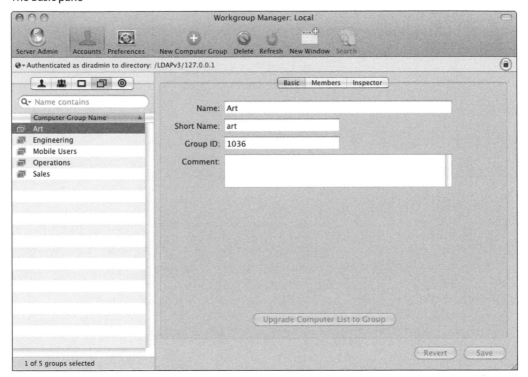

An existing computer list can be upgraded to a computer group by using the button on this page.

The Computer Group Members tab

On the Computer Group Members tab, shown in Figure 10.25, computer accounts and other computer groups can be added to a group's membership, either by using the computer account browser opened by clicking the Add (+) button or the network browser opened by clicking the Ellipsis (...) button. Up to 2,000 computers can be added to a computer group.

Figure 10.25

The Members pane

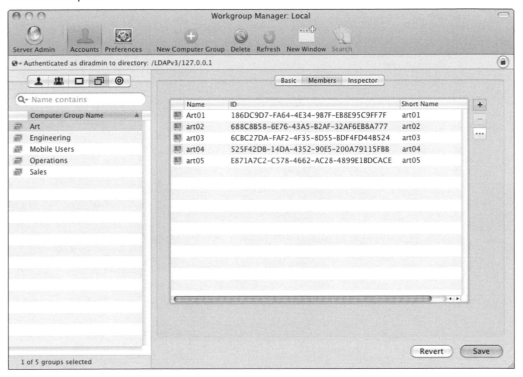

To avoid unpredictable behavior, a group shouldn't add another group to its membership if it's already a member of that group or other subgroups contained by it, creating a loop of group memberships.

The Computer Group Inspector tab

The last tab presented for computer group account records is visible only if the option Show "All Records" tab and inspector is enabled in Workgroup Manager's preferences.

The Computer Group Inspector tab, shown in Figure 10.26, presents a raw listing of all attributes stored in the selected computer group account's directory record. This listing allows administrators to edit attributes, add new values, or add new attributes to the record.

Figure 10.26

The Inspector pane

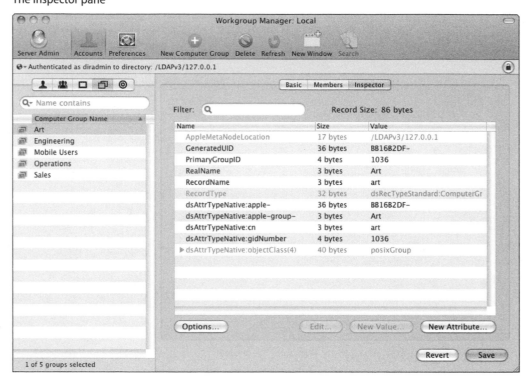

NOTE

Editing the raw attributes of a directory domain user record is an advanced feature that should be done only by users fully aware of what they're doing.

Creating and Configuring Records

After selecting the account record tab of the type of account you want to create in the Accounts List, you can create a new user, group, computer, or computer group account record by using the contextually relevant button in the Workgroup Manager toolbar.

Creating new users and groups

Creating basic new user and group account records within Workgroup Manager involves logging in to the desired domain directory, creating a new account from scratch or using a defined preset, and then saving the record.

To log in to the desired directory domain in Workgroup Manager, follow these steps:

1. **Launch Workgroup Manager and then authenticate with the server.**

2. **Select the desired directory domain by using the pop-up menu appearing after the globe icon in the directory domain authentication strip appearing below the toolbar.** The strip should initially report one of the following:

   - `Authenticated as admin to local directory: /Local/Default`. If this option is shown, Workgroup Manager allows creation of accounts only in the local domain node. To select the network-visible directory domain, click the globe's pop-up menu and then choose `/LDAPv3/127.0.0.1` from the list of directory domains.

   - `Viewing directory: /LDAPv3/127.0.0.1. Not Authenticated`. If this option is shown, authenticate with the `/LDAPv3/127.0.0.1` directory domain by clicking the lock icon at the right end of the strip and then providing the credentials for an account with privileges to administrator the directory domain, such as the diradmin account created during installation. The regular local machine admin account doesn't have administrative privileges for this directory domain.

   - `Authenticated as diradmin to directory: /LDAPv3/127.0.0.1`. If this option is shown, you can begin working with accounts. If you want to work with accounts in a different directory service, choose that domain from the pop-up menu or add the new service by choosing Other and then choosing the directory from the browser of known and configured directory services.

3. **If the desired directory service isn't available in the browser listing, launch System Preferences, click the Accounts pane, choose Login Options (authenticating with the pane if necessary), and then click Edit next to the Network Account Server listing.**

4. **Add the desired directory service here or click Open Directory Utility and then type the service using the customizable settings offered by that application.**

5. **Return to Workgroup Manager to browse for the selected directory service and then authenticate with it.** The directory domain authentication strip reports the selected directory and the administrative user authenticated to that service.

To create a basic new user account in Workgroup Manager, follow these steps:

1. **Launch Workgroup Manager and then authenticate with the desired directory domain.**

2. **Click the User tab in the accounts list by clicking the single user silhouette icon.**

3. **Click New User on the toolbar.** A new user record is created with the name Untitled followed by a number.

4. **Type a unique name and then choose an appropriate short name that won't need to change in the future.** Optionally, supply a graphic for the new user.

5. **Type an initial password and then verify it.**

6. **Click Save.** The new account is ready for use.

To create a basic new group account in Workgroup Manager, follow these steps:

1. **Launch Workgroup Manager and then authenticate with the desired directory domain.**

2. **Click the Group tab in the accounts list by clicking the group silhouette icon.**

3. **Click New Group on the toolbar.** A new group record is created with the name Untitled followed by a number.

4. **Type a unique name and then choose an appropriate short name that won't need to change in the future.** Optionally, supply a graphic for the new group by using an image file hosted on the server that's available to group members.

5. **Click the Members tab, click the Add (+) button to display the listing of users and groups, and then drag desired members into the member list.**

6. **Click Save.** The new group account is ready for use.

To create an account preset in Workgroup Manager, follow these steps:

1. **Launch Workgroup Manager and then authenticate with the desired directory domain.**

2. **Create a new account and then fill it out as a template for subsequent new accounts.** Alternatively, select an existing account in the accounts list representing the type of account you want to generate a preset for and the basic settings you want to supply.

3. **Use the Preset pop-up menu to choose Save Preset.** A sheet drops down asking you to supply a name for the preset.

4. **Create a new account and then choose the saved listing from the Preset pop-up menu.** Its configured settings are applied to the new account.

5. **Give the new account a unique name, short name, and additional details and then save the account.**

6. **To modify an existing preset, use it to create a new account, change the new account as desired, save it as a new preset, and then delete the previous preset.**

Creating new computers and computer groups

Creating new computer or computer group account records within Workgroup Manager similarly involves logging in to the desired domain directory, creating a new account from scratch or using a defined preset, and then saving the record. Managed preferences can then be assigned to the records.

A guest computer account can be created to apply generic managed preferences to computers on the domain that don't have a matching computer record.

To create a new computer account in Workgroup Manager, follow these steps:

1. **Launch Workgroup Manager and then authenticate with the desired directory domain.**

2. **Click the Computers tab in the accounts list by clicking the single box icon.**

3. **Click New Computer on the toolbar.** A new computer record is created with the name Untitled followed by a number.

4. **Type a unique name and then choose an appropriate short name that won't need to change in the future.**

5. **Click the Network tab, type the Ethernet ID (hardware MAC address) of the computer, and then type its IP address if it uses a manually assigned, static address.**

6. **Click Save.** The new computer account is ready for use.

To create a new computer group account in Workgroup Manager, follow these steps:

1. **Launch Workgroup Manager and then authenticate with the desired directory domain.**

2. **Click the Computer Group tab in the accounts list by clicking the double box icon.**

3. **Click New Computer Group on the toolbar.** A new group record is created with the name Untitled followed by a number.

4. **Type a unique name and then choose an appropriate short name that won't need to change in the future.**

5. **Click the Members tab, click the Add (+) button to display the listing of computer and computer group accounts, and then drag desired members into the member list.** Alternatively, click the Ellipsis (…) button to browse for available computers that can be added to the computer group.

6. **Click Save.** The new computer group account is ready for use.

To create a guest computer account in Workgroup Manager, follow these steps:

1. **Launch Workgroup Manager and then authenticate with the desired directory domain.**

2. **Choose Server ⇨ Create Guest Computer from the main menu bar.** A new Guest Computer account appears among other computers in the accounts list. This account can be used to apply generic managed preferences to network machines without a unique computer account.

Managing Account Access and Privileges

Workgroup Manager can be used to reset a user's lost password, set password policy that forces users to maintain a secure password for their accounts, disable user accounts, and assign full or limited administrative access to the directory domain.

To reset a user's password in Workgroup Manager, follow these steps:

1. **Launch Workgroup Manager and then authenticate with the desired directory domain.**

2. **Select the user's account.** Multiple users can be simultaneously selected from the accounts list.

3. **From the Basic tab, type a new password, verify it, and then click Save.** Administrators can't look up a user's lost password. Additionally, changing an account's password doesn't change the user's FileVault password or his or her Keychain login password, which must both be reset manually. Resetting a FileVault password requires an existing master password for FileVault on the client machine.

To set password policy for a user account in Workgroup Manager, follow these steps:

1. **Launch Workgroup Manager and then authenticate with the desired directory domain.**

2. **Select the user's account.** Multiple users can be simultaneously selected from the accounts list.

3. **From the Advanced tab, click Options.** A sheet appears where you can configure the settings as desired to set policy restrictions on the user's login and password:

- Disabling the account on a specific date
- Disabling the account after being inactive for a set number of days
- Disabling the account after a set number of failed login attempts
- Forcing the set password to contain a minimum number of characters

- Requiring a password to be reset by the user after a set number of days
- Requiring the password to be reset after the next login, forcing the user to immediately set a new password for the new account

4. **Click Save.** Administrator accounts are exempt from set password policy rules.

To disable a user's account in Workgroup Manager, follow these steps:

1. **Launch Workgroup Manager and then authenticate with the desired directory domain.**

2. **Select the user's account.** Multiple users can be simultaneously selected from the accounts list.

3. **From the Basic tab, deselect the access account check box.** Alternatively, change the user's password.

4. **Click Save.** The user is no longer able to use the account to log in or access network resources. Removing access is preferred over simply deleting the account because you may need to enable access again later.

To assign a user directory domain privileges in Workgroup Manager, follow these steps:

1. **Launch Workgroup Manager and authenticate with the desired directory domain.**

2. **Select the user's account.** Multiple users can be simultaneously selected from the accounts list.

3. **From the Privileges tab, use the Administrative capabilities pop-up menu to choose full or limited access to directory records.** Full access allows the user to add, edit, or delete any domain records.

4. **If assigning limited access, use the Add (+) button to add user and group accounts the user can administer.** For each account, assign allowed operations by using the check boxes to:

- Manage user passwords
- Edit managed preferences
- Edit user information
- Edit group membership

5. **Click Save.** The user can now log in to Workgroup Manager and authenticate into the directory domain to use the assigned administrative privileges.

Configuring account features

Beginning with a basic user account, a directory administrator can assign additional account features that give the user access to group folders and workgroup wikis, designate a home directory, set up a profile path and home directory for users logging in when using a Windows PC, and enable mail access and print quota limits for a user.

To edit a user's group membership in Workgroup Manager, follow these steps:

1. **Launch Workgroup Manager and then authenticate with the desired directory domain.**

2. **Select the user's account.** Multiple users can be simultaneously selected from the accounts list.

3. **From the Groups tab, use the Add (+) button to add the desired groups to the user's group membership.**

4. **Alternatively, if multiple users are being added to a group, select the group account instead, click its Members tab, use the Add (+) button to display the listing of users and groups, and then drag desired members into the member list.**

5. **Click Save.**

To configure a network home folder for a user account in Workgroup Manager, follow these steps:

1. **Use Server Manager to create a share point with Automount support for home directories.** Enable AFP file sharing for Mac users. NFS may also be used for home directory share points in a mixed environment of Mac OS X and other Unix users. Enable SMB file sharing if Windows users will use the same share point.

2. **Launch Workgroup Manager and then authenticate with the desired directory domain.**

3. **Select the user's account.**

4. **From the Home tab, use the Add (+) button to define settings for the home directory:**

- Share point URL, a file system location pointing to the home directory.

- A path to the home folder within the share point. This can be simply the user's short name or a path of folders that the home folder sits inside. Don't use a leading or trailing slash in this path.

- A full path to the home directory that follows the network share, following this pattern: /Network/Server/[*server hostname*]/Volumes/[*drive name*]/[*share name*]/[*home directory path*].

5. **Optionally, specify a disk quota for the user.** Quota support on the share point volume must be enabled by using Server Admin.

6. **Click Save.** At login, the user should generate a new network home folder.

To configure a Windows profile and home directory in Workgroup Manager, follow these steps:

1. **Launch Workgroup Manager and then authenticate with the desired directory domain.**

2. **Select the user's account.** Multiple users can be simultaneously selected from the accounts list.

3. **From the Windows tab**, specify:

   - A User profile path, a file system location pointing to the profile directory, by using Microsoft's backward slash path syntax, following this convention: `\\[servername]\[share name]\[path to profile]\[username].`

     To use the default `/Users/Profiles` location, leave this field blank. To configure Windows users to maintain a local profile, specify: `C:\Documents and Settings\username.`

   - A login script, if desired, relative to its location inside `/etc/netlogon.`

   - A full path to the home directory that follows the network share, following this pattern: `/Network/Server/[server hostname]/Volumes/[drive name]/[share name]/[home directory path].` To use the same home directory specified under the Home tab for Mac logins, leave this field blank.

4. **Click Save.**

To enable mail access for a user account in Workgroup Manager, follow these steps:

1. **Launch Workgroup Manager and then authenticate with the desired directory domain.**

2. **Select the user's account.** Multiple users can be simultaneously selected from the accounts list.

3. **From the Mail tab, click the Enabled radio button and then specify:**

   - A mail server by its DNS name.

   - Optionally, a mail quota for the user. Setting 0 MB creates an unlimited mailbox.

   - The supported email protocols for the user as POP, IMAP, or both.

4. **Click Save.**

To enable print quotas for a user account in Workgroup Manager, follow these steps:

1. **Launch Workgroup Manager and then authenticate with the desired directory domain.**

2. **Select the user's account.** Multiple users can be simultaneously selected from the accounts list.

3. **From the Print tab, click the All Queues radio button to apply a simple quota setting limiting the number of pages that a user can print over a set number of days.** To define queue limits per print queue for the user, select Per Queue and then select:

    - A printer queue name.

    - A print server by using its DNS name or IP address.

    - Specify queue settings as unlimited printing or set the number of pages that user can print over a set number of days for each queue defined. Use the Add (+) button to set up additional queues for each printer desired.

4. **Click Save.**

Organizing, filtering, and editing domain accounts

Accounts in Workgroup Manager can be organized by using a pool of defined keywords. Search features can be used to filter records based on assigned keywords or other account attributes. Additionally, search queries can be used to define a pool of records that can be batch-updated together.

Multiple records can also be manually selected from the accounts list and edited together.

To use keywords with accounts in Workgroup Manager, follow these steps:

1. **Launch Workgroup Manager and then authenticate with the desired directory domain.**

2. **Select a user's account and then click the Advanced tab.**

3. **Near Keyword, click the Edit button marked with a pencil icon.** A sheet drops down.

4. **Add keywords to the list by using the Add (+) button and then click OK.**

5. **Select accounts to assign them keywords.** Multiple users or computers can be simultaneously selected from the accounts list. To assign keywords, do the following:

    - For user accounts, add keywords by using the Advanced tab.

    - For computer accounts, add keywords by using the General tab.

6. **To add keywords to an account record, click the Add (+) button.** From the list that drops down, select the predefined keywords added in step 4.

7. **To add or change keywords, click the Edit Keywords button and then click OK to save your changes.**

8. **Click Save.**

To filter accounts by using Search in Workgroup Manager, follow these steps:

1. **Launch Workgroup Manager and then authenticate with the desired directory domain.**

2. **Select a user's account and then click the Search button on the toolbar.** A sheet drops down.

3. **Define criteria for the search query filter by using the pop-up menus to supply any combination of the following:**

   - A Record Name that is, contains, starts with, or ends with a given text string. A Record Name is the internal or short name of an account commonly used at the command line, such as admin.

   - A Real Name that is, contains, starts with, or ends with a given text string. A Real Name is the display name of an account used in Mac OS X, such as Administrator. Real or record names can generally be used interchangeably in the graphical interface.

   - A User ID that is, contains, is greater than, or is less than a given number. This is the UID that uniquely identifies each account.

   - A Comment that is, contains, starts with, or ends with a given text string. Comment is a free text field associated with account records in Workgroup Manager.

   - A Keyword that is, contains, starts with, or ends with a given text string. Keywords can be defined and applied to account records in Workgroup Manager.

   - A Group ID that is, contains, is greater than, or is less than a given number. A user account record has a Primary Group ID it's associated with, and each group has a Group ID that identifies its members.

4. **Click Search Now.** Workgroup Manager displays the matching records in the accounts list. The search results can be cleared or the query can be edited by using the two buttons in the query pane.

To batch-edit accounts by using Search in Workgroup Manager, follow these steps:

1. **Launch Workgroup Manager and then authenticate with the desired directory domain.**

2. **Click the Search button on the toolbar to define a search query, as detailed in the previous steps.**

3. **Click the Perform a batch edit on the search results check box.** Optionally, select the options to preview and edit search results before applying changes or to display a summary view of changes and errors.

4. **Click Search Now.** The records matching the search can be batch-edited.

5. **Click Apply Now when finished.** If the preview option was selected, a listing of the affected accounts are presented. If the summary display option was selected, a listing of the changes are presented, including the affected records and fields. You can save a text log of the report by clicking the Save button.

6. **Remove any accounts you don't want to be updated with the changes and then click Apply.**

CROSS-REF

For more on managing preferences in Workgroup Manager, see Chapter 34.

Summary

- Workgroup Manager serves as the main control interface for creating and customizing user, group, and computer accounts and then assigning them managed preferences.

- Part of the Server Administration Software package, Workgroup Manager is installable on any server or desktop Mac system running at least Mac OS X Snow Leopard.

- Workgroup Manager is used with the advanced configuration, replacing the simpler user and group management available within Server Preferences.

- Workgroup Manager presents two primary modes when working with directory domain accounts: working with record details by using the toolbar's Accounts button and assigning managed preferences to accounts by using the Preferences button.

- The application is designed to work with multiple, different directory domains, allowing organizations to group servers and workstations into subdomains and to combine different directory server types, including OpenLDAP and Active Directory, for use with Apple's Open Directory and its managed preferences.

Additional Advanced Admin Tools

Apple supplies a variety of server administration tools that ship with Mac OS X Server on the installation DVD within the Other Installs folder:

- Server Admin is used for enabling and configuring services on the server and managing access to them.

- Workgroup Manager is supplied for working with both local accounts and network-accessible directory domain user, group, and computer account records. It's also used for assigning managed preferences to these accounts.

- iCal Server Utility is used to manage global contact information stored in Open Directory. Prior to Snow Leopard, this application was named Directory.app (not to be confused with Directory Utility).

- Server Monitor is used to monitor the status of Xserve hardware that supports various reporting sensors and, on Xserve (late 2006) models or later, supports Lights-Out Management.

- RAID Admin is used to administer the now-discontinued Xserve RAID appliance.

- System Image Utility is used to create NetBoot, NetRestore, and NetInstall images for network delivery to client machines.

- Command-line tools provide access to the features of Apple's supplied graphical administration applications from Terminal or a remote shell, allowing for remote access administration and configuration by using SSH and the creation of scripted tasks that can be run on a schedule.

In This Chapter

iCal Server Utility

Server Monitor

RAID Admin

System Image Utility

Command-line tools

CROSS-REF

For more on Server Admin, see Chapter 9. For more on Workgroup Manager, see Chapter 10. For more on managed preferences, see Chapter 36.

This chapter describes how these tools can be used, presents an overview of the GUI each uses, and outlines Terminal commands that can be used to perform the same actions programmatically.

iCal Server Utility

In Leopard Server, Apple introduced Directory.app, shown in Figure 11.1, as a client-side tool for browsing shared information about people, groups, locations, and resources defined within the organization's directory service.

Figure 11.1

Directory.app, prior to Snow Leopard Server

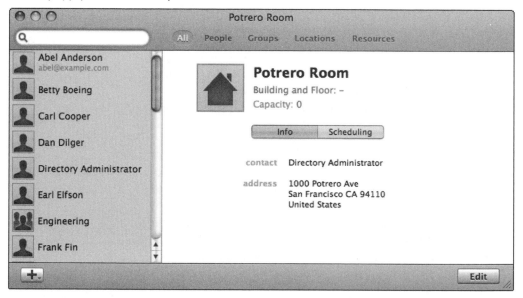

This included looking up a user's photo, manager, direct reports, and the public groups the person belonged to. This same contact information was supplied via the directory contact bindings defined in Directory Utility to other Mac OS X applications, including Address Book, mail for address completion, and iChat buddy listings.

Users could also upload their own contacts into directory services to create *shared contacts*, which might be vendors or clients who don't have a local account but whom other people in the company might want to contact.

Snow Leopard Server changes how user records are managed with the introduction of Address Book Server. Instead of uploading shared contacts and other information into the directory service, Snow Leopard provides a separate data store, limiting users' need to directly access directory records.

CROSS-REF
For more on Address Book Server, see Chapter 28.

For this reason, Directory.app is no longer used to provide client access to account records for users and groups. Instead, users are supposed to look up network contacts via Address Book, which includes the following, as shown in Figure 11.2:

- **All Contacts.** A composite listing of contacts Address Book knows about
- **All Directories.** A set of searchable listings of any user-shared contact listings in addition to Directory Services
- **Directory Services.** A searchable listing of the directory under the All Directory Services umbrella group
- **On My Mac.** The list of local contacts
- **User@server.** The local user's set of network shared contacts

Figure 11.2

Address Book

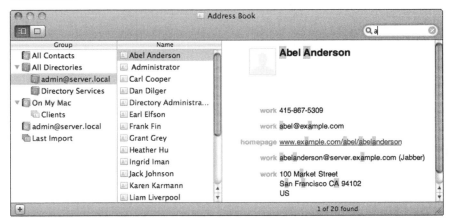

Still missing is any way to define locations, maps, and resources used by iCal Server and stored in the directory. The new iCal Server Utility performs this function; Apple has simply scraped people and groups from the old Directory.app and renamed it, as shown in Figure 11.3.

CROSS-REF
For more on iCal Server, see Chapter 26.

Figure 11.3

iCal Server Utility in Snow Leopard Server

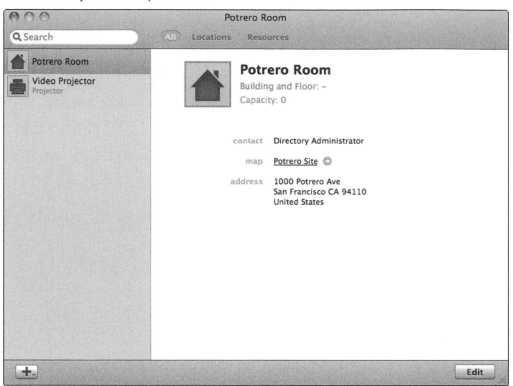

iCal Server uses locations and resources to book rooms and equipment in relation to meetings as well as maps to show where locations and resources can be located:

- **Locations refer to rooms or other landmarks not associated with a specific person and are used to book conference rooms or other places associated with meetings.** Locations can be configured to auto-accept meeting request invitations, enabling users to browse up-to-date availability information and directly book a location for a meeting.

- **Resources refer to shared equipment, such as an automobile, conference phone, copier, digital camera, notebook, printer, projector or projection screen, scanner, or video camera.** By defining resources in the company directory and enabling them to auto-accept meeting request invitations, users can look up what resources are available and schedule their use.

● **Maps to the location or resource are images that an administrator manages within iCal Server Utility.** Maps added to the company directory can be more accurate or detailed than a generated Google map. After being defined, a map can be associated with a location or resource record and subsequently viewed by users. A pushpin can be used to designate a specific location on a map.

To use iCal Server Utility, a system must be bound to the directory.

To add a Network Account Server in Snow Leopard, follow these steps:

1. **Launch System Preferences and then click the Accounts tab.**

2. **Click the lock icon and then authenticate as a local administrator.**

3. **Select Login Options.**

4. **Click Edit Network Account Server.** The sheet shown in Figure 11.4 drops down.

Figure 11.4

The Network Account Server editor sheet

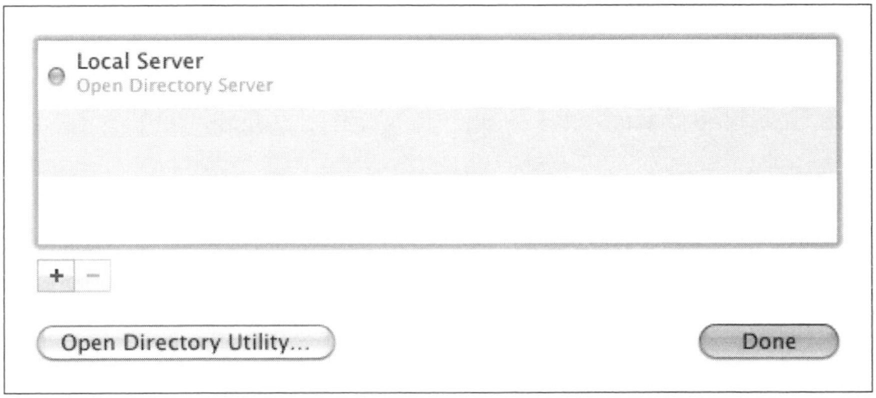

5. **Click the Add (+) button to add the IP address or DNS name of an LDAP, Open Directory, or Active Directory server.**

6. **Authenticate with the server.**

7. **Click Done.** If authentication is successful, the new directory service is added to the list of configured Network Account Servers.

To create a location record in iCal Server Utility, follow these steps:

1. Launch iCal Server Utility. You must have administrative privileges on the directory domain and have your system bound to the directory as a Network Account Server.

2. Click the Add (+) button and then choose New Location.

3. Configure the location's details, as shown in Figure 11.5:

- A unique name and an optional graphic icon
- A primary contact for the location
- A map to the location.(Maps are created separately in iCal Server Utility.)
- An address and phone number for the location
- A building name, floor, and seating capacity for the location
- A note field for additional details

Figure 11.5

Creating a location record in iCal Server Utility

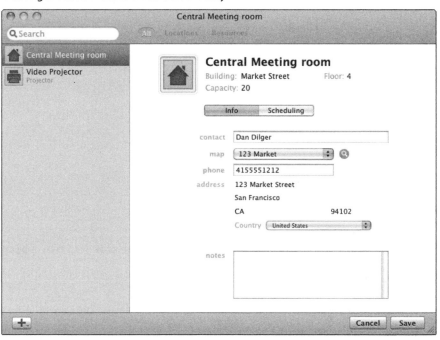

4. Click Save. The location record is saved in the directory, and a new calendar is created to schedule events that users associate with it. The location name auto-resolves for users scheduling it as the location for a new event.

To create a resource record in iCal Server Utility, follow these steps:

1. **Launch iCal Server Utility.** You must have administrative privileges on the directory domain and have your system bound to the directory as a Network Account Server.

2. **Click the Add (+) button and then choose New Resource.**

3. **Configure the Resource's details, as shown in Figure 11.6:**

- A unique name and an optional graphic icon

- A resource type and description field (Types can include automobile, conference phone, copier, digital camera, notebook, printer, projector or projection screen, scanner, or video camera. You can also type in an alternative resource category.)

- An owner for the resource

- A map to the resource (Maps are created separately in iCal Server Utility.)

- An address for the resource

- A note field for additional details

Figure 11.6

Creating a resource record in iCal Server Utility

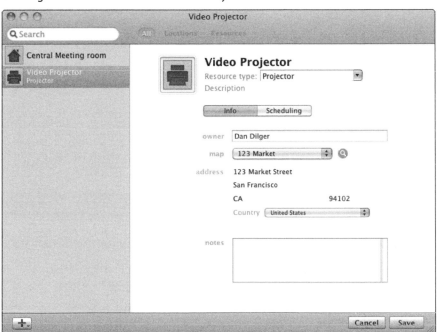

4. **Click Save.** The resource record is saved in the directory, and a new calendar is created to schedule events that users associate with it. The resource name auto-resolves for users scheduling it as an attendee in a new event.

Custom maps can be created in iCal Server Utility to help users find the location of conference rooms or equipment within a campus or floor plan.

To create a map in iCal Server Utility, follow these steps:

1. **Launch iCal Server Utility.** You must have administrative privileges on the directory domain and have your system bound to the directory as a Network Account Server.

2. **Choose Edit Maps from the File menu.** A map editor window, shown in Figure 11.7, opens.

Figure 11.7

Creating a map record in iCal Server Utility

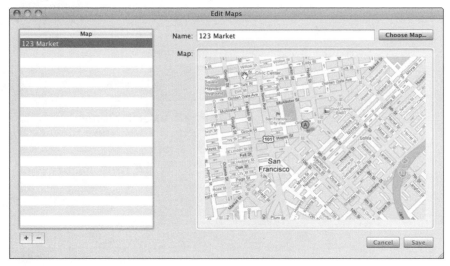

3. **Click the Add (+) button to define a new map with a unique name.**

4. **Click the Choose Map button and then choose any image file.** This can be a Google map screenshot or custom artwork representing a campus or building floor plan.

5. **Click Save.** The map record is saved in the directory and can be attached to location or resource records.

To assign and configure a map for a location or resource, follow these steps:

1. **Launch iCal Server Utility.** You must have administrative privileges on the directory domain and have your system bound to the directory as a Network Account Server.

2. **Select a location or resource record, click the Edit button, and then assign the record a defined map from the pop-up control.**

3. **Use the Detail button marked with an arrow to open the Map editor, shown in Figure 11.8.**

4. **Click the Set Pushpin button to mark a specific location on the map and then use the Zoom control to arrange the graphic placement of the map as desired.**

5. **Click OK.** When a user clicks the map link within a location or resource record, the associated map appears with the pushpin location defined by the administrator. The user can zoom in and out as desired.

Figure 11.8

Configuring a map in iCal Server Utility

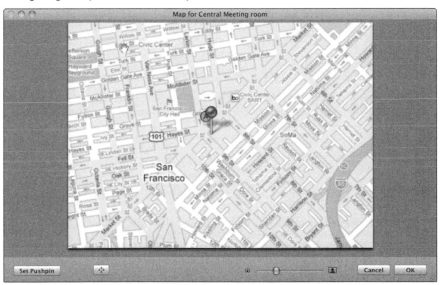

Server Monitor

When using Xserve equipment with support for hardware sensors, Server Monitor allows you to remotely monitor the system's status. You can use it to:

- Start up if the system is an Xserve (late 2006) model or later, which supports Lights-Out Management (LOM) (This feature enables you to connect to the server even when the server is shut down.)
- Shut down and restart servers
- Check component status
- Turn system identifier lights on and off for identification
- Configure the system to send email notifications of system problems or alerts

Server Monitor acts as an interface for `hwmond`, the hardware monitor daemon. This process won't run on any hardware apart from the Xserve and PowerMacs expressly sold as servers.

The application provides only all or nothing access to the server's information. There's also no SACL for Server Monitor, so you can't restrict specific admin users to read-only status or limit groups of admins from accessing all or parts of information presented about the servers.

When using LOM, you must configure a LOM port with a unique address and assign a LOM admin account. This can be done during the initial configuration in Setup Assistant.

LOM Channel 1 attaches to the network by using the same physical port as the Built-in Ethernet 1 (en0), but it requires its own unique IP address. Some Xserve models use a second LOM Channel that similarly works over Ethernet 2 (en1). LOM can't be enabled on a port used with link aggregation.

Monitoring groups of servers

The utility of Server Monitor becomes most evident when you're using it to monitor the health and well-being of a number of different servers, possibly even at various remote sites.

To set up a new Xserve in Server Monitor, follow these steps:

1. **Launch Server Monitor.**

2. **Click Add Server on the toolbar.** The sheet shown in Figure 11.9 drops down.

3. **Type the server address and the username and password of a local server administrator.** You can also browse for available servers via Bonjour from the list below by revealing Available Servers. If your server supports LOM, type the IP address or DNS name of the configured LOM port and then type credentials for the LOM port administrator account.

4. **Choose an update interval from the pop-up menu.** The default is every 10 minutes, but it can be set to 30 seconds; 1, 5, 10, or 30 minutes; or hourly; or it can be disabled for manual updating.

5. **Click OK.** The server is added to the list of servers to monitor.

Figure 11.9

Adding a server to Server Monitor

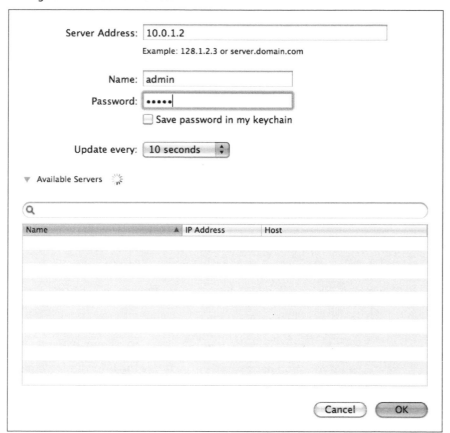

Xserve hardware detail

To get an overall view of the operation of a series of servers, Server Admin presents a status listing for the servers it knows about, with a status summary of colored icons to show the status for each of the various subsystems:

- Green for good
- Yellow for warning condition
- Red for a failure indication

Each subsystem gets an overall color indicator in the server list, with the information tabs below the server listing revealing more information and detail. The icons represent the status of a reporting section:

- Info
- Memory
- Drives
- Power
- Network
- Temperature
- Blowers
- Security

By clicking the Show warning and failures only check box, the server display only indicates yellow warning conditions and red failures.

By clicking the Show detailed status check box, Server Monitor presents additional status indicators for each component, such as each power supply, drive, and so on.

To review an Xserve's basic information in Server Monitor, follow these steps:

1. **Launch Server Monitor.**

2. **Select the server and then click the Info tab, shown in Figure 11.10.**

3. **The information pane displays the following information about the server:**
- IP address
- Name
- Kind
- Up time
- Last update
- OS version
- Processor
- Memory
- Boot ROM
- Serial number
- LOM version

4. **Click the System identifier light button to turn it on.** This can be used to identify a server in a rack.

Figure 11.10

The Info pane in Server Monitor

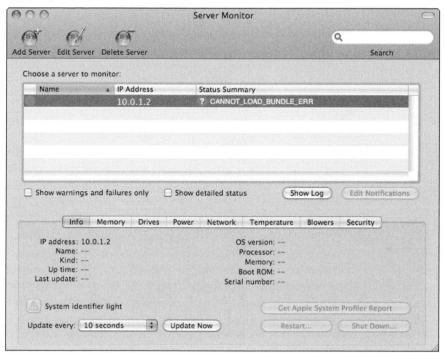

5. **Choose an update interval from the pop-up menu.** The default is every 10 minutes, but it can be set to 30 seconds; 1, 5, 10, or 30 minutes; or hourly; or it can be disabled for manual updating.

6. **Click the Update Now button to refresh the server's information.**

7. **Click Get Apple System Profiler Report to download a comprehensive detail of the server's hardware and installed software.**

8. **Click Show Log to view Server Monitor's interactions with the server.** This isn't the system log for the server; instead, the log shows server status changes, the times at which Server Monitor contacted the server, and whether a connection attempt was successful.

9. **Note the Restart and Shut Down buttons.** Anyone you provide with access to Server Monitor and who is in the admin group can take down the server by pressing a button.

10. **Click Edit Notifications to send out email alerts when specified conditions on the server occur.** Notifications are sent to all the recipients listed; there's no detailed control over who is notified about what events. Notification options are saved within a file at /etc/hwmond.conf.

To review an Xserve's memory information in Server Monitor, follow these steps:

1. **Launch Server Monitor.**

2. **Select the server and then click the Memory tab, shown in Figure 11.11.**

Figure 11.11

The Memory pane in Server Monitor

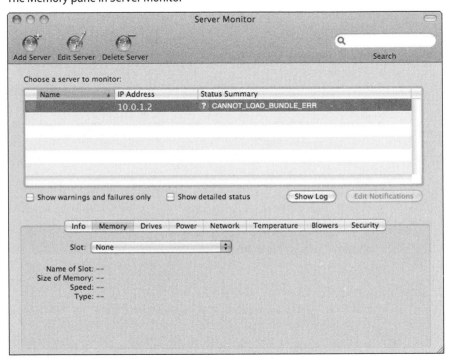

3. **The Memory pane displays information for the server's selected memory slot, as chosen in the pop-up menu:**
   - Name of the slot
   - Size of the memory installed
   - Speed rating
   - Type

To review an Xserve's drive information in Server Monitor, follow these steps:

1. **Launch Server Monitor.**

2. **Select the server and then click the Drives tab, shown in Figure 11.12.**

Figure 11.12

The Drives pane in Server Monitor

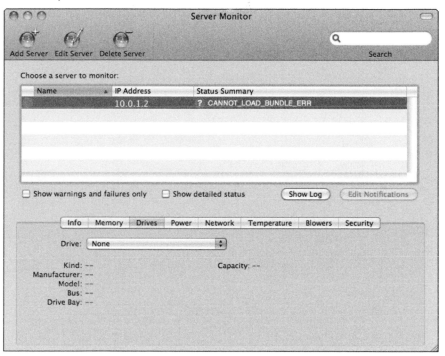

3. **The Drives pane displays information for the server's selected drive, as chosen in the pop-up menu:**
- Kind
- Manufacturer
- Model
- Bus
- Drive bay
- Capacity

To review an Xserve's power information in Server Monitor, follow these steps:

1. **Launch Server Monitor.**

2. **Select the server and then click the Power tab, shown in Figure 11.13.**

Figure 11.13

The Power pane in Server Monitor

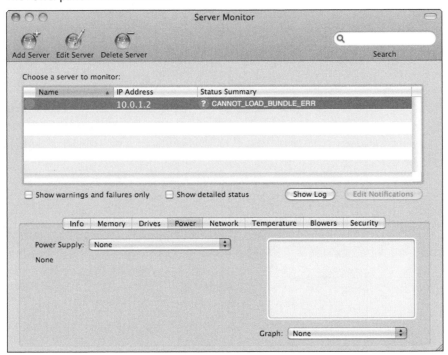

3. **The Power pane displays information for the server's selected power supply (including any external USB UPS units attached), as chosen in the pop-up menu:**
   - Type detail with source, status, and voltage
   - A graph of changes in those events

To review an Xserve's network information in Server Monitor, follow these steps:

1. **Launch Server Monitor.**

2. **Select the server and then click the Network tab, shown in Figure 11.14.**

3. **The Network pane displays information for the selected server's network adapter, as chosen in the pop-up menu:**

- IP address
- Subnet mask
- Ethernet MAC address
- Link status
- Speed
- Duplex setting
- Physical location
- A throughput graph showing either packets in, packets out, kbit/sec in, or kbit/sec out

Figure 11.14

The Network pane in Server Monitor

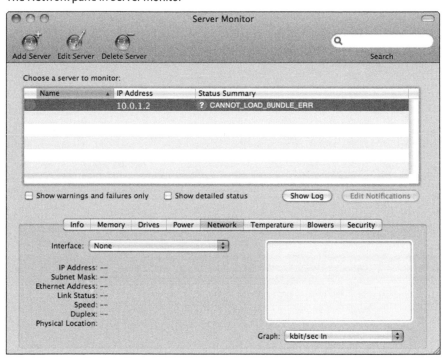

To review an Xserve's temperature, blowers, or security information in Server Monitor, follow these steps:

1. **Launch Server Monitor.**

2. **Select the server and then click the Temperature tab, shown in Figure 11.15.**

3. **The Temperature pane displays information for the server's selected temperature sensor location, as chosen in the pop-up control:**

- Temperature readings in either Fahrenheit or Celsius, as chosen by the radio buttons
- A graph showing temperature readings over time

Figure 11.15

The Temperature pane in Server Monitor

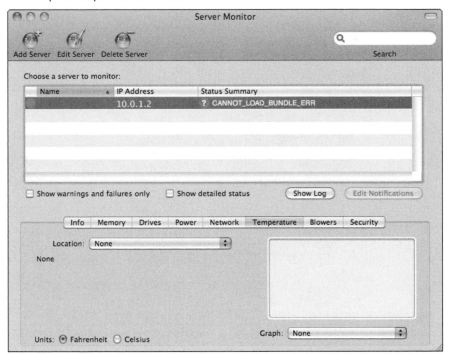

4. **Click the Blowers tab.**

5. **The Blowers pane displays information for the server's selected blower, as chosen in the pop-up menu:**

- RPM running speeds
- A graph showing blower speeds over time

6. Click the Security tab for a report of case intrusion and whether the security lock is engaged.

RAID Admin

When using Apple's now-discontinued Xserve RAID equipment, RAID Admin — shown in Figure 11.16 — allows you to monitor the system's status. RAID Admin is a Java app that runs on Mac OS X, Solaris, Windows, or any other platform that supports Java.

Figure 11.16

RAID Admin

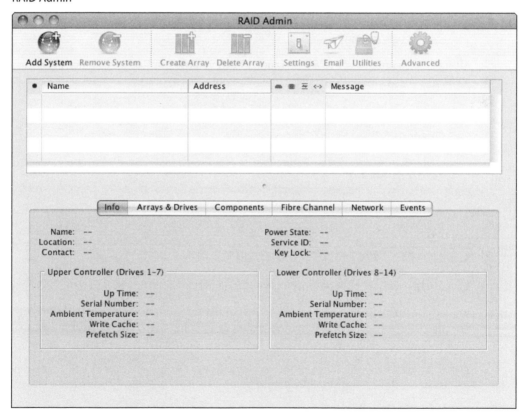

You can use RAID Admin to:

- Create and delete logical disk arrays on the RAID unit
- Check component status

- View an event listing
- Configure the system to send email notifications of system problems or alerts

Apple provides documentation for configuring the Xserve RAID with RAID Admin online at `http://helposx.apple.com/raidR3/english/raidadmin.html`.

System Image Utility

Used with the NetBoot service, System Image Utility allows you to create disk images for:

- **NetBoot.** This acts like a network replacement for a client machine's local hard drive.
- **NetInstall.** This acts like a network replacement for a local DVD drive for installation.
- **NetRestore.** This acts like a network replacement for a local FireWire hard drive used for disk imaging.

After creating images with System Image Utility, you use the NetBoot service in Server Admin to make the images available to client machines and configure them to boot directly from the images.

System Image Utility can also use Automator Action workflows to customize the process of creating images.

CROSS-REF
For more on using NetBoot, NetInstall, and NetRestore images with the NetBoot service, see Chapters 34–35.

Command-Line Tools

Because Mac OS X is built on Unix, many of the administration utilities in Mac OS X Server are actually just a graphical interface for working with command-line utilities.

That allows you to run these commands directly by using the Terminal application, which presents a Unix shell, or an independent execution environment.

A shell provides an interactive programming language interpreter for directly executing commands or creating scripts that programmatically execute a series of commands.

In addition to running the default bash shell on the server directly within a Terminal window, you can also remotely execute commands from an administrative system, configuring and monitoring your servers from another location over a remote shell connection.

You can also programmatically monitor events by using an application that communicates with the server via a remote shell. Apple's Server Admin and other tools typically perform remote administration functions via the command shell, and Server Admin itself acts as a graphical interface for the `serveradmin` command-line tool.

Using the Unix command line

When you open Terminal, you're given a command prompt that presents:

- The name of the system
- The current path of the working directory
- The current username
- A prompt symbol, which looks like this:

When put together, these elements should look like this:

```
server:~ username$
```

When typing commands at the prompt, file system locations are presented as paths, where:

- The user's home directory at `/Users/username` is abbreviated as ~. This appears in the prompt as the working directory `server:~ username$`.
- The current directory is represented as a single dot: . . So typing **./Movies** is identical to specifying `/Users/username/Movies` when the current working directory is ~.
- The parent directory is represented as two dots: .. . So typing **../Movies** is identical to specifying `/Users/username/Movies` when the current working directory is `/Users/username/Photos`.

Unix commands don't recognize spaces or special characters in path names, so any spaces in file or folder names must be escaped by using a backslash before the space or the path may be typed enclosed in quotation marks.

For example, to specify a path including a folder named `Chapter 1`, you'd need to escape the space (`~/Documents/Chapter\ 1`) or use quotes (`"~/Documents/Chapter 1"`).

When you type a command, you must either type the full path of the command or have its location configured within your `PATH` environment variable. This tells the shell the locations of common commands. By default, this is `PATH=/bin:/sbin:/user/bin:/user/sbin:/system/Library/`.

This allows any commands in those folders to be given without their full path name, so the command-line text editor `/usr/bin/pico` can simply be typed as **pico**. To edit a file with Pico, you simply type the command and the path of the file you want to edit. For example, to edit your Apache configuration file, type **pico /etc/apache2/httpd.conf**.

On Mac OS X, Pico is actually linked to the replacement Nano command, so when you type that command, your file is opened by Nano instead, which, of course, is a thousand times better. Some users may be attached to using one of the other text editors that are also supplied with

Mac OS X, including Vi and Emacs. Using Terminal with the default bash shell, you can drag and drop files or folders into a command to have the system type out the path for you. You can also type part of a name and then press the Tab key to auto-complete it. To repeat a previous command, press the up arrow; you can also cycle through previous commands to use one again.

If you're an administrator and need to perform a command as the root user, you can use sudo prior to typing your command in order to authenticate and be granted temporary privileges to operate as root. Be sure you understand what you're doing because even a minor error can cause serious problems that may be difficult or impossible to correct:

- Inadvertent data loss
- Service configuration problems
- Opening security holes

Remember, there's no graphical feedback and fancy global undo features in the world of the command line. However, what you give up in terms of intuitive ease of use you get back in terms of scriptable, concise power that you can apply in very productive ways.

You can obtain the results of one command and pipe them to another to perform simple programs in a single line. Type the vertical bar character |, called pipe, to link commands together.

For example, you could take the results of the `ls` command, which is used to list a directory's contents, and combine it with the `grep` search tool to search through a long folder listing and get only the results you want.

The example `ls -al /usr/bin | grep "nano"` shows how to use commands with:

- **Switches.** In this case, using the `-al` after `ls` to get a directory listing both with any invisible files and in a long format
- **Paths.** Specifying a specific directory to perform a listing on
- **Parameters.** In the example, including the path argument supplied to `ls` to obtain the directory listing and the string given to `grep` to define the desired search
- **Pipes.** Sending the results of the directory listing to the search tool `grep`

The results of this particular listing and search should look like this:

```
-rwxr-xr-x    1 root    wheel      297424 Sep 23  2007 nano
lrwxr-xr-x    1 root    wheel           4 Oct 25  2007 pico -> nano
```

This listing presents the following information on two files in that folder:

- The file mode, which denotes that the first – character indicates the first is a file; the second `l` indicates it's a softlink that points to another file. A directory would be assigned a `d`.

- POSIX file permissions, which present read (r), write (w), execute (x), or no permissions (–), with the first three characters pertaining to the file's user, the second three the group, and the third three to other users. For both, only the owner can write over the files.
- The number of hard links pointing to the file
- Owner and group, which are root and wheel here
- File size in bytes; pico is only 4 bytes because it simply links to nano.
- Modification date
- File name

To get more information on the parameters a command supports, you can look it up by using the man command. For example, typing **man ls** provides a detailed page of instructions on how to use the command and its various options. To exit a man page, type **control z** or press the Q key.

In addition to using pipes to chain commands together, you can use redirects to:

- **Dump the results of an operation into a file.** For example, ls > ~/listing.txt saves the results of a folder listing as the specified file.
- **Append results to the end of a file.** For example, ls >> ~/listing.txt saves additional results of a folder listing without overwriting the file's contents.
- **Import content from a file into an operation.** For example, to search for a word within the file, you can type **grep "nano" < ~/listing.txt**.

This begins to show how the command line can be use to efficiently issue commands that obtain server configuration, write out configurations, and build programmatic scripts that chain together commands to perform powerful tasks.

Remote administration by using SSH

Using the Secure Shell (SSH), you can remotely log in to a server or workstation with SSH remote login enabled to perform shell commands.

SSH offers an encrypted alternative to the insecure Telnet service for remotely connecting to another host over a command-line session. In addition to executing commands, SSH can be used to secure other services; SCP (Secure Copy) and SFTP (Secured File Transfer Protocol) both use SSH to tunnel their data.

Snow Leopard Server's SSH service uses the open-source package OpenSSH. The default port used for SSH is TCP 22, which must be allowed through any firewalls in order to remotely log in to the server.

To initiate an SSH connection to a remote host, type **ssh *admin@server.example.com***, where admin is the user you want to log in as and server.example.com is the name of the host you want to reach. You can alternatively use the system's IP address.

You can also issue remote commands by using SSH in a single line, such as using the command `ssh root@server.example.com shutdown -r now` to remotely shut down and restart the machine.

CROSS-REF

For more on using SSH and configuring the service, see Chapter 19.

Using systemsetup, serveradmin, and networksetup

A variety of machine settings configured in System Preferences can be viewed or set from the command line by using the `systemsetup` tool. Many of these also require using sudo for root permissions. For example, you can:

- Obtain the computer name by typing **sudo systemsetup –getcomputername**
- Set the computer name by typing **sudo systemsetup –setcomputername** *computername*
- Obtain the computer date by typing **sudo systemsetup –getdate**
- Set the computer time by typing **sudo systemsetup –settime** *16:20:00*
- Set a time server by typing **sudo systemsetup -setnetworktimeserver** *ntpserver*
- Set restart after crash by typing **sudo systemsetup -setrestartpowerfailure on**

Configuring services

Many of the functions Server Admin provides are available at the command line by using the `serveradmin` tool, which also requires using sudo for root permissions, including:

- Starting and stopping services:

  `sudo serveradmin start web`
- Presenting a list of the running services:

  `sudo serveradmin list`
- Providing a status detail for a service:

  `sudo serveradmin fullstatus calendar`
- Obtaining a list of available settings for a service:

  `sudo serveradmin settings jabber`
- Configuring settings:

  `sudo serveradmin settings afp:guestAccess = yes`
- Exporting configuration settings to a file:

  `sudo serveradmin settings all > outfile`
- Importing configuration settings from a file:

  `sudo serveradmin settings < outfile`

Configuring network services

Network-related configuration can similarly be performed with the `networksetup` tool. For example, to obtain the current network interface configuration for all ports with their MAC addresses, type **sudo networksetup –listallhardwareports**.

From the hardware report information, you can obtain the IP configuration of a specific port by typing **sudo networksetup -getinfo "Ethernet"**.

To change the IP configuration, type **sudo networksetup -setmanual "Ethernet"** *ipaddress subnetmask router*.

If you need to change your server's IP address, you need to also use the `changeip` command, which updates all the services to recognize the new address. Type **sudo changeip [(*directory|-)]** *old-ip new-ip* [*old-hostname new-hostname*].

For example, to change the Open Directory master from `10.0.0.1` to `10.0.1.1` and change its DNS name from `server.example.com` to `new.example.com`, type **sudo changeip / LDAPv3/127.0.0.1 10.0.0.1 10.0.1.1 server.example.com new.example.com**.

You then need to restart the system, and you also need to change the configuration of clients or replicas configured to use the old address.

User and directory command-line tools

You can create a new user with local administrator permissions from the command line by typing **sudo /System/Library/ServerSetup/serversetup -createUserWithID** *name shortname password uid*.

Managing directory services

To create other users or to give a user domain administrator privileges, you use the `dscl` tool instead, which launches a directory service command-line interactive session.

Within this environment, you navigate through the directory domain rather than the file system, and you can read the configuration of directory keys and append or delete record attributes, including managed client settings.

Managing users

Creating a new account by using `dscl` requires navigating to the directory folder for users, authenticating with the directory, and then manually creating all the elements of the user record created in Workgroup Manager. Follow these steps:

 1. Launch `dscl` **interactively by typing** dscl localhost.

 2. **Navigate to the user directory by typing** cd /LDAPv3/127.0.0.1/Users.

 3. **Authenticate as a directory admin by typing** auth diradmin.

4. **Type your password when prompted.**

5. **Create a new account, specifying a home folder path, by typing the following:**

```
create sjobs HomeDirectory
"<home_dir><url>afp://afp.example.com/Users</
    url><path>sjobs</path></home_dir>"
```

or:

```
create sjobs NFSHomeDirectory
/Network/Servers/nfs.example.com/Users/sjobs
```

6. **Assign a unique user ID by typing** `create sjobs UniqueID 1050`.

7. **Give the account a long username by typing** `create sjobs RealName "Steve Jobs"`.

8. **Specify a user shell by typing** `create sjobs UserShell /bin/bash`.

9. **Assign a password by typing** `passwd sjobs`.

10. **Assign a group membership by typing** append engineering GroupMembership sjobs.

11. **Quit the** `dscl` **session by typing** quit.

12. **Log in to the home folder file server by typing** ssh admin@afp.example.com.

13. **Create a new home folder for the user by typing** sudo createhomedir –s –u sjobs.

Volume, disk image, and file permission tools

Volumes can be mounted from the command line by using the `mount` tool:

- View a list of mounted file systems by typing **sudo mount**.
- Mount a network volume by typing the following:

```
sudo mount_afp afp://username:password@server/share
sudo mount_webdav http://server/path
```

Free space and disk use of a volume and its individual partitions can be found from the command line by using the `df` tool and monitored by using the `diskspacemonitor` command, which uses a setting file at `/etc/diskspacemonitor/diskspacemonitor.conf` to configure how it performs alerts or triggers disk recovery scripts for reclaiming space if set thresholds are reached:

- View disk information by typing **df**.
- Enable disk space monitoring by typing **sudo diskspacemonitor on**.

Disk imaging

You can erase, verify, and repair file systems from the command line by using the `diskutil` tool, which serves as the underlying engine for the Disk Utility application:

- View available disk and drive bay information by typing **diskutil list**.
- Review other features available by typing **man diskutil**.

You can create disk images from the command line by using the `hdiutil` tool and then prepare them for use with Apple Software Restore by using `asr`, which together serve as the underlying engine for System Image Utility.

File system permissions

Snow Leopard Server works with two types of file permissions:

- **POSIX.** These file permissions are based on the three-tiered Unix model of a user, his or her primary group, and everyone else. Each of the three buckets can be allowed or denied permission to read, write, and execute the file or directory.
- **ACLs.** These are designed to be compatible with Windows, enabling a finer granularity of control that defines a rule set that allows or denies a variety of use permissions to any number of different users or groups specified in the list's entries.

In Mac OS X, ACL support can be activated only on HFS+ volumes, and only the AFP and SMB file-sharing protocols provide network file system support for ACLs. Permissions defined by ACLs on files exported by using NFS are enforced by the server but aren't visible and can't be modified by NFS clients.

ACL permissions are defined by ACEs, which define access to the file or folder by specifying a permission rule that includes:

- A user or group account, specified by its universally unique ID number
- The Allow or Deny ACE type
- Thirteen different access permissions, as defined in Apple's ACL model
- Inherited, a flag indicating that the permission was inherited from its parent folder
- Applies to, which indicates how the permission propagates to child files or folders

You can set, change, and verify file system permissions for both POSIX and ACLs from the command line by using the `chmod` tool designed to change mode bits on files:

- To change POSIX permissions by user (u), group (g), and other (o) so the owner has full read (r), write (w), and execute (x) permissions but group and other users don't have write permissions, use one of the following commands:

```
chmod filename 755
chmod filename u=rwx,go=rx
chmod filename u=rwx,go=u-w
```

- To manage ACL permissions, you read, write, or delete ACEs by username or group name. The entry is added to the ACL:
  - Add write permission by user admin by typing **chmod +a "admin allow write"** *file name*.
  - Remove write permissions from user admin by typing **chmod -a "admin allow write"** *file name*.
  - Make inherited permissions explicit by typing **chmod -i** *file name*.
  - Remove inherited permissions by **typing chmod -I** *file name*.
  - Remove the entire ACL by typing **chmod -N** *file name*.
  - Review other features available by typing **man chmod**.

Summary

- iCal Server Utility is used to manage global contact information stored in Open Directory. Prior to Snow Leopard, this application was named Directory.app (not to be confused with Directory Utility).
- Server Monitor is used to monitor the status of Xserve hardware that supports various reporting sensors and, on Xserve (late 2006) models or later, supports Lights-Out Management.
- RAID Admin is used to administer the now-discontinued Xserve RAID appliance.
- System Image Utility is used to create NetBoot, NetRestore, and NetInstall images for network delivery to client machines.
- Command-line tools provide access to the features of Apple's supplied graphical administration applications from Terminal or a remote shell, allowing for remote access administration and configuration by using SSH and the creation of scripted tasks that can be run on a schedule.
- To learn more about how to use command-line tools, start by typing **man man**.

Supplying Core Network Services

DNS Service

S ervers and client computers on a network use IP numbers to address and route the messages sent between them. DNS (Domain Name Service) is used to map those IP addresses (such as `10.0.1.2`) to domain names (such as `server.mycompany.com`) as well as to provide a reverse lookup of hostnames for a given IP address.

While the primary purpose of DNS is to substitute IP address numbers with hostnames that are easier for humans to read and recall, Mac OS X Server and its applications also require a properly configured DNS infrastructure in place to function correctly.

Small organizations operating a single server or setting up their first Mac OS X Server can use the standard configuration to automatically set up DNS that relies on the ISP's existing DNS servers.

CROSS-REF

For more on standard, workgroup, and advanced configuration, see Chapter 3.

However, many organizations might want to configure their own DNS, either because they can't use their ISP's DNS or because they choose not to because of factors such as wanting control over how DNS records changes, how updates are applied, or wanting to keep local DNS records exposed only within the company's private network and not shared publicly to the outside Internet.

This chapter briefly describes how DNS works, what's involved in planning the DNS, how the service is configured within Mac OS X Server, and how to maintain and monitor DNS.

In This Chapter

Introduction to DNS

Planning DNS

DNS setup and configuration

Managing and monitoring DNS

Introduction to DNS

Before the development of the commercial Internet among personal computer users, Apple created AppleTalk as a simple way to network Macs together with expensive shared peripherals, such as the LaserWriter, through the use of a simple plug-and-play cabling system.

AppleTalk used a dynamic numbering system that allowed hosts on the network to automatically discover each other and announce themselves by name so that no separate naming or numbering servers were necessary to centralize the task of handing out numbers and assigning names to each system. However, this method didn't scale up to many thousands of users.

Whereas AppleTalk was really only intended to serve home users and small offices, the Internet Protocol (IP) needed to scale up dramatically to serve the needs of billions of users and devices.

From the beginning, Internet name records associating computer hostnames with their IP addresses were managed by using *host files*, which are simple text documents kept in sync by overwriting them whenever a new system is added to the network.

However, the problem of needing globally unique hostnames for each system — and a unique way of distributing new updates among all the systems on the Internet — begged for a hierarchical system of interconnected name servers because no single server could maintain records of all the hosts on the entire Internet.

Additionally, a distributed naming system was needed to provide the performance and redundancy required to support the critical name-resolution needs of a vast global network operating within the reality of inevitable server downtime and regional network outages.

The DNS hierarchy

DNS answers those needs by acting as a distributed data service of machine name records organized into domain zones.

The DNS mechanism for looking up machines by name begins with a series of top-level domains, including `com` for commercial entities, `mil` for the military, `gov` for government, `edu` for education, `net` for network providers, `org` for other organizations, and country codes for regional domains.

These top-level domains are maintained by Root Name Servers. Within a top-level domain, a specific domain name, such as `apple.com`, can be registered to an organization that then manages the name records within that subdomain, as shown in Figure 12.1.

For example, Apple publishes a series of name records that point to the IP addresses assigned to the company's public servers for outside users to look up via DNS. Other, outside DNS servers point to the Apple authoritative name servers as the source for looking up `apple.com` addresses and may also cache the Apple name records for faster subsequent lookups by the users who access them.

Within Apple, internal DNS servers manage name records for all the local servers, computers, printers, and other devices that need to be located on the network by name, although those internal name records don't need to be made public to outside users.

This hierarchical system of name resolution provides a network of interconnected DNS servers to answer name requests made by clients anywhere in the world. For example, when users type **www.apple.com** into a web browser, the system sends a DNS query to their local DNS server, likely operated by their ISP. If that server doesn't have a record for Apple, it forwards the query up the chain of DNS servers until it reaches a server that does know where `apple.com` is located.

Figure 12.1

The hierarchical structure of DNS provides for an authoritative, distributed mechanism for domain name servers that can answer name queries quickly, minimizing the amount of traffic used to resolve names.

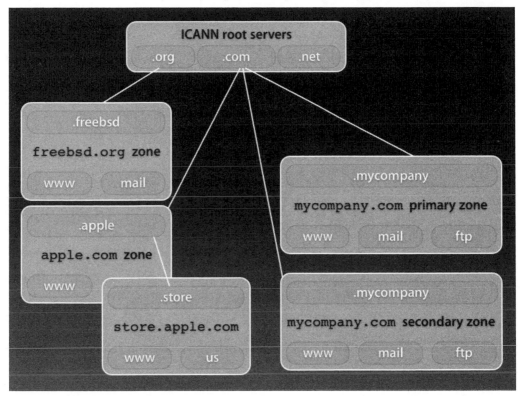

This process may require the query to work all the way back to the Apple authoritative name server that maintains the master, primary listing of the Apple name records. However, to optimize the performance of DNS, other DNS servers frequently cache name record information so that name resolution answers can be found and provided quickly.

Once the name record is located, the IP address assigned to that name is sent back to the original requester to enable his or her system to make an actual request for information by using that IP address — in this case, an HTTP request by the browser to download Apple's public web page and all the resources associated with it.

Without functional DNS, users are stuck unless they happen to know the IP address of every service they want to use. This makes DNS a critical aspect of a properly functioning network.

DNS zones

The DNS records that map names to IP addresses are organized into zones; a single DNS server can host multiple zones. Three types of DNS zones commonly used in Mac OS X Server are:

- **Primary zone.** A primary zone acts as the authoritative name server, with a master list of zone name records.

- **Secondary zone.** A secondary zone is maintained to provide a backup to the primary zone, ensuring that the name records are available even if the primary zone server goes offline. The secondary zone DNS server maintains a list of primary zone servers and contacts them on a regular basis to request a *zone transfer*, or a copy of the primary zone's records. This keeps the secondary zone up to date with any changes made. The secondary zone servers answer requests for name lookups, providing load-balancing for DNS. Their refresh interval can be adjusted depending on how frequently the DNS records in the given zone change.

- **Forward zone.** A forward zone maintains a list of external DNS servers and forwards the name lookups it receives to those outside DNS servers. Although forward zone servers don't make zone transfer requests, they can cache the external lookups that pass through them, providing a quick answer to the next identical lookup request.

NOTE

A forward zone can't be created within the graphical interface of Server Admin, so if you have specialized needs to set one up, you have to dig down into the command line to configure this.

DNS machine records

Each of these zone servers maintains listings of DNS records, which associate a name to an IP address. There are several different types of DNS records, which are designated with a character code:

- **Address record (A).** An A record maintains the IP address for a domain name.

- **Canonical Name record (CNAME).** A CNAME record stores an alias that points to another domain name. This allows a machine to have multiple DNS names, such as providing server `border255.apple.com` with the friendlier alias of `www.apple.com`.

- **Hardware Info record (HINFO).** An HINFO record provides information about the given host's hardware. These aren't supported in Server Admin.

- **Mail Exchanger record (MX).** An MX record points to a zone's mail server. Multiple MX records can be weighted to allow various degrees of priority to be given to a primary mail server.

- **Name Server record (NS).** An NS record stores the zone's authoritative name server, which is the name of the DNS server itself.

- **Pointer record (PTR).** A PTR record provides the reverse lookup domain name for a given IP address. Mac OS X Server automatically generates PTR records when an A record is created.

- **Service record (SRV).** An SRV record indicates the services available from a given host. Microsoft popularized SRV records in Active Directory, which uses them to allow machines to find the Windows domain controller or Exchange Server on the network. They're also used by Bonjour browsing to advertise available services, such as a list of the websites available within an organization. Like MX records, SRV records can provide a priority field.

- **Text record (TXT).** A TXT record responds to its DNS query with a text string. This can be used to provide additional information about a network machine, such as specifying the location, model number, and custom features of a printer. These aren't supported in the Server Admin GUI.

Administrators set up machine records on the primary zone server, which relays the information directly to hosts performing a query, or through secondary zone servers that request a zone transfer of the information for redundancy.

Bonjour and multicast DNS

Although DNS records are usually served unicast from the name server to the single host requesting the information, the specification also defines multicast name record broadcasts. Apple used this capacity to port the dynamic discovery technology in AppleTalk to IP networks.

Branded as Bonjour by Apple (after a naming dispute prevented the company from using the original name of Rendezvous) and released as an open specification under the name Zeroconf, multicast DNS enables machines on the same network to discover each other and get information about the services available from the other hosts on the network without needing a central DNS server to organize and distribute lists of name and service records. Figure 12.2 shows how Bonjour and DNS can work independently or together to help computers discover other machines on the network.

Apple uses Bonjour in iTunes, iPhoto, and with personal web and file sharing to enable computers to advertise shared music libraries, photo albums, websites, and file folders through multicast DNS broadcasts. Mac OS X's iChat also supports discovery of locally available chat buddies by using Bonjour, and both AirPort base stations and Time Machine Server shares advertise themselves to users by using the technology.

Apple also offers Bonjour as an open specification to printers and other devices so their peripherals can be found on the network without needing to set up and manage DNS device records on a central server.

Like AppleTalk, Bonjour is designed to work within a subnet. To work beyond the local subnet, network administrators either need to allow multicast routing, which largely defeats the purpose of having subnets in the first place by allowing broadcast messages to cross the router into other subnets, or need to configure DNS-SD (DNS Service Discovery), also known as Wide Area Bonjour.

Figure 12.2

Bonjour enables host computers to resolve the names and IP addresses of other machines on the network — as well as discover the services they make available — without using a centrally updated DNS server.

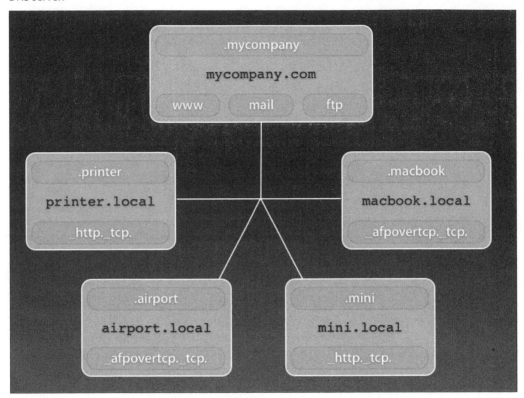

DNS-SD allows systems on different subnets to access dynamically updated name and service records. However, unlike local Bonjour, this isn't configuration-free because of security implications. Users may not want their local services broadcast publicly, and DNS record changes for these services need to be authenticated.

For this reason, DNS-SD is both opt-in and requires a system for authorizing updates. It's possible to implement DNS-SD as a sort of push DNS by setting up and managing DNS-SD record updates via Dynamic DNS, a service that accepts updated information from the client about its IP address after first authenticating with the Dynamic DNS server.

The Apple MobileMe service includes support for tying DNS-SD to a subscriber's account for authentication purposes. Registered systems update their IP addresses as they change, allowing remote users to authenticate and then locate other registered systems across the open Internet.

Planning DNS

Although the idea of matching hostnames to IP addresses may seem like a simple task, DNS administration is complex and requires advanced expertise to optimize and customize the service. The definitive reference on BIND 9, the open-source DNS server software Apple ships with Mac OS X Server, is itself nearly 600 pages.

Mac OS X Server is designed to function as a capable DNS server, and it provides tools to make the task of configuring DNS relatively easy. However, Apple doesn't expose all the options available in BIND through its graphical interface tools. That requires administrators with specialized needs to manually edit BIND's configuration files from the command line.

Proper configuration of DNS is critical to operating a functional server and in particular is important to operating directory services, such as Open Directory or Active Directory from Microsoft, which are themselves core network services supporting other advanced services.

Improperly configured DNS servers can cause major problems for users on the network and can present serious security issues. Without access to correctly functioning DNS, the server won't be able to resolve the names of other servers it might depend on, and network client computers won't be able to reach any other network hosts by name unless they know those devices' IP addresses by heart. That means no mail, web, or other network access works outside of Bonjour-based browsing of local file and print services.

Additionally, because computers trust DNS to point them to secured network services, a fake DNS server or falsified DNS records on the real server can be used to direct users to malicious machines. This demands careful consideration and planning before starting up DNS.

CROSS-REF
For more on Open Directory, see Chapter 21.

Before making plans to set up DNS, it should be evaluated whether local DNS servers are necessary. It may be possible to delegate the task of maintaining name records to the ISP, which already runs its own DNS, or to use an existing DNS that may already be available within the organization.

If there's a real need for a local DNS, plan out how extensive those needs are. Because users on the network are unable to do much of anything without a functional DNS server available, there should be at least two servers providing DNS records for a given zone.

It's also important to determine how many hosts and devices actually need DNS records. For example, depending on how devices are used, Bonjour may provide a suitable alternative to creating DNS name records for shared printers.

DNS Setup and Configuration

You have two options for configuring DNS in Mac OS X Server: using graphical tools from Apple or diving down to the command line to manually edit configuration files.

To configure DNS from Server Admin, first enable the service within the desired server's listing of configured services.

To enable DNS configuration in Server Admin, follow these steps:

1. **Launch Server Admin and then connect to the desired server.**

2. **Select the server listing and then click Settings on the toolbar.**

3. **Click the Services tab.**

4. **Click the check box for DNS.**

5. **Click Save.** DNS should now appear in the list of configurable services for the selected server, as shown in Figure 12.3.

After selecting DNS from the list of services in the Servers list, configure the initial settings from the Zones tab and then choose the desired event logging level from the Log tab or the Log Level pop-up menu in the Settings tab.

DNS configuration files

Because the underlying Unix software that provides most of the core services in Mac OS X Server, including DNS, typically relies on text configuration files, the graphical administration tools from Apple act largely as a specialized interface for editing those files.

There are two problems with this. The first is that the graphical front-end tools don't accommodate every feature administrators might want to use. The second potential problem has been that once administrators make sophisticated manual changes to their configuration files, they're at risk of running into problems using the graphical tools at a later time because those tools may overwrite their custom changes.

To help solve this problem, Apple has in many cases created multiple configuration files with structured portions designed to allow for dual editing with less chance of conflict. A main configuration file, mirroring where settings would be entered in a typical Unix or Linux system, is commonly designed by Apple to accommodate customized editing by hand.

This typically involves creating a special section within the configuration file and designating that portion to be left untouched because it's maintained by tools from Apple. The configuration file may also reference and include a secondary set of configuration files directly maintained by those tools, separating manual configuration editing from automated file updates.

Figure 12.3

DNS configuration in Server Admin

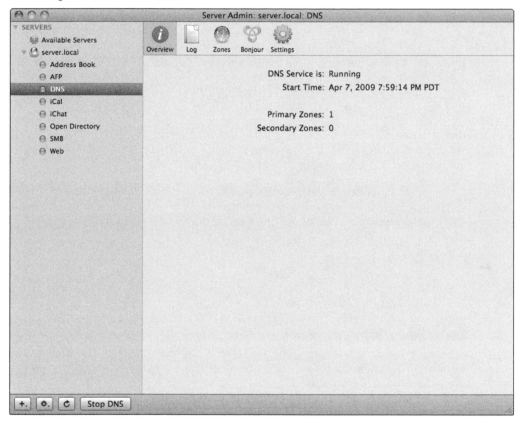

This convention tends to make it easier for administrators to resort to the command line when necessary but leaves the door open to return to using Apple's graphical tools without worrying that their custom modifications might be overwritten.

Apple made this change in the DNS of Leopard Server, which not only enhanced the amount of configuration that could be done within Server Admin but also set up new, structured configuration files that can be edited manually with less potential for conflict with the updates made by administration tools from Apple.

DNS zones

This method of configuration file management is particularly evident when editing zone records. A typical BIND installation is configured on other platforms, such as on Linux, by editing this text file: `/etc/named.conf`.

Manual zone configuration

The BIND background process is `named`, the name daemon. It consults the `named.conf` file, which outlines its global options (specifying a directory of other external files, with configuration information, that are included in DNS configuration), followed by actual DNS zone definitions.

In Mac OS X Server, the `named.conf` file includes the file `/etc/dns/options.conf.apple` for its options configuration, `/etc/dns/loggingOptions.conf.apple` for its logging configuration, and `/etc/dns/publicView.conf.apple` for its zone configuration information, leaving little left to configure in the `named.conf` file itself.

Changes made to the `named.conf` file in Mac OS X Server are used by BIND but aren't reflected in Server Admin. Zones created within Server Admin are instead saved to separate configuration files, which are located at `/var/named/zones`.

This enables administrators to manually modify zone records and have those changes reflected in Server Admin. Users without specialized needs may be able to avoid manually editing files at all, thanks to expanded support for graphical editing of DNS records within Server Admin.

CROSS-REF
For more on using Server Admin, see Chapter 9.

Using Server Admin to create zone records

Creating a new zone record by using the Server Admin application that Apple provides is more intuitive than editing configuration files by hand. It also provides some structure and basic error-checking to prevent users from making inadvertent typos.

A new zone record is needed only when creating a new primary zone to serve DNS records or to set up a secondary zone that assists in serving the DNS records for an existing primary zone. Users who are administering a network that already has external DNS either from the ISP or through their organization likely won't need to configure a DNS zone.

Additionally, there are also types of DNS zone records that Server Admin doesn't allow the graphical tools to create, such as a forward zone. For these and other advanced needs, administrators may need to resort to manual command-line editing, armed with a full reference of the DNS specification.

To create a new primary DNS zone by using Server Admin, follow these steps:

1. **From the DNS pane in Server Admin, click Zones on the toolbar, shown in Figure 12.4.**

2. **Choose Add Primary Zone (Master) from the Add Zone pop-up menu.** This sets up a new example zone in the page's listing of DNS zones. The new zone is assigned the name `example.com`.

Figure 12.4

DNS zone configuration in Server Admin

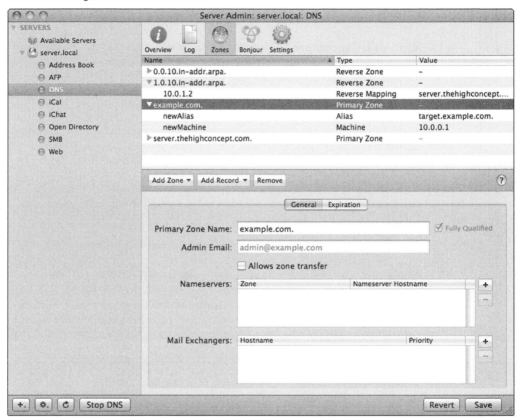

3. **Change the example name to the desired Primary Zone Name.** Be sure to type your zone name before saving the new zone. The name provided needs to be a *fully qualified domain name*, which means it must supply the full domain name to the top-level domain and be followed by a trailing period. For example, if you're creating a new zone named `servers` within the domain `mycompany.com`, the fully qualified domain name for the new zone would be `servers.mycompany.com.`, including the trailing period.

4. **Type the zone's administrator email address.** This can assist others in reporting any problems with the zone.

5. **To allow a secondary zone to request copies of the new primary zone's records, click the Allows zone transfer check box.**

6. **Add the local server as the zone's name server, specifying its fully qualified domain name.** To add a name server, click the Add (+) button and then edit the entry to reflect the hostname of the name server for that zone, which should be the hostname of the local server given that this is a new primary zone master record.

7. **Create Mail Exchanger records for the local mail servers, specifying each by hostname as a fully qualified domain name, and then assign each a priority.** To add a mail exchanger record, click the Add (+) button and then edit the entry to reflect the hostnames of the mail servers for that zone. This may be the local server. Use priority numbers to balance what servers clients should default to using.

8. **Click Save to generate the zone record.** The new zone begins serving the name server and mail exchanger records you created, and you can now begin entering new DNS records for the zone as described in the section later in this chapter.

A secondary zone backs up the primary, hosting a copy of its records to provide failover redundancy. The secondary keeps its records up to date by requesting a zone transfer from the primary zone master at regular intervals.

To create a new secondary DNS zone by using Server Admin, follow these steps:

1. **Make sure the primary zone supports zone transfers.** If the primary zone was created by using Server Admin, click the Allow zone transfer check box within the primary zone's configuration on the DNS server hosting that primary zone. If a different system administers the primary zone, contact the zone administrator for that system to request that zone transfers be allowed.

2. **From the DNS pane in Server Admin, click Zones on the toolbar.**

3. **Choose Add Secondary Zone (Slave) from the Add Zone pop up menu.** This sets up a new example zone in the page's listing of DNS zones. The new zone is assigned the name `example.com`.

4. **Type in the fully qualified domain name of the secondary zone, which must be identical to the primary zone's name.**

5. **Type the zone administrator's email address.**

6. **Click Save to generate the zone record.** The new zone requests a zone transfer of DNS records from the primary master zone and begins serving them as requested by clients.

DNS machine records

Once a primary zone is created, it can be populated with DNS machine and associated records. The same Zones page of the DNS pane used to create a new zone file also allows administrators to add the following types of DNS records to a zone:

- **Alias CNAME records.** These assign a secondary alias name to an existing hostname, which itself must be recorded within a machine A record.
- **A records.** These are conventional DNS entries that link a given hostname to an IPv4 address or to multiple IP addresses.
- **Pointer PTR records.** These allow for the reverse lookup of names by IP address and are automatically created by Server Admin as conventional A name records are added. One new PTR record is created for each IP address assigned to a machine within an A record. PTR records are created in a special *reverse zone*, which is named after the IP subnet, written backward, followed by in-addr.arpa. For example, if your server is 10.0.1.2, Server Admin creates a new reverse zone for it named 1.0.10.in-addr.arpa. and containing a PTR record mapping 10.0.1.2 to the hostname of the server.
- **Service SRV records.** These provide information on how to locate a host providing a specific service on the network, such as a web or directory server, instead of just resolving domain names. Service records are used with Bonjour browsing to advertise available resources to devices that might want to use them. For example, Safari browses for web service records of service type http._tcp to create a dynamic list of available web servers.

NOTE

Zone-related records, including name server (NS) and mail exchanger (MX) records, are created as part of the zone definition rather than added as records within the zone, as is common in other DNS configuration environments, such as Windows Server.

To create new DNS records within a zone by using Server Admin, follow these steps:

1. **From the DNS pane in Server Admin, click Zones on the toolbar.**

2. **Choose a new record type from the Add Record pop-up menu.** The three types available are A records, CNAME alias records, and SRV service records.

To add a new A record:

1. **Type the hostname of the machine, either as its short name with no trailing period, such as** server**, or fully qualified by using the entire name of the zone, such as** server.mycompany.com.**, with a trailing period.** When you add the trailing period, a check mark for Fully Qualified is marked for you to highlight this.

2. **Add an IP address assigned to this machine by clicking the Add (+) button.** Additional IP addresses can be added simultaneously. Each new IP address generates a PTR record within the reverse zone for the subnet of the assigned IP address. New reverse zones are also generated as needed.

To add a new CNAME alias record:

1. **Type an alias name of the machine, either as its short name with no trailing period or fully qualified by using the entire name of the zone with a trailing period.**

2. **Add the destination name that the alias should point to, either as a short name or fully qualified.** For both entries, when you add a trailing period, a check mark for Fully Qualified is marked for you to highlight this.

To add a new SRV record:

1. **Type a service name label used for browsing.**

2. **Add a service type from the drop-down menu of choices or type a custom type.**

3. **Specify a hostname, either by short name with no trailing period or fully qualified by using the entire name of the zone with a trailing period.**

4. **Specify the port number to be used as well as a priority and weight.**

5. **Enter a text field to supply additional information for Bonjour browsing.**

3. **Click Save to add the new records to the zone and begin serving them.**

Three types of DNS records aren't supported in the graphical interface of the Zones page provided by Server Admin. These are created in the definition of the zone itself:

- **Start of Authority (SOA) records.** These describe the characteristics of the zone itself, specifying details such as a serial number (based on the zone record's creation date and the number of times the zone record has been modified) and the following time values, all of which are given default entries during the creation of the zone record. In the standard BIND configuration file generated by Server Admin, these values are given in seconds, whereas in Server Admin, they're presented in hours, as shown in Figure 12.5:

  - **TTL (Time-to-Live).** Expressed within the Server Admin interface as zone is valid for *n* hours. TTL refers to the length of time a DNS response can be cached by another server before the information expires, forcing that server to obtain the information again. Expiring the cache is done to balance the need for up-to-date records against the performance gained by allowing other servers to cache a copy of the record locally.

  - **Refresh.** Expressed as secondary zones should refresh every *n* hours

  - **Retry.** Expressed as if refresh fails, retry every *n* hours

  - **Expire.** Expressed as zone data expires *n* hours after refreshing

- **Name server (NS) records.** These point to DNS servers for the zone and are entered during the creation of the zone record.

- **Mail exchanger (MX) records.** These identify mail servers for the zone and are similarly entered during the creation of the zone record.

Figure 12.5

DNS zone SOA configuration in Server Admin

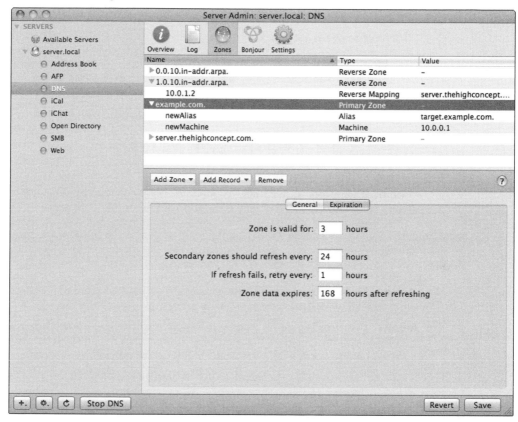

To modify SOA values or NS and MX records for a DNS zone by using Server Admin, follow these steps:

1. **From the DNS pane in Server Admin, click Zones on the toolbar.**

2. **Modify the zone's SOA values.** A zone record's primary zone name and admin email values are part of the SOA record in the actual zone configuration file. To change other values, click the Expiration tab. The values presented here relate to the SOA record's TTL, refresh, retry, and expire values.

3. **Modify the zone's NS records.** To add a new name server, return to the General tab of the zone record and then click the Add (+) button. To change an existing NS record, double-click the name server listing and then update it. To delete an NS record, select the listing and then click the Delete (−) button.

4. **Modify the zone's MX records.** To add a new mail exchanger, click the Add (+) button. To change an existing MX record, double-click a listing and then update it. To delete an MX record, select the listing and click the Delete (–) button.

5. **Click Save to generate new records in the zone.**

There are also additional types of DNS records not supported in the graphical interface provided by Server Admin. To add other types of DNS records, you need to manually edit the DNS configuration files.

Managing and Monitoring DNS

Because the DNS is both critical to the correct operation of the server and also involves network security concerns, it's important to monitor its operation and keep it up to date with the security patches and software updates regularly released for Snow Leopard Server.

In addition to keeping the system up to date, there are three ways to monitor the status of DNS in Server Admin by using the toolbar pages presented for the service in the DNS pane of Server Admin:

- **Review the Overview page for the service.** This shows whether the process is running, when it was started, and how many active zones are being served.

- **Monitor the error log generated by the service on the Log page (shown in Figure 12.6).** To configure the detail logging level desired, click the Settings page of the DNS pane and then select one of the following options from the Log Level pop-up menu:
  - Critical records only critical errors, such as hardware errors.
  - Error records all errors, not including warning messages.
  - Warning records all warnings and errors.
  - Notice records only important messages, warnings, and errors.
  - Information records most messages.
  - Debug records all messages.

- **Monitor the records listed on the Zones page against your documented configuration to detect any unauthorized changes.**

Securing DNS

A variety of security attacks can target DNS. Some can be proactively safeguarded against, whereas others require vigilant monitoring and auditing of records, along with prompt efforts to keep the system up to date with the latest security patches.

Figure 12.6

DNS log level configuration in Server Admin

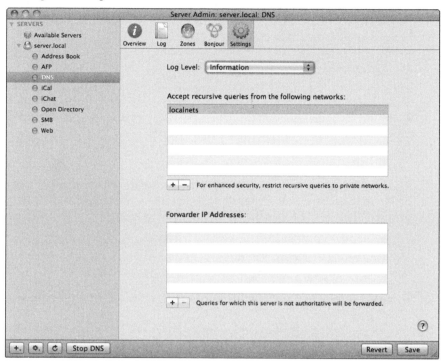

DNS spoofing

In this attack, false DNS information is added to a DNS server's cache, enabling a domain name query to be answered with the IP address of either a malicious server or more benign incorrect information. This can be avoided by keeping up to date with any patches for BIND vulnerabilities and auditing DNS records for accuracy.

Server mining

An outside attacker may pose as a secondary zone to request a zone transfer of the subnet's DNS records to gain information about the machines on the network. This can be blocked by using the firewall to deny incoming TCP connections over port 53 apart from your own secondary zone servers.

CROSS-REF

For more on the firewall service, see Chapter 14.

DNS profiling

A second way attackers may attempt to collect information about your DNS server in order to target an exploit to it involves requesting the version information for BIND, the software which handles DNS. This can be blocked by removing the version information from the configuration file located at /etc/named.conf.

Denial of service (DoS)

In a denial-of-service attack, the DNS server is flooded with requests that overwhelm the server and prevent it from responding to legitimate responses. A firewall rule may be able to block the attack after it begins, but administrators can only monitor network traffic and server availability because a DoS attack can originate from anywhere.

Service piggybacking

If outside hosts find that your DNS server is faster at resolving queries than their own, they may begin using yours, eventually resulting in a problem where your own resources are taxed to provide for more users than they were provisioned to serve.

Administrators can block unauthorized use by external users by limiting *recursion*, which fully resolves domain names to IP addresses, only to local users. Recursion can be limited to specific networks by using the Settings page of the DNS pane in Server Admin.

To limit recursion to specific networks by using Server Admin, follow these steps:

1. **From the DNS pane in Server Admin, click Settings on the toolbar.**

2. **Add the local subnet under Accept recursive queries from the following networks along with any additional networks as desired by clicking the Add (+) button and then typing IP addresses or ranges of networks.**

3. **Click Save to record the change.**

Services depending on DNS

Nearly every service running on the system requires properly configured DNS just to resolve client names and the name of the server itself. There are also other applications of DNS, including service priority for mail, load balancing of other services, and directing multiple names to the same server, either for multihoming multiple aliases to the same host or for the virtual hosting of separate instances of services under different names.

MX records for mail services

For mail service to function properly on the network, administrators must configure DNS with MX records. These special service records were uniquely created to support receiving mail from multiple servers all sharing the same domain address.

For example, mail1.mycompany.com and mail2.mycompany.com can both be assigned MX records that enable the organization to use the email domain @mycompany.com instead of accounting for the actual server names of however many servers may actually be put into service.

Additionally, MX records have a defined priority level that determines which email host gets the highest priority in receiving mail, with the lowest priority level number getting the highest priority. If that server isn't available, the second-highest priority server receives the mail. This allows a backup server to accept and queue mail that can be delivered to the primary server when it becomes available.

Using the previous examples of email hostnames, an administrator would create the following MX record entries in the Zone page of the DNS pane in Server Admin:

- name mail1.mycompany.com priority 10
- name mail2.mycompany.com priority 20

This would ensure that mail1.mycompany.com was first in priority to receive the mail bound for users@mycompany.com.

Round-robin load distribution

To provide a similar level of load distribution to services apart from mail, administrators can assign multiple IP addresses to a single domain name by using multiple A machine records — one for each name. The DNS server subsequently cycles through the series of IP addresses, providing clients with a revolving series of IP addresses in response to their name-to-address lookup query.

For example, to use round-robin address shuffling to spread the load of a website across three servers, where the desired URL is www.mycompany.com and the IP addresses of the servers are 10.0.1.10, 10.0.1.11, and 10.0.1.12, you'd create three A name records for www, one for each address. Clients looking up your URL would get back a response that gave every third user the first IP address, cycling through the addresses so that a third of the traffic is directed to each server.

The DNS server doesn't monitor the server load or its processing capacity; it simply hands out a constantly revolving set of responses to direct users to different servers.

Hosting multiple domain names on the same server

The opposite can also be done to host several services on the same server. By setting up a series of CNAME records that point service name aliases to the same host, those services can later be scaled to multiple separate servers as needed in the future, without any configuration changes on the client end.

For example, a small company might initially set up the following CNAME records to all point to the same server, perhaps server.mycompany.com:

- `www.mycompany.com` for web services
- `ftp.mycompany.com` for FTP file sharing
- `mail.mycompany.com` for mail service
- `vpn.mycompany.com` for VPN access

In the future, those CNAME records could be remapped to independent servers, each with their own hostname, in order to manage the increased load. Client machines wouldn't need to know that www and vpn now pointed to different servers, and no configuration changes would be necessary.

There's nothing special about the specific alias names assigned; www is only the conventional name for a domain's main web server. The company's website could just as well be advertised as being `server.mycompany.com`. However, if the company initially uses only one hostname for each of these services, it would need to roll out extensive configuration changes in the future when it wanted to split those services up across multiple servers.

Virtual domain hosting

A third DNS scenario involves hosting multiple domains on the same server. If a company wanted to maintain web or mail services across two domains by using the same server, such as `mycompany.com` and `opencompany.org`, they'd only need to register both domains and create a duplicate zone for handling the records for each.

Whereas DNS only points both names to the same server, the specific configuration for enabling virtual domains on those services is performed in the web or mail service. For example, the web service could host the same website under both domain names or it could be set up to respond to requests from each domain by using two separate websites.

CROSS-REF
For more on virtual domain hosting in the web service, see Chapter 24.

Using DNS with Bonjour

DNS provides a centralized, administratively managed solution to resolving the IP addresses for hostnames and discovering available services on the network, such as the local mail service or alternative name servers. The Apple Bonjour technology provides a decentralized, automatic alternative method for discovering available services on computers in the local subnet.

Both can be used together. For example, the Bonjour support built into many modern printers allows network users to find and connect to them without necessarily requiring administrators to manage DNS records for them. Administrators can also allow users to advertise their own web and file shares that other users on the local network can browse from the Finder or from the Safari Bonjour listing.

Alternatively, static SRV records on the DNS server can provide Bonjour-style browsing of resources across the entire organization without needing to forward local broadcasts from Bonjour across subnets.

To enable Bonjour browsing by using Server Admin, follow these steps:

1. **From the DNS pane in Server Admin, click Bonjour on the toolbar, shown in Figure 12.7.**

2. **Click the Enable automatic client Bonjour browsing for domain check box.**

3. **Type a domain name for Bonjour browsing, such as** `bonjour.mycompany.com`.

4. **Click Save to record the change.** This makes the records from all primary zones on the server available to the Bonjour browsing domain.

DNS-SD can also be used to provide automatically updated IP address and service availability information across networks.

Figure 12.7

Bonjour configuration in Server Admin

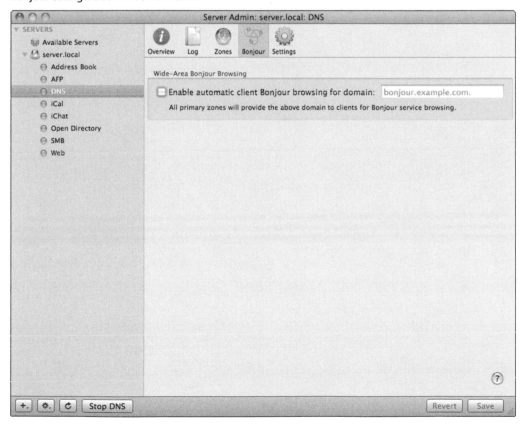

Summary

- Unicast DNS supplies a centralized, administrator-managed service for providing host-name, service, and IP address information for the server and any network clients and also acts as part of the larger hierarchy of the Internet's DNS.

- Multicast DNS, branded by Apple as Bonjour, provides a parallel and complementary mechanism for providing distributed, automatic hostname, service, and IP address information to the local subnet.

- DNS zones define the namespace of a subdomain. They contain a series of DNS records specifying the IP addresses of machines within the domain and the services they provide.

- Special reverse lookup zones with pointer records are used to obtain hostnames from IP addresses. Server Admin automatically creates these when conventional A machine records are entered.

- A primary zone manages an authoritative list of DNS records for the given zone, whereas secondary zones request a zone transfer copy of the primary zone's records to serve as a backup in making those records available.

DHCP Service

Network machines can be configured to obtain a unique IP address and other configuration information from a central DHCP (Dynamic Host Configuration Protocol) server. At startup, they look for a DHCP server, and if found, they request a DHCP lease, which provides the client with an IP address it can use for the length of the lease. The DHCP server may also provide the client machine with other information about the network, such as where it can find DNS or directory servers.

The primary purpose of DHCP is to manage the allotment of IP addresses, which can be a relatively scarce resource. Even when lots of addresses are available, DHCP allows administrators to direct how they're distributed so an organization's network can be divided into manageable subnets.

Small groups operating a single Snow Leopard Server in the standard configuration — or a workgroup configuration server plugged into a larger organization's network — have to rely on existing DHCP services already in place, supplied either by an appliance router such as an AirPort base station or by the local IT department's DHCP servers operating on the network.

In the advanced configuration, Snow Leopard Server can host its own DHCP server. Administrators might already have existing DHCP services in place, so enabling DHCP on the server may not be necessary.

CROSS-REF
For more on standard, workgroup, and advanced configurations, see Chapter 3.

However, the Snow Leopard Server administration tools may make centralizing DHCP services together with the other services running on the server an attractive alternative. Multiple servers can provide DHCP services to the network, ensuring that clients always have access to it, even if the principal server goes offline.

This chapter briefly describes how DHCP works (which involves an introduction to IP addressing conventions), what's involved in planning DHCP services, how DHCP is configured within the Server Admin interface, and how to maintain and monitor the services.

---

13 ▶ **In This Chapter**

Introduction to DHCP

Planning DHCP

DHCP setup and configuration

Managing and monitoring DHCP

Introduction to DHCP

Many end users are familiar with DHCP as being the way to automatically obtain an IP address, gateway router, subnet mask, and DNS server address required to connect a client computer to a network without having to manually supply all those details.

On the server end, DHCP also makes it easier for administrators to automate the distribution of network configuration changes. For example, if the network addressing scheme or the chosen IP address of the network's DNS server changes, DHCP allows administrators to change that information once, allowing all network clients to pick up the new information the next time they obtain a new DHCP lease.

In environments where the local subnet has only a relatively small pool of IP addresses available to use (particularly when there's a high turnover in the number of different users that might need a short-term address), DHCP can manage those address assignments like a librarian, providing DHCP leases on loan to users for a specific period of time and keeping records of which computers have been given a lease. When those leases expire, the IP addresses are returned to the DHCP pool of addresses that can be distributed to new users.

This turnover efficiently distributes IP addresses without requiring manual accounting of which computer is assigned which address. It also typically results in client machines being given different addresses each time they obtain a lease, although specific addresses can also be reserved for a particular system.

For example, servers and other network machines that don't want their IP address to change can be assigned a *static address* on the DHCP server (also called a DHCP reservation or fixed address), which is only ever assigned to that particular system. The system is uniquely identified to the DHCP server by the hardware MAC address of the system's network adapter.

A system with a static DHCP reservation (as opposed to a manually configured IP address) can be automatically kept up to date with changes to other network configuration information provided by the DHCP server (such as a new DNS or LDAP directory server address), making it easier to roll out updates across all machines on the network if they obtain a dynamic or static IP assignment from the DHCP server.

Mac OS X Server can be configured to supply DHCP services by using the graphical interface provided by Server Admin. The core network service is provided by a background process named `bootpd`. It gets its name from BootP, the Bootstrap Protocol, which was the original predecessor to today's DHCP.

BootP was designed to provide diskless Unix workstations with a simple way to find a network image to startup from; Apple used BootP as the basis for its proprietary NetBoot 1.0 protocol, which has since been replaced by NetBoot 2.0, which uses DHCP-based communications.

DHCP builds on and replaces the original BootP to provide machines on the network with initial network configuration information as they start up, resulting in both DHCP and NetBoot being handled by the same process.

CROSS-REF
For more on NetBoot, see Chapter 34.

Planning DHCP

Planning local DHCP services requires an understanding of how IP addresses are organized into subnets to allow machines on different subnets to route messages to each other.

Public versus private IP addresses

An organization may be given a subnet of public IPv4 addresses by its ISP, but actual computers are rarely ever assigned one of these public addresses. In part, this is because IPv4 numbers (the typical addresses that look like 17.251.200.70) are relatively scarce.

Although there are over 4 billion IPv4 numbers that can potentially be assigned, they're sequentially accorded to organizations in batches. Apple was among the first couple dozen companies to obtain a subnet from this pool and was subsequently given a range of 16 million addresses: the entire 17.x.x.x subnet.

Today, there are no more big subnets available to assign, a factor that has prompted the development of IPv6, which uses a new addressing scheme that provides many, many more potential addresses.

Apart from address scarcity, there's also another reason why public IPv4 addresses aren't assigned to individual users: There's little security in place in many IPv4-related protocols to prevent outside attacks on the system.

These two factors have combined to result in most users being assigned private addresses instead. A *private address* can't be reached directly from the outside Internet. That's because Internet routers don't forward packets addressed to private address subnets; instead, packets sent from a private address must be translated to a public address by the router by using NAT.

The router keeps track of the mappings so outside responses (such as a requested web page) can be directed back to the original system. Without this NAT layer, outside hosts couldn't find the machines on the inside network. This also enables the subnet to firewall any incoming traffic that didn't originate from within the private network, blocking any unsolicited traffic, including any attempts by outside attackers to find or exploit vulnerabilities in networked machines.

Subnets

Both public and private IPv4 addresses are organized into subnets, which define a particular range of numbers. Initially, subnets were assigned in huge batches (like the Apple subnet), where the first octet (the first eight bits of the address, represented by the first set of numbers before the first period) was designated as a network number and the rest of the address was a unique host identifier.

This provided 256 networks of more than 16 million hosts. The Internet quickly needed more than 256 huge networks, so this initial scheme was replaced with class addressing, which created networks of various sizes to tailor the subnet size to the user's need:

- Class A provided a few networks (128) with many hosts (over 16 million).
- Class B split a Class A into thousands of networks with 65 thousand addresses each.
- Class C split a Class B into millions of networks with 256 addresses each.

This system posed a number of problems. One was that many companies needed more addresses than a Class C but much less than a full Class B, resulting in many unnecessarily large allocations of IPv4 numbers. Additionally, network routers had to manage increasingly long routing tables to determine how to forward traffic from the local network to one of the millions of networks it might be destined for.

This was later replaced with CIDR (Classless Inter-Domain Routing), which created a flexible way to chop the IPv4 address space into subnets of variable size while also making it far easier to route traffic across the Internet. CIDR ignores the old Class boundaries and instead uses a variable subnet mask to define how large of a subnet a given IP address belongs to.

This also allows an ISP to aggregate the various subnets it assigns to its client companies into supernets so Internet routers can greatly reduce the total number of different networks they have to keep track of in order to successfully direct packets toward their final destination.

This also allows companies to subnet their own ranges of IP addresses to serve their local needs without increasing the number of networks outside routers need to know about because the company's own routers manage those fractional subnets and advertise only a larger supernet to the outside Internet.

DHCP subnets

Subnets can be created within both public and private IP address spaces. Here, I focus on private IP address subnets because configuring public Internet routing falls well outside the scope of setting up DHCP services for a local subnet.

Within an organization, a DHCP server is used for dynamic allocation of an IP address (and other configuration information) for a specific subnet or group of subnets. The configuration of the organization's subnets may be handed down from the IT department or local administrators may themselves need to design subnets as required.

Most small- or medium-sized organizations may need only one subnet; an AirPort base station sets up a single subnet when configured to create a local network and can also optionally act as that subnet's DHCP, DNS, NAT, firewall, and router, managing and securing traffic between that local private subnet and the outside public Internet access it negotiates with an ISP by using a single public address.

Mac OS X Server can perform the same functions. Depending on how much complexity and centralization an administrator wants, a given server can be set up to manage all, part, or none of these core services for the network.

Here, it's assumed that the administrator wants to perform DHCP by using Snow Leopard Server; it's also possible for the server to provide DHCP alongside another device, such as an AirPort, but the redundant overlap in coverage might not be worth enough to warrant duplicative configuration efforts and the possibility for confusion if both systems work slightly differently. A client machine obtains DHCP configuration from whichever server first replies to its query.

The primary private address pool used in commercial networks is the 10.x.x.x subnet, which provides a Class A–style range of over 16 million addresses than can be further carved up into subnets any way an organization wants. Because it's designated as a private address subnet, routers don't attempt to send traffic addressed to a 10.x.x.x subnet over the public Internet.

Another common private network subnet is 192.168.x.x, which is often used by home routers. It provides a range of over 65,000 addresses and can also be cut up into individual subnets, although the 10.x.x.x network may allow organizations more flexibility and easier-to-remember subnet address ranges and subnet mask numbers.

Without being divided into individual subnets, the 10.x.x.x range has a subnet mask of 255.0.0.0, but in many common uses (including the default settings used by the AirPort base station), the private subnet is presented as 10.0.1.x by using a subnet mask of 255.255.255.0, effectively subnetting the 16 million potential addresses down to a more manageable 254 network hosts.

To support additional network machines, organization administrators can create a larger subnet or multiple small subnets connected by routers configured with the appropriate rules to exchange network traffic between the private subnets and the public Internet. The following numbers illustrate how subnets can be partitioned into smaller subnets, with x representing any value from 1 to 254 (with 0 and 255 reserved as the network and broadcast IP addresses in subnet masks of at least 24 bits):

- 10.x.x.x creates a large subnet with over 16 million hosts by using the subnet mask 255.0.0.0.
- 10.0.x.x creates a large subnet with over 64,000 hosts by using the subnet mask 255.255.0.0.
- 10.0.1.x creates a subnet with 254 hosts by using the subnet mask 255.255.255.0.
- 10.0.2.x creates another subnet with 254 hosts by using the subnet mask 255.255.255.0. This pattern can continue through subnet 10.0.254.x.

As these numbers show, the subnet mask acts to cover up the portion of the IP address that describes the subnet itself, leaving behind only the portion of the address unique to a specific machine in that subnet. In the final examples, the subnet mask 255.255.255.0 effectively covers up the values in the first three octets (10.0.1.x), leaving behind the 256 numbers that can uniquely reference specific machines (or are reserved for special uses on the network).

The configuration of subnets used within an organization obviously shapes the way DHCP assigns those IP addresses to the client machines that need them.

Dynamic and static IP addressing

DHCP provides systems with network configuration on startup, but it doesn't necessarily have to provide a dynamic IP address that's subject to change. The service can also assign static addresses to host systems that need them.

Assigning dynamic addresses

Administrators can designate a pool of IP addresses within the subnet to use in assigning client machines on the network that request an address. The assignments can be limited to lease periods of several days or just a few hours. The shorter the lease period, the faster the addresses are returned to make them available to new users.

The pool of dynamic addresses must exclude any IP addresses on the subnet that are manually assigned to devices on the network. This includes the address of the gateway router and any network equipment that doesn't support obtaining an IP address by using DHCP.

It must also not overlap with any pool of addresses assigned by another DHCP server or by a VPN concentrator, which similarly assigns an IP number on the local subnet to any remote machines that need one. How large the DHCP and VPN pools need to be depends on the number of network clients they need to serve at once, a factor that involves the lease period.

Reserving static addresses

Although many network clients don't care what their specific IP address is, servers that need an IP assignment that doesn't change, clients that want a predictable address lease in order to be directly addressable in a server role, and devices such as printers that benefit from having a set address can all have a specific address reserved for them.

Although it's possible to manually assign these machines an IP address and simply exclude these addresses from the DHCP pool, there are reasons for using a static IP reservation from the DHCP pool instead.

Using reserved static addresses ensures that machines obtain other dynamic configuration information provided by the DHCP server, even if they always obtain the same IP address. DHCP also provides network computers with these minimums:

- **The default gateway address of the router.** Used to forward traffic to other networks
- **The addresses of DNS servers.** Provides name resolution services
- **The subnet mask.** Defines the size of the local subnet

In Mac OS X Snow Leopard Server, the DHCP service may optionally also specify:

- **DNS search domains.** Clients append these to the end of unqualified hostnames complete (fully qualify) a DNS name using the supplied domain, such as `company-name.com`.
- **The name, search base, and port number.** For the local LDAP directory
- **Local WINS configuration information.** Used to provide network browsing services to Windows client computers for file and print server discovery

DHCP enables the central updating of this network-related information across client machines on the network, whether they use a dynamic IP address or not.

Planning DHCP subnets

A DHCP server can respond to requests from client computers on multiple subnets. When a client machine configured to use DHCP starts up, it sends a broadcast message to its local subnet and waits for a response from a DHCP server.

If the DHCP server isn't located in the same subnet as the client, the router between the two subnets must be capable of forwarding the client broadcasts and the DHCP server response; broadcast traffic is usually limited only to the local subnet. If forwarding these broadcasts isn't possible on the routers being used, a DHCP server needs to be located in each subnet.

Alternatively, it's also possible for more than one DHCP server to provide addresses for the same subnet, as long as each is distributing a non-overlapping pool of IP addresses. This might be useful to ensure that clients always have access to an address.

If no DHCP server for a subnet is available, a client machine configured to use DHCP makes up its own local link address and subsequently isn't able to access the Internet or most other local services. These addresses are randomly invented by the client within the specially designated private subnet of `169.254.x.x`.

If clients that have been working properly on the network are suddenly assigning themselves these IP addresses, it's because the DHCP server either isn't responding correctly or is out of available IP addresses to assign or because the client machines aren't properly connected to the same subnet as the DHCP server. If a system has never obtained a DHCP address from the server, it may not be properly configured to use DHCP.

DHCP Setup and Configuration

To configure the DHCP service from Server Admin, first enable the service within the desired server's listing of configured services.

To enable DHCP configuration in Server Admin, follow these steps:

1. **Launch Server Admin and then connect to the desired server.**
2. **Select the server listing and then click Settings on the toolbar.**
3. **Click the Services tab.**
4. **Click the check box for DHCP.**
5. **Click Save.** DHCP should now appear in the list of configurable services for the selected server, as shown in Figure 13.1.

Figure 13.1

DHCP configuration in Server Admin

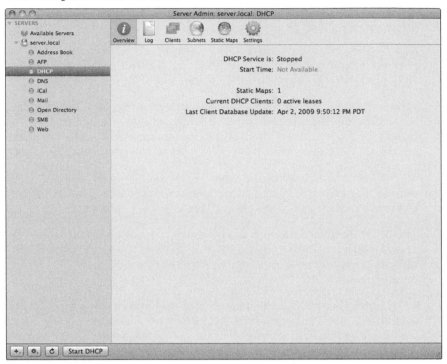

After selecting DHCP from the list of services in the Servers list, configure the initial settings from the Subnet tab and then choose the desired event logging level from the Log Level tab.

Configuring network services in DHCP

To set up a new subnet with DHCP-supplied network settings, follow these steps:

1. **From the DHCP pane in Server Admin, click Subnets on the toolbar.**

2. **Click the Add (+) button.**

3. **Type a name label for the subnet.**

4. **Choose starting and ending numbers for the DHCP pool.** These IP addresses must be a continuous range within the subnet and can't overlap to manually assigned IP addresses currently in use or to other subnet pools on this server or on other DHCP servers or include reserved IP addresses.

5. **Type the subnet mask.**

6. **From the pop-up menu, choose the network interface that will host DHCP.**

7. **Type the gateway router address for the subnet.**

8. **Choose a lease time from the pop-up menu.** This should roughly match the shortest length of time you would expect a typical user on your network to need an IP address lease.

9. **Click Save.**

10. **Enable the new subnet by clicking its check box and click Save.** DHCP should now be actively distributing IP addresses in response to client requests in the newly created subnet, as shown in Figure 13.2.

Figure 13.2

DNS configuration for the DHCP subnet

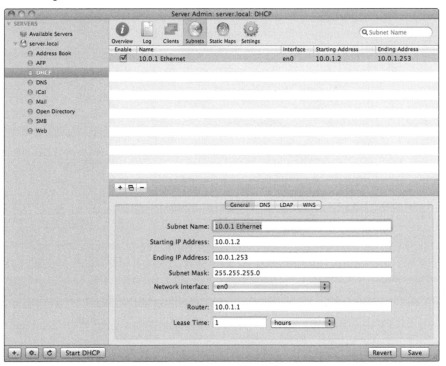

NOTE

Enabling a subnet allows the DHCP server to begin distributing addresses from the designated pool. If the subnet is disabled, the DHCP server doesn't allocate IP addresses, but it continues to serve up other network information (such as any specified DNS or LDAP directory server configuration) to any clients that have been configured to use DHCP with a manual address as long as that client's manual address is within the designated subnet range.

DNS

The DNS information provided by DHCP can be updated to roll out any changes in DNS config-uration across the subnet's machines.

To configure DNS information in DHCP, follow these steps:

1. **From the DHCP pane in Server Admin, click Subnets on the toolbar.**

2. **Click the DNS tab.**

3. **Type at least a primary and secondary DNS server.**

4. **Type the default domain name for the search domain.**

5. **Click Save.** You're prompted to restart the DHCP service. After restarting, DHCP should now provide DNS information for the selected subnet, as shown in Figure 13.3.

Figure 13.3

DNS configuration for the selected DHCP subnet

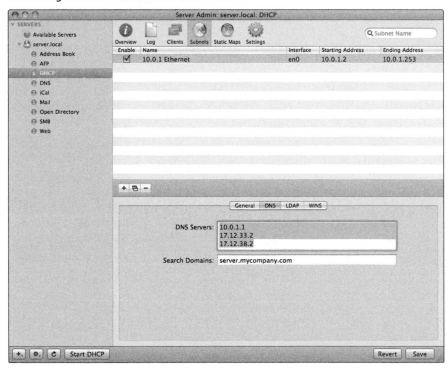

LDAP

Using DHCP to provide LDAP configuration automates the process of setting up directory services for each machine on the subnet. The order of the LDAP servers provided here also determines their search order in automatic Open Directory search policy.

If the DHCP server being configured is also the Open Directory master, its LDAP information should be pre-populated. If another machine is acting as the directory server master, obtain its DNS name or IP address and its search base to supply below.

CROSS-REF
For more on LDAP, Open Directory, and search policy, see Chapter 21.

To configure LDAP directory service information in DHCP, follow these steps:

1. **From the DHCP pane in Server Admin, click Subnets on the toolbar.**

2. **Click the LDAP tab.**

3. **Type the DNS name or IP address of the LDAP domain master.**

4. **Type the search base for LDAP queries.**

5. **If the LDAP server uses a nonstandard port, type that.**

6. **If LDAP over SSL security is enabled and desired, click the check box.**

7. **Click Save.** You're prompted to restart the DHCP service. After restarting, DHCP should now provide LDAP information for the selected subnet, as shown in Figure 13.4.

WINS

If the server is providing services to Windows clients, adding WINS configuration enables those clients to browse for file and print shares. You need:

- **The names or IP addresses of the primary and secondary WINS servers.** This may be the local server if it's supplying SMB file sharing.
- **The NetBIOS Datagram Distribution (NBDD) server.** This forwards broadcasts to other subnets but isn't typically used.
- **The NetBIOS over TCP/IP (NBT) node type.** This is one of the following:
  - **Broadcast (b-node).** Broadcasts for name resolution, the most common node type
  - **Hybrid (h-node).** First checks the WINS server and then broadcasts
  - **Peer (p-node).** Only checks the WINS server for name resolution
  - **Mixed (m-node).** Broadcasts for name resolution and then checks the WINS server

Figure 13.4

LDAP configuration for the DHCP subnet

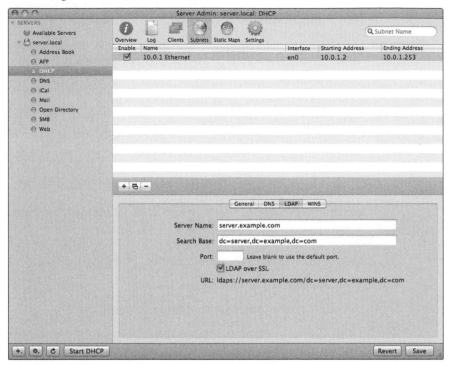

● **The NetBIOS Scope ID.** This isolates NetBIOS communication on a network and is appended to the NetBIOS name of the computer so that machines with the same NetBIOS Scope ID can all communicate, but it's not typically used.

To configure WINS information in DHCP, follow these steps:

1. **From the DHCP pane in Server Admin, click Subnets on the toolbar.**

2. **Click the WINS tab.**

3. **Type a primary and optionally a secondary WINS server.**

4. **Set the node type.** Broadcast (b node) is the most common.

5. **Type an NBDD Server and NetBIOS Scope IP if used.**

6. **Click Save.** You're prompted to restart the DHCP service. After restarting, DHCP should now provide WINS information for the selected subnet, as shown in Figure 13.5.

Figure 13.5

WINS configuration for the DHCP subnet

Setting up a static IP reservation

To assign a system the same consistent IP address from the pool but retain dynamic updates of the other configuration information in DHCP, you can reserve a static IP address for it by speci-fying the system's Ethernet address, sometimes referred to as its MAC address. This is a globally unique hardware serial number of the network interface.

A computer with multiple network interfaces can have multiple IP addresses reserved for it, one per MAC address. For example, a notebook might connect to your network wirelessly or via Ethernet; because each network interface has its own MAC address, you may need to define both if the same user needs a specific IP address regardless of how he or she connects to the network.

To create a static IP reservation, follow these steps:

1. **From the DHCP pane in Server Admin, click Static Maps on the toolbar.**

2. **Click the Add Computer button.**

3. **In the sheet that drops down, type a computer name, a MAC address, and the desired IP address assignment.** Additional reservations can be made for the same machine by using the Add (+) button.

4. **Click OK.** The system is now assigned a static address, as shown in Figure 13.6. No configuration is needed on the client end.

Figure 13.6

IP address reservations within Static Maps of the DHCP configuration

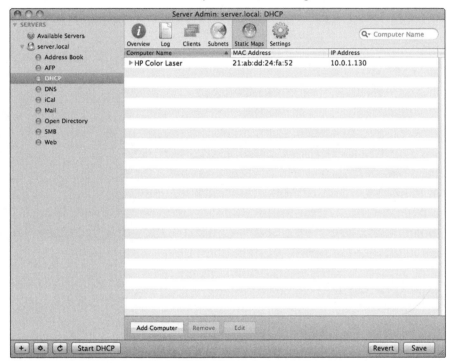

Managing and Monitoring DHCP

The status of the DHCP service can be monitored in Server Admin in three ways by using the toolbar pages presented for the service:

● **Review the Overview page for the service.** This reports whether the process is running, when it was started, how many active leases and how many reservations are listed, and the last time the client database was updated.

- **Monitor the log files generated by the service for error conditions or connectivity problems.** Logs may also help in troubleshooting problems with clients receiving a lease by pinpointing whether the client system can even see the DHCP server or if there's a problem that's occurring after negotiation starts.
- **Monitor the Client List page.** Here, you can review the client computers being assigned DHCP leases by name, MAC address, client ID (a label entered during the client machine's network configuration), assigned IP address, and the remaining time left in the DHCP lease. A check box can be used to display or filter out expired leases.

Troubleshooting common problems

Because most of your users can't do anything without obtaining a DHCP lease, you're quickly informed of any problems. Solving the problem is a simple matter of isolating what the problem is by process of elimination.

No DHCP assignments occurring in a specific subnet

If the DHCP server isn't located in the same subnet as the client, the router between the two subnets must be capable of forwarding the client broadcasts and the DHCP server response; broadcast traffic is usually limited only to the local subnet. If forwarding these broadcasts isn't possible on the routers being used, a DHCP server needs to be located in each subnet.

Client computers not getting DHCP assignments

If no DHCP server for a subnet is available, a client machine configured to use DHCP makes up its own local link address and subsequently isn't able to access the Internet or most other local services. These addresses are randomly invented by the client within the specially designated private subnet of 169.254.x.x.

If clients on the network are assigning themselves these IP addresses, it's because the DHCP server either isn't responding correctly or is out of available IP addresses to assign or because the client machines aren't properly connected to the same subnet as the DHCP server.

Review the DHCP server's logs and records to see if there are available IP addresses in the pool. If not, reduce the lease time and/or create a larger address pool to help ease the IP address shortage.

Add a DHCP server to the local subnet or relay BootP broadcast traffic between the affected subnets. If that's not the issue, seek to resolve a network connectivity problem between clients and the server, starting with a review of the client's DHCP configuration.

Using multiple DHCP servers

More than one DHCP server can be used to provide addresses for the same subnet, as long as each is distributing a non-overlapping pool of IP addresses. This might be useful to ensure that clients always have access to obtaining an address.

The address pools of each server must also not overlap any manually configured IP address assignments or any addresses assigned by the VPN service.

Different DHCP servers offer different features; for example, the DHCP server in the AirPort base station doesn't support distributing LDAP or WINS configuration information or static IP reservations. Clients that need extra configuration information or are set up to use a static IP reservation may obtain a basic DHCP lease from the AirPort instead because machines accept a DHCP lease from the first server that responds to their initial DHCP requests.

An AirPort base station can be configured to simply relay the existing network instead of providing its own DHCP server. This allows wireless clients to obtain their DHCP configuration from the server rather than from the base station.

CROSS-REF
For more on VPN configuration, see Chapter 16.

Summary

- DHCP provides dynamic IP addressing from a pool of available addresses but also distributes DNS, LDAP directory server, and WINS configurations to clients.

- Client machines can be assigned whatever free IP address is available from the pool or a static reservation can be made so they always get the same address. They can also be configured an IP address manually with DHCP, which provides other dynamic configuration information apart from an address or entirely manually, which requires the machine to use an address outside the DHCP server's address pool.

- Multiple DHCP servers can serve the same subnet but only if their address pools don't overlap.

- DHCP clients use broadcast messages to find the server and obtain a lease. If both aren't located in the same subnet, the router must forward broadcast BootP traffic for this to work.

Firewall Service

The firewall service in Mac OS X Server erects a checkpoint barrier to prevent unintended network communications from attacking the server and potentially other machines on the network to obtain private information, maliciously interrupt network services, or use network resources for undesirable purposes.

Apart from the firewall, Snow Leopard Server incorporates a variety of security practices to harden the software from external attacks. Most modern network services require authentication before allowing any communications that could expose any vulnerabilities; and those that don't, such as publicly accessible web services, greatly limit external interaction to specific interfaces that behave in known ways.

Still, the best way to defend against external attacks is to proactively stop them before they can gain access to the network or server. This is the role of the firewall service.

Smaller groups operating Snow Leopard Server in a standard or workgroup configuration are likely to already have some firewall protection in place, supplied either by an appliance router, such as an AirPort base station, or by the organization's firewall installed at the router on the boundary of the public Internet.

Server Preferences enables users to remotely set up firewall services in the AirPort base station or, alternatively, to configure and run the firewall service on the server itself.

In the advanced configuration, Snow Leopard Server can protect the server (and the local network, if the server also acts as an Internet gateway) by using a port filtering *IP firewall*, configured via an advanced firewall configured within Server Admin. This service can manage both incoming and outgoing network traffic at the port level.

The IP firewall service configured within Server Admin isn't supplied by a specific process but rather is a collection of behaviors in the kernel that can be managed by the command-line tools `ipfw` and `sysctl`. Administrators with advanced firewall needs can customize its rules beyond the features presented in Server Admin by manually editing its configuration files.

In This Chapter

Introduction to firewalls

Planning
firewall services

Firewall setup and
configuration

Managing and
monitoring
firewall services

This chapter describes how firewalls work, what's involved in planning firewall services, how the firewall service is configured within the Server Admin interface, and how to maintain and monitor the service.

Introduction to Firewalls

Mac OS X Snow Leopard uses two complementary firewall technologies:

- **An IP firewall that has long been available to filter inbound and outbound network traffic at the port level.** It selectively decides whether to allow traffic or packets through based on the originating IP address or port number and/or the destination address or port.

- **An application firewall that was introduced in Mac OS X Leopard.** It enables the user to selectively allow incoming network traffic to a particular application. It's configured from the Firewall tab of the Security pane within System Preferences.

These two firewalls operate as independent barriers. If the IP firewall allows traffic on specific ports, the application firewall can still restrict which applications can access that traffic. Conversely, even if the application firewall allows network access to a specific application, the IP firewall may block the ports that that application uses.

In Mac OS X Server, graphical configuration of the application firewall isn't available from the Security pane of System Preferences and isn't listed as a feature applicable to server users.

Server Admin provides a graphical interface for the IP firewall to advanced configuration users, and Server Preferences supplies simplified access to the IP firewall for standard and workgroup configuration users. In any server configuration, the command line can also be used to set up IP firewall rules.

Understanding how both firewalls work helps explain why those configuration interface options are presented in the way that they are in Snow Leopard Server (and on Mac desktops).

The Mac OS X Leopard application firewall

Prior to the release of Mac OS X Leopard, the desktop version of the operating system offered a basic configuration interface for the IP firewall service in the Sharing pane of Server Preferences. This simple configuration interface allowed users to selectively filter incoming traffic only by port number. There was no option to set up outgoing filters graphically, although complex rules could be defined manually by editing the IP firewall's configuration files.

Apple removed its graphical interface in Leopard and instead offered a new application firewall. The underlying process behind the former IP firewall is still there and can be configured manually. However, the only graphical configuration interface presented on desktop Macs now is the application firewall in the Security pane of System Preferences. But this isn't available under Mac OS X Server.

The application firewall may appear somewhat similar to the simplified version of the IP firewall presented in the Security pane of Server Preferences, as shown in Figure 14.1, but the two aren't the same thing.

Figure 14.1

IP firewall configuration in Server Preferences

The Mac OS X application firewall is designed to provide a practical level of security that's easy for users to understand and therefore to manage correctly. All users have to know is which applications they want outside users to be able to access. They don't need to know anything about the specific ports those apps might use.

Additionally, with the application firewall set to allow access only to configured applications, only the applications that are granted inbound access are given access; a nefarious spambot can't use an open port on the system to install its own publicly available server.

Additionally, Apple also uses a security certificate to sign all applications that have been granted access so they can't be modified by a rogue attacker and still maintain the same access to inbound network connections. If an application is modified, the system alerts the user to verify whether the changed application should continue to be given inbound access.

The application firewall doesn't limit any outbound connections. Presumably, if a local application is sending data, it's because the user initiated it, making it unnecessary to have a security impediment forcing him or her to approve it. Similarly, the application firewall also allows incoming responses to outbound requests, such as a web page returned in response to a web browser request.

There are scenarios where a user might want to audit what an application is doing or stop it from calling home, such as to check on a license key. There are specialized software tools to flag and filter outbound traffic too, but that lies outside the job of a security-oriented firewall. Apple doesn't offer outbound filtering as a feature of its application firewall.

The application firewall is available to desktop users and can be configured in three ways:

- **Allow all incoming connections.** This leaves all applications open to inbound traffic.

- **Deny inbound connections except for essential services.** This blocks all applications from receiving unsolicited inbound connections (including services that have been enabled elsewhere, such as file sharing, iChat Bonjour messaging, and iTunes music sharing), except those from certain root-level system configuration processes:

  - `configd`, used to implement DHCP and configure local networking
  - `mDNSResponder`, used to implement Bonjour browsing
  - `raccoon`, used to implement IPsec for VPN connections

- **Set access for specific applications and services.** This option allows incoming access by default to all applications that have been signed by a Certificate Authority that the system trusts, which includes all the applications Apple bundles. The method for setting inbound connection access to these applications is based on their origin:

  - Any services that have been enabled elsewhere, such as AFP and SMB file sharing, SSH remote login, VNC screen sharing, and web sharing, are expressly allowed access and must be turned off elsewhere to deny their access. In Snow Leopard Server, this is done within Server Preferences.

  - To manage incoming connection access to a specific signed application, add it to the list and then allow or block an incoming connection from the pop-up menu.

  - For an unsigned application, the system prompts you to allow or deny incoming connection access when you first launch it. Either way, the application is signed and added to the list as allowed or blocked as you choose. This may result in problems for applications that modify themselves while running, which isn't recommended behavior. If a signed app changes itself (or is modified by a rogue process), the system doesn't allow it to launch.

  - Applications recognized by the system that can't be signed prompt the user whether to allow or deny incoming connection access at each launch.

The port filtering IP firewall

Although the application firewall offers a practical security benefit to desktop users (who are likely to be working within the protected domain of an IP firewall on the network, such as an AirPort base station), Mac OS X Server administrators face a variety of different issues that require the sophistication and complexity involved in using the port filtering IP firewall presented in Server Preferences and in Server Admin and configurable from the command line.

Instead of granting inbound access to specific processes by using certificate signing at the application layer of the network stack, an IP firewall examines network traffic at the transport layer. It allows or denies traffic in and out based on a series of prioritized rules entered in the firewall configuration.

TCP and UPD ports

In IP, communications occur over two primary transport protocols:

- **Transmission Control Protocol (TCP).** Establishes connection-oriented communications that require significant overhead to ensure that all data sent is received in a specific order. It's inherently unicast traffic from one source to a single destination.
- **User Datagram Protocol (UDP).** Sends connectionless communications in one direction. It makes no effort to ensure that the data sent is received or arrives in any specific order. It can support multicast messaging to a variety of destinations or broadcast messages that are sent to every host on the local subnet.

Both protocols send data with an assigned *IP port number* and IP address. Just as the IP address targets a specific subnet and machine, the port number targets a specific application or process listening on that machine.

Many port numbers have a common association with a specific application or service, such as port 22 for SSH remote login or port 80 for web servers. The port is used only to direct communications to a known listening application, so services can be assigned alternative ports as needed, as long as both sides agree in advance on which ports to use. For example, although port 80 is the default port for the web service, it can also be configured to listen for requests at other ports.

A single port number can be used for TCP or UDP or a mix of both, and some applications make use of multiple ports. For example, the L2TP VPN service requires UDP on ports 500, 1701, and 4500. The firewall can allow or deny either TCP or UDP or both on a specific port.

Firewall rule priority

The IP firewall in Snow Leopard Server examines traffic and applies its configured rules, either allowing or blocking traffic as required. The rules listed in the firewall's configuration are applied in numerical order. To minimize the risk of inadvertently blocking essential traffic or permissively allowing unintended access, administrators need to manage traffic rules in three basic rule tiers:

- **Allow essential traffic required for network functions.** This includes features such as *loopback* (which sends traffic to the system itself and must therefore not be blocked by the firewall) and is configured using high-priority, low-numbered rules. These basic rules are configured for you and are visible in the Advanced pane of firewall settings in Server Admin.
- **Allow service traffic related to network packets to specific service ports, such as web and mail services.** Permitting traffic to ports with designated, configured services allows the required firewall access on a per-service basis. These services are designated as medium-priority rules and are listed as check boxes in the Service pane of firewall settings in Server Admin.
- **Deny everything else.** Unsolicited packets or traffic are blocked before reaching their destination. A basic set of high-numbered, low-priority deny rules are set by default and are visible in the Advanced pane of the firewall settings in Server Admin.

Planning Firewall Services

Planning firewall services on the server requires stepping back to look at how security is implemented on the entire local network. Snow Leopard Server can act as a firewall for the local network if it serves as the Internet gateway. This allows the server to act as a filter for all traffic, so rules configured in the firewall service impact all machines on that subnet.

However, there are a few reasons to not do this. First, it makes both the server and the local network's firewall a single point of failure. It's not just that both services fail if the server becomes unavailable. The larger problem is that any vulnerability exploited in the firewall may give attackers immediate access to the server.

That makes it more attractive to use an external firewall to protect the network — even a simple one provided by an AirPort base station, for example — and dedicate the firewall service on the server to protect the server itself. In this case, if the external firewall is compromised, attackers hit another barrier they have to overcome before actually gaining access to sensitive data.

Having an external firewall does mean that rules need to be managed in multiple places, so access for new applications may require ports to be opened through each firewall.

In order for the external firewall to offer any real protection for the server, it can't simply pass all traffic to the server's IP address. Many appliance servers offer this capability under the name DMZ server. This essentially opens a hole in the firewall and exposes the machine at the specified IP address to all public traffic without any filtering. This is used as a convenient way to bypass having to open up all the specific ports on the firewall that may be used by the particular machine but defeats all security.

This section describes how to plan for specific, practical firewall uses, resulting in rules that can be added to the firewall service to modify how it works.

Limiting services to local users

One basic reason for enabling the firewall service on the server is to selectively allow or block access to users based on their location or IP address. For example, you may want to limit the web service to only users on the local subnet, creating a private *intranet* that outside users can't access.

Defining address groups and allowing services

This can be done by defining an *address group* for the local subnet and then allowing the web service only to that address group. Because there are default rules that deny everything that isn't expressly allowed, allowing the web service to the local subnet's address group would effectively limit web access only to local users. Server Admin makes it easy to set up new rules by defining address groups and allowing services to them.

Advanced firewall rules

It's also possible to accomplish the same task by manually creating an advanced rule in Server Admin, which is similar to what an administrator would have to type from the command line to create a new rule.

To accomplish the same task of limiting web traffic to local users by using an advanced rule, you need to explicitly specify a series of rule components, including:

- **A priority.** Firewall rules are numbered in order of how they're applied. As previously noted, a rule allowing access to the web service would need to be assigned a lower number to come before the high-number, low-priority rules set to deny everything; otherwise, the new allow rule would have no effect. In Server Admin, setting the priority of advanced rules is done by dragging to reorder the rules.

- **An action.** In this case, to allow; the other primary action is to deny.

- **The protocol involved.** In this case, the web service is TCP, but other services may be UDP or require multiple rules that specify both protocols. Other rules might also specify another protocol, such as ICMP (Internet Control Message Protocol), which relates to sending messages to see if other systems are replying; a firewall administrator might want to deny such requests.

- **The service.** Here, the service is web at port 80; with a nonstandard port or less common service type, you'd need to provide the actual port number the firewall is acting upon.

- **The source address and port.** Here, it would be an address group representing the local subnet audience originating web requests, which is a range of addresses. This might otherwise be a single IP address inside or outside the local subnet.

- **The destination address and port.** Here, it's the IP address of the server, which is the destination of the web requests. This could also be a range of addresses defined by an address group if the traffic destination being filtered were instead anyone on the local subnet.

- **The interface.** This is the network interface where the traffic being filtered is received, such as en0 for the first built-in Ethernet port.

Logging allowed or denied packets

Outside filtering traffic to determine if it should be allowed or denied, a second feature of the IP firewall is to log the traffic that passes through it. The firewall can be configured to log all traffic or can be selectively limited to packets that were either allowed or denied by the firewall.

For example, an administrator might want to log allowed traffic to monitor the websites that users on the network were visiting. Alternatively, he or she might want to only monitor denied traffic in order to troubleshoot issues with traffic being blocked by the firewall.

NOTE

Instead of opening up access to specific IP addresses in the firewall, administrators can provide authenticated access to internal services by using the VPN service, which is described in Chapter 16.

Limiting external access to a specific user

In addition to limiting external access by only allowing services to an address group representing the local subnet, administrators can also grant either a single user or a subnet of IP addresses external access to a local service by simply defining a new address group and then allowing access to the desired service.

Blocking external access to a specific user

Conversely, there may be services publicly opened to the Internet that an administrator might want to selectively block. One example is SMTP mail service, which typically occurs over port 25.

To block a known spammer from sending traffic over SMTP, the spammer's IP address can be assigned to a new address group that's selectively denied access to SMTP services.

Limiting peer-to-peer file sharing and gaming

Another example of a firewall use that administrators might want to incorporate into their plans relates to applications that consume bandwidth, such as file sharing or gaming. In this case, the firewall service can be used to contain that traffic to the inside network by allowing it on the inside local network interface but not on the public-facing network interface.

This requires creating an advanced firewall rule because the standard interface to allow services doesn't enable the user to specify the interface.

Firewall Setup and Configuration

To configure the firewall service from Server Admin, first enable the service within the desired server's listing of configured services.

To enable firewall configuration in Server Admin, follow these steps:

1. **Launch Server Admin and then connect to the desired server.**

2. **Select the server listing and then click Settings on the toolbar.**

3. **Click the Services tab.**

4. **Click the check box for Firewall.**

5. **Click Save.** Firewall should now appear in the list of configurable services for the selected server, as shown in Figure 14.2.

Figure 14.2

IP firewall configuration in Server Admin

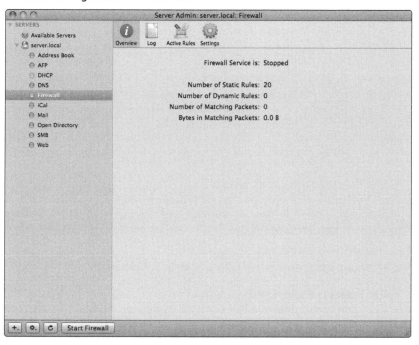

After selecting Firewall from the list of services in the Servers list, the Overview page presents a status listing of the number of active rules as well as the number and size of packets matching those rules.

Administrators can review the initial rules settings from the Active Rules pane, shown in Figure 14.3, and use the Log pane to review reported events.

Figure 14.3

Active firewall rules in Server Admin

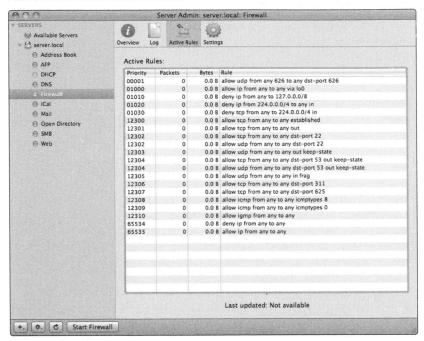

The Settings page presents four tabs, as shown in Figure 14.4:

- **Address Groups.** Individual IP addresses or subnets can be added as new address groups, but there are three created by default:
  - Any, representing all IP addresses
  - The 10.0.0.0/8 private address space
  - The 192.168.0.0/16 private address space
- **Services.** Here, any address groups defined on the previous tab can be given access to all or specifically granted ports.
- **Logging.** Allowed, denied, or all traffic can be logged
- **Advanced.** Here, advanced rules specifying the network interface to be used, protocols other than TCP or UDP, and both incoming and outgoing port and IP addresses or subnets can be defined. Stealth can also be enabled for TCP or UDP traffic so denied traffic won't get a failure notification.

Figure 14.4

The Settings pane in Server Admin

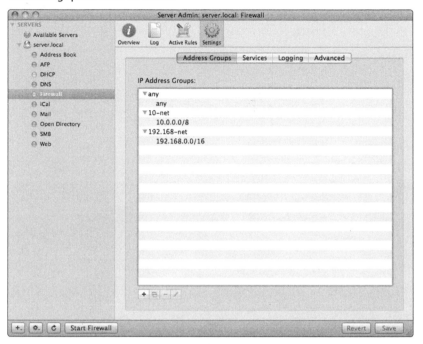

Defining address groups

As previously outlined, the standard way to create rules in Server Admin is to define address groups and then selectively grant allowed access to services, which are shown in Figure 14.4.

To define a new address group, follow these steps:

1. **From the Firewall pane in Server Admin, click Settings on the toolbar.**

2. **Click the Address Groups tab.**

3. **Below the IP Address Groups list, click the Add (+) button to drop down a sheet.**

4. **In the Group name field, type a descriptive group name label.**

5. **Type the address or subnet you want to create rules for.** This can be typed as:

- **A single IP address:** for example, `10.0.2.1`
- **A subnet by IP address and subnet mask:** `10.0.2.0:255.255.255.0`
- **A subnet by IP address and subnet mask in CIDR notation:** `10.0.2.0/24`

6. **Click OK to create the new address group listing.**

7. **Click Save to save the changes.** Move to the Services tab to assign the newly created address group access to the desired services.

Allowing services

Once an address group is created, you can selectively grant allowed access to individual services listed under the Services tab or create a new service entry by specifying a port or range of ports, as shown in Figure 14.5.

Figure 14.5

Services configuration in Server Admin

To allow an address group access to specific services, follow these steps:

1. **From the Firewall pane in Server Admin, click Settings on the toolbar.**

2. **Click the Services tab.**

3. **Select the desired address group from the Editing services for pop-up menu.**

4. **Use the radio buttons to either grant access to all services or to specify specific ports.**

5. **To enable specific ports, click the check box for the desired service.**

6. **If the desired service isn't listed, define a new service.** This can be done by:

    1. **Clicking the Add (+) button to drop down a sheet.**

    2. **Typing a descriptive name label for the service.**

    3. **Typing the port or range of ports that service uses.** Multiple ports can be specified as a sequence, such as 100-200, or as a series, such as 200,210,250.

    4. **Typing the protocol that the service uses, such as TCP, UDP, or TCP and UDP.**

    5. **Clicking OK to save the new service entry.**

7. **Click Save to record the allowed services for the given address group as firewall rules.**

Logging options

From the Logging tab, click the check box to enable logging. Click either or both check boxes to log allowed and/or denied packets. Type a maximum number of packets to log, using 0 to enable unlimited logging. Click Save to save the logging settings.

Advanced firewall rules

In order to create rules that can't be specified by using the standard rule method involving enabling services for defined address groups, use the Advanced tab. Advanced rules allow users to specify additional rule details, including protocols other than TCP and UDP, source ports, and a network interface.

To create an advanced firewall rule, follow these steps:

1. **From the Firewall pane in Server Admin, click Settings on the toolbar.**

2. **Click the Advanced tab, shown in Figure 14.6.**

3. **Click the Add (+) button.** Alternatively, if you want to create a new rule similar to an existing one, select a rule from the list, click the Duplicate button marked with a double window icon, select the duplicate rule, and then click the Edit button marked with a pencil icon. A sheet drops down.

4. **In the Action pop-up menu, choose allow or deny.** Alternatively, choose Other and then type the desired action; for example, Log.

5. **From the Protocol pop-up menu, choose TCP or UDP.** Alternatively, choose Other and then type a custom protocol; for example, ICMP, ESP, or IPENCAP.

6. **From the Service pop-up menu, choose a service.** Alternatively, choose Other to provide a nonstandard service port below as the destination port.

7. **Click the check box to optionally log packets that match the advanced rule.**

Figure 14.6

Advanced firewall rules in Server Admin

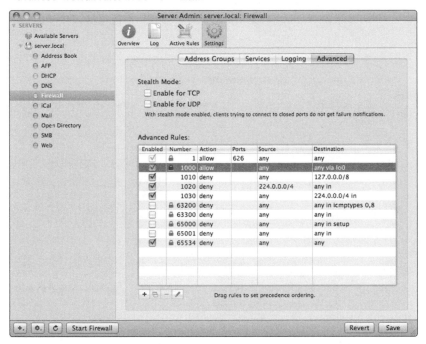

8. **Choose a source of filtered traffic by selecting any or a defined address group from the Source Address pop-up menu.** Alternatively, type the source IP address or subnet by using CIDR notation, such as 10.0.2.0/24.

9. **For a nonstandard service port, type the Source Port number.**

10. **Choose a destination for filtered traffic by selecting any or a defined address group from the Destination Address pop-up menu.** Alternatively, type the source IP address or subnet by using CIDR notation, such as 10.0.2.0/24.

11. **For a nonstandard service port, type the Destination Port number.**

12. **Use the Interface pop-up menu to choose the network interface that the rule is applied to, where In refers to the packets being sent to the server and Out refers to the packets being sent from the server.** Alternatively, choose Other and then type the network interface name, such as en0, en1, fw1.

13. **Click OK to add the new advanced rule to the listing.** Drag the rule to set its priority order among other rules.

14. **Click Save to apply the rule immediately.**

Managing and Monitoring Firewall Services

From the Firewall pane of Server Admin, the Overview page presents a status listing of the number of active rules as well as the number and size of packets matching those rules.

Administrators can review the initial rules settings from the Active Rules pane and then use the Log pane to review reported events within `/var/log/ipfw.log`.

Invalid rule troubleshooting

Rules created in the Advanced tab can accept any input, even if the values aren't valid. When an invalid rule is applied, it logs an error message and then stops. The error doesn't specify which rule is invalid, but this can be determined by reviewing the rules that were loaded prior to hitting the invalid rule:

- Compare the listing of active rules on the Overview page of the Firewall pane with the listing on the Active Rule page.

- Review the configuration file at `/etc/ipfilter/ipfw.conf.apple` to see which rules Server Admin attempted to load. The first rule in this listing that isn't also in the Active Rules list is probably the invalid rule.

- This rule can be disabled from the Advanced tab, which results in it being commented out of the configuration file.

Stealth mode

To prevent intruders from seeing that their attempts to connect are being blocked by the firewall, administrators can enable stealth for either or both TCP or UDP traffic by using the Advanced tab. With this enabled, denied traffic won't get a failure notification.

Adaptive firewall

The IP firewall has an *adaptive firewall* feature that dynamically generates a firewall rule when a user fails to log in after 10 consecutive attempts. The generated rule blocks the user's system for 15 minutes, preventing additional login attempts.

The adaptive firewall feature requires no configuration and is active when the firewall is enabled. The number of dynamic rules in effect is listed on the Overview page of the Firewall pane.

Summary

- The firewall service provides a security barrier by blocking outside intruders from accessing the server or potentially the network (if the server is configured as the network gateway) outside of the selectively allowed ports or applications.

- Mac OS X uses two firewalls: a user-friendly application firewall that selectively allows incoming connections to specific applications and an IP firewall that selectively allows incoming or outgoing traffic based on protocol, IP address, and port number.

- Server Preferences configures the IP firewall for standard and workgroup configurations.

- Server Admin presents a graphical interface for configuring the IP firewall for advanced configuration users. It defines address groups and then allows them access to specific services or, alternatively, allows for advanced rules that define additional access control by interface, port, and protocols to be filtered.

NAT Service

N AT (network address translation) allows companies or individuals to share their public IP address across multiple systems located inside their router, in part to satiate the demand for public IP addresses from the limited number of IPv4 numbers available but also to help shield internal systems from public attacks.

NAT provides two primary features. The first is *IP masquerading*, which is used to enable outside access to the public Internet by devices within a subnet of private internal addresses, such as `10.x.x.x` or `192.168.x.x`.

Without NAT, outside hosts would have no way to route replies back to the original system because private addresses are only valid locally. NAT bridges the security moat that isolates inside systems from external attacks.

A second feature is *port forwarding*, which is used to direct incoming traffic to specific inside hosts. This enables a single public IP address to receive traffic bound for different internal servers, such as mail and web.

The NAT service is provided by the `natd` background process. It acts as an extended function of the IP firewall, which is part of the Mac OS X Server kernel. In addition to allowing, denying, and logging traffic, the firewall can also be configured to divert traffic to NAT. This requires the firewall to be active in order for NAT to work.

CROSS-REF
For more on the firewall service, see Chapter 14.

This chapter describes how NAT works, what's involved in planning NAT services, how the NAT service is configured within the Server Admin interface, and how to maintain and monitor the service.

In This Chapter

Introduction to NAT

Planning NAT services

NAT setup and configuration

Managing and monitoring NAT

Introduction to NAT

As previously noted, Mac OS X Snow Leopard provides two features under NAT:

- **IP masquerading.** This enables multiple inside systems to access the Internet while hiding behind a single public IP address.
- **Port forwarding.** This allows specific types of inbound traffic to be directed to inside servers based on its port, such as port 80 web traffic being forwarded to a web server.

As with firewall services, NAT can be supplied either by Mac OS X Server acting as a network gateway or by an external network device, such as dedicated firewall equipment or a multipurpose appliance, such as an AirPort base station.

However, because NAT actually modifies outbound traffic as it passes through it, multiple layers of NAT can cause complex problems for some network applications. This means NAT should be handled only by one device acting as the network gateway.

For users with basic needs, an AirPort can provide both IP masquerading and port forwarding. However, because the NAT configuration is connected to other network services, including the firewall, DNS, and DHCP, administrators might want to run NAT on the server instead. This provides the following advantages over using the AirPort's built-in services:

- Advanced firewall rule configuration
- DNS caching
- DHCP static reservations
- Support for incoming VPN connections

If none of these features are needed, using an AirPort can simplify the configuration required and take that extra load off the server. If the server does need to be used as a network gateway, the Gateway Setup Assistant can be used to help configure DNS, DHCP, firewall, and NAT services.

Creating private networks

NAT does for network traffic something like what a private branch exchange does for a company's telephone calls. Private IP addresses are similar to private telephone extensions that a company may use for its internal phones. A company may have only one public phone number but can freely assign extensions internally. Other companies can similarly assign the same extension numbers to their own employees, making the extension number itself insufficient for placing a call.

In effect, NAT allows internal users to place calls to outside phone numbers without being dedicated a public phone number. It also enables outside callers to reach specific phone extensions when making inbound calls.

However, NAT differs from a typical phone system in that unsolicited callers can't reach inside users simply by guessing their extension numbers; NAT allows only inbound traffic that's either a response to an internal request or directly provisioned in port forwarding rules.

NAT firewall integration

For NAT to work, it requires the IP firewall to be configured to divert outbound client traffic to it. Any outbound traffic matching the firewall's divert rules are exempted from the remainder of the firewall's rule gauntlet and are instead sent to `natd`.

The NAT process then replaces the outbound traffic's originating address information with a public IP address and records the local private address of its originating system. The modified packets are then sent out through the firewall.

This record-keeping step allows a return response directed back to the public IP address to be routed back to the original system inside the firewall by NAT. For example, a local user at `10.0.1.50` might send a request for a web page. When this outbound request hits the firewall, it diverts the request to `natd`, which changes the request's originating IP address to the company's public IP address instead and records the event in an internal table.

When the public web server responds to the company's public IP address, `natd` looks up the `10.0.1.50` internal address of the original requestor and then sends the response to that system. Neither the local client nor the remote web server needs to know about the IP sleight of hand going on with NAT; ideally, the translation should be invisible.

Problems related to NAT

However, NAT can cause other problems. The stateful records NAT maintains are relatively short-lived, making it necessary to keep connections alive to avoid losing connectivity. Outside hosts can't initiate TCP connections, and stateless UDP transmissions may be blocked.

IPsec encrypts packets, making NAT unable to successfully change the packets' port addressing. Protocols such as FTP and SIP (Session Initiation Protocol, used for video conferencing) use complex communications over multiple ports where the application itself manages addressing. NAT can interfere or block these protocols by modifying the addressing of packages, making them invalid.

To circumvent these problems, a variety of NAT traversal techniques are used to help NAT deal with application-specific issues caused by IP masquerading.

Exposing public services to outside users

Whereas IP masquerading enables clients to obtain a useable IP address to access the outside Internet, port forwarding enables outside users to connect to multiple internal servers by using the same public IP address.

IP masquerading uses dynamic address translation based on state information stored by NAT as outbound requests are made by internal hosts. Port forwarding uses static address translations based on configured rules.

This makes port forwarding more straightforward and less likely to cause problems for inbound services. However, port forwarding can only forward a single port to a single server. That means inbound web traffic on port 80 can only be forwarded to a single web server, so a company with multiple web servers couldn't host them all behind a single IP address by using NAT port forwarding.

Other applications, such as VNC screen sharing or P2P file sharing, turn clients' systems into short-term servers, requiring a dynamic sort of port forwarding to enable multiple inside clients to allow connections from outside systems.

Apple's NAT-PMP (Port Mapping Protocol) allows client applications to dynamically create port forwarding rules to support inbound connections. It's been built into Mac OS X since Tiger and is also supported in modern AirPort base stations.

IP forwarding without NAT

The NAT service can also be used to route traffic without performing any address translation. This is referred to as IP address forwarding. It's used to route traffic between two private subnets where the server acts as a gateway, such as $10.0.1.x$ and $10.0.2.x$, where no IP masquerading is needed.

Planning NAT Services

Because of the widespread practice of using private IP addresses, setting up NAT is essential. Whether it's supplied by the server is a matter of planning. Snow Leopard Server provides a Gateway Setup Assistant to help automatically configure DNS, DHCP, firewall, and NAT services, but this process overwrites any existing configuration.

Alternatives to NAT

Server Admin provides only a minimal interface for configuring NAT, requiring administrators with advanced needs to resort to the command line to edit configuration files manually. This might make it more attractive for users with basic needs for NAT to rely on something like an AirPort or dedicated network equipment to provide the service.

AirPort provides a basic but easy-to-use interface for configuring port mappings, something still lacking in Snow Leopard Server. Using AirPort Utility, the Advanced base station configuration page supplies a Port Mapping pane that allows users to create static NAT mappings, as shown in Figure 15.1.

AirPort also manages dynamic mappings for users within the private network it creates and supports NAT-PMP as well as DHCP allocation.

Other network appliance routers present a similar interface for port mapping, although each router model may support different NAT transversal protocols and may or may not support features such as NAT-PMP.

Figure 15.1

The port mapping configuration sheet presented in AirPort Utility

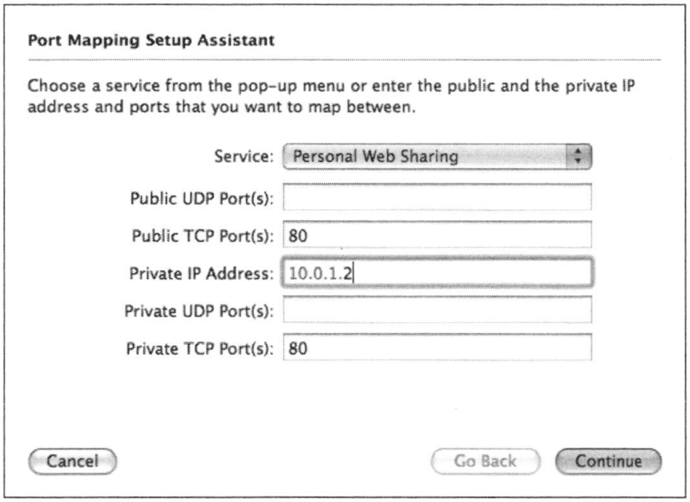

Port Mapping Setup Assistant

Choose a service from the pop–up menu or enter the public and the private IP address and ports that you want to map between.

Service:	Personal Web Sharing
Public UDP Port(s):	
Public TCP Port(s):	80
Private IP Address:	10.0.1.2
Private UDP Port(s):	
Private TCP Port(s):	80

Cancel   Go Back   Continue

Integrating with external NAT services

Additionally, servers operating within a larger organization shouldn't need to supply NAT for the typical purpose of translating addresses between public and private IP addresses, although the NAT service may still be used to route between subnets of private addresses in IP forwarding only mode.

NAT Setup and Configuration

To configure the NAT service from Server Admin, first enable the service within the desired server's listing of configured services.

To enable NAT configuration in Server Admin, follow these steps:

1. **Launch Server Admin and then connect to the desired server.**

2. **Select the server listing and then click Settings on the toolbar.**

3. **Click the Services tab.**

4. **Click the check box for NAT.**

5. **Click Save.** NAT should now appear in the list of configurable services for the selected server, as shown in Figure 15.2.

Figure 15.2

NAT configuration in Server Admin

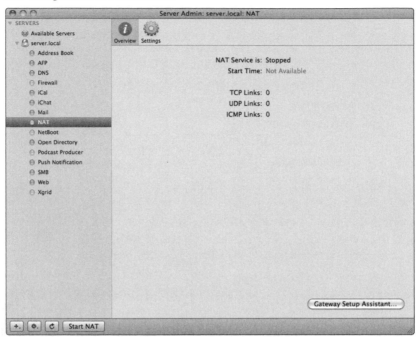

After selecting NAT from the list of services in the Servers list, the Overview page presents a status report of when the service was started and how many links are active by protocol: TCP, UDP, and ICMP.

Administrators can launch the Gateway Setup Assistant to help automatically configure NAT, along with DNS, DHCP, and firewall settings, as shown in Figure 15.3.

The Settings page presents two modes: one to configure the service to support IP forwarding only and the other to additionally provide network address translation. With NAT, the user needs to specify the external, public network interface and can optionally turn NAT-PMP on or off, as shown in Figure 15.4.

Configuring NAT for a LAN

There are a series of steps involved in setting up NAT when using Snow Leopard Server as the gateway for a LAN. Many of these are automated by the Gateway Server Assistant described shortly or may be configured manually as needed.

Figure 15.3

The Gateway Setup Assistant

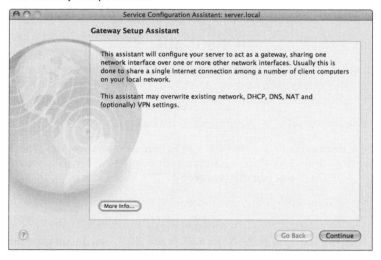

Figure 15.4

The Settings page of the NAT pane

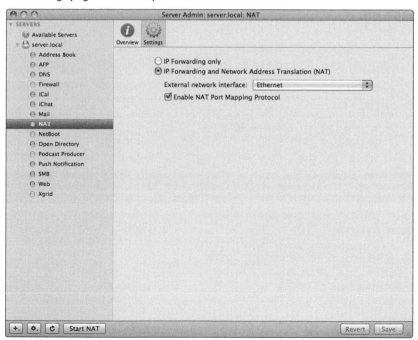

To set up NAT in general terms, follow these steps:

1. **Select the gateway interface.** To act as a gateway, the server needs at least two network interfaces: one for the public WAN and one for the local LAN.

2. **Set up DHCP or static IP addressing for client machines.**

3. **Configure network settings for the server.** The selected WAN interface needs the public IP address, exemplified here as `15.50.10.2`, whereas the local LAN interface needs to match the private subnet of the DHCP, such as `10.0.1.x`.

4. **Enable NAT configuration in Server Admin as previously described.**

5. **From the Settings page of the NAT pane in Server Admin, select IP forwarding and Network Address Translation and then choose the external network interface designated for the public WAN in step 1.**

6. **Configure port forwarding.** This requires editing configuration files and is described shortly.

7. **Start the NAT service by clicking Start NAT in the NAT pane in Server Admin.**

8. **Start the firewall service by clicking Start Firewall in the Firewall pane in Server Admin.** The NAT service can't begin working without an firewall active.

9. **Configure and start DHCP.** Client machines should now be able to access the public network by using their private addresses assigned via DHCP.

Configuring port forwarding

In order for outside hosts to connect to servers with private IP addresses, port forwarding must be configured to assign incoming ports to a corresponding port on the internal IP address of the desired server. This may involve mapping one port to the same port on an inside host, as would be used to forward incoming web requests on the public `15.50.10.2` port 80 to a private web server at `10.0.1.2`, also on port 80.

Alternatively, it may require mapping several individual ports or a range of ports to the corresponding ports of an internal server. It may also map ports on the public IP address to the same ports on multiple servers, such as linking ports 80 and 8080 on `15.50.10.2` to port 80 on two internal addresses: `10.0.1.2` and `10.0.1.3`. This exposes two web servers on one IP address, each using different ports. However, it's not possible to map the same port 80 to two different internal servers.

To configure port forwarding, follow these steps:

1. **Create the file** `/etc/nat/natd.plist` **by using the Apple-supplied template:** `sudo cp /etc/nat/natd.plist.default /etc/nat/natd.plist`.

2. **Edit the file** `/etc/nat/natd.plist` **by using a text editor (Pico in this example) in Terminal:** `sudo pico /etc/nat/natd.plist`.

3. **Add an XML block for each protocol (TCP or UDP) and port to be forwarded, as shown in Listing 15.1.**

Listing 15.1

```
<key>redirect_port</key>
        <array>
        <dict>
                <key>proto</key>
                <string>TCP or UDP</string>
                <key>targetIP</key>
                <string>inside IP address</string>
                <key>targetPortRange</key>
                <string>inside port(s)</string>
                <key>aliasIP</key>
                <string>outside IP address</string>
                <key>aliasPortRange</key>
                <string>outside port(s)</string>
        </dict>
</array>
```

4. **Save the file in Pico by using** Control-X.

5. **Restart the NAT service by using Server Admin or from the command line:**

```
sudo systemstarter stop nat
sudo systemstarter start nat
```

For example, to forward incoming web requests on the public 15.50.10.2 port 80 to a private web server at 10.0.1.2 also on port 80, the added XML would look like Listing 15.2.

Listing 15.2

```
<key>redirect_port</key>
        <array>
        <dict>
                <key>proto</key>
                <string>tcp</string>
                <key>targetIP</key>
                <string>10.0.1.2</string>
                <key>targetPortRange</key>
                <string>80</string>
                <key>aliasIP</key>
                <string>15.50.10.2</string>
```

continued

Listing 15.2 *(continued)*

```
            <key>aliasPortRange</key>
            <string>80</string>
    </dict>
</array>
```

Configuring a gateway without NAT

Servers operating within a larger organization shouldn't need to supply NAT for the typical purpose of translating addresses between public and private IP addresses. The NAT service may still be used to route between subnets of private addresses in IP forwarding only mode.

To set up NAT as an IP forwarding gateway only, follow these steps:

1. **Configure network settings for the server.** The gateway server needs two interfaces configured by using private subnets, such as $10.0.1.2$ and $10.1.2.2$.

2. **Navigate to the Settings page of the NAT pane in Server Admin.**

3. **Select IP forwarding only.**

4. **Click Save and then restart the NAT service.** The gateway should now route traffic between the two subnets.

Using the Gateway Setup Assistant

The Gateway Setup Assistant can automate the process of setting up initial NAT service and configure the appropriate settings for DHCP, DNS, and VPN.

To use the Gateway Setup Assistant to configure settings, follow these steps:

1. **Launch Server Admin and then connect to the desired server.**

2. **Click NAT and then click Overview on the toolbar.**

3. **Click the Gateway Setup Assistant button on the Overview page.** As shown in Figure 15.5, the assistant warns when you begin that running the tool may overwrite existing settings.

4. **Click Continue.**

5. **Choose the WAN public interface from a drop-down menu that presents multiple Ethernet interfaces (if installed), FireWire, and AirPort.**

6. **Click Continue.**

7. **Choose LAN interfaces to share the Internet connection with from the listing presented, including any Bluetooth, Ethernet, FireWire, and Airport interfaces installed apart from the interface already selected to serve as the public WAN interface.**

8. **Click Continue.**

9. **Optionally, enable L2TP VPN service by providing a shared secret.** This is a passphrase that all VPN users need to provide when configuring their connection to the VPN gateway. The supplied passphrase should be secure and shouldn't be the password of an administrator or another user on the server.

Figure 15.5

The Gateway Setup Assistant

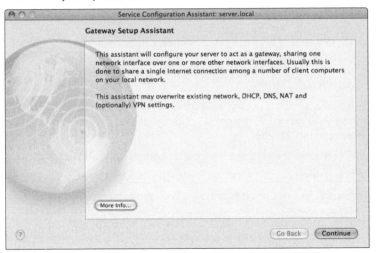

10. **Click Continue.**

11. **Review the configuration summary and then click Continue to confirm the changes.**

12. **Click Close.** The assistant now does the following:

    - Assigns each LAN network interface a private, static IP address, starting at `192.168.0.1`, with each successive interface incrementing the 0 subnet by one: `192.168.1.1`, `192.168.2.1`, and so on

    - Enables the DHCP service to allocate addresses in the `192.168.x.x` range for the LAN interfaces, removing any existing DHCP subnets

- Reserves half the available addresses for VPN use (if activated), leaving `192.168.x.2` to `192.168.x.127` in the DHCP pool and defining `192.168.x.128` to `192.168.x.254` for VPN users
- Enables the firewall service to secure LAN networks, creating address groups for each LAN interface and permitting all traffic from the DHCP address to any destination address
- Enables the NAT service on the LAN interfaces
- Enables DNS configured to cache DNS lookups for improved performance

Once completed, the assistant presents a listing of settings it will configure. Click Continue to accept the settings. As shown in Figure 15.6, the tool makes the following changes to the server settings:

- The selected Ethernet port is designated as a WAN connection by using its existing public IP network settings.
- The selected shared interfaces are assigned private subnet IP addresses, starting with `192.168.1.1`.
- DHCP is enabled for the private subnet, with a pool from `192.168.1.2` to `192.168.1.127` if VPN is turned on; otherwise, it's the entire subnet from `192.168.1.2` to `192.168.1.254`. Any previously configured DHCP settings are overwritten.
- IP firewall is turned on and an Address Group is created for the VPN, allowing access to the private subnet. All incoming public IP traffic is blocked, apart from responses to internal hosts' queries.
- NAT is turned on, with IP masquerading enabled for the `192.168.1.x` subnet.
- VPN is turned on and assigned a pool of IP addresses in the local subnet.
- DNS services are turned on, and caching is enabled to improve performance.

The Gateway Setup Assistant is similar to Internet Connection Sharing in the desktop version of Mac OS X, although it additionally offers to split the DHCP pool to allow space for private IP number assignments made by the VPN service.

Figure 15.6

The Gateway Setup Assistant Confirm Setup page

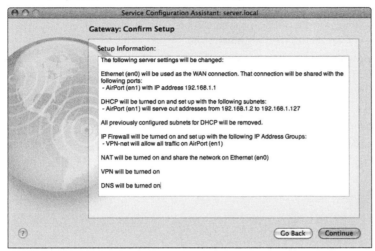

Managing and Monitoring NAT

From the NAT pane of Server Admin, the Overview page presents a status listing of the number of links by protocol. Logging can be enabled with the command `/usr/sbin/natd -log`, resulting in the log file at `/var/log/alias.log`.

If NAT stops working, make sure the firewall service is active; if the firewall service stops, NAT will appear to be running even though it has ceased functioning.

Because NAT is a service provided in conjunction with the firewall, management and monitoring of NAT are related to the firewall service, and the troubleshooting of NAT issues can often best be addressed by making sure the firewall is functioning correctly and properly diverting traffic to the NAT service.

Additionally, many potential problems related to NAT involve protocols that may be incompatible with NAT or require special handling to be used with the service, such as iChat video conferencing. These require addressing issues in the external protocol and can't simply be resolved by the NAT service apart from simply turning it off.

If your organization or service provider is already presenting a level of NAT, running a secondary level of NAT where address translation is already in effect will likely cause problems for applications and protocols that require special efforts to be compatible with NAT.

Summary

- NAT enables the use of private IP addresses with IP masquerading. This allows private addresses to access the public Internet but prevents public addresses from sending unsolicited requests to private IP addresses.

- To allow public Internet users to reach private IP addresses, static port forwarding can be enabled to link a specific incoming port on the public IP address with an internal IP address and port number.

- The NAT service can also be used to set up routing between private IP subnets by using IP forwarding.

- NAT-PMP allows private client computers to dynamically configure port forwarding to support applications that use specific ports impacted by NAT.

VPN Service

16

A VPN enables organizations to provide secured access to the services and resources provided on a local network to authenticated remote users over the public Internet.

A VPN is an encrypted link between two networks that offers the security of a private network at a much lower cost than paying for a dedicated phone line to the remote user. It's a virtual private network in the sense that it uses a low-cost shared network to create a secured link by using encryption, often described as a tunnel that the encrypted traffic passes through.

In addition to supporting individual remote users, a VPN can also be used to establish secure communications between two remote sites, enabling both sides to use their existing Internet access to set up a secure link between the two locations without needing a secondary and expensive dedicated line.

VPNs solve a range of security problems for remote users. Although a firewall can be used to limit access to specific services to outside users, the traffic allowed to pass through the firewall to a remote user must then travel over a public network, where it may be possible to either snoop on the traffic or modify it before it reaches the intended user. False transmissions may also be forged to appear to come from a trusted, known user.

Transport-level authentication, such as SSL/TLS, can be used to secure specific network communications, such as web or email traffic, between a client and a server but requires those applications to be aware of and support SSL/TLS.

VPNs do the same thing for any type of traffic, setting up a special tunneling protocol to encapsulate standard IP traffic and supplying data encryption for the transmissions that pass through that tunnel, keeping the traffic safe from snooping, forgery, and any attempts made to modify the data en route.

This chapter describes how VPN works, what's involved in planning VPN services, how the VPN service is configured within the Server Admin interface, and how to maintain and monitor the service.

16 ▸ In This Chapter

Introduction to VPN

Planning VPN services

VPN setup and configuration

Managing and monitoring VPN

Introduction to VPN

The VPN service in Snow Leopard Server allows remote clients to authenticate and securely connect to the server in order to access services on the private network, which are unavailable to other outside users because they're blocked by the firewall.

Remote users can use the built-in VPN client in Mac OS X or supplied by Windows or any other VPN client software on any platform that supports standard VPN connections.

VPN transport protocols

In order to maintain the broadest range of VPN clients, Mac OS X Server provides support for two different VPN protocols: PPTP and L2TP/IPsec. The service can support either protocol or both at the same time, although each must reserve its own range of IP addresses for remote users.

PPTP (Point-to-Point Tunneling Protocol)

Originally developed by Microsoft, PPTP VPNs may be required to support older machines prior to Windows XP or Mac OS X Panther 10.3. This legacy option is available from Server Admin only while working in the advanced configuration.

It works by setting up a PPP (Point-to-Point Protocol) connection by using GRE (Generic Routing Encapsulation) as its tunneling protocol. In conjunction with GRE, a management session is maintained on TCP port 1723. To use PPTP, both GRE IP protocol 47 and TCP port 1723 must be allowed through the firewall.

NOTE

GRE is an IP protocol designated as 47, similar to TCP (IP protocol 6) or UDP (IP protocol 17), although no port numbers are associated with GRE, as there are with TCP or UDP. Allow GRE traffic by using an advanced rule in the Server Admin Firewall pane by selecting Other as the protocol and then typing GRE.

L2TP/IPsec (Layer 2 Tunneling Protocol using IPsec encryption)

L2TP is an improvement over PPTP based on technology from Cisco. It's also an IETF standard.

This VPN protocol is preferred for its enhanced security and is configurable from both Server Admin and within Server Preferences for servers in standard or workgroup configuration.

CROSS-REF

For more on setting up L2TP VPN services by using Server Preferences, see Chapter 7.

L2TP/IPsec works by first setting up an Internet Key Exchange (IKE) over UDP port 500, which exchanges a shared secret or certificate to authenticate both parties. IKE also uses UPD port 4500 for NAT transversal if the VPN server is sitting behind NAT.

L2TP tunnels traffic using UDP port 1701, and IPsec encapsulates this traffic by using ESP (Encapsulating Security Payload). To use L2TP, ESP IP protocol 50 and UDP ports 500, 4500, and 1701 must be allowed through the firewall.

Authentication methods

Mac OS X Server's PPTP VPN uses Microsoft's Challenge Handshake Authentication Protocol version 2 (MS-CHAPv2) to authenticate remote users by a username and password, which supplies reasonable security as long as the designated passwords used aren't weak. New in Snow Leopard Server, PPTP now also supports Kerberos authentication.

The L2TP VPN provides superior transport encryption by using IPsec and supports both Kerberos and, optionally, MS-CHAPv2 for authentication.

Kerberos provides SSO authentication by using a Key Distribution Server authority, which is supplied in Mac OS X Server in conjunction with Open Directory. It uses a secret key system to authenticate both the user to the server and the server to the user. This is superior to the encoded passwords sent over the network by MS-CHAPv2.

CROSS-REF
For more on Kerberos, see Chapter 20. For more on Open Directory, see Chapter 21.

To initiate a secure session via IPsec, L2TP additionally requires a shared secret or, optionally, a security certificate. The shared secret is known to both the server and the client and serves as a trust token to initiate the VPN session. The actual authentication of the VPN user is handled by Kerberos or, alternatively, by using an MS-CHAPv2 username and password.

Both PPTP and L2TP can also now be configured to use RADIUS authentication in Snow Leopard Server, obtaining the same user access as AirPort base stations.

CROSS-REF
For more on RADIUS authentication, see Chapter 17.

Remote access for mobile devices

Snow Leopard Server provides a new third option related to VPN service, which Apple calls Mobile Access and which appears as its own pane in Server Admin.

Instead of using conventional VPN tunneling to encapsulate all types of network traffic between a remote user and the local server, Mobile Access uses SSL to encrypt specific types of web and mail traffic used by the iPhone and iPod touch.

This allows mobile users to securely access internal websites, email, contacts, and calendar information on the local server via a proxy that relays encrypted data using an SSL certificate.

Planning VPN Services

Choosing a protocol and authentication method for the VPN service depends on the clients you need to support. If you have legacy PC clients running anything older than Windows XP or Macs running anything prior to Mac OS X 10.3 Panther, you need to configure the PPTP VPN.

L2TP is preferred for its enhanced security, but Mac OS X Server can be used to configure and provide both PPTP and L2TP VPN services at the same time within Server Admin.

Kerberos authentication, and therefore L2TP, is required in order to use the VPN service in an environment where directory services are provided by the Microsoft Active Directory or a Linux OpenLDAP server.

Network limitations

The L2TP and PPTP VPN services are each configured to manage a pool of IP addresses, which are dynamically assigned to remote users when they connect, within the local subnet, similar to DHCP.

These IP address pools must not overlap each other, any static assignments on the local network, the pool of addresses managed by the server's DHCP service, or any other DHCP service operating on the network.

Additionally, the local subnet can't overlap with the private subnet being used by remote users. For example, if the local subnet is `10.0.1.0/24` (and therefore using addresses between `10.0.1.1` and `10.0.1.254`), any remote users who try to connect must use a different subnet, either something like `10.0.2.0/24` (using addresses between `10.0.2.1` and `10.0.2.254`) or `192.168.0.0/16` (using addresses between `192.168.0.1` and `192.168.0.254`).

The remote subnet also can't partially overlap the local subnet by using something like `10.0.0.0/16` (which assigns addresses between `10.0.0.1` and `10.0.254.254`) because it's a supernet of `10.0.1.0/24`.

If the remote and local subnets overlap, the remote system can't properly route traffic to the local network because it ends up with two IP addresses in the same subnet.

A remote client system is typically configured to connect to the VPN and direct all outbound traffic through the VPN to the private network. It can optionally be configured with routing definitions so that only traffic to the private network passes through the encrypted VPN and other Internet requests are directed out its standard route to the Internet. This conserves efforts the server has to make to encrypt the remote user's traffic.

Hardware VPN appliances

An alternative to consider in setting up VPN service is a dedicated hardware appliance. If you expect to support many concurrent remote users, the VPN service imposes a significant load on the server and may likely result in dropped connections.

A hardware VPN concentrator supports hundreds of users, removing that extra processing effort from the server and improving overall reliability. It's important to make sure that any VPN hardware you consider is supported by the built-in client in Mac OS X or you may need to install a third-party VPN client at considerable expense.

Unlike firewall, NAT, and DHCP services, the AirPort base stations don't support VPN service. If your server is participating in a larger organization, VPN services for your network are likely already available.

If using a hardware VPN isn't an option, using routing rules to minimize the amount of remote traffic that travels over the VPN helps, as does using Mobile Access as a lightweight alternative to VPN access for iPhone and iPod touch users.

VPN Setup and Configuration

Configuring VPN settings requires a plan for enabling PPTP, L2TP, or both services — along with collecting information about your current network settings and the type of authentication you'll be using — and may require changes to your firewall configuration to allow incoming VPN traffic from remote users.

Server Preferences

A simplified interface for configuring the VPN service is presented in Server Preferences. This only supports L2TP clients and doesn't support RADIUS authentication, load balancing, or custom network routing definitions.

Server Admin

To configure the more advanced options available in VPN service from Server Admin, first enable the service within the desired server's listing of configured services.

To enable VPN configuration in Server Admin, follow these steps:

1. **Launch Server Admin and then connect to the desired server.**
2. **Select the server listing and then click Settings on the toolbar.**
3. **Click the Services tab.**
4. **Click the check box for VPN.**
5. **Click Save.** VPN should now appear in the list of configurable services for the selected server, as shown in Figure 16.1.

Figure 16.1

VPN configuration in Server Admin

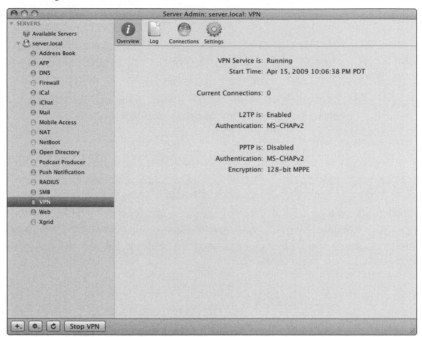

After selecting VPN from the list of services in the Servers list, the Overview page presents a status report of when the service was started, how many active users are connected, which protocols are enabled, and what type of encryption each uses.

The Log page of the VPN pane in Server Admin presents a listing of the events recorded in /var/log/ppp/vpnd.log. The Connections page shows all the currently connected remote users for both PPTP and L2TP, along with their remote IP addresses and the IP address the VPN service has assigned them on the local subnet, as shown in Figure 16.2.

The Settings page presents four tabs for configuring the VPN service:

- **L2TP.** For configuring the IP assignment pool, option load balancing, authentication method, and shared secret for IPsec

- **PPTP.** For configuring the IP assignment pool, authentication method, and the option to use low-security, 40-bit encryption to support older clients

- **Client Information.** For providing DNS servers and search domains to remote users as well as configuring routing definitions to manage what traffic remote users send over the VPN connection

- **Logging.** To enable more verbose event recording

Figure 16.2

VPN connections in Server Admin

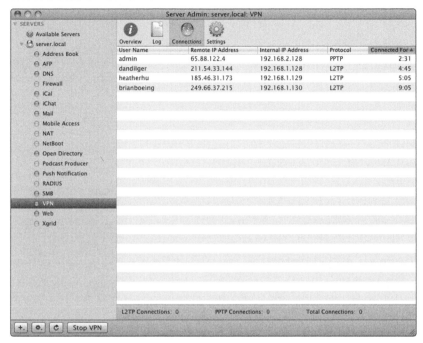

A series of steps are involved in setting up VPN services on Snow Leopard Server.

To set up a VPN in general terms, follow these steps:

1. **Select the protocol needed and the type of authentication desired.** L2TP is preferable, but you may need to also enable PPTP if you have older VPN clients to support. If
   you're already using RADIUS to manage wireless clients, you can also use it to streamline VPN authentication. You can use Kerberos if you have a directory service infrastructure based on Open Directory, Active Directory, or LDAP; otherwise, you need to
   use basic MS-CHAPv2.

2. **Configure all firewalls to allow the traffic as required.** For L2TP, allow ESP IP protocol 50 and UDP ports 500, 4500, and 1701. For PPTP, allow GRE IP protocol 47 and TCP
   port 1723. Create Advanced rules in the Firewall pane to allow this traffic. Optionally,
   VPN traffic can only be allowed for the specific IP addresses of VPN users by using an IP
   Address Group if those addresses are known; however, remote road warriors may frequently need to connect from alternative, unpredictable locations.

3. **Configure VPN settings for the server.** Designate an available range of local IP addresses for each VPN service enabled, and make sure these don't overlap the addresses being used by DHCP or any manual assignments. For L2TP, provide a secure shared secret or generate a certificate. Specify DNS and then type custom routing definitions as desired.

4. **Configure VPN client settings.** Mac OS X clients can use a configuration file to automate this setup, whereas Windows users need to follow instructions for typing the configuration manually.

To configure VPN settings for L2TP, follow these steps:

1. **Select the Settings page from the VPN pane in Server Admin.** The default tab displayed is L2TP, as shown in Figure 16.3.

2. **Click the check box to enable L2TP over IPsec.** Supply a range of local IP addresses for remote users to use that is large enough to accommodate the total number of concurrent connections you expect to maintain. This pool must not overlap any manual or DHCP IP address assignments.

3. **Optionally, enable load balancing by typing the IP address of a cluster server.**

4. **Select a PPP authentication method.** If your system is bound to a Kerberos authentication server, select Kerberos. Otherwise, choose MS-CHAPv2. Alternatively, select RADIUS and then type the IP addresses and shared secrets for the primary and secondary RADIUS servers.

5. **Supply a shared secret or certificate for IPsec authentication.** If you don't have a certificate to use, you can supply a simple shared secret password. It should be at least eight alphanumeric characters and include punctuation but no spaces. This shared secret (or certificate) is also used to configure VPN clients and must be kept secret by users to provide security as a token of trust between the client and server.

6. **Click the Client Information tab and then type the DNS servers for the local subnet and any search domains.** Add network routing definitions to limit the amount of traffic remote users direct over the VPN connection by following the steps outlined shortly.

7. **Click Save.** L2TP over IPsec should now accept incoming requests.

Figure 16.3

L2TP VPN configuration in Server Admin

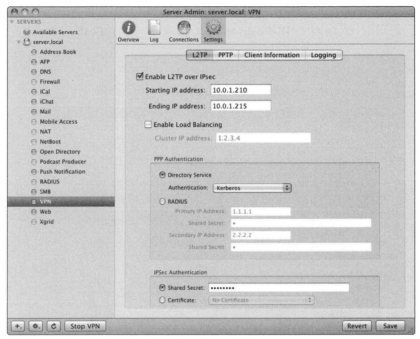

To configure VPN settings for PPTP, follow these steps:

1. **Select the Settings page from the VPN pane in Server Admin.** The default tab displayed is L2TP; select PPTP, shown in Figure 16.4.

2. **Click the check box to enable PPTP.** Type a range of local IP addresses for remote users to use that is large enough to accommodate the total number of concurrent connections you expect to maintain. This pool must not overlap any manual or DHCP IP address assignments or the range specified for L2TP VPN users.

3. **Optionally, allow 40-bit encryption but only if you have older clients that require this.** Reducing encryption security from 128-bit to 40-bit is a major drop in the effective security you're providing for VPN traffic.

4. **Select a PPP authentication method.** If your system is bound to a Kerberos authentication server, select Kerberos; otherwise, choose MS-CHAPv2. Alternatively, select RADIUS and then type the IP addresses and shared secrets for the primary and secondary RADIUS servers.

5. **Click the Client Information tab.** Type the DNS servers for the local subnet and any search domains. Add network routing definitions to limit the amount of traffic remote users will direct over the VPN connection by following the steps outlined shortly.

6. **Click Save.** PPTP should now accept incoming requests.

Figure 16.4

PPTP VPN configuration in Server Admin

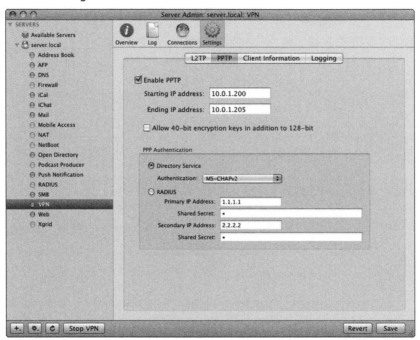

By default, the VPN connection for remote users serves as their default gateway, meaning that all their network traffic forwards through the VPN tunnel.

This includes any public requests for resources, such as web pages, which are forwarded out to the public Internet via the local private network's gateway and are returned through it again and directed back to the remote user through the VPN connection.

This behavior can be customized by configuring custom routing definitions to explicitly limit VPN traffic to include only traffic that needs to use the VPN, leaving everything else to use the remote user's standard gateway to the Internet.

To configure custom network routing definitions, follow these steps:

1. **Click the Client Information tab from the Settings page of the VPN pane in Server Admin, as shown in Figure 16.5.**

Figure 16.5

Custom routing definitions

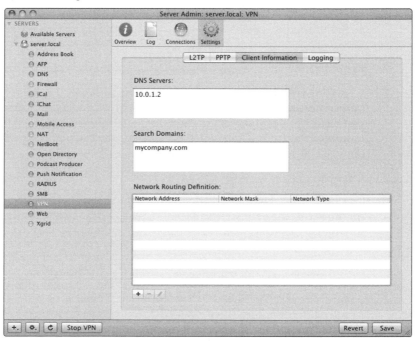

2. **In the Network Routing Definition section, click the Add (+) button and then type an IP address and network mask matching the range of IP addresses you want remote users to route over the VPN connection; for example,** `10.0.1.0` **with subnet mask** `255.255.255.0.`

3. **Select Private to direct this traffic over the VPN connection and then click OK.**

4. **To exclude a portion of a designated private range, add a new route, specifying Public.** This directs that specific traffic to the remote system's local gateway. For example, to prevent a single IP address from using the VPN tunnel, you could specify `10.0.1.100 255.255.255.255` as a Public route. There's no need to define specific public routes, however, because any traffic that doesn't match the designated rules is directed to the remote user's public gateway rather than through the VPN tunnel.

5. **Click Save.** The new routing should now be in effect for all VPN users.

For users to connect to the VPN, they need the DNS name or public IP address of the server, the certificate or shared secret to use L2TP, and their network account and password to log in to either PPTP or L2TP. Once they connect, they should be assigned a DNS server and IP address from the designated VPN pool.

To configure Mac OS X VPN clients, follow these steps:

1. **Select Network from System Preferences.**

2. **Click the Add (+) button, specify VPN as the interface and L2TP over IPsec or PPTP as the VPN type, type a descriptive label for the service name, and then click Create.**

3. **Type the VPN server name and network account name for the user.**

4. **Click Authentication Settings and then type the shared secret under machine authentication or, alternatively, select Certificate and then select the installed certificate.** Under user authentication, type the password or leave this blank to be prompted for the password when connecting. Alternatively, select Kerberos if the client machine is bound to the directory server.

5. **Click OK.**

6. **To share this same configuration with other users, click the Action button marked with the gear icon and then choose Export Configurations from the pop-up menu.** Optionally, select both Export user configurations and Include items from the user's keychain to include the username and password settings supplied. You can also select both Export the machine configuration and Include items from the system keychain to include the shared secret or certificate as part of the configuration file.

7. **Secure access to the resulting configuration file because it includes everything required to connect to the VPN.** Mac OS X users can double-click the file to automatically set up their system to connect to the VPN, needing only to supply their own network username and password, unless they'll all be using Kerberos authentication via the directory service.

Managing and Monitoring VPN Services

From the VPN pane of Server Admin, the Overview page presents a status report of when the VPN service was last started, how many active users are connected, which protocols are enabled, and what type of encryption each is using.

The Log page of the VPN pane in Server Admin presents a listing of the events recorded in `/var/log/ppp/vpnd.log`. The details of logging can be adjusted from the Logging tab of the Settings page. Selecting Verbose logging also increases the size of the log file.

When troubleshooting a failed connection in the VPN service, the logs show how far the client gets before running into a problem. This should indicate if the problem lies with blocked VPN ports in the firewall, NAT transversal problems, an account or client configuration issue, or a routing problem related to the IP subnets on either side of the VPN connection.

The Connections page of the VPN service page in Server Admin shows all the currently connected remote users for both PPTP and L2TP, along with their remote IP addresses and the IP addresses the VPN service has assigned them on the local subnet.

To limit VPN access to specific users by using ACLs, follow these steps:

1. **From Server Admin, select the server name of the VPN server.**

2. **Click Settings on the toolbar and then click the Access tab, shown in Figure 16.6.**

Figure 16.6

VPN service access control

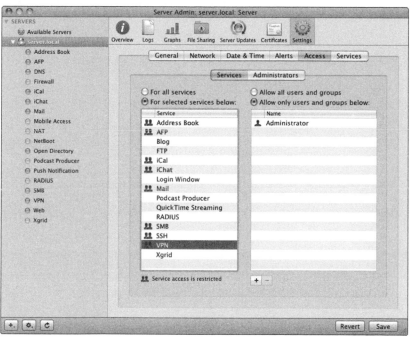

3. **From the Services tab within Access, select the VPN service from the left column.**

4. **Click the Allow only users and groups below radio button.**

5. **Click the Add (+) button.** A Users & Groups sheet opens.

6. **Drag users or groups to the access list on the right to define who has VPN access.**

7. **Click Save.** VPN access is now limited to the selected users.

Summary

- VPN is used to enable remote users to authenticate and gain access to local network resources through the firewall.

- L2TP over IPsec is the preferred method for connecting over the VPN, although PPTP may be required for compatibility with older systems.

- The remote user needs to get a local IP address that's routable from his or her remote location and also valid and not conflicting with any IP assignments on the local network.

- Mac OS X client configuration files can be used to simplify client setup, but the files must be secured because they contain all the information needed to connect to the VPN remotely.

RADIUS Service

RADIUS enables organizations to centrally secure access to network services, including wireless networks and VPNs.

Originally designed as an AAA (Authorization, Authentication, and Accounting) server for authenticating, authorizing, and accounting dial-up users, the RADIUS protocol is used in Snow Leopard Server to manage user access to both external AirPort base stations and the VPN service by using the account information stored in Open Directory.

Supporting RADIUS allows AirPort base stations to tie into third-party authentication systems that use the RADIUS standard; these were originally managed as stand-alone authentication servers but are now more commonly tied into an organization's LDAP directory server infrastructure, such as Microsoft's Active Directory.

Apple's RADIUS implementation leverages the freeRADIUS open-source package. Mac OS X Server integrates the software to use Open Directory for its authentication.

Apple provides RADIUS support in Mac OS X Server almost exclusively to manage users of AirPort base stations, but because it's based on familiar open-source software, it can also be adapted to act as the authentication server for other devices that support RADIUS, such as an external VPN concentrator, a network switch supporting the 802.1X protocol for authenticating wired port access, or other types of Network Access Servers.

This chapter describes how RADIUS works, what's involved in planning RADIUS services, how the RADIUS service is configured within Mac OS X Server's Server Admin interface, and how to maintain and monitor the services.

In This Chapter

17

Introduction to RADIUS

Planning RADIUS services

RADIUS setup and configuration

Managing and monitoring RADIUS

Introduction to RADIUS

If you manage a number of wireless base stations, the RADIUS authentication service in Mac OS X Server can both greatly simplify administration and provide improved security. In addition to Apple's AirPort products, many other commercial-quality Wi-Fi base stations also support the RADIUS standard.

Securing Wi-Fi access using directory services

When AirPort base stations are configured to use RADIUS, access to the wireless network is managed centrally instead of against the internal account database on a base station itself. Both methods use WPA2 (Wi-Fi Protected Access 2) authentication, which replaced the less-secure and now deprecated WEP (Wired Equivalent Privacy), and the original, interim WPA specification, which didn't support the stronger AES (Advanced Encryption Standard) block cipher specified in the 802.11i standard for wireless security.

The authentication performed by an AirPort base station itself is referred to as WPA2-Personal or WPA2-PSK (Pre-Shared Key) and requires the user to only type a simple wireless network passphrase. In contrast, centralized authentication employing a RADIUS server is designated as WPA2-Enterprise and requires the user to present both a username and a password, along with specifying an authentication protocol.

When a wireless user attempts to connect to a wireless network supporting WPA2-Enterprise, the user is first given unauthenticated, limited access to the network in order to present his or her credentials. The user's credentials are then passed from the base station to the RADIUS service via a security standard designated as 802.1X, which supports a variety of different encryption methods under the Extensible Access Protocol (EAP).

The RADIUS service then consults Open Directory to authenticate the user and determine if he or she is authorized to access the network. If the user supplies the correct password and is among the users who have been granted access, RADIUS tells the base station to initiate an authenticated connection; if the wrong credentials are presented or the user hasn't been granted access to the wireless network, his or her attempt to connect to the network is denied.

Snow Leopard Server's VPN service can also use RADIUS as its authentication server, enabling the service to authenticate against the same, centralized RADIUS server as an organization's AirPort base stations, whether or not that RADIUS authentication is being handled by Snow Leopard Server or a third-party system.

CROSS-REF
For more on VPN, see Chapter 16.

Alternatives to using RADIUS

Outside of using RADIUS, AirPort base stations must be configured manually with simpler shared password security and/or MAC network hardware address limitations to control access to specific computers. This is significantly more work and requires constant attention to administering access control in multiple places.

For VPN services, Snow Leopard Server can achieve the same centralized authorization and access control by specifying Kerberos authentication for VPN access directly within Server Admin; in Mac OS X Server, RADIUS simply acts as a mechanism for authenticating network users by using Open Directory and Kerberos security.

CROSS-REF
For more on Kerberos, see Chapter 20. For more on Open Directory, see Chapter 21.

Planning RADIUS Services

Because RADIUS relies on Kerberos and Open Directory for its authentication, planning for RADIUS in Snow Leopard Server is simplified largely to the point of deciding to turn the service on and configure services to use it.

Configuring the RADIUS server by using the supplied tools requires setting up the service with at least one AirPort base station. Again, Apple supplies RADIUS support primarily as a way to substitute the built-in password control in the AirPort base stations with a directory services–backed, central authentication system.

If you don't have AirPorts to manage, it's unlikely you want to activate and use RADIUS, although it's possible to use the service with other third-party Network Access Server devices that support RADIUS after some custom configuration work.

Working with AirPort base stations

AirPort base stations can be manually configured to use RADIUS authentication by using AirPort Utility, from the Access tab, and specifying RADIUS as the MAC address access control type, as shown in Figure 17.1.

However, the configuration tools within Snow Leopard Server make it easier to configure several AirPort base stations at once. As many as 64 base stations can be added within the RADIUS Service Configuration Assistant, which is launched from the Overview page of the RADIUS pane inside Server Admin, as shown in Figure 17.2.

The Configuration Assistant asks the administrator to specify a security certificate and then presents a listing of available AirPort base stations on the network. Each base station requires the configured password of the device to be added to the list of selected base stations that will use RADIUS.

The assistant then presents the option of allowing base station access to all users or limiting access to specific groups. Once this is completed, the assistant shows a confirmation listing of the settings chosen and asks the user to commit the changes, which are then pushed out to the base station units as a configuration update.

Apart from using the assistant, it's also possible within Server Admin to add base stations manually by IP address or to browse for available base stations. Adding a new base station configures the unit to use WPA2-Enterprise for client authentication via EAP-TTLS (Extensible Authentication Protocol-Tunneled Transport Layer Security). It also sets a random shared secret for setting up a trust relationship between the base station and the RADIUS service.

Figure 17.1

RADIUS configuration in AirPort Utility

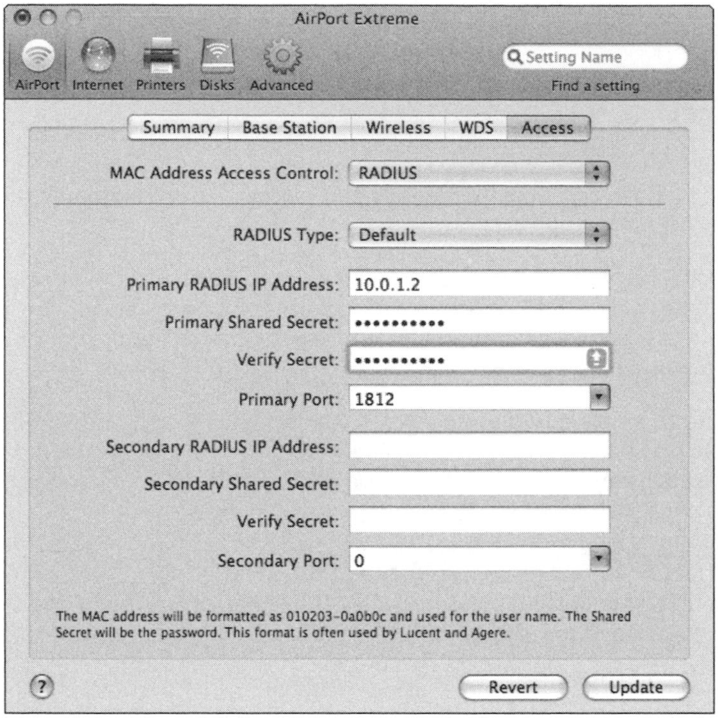

EAP-TTLS extends TLS to establish a secure connection prior to authenticating the user. The protocol uses a Certificate Authority–signed PKI (Public Key Infrastructure) certificate (either acquired from a Certificate Authority or self-signed by Mac OS X Server) to initially authenticate the server with the client.

After the client accepts the server's certificate, the server then sets up a secured connection and authenticates the client through that tunnel. When using EAP-TTLS, the client doesn't need to authenticate with the server first, simplifying configuration because PKI user certificates don't need to be preinstalled on every user's system.

The tunnel in EAP-TTLS protects the user's account name from being exposed in cleartext and helps prevent a man-in-the-middle attack from occurring during authentication.

Figure 17.2

RADIUS AirPort configuration in Server Admin

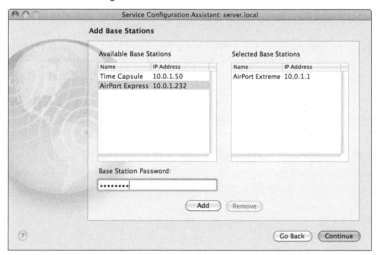

Planning to use security certificates

Snow Leopard Server simplifies the process of setting up and managing PKI certificates. Once a certificate has been either obtained from a Certificate Authority or generated by Snow Leopard Server itself, Server Admin makes it easy to specify it for use in the services that make use of TLS certificates.

Apple commonly refers to SSL certificates throughout the Server Admin interface, although the modern version of Netscape's original SSL specification is now officially referred to as TLS by the IETF standards body.

Using Certificate Assistant, which can be launched from the Certificates page of a server's main pane in Server Admin, administrators can import a private key and public certificate from a Certificate Authority or generate custom, self-signed certificates created by the server.

The certificate acts as a public key; instead of using a simple password or shared secret between the server and the client to encrypt transactions — a method that requires some way to securely distribute the password in advance — public-key cryptography uses a secret private key on the server to encrypt data that can be decrypted by the client by using the public certificate.

The public certificate doesn't need to be secured because it can't be used to forge messages that appear to originate from the server the way a simple password could; it only acts as a decoding key. This enables the client to trust that the information it decrypts by using the public certificate came from the server and wasn't altered along the way. The client must have some basis for trusting that the server's certificate is valid: Either the user must explicitly trust the self-signed certificate it obtains from the server or a trusted Certificate Authority must verifiably sign the certificate, where *sign* means encrypt by a Certificate Authority so the certificate can be decrypted by the Certificate Authority's public certificate.

Mac OS X and other client operating systems ship with a variety of root certificates, which Apple trusts on behalf of the user. Organizations can also install their own root certificate on client machines so those machines automatically trust self-signed certificates the organization creates.

If a client machine lacks a root certificate to verify a given public certificate as being valid, the user has to manually accept the certificate before his or her system can use it.

CROSS-REF

For more on creating and working with certificates in Server Admin, see Chapter 9. For more on PKI certificate security, see Chapter 20.

RADIUS Setup and Configuration

In order to use RADIUS for centralized authentication, the service itself must be set up and turned on, an SSL certificate must be supplied, wireless base stations must be configured to use RADIUS, and individual users and groups must be authorized to use the service.

To configure the RADIUS service from Server Admin, first enable the service within the desired server's listing of configured services.

To enable RADIUS configuration in Server Admin, follow these steps:

1. **Launch Server Admin and then connect to the desired server.**
2. **Select the server listing and then click Settings on the toolbar.**
3. **Click the Services tab.**
4. **Click the check box for RADIUS.**
5. **Click Save.** RADIUS should now appear in the list of configurable services for the selected server, as shown in Figure 17.3.

After selecting RADIUS from the list of services in the Servers list, the Overview page presents a status report of when the service was started and how many base stations are configured to use it. There's also a button to launch the RADIUS service configuration assistant.

The Logs page of the RADIUS pane in Server Admin presents a listing of the events recorded in /Library/Logs/ppp/radiusconfig.log and /var/log/radius/radius.log.

Figure 17.3

The RADIUS pane in Server Admin

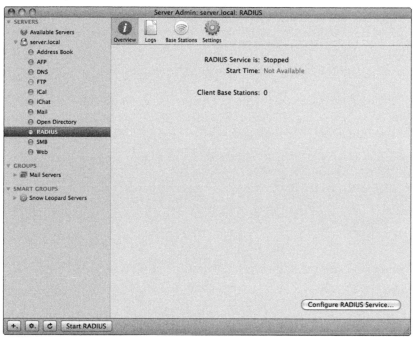

The Base Stations page, shown in Figure 17.4, shows all the currently connected configured AirPort devices set up to use RADIUS for user authentication, enables administrators to add new base stations, and presents a button to save an Internet Connect file for simplifying Mac OS X client machine configuration for accessing the wireless network by using 802.1X and the certificates that WPA2-Enterprise uses.

The Settings page presents a drop-down menu for selecting the public certificate to use for RADIUS as well as a button link for specifying the users or groups to be authorized for access. It also presents a check box for archiving the radiusconfig.log file every set number of days.

A series of steps are involved in setting up RADIUS on Snow Leopard Server.

To set up a RADIUS in general terms, follow these steps:

1. **Obtain SSL certificates to be used for RADIUS.** Certificates can be purchased from a commercial Certificate Authority, such as Verisign, or Snow Leopard Server's certificate assistant can be used to generate a self-signed certificate.

2. **Configure AirPort base stations to use RADIUS.** This can be done manually in Server Admin or by using the configuration assistant.

3. **Select the users or groups to be given authorized access by RADIUS.**

4. **Configure other services that will use RADIUS authentication.** Mac OS X Server's VPN service as well as other third-party VPN and 802.1X secured networking hardware can also be configured to use RADIUS for user authentication.

5. **Turn RADIUS on.** Once activated, AirPorts and other devices can grant access to authorized users by using directory services.

Figure 17.4

The RADIUS Base Stations page in Server Admin

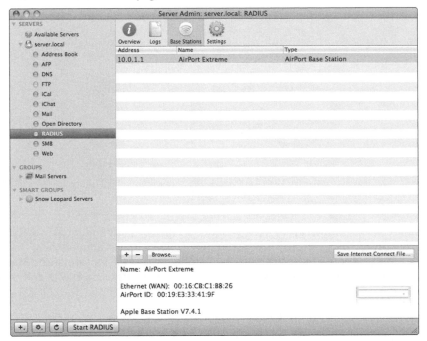

These steps can be automated by using the RADIUS configuration assistant, which leads you through the steps of selecting a certificate, adding base stations, and selecting the allowed users. The assistant can be launched from the Overview page of the RADIUS pane in Server Admin.

If you need to customize any of these steps or edit settings after the fact, the same tasks can be performed within Server Admin outside of the assistant.

To manually configure certificate settings for RADIUS, follow these steps:

1. Click the Settings page from the RADIUS pane in Server Admin.

2. From the pop-up menu, select an installed certificate or choose Manage Certificates to create or import a certificate for use with RADIUS.

3. If you choose Manage Certificates, click the Add (+) button to either Create or Import a certificate identity:

- **Create a Certificate Identity.** This launches the Certificate Assistant, as shown in Figure 17.5.

- **Import a Certificate Identity.** This presents a target for dragging in a private key and public certificate acquired from a Certificate Authority.

Figure 17.5

The Certificate Assistant in Server Admin

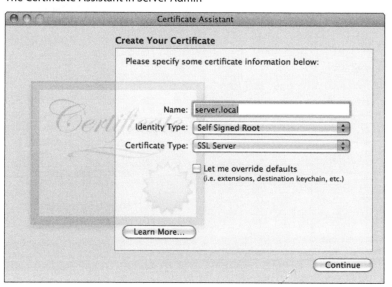

4. After creating or importing the desired certificate identity, return to the Settings page of the RADIUS pane in Server Admin to select the desired RADIUS certificate from the pop-up menu.

5. Click Save.

To manually configure AirPort base stations to use RADIUS, follow these steps:

1. **Click the Base Stations page from the RADIUS pane in Server Admin.**

2. **To manually add a base station by IP address, click the Add (+) button and then type the following details into the sheet that appears:**

- Name of the base station unit (not the wireless network name)
- Type of base station, specifying the model
- IP address of the AirPort
- Shared secret used to allow the server and base station to trust each other (this isn't used for encryption but should still be kept private)
- Verify that the shared secret was typed properly.

3. **Alternatively, browse for base stations and then click Browse to open a sheet with all the local base stations visible on the network, as shown in Figure 17.6.** Simply select the desired base station, type its unit administration password, and then click Add. The base station is configured with a random shared secret and appears in the list among other base stations. Each base station unit must be entered individually.

Figure 17.6

The AirPort base station browser in Server Admin

Choose an AirPort Base Station:

Name	IP Address
Time Capsule	10.0.1.50
AirPort Express	10.0.1.232
AirPort Extreme	10.0.1.1

Name: AirPort Extreme

Ethernet (WAN): 00:16:CB:C1:B8:26
AirPort ID: 00:19:E3:33:41:9F

Apple Base Station V7.4.1

Base station password:

Adding an AirPort Base Station will configure it to use WPA2 Enterprise for client authentication via TTLS. It will also set a random Shared Secret for communication between the base station and the RADIUS service on the server.

Cancel   Add

Once the desired base stations are all configured to use RADIUS, you can use the Save Internet Connect File button to generate a configuration file for setting up Mac OS X desktop computers to access the WPA2-Enterprise settings of the wireless network.

This simplifies the client configuration process, which would otherwise require manually typing the network name and specifying the type of 802.1X encryption to be used. Users can optionally type their username and password into their AirPort configuration or type it when connecting.

To manually configure the users authenticated via RADIUS, follow these steps:

1. **From Server Admin, select the server name of the RADIUS server.**

2. **Click the Settings page and then click the Access tab, as shown in Figure 17.7.**

Figure 17.7

RADIUS user authentication in Server Admin

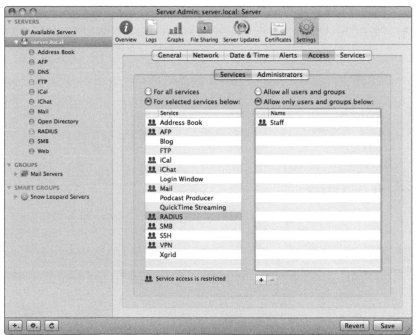

3. **From the Services tab within Access, select the RADIUS service from the left column.**

4. **Above the right-hand column, click the Allow only users and groups below radio button.**

5. **Click the Add (+) button.** A Users & Groups sheet opens.

6. **Drag users or groups to the access list on the right to define who has RADIUS access.**

7. **Click Save.** RADIUS access is limited to the selected users for all devices that use RADIUS for authentication.

For users to connect to a RADIUS-secured Wi-Fi network, they can simply browse for the wireless network name and then type their network account name and password.

Managing and Monitoring RADIUS

From the RADIUS pane of Server Admin, the Overview page presents a status report of when the VPN service was last started and how many client base stations are configured to use the service.

The Logs page of the RADIUS pane in Server Admin presents a listing of the service-related events recorded in `/var/log/radius/radius.log` and configuration-related events saved to `/Library/Logs/ppp/radiusconfig.log`. The archiving of event logs can be managed from the Settings page.

When troubleshooting a failed connection in the RADIUS service, the logs may help indicate whether the problem is between the user and the base station or whether it's related to RADIUS authentication between the base station and the server.

Summary

- RADIUS is used to enable wireless base station users to authenticate and gain access to wireless networks by using their directory services user account and password (WPA2-Enterprise) rather than using a simple shared network password to manage network access on the base station itself (WPA2-Personal).
- Snow Leopard Server's WPA2-Enterprise implementation uses an 802.1X configuration that specifies EAP-TTLS authentication.
- The EAP-TTLS encryption RADIUS uses requires a certificate, either obtained from a commercial Certificate Authority or generated by Certificate Assistant within Snow Leopard Server.
- Once configured for AirPort base stations, RADIUS can also be used to authenticate VPN users or other Network Access Server devices supporting 802.1X security.

Xgrid Service

Xgrid is a feature of Mac OS X Snow Leopard Server that simplifies the creation, deployment, and management of computational grids, which distribute jobs across multiple computers to employ the idle capacity of those machines to perform complex tasks.

Xgrid enables users to submit jobs to be processed by a centrally managed cluster or by an ad hoc grid of Xgrid agent systems that are made available to handle jobs managed by an Xgrid controller.

Xgrid can be used to turn an organization's desktop machines into a distributed grid with super computing power at very little cost.

Because the Xgrid agent software is preinstalled with Mac OS X Leopard or later systems and is available for previous versions of the operating system, client systems are ready to be activated to turn their idle processors into a productive computing system cluster.

Apple notes the following features for Xgrid:

- Easy grid configuration and deployment
- Simple and flexible job submission
- Automatic controller discovery by agents and clients
- A flexible architecture based on open standards
- Support for the Unix security model, including password or Kerberos SSO authentication
- Choice between a command-line interface or an API-based model for grid interaction

This chapter describes how Xgrid works, what's involved in planning computational grid deployment, how it's configured, and how to maintain and monitor grids.

Introduction to Xgrid

When jobs are submitted, Xgrid breaks the jobs down into multiple tasks and distributes them among multiple nodes. These nodes can be:

- Desktop Macs running Mac OS X Tiger v10.4 or later
- Mac servers running Mac OS X Tiger Server v10.4 or later

Because many systems sit idle during the day, in the evening, or on weekends, the application of these systems into a computational grid is referred to as *desktop recovery*.

Building grids from otherwise idle systems enables you to greatly improve computational capacity without any new hardware purchases. The Xgrid software included with Mac OS X Server makes grid configuration straightforward.

Systems in a cluster are typically homogeneous, co-located, and strictly managed. In contrast, an ad hoc grid can be loosely coupled, located anywhere, and doesn't necessarily need to be identically configured or have the same specifications.

Large rendering or simulation jobs can be distributed across all the systems in an office overnight; the same systems can also be used to augment a dedicated computational cluster available to Xgrid clients at all times.

Xgrid components

Xgrid handles collections of execution instructions that can include data and executables. It can run scripts, utilities, custom software, and anything that doesn't require any user interaction.

Distributed processing in Xgrid is handled through a three-tiered model that:

- Accepts tasks from a client
- Triages them through a controller
- Executes them on available agents

Agents

Xgrid agents handle the computational tasks of a job. In Mac OS X, the Xgrid agent software is turned off by default, but when an agent is enabled from the Sharing pane of System Preferences, shown in Figure 18.1, it activates at next startup and looks for a controller it can register with to receive any available tasks.

An agent can use Kerberos authentication to register with the controller, can use regular password authentication, or can be configured to not use any authentication. This exposes the agent to the potential of allowing unauthorized access.

The controller sends the agent instructions and data related to jobs the controller is managing. The agent handles the assigned tasks and returns the results back to the controller.

By default, agents seek to bind to the first available controller found. An agent can only bind to a single controller. You can alternatively configure the agent to bind to a specific controller, as shown in the Sharing pane configuration sheet in Figure 18.2.

Figure 18.1

Xgrid Agent configuration in System Preferences

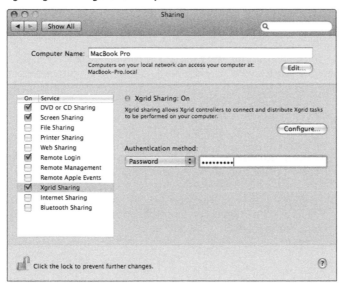

Figure 18.2

Xgrid agent binding options

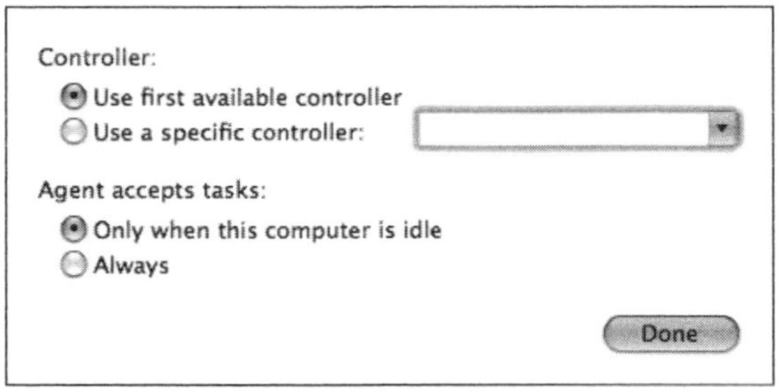

You can specify whether an agent is always available or limit it to accepting jobs only when the system is idle. The agent is considered idle when it has no mouse or keyboard input; it doesn't factor in actual CPU or network activity.

If a user begins work on an agent system currently running a grid task, the agent continues to perform the task until it's finished.

The default agent setting on Mac OS X Server is to run as a dedicated agent, while the desktop Mac OS X settings are configured by default to only accept tasks when the system has had no user input for 15 minutes.

Clients

Any system can act as an Xgrid client as long as it's minimally running at least Mac OS X Tiger v10.4 or later and has a network route to the Xgrid controller. A client can generally connect only with a single controller.

Depending on the controller's configuration, the client must authenticate with a domain password or via Kerberos SSO before submitting a job to the grid.

A client user submits a job to the controller by using the Xgrid command-line tool. The job can target a specific Xgrid controller or use Bonjour's multicast DNS to dynamically discover an available controller.

When the job is completed by its assigned agent, the controller notifies the client, and the client can then retrieve the results of the job from the controller.

Controllers

An Xgrid controller accepts jobs from clients and manages communications between the computational agent resources of the grid. Acting as a controller requires Mac OS X Leopard Server v10.5 or later.

The controller advertises its presence on the network via Bonjour and accepts connections from clients and agents. Clients submit jobs to the controller, which parcels the jobs out into tasks, assigns the tasks to available agents, accepts the results of the task back, and notifies the client that the job is complete, enabling the client to obtain the results of the job.

Multiple Xgrid controllers can be running on the same subnet, but there can only be one controller of a given grid. Clients typically deal with a single controller, and agents are bound to either the first controller found or to the specific controller they're assigned to bind with.

A controller can manage any number of available agents; Apple reports having tested Xgrid to work with as many as 128 agents per controller. There are no software limits on the number of agents a controller can use.

Computational grids

Xgrid provides a lot of flexibility in how it can be deployed. There are three main types of computational grids:

- Xgrid clusters
- Local grids
- Distributed grids

Xgrid clusters

Systems in a cluster are dedicated to computation. They're often deployed co-located in the same rack with high-performance networking interconnects and managed for optimum performance.

They commonly have identical hardware specifications for their processor, RAM, and disk storage and are set up to run the same versions of their software.

Each cluster server runs Xgrid agent software, and the head node operates as an Xgrid controller.

Because the systems are dedicated for computational tasks, they're always online and ready, job failure rates are usually very low, and they don't need to share their available resources with other general user tasks.

Cluster configuration grids are subsequently the most efficient model of distributed computing but also the most expensive.

Local grids

Idle systems within a managed environment available to a company or university computer lab are easily assembled into a grid for desktop recovery.

Because the systems are managed by a single organization and are available on the same LAN, they can provide good network performance and substantial manageability for use by Xgrid as members of a local grid.

However, jobs running on these systems may be interrupted as they resume regular use or are reset or disconnected from the network. This can cause Xgrid tasks to fail, resulting in the Xgrid controller needing to reassign the failed tasks to another available agent.

The performance of a local grid depends on how many agents are available, the failure rate of jobs because of interruptions, and the capacity of individual machines to contribute their resources toward computational productivity.

Distributed grids

Xgrid can also be used to allow other systems to donate time to the computational grid, forming a distributed grid.

A user can configure the Xgrid agent on his or her system to specify the IP address or hostname for an Xgrid controller, dedicating his or her available CPU time to that controller's grid regardless of where the controller is located.

The controller administrator doesn't need to have any direct management control or knowledge of the agent system to be able to tap into its available processing capacity.

Because of the greater amount of unmanaged chaos introduced by random Xgrid agent participants, a distributed grid can experience very high failure rates for jobs but also lack any administrative burden for the grid owner.

In very large jobs, high rates of task failures may not be a significant problem if failed tasks can be quickly reassigned to other available agents.

Additionally, because data is being sent over the Internet rather than over a local network, the network performance of agents connected to a distributed grid can become an issue.

Distributed grids subsequently offer the least efficient model of distributed computing but are also the least expensive.

Xgrid Admin

After configuring an Xgrid controller, you can use Xgrid Admin to manage the grid. Xgrid Admin — supplied with the Server Admin tools installed on Snow Leopard Server within the `/Applications/Server` folder and available for installation on an administrative computer by using the server tools package on the installer DVD — can manage multiple logical grids on each controller. Agents can only belong to one grid and must finish their assigned tasks before being moved between grids.

Xgrid Admin is used to:

- Check the status of a grid and its activity, including the number of agents working and available, processing power in use and available on each, and the number of jobs running and pending
- Add or remove controllers from its management console
- Add or remove computational grids on each controller
- See a list of agents in a grid and the CPU power available and in use for each agent
- Add or remove agents in a grid
- See a list of jobs in a grid, the date and time each job was submitted, current progress, the active CPU power for the job, and tasks
- Remove jobs in a grid
- Stop a job in progress
- Restart a job that was stopped or is complete

The Overview page of Xgrid Admin, shown in Figure 18.3, presents a list of controllers in its source list, along with a sublisting of logical grids created on that controller.

Figure 18.3

The Xgrid Admin Overview page

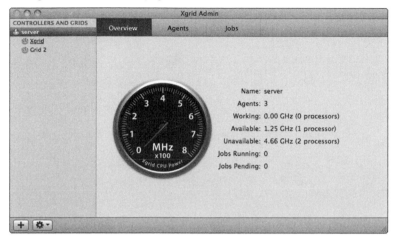

The main pane of the application shows the name of the selected controller or grid and lists its current status, including:

- The number of assigned agents available
- The number of working processor cores and the total GHz in use
- The number of available processor cores and the total GHz available
- The number of unavailable processor cores and the total GHz represented
- The number of jobs running
- The number of jobs pending

Additional grids can be created on a controller by using the Add (+) button to choose Add Grid from the pop-up menu. Name the grid, and it appears in the list under the selected controller.

Additional controllers can be monitored by adding them with the Add (+) button and choosing Add Controller from the pop-up menu. Type the DNS name or IP address of the controller, authenticate to it, and then it appears in the source list with its defined grids.

The Action button is used to disconnect a selected controller or remove it from the list. If you select a grid, you can rename it, remove it, or make it the default grid. The default grid for a controller is underlined in the list.

The Agents page, shown in Figure 18.4, presents a listing of agents connected to the selected controller or grid. Each agent has a graphical status indicator:

- Clear means the agent is offline.
- Green means the agent is working.
- Yellow means the agent is available but not running.
- Red means the agent is unavailable.

Figure 18.4

The Xgrid Admin Agents page

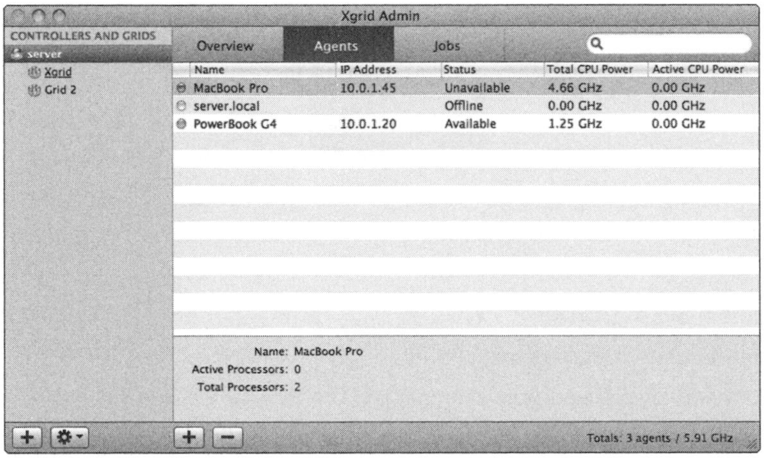

Controls below the agent listing allow you to add or remove agents from a grid or controller.

The Jobs page, shown in Figure 18.5, presents a listing of jobs running or queued up on the selected controller or grid. Each job has a graphical status indicator:

- Clear means the job is pending.
- Gray means the job is submitting.
- Green means the job is running.
- Red means the job has failed or cancelled.
- Blue means the job is complete.

Controls below the job listing allow you to add, remove, stop, or pause jobs from the selected grid or controller.

Figure 18.5

The Xgrid Admin Jobs page

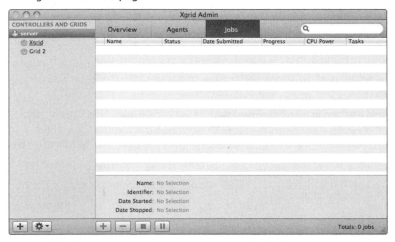

Planning Xgrid Distributed Processing

In preparing to set up Xgrid, you need to evaluate your security, hardware, and networking needs. Consider the types of tasks your distributed processing grid will accept, the sensitivity of any data being used, the degree of control you exercise over available agents, and whether you already have strong authentication systems in place.

The minimum agent hardware and networking resources required will also depend on the type, complexity, and volume of distributed jobs you'll be performing across the grid.

Security

Xgrid communications between the controller and its clients and agents can be configured to require authentication or not use any.

Authentication settings for the Xgrid controller are configured by using Server Admin, with separate authentication settings for agents and clients. Both can be configured to use:

- **SSO Kerberos authentication.** This is the preferred setting, as it enables users to authenticate against their directory accounts and offers SSO. Kerberos is the natural choice if:
  - You already have Kerberos in use.
  - You have administrative control over all agents and clients in use.
  - The jobs you run require special privileges, such as local, network, or SAN file system access.

To use Kerberos authentication, the Xgrid controller must be configured for Kerberos, must be in the same realm as the server running the Kerberos domain controller system, and must be bound to the Open Directory master. Each Xgrid participant must have a Kerberos principal. The clients and agents obtain ticket-granting tickets for their principal, which is used to obtain a service ticket for the controller service principal. The controller looks at the ticket granted to the client to determine the user's principal and verifies it with the relevant SACLs and groups to determine privileges. Agents use the host principal, and the controller uses the Xgrid service principal, found in the `/etc/krb5.keytab` file.

- **Password authentication defined within Server Admin.** This uses a simple shared secret that each client provides rather than unique passwords for individual users that Kerberos manages. You may be unable to require Kerberos authentication because:

  - You may lack a Kerberos server or your realm may not trust potential Xgrid clients.

  - You want to use agents across the Internet or that are outside your control.

  - You may want to operate an ad hoc grid without the ability or resources to configure trust relationships with your agents.

- **No authentication.** Not using authentication is appropriate only for testing in a private network at home or in a lab that's inaccessible from any untrusted systems or when none of the jobs or the computers contain sensitive or important information.

Hardware and network requirements

To act as an agent in a grid, Xgrid requires Mac OS X Tiger v10.4 or later. Agents need to be fast enough and have enough RAM and storage to offer significant available processing power compared to their potential for job failure. They also need to have a suitably fast network connection.

Xgrid agents handling the distributed processing of Podcast Producer workflows need a graphics card capable of supporting Quartz Extreme.

CROSS-REF
For more on Podcast Producer, see Chapter 30.

The number of Xgrid node agents you need and can use depends on your workload:

- The number of jobs you'll be handling
- The submission schedule for rush hour jobs
- The type and complexity of jobs being managed, which determines both the time needed to complete a job and how many of its tasks can be performed in parallel

The more Xgrid nodes you use, the more network bandwidth you need. For some tasks, an Xsan shared file system may be required to provide the necessary bandwidth to process the data between nodes.

The minimum requirements for a server to function as an Xgrid controller is Mac OS X Tiger Server v10.4 or later and network access.

To work with multiple Xgrid agents, you need fast network connectivity and access to enough fast storage to accommodate the size of the jobs and their data you're computing.

The primary requirement for a controller is that it must be network-accessible to clients and agents. If access to port 4111 is blocked by the organizational firewall, the controller may need to be located outside in a DMZ.

If the controller can be located on the same subnet, clients and agents can discover the controller via Bonjour. If that's not possible, the controller needs a static IP address and/or the appropriate DNS entries to allow proper name resolution.

Xgrid Setup and Configuration

To configure Xgrid within Server Admin, first enable the service within the desired server's listing of configured services and then do the following:

- Run the configuration assistant.
- Review controller settings.
- Review server agent settings.
- Configure service access settings.
- Configure client agents.

To enable Xgrid configuration in Server Admin, follow these steps:

1. **Launch Server Admin and then connect to the desired server.**

2. **Select the server listing and then click Settings on the toolbar.**

3. **Click the Services tab.**

4. **Click the check box for Xgrid.**

5. **Click Save.** Xgrid should now appear in the list of configurable services for the selected server, as shown in Figure 18.6.

Figure 18.6

The Xgrid pane in Server Admin

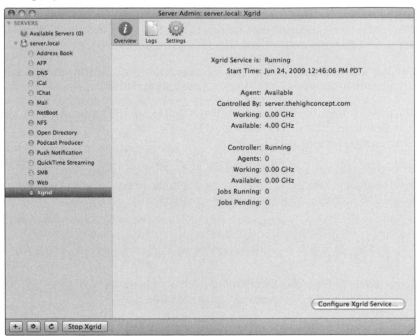

Configuring the Xgrid service

The required steps needed to set up Xgrid can be automatically configured by using the Service Configuration Assistant launched from the Xgrid pane in Server Admin.

To configure initial Xgrid services using the assistant, follow these steps:

1. **Launch Server Admin and then connect to the desired server.**

2. **Click Xgrid.**

3. **Click the Overview tab and then click Configure Xgrid Service.** The assistant, shown in Figure 18.7, opens.

4. **Click Continue.**

5. **Click one of the following radio buttons, shown in Figure 18.8, and then click Continue:**

- **Host a Grid.** This configures the server as an Xgrid agent and controller and sets up a network file system.

- **Join a Grid.** This only sets up the Xgrid agent and searches for a controller on the network to bind itself to.

Figure 18.7

The Service Configuration Assistant

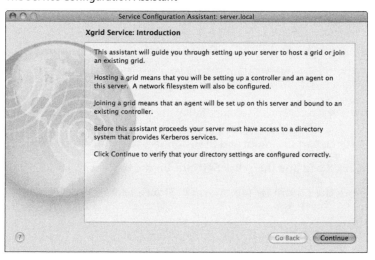

Figure 18.8

Choosing a configuration in the assistant

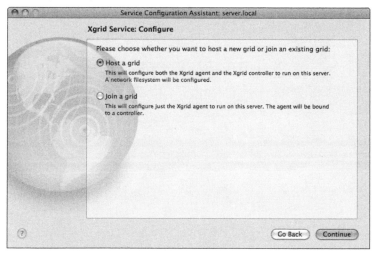

6. **Authenticate as a directory administrator to configure the shared file system.** You can delay configuration by leaving this blank.

7. **Click Continue.**

8. **Confirm the settings overview presented and then click Continue.**

9. **Click Close to complete the assistant.**

Configuring an Xgrid controller

Because the configuration assistant sets up your entire configuration for you, you probably only need to review the settings in Server Admin.

To review the Xgrid controller settings, follow these steps:

1. **Launch Server Admin and then connect to the desired server.**

2. **Click Xgrid and then click Settings on the toolbar.**

3. **Click the Controller tab, shown in Figure 18.9.**

Figure 18.9

Configuring the Xgrid controller in Server Admin

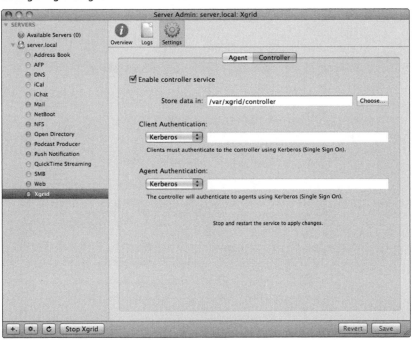

4. **Click the Enable controller service check box.**

5. **Choose the data store location that saves shared data between agents and clients.** The default location is `/var/xgrid/controller`.

6. **Choose a Client Authentication from the pop-up menu.** The options are:
   - Kerberos authentication
   - Password, using the supplied shared secret
   - No authentication

7. **Choose an Agent Authentication from the pop-up menu.** The options are:
   - Kerberos authentication
   - Password, using the supplied shared secret
   - No authentication

8. **Click Save.**

Configuring an Xgrid agent

Because the configuration assistant sets up your entire configuration for you, you probably only need to review the settings in Server Admin.

To review the Xgrid agent settings, follow these steps:

1. **Launch Server Admin and then connect to the desired server.**

2. **Click Xgrid and then click Settings on the toolbar.**

3. **Click the Agent tab, shown in Figure 18.10.**

4. **Click the Enable agent service check box.**

5. **Choose the controller to use:**
   - **Use first available controller.** This discovers the controller via Bonjour and binds to the first available system.
   - **Use a specific controller.** If your server is configured to act as the controller, it pre-populates this field with the local address.

6. **Click the radio button for one of the Agent accepts tasks options:**
   - **Only when this computer is idle.** Waits for 15 minutes of no user input.
   - **Always.** The default setting for the server. It accepts and begins work on all available tasks queued up by the controller.

7. **Choose the Controller Authentication method from the pop-up menu.** The options must match the controller settings and are:
   - Kerberos authentication, the default for the server

- Password, using the supplied shared secret
- No authentication

8. **Click Save.**

Figure 18.10

Configuring the Xgrid agent in Server Admin

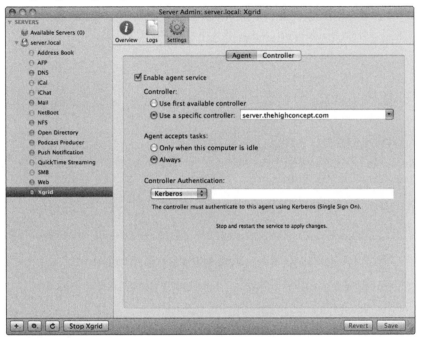

To limit access to the Xgrid service in Server Admin, follow these steps:

1. **From Server Admin, select the server name of the contact server.**

2. **Click Access on the toolbar and then click the Services tab, shown in Figure 18.11.**

3. **From the Services pane within Access, click the Xgrid service in the left column.**

4. **Click the Allow only users and groups below radio button above the right column.**

5. **Click the Add (+) button.** The Users & Groups sheet opens.

6. **Drag users or groups to the access list on the right to define users who can have Xgrid access.**

7. **Click Save.**

Figure 18.11

Configuring access to the Xgrid service in Server Admin

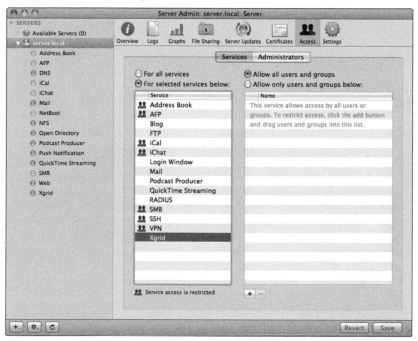

To configure client systems as Xgrid agents, follow these steps:

1. **Launch System Preferences.**

2. **Click the Sharing icon.**

3. **Click the Xgrid Sharing: On radio button.**

4. **Choose an Authentication method to match the Xgrid controller:**

- Kerberos authentication, the default for the server
- Password, using the supplied shared secret
- No authentication

5. **Click Configure.** A sheet drops down.

6. **Choose the controller to use:**

- **Use first available controller.** This discovers the controller via Bonjour and binds to the first available system at boot. This is the default setting.
- **Use a specific controller.**

7. **Click a radio button for one of the Agent accepts tasks:**

  - **Only when this computer is idle.** Waits for 15 minutes of no user input. This is the default setting for client systems.

  - **Always.** Accepts and begins work on any available tasks sent by the controller.

8. **Click Done.**

You can also roll out managed preferences for machines configured to use your directory server that enable and configure Xgrid sharing.

CROSS-REF

For more on managed preferences, see Chapter 36.

Managing and Monitoring Xgrid Services

Xgrid Admin is used to manage and monitor jobs and available agents on your controllers' grids.

To review the Xgrid controller status, follow these steps:

1. **Launch Xgrid Admin.**

2. **Type the name of the controller you want to monitor and then authenticate with it if you're prompted.** If you're not prompted, click the Add (+) button and then choose Add Controller from the pop-up menu.

3. **Click the Controller server icon.** From the Overview tab, the status report shows:

  - The number of assigned agents available

  - The number of working processor cores and the total GHz in use

  - The number of available processor cores and the total GHz available

  - The number of unavailable processor cores and the total GHz represented

  - The number of jobs running

  - The number of jobs pending

4. **To remove a controller from the listing, select the controller, click the Action button marked with a gear icon, and then choose Remove Controller from the pop-up menu.**

5. **To add additional grids to your controller, click the Add (+) button, choose Add Grid from the pop-up menu, and then type a name for the new grid.**

6. **To remove a grid from your controller, select the grid, click the Action button marked with a gear icon, and then choose Remove Grid from the pop-up menu.**

To review the Xgrid agent status, follow these steps:

1. **Launch Xgrid Admin.**

2. **Type the name of the controller you want to monitor and then authenticate with it if you're prompted.**

3. **Click the server icon of the controller or grid you want to monitor agents on from the source list.**

4. **Click Agents.** This page presents a status report that shows all known agents and shows the following information for each:

- The configured agents by name
- The IP address of each agent
- The current status of the agent
- The total CPU power in GHz available to the agent
- The active CPU power in GHz currently in use for Xgrid tasks

Selecting an agent listing presents additional detail in the pane below it:

- The number of active processor cores
- The number of available processor cores

Individual agent listings are also marked with colored indicators to make their current status more obvious:

- Clear means the agent is offline.
- Green means the agent is working.
- Yellow means the agent is available but not running.
- Red means the agent is unavailable.

5. **To add additional agents to your selected controller or grid, click the Add (+) button and then type a name for the new agent.**

6. **To move an agent from one grid or controller to another, you have to remove the agent and then add it manually.** You can't drag agents between grids to reassign them. Some agents may specify a specific controller in their binding configuration, making it impossible to reassign them.

7. **To remove an agent from your selected controller or grid, select the agent and then click the Delete (–) button.**

To review the Xgrid job status, follow these steps:

1. **Launch Xgrid Admin.**

2. **Type the name of the controller you want to monitor and then authenticate with it.**

3. **Click the server icon of the controller or grid you want to monitor jobs on from the source list.**

4. **Click Jobs.** This page presents a status report that shows all current jobs and shows the following information for each:

- Job name
- Current status of the job
- Date it was submitted
- Current progress
- CPU power it's currently consuming
- Number of tasks involved

Selecting a job listing presents additional detail in the pane below it:

- The job's identifier number
- Time stamp showing when it was started
- Time stamp showing when it was stopped

Individual job listings are also marked with colored indicators to make their current status more obvious:

- Clear means the job is pending.
- Gray means the job is submitting.
- Green means the job is running.
- Red means the job has failed or cancelled.
- Blue means the job is complete.

Controls below the job listing allow you to remove, stop, or pause jobs from the selected grid or controller. You can't move jobs between grids or between controllers.

Monitoring Xgrid logs

System, controller, and agent logs for Xgrid are available from the Logs page of Server Admin's Xgrid pane, shown in Figure 18.12:

- The Xgrid System Log, located at `/var/log/system.log`
- The Xgrid Controller Log records error messages generated by `xgridcontrollerd`, located at `/Library/Logs/Xgrid/xgridcontrollerd.log`.
- The Xgrid Agent Log records error messages generated by `xgridagentd`, located at `/Library/Logs/Xgrid/xgridagentd.log`.

Figure 18.12

The Logs page of the Xgrid pane

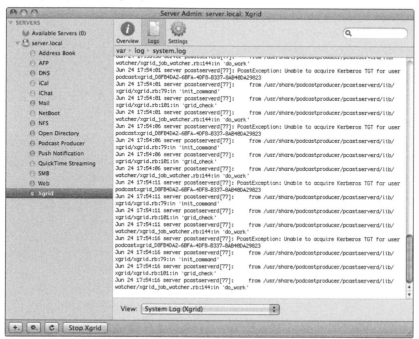

Summary

- Mac OS X Server supplies an Xgrid service for setting up a controller to manage computational grids of agents. Clients can submit jobs to the grid controller and obtain notifications when the jobs are complete.

- Grids can range from clusters of dedicated machines to local grids that use the idle capacity of managed workstations in an organization to distributed grids that aggregate whatever machines they can gain access to, with each type offering a different balance between deployment cost and overall efficiency.

- Mac clients starting with Tiger can be assigned to a grid as agents by enabling Xgrid sharing in System Preferences. Some tasks may require specialized hardware on the agent. For example, Podcast Producer submits tasks that require the agent to have graphics processors capable of handling Quartz Extreme.

- Xgrid Admin can be used to view the status of grid controllers, agents, and jobs.

19 Other Network Services

S now Leopard Server runs a variety of other important core network services, some of which are required to properly run a Mac OS X Server environment. This chapter describes how these additional core services work, what's involved in planning them, how the services are configured, and how to maintain and monitor them.

Introduction to Other Network Services

Snow Leopard Server has other network services that are vital to properly running Mac OS X Server. These services include:

- Network Time Protocol (NTP) for syncing network time services
- Simple Network Management Protocol (SNMP) for event logging
- Secure Shell (SSH) for remote login
- Virtual Network Computing (VNC) for remote screen sharing
- Remote Management for use with Apple Remote Desktop

In This Chapter

Introduction to other network services

Managing and monitoring other network services

Network Time Protocol

NTP synchronizes network clocks using UTC (Coordinated Universal Time), a global standard for tracking the mean solar time maintained by the Royal Observatory in Greenwich. UTC compensates for the slowing of Earth's rotation by adding leap seconds at irregular intervals to the time calculated by atomic clocks in order to reflect the time maintained as Greenwich Mean Time (GMT).

Authoritative NTP servers, referred to as Stratum 1 servers, maintain the current UTC time. Secondary servers, known as Stratum 2 and 3 servers, regularly request the time from Stratum 1 servers and estimate the delay in sending and receiving updates, using this calculation to set their own clocks and to serve accurate time signals to other systems. Time estimates are kept accurate to a nanosecond.

Client computers use NTP to request the time from these servers, convert the UTC time to their set time zone, and then use this to correct their local clock settings. Apple provides a Stratum 2 time server at `time.apple.com`, and Macs are set by default to automatically update their internal clocks to this server. NTP uses UDP port 123.

By enabling NTP on Mac OS X Server, the local server can keep its clock in sync with Apple or any other authoritative NTP server and also provide a local NTP time service for client computers to use. Clients can be configured to use the local server within the Time & Date pane of System Preferences or this setting can be applied as a managed preference.

CROSS-REF
For more on using managed preferences, see Chapter 36.

NTP is enabled by default on Snow Leopard Server, and the system is configured to obtain its time settings from Apple's server.

Configuring client computers to obtain their time from the local server rather than over the Internet isn't critical, but client computers should have their clocks set automatically instead of simply having their time and date settings in System Preferences set manually.

Choosing to configure network clients to obtain their time from the local server may help reduce unnecessary outbound traffic.

To check the status of a server's NTP configuration in Server Admin, follow these steps:

1. **Launch Server Admin and then connect to the desired server.**

2. **Select the server listing and then click Settings on the toolbar.**

3. **Click the General tab, shown in Figure 19.1.** Note the selected check box for NTP.

4. **Click the Date & Time tab.** Note the check box for Set date & time automatically. By default, it's set to `time.apple.com`.

5. **To update any changes, click Save.** Clients may access NTP on the local server to set their own clocks.

To manually set local systems to obtain their time from the local server, follow these steps:

1. **Launch System Preferences and then select the Date & Time pane.**

2. **Click the Set date & time automatically check box.** By default, it's set to `Apple Americas/US (time.apple.com)` or the corresponding server for Asia or Europe.

3. **Specify the local time server by using its DNS name, such as** `server.example.com`. The local system now acquires its time from the server.

Figure 19.1

The General pane in Server Admin

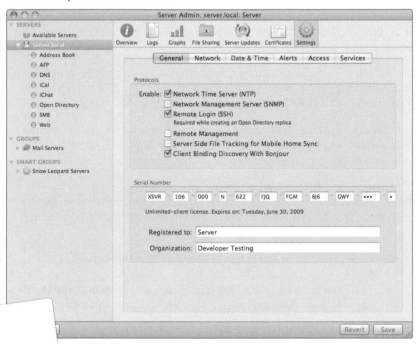

...ork Management Protocol

...ed method for reporting events to a centralized management server. An
...ce (also called a network element) uses a software agent to report a config-
...cal variables representing the device's current status to a network man-
...system (NMS).

In the case of Snow Leopard Server, the agent is a process called snmpd, derived from the
open-source package Net-SNMP. The agent is preinstalled but not configured; before turning
the service on in Server Admin, a command-line configuration tool named snmpconf must be
used to generate two configuration files:

- snmpd.conf, which configures access control for the service and the general system
  setup of the server, including its location and some contact information
- snmp.conf, which sets up the service to use that same access control information

A variety of Object Identifiers (OIDs) can be configured to report variables such as RAM use,
disk capacity, network throughput, CPU load and temperatures, and even a list of running
processes. This information is reported to an NMS, such as InterMapper, Lithium, or the free RRDtool,

each of which can centrally monitor a variety of SNMP-managed devices across an organization, including network switches, uninterruptible power supplies, printers, client computers, firewalls, routers, and AirPort base stations.

Snow Leopard Server supports SNMP v1, SNMP v2c, and SNMP v3 over either IPv4 or IPv6; the default access protocol is SNMP v2. The default ports used by SNMP are UDP 161 and 162.

The default read-only community string is public, so configuring access control for the service is important to do before enabling it; otherwise, anyone with a network route to the server can obtain and read a variety of configuration and status information.

SNMP is disabled by default on Snow Leopard Server, and the system must be configured before activating the service because its initial settings are neither secure nor very useful for reporting data.

Choosing to enable SNMP largely relates to whether you currently operate remote management features for other devices. Adding Snow Leopard Server to an existing SNMP NMS is fairly easy to do by simply running though the command-line assistant used to configure its reporting settings and set its access control.

To configure and activate SNMP for the server, follow these steps:

1. **Prior to activating the SNMP service, open Terminal and then configure SNMP by typing** sudo /usr/bin/snmpconf –i. The tool presents a menu of files to configure.

2. **Type** 1 **to set up** snmpd.conf. A menu of settings appears.

3. **Type** 1 **to enter Access Control Setup.** Minimally, specify a community name to add read-only access. The default setting is public. Assign a community name to match your other SNMP managed devices. Optionally, you can also specify a hostname or network address to accept this community name from to restrict access to a specific NMS.

4. **Type** finished **to return to the file configuration menu.**

5. **Type** 5 **to provide System Information Setup.**

6. **Type** 1 **to specify the physical location of the machine and then type an identifying label for the server, such as** West Server Room, Rack 5, Unit 1.

7. **Type** 2 **to supply contact information for the administrator and to supply a contact name, phone number, and email address as appropriate and then press Return.**

8. **Type** 3 **to define a proper value for the** sysServices **object and then supply values to answer the following questions by using** 0 **for no and** 1 **for yes:**

   - Does this host offer physical services (eg, like a repeater) [answer 0 or 1]: 0
   - Does this host offer datalink/subnetwork services (eg, like a bridge): 0

- Does this host offer internet services (eg, supports IP): 1
- Does this host offer end-to-end services (eg, supports TCP): 1
- Does this host offer application services (eg, supports SMTP): 1

9. **Type** finished **to complete** sysServices **and then type** finished **again to exit** snmpd.conf**.** The tool again presents a menu of files to configure.

10. **Type** 3 **to set up** snmp.conf**.** A menu of settings appears.

11. **Type** 1 **to enter Default Authentication Options.**

12. **Type** 3 **to supply the default** snmpv1 **and** snmpv2c **community name to use when needed and then type the community name you supplied in step 3.**

13. **Type** finished **to complete** defcommunity**, type** finished **again to exit** snmp.conf**, and then type** quit **to exit the tool.**

14. **Launch Server Admin and then connect to the desired server.**

15. **Select the server listing and then click Settings on the toolbar.**

16. **Click the General tab and then click the SNMP check box.**

17. **Click Save.** The server should now begin reporting its configuration to the NMS by using the community name specified.

Secure Shell

SSH remote login offers an encrypted alternative to the insecure Telnet service for remotely connecting to another host over a command-line session. In addition to executing commands, SSH can be used to secure other services; SCP (Secure Copy) and SFTP (Secured File Transfer Protocol) both use SSH to tunnel their data.

Snow Leopard Server's SSH service uses the open-source package OpenSSH. The default port used for SSH is TCP 22, which must be allowed through any firewalls in order to remotely log in to the server. SSH is strongly preferred over Telnet because the former sends all its communications over the Internet in cleartext, including the username and password used to log in. For this reason, although Telnet is installed, it's disabled by default.

Public-key cryptography

SSH uses public-key encryption to secure the remote login session before the user's credentials are submitted to the server. It can also optionally use public-key authentication to avoid the need to ever present a username and password, a feature that allows automated processes to open a secured SSH connection in the background without user interaction.

In public-key cryptography, two parties that want to communicate securely don't need to initially exchange secret passwords in advance of beginning a secured session. Instead, both parties use a secret *private key* they maintain locally and a matching *public key* that doesn't need to be kept secret.

The public key is used to encrypt data that can subsequently be decrypted only by its corresponding private key. Because the public key can't decrypt the messages it encrypts, it doesn't need to be kept secret like a normal password does.

In an SSH session, the server presents its *fingerprint*, or public key, to the client attempting to log in, which also supplies its own public key to the server. After the two systems exchange their public keys, they can begin sending encrypted messages to each other, confident that a third party can't secretly intercept, read, or respond to their messages, even if it were able to obtain the public keys.

If a third-party "man in the middle" attempts to pretend to be one of the two parties, the network identity of that third party first flags the impostor's attempt as illegitimate because the client records the location of the server when accepting its public key and associates the two.

Additionally, the third party can be challenged to decrypt a message scrambled by using a private key and respond with a new message scrambled with the opposite private key, something it can't do if it can access only the public keys. Only the two systems can decrypt each other's messages, using the secret private keys created to complement their public keys. With a secured session initiated, the client and server each combine their private key with the public key they've obtained to create a *session key*, which can be used to more efficiently encrypt messages between them. The session key works like a conventional password and must be kept secret.

Public-key authentication

The initial public-key encryption session proves only that the client and the server are the same entities throughout the session; this provides confidentiality, but it doesn't actually authenticate the user because any entity could generate a private- and public-key pair and begin confidential communications with the server, whether they're a known and authorized user or not.

To actually authenticate, the client can use the newly secured channel to send his or her account password to the server. The client may also authenticate by using public keys; this requires that the client initially authenticate as a known user and then deliver his or her public key to the server.

The server maintains the client's public key in the user's account, saving it to a `/.ssh/` folder within the user's home directory. At subsequent logins, the user only needs to provide an account name; the server looks up the user's public SSH key that it maintains on file and then uses it to challenge the remote client to decrypt a message scrambled with it. Legitimate users can unscramble the challenge by using their private key, proving that they're the same entity who initially authenticated with the server and who provided the server with the public key associated with the users they claim to be.

NOTE
If the authenticating user's home directory is encrypted with FileVault, the server can't obtain the user's public key unless the user is already logged in to the server.

Kerberos authentication

In Mac OS X, SSH can also use Kerberos to handle SSO authentication for a user who's already successfully logged in to his or her Open Directory account if the directory domain has enabled Kerberos authentication.

CROSS-REF
For more on using Open Directory and Kerberos, see Chapter 21.

SSH is enabled by default on Snow Leopard Server, and the system must be configured to support SSH in order to act as an Open Directory replica.

Because SSH was designed with security in mind, there's little reason for blocking or deactivating the service. Instead, it may likely be used to secure access to other services that don't supply similar levels of encryption. For example, VNC traffic can be tunneled through an SSH connection to secure a screen-sharing session. To enable public-key authentication for remote users, they must generate a private- and public-key pair and copy the public key to their user folder on the server.

To check the status of a server's SSH configuration in Server Admin, follow these steps:

1. **Launch Server Admin and then connect to the desired server.**

2. **Select the server listing and then click Settings on the toolbar.**

3. **Click the General tab.** Note the selected check box for SSH.

4. **To update any changes, click Save.** Clients may log in remotely by using SSH.

To limit access to SSH remote login to specific users in Server Admin, follow these steps:

1. **Launch Server Admin and then connect to the desired server.**

2. **Select the server listing and then click Settings on the toolbar.**

3. **Click the Access tab and then click the Services tab.**

4. **From the Services pane within Access, shown in Figure 19.2, click the For selected services below radio button above the left column and then choose SSH from that list.**

5. **Above the right-side column, click the Allow only users and groups below radio button and then click the Add (+) button under the right-side column of allowed users.** A Users & Groups sheet opens.

6. **Drag users or groups to the access list on the right to limit SSH login to those users.** Administrative users can always log in by using SSH.

7. **Click Save.**

Figure 19.2

Managing access to SSH in Server Admin

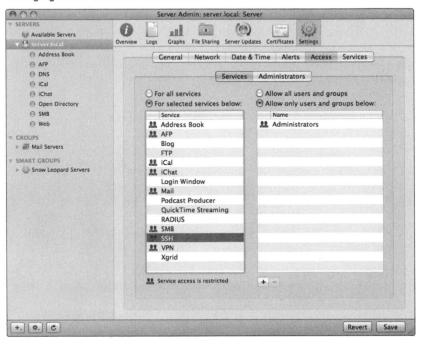

To initiate an SSH session to a remote server, follow these steps:

1. Launch Terminal and then type ssh *admin@server.example.com* **by using the desired username in place of** *admin* **and the desired server name or address.** If this is the first time you're connecting to this host, you're presented with this message:

```
The authenticity of host 'server.example.com (10.0.1.2)'
   can't be established. RSA key fingerprint is 74:ef:41:7e:
   ce:8e:d2:7a:ec:61:7b:42:6b:6e:fe:bc.
Are you sure you want to continue connecting (yes/no)?
```

2. Type yes **to accept the server's public key, which is subsequently saved locally to** /Users/username/.ssh/known_hosts.

3. Type the password when prompted for the user specified. You should now have the remote access equivalent of working from the server's local command line. If the server's IP address or public key is ever changed, you receive this warning:

```
@@@@@@@@@@@@@@@@@@@@@@@@@@@@@@@@@@@@@@@@@@@@@@@@@@@@@@@@@@@@@@@
@    WARNING: REMOTE HOST IDENTIFICATION HAS CHANGED!    @
@@@@@@@@@@@@@@@@@@@@@@@@@@@@@@@@@@@@@@@@@@@@@@@@@@@@@@@@@@@@@@@
```

```
IT IS POSSIBLE THAT SOMEONE IS DOING SOMETHING NASTY!
Someone could be eavesdropping on you right now (man-in
the-middle attack)! It is also possible that the RSA host
key has just been changed.
The fingerprint for the RSA key sent by the remote host is
74:ef:41:7e:ce:8e:d2:7a:ec:61:7b:42:6b:6e:fe:bc.
Please contact your system administrator. Add correct host
key in /Users/username/.ssh/known_hosts to get rid of this
message.
Offending key in /Users/username/.ssh/known_hosts:1
RSA host key for 10.0.1.2 has changed and you have
requested strict checking. Host key verification failed.
```

4. **To obtain an updated public key to connect to the server, delete the offending key fingerprint entry in** /Users/username/.ssh/known_hosts **at the line number specified after the colon and then connect again.**

To create a private- and public-key pair for a user for SSH authentication, follow these steps:

1. **Launch Terminal and then type** ls –ld ~/.ssh **to see if your local user folder contains a directory for storing SSH keys.** If the folder doesn't yet exist, create it by typing **mkdir ~/.ssh** and then typing the directory as **cd ~/.ssh**.

2. **Type** ssh-keygen -b 1024 -t rsa -f id_rsa -P " **to generate a key pair by using 1024-bit RSA keys.** The private key is named id_rsa, and no password is assigned to it, enabling the user to log in to a server without typing a password to enable use of the private key.

3. **Copy the public key into the local authorized key file by typing** cat id_rsa.pub >> authorized_keys2.

4. **Change permissions on the private key to restrict access to the user and group by typing** chmod go-rwx ~/.ssh/.id_rsa.

5. **Upload the authorized keys file to the** .ssh **folder within the user's home folder on the server by typing the secure file copy command** scp authorized_keys2 username@server.example.com:~/.ssh/. Subsequent SSH connections don't prompt this user for a password because the installed keys handle authentication instead.

Virtual Network Computing

VNC is a remote screen-sharing protocol originally developed in a joint effort by Oracle and Olvetti to create a thin client Network Computer tablet to serve as a highly portable terminal.

The technology behind the device was acquired by AT&T, which scuttled the hardware research but released the software as an open-source project. VNC enables any operating system to view or control a remote display that another host serves up.

Apple added VNC viewer support to Mac OS X Leopard under the name Screen Sharing. It earlier incorporated a VNC server into Mac OS X to support Apple Remote Desktop, which uses VNC to enable administrators to remotely view or control desktops of configured clients.

Mac OS X's VNC server is configured from the Sharing pane of System Preferences by turning on Screen Sharing and providing a session password that clients must type to remotely view the local display. Access can also be limited to specific hosts.

Screen Sharing is hidden away in `/System/Library/CoreServices/`. Launching a VNC session can be performed via the Finder by using the browse list of computers populated by Bonjour. A Mac with Screen Sharing turned on advertises itself over Bonjour, enabling remote users to discover and connect to the system's VNC server via the Share Screen button presented in the Finder.

Other systems supporting VNC, including everything from Windows PCs to mobile phones, may be connected to manually by using a VNC URL — such as `vnc://server.example.com` in Safari — by using the Finder's Go to Server feature or by manually launching the Screen Sharing application and then typing its DNS name or IP address. VNC uses TCP port 5900.

Mac OS X Server enables VNC by default when booting up from its installer DVD to enable remote installation and configuration. For this reason, access to the server should be secured because all that's needed to connect to it via VNC is the server's IP address and its serial number, which is used as the new machine's VNC password.

CROSS-REF
For more on remote installation by using VNC, see Chapter 6.

VNC is enabled by default on Snow Leopard Server. The system is initially configured to encrypt keystrokes and passwords but can be set to encrypt all traffic by using Screen Sharing preferences. Additional encryption is more secure in exchange for not being as fast.

If you're not using a management tool, such as Apple Remote Desktop, VNC provides a simple and free option for remotely accessing Snow Leopard Server — but lacks the ability to remotely restart a server that isn't responding, for example — and provides no reporting or automated configuration features.

To check the status of a server's VNC configuration, follow these steps:

1. **Launch System Preferences on the server.**

2. **Click the Sharing pane, shown in Figure 19.3, and ensure that Screen Sharing is selected.** If it's not, click its radio button, click the Computer Settings button, and then assign a password to allow VNC viewers to control the screen.

3. **Save the settings by closing the System Preferences window.**

Figure 19.3

Enabling VNC Screen Sharing in System Preferences

Remote Management

In addition to the screen-sharing features available through VNC, Snow Leopard Server also supports Remote Management, an additional layer of control that enables administrators to manage machines on the network by using Apple Remote Desktop.

Beyond simply viewing or controlling a remote system's display, Remote Management enables an administrator to perform certain tasks directly, some of which are either not possible to do from a shared screen or are faster to do without direct console interaction.

Apple Remote Desktop can send commands that Macs configured with Remote Management can respond to, such as:

- Sleeping, waking, restarting, or shutting down one or multiple systems, either immediately or after allowing the local user to save any open work
- Logging out the current user
- Emptying the trash for all users on a system
- Opening files and applications on one or multiple systems
- Upgrading Apple Remote Desktop Client software on a group of Macs
- Setting the startup disk to a local disk or partition or selecting from a list of NetBoot or Network Install images

Apple Remote Desktop can also use SSH to send commands to a group of Mac OS X systems to:

- Execute commands as the current user or a specified user
- Set System Preferences in the Network, Energy Saver, and Date & Time panes via command-line tools
- Configure custom scripts and apply them across computers as desired

Because Apple Remote Desktop also uses VNC for basic screen sharing, activating Remote Management on Mac OS X Server overrides the VNC settings. For client computers, activating VNC can similarly only be done if Remote Management is turned off.

Remote Management is based on the WBEM (Web-Based Enterprise Management) standard and uses TCP port 3283. However, Apple's implementation of WBEM (the basis of Remote Management) isn't exposed for easy use with alternative management applications.

Remote Management is in some ways a modern superset of the remote reporting and control features associated with SNMP.

Remote Management is disabled by default on Snow Leopard Server. Turning the service on disables VNC because the service is intended for use with Apple Remote Desktop, which provides both VNC screen sharing and a superset of additional reporting and automated configuration features as well as the ability to send commands that can act across a variety of systems.

To check the status of a server's remote management configuration, follow these steps:

1. **Launch Server Admin and then connect to the desired server.**

2. **Select the server listing and then click Settings on the toolbar.**

3. **Click the General tab.** Note the deselected check box for Remote Management. Enabling Remote Management interrupts the existing operation of VNC.

4. **To update any changes, click Save.**

Managing and Monitoring Other Network Services

The Logs page of the selected server pane in Server Admin presents two logs that record events related to these other network services:

- The System Log at `/var/log/system.log` reports VNC configuration changes and also receives any errors reported by NTP.
- The Secure Log at `/var/log/secure.log` reports SSH and VNC connection activity.

SNMP logs are written to `/var/log/snmpd.log`, which is available through `Console.app`, System Profiler, or from the command line.

Once configured, NTP runs on autopilot, whereas SNMP, VNC, and Remote Management are all services largely managed on the client end, either by the SNMP NMS, the VNC viewer, or Apple Remote Desktop.

Summary

- NTP time synchronization is critical for a variety of network services and impacts how files and log entries are dated and how sync changes are resolved. Clients can be configured to obtain a time sync from Snow Leopard Server via NTP.

- SNMP support allows Snow Leopard Server to integrate into existing network management systems that monitor service uptime and keep tabs on network equipment, watching for problems than might need to be addressed.

- SSH enables remote users and scripted tasks to securely communicate with the server and authenticate by using passwords, shared keys, or Kerberos.

- VNC and Remote Management enable administrators to remotely control servers without requiring a local console and display. VNC is activated during installation to enable remote setup. The Remote Management service can be enabled for use with Apple Remote Desktop.

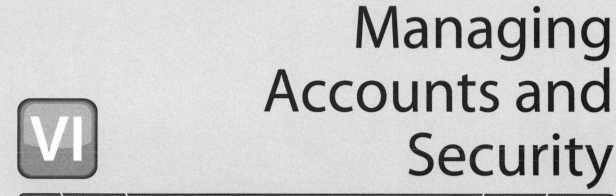

Managing Accounts and Security

Introduction to
Mac OS X Server Security

Mac OS X Snow Leopard Server builds on its highly regarded Unix foundation with a variety of software packages that are openly available to third-party security vetting.

Apple's operating system also incorporates some of the latest technology in the field of security hardening, including:

- Sandboxing, based on TrustedBSD's Mandatory Access Control (MAC) framework, to lock down the permissions of specific processes

- Application signing by using public-key signatures to help identify when code has been tampered with and to block maliciously altered code from inheriting the permissions of the original application

- Address Space Layout Randomization (ASLR), a feature that makes it much more difficult for malicious code to predict useful memory addresses to target

- Support for Non-eXecutable (NX) CPU enforcement that blocks exploits from injecting malicious executable code into memory and tricking the application to run it as it if were its own instructions

Besides the security features built into the operating system, there are a variety of security issues that only the user can address. No amount of software security can prevent a disgruntled employee from opening up a server and physically stealing its hard drive storage.

Similarly, nothing in the operating system can prevent a stack of backup media archives from being lost in the same disaster that destroyed the original data or from walking out the door in the hands of a thief.

Security involves a wide range of measures taken to safeguard user and company data for authorized users, to protect the privacy and confidentiality of communications, and to isolate systems and networks from malicious attacks and attempts to steal information.

This chapter introduces a variety of security principles related to operating a server, describes what's involved in planning for security, and provides suggestions on how to maintain and monitor the security of the server.

Hardening Local Server Security

Although often overlooked as a security subject, the physical security of a server is a very important consideration. Users who have physical access to the server should be assumed to have almost complete control of the system and any data on it.

Even in the case of an appropriately configured server, a user with physical access can:

- Restart the system from an external drive, bypassing the installed operating system's configured security restrictions
- Boot the system from an install disc and then reset the assigned administrator password
- Steal its internal disk media or surreptitiously duplicate the data by using an attached drive
- Boot the server into Target Mode and then copy its data to another system
- Install a USB keylogger to record every character typed on the keyboard to obtain sensitive account passwords

Servers should be kept in a secure location where access to the room can be restricted, access to the console can be limited, and physical access to the inside of the system can be locked down.

Firmware secured startup

Additional steps can be taken to help secure the server even if some physical access is obtained. A firmware password can be used to prevent the server from booting to specific types of volumes unless the set password is supplied.

The Firmware Password Utility on the Mac OS X Snow Leopard Installer DVD can be used to set this password, which is required before performing firmware boot commands, including the ability to:

- Use the C key to start up from an optical disc
- Use the N key to start up from a NetBoot server
- Use the T key to start up in FireWire target disk mode
- Use the D key to start up from the Diagnostic volume of the Install DVD
- Start up a system in Single-user mode by pressing ⌘+S during startup. Single-user mode bypasses the entire user login system and effectively gives the user root access to the entire system.
- Reset the system's Parameter RAM (PRAM) by pressing ⌘+Option+P+R during startup
- Start up in Verbose mode by pressing ⌘+V during startup
- Start up in Safe Boot mode by pressing the Shift key during startup
- Launch the Startup Manager by pressing the Option key during startup

When using a firmware password, it's important to keep in mind that users with physical access to the server can reset it by turning the system off, removing installed RAM, and resetting the system's PRAM three times. It's also possible to obtain the firmware password by using a software utility if the server is running.

This means that using a firmware password may help limit access attempts but isn't infallible, particularly if users can open up the machine or access its console.

Physical port security

Users with access to the physical ports on the server can potentially mount drives, install network interfaces, attach keyloggers to monitor keyboard input, and gain access to data in system memory.

An unused physical interface, such as FireWire, can be disabled in software by disabling its kernel extension located at `/System/Library/Extensions/IOFireWireFamily.kext`. Removing driver support for FireWire prevents the use of any FireWire external drives for any purpose, including backups or troubleshooting you may want to perform in the future, until the drivers are replaced and the system is rebooted.

Likewise, the use of USB storage devices, such as USB hard drives and dongle flash drives, may be similarly disabled independently from other classes of USB functionality, including keyboard and mouse access, by removing the kernel extension located at `/System/Library/Extensions/IOUSBMassStorageClass.kext`.

The system must be restarted after removing a kernel extension for the change to take effect. A disabled kernel extension may be reinstalled by a future Apple Software Update seeking to update the file.

Access to other physical ports that are being used and can't be disabled should be physically blocked, particularly if access to the server's location can't be rigorously controlled. This includes access to keyboard cables and any available front- and rear-facing ports, such as USB, SCSI, FireWire, and console serial ports, and any hub ports that may be accessible from attached devices, such as USB ports supplied on the keyboard.

Physical network ports on the server should also be secured to prevent the server from being connected to a dummy network. The network itself must also be secured, without any open, active ports that may be used to launch attacks on the server.

Wireless security

Wireless network interfaces, including Bluetooth and Wi-Fi, can both serve as vectors for attack. Neither is suitable for use on a secured server.

If your server shipped with Bluetooth and AirPort Wi-Fi interfaces, you can unplug the wireless hardware internally or remove the interfaces in software by disabling the following kernel extensions for Bluetooth and Wi-Fi interfaces:

- `/System/Library/Extensions/IOBluetoothFamily.kext`
- `/System/Library/Extensions/IOBluetoothHIDDriver.kext`

- `/System/Library/Extensions/AppleAirPort.kext`
- `/System/Library/Extensions/AppleAirPort2.kext`
- `/System/Library/Extensions/AppleAirPortFW.kext`

Wireless access can be provided to users via external wireless access points and secured with 802.1X Network Access Control by using the RADIUS service.

CROSS-REF
For more on the RADIUS service, see Chapter 17.

Audio- and video-recording security

To prevent unauthorized audio and video recording by using the server's built-in audio inputs and video camera interfaces, you can disable the following kernel extensions:

- `/System/Library/Extensions/AppleOnboardAudio.kext`
- `/System/Library/Extensions/AppleUSBAudio.kext`
- `/System/Library/Extensions/AudioDeviceTreeUpdater.kext`
- `/System/Library/Extensions/IOAudioFamily.kext`
- `/System/Library/Extensions/VirtualAudioDriver.kext`
- `/System/Library/Extensions/Apple_iSight.kext`
- `/System/Library/Extensions/IOUSBFamily.kext/Contents/PlugIns/AppleUSBVideoSupport.kext`

Camera and microphone hardware can also be disabled internally.

Securing local account login

Local login to the server can be configured to provide an access warning, including a notice of the server's ownership, a prohibition against unauthorized access, and a reminder to authorized users that login implies consent to monitoring.

This warning appears in the local login window and for remote access users and is set by typing this command:

```
sudo defaults write /Library/Preferences/com.apple.loginwindow
    LoginwindowText "This system belongs to X Corporation. Use
    of this system implies consent to monitoring. Unauthorized
    use of this system will be prosecuted."
```

User accounts in Mac OS X are given access based on whether they're assigned administrative access to the local system, whether the account includes managed preferences or parental controls, and whether the account is a guest account:

- The root user has unrestricted access to the system.
- An administrator user has full control of computer configuration.
- A standard non-administrator user has nonprivileged user access.
- A managed non-administrator user has restricted access based on the managed preferences assigned to his or her account in the network directory.
- A guest user has restricted access with no password. When the user logs out, all of his or her home folder information is deleted. Guest login is disabled by default and applies only to desktop users.

Acting as a root user

Root login is disabled by default to prevent its misuse. If multiple administrators log in to the system as the root user to perform tasks that require root access, there's no record of which individual performed a specific task.

To allow root access without making every administrator log in as root, individual administrative users can perform commands as the root user by issuing the sudo command, which, when used without a target user, assumes the root user.

Every time an administrative user invokes sudo, the event is logged for security purposes. After typing **sudo** prior to a command, the user is asked to type his or her password. If that account has administrative access, the user is granted a window of time to issue commands acting as the root user, which is 5 minutes by default. After that period expires, the user must authenticate again if reissuing a sudo command.

Acting as an administrative user

Administrative users should log in only with the amount of privileges they need during their login session. This would mean that an administrator logging in to a server to check email or browse the web would do so by using a standard non-administrative account.

Routinely logging in as an administrative account to perform non-administrative functions bypasses the operating system's security safeguards designed to prevent an accidental modification of system preferences without being required to authenticate. It also provides malicious attackers with a greater opportunity to access resources that would otherwise flag a request for authentication.

Local administrative users can perform powerful configuration tasks with serious security implications on the server. These include:

- Creating new user accounts
- Adding other users to the Admin group, granting them administrative access

- Changing the FileVault master password, which can be used to decrypt users' encrypted home directories
- Enabling or modifying file sharing and access
- Modifying firewall and network configuration
- Installing system software, including user applications that require system level access

Users in both the local accounts database and the network directory domain can be assigned local administrative access to the server. From Workgroup Manager, local and directory domain accounts can be assigned administer-this-server privileges from the Basic tab of their user record, as shown in Figure 20.1.

Figure 20.1

Assigning local administrative rights on the server in Workgroup Manager

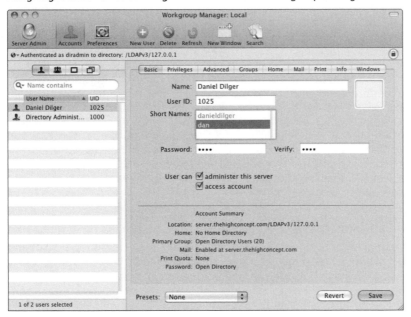

CROSS-REF
For more on working with user accounts in Workgroup Manager, see Chapter 10.

Acting as a limited administrative user

Administrative access to configure and monitor services can be customized by using Server Admin to define SACLs by using the Administrators tab within the Access pane of the server's Settings page, shown in Figure 20.2.

Figure 20.2

Assigning SACLs to define service configuration permissions in Server Admin

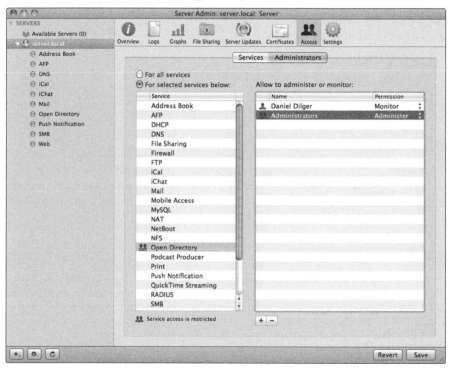

SACLs can be used to selectively allow full administrative configuration rights or read-only monitor access to view settings and status information for services running in Server Admin. These SACLs operate on a system level, so they also restrict command-line service configuration access.

CROSS-REF

For more on using SACLs in Server Admin, see Chapter 9.

Acting as a non-administrative user

Logging in to the server as a non-administrative user when not performing any actions that require administrative privileges is recommended to avoid inadvertently making configuration changes.

Non-administrative users may be associated with managed preferences defined within Workgroup Manager, resulting in a *managed user*. Such a managed, non-administrative account can be used to restrict access to applications and System Preference settings as well as to impose Parental Control time-use limitations, hardware access restrictions, and other settings that may be useful in defining the security policy of users logging in to a server.

CROSS-REF

For more on using managed preferences, see Chapter 36.

Securing User Data

Network administrators commonly provide users with a home folder hosted on the server. Snow Leopard Server supports home folders for users on different client platforms and enables FireVault encryption for Mac users. Server administrators must secure users' home folders and the credentials users supply to access the server.

Managing home folders

Network users are assigned a home folder in their account record in Workgroup Manager under the Home tab. Home folders may be stored on the same server that hosts the directory domain or may be distributed across multiple file-sharing servers to balance the user load.

CROSS-REF

For more on configuring home folder settings in Workgroup Manager, see Chapter 10.

Home folders for Mac users

For Mac clients, the preferred protocol for hosting home folders is AFP, which supports authentication-level access security. Mac home directories can also be hosted on NFS exports, particularly in cases where the server also supports Unix clients.

However, NFS manages access control to exported home folders only by user ID or client IP address; it doesn't support user authentication.

Home folders for other clients

Apart from hosting NFS exports for Unix clients, many Mac OS X Server installations may have needs to serve home folders to Windows users. Windows clients require hosting file shares by using SMB.

Mac OS X Server is configured by default to share a user's same home folder as AFP, when the user logs in from a Mac, or SMB, when the user logs in from Windows, a feature known as virtual share points. This is configured under the Advanced tab of the SMB service's Settings page in Server Admin.

CROSS-REF

For more on configuring share points in Server Admin, see Chapter 9. For more on AFP, NFS, and SMB file sharing, see Chapter 22.

Choosing a home folder type

Workgroup Manager and client configuration combine to create a variety of different options for setting up users' home folders:

- **Local home folders exist for users created on the server.** These are identical to the local /Users/username folders created on the desktop and abbreviated as ~/.

- **No home folder is the default option for network users.** However, this isn't very useful because network users who log in can't work from a home directory.

- **Network home folders are the obvious solution.** When users log in with a home folder configured for them on an automountable network file share, they can save their files and preferences to the network location, just as they would to their local ~/ home folder. The problem with network home folders is that this places a significant burden on the network, which must be fast enough to support constant updates and the potentially large files users keep in their home folders. Mobile users connected via a wireless network are likely impacted the greatest by this additional overhead related to their home folder access.

- **Mobile accounts seek to solve this issue by enabling the user to maintain a local copy of the network home folder for performance purposes.** Mobile accounts also cache any managed preferences and the user's authentication information, enabling the user to log in to the system when not connected to the network and ensuring that managed preferences continue to be applied.

- **Portable Home Directories enhance mobile accounts by allowing the locally stored copy of the network home folder to be automatically synced at login and logout during the user's session or manually.** This keeps the mobile system up to date with files that may be copied to the network home folder by the user while working on a desktop system.

- **External accounts are a special form of mobile account where the user's home folder is stored on an external drive.**

Mobile accounts, including Portable Home Directories, offer a variety of advantages over using simple network home folders:

- **Applications can work with their cache files locally instead of having to copy temporary files across the network to a network home folder.** Some applications have compatibility issues with saving files to a network home directory because they expect to be saving items to a local home folder.

- **Mobile accounts create less network overhead.** Cache files aren't being regularly copied to the network home directory, and any synced files are efficiently updated only when changes are made.

- **Mobile users can access their system without the network by using cached authentication.** With a Portable Home Directory, they can work with their files offline and then sync them to their network home on the server after reconnecting.

Mobile accounts also offer a couple of advantages over using a local home folder:

- **Mobile accounts can be individually managed.** Managed preferences for users with local accounts can be applied only on a machine level, where settings are applied to all user accounts on the mobile system. Mobile accounts can be individually managed just like network accounts.

- **Mobile users with Portable Home Directories can restore their home directory after data corruption, equipment failure, or loss by downloading their synced network directory from the server to a new system.** Local home folders must rely on the availability of an external backup.

FileVault home folder encryption

The contents of local and mobile home folders can be encrypted with FileVault to make sensitive data worthless to a thief, even if the server's storage media are stolen from the machine.

FileVault works with local user accounts on the server and with the home folders of network users stored locally on the client as a Portable Home Directory. Each user's folder is saved as a sparsebundle disk image scrambled by using AES-256 encryption.

NOTE

In Mac OS X, a bundle is a folder and its contents that act as and appear to be a single file. A *sparsebundle* is a folder that acts similar to a sparsefile, which is a disk image that expands dynamically to accommodate the growth of the data it contains. FileVault uses a sparsebundle to enable an encrypted home folder to work as a single file while retaining the benefits of a folder structure, primarily to enable efficient incremental backups by Time Machine of only data that has changed.

The sparsebundle design of FileVault enables an encrypted home folder to efficiently grow in proportion to its need instead of starting out larger than necessary and requiring manual expansion. However, if a large number of files stored within the sparsebundle are deleted, it takes some time for the sparsebundle to shrink back down to an optimized size.

Network encrypted disk images

Users planning to generate large amounts of temporary, sensitive working files should create a separate encrypted disk image outside of their home directory. Encrypted read/write disk images can be created by using Disk Utility.

After an encrypted disk image is created to protect files or folders stored on a network volume, the disk image can be mounted by a network user, which has the side effect of protecting the data transmitted over the network between the client and the disk image on the server by using AES-256 encryption.

The encrypted disk image must be mounted by only one system at a time in order to prevent irreparable corruption in the disk image's content.

Securing certificates and other credentials

In addition to encrypting files and folders, network users also have credentials to secure: passwords, certificate identities, and secured notes. With all the passwords and identity information for users to store, there's a risk that users will either forget their credentials or write them down in nonsecure ways that enable easy theft.

Mac OS X Keychain

Apple's solution to password overload is another password: the one that secures the keychain. Mac OS X offers to maintain users' passwords within the primary keychain stored by default at `~/Library/Keychains/login.keychain`.

Any number of additional keychains can be created, each with its own list of items. A default keychain can be designated from within Keychain Access, shown in Figure 20.3, which also lists all the user's keychains and provides access to their stored items.

Each item in a keychain maintains an ACL that designates access to specific applications. Access to the keychain item value can be set to force the application to require the user to supply the keychain's password first.

The secure, encrypted storage of passwords in keychains enables users to create longer and more complex passwords, which are subsequently more secure, without the problem of users forgetting passwords or having to rely on insecure memory aids such as writing the passwords down. This balances security with convenience in a positive way.

Figure 20.3

Keychain Access

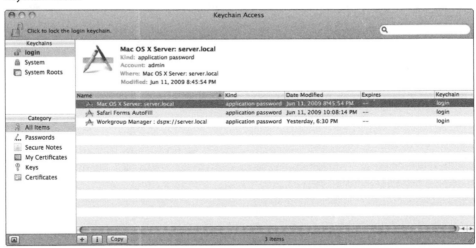

Portable keychains

Keychains can be saved to an external drive, such as a USB thumb drive, to create a secondary level of security. Additionally, a biometric thumb drive can provide a third level of credentialing, where the user combines three separate identity factors:

- What you have, a physical device like the thumb drive storing a keychain
- What you know, represented by the password locking the keychain
- What you are, based on the biometric thumb reader

Multi-factor authentication applies diversity to secure mobile users so theft of a laptop wouldn't in itself expose FileVault-secured data; the external keychain storage and locked keychain password both help make it increasingly less likely that data would be inadvertently exposed.

Smart cards

Mac OS X supports smart cards used by third-party readers as a sort of physical, mobile keychain. Although new passwords can't be added to a smart card, the card itself can be accessed as a credential by any application that supports keychains.

Like other keychains, a smart card can be locked by using a PIN, which requires that the same PIN be supplied to unlock and use the smart card for authentication. As with a keychain file saved to an external USB drive, a smart card acts as a "what you have" factor to enhance the security of authenticating users.

Certificate identities

A certificate identity is represented by a document that binds a public key to an individual or business by using a digital signature. The signature may be:

- Self-signed by the issuer, where no higher authority is involved to validate that the public key and identity are legitimately linked together; the issuer simply asks the user to trust that the public key it has received from the issuing individual or company is valid and hasn't been tampered with.

- Signed by a Certificate Authority, where a reputable company validates that the public key does indeed come from the identity it's associated with and that the public key hasn't been tampered with since the validation was made.

Mac OS X and other client operating systems ship with a variety of root certificates that are trusted by Apple on behalf of the user. These root certificates allow client systems to automatically trust new certificates they received that have been signed by one of those Certificate Authorities.

Organizations can also install their own root certificate on client machines so their client machines automatically trust any self-signed certificates the organization creates, acting in the role of a Certificate Authority.

Implicit trust of a root certificate, which is simply a Certificate Authority's self-signed certificate, allows the Certificate Authority to subsequently sign additional certificates with a signature that the client system can verify against the root certificate's public key.

If a client machine lacks a root certificate to verify that a given certificate is valid, the user has to manually accept the certificate before his or her system can use it. In some cases, a system may refuse to accept a certificate if it's not signed by a known Certificate Authority with a verifiable root certificate that the system already trusts.

Once accepted as legitimately identifying an authority, a certificate acts as a public key; instead of using a simple password or shared secret between the server and the client to encrypt transactions, a method that requires some way to securely distribute the password in advance, public-key cryptography uses a secret private key on the server to encrypt data that the client can decrypt in conjunction with the client's private key.

The public key doesn't need to be secured because it can't be used to forge messages that appear to originate from the server the way a simple password could; it acts only as a decoding key for encrypted messages from the server. This allows the remote server to negotiate a session key to the client under the confidentially secured cover of encrypted messages.

This use of certificates enables the client to trust that the information it decrypts (by using the public key contained in the certificate) actually came from the server and wasn't altered along the way. The client must have some basis for trusting that the server's certificate is valid; either the user must explicitly trust the self-signed certificate it obtains from the server or the certificate must be verifiably signed by a trusted Certificate Authority, where *signed* means encrypted by a Certificate Authority so the certificate can be decrypted by using the Certificate Authority's own public key contained in its root certificate.

The Certificates page in Server Admin, shown in Figure 20.4, shows a listing of installed certificate identities. Under the listings, an Add (+) button opens a pop-up menu that offers to:

- Import an existing certificate identity obtained from a Certificate Authority
- Create a new certificate identity, a process that involves creating a self-signed certificate by using the Mac OS X Certificate Assistant

Figure 20.4

The Certificates page in Server Admin

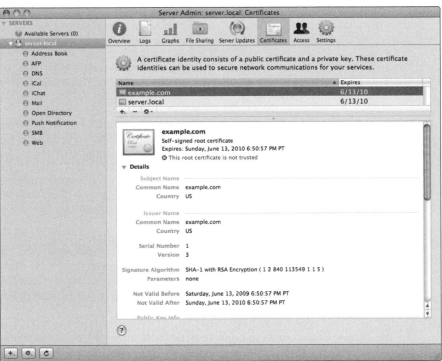

An Action menu (a button with a gear icon on it) offers to replace a self-signed certificate with a Certificate Authority–signed one or to renew an expiring certificate. This enables administrators to start off with their own self-signed certificate and then replace it with a Certificate Authority–signed identity in the future.

To request a Certificate Authority–signed version of your own certificate, the Action button also offers to generate a CSR (Certificate Signing Request), which can be submitted to a Certificate Authority in order to obtain a signed version of the locally generated certificate. Essentially, the Certificate Authority encrypts your certificate with its own private key, enabling third parties who trust the Certificate Authority to also trust your Certificate Authority–signed certificate.

Public Key Infrastructure

Legitimacy in certificate security is predicated on managing which root certificates are trusted. If a user readily accepts a root certificate created by a malicious attacker, that client system subsequently trusts any certificates signed by that malicious root certificate, giving the user a completely false sense of security.

PKI (Public Key Infrastructure) is a set of policies, software, and procedures that determines how to verify that a certificate is valid in establishing that a public key does belong to a given identity (whether an individual or an organization) and what exactly the certificate is designed to do.

The PKI in Mac OS X Server can generate and certify identities for a variety of purposes, but the most common use is in creating certificates used to secure SSL connections between clients and services, such as:

- Mail
- Websites
- Wiki and blog collaboration services
- Address Book Server
- iCal Server
- RADIUS authentication
- Directory services

The public key contained in a certificate is restricted to a set of allowed uses in its certificate extensions section, such as:

- Email signing
- Message encryption
- Signature verification
- SSL server authentication
- IPsec encryption
- Code signing
- Client authentication

It's possible to create a single certificate with multiple defined uses, but creating a certificate for multiple uses is also less secure. Certain certificates are restricted to very specific uses. For example, Apple issues MobileMe certificates that are limited entirely to authenticating the client for iChat signing and encryption.

A certificate is also designated as valid for only a limited time. Once it expires, it must be replaced with a new certificate. A signing Certificate Authority can also revoke a certificate prior to its expiration. A certificate contains the URL of a revocation center with the authority to invalidate it, enabling clients to check that the certificate is still valid.

CROSS-REF
For more on creating certificates in Server Admin, see Chapter 9.

Securing Shared Data

In addition to safeguarding individuals' data and credentials, server administrators also manage security for shared data accessed over the network. This requires managing:

- Authentication, which is verifying an individual's identity
- Authorization, which is verifying that an authenticated individual has the authority to perform a specific action

Authentication

In general terms, a system verifies your identity only if you can provide both a username and a password because simply knowing a username doesn't uniquely prove you're that person to the system.

Once the system has authenticated you, the operating system can then determine what access to services and files you should have based on the defined permissions for files, folders, and services.

Security and directory services

Each system on the network manages its own local authentication and authorization when users log in and attempt to access local files. In order to provide shared network services, however, a server may participate in a network domain with a directory that provides centralized authentication services for all the members of the domain.

There are a number of ways users may be authenticated in Mac OS X Server:

- **Authentication by using Crypt Passwords stored in user accounts is a legacy authentication method related to user accounts that have migrated from early versions of Mac OS X Server.** Passwords are hashed and stored within the directory's user account records. This doesn't support the use of modern network-secure authentication protocols, such as Kerberos, or the configuring of password security policy.

- **Open Directory authentication stores passwords outside the LDAP directory by using the Apple Password Server, which is based on the SASL (Simple Authentication and Security Layer) protocol.** Open Directory supports a variety of authentication methods, including:
  - APOP (Authenticated POP3) for clients using POP3 for incoming mail service. APOP stores a recoverable password.
  - CRAM-MD5
  - Kerberos
  - Microsoft's LAN Manager for legacy Windows 95 clients
  - Microsoft's NTLMv2 for modern Windows clients
  - Microsoft's MS-CHAPv2 for VPN service clients
  - NSA SHA-1
  - WebDAV-Digest, for web service clients. It stores a recoverable password.

  A subset of Open Directory's authentication methods can be selectively enabled to enhance the security of password storage on the server by using the Policies/Authentication tab of the Open Directory pane's Settings page in Server Admin, shown in Figure 20.5. For example, if you're not providing any Windows services, LAN Manager and NTLMv2 can be disabled to avoid storing passwords that use these authentication methods on the server. This prevents an attacker who gains access to the password database from exploiting weaknesses in these authentication methods to crack users' passwords.

  Open Directory authentication also enables administrators to set password policy, such as a minimum password length or complexity, for all users or for individual account records stored in a particular directory.

- **RADIUS authentication to secure wireless networks and VPN services.** This method provides compatibility with external network devices, such as wireless base stations that support the interoperable RADIUS protocol. The RADIUS service itself authenticates users against Open Directory.

- **Kerberos v5 authentication.** Mac OS X Server supports using Kerberos authentication within Open Directory for integration into existing Kerberos realms. The Key Distribution Center (KDC) in Mac OS X Server also uses the password policies you set up on the server. Kerberos requires using Open Directory passwords. A variety of services in Mac OS X are *kerberized* to support Kerberos authentication, which enables the user to sign in once and use that same authentication session to subsequently authenticate behind the scenes with services, including:
  - Address Book Server
  - AFP
  - Apache
  - FTP
  - iCal Server

- iChat Server
- Mail
- SMB
- SSH
- VPN
- **Third-party LDAP authentication may be used to leverage an existing Microsoft Active Directory or another LDAPv3 directory service infrastructure already in place.**

CROSS-REF

For more on Open Directory and Kerberos, see Chapter 21. For more on RADIUS, see Chapter 17.

Figure 20.5

Configuring supported authentication types for Open Directory in Server Admin

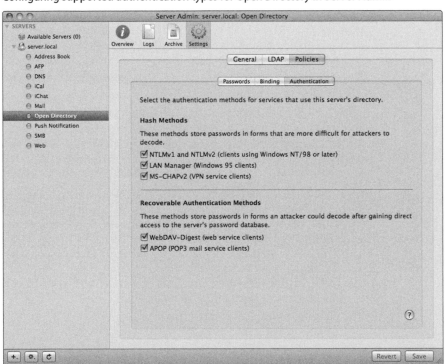

Setting global security policy in Server Admin

To enhance authentication security, administrators may define security policy that sets a minimum duration, length, and complexity for users' Open Directory passwords.

In Server Admin, password policy can be set globally from the Policies/Passwords pane within the Open Directory pane's Settings page, shown in Figure 20.6. Check boxes enable policy restrictions that can disable the account:

- On a specific date
- After being used for a set number of days
- After being inactive for a set number of days
- After a set number of failed login attempts

Figure 20.6

Setting global password policy in Server Admin

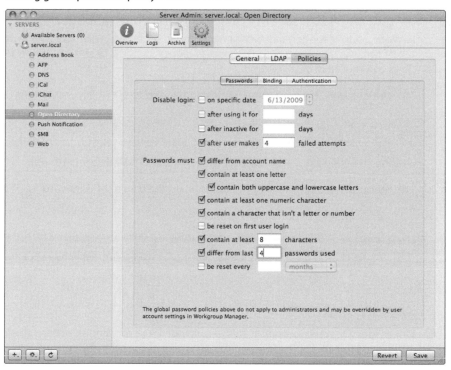

The pane can also set password policy, forcing the user's set password to:

- Differ from the account name
- Contain at least one letter
- Contain both uppercase and lowercase letters
- Contain at least one numeric character
- Contain at least one character that isn't a letter or number
- Be reset after the next login, forcing the user to immediately set a new password for the new account
- Contain a minimum number of characters
- Differ from the last set number of passwords used
- Be reset by the user after a set number of days, weeks, or months

Global password policies aren't applied to administrator accounts.

Setting individual security policy in Workgroup Manager

In Workgroup Manager, password policy can be set for an individual user under the Advanced tab of the user's account record, shown in Figure 20.7. These settings override the global settings configured in Server Admin.

The Options button opens a sheet that can be used to set policy restrictions on the user's login:

- Disabling the account on a specific date
- Disabling the account after being inactive for a set number of days
- Disabling the account after a set number of failed login attempts

The sheet can also set password policy, forcing the user's set password to:

- Contain a minimum number of characters
- Be reset by the user after a set number of days
- Be reset after the next login, forcing the user to immediately set a new password for the new account

Authorization

Once Open Directory authenticates a user, individual services can determine if the user is authorized to access files and services or administer settings by consulting:

- POSIX permissions or ACLs for file system access
- SACLs that define allowed users and administrators

Figure 20.7

Assigning individual password policy in Workgroup Manager

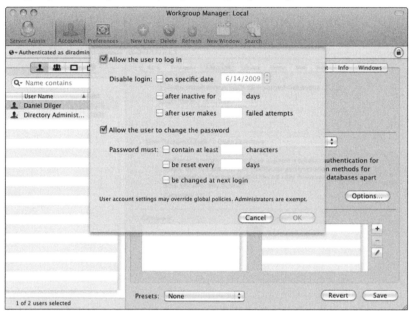

File access permissions

Snow Leopard Server works with two types of file permissions:

- POSIX file permissions are based on the three-tiered Unix model of a user, his or her primary group, and everyone else. Each of the three buckets can be allowed or denied permission to read, write, and execute the file or directory, with each bucket providing at least as much access as the previous one; in other words, the owner has the most access, the group may have less, and the rest of the world may be further restricted.
- ACLs are designed to be compatible with Windows and enable a finer granularity of control that defines a rule set that allows or denies a variety of use permissions to any number of different users or groups specified in the list's entries.

In Mac OS X, ACL support can be activated only on HFS+ volumes, and only the AFP and SMB file-sharing protocols provide network file system support for ACLs. Permissions that ACLs define on files exported by using NFS are enforced by the server but aren't visible to and can't be modified by NFS clients.

ACL permissions are defined by ACEs, which define access to the file or folder by specifying a permission rule that includes:

- A user or group account, specified by its universally unique ID number
- The Allow or Deny ACE type
- Thirteen different access permissions as defined in Apple's ACL model
- Inherited, a flag indicating that the permission was inherited from its parent folder
- Applies to, which indicates how the permission propagates to child files or folders

Inheritance and precedence

In addition to explicit permissions assigned to a file or folder, there may also be inherited permissions that trickle down from a containing folder. Inherited permissions are used to enable administrators to broadly set permissions across a wide range of files instead of explicitly needing to assign file permissions to each file individually.

The Applies to field of the ACE sets inheritance rules. There are four options:

- Apply to this folder
- Apply to child folders (subfolders)
- Apply to child files (files in this folder)
- Apply to all descendants

When a new file or folder is created, the Mac OS X kernel determines its effective permissions based on the inheritance settings of its parent folder. After creating a new ACE permission that applies to child items, those inherited permissions must be propagated before the containing folders and files below it in the file system hierarchy inherit the assigned permissions. Only the entire ACL can be propagated, not an individual ACE.

A file with inherited permissions can't change those permissions until they're made explicit.

To determine what type of access a user has to a shared file or folder, Snow Leopard Server evaluates the file's or folder's ACEs, followed by its designated POSIX permissions. It then applies the following rules of precedence to determine the effective permissions for a given user:

- **Without defined ACEs, POSIX permissions apply.**
- **With ACEs, rule order is important.** If a file or folder has defined ACEs, the kernel starts with the first ACE in the ACL and works through the list until the requested permission is satisfied or denied. ACE order can be changed from the command line by using the `chmod` command.
- **Deny permissions override others.** Server Admin lists Deny permissions above Allow permissions because Deny permissions have precedence. When evaluating permissions, once a Deny permission is encountered, the system ignores any remaining permissions assigned to the user and simply denies permission. For example, if a user is allowed read permissions in one ACE but belongs to a group denied read permissions in another, Server Admin reorders the permissions so the Deny permission comes first to highlight that the system enforces the Deny rule.

● **Allow permissions are composite.** The system defines a user's permissions as a combination of all the permissions assigned to the user, including standard POSIX permissions.

CROSS-REF
For more on using file permissions to secure file shares, see Chapter 22.

Service access permissions
Snow Leopard Server uses SACLs to manage access to and configuration of services running on the server.

Using SACLs to manage access to services
Users and groups can be selectively allowed access to all or specific services by using the Services tab of the Access pane of the server's Settings page in Server Admin, shown in Figure 20.8.

Figure 20.8

SACL configuration for user and group access to individual services in Server Admin

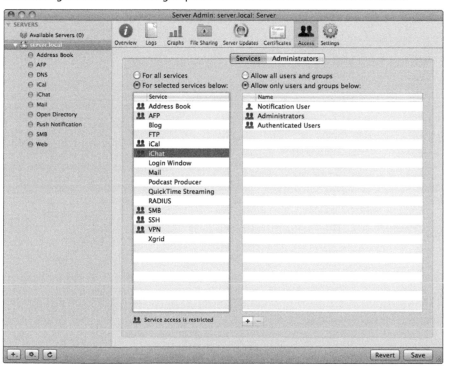

Using SACLs to manage access to Mobile Access services

Users and groups can also be selectively granted access to secure mail, web, Address Book, and iCal services made available through the Mobile Access service from the Access page of the Mobile Access pane in Server Admin, shown in Figure 20.9.

Figure 20.9

Mobile Access SACL configuration for users and groups in Server Admin

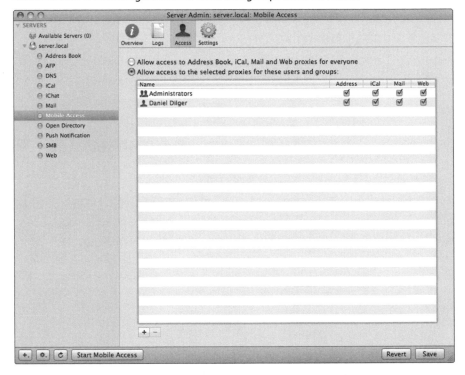

Using SACLs to manage administrative access to services

Using the Administrators tab of the Settings page of the server in Server Admin, shown in Figure 20.10, users and groups can be selectively allowed either:

- Administer access to configure the settings of all or specific services
- Monitor access to view the configuration settings of all or specific services

This enables users to monitor or configure individual services without needing full administrative control of the server itself.

SACLs aren't limited to managing administrative access within Server Admin but work on a system level to also control access to command-line utilities. However, access to Unix configuration files are not protected by SACLs and must therefore instead be managed by using POSIX or ACL file system permissions.

Figure 20.10

SACL configuration for user and group administrative access to services in Server Admin

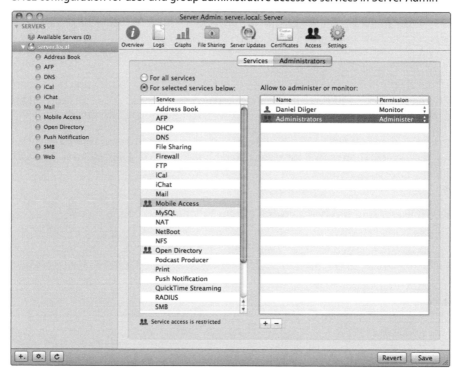

Securing backups

Access to server backups, including Time Machine Server file shares that store users' backups, should be considered equivalent to access of the server's primary copy of the same data, even if some measures are taken to physically lock or password-protect the backup archives.

Moving a copy of backups offsite is a critically important element of any backup plan but also a potential security risk. The private data stored on backups is likely carefully secured on the server, but once taken offsite, the hard drives or other storage media are much easier to steal or potentially even modify with malicious intent.

For this reason, adequate security measures must be taken to make sure that backups are treated as carefully as server equipment and safeguarded with the same degree of access control as the primary server resources they're providing a backup for.

Securing Transports with Encryption

Once data leaves the local network and ventures out across the open Internet, additional security measures are required to safeguard sensitive data. Encrypting data traveling via network transport protocols lets remote users access local resources without exposing private data.

VPN

A VPN enables organizations to provide secured access to the services and resources provided on a local network to authenticated remote users over the public Internet.

A VPN is an encrypted link between two networks that offers the security of a private network at a much lower cost than paying for a dedicated phone line to the remote user. It's a VPN in the sense that it uses a low-cost shared network to create a secured link by using encryption, often described as a tunnel that the encrypted traffic passes through.

Mac OS X Server supports two methods of conventional VPN remote access:

- **PPTP** (Point-to-Point Tunneling Protocol)
- **L2TP/IPsec** (Layer 2 Tunneling Protocol using IPsec encryption)

CROSS-REF
For more on the VPN service, see Chapter 16.

SSL

SSL is a standard originally created by Netscape for allowing web servers to secure a confidential connection with a user, encrypt transmissions, and authenticate as a trusted entity.

Netscape's SSL 3.0 formed the basis of the IETF TLS specification, which has since technically replaced SSL. However, TLS is still commonly referred to as SSL, particularly by Apple within its Server Admin interface.

SSL works by using public-key cryptography. The server retains a private key and publishes a public key to users in the form of an SSL certificate. Information that the public key encrypts within the certificate can be decrypted only by using the private key.

This enables users who trust the public-key certificate — which is often itself signed by a trusted third-party Certificate Authority to enable clients to automatically trust that the website identity listed in the certificate legitimately sent it — to:

- Generate a random number
- Encrypt it with the server's public key
- Send the result to the server

Only the server can decrypt this information via its secret private key. This exchange enables the server and client to create session keys for further encrypted communications. No third parties can intercept and decrypt the initial exchange of the encrypted random number, so the keys generated on both ends enable the client and server to continue confidential, encrypted communications.

Securing web access

For web clients, this results in a security upgrade from HTTP to encrypted HTTPS, allowing the client to provide private information, such as login information, and receive private information in response, such as banking details.

To support SSL, the server must generate its own self-signed certificate identity (which clients have to assume trust in) or obtain a signed version of that identity endorsed by a Certificate Authority, a step that enables clients to automatically trust the server's public-key certificate as reputable if it matches the URL it was received from by the client.

SSL can then be activated on the web server by using the Security pane within the Sites page.

CROSS-REF

For more on configuring SSL within the web service, see Chapter 24.

Securing access with other services

SSL is also used to secure access to other services in Mac OS X, including:

- LDAP directory services in the Open Directory service, configured on the Settings page within the LDAP tab of Server Admin
- Address Book Server, configured on the Settings page of the Authentication tab
- iCal Server, configured on the Settings page of the Authentication tab
- iChat Server, configured on the Settings page of the General tab
- IMAP, POP, and SMTP mail services, configured on the Settings page of the Advanced/ Security tabs
- Mobile Access, configured on the Settings page by using the Advanced button

- VPN authentication, configured on the Settings page under the L2TP and PPTP tabs
- RADIUS authentication, configured on the Settings page
- Podcast Producer capture, configured on the Settings page of the General tab

Securing Applications and Preferences

Mac OS X Server security can also be extended to users' computers by using technologies available in the client operating system that can be managed by network policy set in Workgroup Manager and enforced through directory services.

Application signing

Beginning with Mac OS X Leopard, Apple uses application signing to enable developers to digitally sign code by using a Certificate Authority–signed certificate with the key usage of commercial code signing. This step hermetically seals the application, preventing malicious efforts to tamper with its code.

Once an application is signed, the system can trust that the code hasn't changed since it was installed, enabling the Mac OS X application firewall to safely grant the program inbound network access at the user's request. If an application isn't signed, the application firewall attempts to sign the application itself.

The system also asks the user for his or her consent only to allow an updated version of a signed application, similarly signed by the same certificate, to assume the same keychain access as the previous application. This prevents the user from being repeatedly inundated with requests to grant updated applications the same access to the keys that previous versions of the software have stored.

The system also uses application signing to limit access to specific security-related APIs and to control access to applications as defined by parental controls or managed preferences.

CROSS-REF
For more on the application firewall in Mac OS X Server, see Chapter 14.

Managed preferences

Configured within Workgroup Manager, managed preferences enable administrators to either set or force specific configurations for network users, groups of users, or computers or across groups of computers.

Using managed preferences, an organization can centrally automate the setup of a customized user environment tailored to specific users or defined computers. Managed preferences can also be used to enforce security policy, preventing users from installing or launching applications and even turning off hardware features, such as Bluetooth or optical disk burning.

CROSS-REF

For more on using managed preferences, see Chapter 36.

Summary

- Physical security of the server, including access to cables, ports, and opening the case, is a frequently overlooked security issue. Physical access to the server can be exploited to work around a variety of security mechanisms, including file system access controls.

- Unnecessary server hardware, including wireless interfaces, ports accepting mass storage devices, and audio/video capabilities, or software can be disabled o harden the server's security profile.

- Administrators should log in to the server with the least amount of user privilege they need.

- Client users with mobile accounts can secure their home folder data by using FileVault and create additional encrypted disk images on server shares for efficiently storing confidential data.

- The Mac OS X Keychain can simplify the use of multiple passwords, making it easier for users to employ secure passwords and take advantage of multi-factor authentication.

- Authentication systems, including Open Directory, only verify identity; they don't authorize the user with specific permissions.

- File permissions and SACLs can be used to shape users' access permissions to files and services on the system.

- Mac OS X includes VPN services to secure remote users' access to local resources.

- SSL certificates are used to secure access to a variety of services in Snow Leopard Server by setting up confidential transactions to establish encrypted security with users.

Using Open Directory

M ac OS X Server uses Open Directory to handle its network directory services, which act as a central store for information about users, groups, computers, and other network resources in an organization.

As an authoritative repository of network information, the directory services records Open Directory makes available are used to:

- Enable users and services to look up available network resources, such as printers, web servers, or file system mounts

- Authenticate users' identities for login to network systems and to access services

- Allow services to obtain authenticated users' identity information, enabling the services to evaluate requested access authorization

- Provide and manage account details for network users, such as their mail service configuration, home folder settings, and quota limitations on print, mail, and home folder shares

- Enforce managed preferences settings to define and restrict the configuration and environment allowed for network users, groups, and computers

In addition to serving as the primary network directory domain for Mac OS X Server, Open Directory also acts as the abstraction layer that sits between processes that need directory information and various sources of that information, which may include:

- Any number of different Open Directory domains on the network

- Third-party LDAP directory servers, including Microsoft's Active Directory, Novell's eDirectory, or OpenLDAP

- A local directory domain

- Sun's NIS or local BSD configuration files

- Services dynamically advertised by Bonjour, SMB/WINS, or SLP

- Another source enabled by using an Open Directory plug-in

This chapter describes how Open Directory works, what's involved in planning for directory services, how it's configured, and how to maintain and monitor directory services.

Introduction to Open Directory

Directory services supply a centralized repository of information about a network domain, its users, computers, defined groups, and available services. A look at how Open Directory developed can help in understanding how the system works and how it supports interoperability with other directory services.

Directory service origins: NIS, NetInfo, NT domains

Essentially, directory services are an outgrowth and expansion of the simple naming services provided by DNS, which delivers an authoritative system limited to looking up hostnames and service records across the Internet.

DNS replaced the role of static host files stored on each computer at /etc/hosts, with a network service that could provide dynamic updates for IP address assignments to any systems that needed the information.

NIS

In the mid-1980s, Sun developed NFS as a protocol to access files stored on a remote computer. A problem that needed to be addressed was that different clients on the network needed to share consistent user and group identification information for NFS-shared files in order to manage access permissions.

At the time, Unix systems all stored their user and group information in a series of flat files following a basic outline, with some variations in naming conventions:

- /etc/passwd is a list of users, their user and group IDs, the location of their home directories, and, originally, each user's password but later was typically a reference to a shadow password file.

- /etc/master.passwd is a shadow password list of users' passwords removed from the passwd file and encrypted with a hash to enhance security.

- /etc/group is a list of groups and their members.

Sun's complementary NIS (Network Information Service) updated client systems' static flat file sources of information about known users and groups with an automated service. Existing processes didn't typically need to know anything about NIS because they could continue to consult the configuration information in /etc flat files; NIS simply kept that information up to date.

Among problems with NIS is the fact that distributing passwords over the network isn't very secure, even if they're hashed with basic encryption. Pushing out constant file updates to hosts on the network was also inefficient and resource-intensive. However, NIS did become the common way to provide directory services for Unix systems.

NetInfo

In the late 1980s, NeXT introduced NetInfo, a system that replaced how Unix processes ask for directory information. Instead of constantly updating the old static information sources, NetInfo replaced them with a directory database on each system. Processes looking up a user or host-name would have their request redirected to the NetInfo database.

The advantage to this system was that multiple levels of external databases of directory information could also be consulted by using the same system. A process that needed to know about available printers, users, or hostnames could consult NetInfo, and if the information couldn't be found in the local database, the system could direct the query to other NetInfo domains maintained by servers in the organization until the answer was found, just like a DNS query.

There were also problems with NetInfo; it was negatively associated with NeXT as a proprietary, nonstandard system in the Unix world. It also had some technical problems. If a DNS lookup failed, other requests for information could end up stalled behind it. If the local NetInfo database became corrupted, users couldn't even log in to the machine without manually tracking down and deleting the NetInfo database, which would wipe out the local user database.

Apple took the concept of NetInfo and modernized it in Mac OS X, first making it open source and eventually replacing the local NetInfo database with standard XML configuration files beginning with Mac OS X Leopard.

In addition to deprecating the directory database design, Apple also dropped the NetInfo name and began using the title Directory Services instead.

Conceptually, however, the new Open Directory performs the same role in Mac OS X that the old NetInfo did: It abstracts away the differences in various implementations of directory services so processes don't need to know anything apart from how to talk to Mac OS X's Directory Services.

NT domains

Microsoft implemented its own directory domain system for Windows NT in the mid-1990s, which used a Primary Domain Controller to authenticate domain logins and network services for Windows NT client machines bound to the domain.

Backup Domain Controllers could be set up to act as replicas to balance the load for directory service requests from clients. However, a local network could only support one NT domain, and Windows clients could also only support being bound to a single domain.

Local Windows user account information is stored in the Windows Registry database. As with NetInfo, any corruption in the Registry database can render the machine unbootable. The Windows Registry is even more fragile because of the fact that many applications, utilities, and processes set and change registry values directly as compared to NetInfo, where direct manipulation of its data was extremely rare.

NT domains were entirely proprietary to Microsoft, but the development of the Samba open-source project has made it possible for Unix-like operating systems to participate in or even serve as a domain controller for Windows clients, a feature Apple has integrated into its directory services architecture in Mac OS X Server.

Modern directory services: X.500 and LDAP

Parallel to the development of NIS and NetInfo in the 1980s, the International Telecommunication Union (ITU) began work on defining standards for email messaging (X.400) and directory services (X.500).

X.500

The X.500 standard envisioned publishing organizations' directory information by using the Directory Access Protocol (DAP) in order to facilitate email services, enabling users and other entities to be looked up by a Distinguished Name, just as computer hosts could be looked up by their fully qualified domain name by using DNS.

A Distinguished Name (dn) is composed from a Relative Distinguished Name, which may be expressed as a Common Name (cn), combined with a path of other entities, including Domain Components (dc), which are patterned after the organization's DNS domain. For example, a user's Distinguished Name might be expressed as:

```
dn: cn=Daniel Dilger,dc=example,dc=com
```

An X.500 directory might be organized in any tree structure that makes sense to an organization and would likely contain lots of private information, making organizations unlikely to want to expose it to public access in the manner of DNS. DAP was also a heavyweight protocol in that it was complex and difficult to support and was tied to the ITU's OSI network stack rather than TCP/IP, which had become far more popular with the emergence of the commercial Internet.

Novell Directory Services (NDS) implemented X.500 for DOS users in 1993, and Microsoft released Exchange Server in 1996 with X.500 directory services to manage its email users.

LDAP

Responding to criticisms of DAP, the IETF developed LDAP, initially for accessing X.500 directories by using the TCP/IP network stack and eventually for actually implementing directory services.

In Windows 2000, Microsoft migrated Exchange Server's X.500 directory service to replace NT domains and act as the preferred directory services system for Windows servers under the new name Active Directory.

Open Directory and LDAP

In Mac OS X Jaguar Server 10.2, Apple introduced Open Directory as a Mac OS X framework for working with information from a variety of directory services.

Jaguar Server's Open Directory 1.0 continued to use a NetInfo directory domain but added support for MIT's Kerberos authentication by incorporating a Kerberos key distribution center (KDC) and the alternative capacity to join an existing Kerberos realm.

The release also enabled the storage of user passwords in a separate Authentication Manager outside the directory instead of using crypt passwords stored in the directory domain database, as previous versions of NetInfo had.

The following year, Panther Server 10.3 replaced its NetInfo database with an LDAP directory based on the open-source OpenLDAP project and stored by using Berkeley DB. It also replaced Authentication Manager with the new Apple Password Server for securely storing directory users' passwords in a manner compatible with a variety of different authentication mechanisms.

Panther Server also incorporated support for using Samba 3 to provide NT domain controller services to Windows users by using the same directory information Open Directory managed. The following release added support for joining Active Directory domains as a member server.

With the release of Mac OS X Leopard Server, support for NetInfo was eliminated completely, and even local directory domain information was stored in XML files rather than in a NetInfo database.

Directory domains

In any directory service, a series of records needs to be maintained by a directory server. In Mac OS X, those records may be stored in:

- A local domain accessible only by local users and processes, described as `/Local/Default` and saved as XML files at `/var/db/dslocal/`
- Local flat files in legacy use by the BSD subsystem and NIS, described as `/BSD/Local` and stored in the standard Unix files within `/etc`
- A network-visible directory domain made available to any authorized users, described as being within the LDAPv3 node, such as the designation `/LDAPv3/127.0.0.1`

Mac OS X systems can bind to multiple directory domains by adding a Network Account Server from the Login Options page of the Accounts pane in Mac OS X Snow Leopard's System Preferences, shown in Figure 21.1.

Workgroup Manager allows users with administrative access to a directory domain to view and edit records. It can be used to work with account records in the server's local domain or in its network-visible directory domain.

CROSS-REF
For more on using Workgroup Manager, see Chapter 10.

Figure 21.1

Configuring a Network Account Server in System Preferences

Search policy

Systems running Mac OS X use a defined search policy or search path to look up information published by directory services that the system is configured to use. By default, a Mac OS X system consults only its local domain. This means the system knows only about users, groups, and other entities created in its local accounts record.

When users and groups are created in the Accounts pane of System Preferences, they're being defined in the local domain and are available for use only on that system. In other words, remote users can only log in to a system via SSH or personal file sharing by using accounts that have been defined on that system's local domain.

Multiple levels of search policy

In order to share accounts across a network so they can be used to log in to any system and access resources on multiple servers, a shared pool of account information has to be served by a network-visible directory domain. Computers join the domain and add it to their search policy.

This is something like autonomous counties joining to form a state. The counties might have local politicians that exercise authority within their county, but state politicians have authority across the entire state.

Similarly, local users defined in the local domain of a computer can be used only on that system, whereas network accounts defined in the shared directory domain could be used to log in to any system connected to the domain.

Additional levels of search policy can be created with hierarchical levels of directory domains. This is like states joining to form a federation.

A practical example of using multiple levels of search policy would be defining individual directory domains to serve regional offices within an organization and a second directory domain that defines users with access across the entire company. Systems would have three levels in their search policy:

- Their local domain
- The regional directory domain
- The company directory domain

This structure enables administrative delegation, so each regional directory can and only needs to manage the accounts relevant to it. Changes that need to be applied across the scope of the entire company could also be made in one place and still be visible to all users, thanks to the search policy.

Once a search finds an answer, it stops looking. For example, if a local system looks up a user and finds a matching account in the local domain, it doesn't continue searching available directory domains over the network.

Automatic search policy

Mac OS X can be configured with automatic search policy. This allows the system to obtain the address of the local LDAP directory server from DHCP when the system gets its IP assignment.

The specified LDAP server is automatically added to the system's search policy, enabling network users that the directory server defines to authenticate for local login. This is flexible and convenient because the system can automatically join a domain when connecting to one network and then adjust the search policy upon joining a new directory domain when connecting to another network — all without any manual configuration for the user to manage.

There's also a security risk in using automatic search policy because a system configured to automatically join any network via DHCP and obtain LDAP configuration settings could be duped into using a malicious DHCP server, particularly if the system is also set to automatically join any open Wi-Fi network that becomes available.

Custom search policy

Mac OS X systems can also be configured with a custom search policy, which allows the user to determine the search order for directory domains.

One common example is defining Mac OS X machines to first authenticate with an Active Directory domain as a user and then obtain managed preferences configuration from an Open Directory domain on a workgroup or computer level.

With a custom search policy, once a user disconnects from a network, the directory domain is no longer available to obtain authentication or managed preferences information. However, using a locally cached mobile account, the user's network directory account is mirrored locally, enabling the user to log in and use cached managed preferences settings without needing any access to the directory server.

Search policy for authentication and contacts

Mac OS X maintains two separate search policies for specifying the order in which available directory domains are accessed to obtain different kinds of information:

- The Authentication search policy is used to define how to obtain administrative data, including user authentication information.

- The Contacts search policy is used to define how to obtain names, addresses, and other contact information from the directory.

Each can be configured independently by using one of three options:

- Automatic, which sets search policy via DHCP settings

- Local directory, which consults only the local directory domain

- Custom Path, which enables the user to set the search order of configured directory domains

Search policy is set by using Directory Utility, shown in Figure 21.2, which can be launched from the Network Account Server editor available from the Login Options page of the Accounts pane in Mac OS X Snow Leopard's System Preferences.

Figure 21.2

Configuring search policy by using Directory Utility

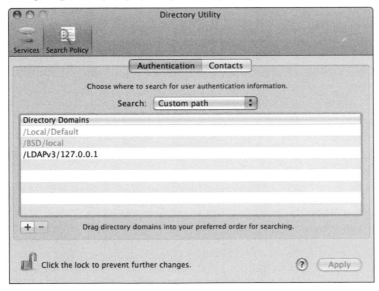

Open Directory authentication

Open Directory supports a variety of authentication methods for supporting different network services, each of which has developed around different standards. Authentication shouldn't be confused with authorization:

- Authentication is verifying an individual's identity, done by comparing the username and password a user offers with the system's record of what it should be.
- Authorization is verifying that an authenticated individual has the authority to perform a specific action.

Open Directory provides user authentication for network services so that each service doesn't have to each manage its own list of users and passwords. It also provides information about the user, such as group memberships, that the service can evaluate in determining whether the user is authorized to perform an action.

For example, a file-sharing service might provide a user's supplied credentials to determine if they're valid. Open Directory maintains the user's record in its LDAP directory and stores an encrypted copy of the user's password in a special Password Server database. It can compare the password the user supplied with its own records and authenticate the user to the file-sharing service.

However, the file-sharing service itself needs to determine if the authenticated user is authorized to access the files it's requesting. The file-sharing service first uses its SACL to decide whether the user is authorized to access the service. It may subsequently request additional information from Open Directory to determine whether the user's group membership allows it authorized access to the requested files, evaluating the relevant POSIX permissions and ACLs in the file system.

Authentication methods

How a service authenticates depends on the authentication methods it knows how to use. Because different services in Mac OS X Server are often based on open-source projects that have developed independently, Open Directory supports a variety of different authentication options.

When a service authenticates a user, Open Directory negotiates the use of the strongest possible authentication protocol.

Open Directory stores passwords outside its LDAP directory by using the Apple Password Server, which is based on the SASL protocol.

SASL is an abstraction layer designed to match authentication methods with application protocols, so network services that support SASL can conceivably support any authentication methods that also support SASL.

Open Directory supports a variety of authentication methods, including:

- APOP (Authenticated Post Office Protocol), for clients using POP to access the local mail service. APOP stores a recoverable password.
- CRAM-MD5

- MIT Kerberos v5 via the Generic Security Services Application Program Interface (GSSAPI)
- Microsoft LAN Manager for legacy Windows 95 clients
- Microsoft NTLMv2 for more modern Windows clients
- Microsoft MS-CHAPv2 for VPN service clients
- NSA SHA-1
- WebDAV-Digest, for web service clients. It stores a recoverable password.

A subset of Open Directory's authentication methods can be selectively enabled to enhance the security of password storage on the server by using the Policies/Authentication tab of the Open Directory pane's Settings page in Server Admin.

For example, if you're not providing any Windows services, LAN Manager and NTLMv2 can be disabled to avoid storing passwords on the server by using these authentication methods. This prevents an attacker who gains access to the password database from exploiting weaknesses in these authentication methods to crack users' passwords.

NOTE

Under NetInfo, user passwords were stored in the directory domain database itself. These are called *crypt passwords* and are retained only for legacy compatibility reasons. Any accounts using a crypt password can support only basic authentication. Modern account records created since Mac OS X 10.1 are assigned Open Directory passwords instead.

Kerberos authentication

The ideal authentication method for services in Mac OS X Server is Kerberos. That's because Kerberos is designed to deliver a variety of unique security features, including:

- SSO to allow users to authenticate with the system once. Then, they obtain a ticket-granting credential that enables them to obtain subsequent tickets to authenticate with services over a period of time without having to re-enter their passwords throughout the configured session period, similar to obtaining an amusement park day pass that allows its bearer entry to any attraction without presenting an individual pass for each ride.
- Mutual authentication proves the identity of both the client and the server to prevent malicious attackers from posing as legitimate network services.
- Passwords aren't sent over the network; instead, the system exchanges signed tickets that can't be decrypted to obtain a password.
- Time sensitivity in transactions helps prevent replay attacks.

The problem with deploying Kerberos has been that it requires a lot of complex integration work. This has historically limited Kerberos to large organizations, such as universities:

- Kerberos requires installing a KDC password database and registering all the servers and clients to use it.

- Kerberos requires integration with an existing directory system because Kerberos itself doesn't manage information such as a user's group memberships or home folder location. The tools for managing Kerberos and managing directory services have historically been different.

- Kerberos requires support in both server and client software, which has been hit or miss. Different vendors may implement elements of the standard differently.

- Some network protocols were designed to use only traditional challenge-response authentication methods and need some adapting mechanism to work with Kerberos.

Mac OS X makes it easy to deploy Kerberos by delivering a KDC integrated with Open Directory and providing an integrated suite of network services as well as server and client software that's all Kerberized to work with the authentication system.

Serving directory domains

Once Kerberized, an Open Directory master acts as a Kerberos *realm*, or authentication domain. The name of a Kerberos realm is shouted in all caps to distinguish it from lowercase DNS names. Within the realm are users and services, which are both referred to as *principals*.

In Kerberos v5, names of realms and principals are expressed in these forms:

- Realm: `EXAMPLE.COM`
- User principal: `danieldilger@EXAMPLE.COM`
- Service principal: `afpserver/server.example.com@EXAMPLE.COM`

Open Directory server roles

Mac OS X Server can act as an authenticating directory server in the role of one of the following:

- **Open Directory master.** As the first server to set up a directory domain, it acts as the primary owner of the domain's LDAP directory records, the Password Server database, and, optionally, a Kerberos KDC. This role is configured from the Settings page of the Open Directory pane in Server Admin.

- **Open Directory replica.** It acts as a read-only backup to share the load in serving a directory domain. A master can manage 32 replicas. This role is configured from the Settings page of the Open Directory pane.

- **Open Directory relay.** A relay is a replica with replicas of its own. Using multiple tiers of replicas limits the number of replicas a master has to update while allowing a large number of replica servers in total. A relay replica can have 32 replicas of its own, creating the potential for 1,056 replicas in two tiers (32 × 32 replicas + 32 relay replicas), where no master or relay needs to manage more than 32 replicas. This role is configured from the Settings page of the Open Directory pane.

- **Primary Domain Controller (PDC).** This is an Open Directory master configured to serve Windows clients joined to its NT domain. This role is configured from the Settings page of the SMB pane in Server Admin.

● **Backup Domain Controller (BDC).** This is an Open Directory replica configured to serve Windows clients joined to its NT domain, assisting a Primary Domain Controller. This role is configured from the Settings page of the SMB pane in Server Admin.

Managed preferences

Configured within Workgroup Manager and stored in an Open Directory domain, managed preferences enables administrators to either set or force specific configurations for network users, groups of users, or computers or across groups of computers.

Using managed preferences, an organization can centrally automate the setup of a customized user environment tailored to specific users or to defined computers. Managed preferences can also be used to enforce security policy, preventing users from installing or launching applications and even turning off hardware features, such as Bluetooth or optical disc burning.

CROSS-REF
For more on using managed preferences, see Chapter 36.

Planning Directory Services

If you manage a small network with users who have only limited needs for network services, you may not need to assume the extra effort of administering a directory server. It's possible to simply have users log in to their systems by using local user accounts and to create a duplicate series of local accounts on the server they can use for file sharing.

However, the benefits of creating a directory domain rapidly increase in proportion to the number of duplicate local accounts you need to manage. Additionally, there's now little extra work involved in setting up a network directory, and doing so unlocks a variety of useful services bundled with Snow Leopard Server.

Having one account per user managed in a central location enables you to use network home folders for users, simplifying backup. If you manage both Mac and Windows clients, the directory integration features in Mac OS X Server enable you to share accounts across platforms.

Strategic deployment

Your deployment plans for directory services depend on your current circumstances, whether building from scratch, expanding, or integrating into an existing directory services infrastructure:

● **If you have no current directory services in place, you should configure an Open Directory master and should consider setting up an Open Directory replica for failover.** Once your directory is up and running, any downtime a single directory server experiences will interrupt all your network services.

- **If you need to supply directory services across a wide area, you need to plan out strategic deployment of multiple replicas.** Depending on the number of users you'll support, the number of different sites, and the network bandwidth available between sites (whether floors in a building, buildings on a campus, or regional offices around the country), you may need to set up replica servers at each location or, potentially, multiple replicas at locations where network speed limits the link between the master and the replica to the extent that a local failure would slow directory access to the point of being unusable.

- **If your organization already operates directory services, you can set up your local server as a replica or a workgroup configuration server that imports users from the existing directory service.** If your organization already operates an Active Directory or Open Directory domain, even if you lack the permission to edit accounts in the corporate directory domain, you can also set up Mac OS X Server to use cross-domain authentication via Kerberos. This enables your server to accept and validate a user's Kerberos authorization tickets granted by the corporate directory domain.

Capacity planning

The number of users you plan to support per directory server also factors into your plans, and how they work has a big impact on their needs:

- Users who work on a single system all day, such as administrators and graphic artists, put very limited demands on the directory server.

- Users who log in and out of multiple systems, such as students regularly moving between classes in a lab, have a much larger impact.

Depending on the behaviors of the users you're supporting and, in particular, their login and logout patterns and frequencies, you can divide up the thousand simultaneous connections Apple rates for a dedicated Open Directory server among the peak concurrent logins you expect to handle and calculate the number of replicas you need to deploy at each location.

Another factor to consider is whether your Open Directory server will run other tasks or be solely dedicated to performing authentication and LDAP lookups. Use of SSL encryption, the number of replicas a master or relay has to keep updated, and the speed of the network also factor into your needs assessment.

CROSS-REF
For more on hardware and capacity planning, see Chapter 4.

Security planning

In addition to capacity planning, you also need to include a detailed review of security in your deployment plans. Physical security of the directory server is critically important because access to the system could lead to a compromise of the entire network's security.

Although the system never gives passwords back to users, not even to the root user of the system, it's possible for attackers who gain physical access to the password database to extract forms of the users' passwords used to support certain authentication methods.

For this reason, you may decide to turn off support for authentication methods that store unencrypted or simple hash passwords in the Password Server database if the potential for the theft of the server's Password Server database outweighs the convenience of using a broader range of authentication methods. At the same time, consider the implications of your decisions.

For example, turning off support for APOP, which is used to securely authenticate POP3 mail users — because of fears that an attacker might physically break into your server and steal a copy of your Password Server's database to obtain users' recoverable APOP passwords — might actually result in a larger security risk; users connecting with simple password authentication instead will expose their passwords in a manner far easier for malicious attackers to obtain than stealing the server's database.

You should also consider that backup copies of your directory server are as valuable and at least as vulnerable to theft or misuse as the copy you're serving. Data backups should be closely monitored and kept under the same security practices as the server itself.

CROSS-REF
For more on security planning, see Chapter 20.

Directory Services Setup and Configuration

To operate basic directory services, you need:

- A registered domain name for your server and properly configured DNS records
- A deployment plan for setting up new services or integrating into existing services
- Plans that outline a single domain or multiple tiers of domains with a set search policy
- A directory database backup and recovery plan
- Outlined client platform support for Mac and Windows users
- User account information for your users, groups, and computers
- Sufficient storage for the LDAP directory stored on the server
- An SSL certificate if you plan to support secure remote transport of LDAP requests
- A policy covering password strength and authentication methods

Setting up the Open Directory service requires enabling the service in Server Admin and then doing the following:

- Configuring directory services to operate as an Open Directory master
- Setting up backup directory services to operate as an Open Directory replica or an Open Directory relay if you're configuring more than 32 replicas

- Configuring Windows domain services by setting up a Primary Domain Controller
- Setting up backup Windows domain services so Open Directory replicas can serve as Backup Domain Controllers
- Configuring advanced directory service settings
- Configuring servers and clients to connect to directory services for authentication and contact information

To enable directory service configuration in Server Admin, follow these steps:

1. **Launch Server Admin and then connect to the desired server.**

2. **Select the server listing and then click Settings on the toolbar.**

3. **Click the Services tab.**

4. **Click the check box for Open Directory.**

5. **Click Save.** Open Directory should now appear in the list of configurable services for the selected server, as shown in Figure 21.3.

Figure 21.3

Enabling the Open Directory pane in Server Admin

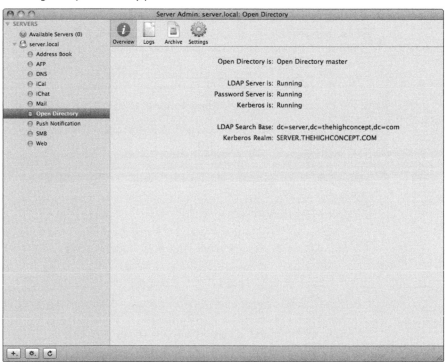

Creating an Open Directory master

An Open Directory master acts as the primary owner of the domain's LDAP directory records, the Password Server database, and, optionally, the Kerberos KDC.

Prior to becoming an Open Directory master, Mac OS X Server may be configured as:

- **A Standalone Directory Server.** This doesn't provide a network-visible directory domain; it only maintains local accounts for use on the server. Promoting a Standalone Directory Server to an Open Directory master simply expands its capabilities.

- **A member of another directory service.** If a Standalone Directory Server is already connected to another directory, upgrading it to an Open Directory master simply expands its capabilities. The server remains connected to the other directory services and simply searches its own directory for information first before searching the external directory.

- **An existing Open Directory master.** To destroy an existing master and set it up as the new master of a pristine new directory domain, you simply demote the master to a Standalone Directory Server and then set it up again as an Open Directory master.

- **An existing Open Directory replica.** A replica can be promoted to an Open Directory master of the same domain to replace the failed master or it can be destroyed to set it up as the new master of a pristine new directory domain or a new replica of a new master. To promote an existing replica to become the new master of the existing directory domain, you simply change the replica's role to Open Directory master. Other replicas of the old master must be destroyed and reinstated as replicas of the new master. To destroy an existing replica and set it up as the master of a pristine new directory domain, you simply demote the replica to a Standalone Directory Server and then set it up again as an Open Directory master.

To promote a server to an Open Directory master in Server Admin, follow these steps:

1. **Launch Server Admin and then connect to the desired server.**

2. **Select Open Directory and then click Settings on the toolbar.**

3. **Click the General tab, shown in Figure 21.4.**

4. **Click Change next to the designated Role:**
   - If the server is currently a Standalone Directory Server, you can promote it to an Open Directory master.
   - If the server is currently an Open Directory master, you must demote it to a Standalone Directory Server before you can set it up as a new Open Directory master.
   - If the server is currently an Open Directory replica or relay, you can promote it to the Open Directory master of the domain to replace the failed master.
   - If the server is currently an Open Directory replica or relay, you can alternatively demote it to a Standalone Directory Server before setting it up as a new Open Directory master unaffiliated with the previous domain.

5. **Choose Open Directory master and then click Continue.**

Figure 21.4

The General pane of the Open Directory pane in Server Admin

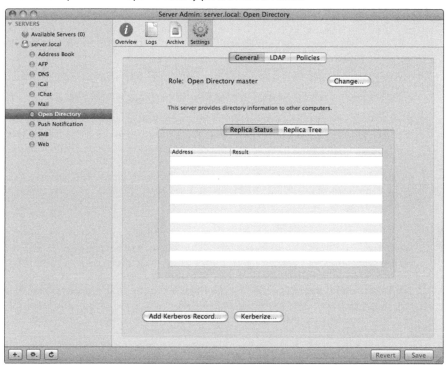

6. **Create an account for the primary directory administrator for the new directory:**

   - **Name.** The default is Directory Administrator. If you plan to operate multiple domains, create administrator account names for each domain; each account name should be unique and descriptive.

   - **Short name.** The default is diradmin; select something unique and descriptive instead.

   - **User ID.** The default is 1000. Select a UID below 100 if you don't want the directory administrator account name to show up in the login window.

   - **Password.** Use a secure password to protect access to your user records. Although the directory administrator account can't be used to retrieve users' domain passwords, it can change passwords to a known value.

7. **Click Continue.**

8. **Type the master domain information for the new directory domain:**

   - **Kerberos Realm.** The default is your server's DNS name in all capital letters.

   - **Search Base.** Leave blank to use the LDAP directory's default search base suffix based on the server's DNS name or add additional entries if needed.

9. **Click Continue.**

10. **Review the settings and then click Continue to create the Open Directory master.**

11. **Click Done.** LDAP, Password Server, and Kerberos services should now appear as running on the Overview page of the Open Directory pane in Server Admin, as shown in Figure 21.3.

Creating an Open Directory replica or relay

An Open Directory replica or relay acts as a read-only backup of the domain's LDAP directory records, the Password Server database, and, optionally, the Kerberos KDC to support the job of the Open Directory master in providing authentication directory information.

If the Open Directory master fails, client systems using it switch to using an available replica. When functioning normally, the Open Directory master sends regular updates to any configured replicas.

During this replication period, the master can't provide authentication or other directory services itself, so plan to perform the initial deployment of replica servers at a time when the replication won't impact network users. Performing replication over a slow link may take some time.

When setting up multiple replicas, you must allow the master to finish replication with each; if you attempt to perform multiple replications at once, the others will fail until the primary replica finishes. Masters and replicas must be kept in sync by using an NTP time server.

To balance the replication load on a master, Leopard Server limited the number of replicas a master could be assigned to 32 and introduced the Open Directory relay, which is a replica that allows replicas. This enables a large number of potential replicas while sharing the replication load. In other respects, a relay and a replica are identical.

Replica creation requires enabling SSH on the master and then making sure that the SSH SACL doesn't limit remote access only to specific administrators because this blocks the replication setup. You can temporarily suspend SSH SACL limitations in Server Admin. Any firewalls in place between the master and the new replica must also allow SSH traffic over port 22.

CROSS-REF

For more on the NTP and SSH services, see Chapter 19. For more on firewall configuration, see Chapter 14.

Prior to becoming an Open Directory replica, Mac OS X Server may be configured as:

- **A Standalone Directory Server.** This doesn't provide a network-visible directory domain; it only maintains local accounts for use on the server. Promoting a Standalone Directory Server to an Open Directory replica simply expands its capabilities.

- **A member of another directory service.** If a Standalone Directory Server is already connected to another directory, upgrading it to an Open Directory replica simply expands its capabilities. The server remains connected to the other directory service and simply searches its own directory for information first before searching the external directory.

- **An existing Open Directory master.** To destroy an existing master and set it up as a replica of another directory domain, you simply demote the master to a Standalone Directory Server and then set it up as a new Open Directory replica.

- **An existing Open Directory replica.** An existing replica must be destroyed to set it up as the replica of another directory domain or as a replica of another replica that's been promoted to serve as the existing directory domain's Open Directory master. To destroy an existing replica and set it up as a replica of a new master, you simply demote the replica to a Standalone Directory Server and then set it up again as an Open Directory replica.

To promote a server to an Open Directory replica in Server Admin, follow these steps:

1. Launch Server Admin and then connect to the desired server.

2. Select the Open Directory and then click Settings on the toolbar.

3. Click the General tab.

4. Click Change next to the designated Role:

- If the server is currently a Standalone Directory Server, you can promote it to an Open Directory replica.

- If the server is currently an Open Directory master, replica, or relay, you can destroy its current role by setting it up as a new Open Directory replica.

5. Choose Open Directory replica and then click Continue.

6. Type the account information for the existing Open Directory master you want to replicate. To create a replica of a relay replica, use the relay's information instead:

- IP address or DNS name of the Open Directory master or relay

- Root password of the Open Directory master

- Short name of a Domain Administrator on the Open Directory master

- Domain Administrator account password

7. Click Continue.

8. Review the settings and then click Continue to create the Open Directory replica.

9. Click Done. LDAP, Password Server, and Kerberos services should now appear as running on the Overview page of the Open Directory pane in Server Admin, as shown in Figure 21.3. The new replica is also listed under the Replica Tree tab of the General pane of the Open Directory pane's Settings page in Server Admin, as shown in Figure 21.5.

Figure 21.5

The Replica Tree pane of the Open Directory pane in Server Admin

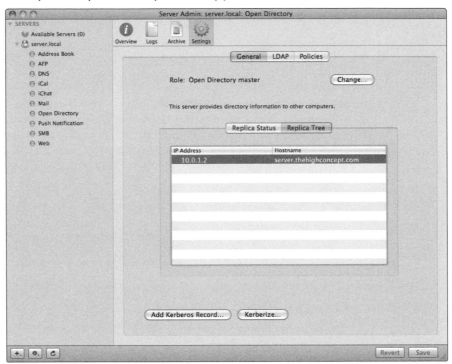

Once an Open Directory replica is created, servers and clients configured to use the Open Directory master automatically connect to an available replica if the master can't be reached.

Systems can also be manually configured in their search policy to use the replica or they can be automatically assigned the replica's IP address as their primary LDAP server by using DHCP.

CROSS-REF

For more on DHCP configuration, see Chapter 13.

Retiring an Open Directory replica or relay

To properly retire a relay, it must be connected to the Open Directory master during its retirement or the master will continue to try to replicate with the missing relay.

To retire a server as an Open Directory replica in Server Admin, follow these steps:

1. **Launch Server Admin and then connect to the desired server.**

2. **Select the Open Directory and then click Settings on the toolbar.**

3. **Click the General tab.**

4. **Click Change next to the designated Role.** If the server is currently an Open Directory replica or relay, you can retire it from service by making it a Standalone Directory Server.

5. **Choose Standalone Directory Server and then click Continue.**

6. **Click Done.** The replica is now removed from the Open Directory master's list of relays in the Replica Tree pane.

Acting as a Primary Domain Controller

Mac OS X Server can host an NT domain for Windows users and provide them with domain login and authentication services, including Windows file and print services, hosted user profiles, and home folders.

The system uses the same network-visible directory domain to support Windows users, so accounts created in Workgroup Manager can be used for logging in to both Macs and PCs. By default, users' home folders are set up to be the same location on both platforms, making it easier for users who work across platforms to work with the same documents.

This also means that to act as a Primary Domain Controller, the server must be configured as an Open Directory master.

Prior to becoming a Primary Domain Controller, Mac OS X Server may be configured as:

- **An Open Directory Standalone Directory Server configured as a Standalone Server in the SMB service.** This doesn't provide a network-visible directory domain or an NT domain; it only maintains local accounts for use on the server. This enables Windows users to access file and print services on the server, but they can't authenticate to log in to a Windows domain. The server can't host user profiles or home folders either. Promoting a Standalone Directory Server to an Open Directory master enables you to promote the server from a Standalone Server to a Primary Domain Controller within the SMB service.

- **An Open Directory Standalone Directory Server configured as a Domain Member in the SMB service.** This doesn't provide a network-visible directory domain or an NT domain; it only maintains local accounts for use on the server. However, as a Domain Member, the server is connected to another server acting as a Primary Domain Controller, enabling it to host user profiles and home folders for users authenticated by the Primary Domain Controller, in addition to providing basic Windows file and print services. Promoting a Standalone Directory Server to an Open Directory master enables you to also promote the server from a Domain Member to a Primary Domain Controller within the SMB service. However, an NT domain can have only one Primary Domain Controller, so the server also needs to create a new NT domain.

● **An existing Open Directory master configured as a Standalone Server in the SMB service.** This can be upgraded to a Primary Domain Controller.

● **An existing Open Directory master configured as a Domain Member in the SMB service.** This can be upgraded to a Primary Domain Controller. However, an NT domain can have only one Primary Domain Controller, so the server also needs to create a new NT domain.

● **An existing Open Directory replica configured as a Standalone Server or Domain Member in the SMB service.** This can't be upgraded to a Primary Domain Controller but can be designated as a Backup Domain Controller.

To determine the configured role of a server in Server Admin, follow these steps:

1. **Launch Server Admin and then connect to the desired server.**

2. **Select the Open Directory and then click Settings on the toolbar.**

3. **Click the General tab.**

4. **View the designated Role:**

● If the server is currently a Standalone Directory Server, you must promote it to an Open Directory master prior to configuring it as a Primary Domain Controller.

● If the server is currently an Open Directory master, you can set it up to serve as a Primary Domain Controller from the SMB service.

● If the server is currently an Open Directory replica or relay, it can't act as a Primary Domain Controller but can be configured as a Backup Domain Controller.

To promote a server to a Primary Domain Controller in Server Admin, follow these steps:

1. **Launch Server Admin and then connect to the desired server.**

2. **Select the SMB service and then click Settings on the toolbar.**

3. **Click the General tab, shown in Figure 21.6.**

4. **Choose an option for the designated Role from the drop-down menu:**

● A Standalone Server can be promoted to a Primary Domain Controller, creating a new NT domain.

● A Domain Member can be promoted to a Primary Domain Controller, creating a new NT domain.

5. **Choose Primary Domain Controller.**

Figure 21.6

The General pane of the SMB pane in Server Admin

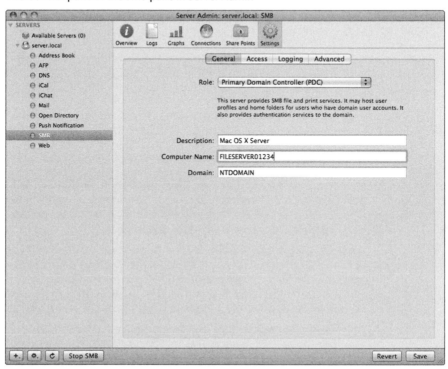

6. **Type the domain information for the new Primary Domain Controller:**
   - Description is visible to Windows clients.
   - Computer Name is the NetBIOS name of the server. It can't contain more than 15 characters or any special characters or punctuation.
   - Domain is the new NT domain you're creating. It can't contain more than 15 characters, can't be WORKGROUP, and can't be the same as any existing NT domain on the network.

7. **Click Save.** You're prompted to type a directory administrator account. You can't use a regular local administrator account to set up a Primary Domain Controller.

CROSS-REF

For more on using Windows with Mac OS X Server, see Chapter 2. For more on configuring the SMB service, see Chapter 22.

Acting as a Backup Domain Controller

A Backup Domain Controller acts as a read-only backup of NT domain directory records to support the job of the Primary Domain Controller in providing authentication and directory information to Windows clients.

If the Primary Domain Controller fails, Windows clients using it can switch to using an available Backup Domain Controller. When functioning normally, the Backup Domain Controllers receive regular updates via the replication of the Open Directory master to an Open Directory replica.

This also means that to act as a Backup Domain Controller, a server must be configured as an Open Directory replica.

Prior to becoming a Backup Domain Controller, Mac OS X Server may be configured as:

- **An Open Directory Standalone Directory Server configured as a Standalone Server in the SMB service.** Promoting a Standalone Directory Server to an Open Directory replica enables you to promote the server from a Standalone Server to a Backup Domain Controller within the SMB service.

- **An Open Directory Standalone Directory Server configured as a Domain Member in the SMB service.** Promoting a Standalone Directory Server to an Open Directory replica enables you to also promote the server from a Domain Member to a Backup Domain Controller within the SMB service. The Backup Domain Controller can join the NT domain it was formerly only a member of, now in a controller role.

- **An existing Open Directory master configured as a Standalone Server or Domain Member in the SMB service.** This can't be upgraded to a Backup Domain Controller but can be promoted to act as a Primary Domain Controller. This also creates a new NT domain.

- **An existing Open Directory replica configured as a Standalone Server or Domain Member in the SMB service.** This can be upgraded to serve as a Backup Domain Controller.

To determine the configured role of a server in Server Admin, follow these steps:

1. Launch Server Admin and then connect to the desired server.

2. Select the Open Directory and then click Settings on the toolbar.

3. Click the General tab.

4. View the designated Role:

- If the server is currently a Standalone Directory Server, you must promote it to an Open Directory replica prior to configuring it as a Backup Domain Controller in the SMB service. A Primary Domain Controller for the NT domain must also already exist.

- If the server is currently an Open Directory master, you can't set it up to serve as a Backup Domain Controller.

- If the server is currently an Open Directory replica or relay, it can be configured as a Backup Domain Controller from the SMB service.

To promote a server to a Backup Domain Controller in Server Admin, follow these steps:

1. **Launch Server Admin and then connect to the desired server.**

2. **Select the SMB service and then click Settings on the toolbar.**

3. **Click the General tab.**

4. **Click Change next to the designated Role:**

- A Standalone Server can be promoted to a Backup Domain Controller if a Primary Domain Controller is already in place.

- A Domain Member can be promoted to a Backup Domain Controller to serve the NT domain that it was formerly only a member of.

5. **Choose Backup Domain Controller.**

6. **Type the domain information for the new Backup Domain Controller:**

- Description is visible to Windows clients.

- Computer Name is the NetBIOS name of the server. It can't contain more than 15 characters or any special characters or punctuation.

- Domain is the NT domain of the existing Primary Domain Controller.

7. **Click Save.** You're prompted to type a directory administrator account. You can't use a regular local administrator account to set up a Backup Domain Controller.

Configuring advanced LDAP settings

LDAP connections between the Open Directory server and clients can be configured to:

- Support SSL for encrypted communications

- Limit the number of LDAP search results the server returns to help prevent denial-of-service (DoS) attacks by malicious users who send multiple queries to overwhelm the server

- Limit the LDAP search timeout interval to help prevent DoS attacks by malicious users who send complex queries to keep the server busy

To configure advanced LDAP options in Server Admin, follow these steps:

1. **Launch Server Admin and then connect to the desired server.**

2. **Select Open Directory and then click Settings on the toolbar.**

3. **Click the LDAP tab, shown in Figure 21.7.**

4. **Configure LDAP options:**

- Enable SSL for encrypted communications by using the check box and then supply an SSL certificate.

- Set a maximum limit for the number of LDAP search results the server returns. The default value is 11,000.

- Set a search timeout interval in seconds, minutes, or hours. The default setting is one minute.

5. **Click Save.**

Figure 21.7

The LDAP pane of the Open Directory pane in Server Admin

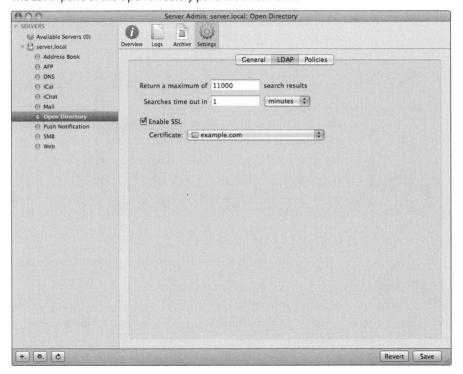

CROSS-REF

For more on creating and using certificates in Server Admin, see Chapter 9.

Server and client configuration using Directory Utility

Mac OS X systems can bind to multiple directory domains by adding a Network Account Server from the Login Options page of the Accounts pane in Mac OS X Snow Leopard's System Preferences.

To configure additional settings related to directory services, Snow Leopard's Network Account Server editor launches Directory Utility, which is used to:

- Configure access to multiple Open Directory domains or other LDAP directories, including setting LDAP mappings and requiring SSL support
- Enable and add an Active Directory domain to the authentication search path
- Enable and use Network Information Services (NIS)
- Define search policy for authentication and contact information for the configured directory services

To add a simple Network Account Server in Snow Leopard, follow these steps:

1. **Launch System Preferences and then click the Accounts tab.**

2. **Authenticate by clicking the lock icon and authenticating as a local administrator.**

3. **Select Login Options.**

4. **Click Edit Network Account Server.** A sheet drops down, shown in Figure 21.8.

Figure 21.8

The Network Account Server editor sheet

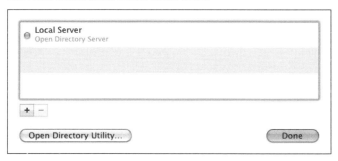

5. **Click the Add (+) button to add the IP address or DNS name of an LDAP, Open Directory, or Active Directory server.**

6. **Authenticate with the server.**

7. **Click Done.** If authentication is successful, the new directory service should appear in the list of configured Network Account Servers.

To configure advanced directory services in Directory Utility, follow these steps:

1. **Launch System Preferences and then click the Accounts tab.**

2. **Authenticate and then select Login Options.**

3. **Click Edit Network Account Server.**

4. **Click the Open Directory Utility button.**

5. **From the Services page of Directory Utility, shown in Figure 21.9, click the lock icon and authenticate as a local administrator.**

Figure 21.9

The Services page of Directory Utility

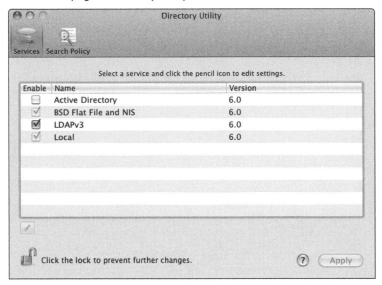

6. **Enable individual services as described shortly and then click Apply.**

To enable support for Active Directory in Directory Utility, follow these steps:

1. **From the Services page of Directory Utility, click the Active Directory check box.**

2. **Double-click the listing to open the configuration dialog box.** A sheet drops down.

3. **Optionally, type the name of the Active Directory Forest.** By default, this is set automatically.

4. **Type the name of the Active Directory domain.**

5. **Type a name for the local system as Computer ID.** This becomes a computer record in Active Directory.

6. **Click the Show Advanced Options triangle and then click the User Experience tab, as shown in Figure 21.10.**

Figure 21.10

The User Experience pane in Directory Utility

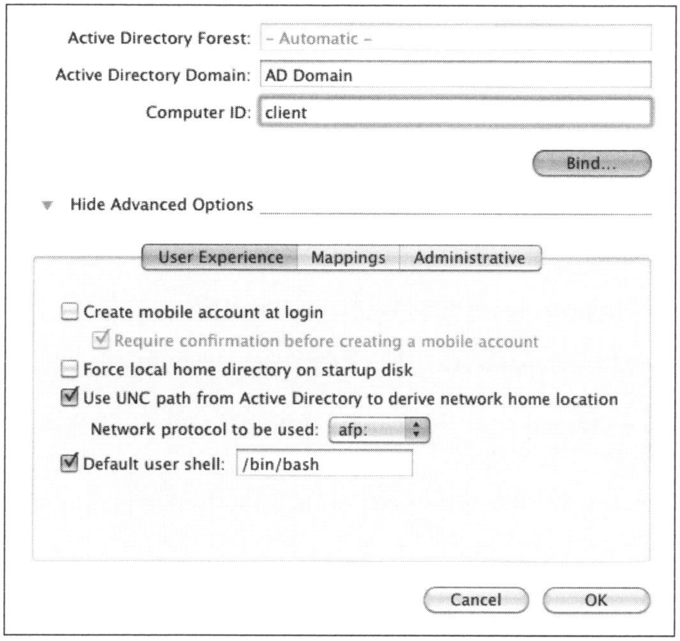

Active Directory Forest:	– Automatic –
Active Directory Domain:	AD Domain
Computer ID:	client

Bind...

▼ Hide Advanced Options

| User Experience | Mappings | Administrative |

☐ Create mobile account at login
    ☑ Require confirmation before creating a mobile account
☐ Force local home directory on startup disk
☑ Use UNC path from Active Directory to derive network home location
    Network protocol to be used: [afp: ◆]
☑ Default user shell: [/bin/bash]

Cancel   OK

7. **Click the Create mobile account at login check box.** A mobile account uses a local home folder on the system's startup volume. The user also has a network home folder as defined in Active Directory. A mobile account also locally caches the user's Active Directory authentication credentials, enabling the user to log in by using the Active Directory account even when the directory server is unavailable.

8. **Click the Use UNC path from Active Directory to derive network home location check box to enable a path stored in Microsoft's** \\server\share\user **notation to be translated to the standard** afp://server/share/user **for mounting by Mac OS X.**

9. **From the pop-up menu, choose the network protocol used for network home folders.** The default is SMB, but if the network home file server supports AFP, you can choose that instead for the Mac's home folder.

10. **Configure a default user shell if desired.**

11. **From the Mappings tab, you can remap the default settings for user ID numbers to Active Directory attributes that you specify.** If left alone, the Active Directory plug-in dynamically generates a unique user ID and a primary group ID from the account's Globally Unique ID (GUID) in Active Directory. The generated user ID and primary group ID are the same for each user account, even if the account is used to log in to different systems.

12. **From the Administrative tab, you can set a preferred domain server and assign local administration privileges to Active Directory groups.** By default, the `domain admins` and `enterprise admins` groups are granted local administrative access. You can also allow authentication from any domain in the forest by clicking the check box.

13. **Click Bind and then authenticate as a local administrator.** The system configures the computer account for the system in Active Directory and begins allowing authentication and local login by Active Directory accounts. Apple's Active Directory plug-in uses LDAP to access Active Directory user accounts and Kerberos for authentication; it doesn't use Microsoft's proprietary Active Directory Services Interface (ADSI) for directory browsing or authentication.

14. **Click OK to save the settings for Active Directory.**

To enable support for Unix flat files and NIS in Directory Utility, follow these steps:

1. **From the Services page in Directory Utility, click the BSD Flat File and NIS check box.**

2. **Double-click the listing to open the configuration pane, shown in Figure 21.11.**

Figure 21.11

BSD flat file and NIS configuration in Directory Utility

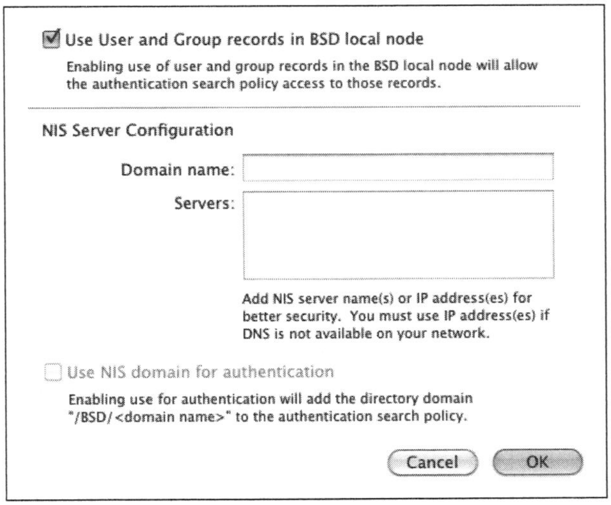

3. **Click the Use User and Group records in BSD local node check box.** This allows the system to access any account and resource information defined in Unix-style text files. The information can't be edited in Workgroup Manager but can be modified by using command-line tools. BSD flat files include:

- `/etc/master.passwd` for usernames, passwords, IDs, and primary group IDs
- `/etc/group` for group names, IDs, and members
- `/etc/fstab` for NFS mounts
- `/etc/hosts` for computer names and addresses
- `/etc/networks` for network names and addresses
- `/etc/services` for service names, ports, and protocols
- `/etc/protocols` for IP protocol names and numbers
- `/etc/rpcs` for Open Network Computing RPC servers
- `/etc/printcap` for printer names and capabilities
- `/etc/bootparams` for bootparam settings
- `/etc/bootp` for bootp settings
- `/etc/aliases` for mail aliases and distribution lists
- `/etc/netgroup` for network-wide group names and members

4. **Add an NIS domain name and NIS server names or IP addresses.**

5. **Click the Use NIS domain for authentication check box.**

6. **Click OK to save the settings for NIS.**

To configure support for LDAP in Directory Utility, follow these steps:

1. **From the Services page of Directory Utility, double-click LDAPv3 to open the configuration pane, shown in Figure 21.12.**

2. **Click the check boxes for the defined LDAP servers you want to enable.**

3. **Add another LDAP directory by using the New or Duplicate button.**

4. **Click the SSL check box for LDAP servers that support encryption.**

5. **From the pop-up menu, choose the schema mappings for the LDAP directory:**

- As supplied by the server
- Using Active Directory schema mappings
- Using Open Directory schema mappings
- Using schema mappings typical for Linux directory servers (RFC 2307)

Enter the search base for the LDAP server when prompted.

6. **Click Edit to set advanced LDAP options, including:**
- The use of a custom TCP port
- Customized attribute mappings
- User authentication settings
- Security policy, such as disabling cleartext passwords, digitally signing packets, encrypting packets, and blocking man-in-the-middle attacks

7. **Click OK to leave the advanced editing window.**

8. **Click OK to save the settings for LDAP servers.**

Figure 21.12

LDAP configuration in Directory Utility

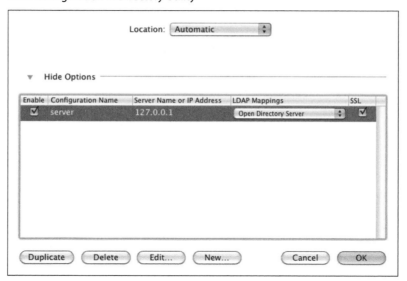

To configure a search policy in Directory Utility, follow these steps:

1. **Launch System Preferences and then click the Accounts tab.**

2. **Authenticate and then select Login Options.**

3. **Click Edit Network Account Server.**

4. **From the Search Policy pane, shown in Figure 21.13, click the lock icon and then authenticate as a local administrator.**

5. **For both Authentication and Contacts, choose one of the following from the Search pop-up menu:**

   - Automatic, which sets search policy via DHCP settings
   - Local directory, which only consults the local directory domain
   - Custom Path, which enables the user to set the search order of configured directory domains. You can drag to reorder the configured directory domains.

6. **Click Apply.**

Figure 21.13

The Search Policy pane of Directory Utility

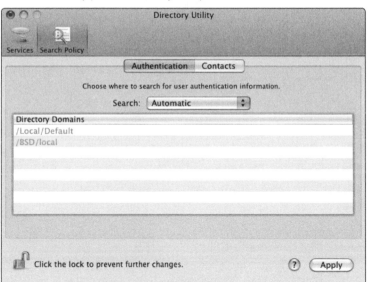

Managing and Monitoring Directory Services

The Overview page of the Open Directory pane in Server Admin presents a status report that includes:

- The current Open Directory role of the server
- Whether the LDAP Server is running
- Whether the Password Server is running
- Whether Kerberos is running
- The LDAP search base
- The Kerberos realm name

Monitoring directory service logs

The Logs page of the Open Directory pane, shown in Figure 21.14, presents a listing of the events for each service component, including:

- The Directory Services Server Log at `/Library/Logs/DirectoryService/DirectoryService.server.log`
- The Directory Services Error Log at `/Library/Logs/DirectoryService/DirectoryService.error.log`
- The stand-alone LDAP service configuration log at `/Library/Logs/slapdconfig.log`
- The stand-alone LDAP service log at `/var/log/slapd.log`
- The Kerberos Server Log at `/var/log/krb5kdc/kdc.log`
- The Kerberos Administration Log at `/var/log/krb5kdc/kadmind.log`
- The Password Service Server Log at `/Library/Logs/PasswordService/ApplePasswordServer.Server.log`
- The Password Service Error Log at `/Library/Logs/PasswordService/ApplePasswordServer.Error.log`
- The Password Service Replication Log at `/Library/Logs/PasswordService/ApplePasswordServer.Replication.log`

Figure 21.14

The Logs page in the Open Directory pane in Server Admin

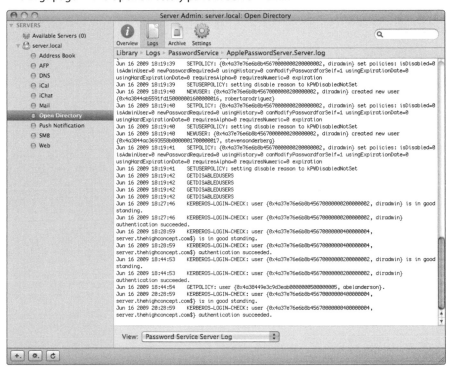

Managing directory accounts in Workgroup Manager

Open Directory records and other LDAPv3 domains allowing write access can be viewed and edited using Workgroup Manager.

Active Directory, BSD flat files, NIS domains, and LDAPv2 domains can be viewed in Workgroup Manager, but those records can't be edited.

Managed preferences

Configured within Workgroup Manager, managed preferences enable administrators to either set or force specific configurations for network users, groups of users, or computers or across groups of computers in the directory domain.

Using managed preferences, an organization can centrally automate the setup of a customized user environment tailored to specific users or to defined computers. Managed preferences can also be used to enforce security policy, preventing users from installing or launching applications and even turning off hardware features, such as Bluetooth or optical disk burning.

CROSS-REF
For more on using managed preferences, see Chapter 36.

Importing records

Workgroup Manager can import user, group, computer, and computer group accounts into an Open Directory domain, either from an exported list generated by the program as a backup or from an XML or a tab- or comma-delimited text file set to contain a series of accounts to import.

An Open Directory domain can import up to 200,000 records from a file. Workgroup Manager can import only files that use Unix line breaks.

To import records into Open Directory by using Workgroup Manager, follow these steps:

1. **Launch Workgroup Manager and then authenticate with the desired directory domain.**

2. **Choose Import from the Server menu.** Select an import file from the file dialog box, shown in Figure 21.15.

3. **Choose what to do when the short name of an imported account matches an existing account by using the Duplicate Handling pop-up menu:**
   - Overwrite existing record.
   - Ignore new record ignores the duplicate account in the import file.
   - Add to empty fields merges information from the import file into the existing account in cases where a record attribute had no value.
   - Append to existing record appends data to existing data for a specific multi-value attribute in the existing account. Duplicates aren't created. You can use this option when importing members into an existing group.
   - Don't check for duplicates disables duplicate checking to decrease the time required for the import of pre-vetted information, but it can result in bad records and unexpected results if there are any duplicates.

4. **Click the Preset for Users check box to use a predefined account record preset from the pop-up menu for imported users.** If a setting is specified in the preset but not in the import file, the value in the preset is used; otherwise, the value in the import file is used.

Figure 21.15

Open Directory record import by using Workgroup Manager

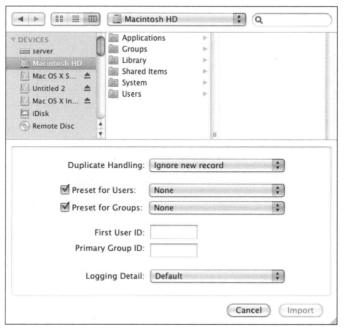

5. **Click the Preset for Groups check box to use a predefined account record preset from the pop-up menu for imported groups.** If a setting is specified in the preset but not in the import file, the value in the preset is used; otherwise, the value in the import file is used.

6. **Type a First User ID for new user accounts without user IDs in the import file.** New User IDs are sequentially assigned for other accounts without user IDs.

7. **Type a Primary Group ID to assign to new user accounts for users that have no primary group ID in the import file.**

8. **Choose a logging detail level from the pop-up menu.** An import log is created at ~/Library/Logs/ImportExport/.

9. **Click Import.** Imported records with plaintext passwords can be imported. However, files exported from Workgroup Manager aren't exported with passwords because passwords aren't stored in LDAP. Passwords can't be exported from the Password Server or KDC. However, the entire Open Directory domain can be exported to an encrypted file by archiving and restoring Open Directory rather than exporting and importing records from the directory using Workgroup Manager. Password policy can be set to require users to change their passwords at first login.

To set user password policy using Workgroup Manager, follow these steps:

1. **Launch Workgroup Manager and then authenticate with the desired directory domain.**

2. **Select account records in the directory domain.** The accounts must use an Open Directory password.

3. **Click the Advanced tab.**

4. **Click the Options button to open a sheet, shown in Figure 21.16, that can be used to set policy restrictions on the user's login:**
   - Disabling the account on a specific date
   - Disabling the account after being inactive for a set number of days
   - Disabling the account after a set number of failed login attempts

   The sheet can also set password policy, forcing the user's set password to:
   - Contain a minimum number of characters
   - Be reset by the user after a set number of days
   - Be reset after the next login, forcing the user to immediately set a new password for the new account

5. **Click Save.**

Figure 21.16

Defining login and password policy in Workgroup Manager

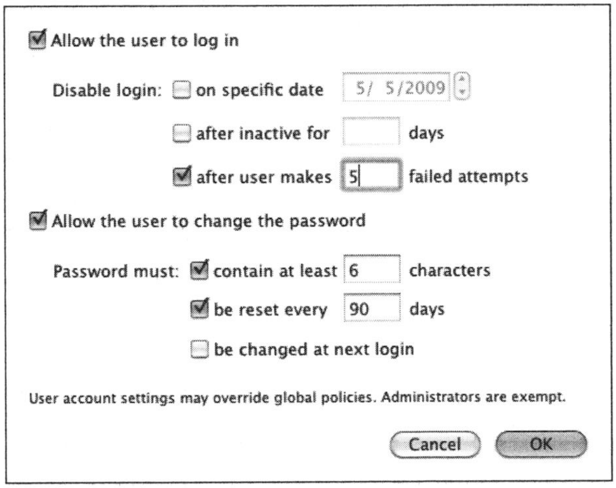

CROSS-REF
For more on using Workgroup Manager, see Chapter 10.

Managing Open Directory policy

Open Directory account password policy can also be set on a global level, along with binding and authentication policy, from the Open Directory pane of Server Admin.

To set global password policy using Server Admin, follow these steps:

1. **Launch Server Admin and then connect to the desired server.**

2. **Select Open Directory and then click Settings on the toolbar.**

3. **Click the Policies tab and then click the Passwords tab, shown in Figure 21.17.**

4. **Click the check boxes to enable policy restrictions to:**
   - Disable the account on a specific date
   - Disable the account after being used for a set number of days
   - Disable the account after being inactive for a set number of days
   - Disable the account after a set number of failed login attempts

   The pane can also set password policy, forcing a user's set password to:
   - Differ from the account name
   - Contain at least one letter
   - Contain both uppercase and lowercase letters
   - Contain at least one numeric character
   - Contain at least one character that isn't a letter or number
   - Be reset after the next login, forcing the user to immediately set a new password for the new account
   - Contain a minimum number of characters
   - Differ from the last set number of passwords used
   - Be reset by the user after a set number of days, weeks, or months

5. **Click Save.** Global password policies aren't applied to administrator accounts and can be overridden by user account settings specified in Workgroup Manager.

Figure 21.17

The Passwords pane of the Open Directory pane in Server Admin

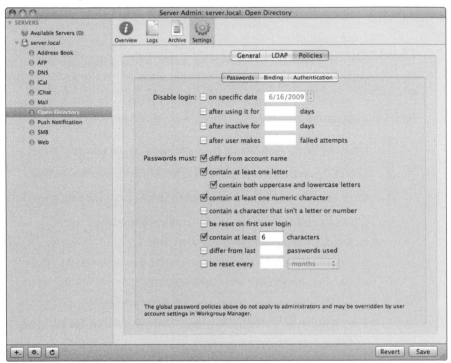

Managing binding policy

An Open Directory master can be configured to permit or require authenticated or *trusted binding* between the LDAP directory and client computers. Open Directory replicas automatically inherit the master's binding policy. Trusted LDAP binding is mutually authenticated; the client computer authenticates to LDAP by using a directory administrator's credentials, and the LDAP directory uses an authenticated computer record created in the directory when trusted binding is configured.

Client users can be configured to use either of two methods for trusted binding, which may both be enabled on the server but shouldn't be used together:

- Encrypt all packets (requires SSL or Kerberos)
- Enable authenticated directory binding

If the security policy of the LDAP directory of an Open Directory master is changed, all client systems bound to the directory must be disconnected and reconnected as a Network Account Server by using Directory Utility.

To set binding security policy by using Server Admin, follow these steps:

1. **Launch Server Admin and then connect to the desired server.**

2. **Select Open Directory and then click Settings on the toolbar.**

3. **Click the Policies tab and then click the Binding tab, shown in Figure 21.18.**

Figure 21.18

The Binding pane of the Open Directory pane in Server Admin

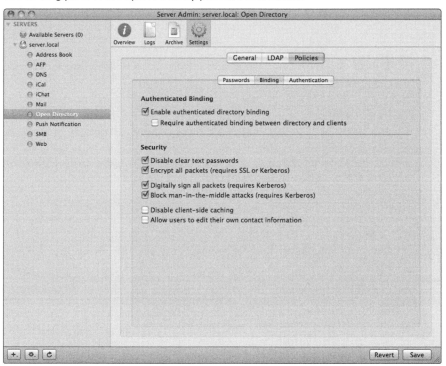

4. **Click the Enable authenticated directory binding check box.** Optionally, click the Require authenticated binding between directory and clients check box.

5. **Click one — and only one — of the following check boxes:**

   - Disable cleartext passwords. This prevents clients from sending passwords as cleartext if the passwords can't be validated by using any secure authentication method that sends an encrypted password.

   - Encrypt all packets (requires SSL or Kerberos). This requires the LDAP server to encrypt all directory data by using either SSL or Kerberos before sending it to client computers.

   - Digitally sign all packets (requires Kerberos). This certifies that LDAP directory data can't be intercepted and modified by a third-party attacker.

   - Block man-in-the-middle attacks (requires Kerberos). This protects against a third-party attacker posing as the LDAP server.

   - Disable client-side caching. This prevents client systems from caching LDAP data locally.

   - Allow users to edit their own contact information. This permits users to change contact information on the LDAP server.

6. **Click Save.** After changing security policy, all LDAP clients must leave and then rejoin the domain.

Managing authentication policy

A subset of Open Directory's authentication methods can be selectively enabled to enhance the security of password storage on the server. For example, if you're not providing any Windows services, LAN Manager and NTLMv2 can be disabled to avoid storing passwords on the server by using these authentication methods.

This prevents an attacker who gains access to the password database from exploiting weaknesses in these authentication methods to crack users' passwords. Disabling authentication methods doesn't increase the security of passwords being transmitted over the network; only the password storage security is affected.

Disabling authentication methods may force users to configure their client software to send passwords over the network in cleartext, compromising password security in a more serious manner.

To set authentication policy by using Server Admin, follow these steps:

1. **Launch Server Admin and then connect to the desired server.**

2. **Select Open Directory and then click Settings on the toolbar.**

3. **Click the Policies tab and then click the Authentication tab, shown in Figure 21.19.**

Figure 21.19

The Authentication pane of the Open Directory pane in Server Admin

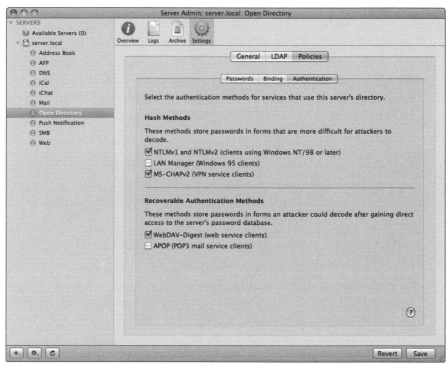

4. **Click the following check boxes to selectively enable the authentication methods you want to use.** Hash methods store passwords in the database in a form that can be attacked to obtain the password, if the attacker were able to obtain the Password Service database:

- Microsoft NTLMv1 and NTLMv2 for more modern Windows clients
- Microsoft LAN Manager for legacy Windows 95 clients
- Microsoft MS-CHAPv2 for VPN service clients

  Recoverable authentication methods store passwords in the database in a form that can be recovered to obtain the password, if the attacker were able to obtain the Password Service database:

- WebDAV-Digest for web service clients
- APOP (Authenticated Post Office Protocol) for clients using POP to access the local mail service

5. **Click Save.** After disabling an authentication method, its hash is removed from the password database the next time the user authenticates. After enabling an authentication method that was disabled, every Open Directory password must be reset, either by a directory administrator or by the user, in order to add the newly enabled authentication method's hash to the password database.

Archiving and restoring Open Directory data

To back up domain directory records and authentication passwords, Open Directory data can be archived to an encrypted disk image, which contains:

- LDAP directory database and configuration files
- The Open Directory Password Server database
- The Kerberos keytab, database, and configuration files
- The local directory domain and the shadow password database

This archive serves as a full backup of the Open Directory master. Because replicas are identical to the master, there's no need to separately back up Open Directory replica servers. After restoring the archive to an Open Directory master, all replicas have to be re-created.

For this reason, if you need to restore a failed Open Directory master, it may make more sense to promote an Open Directory replica to replace the master instead. The replica may be more up to date than the archive, and the replica is already operating. In either case, all replicas must be re-created.

To archive an Open Directory master, follow these steps:

1. **Launch Server Admin and then connect to the desired server.**

2. **Select Open Directory.**

3. **Click Archive on the toolbar, as shown in Figure 21.20.**

4. **Click the Choose button to select a location for archiving.**

5. **Click Archive.** From the sheet that drops down, type an archive name for the disk image and a file encryption password.

6. **Click OK.** The resulting encrypted disk image should be safeguarded with security precautions equivalent to the server itself.

To restore an archive to an Open Directory master, follow these steps:

1. **Launch Server Admin and then connect to the desired server.**

2. **Select Open Directory.**

3. **Click Archive on the toolbar.**

4. **Click the Choose button to select a file to restore from.**

5. **Click Restore.** From the sheet that drops down, choose one of the following:

- **Merge.** Imports the archive's data into the existing directory and password data-bases. If any conflicts are encountered during the merge, the existing record takes precedence and the archive record is ignored. Restore conflicts are recorded in the LDAP service configuration log file at /Library/Logs/slapconfig.log.

- **Restore.** This deletes the existing directory and password databases and replace them with the archive's data.

6. **Type the original archive encryption password and then click OK.** All replicas need to be re-created.

Figure 21.20

The Archive page of the Open Directory pane in Server Admin

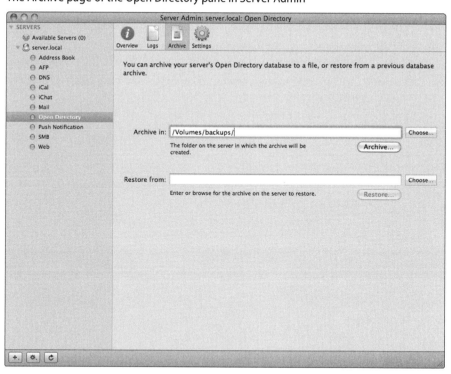

Summary

- Directory services provide centralized accounts, authentication, service, and contact information to network users.

- Mac OS X's Open Directory enables systems to use directory services information from multiple domains by using multiple protocols, allowing the operating system to integrate into an existing infrastructure as well as provide its own directory services.

- Search policy determines the order in which the system queries the network directory servers it's configured to use.

- Open Directory supports a variety of authentication methods to negotiate the most secure protocol available when working with different applications and network services.

- Open Directory incorporates support for Kerberos authentication, which offers secure mutual authentication without sending passwords across the network.

- An Open Directory domain is hosted by a primary master by using relays and replicas to provide distributed services to balance the load across organizations.

- Integrated support for Windows clients allows Open Directory servers to support authenticated login to network PCs in the role of a Windows domain controller.

- Mac OS X clients and servers are configured to bind to directory services by using Directory Utility.

Providing File-Sharing, Mail, Collaboration, and Media Services

VII

File-Sharing Services

O ne of the primary features of Snow Leopard Server relates to file sharing, which is the simple act of making elements on the server available to network users.

In addition to conventional file-sharing protocols used both to serve documents and to host features, such as home directories, there are also a variety of other advanced network services based on specialized file sharing, some of which are discussed in other chapters.

The primary file-sharing protocols supported in Snow Leopard Server for sharing documents among users and groups are:

- Apple Filing Protocol (AFP) is targeted to Macs.
- Server Message Block (SMB) is used to support Windows.
- Network File System (NFS) is common in Unix environments.
- File Transfer Protocol (FTP) is a standard Internet file service.

Web services are also a form of file sharing that employs HTTP as its file-sharing mechanism.

The WebDAV protocol expands on the basic web server to additionally allow users to edit and create new documents within a web share.

A variety of other specialized, advanced services in Snow Leopard Server are also based on HTTP and WebDAV file sharing, including wikis, blogs, webmail, iCal Server, and the new Address Book Server, but this chapter focuses on document file sharing.

CROSS-REF
For more on using web services in general, see Chapter 24. For more on wikis, blogs, and webmail, see Chapter 25. For more on Calendar Server, see Chapter 26. For more on Address Book Server, see Chapter 28.

Other advanced file-sharing features in Mac OS X Server built on or integrated into the conventional document file-sharing protocols, such as AFP and SMB, include:

- **Spotlight Server.** Indexes documents on AFP and SMB file shares to support fast search by network client users
- **Time Machine Server.** Advertises AFP file shares capable of supporting the features required to store network users' backups

In This Chapter

Introduction to
file-sharing services

Planning file services

File service setup
and configuration

Managing and
monitoring file services

This chapter describes how the conventional file-sharing protocols supported in Snow Leopard Server work, what's involved in planning file-sharing services, how they're configured, and how to maintain and monitor the services.

Introduction to File-Sharing Services

A variety of different mechanisms for sharing files over networks have developed in parallel. Each reflects the design goals of its creator, whether it was a company, such as Apple, Microsoft, or Sun, or the community working with the IETF to define a standard that developed alongside other Internet protocols.

In each case, the engineering decisions made have resulted in a differentiating series of unique characteristics for each of these protocols, including:

- The speed, efficiency, and simplicity of the protocol
- The amount of security designed into the protocol
- Compatibility with various client operating systems
- The amount of overhead employed to deliver advanced user features
- Support for specific features in Snow Leopard Server

Apple File Service

Apple originally developed AFP as a component of its AppleShare server in the late 1980s, serving as its file-sharing application and presentation layer protocol matched with an underlying session and transport layer protocol called AppleTalk. For this reason, AFP was originally called the AppleTalk Filing Protocol.

However, with the release of AppleShare IP in the mid-1990s, Apple adapted AFP 2.0 to work over TCP/IP (by using TCP port 548), and since then, AppleTalk has been deprecated as a transport protocol.

Mac OS X has always lacked any support for using AppleTalk as a transport for AFP file sharing. AppleTalk now serves only as a discovery mechanism for browsing available servers, a role that's now being taken over by Bonjour.

AFP versions in Mac OS X Server

As a file-sharing protocol, AFP has been upgraded several times since then in order to add support for new features. AFP 3.0 was released alongside Mac OS X Server 10 to add support for POSIX file permissions, file names greater than 31 characters, and Unicode UTF-8 file name encodings, for example.

Jaguar Server introduced AFP 3.1, with support for Kerberos authentication, AFP connections secured by SSH encryption, and automatic client reconnect, a feature that enables the server to reconnect with idle Mac clients that have gone to sleep.

Although Mac OS X Server disconnects idle clients to conserve resources, you can configure the server to retain information on the client sessions, allowing the client system to reconnect and access their open files on the file share without suffering data loss.

Tiger Server introduced AFP 3.2 with support for extended attributes, including ACL file permissions, as well as 64-bit file sizes. Leopard Server's AFP 3.3 added at least three other AFP command extensions related to supporting Spotlight search and Time Machine Server.

The Apple File Service is the only component of Mac OS X Server actually bound by the product's ten-user or unlimited-user licensing terms. That means the ten-user version of the product sets a limitation only on concurrent AFP users, but any number of users can connect to its directory services; SMB, NFS, FTP, or WebDAV file services; wiki collaboration; email; calendar; and other services.

Third-party AFP servers

Apart from Mac OS X Server, AFP file sharing can also be hosted by other servers, such as ExtremeZ-IP for Windows or the open-source Netatalk package commonly used by Linux servers and many server appliances.

However, the specific AFP features supported by these third-party implementations often don't match those of Apple's currently shipping version, resulting in the potential for compatibility problems that may be difficult to troubleshoot.

Microsoft's archaic Services for Macintosh, which only supported AFP 2.2 features but was bundled with Windows Server and frequently used by Windows shops to enable file-sharing support for Mac users, was recently dropped from Windows Server 2008 for this reason.

AFP: made for Macs

In terms of speed, efficiency, and simplicity, AFP involves the most overhead of the file-sharing protocols used on Mac OS X Server. On the flip side, however, this results in AFP also delivering a richer user experience, more robust security, and customized support for unique Mac features.

On the client side, AFP is largely only supported natively by Macs, making Snow Leopard Server's other protocols important for supporting a variety of different client platforms. What Macs get from using AFP over other file-sharing protocols is full support for the unique conventions in the Mac's HFS+ file system, such as creator codes and resource forks.

Additionally, Apple has extended AFP to support new features, from Spotlight server-side search indexing to acting as a repository for Time Machine Server backups.

In the case of Time Machine Server, the network file server isn't just hosting a simple backup file. it must also ensure that the data being copied to the archive is actually copied successfully and that the process can recover from any network interruptions. This is a new feature that requires support within the network file system protocol. Other protocols that aren't designed to address this issue can't ensure that a successful backup has occurred.

There are many other examples of Mac-related features unique to AFP, including Unix quotas, ACLs, and other extended attributes. Because the protocol is proprietary to Apple, the company can extend it as it chooses, enabling the company to offer competitive and differentiated features.

This also allows Apple to incorporate features from other vendors. For example, since Tiger Server, Apple has been incorporating support for ACL file permissions by using conventions compatible with those used by Microsoft in Windows.

AFP security

In terms of security, AFP supports the use of encrypted passwords with Kerberos authentication as well as incorporating support for either optional or required data encryption by using SSH.

NFS can also support both, but the SMB protocol used by Windows File Sharing supports only password encryption; data isn't encrypted, exposing all communications during transmission. The FTP service doesn't encrypt passwords or data. This demands that SMB or FTP be wrapped in external layers of security, either by using a VPN or tunneling through SSH.

When examining security, the legacy and architecture of a network file system protocol are also important to consider. Apple's AFP was designed to operate over local networks where a certain level of innate security was assumed. After the emergence of the commercial Internet, Apple had to add authentication mechanisms and support for encrypting connections, but both tasks were fairly straightforward because AFP was used largely only for basic file sharing.

In contrast, Microsoft's SMB wasn't purely a way to connect to file shares. It also made assumptions that the networks it used were secure, but SMB also enabled all sorts of IPC (Interprocess Communication) between applications, creating a security mess where simply adding basic authentication wasn't enough to straighten out the loops of spaghetti security.

Although an SSH encrypted AFP file server can be exposed to the Internet with only limited risk, no competent administrator would expose SMB's ports to the open Internet because of the wildly dangerous security implications of doing so.

This makes it comically ironic that Microsoft attempted to position its legacy SMB file-sharing protocol as CIFS (Common Internet File System) in an effort to compete with Sun's NFS for the title of the Internet's file system.

Windows File Service

Mac OS X's file, print, and directory domain services for Windows users are almost entirely provided by Samba, an open-source package designed to emulate how SMB works on Windows. As noted in the previous section, SMB isn't just a simple file-sharing protocol.

Much like AppleTalk on the Mac prior to the widespread use of TCP/IP on PCs, Microsoft developed its own network stack for DOS and Windows users. SMB (originally developed by IBM) fit into the networking system used by DOS PCs in a roughly similar, application-level position to AFP, sitting on top of Microsoft's NBF (NetBIOS Frames) transport-level protocol.

Just as Apple transitioned AFP from AppleTalk to TCP/IP in AppleShare IP and deprecated AppleTalk in Mac OS X, Microsoft similarly transitioned SMB from NBF to NBT (NetBIOS over TCP/IP) in Windows 2000 and subsequently removed legacy NBF support from Windows XP.

A third-party SMB server

However, SMB isn't a simple protocol that other vendors can easily implement. In practice, it's inextricably tied to these Microsoft services:

- **Windows NT domain system.** Used for authentication
- **WINS (Windows Internet Name Service).** Used for network hostname lookup and service discovery across subnets
- **MSRPC (Microsoft Remote Procedure Call).** Used for interprocess communications between network clients and servers; this serves as the basis for NT domains and MAPI communications between Exchange Server and Outlook, for example

In order to deliver support for accessing and serving Windows file and print services from Unix, the Samba project has spent the last couple of decades reverse-engineering Microsoft's suite of interrelated technologies, none of which were designed to be implemented on anything other than Windows. There's also limited accurate documentation of SMB and related protocols.

The complications related to creating a flawless AFP implementation even as Apple itself keeps changing the protocol to serve its needs are completely eclipsed by the harrowing task of figuring out how the components related to SMB work even as Microsoft directs its future in new directions. Since Windows 2000, SMB has shifted toward using the following:

- **Windows Active Directory.** Used for authentication
- **DNS.** Used for network hostname lookup and service discovery

Apple incorporated Samba into Mac OS X for both simple Windows file and print sharing on the desktop and support for hosting NT domains in Mac OS X Server. This support enables Windows PCs to log in to Snow Leopard Server, obtain a roaming profile and assigned home directory, and authenticate to other services.

Samba support in Mac OS X Server is integrated into Open Directory and Kerberos, allowing administrators to manage directory users' Windows login information as a component of their network account rather than as an independent, separate account within a different system.

Using SMB on Macs

Windows file and print sharing is built into Windows PCs. It's also commonly supported by many Linux distributions. Macs also incorporate client support for Windows file and print sharing by using the same Samba software. However, Macs still prefer using AFP.

File system features that aren't natively supported in SMB, including resource forks and rich metadata, require a kludge to retain that information. Mac OS X uses separate invisible files as a workaround when using SMB shares, which isn't ideal for Windows users who browse the same share with settings to make all files visible; this extra support for Mac features not natively available under SMB results in a lot of litter.

Additionally, if the file is edited or moved by another client unaware of the invisible extra data, it may be lost. Some Mac applications may also make assumptions about a network share that may fail if it doesn't act like an AFP share.

Macs accessing a share served by both AFP and SMB may ignore ACL file permissions when connecting as an SMB share. Another issue with sharing the same files under different protocols is that users accessing the same files via a different sharing protocol concurrently may overwrite *oplocks* (the opportunistic locking feature of SMB that allows an application to lock a file while it uses it, storing a local cache for performance reasons) if they're enabled, resulting in lost data.

SMB security

Because Mac OS X's Samba SMB only implements password encryption and doesn't secure the data being transmitted, you definitely won't want to open up SMB's ports to the Internet. Remote clients either need to use a VPN or establish an SSH tunnel to remotely access Windows file shares.

Conversely, when serving SMB shares to PC clients running Vista, you may run into a problem where Vista fails to negotiate Kerberos authentication. This is because Vista attempts to request a service ticket referencing the Mac OS X Server by its short name or basename rather than the server's FQDN (Fully Qualified Domain Name).

Apple's Active Directory plug-in only registers Service Principal Names (SPNs) by the FQDN when it binds the server to Active Directory. This issue can be remedied by adding a CIFS service principal that connects the server's short name to the Active Directory attribute `service-PrincipalName` by using this command: `C:\setpn -A cifs/shortname shortname`.

Network File Service

Developed by Sun, NFS is commonly used to deliver shared files to Unix systems. Mac OS X Server supports sharing files via NFS, and Mac clients can access NFS shares both for basic document access as well as for hosting their network home folders.

In NFS terminology, a shared volume is an *export*. It can be made available to specific systems by IP address segment or exported to World, which allows any host to access the share.

Because the protocol is openly documented in an Internet RFC (Request for Comment), implementing NFS is far easier and less problematic than trying to deliver a clone of a proprietary system under continuous private development, such as AFP or SMB.

There are still reasons why Mac users prefer to use AFP shares over NFS. One is that NFS doesn't support all the same features. For example, the NFS service in Mac OS X recognizes only POSIX-style file permissions. The server enforces ACLs internally, but these can't be set or read by NFS clients.

The preferred method for secure access to NFS is using Kerberos authentication, a feature that's supported only by Macs running Leopard or later.

FTP Service

FTP was developed as a simple way to transfer files between Internet hosts. It's commonly used for downloading software or uploading files to a remote web server.

FTP supports two types of users:

- Authenticated or real users who log in with their network account.
- Guest users who log in as anonymous and by convention use their email address as their password (for convenience in contacting the user; it's not ever actually verified).

Once logged in, FTP users gain default access to the FTP Root, which is located at `/Library/FTPServer/FTPRoot/`.

Guest users by default aren't allowed to delete, overwrite, rename, or change the permissions of any files and can upload new files only to the uploads folder within the FTP Root. If this folder is removed, guests only have read access.

Mac OS X Server can specify three different sharing configurations for FTP:

- **FTP Root and Share Points.** This makes available the files in the FTP Root directory as well as any other share points designated to support FTP. Authenticated users see their home folders with a link to the shared FTP Root, whereas guests see only the FTP Root itself. Within the FTP Root, symbolic links to other FTP share points also make those available to all users.
- **Home Folder with Share Points.** This is largely the same, but authenticated users instead see the FTP Root as their starting point, with a link to their home folders within a Users folder inside the FTP Root that acts as a symbolic link to their user folders.
- **Home Folder.** This gives authenticated users access to only their home directory, with no links to the FTP Root or any other FTP share points. Guest users continue to see the FTP Root and any designated FTP share points.

Support for resource forks is maintained by Mac OS X Server by automatic MacBinary III encoding of files as they're uploaded, a feature that converts files with resource forks (and other Mac-specific information, such as type and creator codes) as they're uploaded and then restores them again at download. Files may also be automatically compressed and decompressed by adding a file suffix, such as `.Z` or `.gz`, to the name at upload and then requesting the file without the suffix at download.

FTP on Mac OS X Server is also integrated with Kerberos authentication but sends all files in the clear after authenticating, so to secure any FTP transfers that involve private data, they should be performed within an SSH tunnel.

Spotlight Server

Mac OS X's file search feature, named Spotlight, indexes local files by using a process named `mdimporter` (metadata importer), which analyzes files to build a data store of search-worthy metadata attributes.

The `mds` (metadata server) process can then use this information to rapidly provide query results to users searching for content, specific file attributes, file names, and similar criteria.

Spotlight Server manages the indexing of server file shares. The background components of Spotlight run under a special user in Mac OS X Server, and file access is granted to this user via ACL file permissions.

Spotlight Server adds some additional overhead to the file server to manage an index of the files in share points where Spotlight has been turned on. If users aren't actually using this feature, it can be disabled to conserve this extra effort. Spotlight Server is configured within Server Admin when setting up a share point.

Spotlight should be turned on only for shares being served by AFP or SMB. If Spotlight is activated and then these file-sharing protocols are turned off, the indexes Spotlight created won't be searchable by network users.

Spotlight search is also only available to Mac OS X clients, so if a given share point is being made available only to Windows users, Spotlight should be turned off for that share point.

Time Machine Server

Time Machine is also a desktop feature in Mac OS X. It uses the system's `FSEvents` mechanism for tracking file system changes and uses this to perform regular incremental backups.

Desktop systems can be configured to save these backups to an external drive or to a network volume that supports AFP (such as Snow Leopard Server's Apple File Service) or WebDAV (such as an AirPort base station with a shared disk) by using some special conventions to ensure that data copied to the network share is actually written out.

This is important because Time Machine writes to a sparsebundle disk image in order to maintain a secure HFS+ file system on the network server. If the computer being backed up were to lose its network connection, it could leave the backup file in an unknown state.

Time Machine Server, as a feature in Mac OS X Server, supports the communication necessary to keep backups accurate. It also sets appropriate file permissions on the share point and initiates advertising the share as a potential backup destination volume for Time Machine users via Bonjour.

In contrast to Spotlight Server, activating Time Machine Server on a share point in Server Admin doesn't cause any significant increase in processor use because the work involved in Time Machine backups is performed on the client side. However, activating the service on the server and setting up clients to use it obviously result in increased disk use.

CROSS-REF
For more on using Time Machine Server, see Chapter 38.

Planning File Services

Successful deployment of file services requires some advanced planning, including:

- Which file service protocols you need to configure to support your audience of users
- What special file service features you need to configure
- How you manage access to files and share points
- How much and what kind of storage your file services need
- What level of service availability your users need
- What hardware is needed to support the level of service required

File service protocols

The protocols you need to configure depend on the client platforms you need to support. Although most client systems can be set up to support any file-sharing protocol with the appropriate third-party software, it's easier and more efficient to serve your clients their native protocol:

- **AFP.** For local Mac users
- **SMB.** For local Windows users
- **NFS.** For local Unix users
- **FTP or WebDAV.** For Internet clients

This requires the least effort in managing client software and centralizes configuration and software updates on the server.

Mac OS X Server makes it relatively easy to activate the desired protocols for a given file share all in one administrative location; other server platforms or appliances may require you to configure each service separately and define the same share points for each service independently.

Special file service features

Outside of basic file sharing, you may also want to configure special services for your shares:

- **Automounts.** For enabling clients in the directory domain to find and mount shares
- **Home folders or group folders.** For network users and groups
- **Spotlight Server.** For searching
- **Time Machine Server.** For support for user backups
- **Specialized file services.** For using FTP or WebDAV

Supporting Automounts and home folders requires a configured directory domain with accounts for users, groups, and computers. Computers must be bound to the domain in order to log in and access resources.

An Open Directory domain can be used with Kerberos to enable SSO for users, enabling them to log in to their system once and subsequently remain authenticated while connecting to various network resources without needing to repeatedly present their credentials.

Supporting Spotlight search features requires accommodating the extra hardware-processing overhead. Supporting Time Machine Server demands significantly more disk storage resources compared to basic user file sharing.

Choosing to support FTP and WebDAV uploads and downloads requires an understanding of the type and sensitivity of data your users might work with; FTP is commonly used to upload changes to a web host, for example, where the possibility of public files being sniffed during upload is probably not an issue. However, it would be a mistake to open up company files to public FTP access because it's not a secure protocol, even when authenticated login is used.

Managing access to files and share points

Planning access control for files and share points involves authorizing share access to specific users or groups of accounts as well as defining the file-level permissions each user will have.

By creating function-based groups of network accounts, you can manage access to files as defined by memberships in groups that represent the needs of related users instead of by assigning complex individual access rules for each user. This results in a manageable, understandable security policy that's easy to adjust by making one change to a group's permissions rather than having to update all the individual users involved.

Similarly, a user can be allowed or denied access to a variety of resources by simply adding or removing him or her from a group rather than needing to make a variety of permission changes to all the involved resources in relation to that individual user's account.

Ownership and permissions

File privileges are a combination of assigned ownership and permissions. A user is assigned ownership of the files he or she creates. Where that file is created also results in defining what permissions are assigned to it. By default, a new file obtains permissions based on the enclosing folder. When creating a share point, make sure that its assigned permissions are appropriate for the needs of the user.

A file created within a share is not only assigned permissions matching the share but retains those permissions even if the file is moved elsewhere. For example, if a user creates a file inside a share with restricted permissions, moving the file to a public share doesn't automatically give every other user wide-open permissions. The file's owner or an administrator will need to change the file's assigned permissions.

Conversely, if a user copies a file into another user's drop box, the file doesn't assume the permissions of that folder; however, access to the file does change because the file permissions of the drop box folder allow only the owner to access the files within it, regardless of the set permissions of the files themselves.

Using ACLs and POSIX permissions

Snow Leopard Server works with two types of file permissions:

- **POSIX.** These file permissions are based on the three-tiered Unix model of a user, his or her primary group, and everyone else. Each of the three buckets can be allowed or denied permission to read, write, and execute the file or directory.

- **ACLs.** These are designed to be compatible with Windows and enable a finer granularity of control that defines a rule set that allows or denies a variety of use permissions to any number of different users or groups specified in the list's entries.

In Mac OS X, ACL support can be activated only on HFS+ volumes, and only the AFP and SMB file-sharing protocols provide network file system support for ACLs. Permissions defined by ACLs on files exported by using NFS are enforced by the server but aren't visible to and can't be modified by NFS clients.

ACL permissions are defined by ACEs (access control entries), which define access to the file or folder by specifying a permission rule that includes:

- A user or group account specified by its universally unique ID number
- The Allow or Deny ACE type
- Thirteen different access permissions as defined in Apple's ACL model
- Inherited, which is a flag indicating that the permission was inherited from its parent folder
- Applies to, which indicates how the permission propagates to child files or folders

Inheritance and precedence

In addition to explicit permissions assigned to a file or folder, there may also be inherited permissions that trickle down from a containing folder. Inherited permissions are used to enable administrators to broadly set permissions across a wide range of files instead of explicitly needing to assign file permissions to each file individually.

Inheritance rules are set by the Applies to field of the ACE, which has four options:

- Apply to this folder
- Apply to child folders (subfolders)
- Apply to child files (files in this folder)
- Apply to all descendants

When a new file or folder is created, the Mac OS X kernel determines its effective permissions based on the inheritance settings of its parent folder. After creating a new ACE permission that applies to child items, those inherited permissions must be propagated before the containing folders and files below it in the file system hierarchy inherit the assigned permissions. Only the entire ACL can be propagated, not an individual ACE.

A file with inherited permissions can't change those permissions until they're made explicit.

To determine what type of access a user has to a shared file or folder, Snow Leopard Server evaluates the file's or folder's ACEs, followed by its designated POSIX permissions. It then applies the following rules of precedence to determine the effective permissions for a given user:

- **Without defined ACEs, POSIX permissions apply.**
- **With ACEs, rule order is important.** If a file or folder has defined ACEs, the kernel starts with the first ACE in the ACL and works through the list until the requested permission is satisfied or denied. ACE order can be changed from the command line by using the chmod command.
- **Deny permissions override others.** Server Admin lists Deny permissions above Allow permissions because Deny permissions have precedence. When evaluating permissions, once a Deny permission is encountered, the system ignores any remaining permissions assigned to the user and simply denies permission. For example, if a user is allowed read permissions in one ACE but belongs to a group denied read permissions in another, Server Admin reorders the permissions so that the Deny permission comes first to highlight that the system enforces the Deny rule.
- **Allow permissions are composite.** The system defines a user's permissions as a combination of all the permissions assigned to the user, including standard POSIX permissions.

CROSS-REF
For more on setting ACL file permissions in Server Admin, see Chapter 9.

How much and what kind of storage

When planning for capacity, it's important to ensure that the amount and type of storage you select will not only serve your immediate needs but also your short-term growth requirements. It also needs to be able to scale with your long-term requirements.

If your chosen storage solution can't keep up with your needs for growth, you may likely find yourself needing to replace it, at considerable expense, rather than being able to grow along with it. The need to start over and develop a new storage plan after implementing your file-sharing system will likely end up costing more than if you had slightly overbuilt your system but ended up with a foundation that supported future growth.

Using RAID storage

One aspect of storage planning related to a disk-intensive activity such as file sharing involves RAID (redundant array of inexpensive disks), a technology that allows administrators to configure specialized volumes that do one of the following:

- Span multiple drives to create a single logical volume from multiple physical disks in order to deliver cost-effective storage by avoiding the need to use the most expensive, largest capacity drives currently in production.

- Stripe data across multiple drives to segment files that appear on a single logical volume across multiple physical disks in order to deliver top disk performance while avoiding the need to use the most expensive, fastest drives currently in production.

- Duplicate redundant data by mirroring data that appears on a single logical volume across another or multiple physical disks in order to deliver more reliability than the most expensive drives can promise.

- Combine these aspects of storage size, performance, and high availability as needed.

Using SAN storage

Another aspect of storage planning relates to the technologies used to connect the server to the storage device. The names of these technologies are often used incorrectly, even in Apple's server documentation, but the terminology used is less important than understanding how each works and recognizing what advantages and drawbacks each has:

- **Direct-attached storage (DAS).** This refers to volumes connected as local devices via direct local interfaces, such as internal SATA or SAS drives or external SCSI, USB, or FireWire devices. A DAS volume may be either a freestanding drive or a JBOD (just a bunch of disks) or a RAID unit exposing itself as a DAS volume with a SCSI, FireWire, or USB interface.

- **Network-attached storage (NAS).** This refers to a network volume served by a free-standing appliance server, often containing a RAID array or simply a collection of drives. A NAS unit serves its volumes to network clients by using a network file system, such as NFS or SMB (CIFS), although some also support AFP. Regardless of the network file system used, a NAS device always appears to be a network share to client computers.

- **Storage area network (SAN).** This refers to a storage device, typically a RAID array, which connects to servers or workstations by using a specialized network interface, often Fibre Channel or iSCSI, a standard that uses SCSI signaling over IP networking. Rather than appearing as a network share, however, the device appears to be a locally attached disk volume. In other words, SAN clients have block-level access to the SAN device rather than file level access, as they would with NAS. Multiple clients can connect to a single SAN over the same storage network, but because each system connects as if it were a locally attached drive, the SAN needs special management software to prevent the connected systems from overwriting each other's data.

Apple markets its Xsan clustered file system for use with SAN devices, making it the alternative of choice for Snow Leopard Server users. Apple's Xsan is based on Quantum Corporation's StorNext File System, making it compatible with StorNext's client software for other platforms. Apple licenses Xsan for far less than other available clustered file systems.

Service availability and hardware needs

In addition to planning adequate disk capacity, your file services plan also needs to accommodate service availability. Remember that many of the other services you provide to network users are dependent on access to file shares; if your file services fall offline, your users may likely even lose the ability to successfully log in and connect to their home folders.

This makes file services a particularly critical piece of your network plans. Planning for high availability in file services involves the following:

- **Planning for IP failover.** This way, a replacement server is available and ready to take over a failed system's roles, helping to mitigate any hardware failures that do occur.

- **Spreading out the server workload.** Thus, an unanticipated hardware failure only has an impact on a limited number of users or a specific service. This avoids inadvertently setting up a single point of failure that can bring down your entire network.

- **Incorporating fail resistant redundancy measures.** Achieve this by using RAID to accommodate a failed drive, using a UPS (Uninterruptible Power Supply) and backup power source to accommodate power failures, and using redundant cooling systems and power supplies to enable systems to continue working even after a component stops.

- **Maintaining an appropriate server environment.** Server components are thus less likely to fail or to be destroyed by accident. This includes enforcing secured access and keeping the area clean and dry, with adequate climate control for both temperature and humidity levels and appropriate cable management.

CROSS-REF
For more on advanced planning for hardware needs, see Chapter 4.

File Service Setup and Configuration

To set up file-sharing services from Server Admin, first enable the file-sharing protocol services, as needed, within the desired server's listing of configured services and then do the following:

- Configure each protocol's services.
- Create share points.
- Configure share point properties.
- Configure share point file permissions.
- Turn on each file service as needed.
- Configure client access.

CROSS-REF

For more on working with share points, Automounts, and home directories in Server Admin, see Chapter 9.

Apple File Service

To configure the Apple File Service from Server Admin, first enable the AFP service within the desired server's listing of configured services.

To enable AFP configuration in Server Admin, follow these steps:

1. Launch Server Admin and then connect to the desired server.

2. Select the server listing and then click Settings on the toolbar.

3. Click the Services tab.

4. Click the check box for AFP.

5. Click Save. AFP should now appear in the list of configurable services for the selected server, as shown in Figure 22.1.

Figure 22.1

The AFP pane in Server Admin

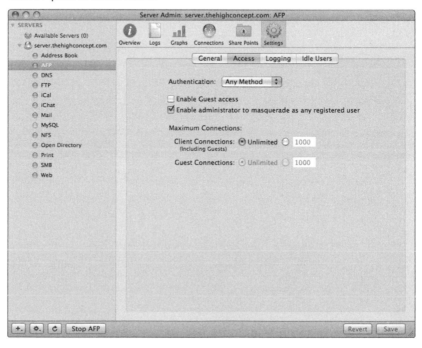

After selecting AFP from the list of services in the Servers list, the Overview page presents a status report of when the service was started, the current network throughput it's using, the current active connections, and whether guest access is activated.

The Logs page of the AFP pane presents a listing of the events recorded in:

- The Apple File Service Access Log (if activated; it's off by default) located at `/Library/Logs/AppleFileService/AppleFileServiceAccess.log`
- The Apple File Service Error Log (which is enabled by default) located at `/Library/Logs/AppleFileService/AppleFileServiceError.log`

The Graphs page of the AFP pane presents a chart representing either the average number of connected users or the network throughput in use over the selected time period.

The Connections page of the AFP pane, shown in Figure 22.2, shows all the currently connected AFP clients by username, status, and network address and indicates how long each has been connected and how long each has been idle.

Figure 22.2

The Connections page of the AFP pane

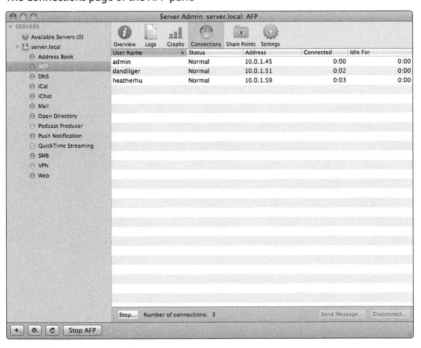

A selected user in the connections list can be disconnected or the administrator can send him or her a message. The client user can't respond to the message, so this feature is primarily intended to notify users that the service will be going offline and that they need to close any open files to avoid data loss.

The Share Points page of the AFP pane, shown in Figure 22.3, is identical to the File Sharing page of the general server pane within Server Admin as well as the Share Points pages within the Server Admin panes for configuring other file-sharing protocols, such as SMB and NFS.

CROSS-REF

For more on setting up share points, file permissions, and disk quotas in Server Admin, see Chapter 9.

Figure 22.3

The Share Points page of the AFP pane

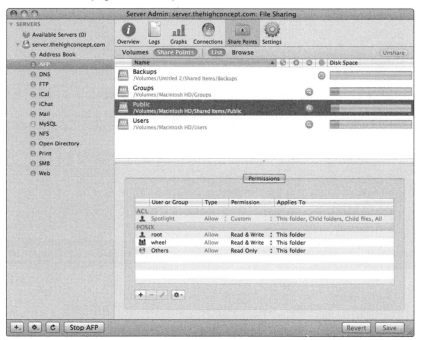

The Settings page of the AFP pane presents four tabs:

- **General.** Presents a field for typing a greeting message that's presented to users at first login. A pop-up menu presents the option to present a custom text encoding for older clients that don't support Unicode.

- **Access.** Sets the authentication method, which can be Standard, Kerberos, or Any (either). It also provides a check box to enable guest access (off by default) and to allow an administrator to masquerade as any registered user. A maximum connections section enables the administrator to set the peak number of concurrent connections allowed by all users and, separately, by guest users. By default, this is set to unlimited.

- **Logging.** Allows the administrator to enable the access log and to configure what access events are logged. This creates significant extra overhead and logging files, so the access log is turned off by default, and enabling it activates the option to archive the logs every set number of days. A separate control enables error log archiving.

- **Idle Users.** Presents a setting that allows sleeping clients to be disconnected as idle but retains the clients' sessions for a set number of hours (24 being the default). This enables users to automatically reconnect after waking without losing their open documents. A second setting enables idle users to be disconnected after a set time and allows separate exceptions for guest users, administrators, registered users, and idle users with open files. A field offers to supply a disconnect message for idle users that support presenting such a message.

To manually configure the users allowed access to the AFP service, follow these steps:

1. **From Server Admin, select the server name of the AFP server.**

2. **Click the Settings page and then click the Access tab.**

3. **From the Services pane within Access, select the AFP service from the left column.**

4. **Click the Allow only users and groups below radio button.**

5. **Click the Add (+) button.** A Users & Groups sheet opens.

6. **Drag users or groups to the access list on the right to define who has AFP access.**

7. **Click Save.** AFP access is thus limited to the selected users.

Windows File Service

To configure the Windows File Service from Server Admin, first enable the SMB service within the desired server's listing of configured services.

To enable SMB configuration in Server Admin, follow these steps:

1. **Launch Server Admin and then connect to the desired server.**

2. **Select the server listing and then click Settings on the toolbar.**

3. **Click the Services tab.**

4. **Click the check box for SMB.**

5. **Click Save.** SMB should now appear in the list of configurable services for the selected server, as shown in Figure 22.4.

Figure 22.4

The SMB pane in Server Admin

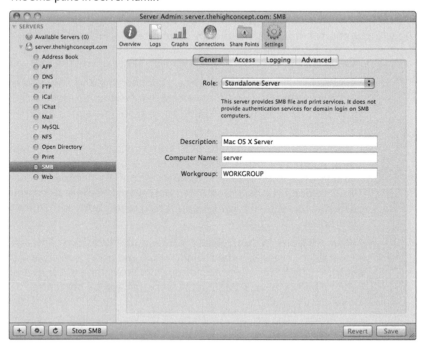

After selecting SMB from the list of services in the Servers list, the Overview page presents a status report of when the service was started, the current active connections, and whether guest access is activated.

The Logs page of the SMB pane presents a listing of the events recorded in:

- The SMB File Service Log compiled by Samba of all file-sharing events, located at `/var/log/samba/log.smbd`
- The SMB Name Service Log, Samba's WINS browsing events, located at `/var/log/samba/log.nmbd`

The Graphs page of the SMB pane presents a chart representing average connected users over the selected time period.

The Connections page of the SMB pane shows all the currently connected SMB clients by username, network address, and how long each has been connected. A button allows a selected user in the connections list to be disconnected.

The Share Points page of the SMB pane is identical to the File Sharing page of the general server pane within Server Admin as well as the Share Points pages within the Server Admin panes for configuring other file-sharing protocols, such as AFP and NFS.

The Settings page of the SMB pane presents four tabs:

- **General.** Sets the role the local server will play as one of the following:
  - **Standalone Server.** Provides basic Windows file and print services without supporting authentication services for Windows domain login for PCs. The server is assigned a name and description and a Workgroup membership, which associates it with other computers for browsing purposes.
  - **Domain Member.** Supports both Windows domain login (including support for hosting roaming profiles and network home directories) and standard Windows file and print services, obtaining its authentication services from another server acting as the Primary Domain Controller. Domain members and controllers are assigned a Domain rather than a Workgroup, which serves both authentication and browsing purposes.
  - **Primary Domain Controller.** Provides authentication services for Windows domain login and standard Windows file and print services as well as serving authentication requests from other Domain Members. To serve as a Primary Domain Controller, a Mac OS X Server must also be configured as an Open Directory master.
  - **Backup Domain Controller.** Acts as a secondary replica to the Primary Domain Controller and serves as a backup and automatic failover for the Primary Domain Controller if it ever falls offline. To serve as a Backup Domain Controller, a Mac OS X Server must also be configured as an Open Directory peplica.
- **Access.** Sets the authentication methods, which can be set to allow:
  - **LAN Manager.** Least secure but required to support Windows 95 clients
  - **NTLM.** The original NT version of LAN Manager, which is now obsolete and only useful if you have NT clients earlier than NT 4 SP4
  - **NTLMv2 & Kerberos.** The most secure option but requires at least Windows NT 4 SP4 or Windows 98

  The Access page also provides a check box to enable guest access (off by default) and to set a maximum number of concurrent user connections.
- **Logging.** This allows the administrator to set the logging level to low, medium, or high to balance the need for reporting events with the logging resources consumed.
- **Advanced.** This presents a setting for enabling the server to act as a Workgroup Master Browser (if acting as a stand-alone server) or a Domain Master Browser (if attached to a Windows domain). The following settings are available for WINS Registration:
  - **Turned off.** The default setting, preventing the server from using or providing WINS services for NetBIOS name resolution

- **To support enabling WINS locally.** Acts as a WINS server for providing NetBIOS name resolution
- **To register with another WINS server.** For NetBIOS name resolution. WINS is analogous to DNS within the Windows domain world.

Finally, a check box offers to enable virtual home folders and is on by default. This allows Windows users to log in and access the same home folder share point configured for Mac users. If disabled, a separate SMB share point must be configured, and Windows users must be configured to use this under the Windows tab of their account within Workgroup Manager.

CROSS-REF

For more on setting Windows account details in Workgroup Manager, see Chapter 10.

To manually configure the users allowed access to the SMB service, follow these steps:

1. From Server Admin, select the server name of the SMB server.

2. Click the Settings page and then click the Access tab.

3. From the Services tab within Access, select the AFP service from the left column.

4. Click the Allow only users and groups below radio button.

5. Click the Add (+) button. A Users & Groups sheet opens.

6. Drag users or groups to the access list on the right to define who has SMB access.

7. Click Save. SMB access is thus limited to the selected users.

Network File Service

To configure the Network File Service from Server Admin, first enable the NFS service within the desired server's listing of configured services.

To enable NFS configuration in Server Admin, follow these steps:

1. Launch Server Admin and then connect to the desired server.

2. Select the server listing and then click Settings on the toolbar.

3. Click the Services tab.

4. Click the check box for NFS.

5. Click Save. NFS should now appear in the list of configurable services for the selected server, as shown in Figure 22.5.

Figure 22.5

The NFS pane in Server Admin

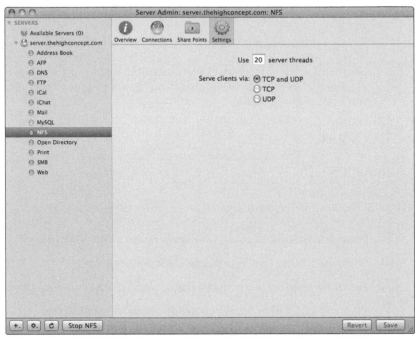

After selecting NFS from the list of services in the Servers list, the Overview page presents a status report showing if the service is running as well as the status of a variety of related processes: `nfsd`, `portmap`, `rpc.lockd`, and `rpc.statd`.

NFS presents no Logs or Graphs pages, but the Connections page shows all the currently connected NFS clients by username and network address and how long each has been idle, how many NFS requests each has made, and the number of bytes that each user has read and written.

The Share Points page of the NFS pane is identical to the File Sharing page of the general server pane within Server Admin as well as the Share Points pages within the Server Admin panes for configuring other file-sharing protocols, such as AFP and SMB.

The Settings page of the SMB pane presents a control to specify the top number of server threads that will run within the `nfsd` process, which is set to 20 by default. The more threads allowed, the more concurrent connections the service can handle.

A second option selects the transport protocols supported under NFS:

- **TCP and UDP.** The default and most flexible
- **TCP.** Forces all clients to use the connection-oriented, error-correcting, higher performance option of TCP, which also puts more work on the server

● **UDP.** Forces all clients to use the connectionless, correctionless datagram protocol, which is more efficient for the server but doesn't work well for remote clients

FTP File Service

To configure the FTP File Service from Server Admin, first enable the service within the desired server's listing of configured services.

To enable FTP configuration in Server Admin, follow these steps:

1. **Launch Server Admin and then connect to the desired server.**

2. **Select the server listing and then click Settings on the toolbar.**

3. **Click the Services tab.**

4. **Click the check box for FTP.**

5. **Click Save.** FTP should now appear in the list of configurable services for the selected server, as shown in Figure 22.6.

Figure 22.6

The FTP pane in Server Admin

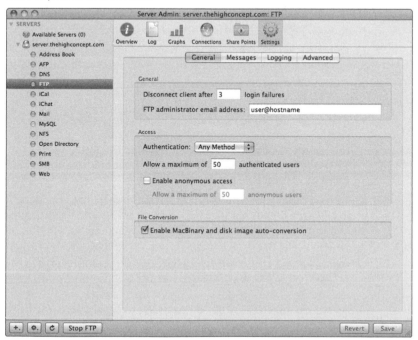

After selecting FTP from the list of services in the Servers list, the Overview page presents a status report showing if the service is running and how long it's been up, the current authenticated and anonymous connections, and whether anonymous FTP is enabled.

The Log page of the FTP pane in Server Admin presents a listing of the events recorded in the FTP log located at `/Library/Logs/FTP.transfer.log`.

The Graphs page of the FTP pane presents a chart representing average connected users over a selected time period.

The Connections page of the FTP pane shows all the currently connected FTP clients by username and type (authenticated or anonymous) as well as their activity.

The Share Points page of the FTP pane is identical to the File Sharing page of the general server pane within Server Admin as well as the Share Points pages within the Server Admin panes for configuring other file-sharing protocols, such as AFP and SMB.

The Settings page of the FTP pane presents four tabs:

- **General.** Sets a preference for disconnecting clients after a set number of login failures (three by default) and allows an administrative email address to be supplied to users. An authentication section sets support for Standard, Kerberos, or Any and sets a threshold on the number of authenticated and anonymous users who may connect. A check box also enables support for anonymous logins. A file conversion option enables the feature for performing MacBinary or compression on the fly for uploads and downloads.

- **Messages.** Sets a welcome and banner message

- **Logging.** Allows the administrator to log the uploads, downloads, FTP commands, and rule violation attempts of either anonymous or authenticated users or both

- **Advanced.** Presents the option of choosing between the three different sharing configurations for FTP:

  - **FTP Root and Share Points.** Makes available the files in the FTP Root directory as well as any other share points designated to support FTP. Authenticated users see their home folders with a link to the shared FTP Root, whereas guests see only the FTP Root itself. Within the FTP Root, symbolic links to other FTP share points also make those available to all users.

  - **Home Folder with Share Points.** This is largely the same, but authenticated users instead see the FTP Root as their starting point, with a link to their home folders within a Users folder inside the FTP Root that acts as a symbolic link to their user folders.

  - **Home Folder.** Gives authenticated users access to their home directory only, with no links to the FTP Root or any other FTP share points. Guest users continue to see the FTP Root and any designated FTP share points. The FTP Root field of the Advanced tab enables the administrator to set a different folder location.

Managing and Monitoring File Services

File-sharing services involve a combination of storage hardware, operating system–enforced file access permissions, and the server software that shares files over the necessary protocols.

Managing file storage hardware

How you manage the storage hardware portion depends on the hardware technologies you choose to deploy to serve your needs. Mac OS X Server provides tools to monitor disk use and throughput of directly attached storage devices, and system logs and SMART disk device monitoring may help to identify hardware problems as they begin to occur.

Disk Utility can be used to monitor and verify the health of disks and volumes and also offers to create software RAID volumes that span, stripe, or mirror volume data across multiple disks by using either HFS+ or ZFS storage pools.

However, the utility of software volume management is limited because it leaves the operating system to manage multi-disk volumes. ZFS should still be considered experimental, so basing your production file-sharing system on it would be risky, to say the least.

RAID storage

Hardware RAID devices offload the work of managing component disks to a separate RAID controller. This frees the operating system from managing that extra overhead, increasing peak performance and response times.

Dedicated RAID devices may likely also provide more sophisticated options for advanced RAID configurations, along with tools for managing and monitoring their volumes.

For example, Apple's discontinued Xserve RAID shipped with RAID Admin software (still bundled in the Mac OS X Server administration tools) for remotely monitoring components, disks, and arrays, along with tracking internal temperatures and network statuses.

SAN storage

When using a SAN device (such as the Xserve RAID or the Promise Vtrak RAID Apple endorsed as its replacement) for full-blown SAN storage, use the Xsan clustered file system and its Xserve Admin management tool to create volumes and monitor SAN health.

Monitoring IP failover

Apple's Xsan allows multiple servers to access a storage device or to share access to the same data on the device, an important component of IP failover systems.

Although it's possible to set up a failover server that constantly mirrors the data being used on the primary server, a SAN configuration enables both the primary and backup servers to access the same shared data managed by the SAN. This allows the backup to take over the primary's functions without any delay and with much less likelihood of data lost before it has the opportunity to be synced to the backup server.

In an IP failover system, a primary server and a secondary backup are connected to the same network via Ethernet and interconnected via FireWire as a second, private IP network interface.

The primary server broadcasts a heartbeat signal every second over both network interfaces by using the `heatbeatd` process. The secondary backup server listens for the signals on both interfaces by using a `failoverd` process.

The two IP addresses of the backup server are specified on the master as the destination addresses for its heartbeat pings by editing the `FAILOVER_BCAST_IPS` line of the master server's `/etc/hostconfig` file (which must be done as the root user).

For example, if the master were configured to use 10.0.1.2 for Ethernet and 10.1.0.1 for FireWire and the backup were configured to use 10.0.1.3 for Ethernet and 10.1.0.2 for FireWire, the master primary would be configured as `FAILOVER_BCAST_IPS="10.0.1.3 10.1.0.2"`.

The secondary backup server also needs to be configured with the two network interfaces it will be listening to for the master server's heartbeat signals. In `/etc/hostconfig`, the following two lines need to be added, representing the primary network interface `en0` and the secondary FireWire interface:

```
FAILOVER_PEER_IP_PAIRS="en0:10.0.1.2"
FAILOVER_PEER_IP="10.1.0.1"
```

Both servers must be restarted, and the FireWire connection should be left unconnected until they restart. Once attached, the backup begins listening for heartbeats on both interfaces; the loss of a heartbeat signal on only one interface is interpreted as a false alarm.

If the primary server goes offline, the secondary takes over its assigned IP address and begins servicing incoming requests. The secondary server's services must be configured identically in order to stand in for the primary. Using shared SAN storage ensures that the data it serves is also identical, although it's also possible to keep the two servers' data in sync by using `rsync`.

Failover events are logged at `/Library/Logs/failoverd.log`, which can be read by using the Console app or accessed from the command line.

Using access control entries

Above the hardware level, file sharing is managed via ACLs of permission rules. In order to effectively manage permissions across a file system, administrators can set inherited rules and then propagate the permissions across the files and folders contained within the volume or share by using Server Admin.

Once inherited ACL permissions are propagated, access control exceptions can be made for specific subfolders by making their inherited permissions explicit and then changing those permissions as desired.

Managing share points

Although Mac OS X Server presents separate configuration panes for each of the file-sharing protocols it supports in Server Admin, it provides a consistent share point configuration interface across all of them, enabling administrators to concentrate on the files they want to share rather than on the software details related to what service is actually managing which shares.

Automount share points

By defining share point mounts in the Open Directory domain, administrators can set up shares that users can mount automatically. Mac OS X users mount special shares in their Network domain, which allows applications and library files — such as Color Sync profiles and fonts — to be stored on the network and incorporated by users without explicit installation steps.

Network home folders

Using a directory domain also allows users to log in to a home directory stored on the network or, alternatively, a Portable Home Directory where files are retained locally for performance but still synced with the network home directory. This enables mobile users to keep files in sync with desktops via the same network home folder.

Integration between the Apple File Service and Samba enables Windows users to access the same directory via SMB that they see when logging in to a Mac by using AFP. This enables easy and convenient support for file access between platforms for individuals who use both.

CROSS-REF
For more on working with share points, Automounts, and home directories in Server Admin, see Chapter 9.

Monitoring file service performance

Individual file-sharing protocols present file service performance data in their Graphs page within Server Admin, and overall performance of the server can be monitored from the server pane's Overview page.

Monitoring performance and resource utilization over time can help in planning to prevent saturated disk storage resources and to ensure that network and server CPU resources are sufficient for immediate and short-term future needs.

Summary

- Mac OS X Server provides file-sharing support for a variety of common protocols to support users on different platforms: AFP for Mac users, SMB for Windows users, and NFS for Unix platforms.

- Apple has built special support into AFP and other protocols to handle advanced features, such as Spotlight server-side indexing for fast network search, and support for Time Machine Server as a specialized, fault-tolerant repository for backup files.

- Additional, specialized file-sharing protocols serve other needs, such as FTP for software uploads and downloads or website file maintenance.

- HTTP and WebDAV provide the file-sharing protocol support for a variety of other advanced services in Mac OS X.

- In addition to software configuration, file-sharing services demand appropriate hardware suited to serving files, a task that may involve using an external DAS or a SAN, both of which commonly use RAID to supply cost-effective capacity, performance, and redundancy for data safety.

- ACLs provide an important level of flexible user access control for documents and folders being shared to network users.

Mail Services

Mac OS X Snow Leopard's mail service provides standards-based email messaging with new support for push notifications, Mobile Access, and significantly faster performance and improved compatibility.

In 2003, Apple released Mac OS X 10.3 Panther Server by using the open-source Cyrus server for clients' inbound email service. In Snow Leopard Server, Apple now uses the Dovecot open-source project to provide clients with inbound email services.

The move to the new mail engine is based on Dovecot's performance, which Apple says is not just faster than mail services in Leopard Server but also eclipses high-end, enterprise-class mail servers, citing benchmarks that rate it as soundly outperforming the Sun Java Messaging Server. Dovecot also provides strict adherence to standard mail delivery protocols, enhanced scalability to handle more users, and better data reliability with new features, including automatic self-healing data corruption detection and repair.

Snow Leopard's mail services also include junk mail filtering by using SpamAssassin's message text analysis to rate the probability of a mail item being unsolicited junk to help users sort noise out of their mailboxes.

Virus detection and quarantine services are provided by ClamAV, which works to detect viruses and then either bounce infected messages back to the sender, delete the message, or quarantine it and then notify the administrator for review.

Snow Leopard also delivers enhanced support for secure delivery to desktop and mobile users by using SSL encryption, new push notification of new messages, and new server-side rules for managing mailbox folders and vacation messages. There's also improved support for mail server clustering to spread messaging services across multiple servers by using automatic failover to gracefully accommodate hardware failures.

This chapter describes how the mail service works, what's involved in planning, how the service is configured, and how to maintain and monitor the mail service.

Introduction to Mail Service

Snow Leopard's mail service sends and receives mail messages by using standard Internet mail protocols:

- Simple Mail Transfer Protocol (SMTP, RFC 5321) to send and transfer mail between servers
- Internet Message Access Protocol (IMAP, RFC 3501) for client mail access that maintains the user's mailbox on the server for centralized access from multiple clients, including webmail
- Post Office Protocol (POP, RFC 1939) for simple mail access for clients that manage their email locally on a single system

The designations of incoming and outgoing mail service are relative to the end-user client, which specifies both an incoming POP or IMAP mail server to obtain new messages from the server and an outgoing SMTP mail server for sending messages out to other users on the same server, within the same organization, or to the Internet. Relative to the server, SMTP handles all outside mail in both directions as well as accepting messages from local clients for local or outside delivery, whereas POP and IMAP handle only the local delivery of new messages to clients.

Outgoing SMTP mail

SMTP handles mail transfer between servers as well as delivery of outbound mail to other domains on the Internet and incoming mail delivery for local users. SMTP is performed by a Mail Transfer Agent (MTA).

In Snow Leopard Server, the MTA is Postfix, an open-source project that originated within IBM in the late 1990s. Postfix addresses speed, simplicity, and security issues related to the widely used Sendmail MTA, which was developed at UC-Berkeley in the 1980s.

If an MTA is unable to reach another server directly for delivery of messages addressed to that server's domain, it seeks to relay the messages to another server. Spammers frequently use this relay mechanism to dupe an unwitting SMTP server to send out their junk mail, potentially resulting in that server being blacklisted for supporting the delivery of spam. Securing SMTP by requiring user authentication helps prevent this problem.

Incoming mail service

IMAP and POP deliver messages from the local mail server to desktop or mobile clients. These services are performed by a Mail Delivery Agent (MDA), which in Snow Leopard is now handled by the new Dovecot engine. Apple and Dovecot have both historically referred to the MDA role as a Local Delivery Agent (LDA) instead; the two terms are synonymous in referring to a mail service component that delivers messages to clients. Client mail applications running on a local system are referred to as a Mail User Agent (MUA).

Clients can be configured to use only IMAP, only POP, or either of the protocols to connect to the server from the mail applications they use. Each protocol works differently, so users should be informed of the merits of each and the potential for unexpected mailbox changes if both protocols are enabled and used on different clients.

IMAP

The IMAP mail service stores users' mail in a mailbox maintained on the server. Clients can then access and organize folders of their messages in this IMAP mailbox as if it were stored locally on their system. In reality, the client mail application actually maintains a cached copy of the mailbox on the server.

IMAP synchronizes changes the user makes locally to the server mailbox store, enabling users to work with their mailbox from multiple computers and see the same messages from each. Users can also access their server mailbox from a browser by using webmail, which requires the web server to access the user's mailbox via IMAP.

The Dovecot open-source project serving as Snow Leopard Server's new mail engine is known for its focus on security as well as full compliance with the latest IMAP4rev1 specifications. According to testing cited by `imapwiki.org`, the latest version of Dovecot fully passed a battery of over 440 IMAP tests, whereas Cyrus, the popular IMAP software Apple has been using in Leopard Server, failed at least a couple-dozen tests.

The IMAP implementations used in Gmail, IBM's Notes Domino, the Kerio Mail Server, and the Sun Java Messaging Server (currently used by Apple for its MobileMe cloud services) were also all reported to have unreliable behavior when checking messages, bugs in updating flags on atomic items in mailboxes, and multiple failures in scripted testing of their compatibility with the IMAP standard.

Strict adherence to IMAP is as important in email software as web standards compliance is in a web server or browser. In many cases, it's even critical because poor implementation of standards on the web usually only results in improperly formatted pages or flaws in using web applications, whereas errors in IMAP can result in email data loss.

Dovecot also supports workarounds for several known bugs in various IMAP and POP3 clients. However, because the workarounds may increase the work that the server performs, it's possible to disable them.

According to the Dovecot project's website, the software is also "among the highest performing IMAP servers," using self-optimizing, transparent indexing of mail folders that support modification by multiple concurrent users.

POP

In contrast to IMAP, the POP mail service acts as a simpler mechanism for delivering new mail messages. Once a user checks his or her messages, the mail items are actually downloaded locally and typically purged from the server. This means that a user who checks mail from different mail clients on different systems by using POP likely ends up with a different set of messages on each, with no way to synchronize those messages together. Users who access POP email from multiple clients typically need to configure all but one of the mail clients they use to leave mail on the server rather than purging all messages every time mail is checked.

Additionally, if the client's mailbox on his or her local disk is lost or corrupted, there's no cached copy left on the server to recover. That means users need to maintain vigilant backups of their local system. With IMAP, a lost or corrupted local mailbox can simply be replaced with a fresh copy from the server.

Whereas IMAP offers significant advantages for users who check mail from different systems, POP connections put less of a load on the server because the process of checking for new mail in a transitory fashion is much less computationally intensive than continually syncing the mailbox with the server, as IMAP does.

Maintaining an IMAP mailbox for users may also result in much larger storage demands, as there's no provision for regularly purging the user's mail locally. This can be managed via mailbox quotas.

Users who have an IMAP mailbox should be informed that using POP to check messages from a different email client results in messages being pulled off the server and saved locally to the POP client unless it's specifically configured to leave a copy of read messages on the server.

Push notifications

The mail service in Snow Leopard also incorporates support for the push notification service. Enabling push messaging is as simple as designating the push server, which by default is the local mail server. Push messaging uses update notifications pushed from the server that ping the remote client to indicate that new messages are available for download. This is far more efficient than having the mobile client regularly log in to the server to check for new mail messages.

Outgoing SMTP mail is always pushed on demand by the client, so push notifications relate only to incoming mail. Mac OS X Snow Leopard uses the XMPP Publish/Subscribe feature to deliver push, which works by delivering a standard instant message. Alternative push messaging systems, such as Microsoft's Direct Push in Exchange ActiveSync, rely on long-lived HTTP requests maintained by the client, which are less efficient.

CROSS-REF
For more on the push notification service, see Chapter 33.

SSL and Mobile Access

The mail service supports securely encrypted connections with clients by using SSL for both incoming and outgoing mail. In addition, the mail service can be configured to work with the new Mobile Access service running on a separate server.

SSL is a standard originally created by Netscape for allowing web servers to secure a confidential connection with a user, encrypt transmissions, and authenticate as a trusted entity. Netscape's SSL 3.0 formed the basis of the IETF TLS specification, which has since technically replaced SSL. However, TLS is still commonly referred to as SSL, particularly by Apple within its Server Admin interface.

SSL works by using public-key cryptography. The server retains a private key and publishes a public key to users in an SSL certificate. Information encrypted by the public key can be decrypted only by using the server's private key. This enables users who trust the certificate (which is often itself signed by a trusted third-party Certificate Authority) to generate a random number, encrypt it with the server's public key, and send the result to the server. Only the server can decrypt this information via its secret private key. This exchange enables the server and client to create session keys for further encrypted communications. No third parties can intercept and decrypt the initial exchange of the encrypted random number, so the keys generated on both ends enable the client and server to continue confidential, encrypted communications.

To support SSL, the mail server must generate its own self-signed certificate identity (which clients have to assume trust in) or obtain a signed version of that identity endorsed by a Certificate Authority, a step that enables clients to automatically trust the server's certificate as reputable if it matches the identity of the mail server. Snow Leopard's Mobile Access service acts as a reverse proxy to enable remote clients and mobile users to securely connect to and access resources inside an organization's firewall via SSL, including mail services, websites, collaboration features, contacts in Address Book Server, and calendars hosted by iCal Server.

CROSS-REF
For more on Mobile Access, see Chapter 32.

Planning Mail Services

If you're migrating existing mail service to Snow Leopard Server, your plans will include moving to the new Dovecot. If you're initiating new mail service, the default installation of Snow Leopard Server uses Dovecot and Postfix. To use a different underlying MTA for your mail services, such as Sendmail, you need to turn off Postfix in Server Admin and configure Sendmail manually.

To set up basic mail service, you need:

- A registered domain name for your mail server and properly configured DNS MX (mail exchanger) records
- Defined user accounts for all mailbox users, with activated email service settings configured under the Mail tab of the account records in Workgroup Manager
- Sufficient storage for user mailboxes stored on the server

- Plans for supporting IMAP, POP, or both protocols for mail clients
- Configured web services and customized webmail if you plan to offer web access
- An SSL certificate if you plan to support secure remote transports to accommodate less-secure authentication methods
- Policy covering junk mail filtering and the handling of discovered viruses

Configuring DNS for email services

For Internet mail service to function properly on the network, administrators must configure DNS with MX, or mail exchanger records. These special service records were uniquely created to support receiving mail by using multiple servers all sharing the same domain address.

For example, `mail1.example.com` and `mail2.example.com` can both be assigned MX records that enable the organization to use the email domain `@example.com` instead of accounting for the actual server names of however many servers are actually put into service.

Additionally, MX records have a defined priority level that determines which email host gets the highest priority in receiving mail, with the lowest priority level number getting the highest priority. If that server isn't available, the second-highest priority server receives the mail. This allows a backup server to accept and queue up mail that can be delivered to the primary server when it becomes available.

Using the previous examples of email hostnames, an administrator would create the following MX record entries in the Zone page of Server Admin's DNS, shown in Figure 23.1:

- name `mail1.example.com` priority `10`
- name `mail2.example.com` priority `20`

This would ensure that `mail1.example.com` was first in priority to receive the mail bound for `users@example.com`. You may alternatively want to have your ISP set up and maintain the necessary MX records for your domain instead of handling your DNS records locally. You don't need MX records set up to provide only local mail service.

CROSS-REF
For more on configuring DNS, see Chapter 12.

Storage options for mail

The outbound mail is temporarily stored at `/var/spool/postfix/` and may be relocated to another local volume by using a symbolic link. User mailboxes are stored in directories within `/var/spool/imap/dovecot/mail/` as a series of discrete files, backed by an index listing of incoming messages stored within a small Berkeley DB database; the actual content of mail messages isn't stored in the database.

Figure 23.1

MX record DNS configuration in Server Admin

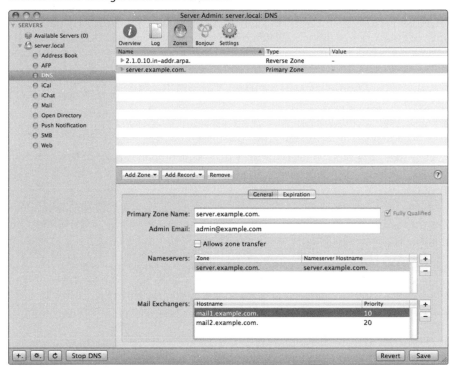

Storing mailbox messages as discrete files greatly simplifies the mail store in comparison to the approach Microsoft Exchange Server takes, which stores all messages, including all file attachments, of all user mailboxes within a giant database.

The number of mailbox messages the server can store is limited only by:

- The size of the storage volume
- The size of individual messages, most of which comes from file attachments
- The volume formatted block size, which defines the minimum size of the files the volume can store

Because the default storage location is on the boot drive, administrators supporting many users with large mailboxes need to plan for mail storage accordingly. The mail store can alternatively be:

- Spread across multiple volumes by using independent mail store partitions
- Stored on an Xsan cluster
- Stored on a mounted remote file system on another server

Mail stores across volumes

The mail store can be defined to use additional new volumes without interrupting existing users. However, mail for existing users won't automatically be moved to the newly defined mail stores; individual users must be configured to use the new stores in the Mail tab of their user records within Workgroup Manager. Removing an existing mail store doesn't delete the messages it contains but does make them inaccessible to users whose mailboxes are stored at that location.

If more than one mail store partition is defined, the mail store location of a particular individual's account mailbox is presented:

- Within the Mail pane of the user's account records in Workgroup Manager
- Under the Accounts tab of the Mail pane's Maintenance page in Server Admin

Mail stores on Xsan

If you define your mail store by using Apple's Xsan file system, you can cluster multiple mail servers that all share the same mail store to achieve top performance and provide automatic failover for hardware redundancy.

In a cluster configuration, the node mail servers all share a single mail store, whereas each cluster node server maintains its own mail index database. Each node server also maintains its own SMTP spool file. If a server node were to go offline, another node in the cluster automatically takes over the failed server's spool file and records the failover event in its log files.

Mail stores on remotely mounted volumes

Maintaining the server's mail store on a remotely mounted volume rather than on directly attached storage or a storage area network incurs the extra overhead of the network and as a result impacts overall performance.

Apple also recommends against using NFS when using a remotely mounted file system.

Backing up and restoring mail stores

Because mail stores store messages as normal files, it's easy to back up the mail service's data by simply duplicating each mail store. Restoring mail service data is similarly a matter of replacing it with a backup copy.

Backups can target individual mailboxes represented as storage folders within the mail store or include the entire mail store. Incremental backups of the mail store can be performed to provide a fast and efficient backup that needs to copy only the small index database file and any new or changed individual message files created or modified since the last backup.

When performing a backup or restore operation, the mail service should be stopped to prevent the index database file from falling out of sync with the mail store contents.

Mail store configuration is performed by using the Advanced/Data Store tab of the Mail pane's Settings page in Server Admin.

Supporting POP and IMAP

By default, the mail service activates both POP and IMAP local mail delivery protocols for users. Depending on your needs, you may want to disable one or the other:

- If you plan to provide only basic email delivery for lots of users with the least server resources possible, you might choose to exclusively serve POP mail.

- If you want to provide a full service mailbox for users and provision webmail service, you need to enable IMAP. Unless your users need to access email from older clients that can support only POP, you might want to serve IMAP exclusively to prevent confusion or the inadvertent download and purging of a user's mailbox on the server.

If you're not providing mail service to users, you can still configure your server to act as only an outgoing and relay SMTP server and simply turn off POP and IMAP. The system still accepts mail addressed to any local users, but users won't be able to check their messages from standard mail client software until POP or IMAP is enabled.

Without enabling POP or IMAP, users' messages can be forwarded to `/var/mail` to allow terminal access to messages on the server by using Unix utilities such as Elm or Pine. Once you configure messages to forward to that location, however, they won't become available for delivery by Dovecot even if POP and IMAP are subsequently enabled. POP and IMAP are configured from the General pane of the Mail pane's Settings page in Server Admin.

Webmail services

Webmail in Mac OS X Server is delivered by SquirrelMail 1.4.17, an open-source PHP package. Using webmail requires IMAP mail service to be enabled because webmail itself is just an interface to the mail server, and it doesn't support accessing email using POP. The webmail service is enabled by using the Web Services pane of the Web pane's Sites page in Server Admin, shown in Figure 23.2. By default, Snow Leopard Server expects to use the local mail server, but webmail can be configured to access IMAP mailboxes served by a mail service running on a separate server.

The webmail configuration is stored within `/etc/squirrelmail/config/config.php`, which can be edited either manually or by using a Perl configuration script by using this command:

```
sudo /etc/squirrelmail/config/conf.pl
```

Figure 23.2

The Sites page of the Web pane in Server Admin

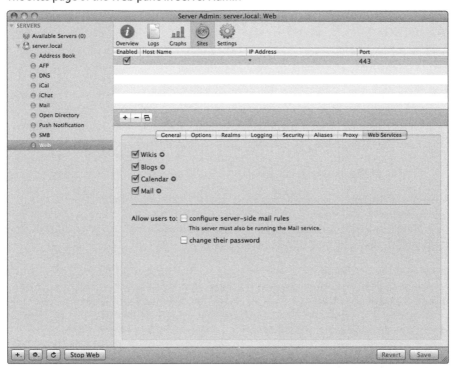

Either way, various elements of the webmail service can be configured, including:

- The service's organization name
- Site logo presented at login
- Mail server settings
- Location of special IMAP folders, such as sent items, drafts, or trash
- Plug-ins and language encoding features
- Themes and appearance settings

Webmail is linked from the wikis and blogs pages but directs to the separate site located at `www.example.com/webmail/src/login.php`. The service must be manually customized to appear cohesive with other web collaboration services.

CROSS-REF

For more on configuring webmail, see Chapter 25.

Securing mail

The mail service supports optional or mandatory SSL transport encryption as well as the use or requirement of secure user authentication methods for both SMTP and local delivery of POP and IMAP.

Using or requiring SSL transport encryption

SLL doesn't automatically provide secure authentication; it only enables confidential transfers between MTA servers or between the LDA server and clients. User authentication methods are selected separately. In other words, you can operate an open-relay SMTP server that enforces SSL security to confidentially accept spam from unauthenticated users under the protection of encryption without achieving any effective security. SSL must be used together with authentication, which is described shortly.

The mail server can be configured to either support or require SSL connections in order to ensure that its communications are confidential. Separate settings apply to:

- SMTP MTA communications between mail servers
- IMAP and POP LDA communications between the server and clients

For both local IMAP and POP and outbound SMTP mail protocols, the mail service supports three options for SSL:

- **Don't Use.** Leaves SSL off and unavailable
- **Use.** Enables clients or other servers that support SSL to request an SSL connection. Clients and other servers that don't request SSL can still talk to the server by using an unencrypted connection.
- **Require.** Forces clients and other servers to support SSL and doesn't allow unencrypted connections with client mail applications or other mail servers that don't support SSL

Using or requiring SSL requires supplying an SSL certificate identity.

CROSS-REF
For information on creating and working with SSL certificates, see Chapter 9.

SSL settings are configured under the Advanced/Security tab of the Mail pane's Settings page in Server Admin.

Using or requiring authentication for SMTP

SMTP is required for accepting mail from outside hosts and relaying outbound messages from local users; if you only want to deliver mail messages for your local users, you can configure your users to send their outbound email to your ISP or organization's SMTP servers.

There are two sources of mail traffic that can request SMTP use:

- Mail delivery from outside servers, addressed to local users
- Mail relay from a server or local user seeking to pass messages to the local server for relay and delivery to users on a third-party server

Mail relay is an important feature because there are times when a mail server can't directly reach the server of the addressed recipient. It then relays the message to another server. However, this relay mechanism also makes it easy for spammers to flood messages through an open relay to deliver unsolicited bulk emails, usually with faked headers that obscure their origin.

This not only puts an extra burden on the mail service but may also associate this spam with the SMTP server acting as an on-ramp to the Internet superhighway, resulting in the server being blacklisted. By forcing users to authenticate in order to relay mail, you can help prevent mail service abusers from sending mail through your system.

Requiring SMTP authentication doesn't prevent mail delivery for your users because the server can continue to accept and deliver local messages addressed to them. It requires authentication only for SMTP relay.

As is the case with SSL, the mail service similarly supports a series of options for configuring security for the SMTP service, ranging from strict to none at all:

- **Mandatory secure SMTP authentication requires all users to present credentials for a specific, secure authentication method, such as Kerberos.** If you provide Kerberos support to all your users, you can demand they use it to achieve the greatest possible security by making it the only option in the list of allowed SMTP authentication methods.

- **Alternative secure SMTP authentication allows users to present credentials for any one of the enabled secure authentication methods.** If you support a variety of clients, you may want to support both Kerberos and CRAM-MD5, for example.

- **Require or allow less-secure SMTP authentication enables users to present credentials by using a less-secure authentication method.** Selecting only one method requires users to use it specifically. PLAIN authentication sends the user's password in the clear, and Login authentication uses a weak crypt hash that's only slightly better. However, by enabling even basic authentication, you can support a greater number of clients and still thwart open relay of spam from unauthenticated users. The security risk of using these less-secure passwords can be addressed by using SSL encryption to keep this exchange confidential. Not requiring the use of SSL yet allowing less-secure authentication methods exposes your users' account passwords and could enable malicious users to assume their identities to gain full access to their mailbox and other available server resources.

- **No SMTP authentication turns your system into an open relay and allows anyone to push mail through your server.**

SMTP authentication options are configured under the Advanced/Security tab of the Mail pane's Settings page in Server Admin.

Restricting access to SMTP

In addition to requiring authentication, you can also secure your SMTP service by restricting the hosts that can connect to your server. You can:

- **Accept unauthenticated SMTP relay only from select servers, subnets, or domain names.** Approved servers and clients can relay mail through your server without authenticating. Any servers or clients not on the list can't relay mail without authenticating. Any hosts can still deliver mail addressed to your local users without authenticating. This option provides an exception for specific, known systems that don't support SMTP authentication.

- **Refuse SMTP connections from select servers, subnets, or domain names.** You can block known mail abusers by adding them to your own list of rejected hosts, which refuses all messages from those hosts.

- **Refuse mail from blacklisted servers.** This option uses a listing published by a Real-time Blackhole List (RBL) server to automatically reject messages from known open relays of junk mail. Enabling this option may result in blocking some valid mail.

- **Filter SMTP connections by using the firewall service.** This option blocks known mail abusers by IP address or subnet before even initiating a connection with the mail server. An advanced rule can be set to deny traffic on SMTP TCP port 25 from the desired source to the destination of the mail server.

SMTP relay settings to accept and refuse connections from specific hosts or to use RBL listings can be configured from the Relay tab of the Mail pane's Settings page in Server Admin.

CROSS-REF

For more on the firewall service, see Chapter 14.

Using and requiring secure authentication for POP and IMAP

Unlike SMTP mail relay, access to users' mailboxes via POP or IMAP has, of course, always required authentication. However, steps can be taken to use more-secure user authentication mechanisms:

- **Mandatory secure POP or IMAP authentication requires all users to present credentials for a specific, secure authentication method, such as Kerberos.** If you provide Kerberos support to all your users, you can demand they use it to achieve the greatest possible security by making it the only option in the list of allowed authentication methods for POP and IMAP.

- **Alternative secure POP and IMAP authentication allows users to present credentials for any one of the enabled secure authentication methods:**
  - If you support a variety of different POP clients, you may want to support Kerberos, CRAM-MD5, and APOP.
  - If you support a variety of different IMAP clients, you may want to support both Kerberos and CRAM-MD5.
- **Require or allow less-secure POP authentication enables users to present credentials by using a less-secure authentication method.** Selecting only one method requires users to use it specifically:
  - PLAIN authentication sends the user's password in the clear.
  - Login authentication uses a weak crypt hash that's only slightly better.

By allowing basic authentication, you can support a greater number of clients; the security risk of using these less-secure authentication methods can be addressed by using SSL encryption to keep the password exchange confidential. Not requiring the use of SSL yet allowing less-secure authentication methods exposes your users' account passwords and could enable malicious users to assume your users' identities to gain full access to their mailboxes and other available server resources.

POP and IMAP authentication options are configured under the Advanced/Security tab of the Mail pane's Settings page in Server Admin.

Managing junk mail and viruses

Once mail is accepted for delivery to local users, the mail service can screen messages for junk mail filtering and virus detection. The server doesn't screen messages it relays between other servers.

SpamAssassin junk mail filtering

The mail service performs junk mail filtering by using SpamAssassin to analyze the text content of a message and assign it a junk mail probability rating. Because detection can offer only limited accuracy, by default, the server doesn't throw out mail suspected to be spam.

Instead, the message is marked with a junk mail rating that the user's mail client can evaluate in the manner configured by the user, either flagging the item as suspected spam or automatically delivering it to a junk mail folder for subsequent review.

SpamAssassin analyzes messages by using Bayesian mail filtering, which determines a junk mail rating statistically by word frequency in comparison to both known junk mail messages and known valid mail. The more messages the system has to compare against, the better its ratings can be. Therefore, the training process improves over time and adapts to changes made by junk mail senders. You can also manually or automatically train the system as described later in this chapter.

The mail system administrator can set a desired level of aggressiveness in interpreting mail as spam, which determines how many junk mail flags a message must raise before it's considered to be junk mail. Settings range from 1 to 40, with the default being 6. Segments of the aggressiveness range are labeled as:

- **Aggressive.** Brands mail as junk with just a few flags
- **Moderate.** Requires more evidence to mark a message as junk
- **Cautious.** Sets a high bar of many flags before designating mail as junk

Once scored, messages are, by default, delivered to the user with the server's junk mail rating via a special X-Spam-Level email header that the client can interpret.

An optional subject tag can also be supplied to prominently flag the message as suspicious. The default option is to add ***JUNK MAIL*** to a message's subject line. Junk mail can also be encapsulated as an attachment to hide what might be offensive content in suspected spam messages yet still make the message available to the user if its junk status happens to be a false positive.

Alternatively, junk messages can also be:

- **Bounced.** Sends the junk message back to the sender. A notification of the event can be sent to a supplied email address.
- **Deleted.** Removes the message without delivery. A notification of the event can be sent to a supplied email address.
- **Redirected.** Quarantines the junk message to a mailbox other than the addressed recipient.

The junk mail filter can also be set to screen out messages in specific languages and from specific locales. Your mail service plans should accommodate determining the languages and locales of valid emails your users might potentially receive email from in order to help prevent false positives in spam detection based on character encodings.

Junk mail settings are configured under the Filters tab of the Mail pane's Settings page in Server Admin.

ClamAV virus detection

The mail service uses ClamAV to scan mail messages for viruses by using regularly updated virus definitions obtained through the free FreshClam service. Suspected viruses are managed similarly to junk mail, although the default behavior is to delete the virus because the accuracy in screening confidence is higher, and the risk of delivering a known virus outweighs the potential of missing a valid email.

As with junk mail, messages with detected viruses can be handled in a variety of ways:

- **Bounced.** Sends the message back to the sender. A notification of the event can be sent to a supplied email address, and the recipient can also be notified.

- **Deleted.** Removes the message without delivery to `/var/virusmails/`. This is separate from deleted junk mail, enabling the system to routinely delete viruses while preserving junk mail for review. A notification of the event can be sent to a supplied email address, and the recipient can also be notified.

- **Redirected.** Quarantines the virus message to a mailbox other than the addressed recipient.

The virus definitions ClamAV uses are updated by a process called `freshclam` at a regular interval set by the administrator. The default setting is four times per day.

Virus filtering settings are configured under the Filters tab of the Mail pane's Settings page in Server Admin.

Server-side message filtering

Snow Leopard introduces new server-side message filter integration that enables a client to submit configuration rules that are performed on the server. This enables the server to do things such as respond to incoming messages with an out-of-office or vacation message instead of needing a client program to be left open to respond to mails.

Other server-side filter actions can perform tasks, such as:

- Directing mails to a specific mailbox based on matching rules for the sender, subject line, or other header information

- Forwarding matching mails to a different email address

- Discarding matching emails to the trash

- Highlighting messages with flags based on various rule criteria

Server-side mail filtering uses Sieve, a scripting language codified in RFC 5228 for defining extensible filtering rules simply and securely, with no capacity for executing potentially dangerous external programs.

Server-side mail filtering is enabled from the Filters tab of the Mail pane's Settings page in Server Admin.

Mailing lists

Mac OS X supports two types of mailing lists for addressing multiple users in a group:

- **Groups-based mailing lists are based on directory-defined groups.** Once enabled, members in the group receive emails sent to the group's email address, which is based on the short name of the group. The mailing lists are synchronized with group membership changes in the directory.

- **Mailman-based mailing lists are managed by the Mailman 2.1.12rc1 open-source package and work as standard Unix-style mailing lists; any individuals using any email address can subscribe to the mailing list and begin receiving messages.** Mailman lists aren't synchronized with directory groups, and new members can join or leave at any time. Mailman also uses its own master password unaffiliated with any directory account to manage list administration features.

Both types of mailing lists are enabled and configured from the Mailing Lists pane of the Mail pane's Settings page in Server Admin. Mailman also supplies a web configuration page for managing lists and other settings at `www.example.com/mailman/listinfo/`.

Local host aliases and virtual hosting

Snow Leopard's mail service supports two options for hosting multiple domain names on the same server:

- Local host aliases enable the server to receive mail for users under different hostnames. Mail to either address — such as `@example.com` and `@anotherexample.com` — is sent to the same mailbox. A company might use local host aliases to receive email at long and short versions of the company name.

- Virtual hosting enables the server to receive mail for users of different domain names independently, so mail to the same name at different domains is delivered to separate mailboxes. That means the same `@example.com` and `@anotherexample.com` would be treated as unrelated users on two different virtual mail servers. An ISP might choose to host several virtual hosts on the same server.

Both local host aliases and unique virtual hostnames can be used at the same time, but once virtual hosting is enabled, all mail aliases, email addresses for local host aliases, and mail addresses associated with the virtual hostname must be fully qualified.

In contrast, without virtual domains active, every short name typed for a user in Workgroup Manager works as an email address for the primary domain and any defined local host aliases.

For example, if you create a user named Daniel with the short names daniel and dan and the server uses both `example.com` and `anotherexample.com` as domain aliases, the following email addresses are all valid and all direct to the same user's mailbox:

- dan@example.com
- daniel@example.com
- dan@anotherexample.com
- daniel@anotherexample.com

However, if you enable virtual hosting, any additional short names defined for each user must contain the username as well as the domain for all mail domain names you expect the user to receive mail under, both for aliases and for virtual host addresses.

User Daniel would need to have the full `dan@example.com` specified as an alternative short name in order to also receive email under that address, and `daniel@anotherexample.com` would also have to be specified as a short name, even if `@anotherexample.com` were defined as a local host alias and not a virtual domain.

Local host aliases and virtual hosting are enabled and configured from the Advanced/Hosting pane of the Mail pane's Settings page in Server Admin.

Mail Service Setup and Configuration

Setting up mail service requires enabling the mail service in Server Admin and then doing the following:

- Configuring basic mail services, such as enabling the desired delivery protocols, securing the SMTP service, and activating junk mail and virus filtering, server-side rules, and logging preferences.
- Configuring advanced mail settings, including authentication and encryption settings, virtual hosting, mail store settings, and mail service clustering
- Setting up user accounts to enable mail in Workgroup Manager
- Configuring mail clients

To enable mail service configuration in Server Admin, follow these steps:

1. **Launch Server Admin and then connect to the desired server.**

2. **Select the server listing and then click Settings on the toolbar.**

3. **Click the Services tab.**

4. **Click the check box for Mail.**

5. **Click Save.** Mail should now appear in the list of configurable services for the selected server, as shown in Figure 23.3.

Figure 23.3

Enabling the Mail pane in Server Admin

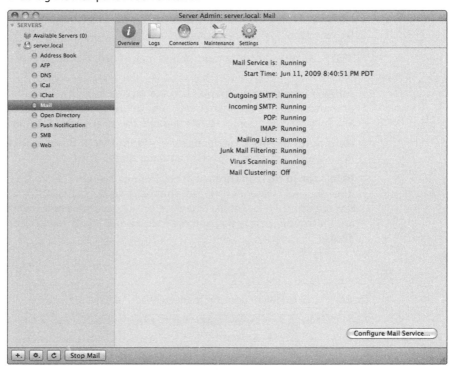

Configuring basic mail services

Much of the basic configuration of the mail service can be performed by using the Mail Service Configuration Assistant, which is launched from the Overview page of the Mail pane in Server Admin.

To perform mail service configuration by using the assistant, follow these steps:

1. **Launch Server Admin and then click Mail.**

2. **Click the Overview page of the Mail pane.**

3. **Click Configure Mail Service to launch the assistant and then click Continue to begin.**

4. **Click the check boxes to enable the following services from the assistant, as shown in Figure 23.4:**

- **POP.** For simple client mail downloads

- **IMAP.** For synchronized user mailboxes and webmail support

- **SMTP.** Allow users to send outbound mail to other local users or to users on other domains

- **Allow incoming mail.** Enables users to receive mail from outside hosts. Specify a domain name to be used in users' email addresses and the mail server's hostname as a fully qualified domain name. Disable this to suspend the inbound SMTP queue.

- **Hold outgoing mail.** Suspends the outbound SMTP queue until you remove the hold, which subsequently sends all waiting messages

- **Relay outgoing mail through host.** Defines a server that your server will send all its outbound messages through. Your organization's firewall or your ISP might require using a relay server. However, if you use a relay server without the server administrator's permission, it may result in your server being cited for mail service abuse.

Figure 23.4

The Mail Service Configuration Assistant in Server Admin

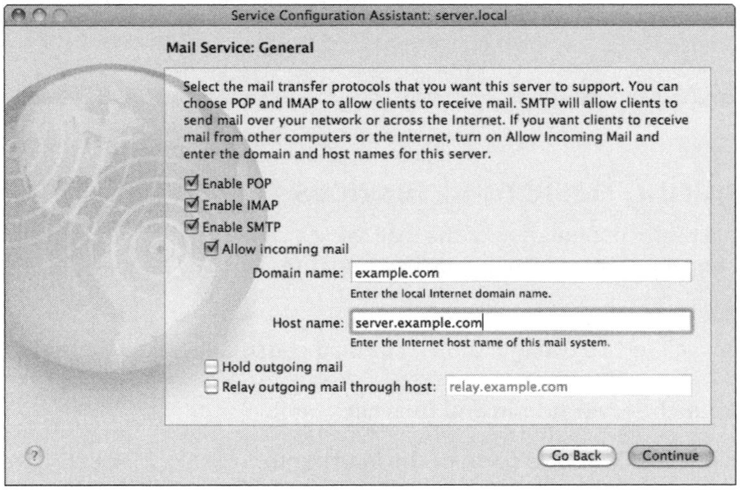

5. **Click Continue.**

6. **Use the controls to set junk mail and virus filtering rules:**

- Enable scanning for junk mail and set a junk mail score. The system delivers junk mails with an X-SPAM header to assist client mail applications in screening out email as configured by the user.

- Enable scanning for viruses.

- Configure the fate of infected messages: deleted, bounced, or redirected to a quarantine mailbox.

- Enable virus definition updates and set an update interval.

7. **Click Continue.**

8. **Use the controls to set authentication methods:**

- Enable secure authentication methods supported by your email clients and your password server.

- Enable nonsecure authentication if you have clients that support only basic password authentication. If you enable this, you should provide SSL encryption to secure the password transaction because it's otherwise sent in the clear or with only a minimal crypt hash.

9. **Click Continue.**

10. **Set the location of the mail database and message store:**

- Enable default mail store location to store messages on the local server's boot drive at `/var/spool/imap/dovecot/mail`.

- Deselect the check box to select an alternative location for the mail store.

- Specify local host alias names for the mail server to enable the server to accept mail for users with different hostnames, such as `@example.com` and `@another example.com`. Email sent to the same username at either address is delivered to the same mailbox.

11. **Click Continue.** The assistant provides a summary of all the settings it's about to configure.

12. **Click Continue to accept the settings and then click Done.**

Once basic settings are performed by using the assistant, additional settings can be configured in Server Admin by using the Settings page.

To configure additional general mail service settings, follow these steps:

1. **Launch Server Admin and then click Mail.**

2. **Click Settings on the toolbar.**

3. **Click the General tab, shown in Figure 23.5.**

4. **Edit the Domain name and Host name of the mail server to match those typed in the assistant.**

Figure 23.5

The General pane Server Admin's Mail pane

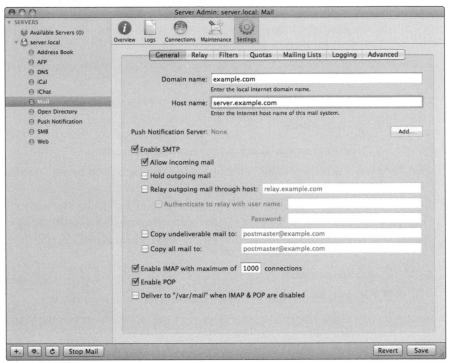

5. **Select a Push Notification Server.** This may be the local server or any other Snow Leopard Server handling the push notification service. Use the Add button to specify the location of the server.

6. **Optionally, type credentials for SMTP authentication with the relay selected in the assistant.** You can also edit the other SMTP configurations the assistant performs.

7. **Type an email address to send undeliverable mail to.**

8. **Type an email address to copy all mail to.** This performs a blind carbon copy of all incoming and outgoing email to a designated mailbox for archiving or monitoring.

9. **Configure a set number of concurrent IMAP connections allowed.** You can also enable or disable POP and IMAP services as configured in the assistant.

10. **Enable alternative delivery** to /var/mail **if both IMAP and POP are disabled in order to allow terminal access to messages using Unix tools rather than local delivery to email clients.**

11. **Click Save.**

To configure additional SMTP relay settings, follow these steps:

1. **Launch Server Admin and then click Mail.**

2. **Click Settings on the toolbar.**

3. **Click the Relay tab, shown in Figure 23.6.**

Figure 23.6

The Relay pane in Server Admin's Mail pane

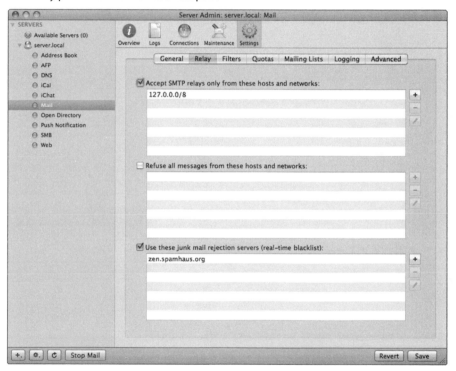

4. **Click the Accept SMTP relays only from these hosts and networks check box and then type IP addresses, subnets, or domain names for any hosts you want to allow to relay mail through your server without authenticating.** Click the Add (+) button to type a host or use the Edit button with a pencil icon to change existing entries. Any servers or clients not on the list can't relay mail without authenticating. Any hosts can still deliver mail addressed to your local users without authenticating.

5. **Click the Refuse all messages from these hosts and networks check box to block SMTP connections from select IP addresses, subnets, or domain names.** Add any known mail abusers to your own list of rejected hosts, which refuses all messages from those hosts. Click the Add (+) button to type a host or use the Edit button with a pencil icon to change existing entries.

6. **Click the Use these junk mail rejection servers check box to refuse mail from blacklisted servers.** This option uses listings published by a RBL server to automatically reject messages from known open junk mail relayers. Enabling this option may result in blocking some valid mail. The default RBL server is `zen.spamhaus.org`. Click the Add (+) button to type a new RBL server or use the Edit button with a pencil icon to change an existing entry.

7. **Click Save.**

To configure additional filtering settings, follow these steps:

1. **Launch Server Admin and then click Mail.**

2. **Click Settings on the toolbar.**

3. **Click the Filters tab, shown in Figure 23.7.**

Figure 23.7

The Filters pane in Server Admin's Mail pane

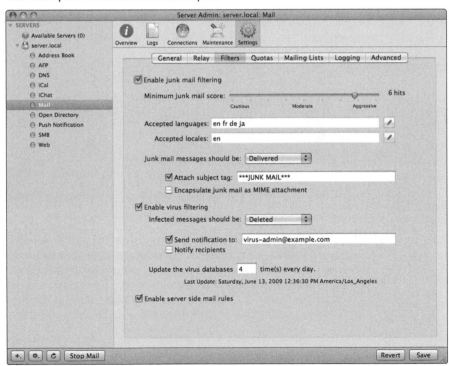

4. Click the Enable junk mail filtering check box and then set the minimum junk score for messages.

5. **Add accepted languages to avoid valid foreign messages from being rejected as spam.** Click the Edit button labeled with a pencil icon to change existing entries.

6. **Add accepted locales to avoid valid foreign messages from being rejected as spam.** Click the Edit button labeled with a pencil icon to change existing entries.

7. Use the pop-up menu to select what should be done with identified junk mail:

- **Delivered.** Sends junk emails with an X-SPAM header that identifies the item's junk mail score to the user's email client for processing as the client has configured. An optional subject tag can also be supplied to prominently flag the message as suspicious. The default option is to add ***JUNK MAIL*** to a message's subject line. The junk mail can also be encapsulated as an attachment to hide what might be offensive content in the suspected spam message.

- **Bounced.** Sends the junk message back to the sender. A notification of the event can be sent to a supplied email address.

- **Deleted.** Removes the message without delivery. A notification of the event can be sent to a supplied email address.

- **Redirected.** Quarantines the junk message to a mailbox other than the addressed recipient

8. Click the Enable virus filtering check box.

9. Use the pop-up menu to select what should be done with identified virus mails:

- **Deleted.** Moves the message without delivery to `/var/virusmails/`. This is separate from deleted junk mail, enabling viruses to be routinely deleted while preserving junk for review. A notification of the event can be sent to a supplied email address, and the recipient can also be notified.

- **Bounced.** Sends the message back to the sender. A notification of the event can be sent to a supplied email address, and the recipient can also be notified.

- **Redirected.** Quarantines the virus message to a mailbox other than the addressed recipient

10. **Set an update interval for virus definitions.** The default is four times per day, but Apple recommends daily updates.

11. **Click the Enable server side mail rules check box.** This supports Sieve email filtering for features such as vacation message replies, automatic mailbox organization, and message flagging.

12. Click Save.

Configure message and mailbox quotas

Mailbox quotas are set within the Mail pane of each user's account record in Workgroup Manager. Global settings in Server Admin limit individual message sizes and set warning thresholds when a mailbox nears its quota.

To configure mailbox quota in Workgroup Manager, follow these steps:

1. Launch Workgroup Manager and then authenticate with the directory domain.

2. Select user records to assign a mailbox quota.

3. Click the Mail tab, shown in Figure 23.8.

Figure 23.8

The Mail pane in Workgroup Manager

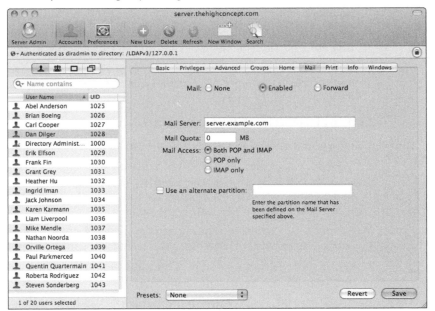

4. Set a Mail Quota for the user, in megabytes.

5. Click Save.

To configure quota settings in Server Admin, follow these steps:

1. Launch Server Admin and then click Mail.

2. Click Settings on the toolbar.

3. **Click the Quotas tab, shown in Figure 23.9.**

4. **Click the Refuse messages larger than check box to reject messages larger than a set size.** The default limit is 10 MB.

5. **Click the Enable quota warnings check box.** Type a percentage threshold for warning users.

6. **Click Edit Quota Warning Message to type email content that the user receives when the target percentage of the mailbox quota is reached.**

7. **Click the Disable a user's incoming mail when they exceed 100% of quota check box.**

8. **Click Edit Over Quota Error Message to type email content that the user receives when the mailbox quota is reached.**

9. **Click Save.**

Figure 23.9

The Quotas pane in Server Admin's Mail pane

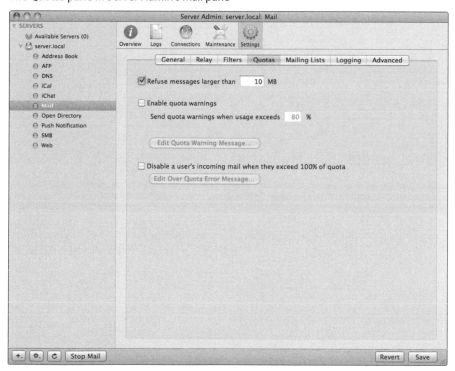

Configure mailing list settings

The mail service in Mac OS X Server supports enabling both workgroup email addresses based on a directory group membership and Unix-style Mailman mailing lists that any user can subscribe to or configure as an administrator with the appropriate password.

To configure mailing list settings in Server Admin, follow these steps:

1. **Launch Server Admin and then click Mail.**

2. **Click Settings on the toolbar.**

3. **Click the Mailing Lists tab, shown in Figure 23.10.**

Figure 23.10

The Mailing Lists pane in Server Admin's Mail pane

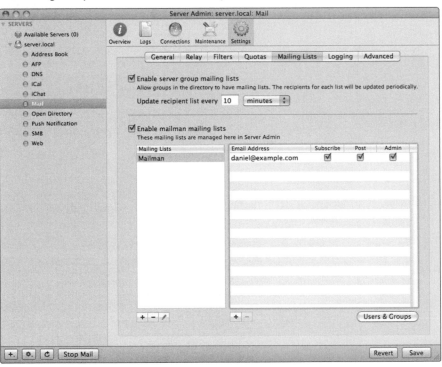

4. **Click the Enable server group mailing lists check box to create email addresses for directory groups.** Group membership is regularly updated. You can specify how quickly the recipient list is updated by typing an update interval. Create new groups and then edit their memberships in Workgroup Manager to create and edit workgroup mailing lists.

5. **Click the Enable mailman mailing lists check box to allow a designated administrator to create lists anyone can join and receive emails from.** Once enabled, you're prompted to provide a master password used by administrators working with Mailman lists. Type the email addresses of administrators you want to be able to create lists on the system.

6. **Create new mailing lists by using the Add (+) button or use the Edit button with a pencil icon to change existing lists.**

7. **Select mailing list members and use the check boxes to set their roles for the selected lists:**

- Subscribe means the user receives emails sent to the list.
- Post means the user can send messages to the list.
- Admin means the user can change list membership and other settings.

8. **Click Save.**

Configure logging settings

Components of the mail service can be set to log events with user-configured details.

To configure logging settings in Server Admin, follow these steps:

1. **Launch Server Admin and then click Mail.**

2. **Click Settings on the toolbar.**

3. **Click the Logging tab, shown in Figure 23.11.**

4. **Select logging levels for:**

- SMTP logs, reported by Postfix
- IMAP and POP logs, reported by Dovecot
- Junk Mail/Virus logs, reported by Amavis, the Perl glue software that interfaces Postfix with SpamAssassin and ClamAV

 The default logging level is Critical, which logs events that typically require prompt administrative action. Increasingly detailed logs of events are maintained by error, warning, notice, information, and debug settings.

5. **Click the Archive logs every check box and then type an archiving period, which is set to one day by default.**

6. **Click Save.**

Figure 23.11

The Logging pane in Server Admin's Mail pane

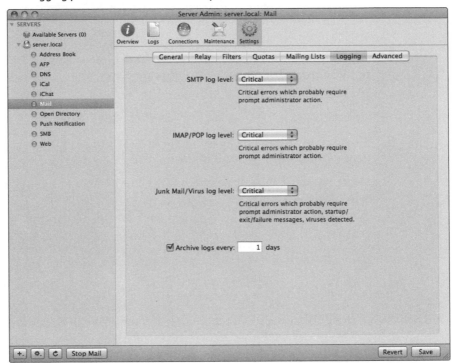

Advanced mail configuration

Once basic configuration of the mail service is completed, advanced settings may be config-ured, including the use of SSL and the desired authentication methods to be supported; local host and virtual hosting settings; a custom location for the mail store; and junk- and virus-filtering settings.

Configure SSL and authentication settings

The authentication methods you enable for the mail service need to balance your security requirements with the authentication types your users' existing mail clients support. If you choose to enable less-secure authentication methods, you should use or require SSL transport layer security to protect passwords that would otherwise be sent with little or no security.

To configure security settings in Server Admin, follow these steps:

1. **Launch Server Admin and then click Mail.**

2. **Click Settings on the toolbar.**

3. **Click the Advanced tab and then click the Security tab, shown in Figure 23.12.**

4. **To allow only strong authentication methods, click the following check boxes:**

- Kerberos and CRAM-MD5 for SMTP authentication
- Kerberos, CRAM-MD5, and APOP for IMAP/POP authentication

5. **To allow weak authentication methods for greater compatibility with a wider array of email clients, you can also enable:**

- Login and PLAIN for SMTP authentication
- Login, PLAIN, and Clear for IMAP/POP authentication

  If you enable weak encryption methods, you should strongly consider at least enabling the use of SSL and ideally determine if your clients can support required use of SSL. Without using SSL to secure email authentication, Login, PLAIN, and Clear passwords are highly vulnerable to interception by malicious users.

6. **To configure the use or requirement of SSL to secure authentication:**

- Choose Use for both SMTP and IMAP/POP SSL settings from the pop-up menu to support client or server requests to establish an SSL encrypted connection. Supporting SSL requires supplying a certificate identity from the second pop-up menu.
- Choose Require for both SMTP and IMAP/POP SSL settings from the pop-up menu to require clients and servers to establish an SSL encrypted connection and refuse any non-encrypted connections. Requiring SSL requires supplying a certificate identity from the second pop-up menu.

7. **Click Save.**

CROSS-REF

For information on creating and working with SSL certificates, see Chapter 9.

Figure 23.12

The Advanced/Security pane in Server Admin's Mail pane

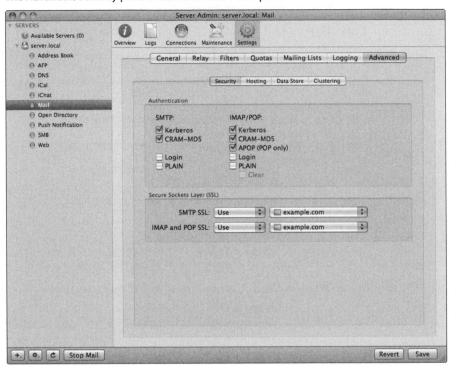

Configure local host alias and virtual hosting settings

As introduced earlier, Snow Leopard's mail service supports two options for hosting multiple domain names on the same mail server:

- Local host aliases enable the server to receive mail for the same user under different hostnames.

- Virtual hosting enables the server to receive mail for a username under different domain names independently.

To configure hosting settings in Server Admin, follow these steps:

1. **Launch Server Admin and then click Mail.**

2. **Click Settings on the toolbar.**

3. **Click the Advanced tab and then click the Hosting tab, shown in Figure 23.13.**

Figure 23.13

The Advanced/Hosting pane in Server Admin's Mail pane

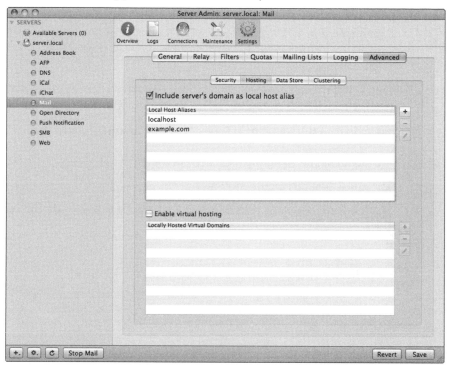

4. **Click the Include server's domain as local host alias check box and then click the Add (+) button to type a new alias.** Use the Edit button marked with a pencil icon to edit existing entries. Each virtual domain requires an MX record to properly direct mail to the server. Conversely, every name that resolves to your mail server IP address should be listed here as a local host alias unless it's intended to be used as a virtual host.

5. **Click the Enable virtual hosting check box.** Click the Add (+) button to type a locally hosted virtual domain. Use the Edit button (marked with a pencil icon) to edit existing entries. Each virtual domain requires an MX record to properly direct mail to the server. You should never list a local host alias domain as a virtual domain.

6. **Click Save.**

Configure mail data store settings

The mail server stores a small index database and a potentially substantial mail store of flat files representing each mailbox as a folder hierarchy storing individual mail messages as discrete files.

Additional mail stores can be defined anywhere on the local file system, including directly attached storage and SAN volumes as well as locally mounted network shares.

Additional mail stores augment the service and don't automatically replace or interrupt the use of existing mail stores. Newly defined mail stores are given a partition name that users can be assigned to use in Workgroup Manager. Once assigned, the user's mail is stored at the new location.

Deleting a mail store partition location in Server Admin doesn't delete its mail but only makes the messages unavailable to any users configured to use it.

To configure data store settings in Server Admin, follow these steps:

1. **Launch Server Admin and then click Mail.**

2. **Click Settings on the toolbar.**

3. **Click the Advanced tab and then click the Data Store tab, shown in Figure 23.14.**

Figure 23.14

The Advanced/Data Store pane in Server Admin's Mail pane

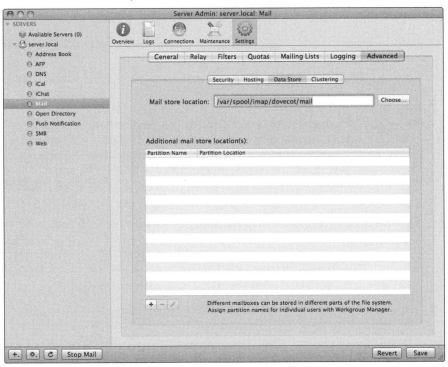

4. Configure a new location for the primary mail store by clicking the Choose button. The default location is `/var/spool/imap/dovecot/mail`.

5. Enable additional mail store locations by clicking the Add (+) button to set up a new partition. Use the Edit button marked with a pencil icon to edit existing entries. Creating a new mail store location requires:

- Supplying a partition name
- Providing a mail store location on the local file system

6. Click OK to create the new mail store.

7. Click Save. The new mail store is now available to assign to users in Workgroup Manager.

To configure clustering in Server Admin, follow these steps:

1. Launch Server Admin and then click Mail.

2. Click Settings on the toolbar.

3. Click the Advanced tab and then click the Clustering tab.

4. Click the Change button to launch the Service Configuration Assistant, shown in Figure 23.15.

5. Three options are presented:

- **Standalone Mail Server with no clustering support.** This migrates an existing clustered mail server data store to a locally defined location.

- **Join a Mail Cluster to add the server to an existing mail cluster or to move the server to a different cluster.** This requires selecting a shared Xsan mail data store that the cluster uses.

- **Create a new Mail Cluster and join it to set up a new cluster.** This requires creating a shared Xsan mail data store to be used by the cluster.

6. Once the cluster's shared data store is configured, the configuration utility walks you through the standard mail configuration steps. All cluster members must share the same configuration, so any changes made to mail server settings, including SMTP, POP, IMAP, and logging, affect all servers in the cluster.

7. Click Save.

Figure 23.15

The Service Configuration Assistant

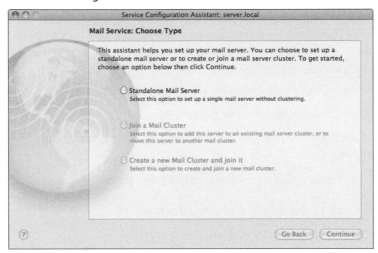

Training the junk mail spam filter

You can manually train the junk mail filter to better differentiate spam from valid emails from the command line by feeding it examples of both.

To train the junk mail filter manually, follow these steps:

1. **Select a mailbox folder containing 200 messages of known junk mail.**

2. **Launch Terminal.**

3. **Run the training tool to analyze the known junk mail by typing** `sa-learn --showdots --spam <junk mail folder>/*`.

4. **Select a mailbox folder with 200 valid emails.**

5. **Run the training tool to analyze the known valid mail by typing** sa-learn --showdots --ham <junk mail folder>/*.

6. **Repeat the training as needed by using false positives as examples of valid email by using the** `--ham` **command and by using missed junk messages as examples by using** `--spam`**.**

You can also train the junk mail filter automatically to better differentiate spam from valid emails by having users submit examples to folders that the mail service will analyze itself periodically.

The server runs a cron job daily at 1 a.m. to scan two specially named mailboxes. The job runs SpamAssassin's `sa-learn` tool on the contents of the two mailboxes and then uses the scans to improve its adaptive junk mail filter.

To train the junk mail filter automatically, follow these steps:

1. **Create two accounts with mailboxes called** `junkmail` and `notjunkmail`.

2. **Tell users to forward spam the system doesn't recognize to** `junkmail@example.com` **and to send their false positive valid emails labeled as possible junk mail to** `notjunkmail@example.com`. The cron job automatically trains the junk mail filter.

3. **Delete the messages in the two accounts daily.**

Granting mail access to users

Once mail service configuration is complete, you need to assign individual user accounts access to email and provide users with configuration settings for their clients.

To enable and configure mail service in Workgroup Manager, follow these steps:

1. **Launch Workgroup Manager and then authenticate with the directory domain.**

2. **Select user records to configure for mail service.** You can batch-configure a manual selection or the results of a search.

3. **Click the Mail tab.**

4. **Click the Enabled radio button to grant the user's mail service.**

5. **Type the hostname of the mail server.**

6. **Type a mail quota for the user's mailboxes, in megabytes.**

7. **Click one of the following radio buttons to enable protocol access for the selected users:**

- **Both POP and IMAP.** Enables users to use either or both protocols depending on their mail clients and preferences. Users should be advised of how each works and the potential for mailbox sync issues when using both.

- **POP only.** Restricts users to the more lightweight protocol, which likely significantly reduces their mailbox footprint in the mail store

- **IMAP only.** Ensures users' mailboxes remain on the server for easy backup and mail restoration if clients lose their local data

8. **Click the Use an alternate partition check box to specify the name of a new mail store partition created in Server Admin.** Groups of users can be assigned different mail stores as service scales up or as classes of students cycle through the mail system.

9. **Click Save.** The users are now provisioned for mail service.

Users' primary email addresses are their first short name at (@) the primary domain name of the mail server. Additional email aliases can be created for users by adding additional short names under their user accounts' Basic tab in Workgroup Manager, shown in Figure 23.16.

Figure 23.16

Typing short names in Workgroup Manager's Basic pane

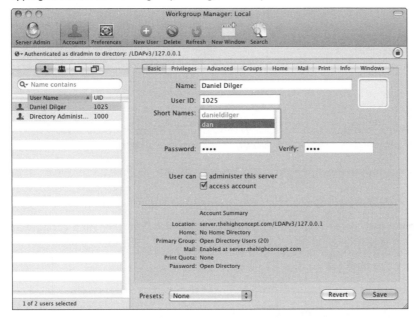

If virtual mail hosting isn't enabled from the Advanced/Hosting pane of the Settings page of Server Admin's Mail pane, simple short names can be added to users' records. Any additional local host aliases assigned to the mail service also result in alternative email addresses for the user.

If virtual mail hosting is enabled, creating alternative email addresses requires specifying the full domain name appended to any short names to fully qualify which mail service the address is to be used with. This means that any short names you want to use as email aliases must be typed in Workgroup Manager in the form `shortname@example.com`.

To configure mail service for clients, follow these steps:

1. **Compile account requirements for users:**

   ● **For IMAP or POP service:** Type the server name and the minimum authentication method users need to configure in their mail client. If you don't have the capacity to limit users to a mail client supporting a secure authentication mechanism such as Kerberos or CRAM-MD5 and subsequently need to support plaintext password authentication, you should minimally encourage users to configure SSL support and, ideally, force them to use it.

- **For SMTP service:** Type the server name of either your local SMTP server or your organization's or ISP's designated SMTP relay. Mobile users may be forced to use an ISP's own SMTP server when working from home or other locations where the local provider restricts its users from contacting other SMTP servers over port 25. If this is a problem, you can use Mobile Access to provide remote users with secure proxy access to your local mail service. For users contacting your SMTP server, provide the minimum authentication method users need to configure in their mail client. If you don't have the capacity to limit users to a mail client supporting a secure authentication mechanism such as Kerberos or CRAM-MD5 and subsequently need to support plaintext password authentication, you should minimally encourage users to configure SSL support and, ideally, force them to use it.

- **For webmail:** Supply the web address for checking mail online. Webmail is enabled under the Web Services tab of the Web pane's Sites page in Server Admin. The service is configured manually as a PHP web application.

2. **Inform users of the differences between IMAP and POP if you enable both services on the server and in users' account records in Workgroup Manager.**

3. **Inform users of the importance of enabling SSL in their mail client configuration if you lack the circumstances to enforce SSL and you need to allow the use of simple password authentication.** Certain clients, such as Mac OS X Mail, automatically negotiate the use of SSL and the most secure authentication method available on the server if the account setup assistant is used. However, if users set up their accounts manually, they may not recognize the options available to them.

Managing and Monitoring Mail Services

The Overview page of Server Admin's Mail pane presents a status report that includes:

- Whether the service is currently active
- When the service was started
- Whether outgoing SMTP is currently active
- Whether incoming SMTP is currently active
- Whether POP is currently active
- Whether IMAP is currently active
- Whether mailing lists are currently active
- Whether junk mail filtering is currently active
- Whether virus scanning is currently active
- Whether mail clustering is currently active

Monitoring mail service logs

The Logs page of the Mail pane, shown in Figure 23.17, presents a listing of the events for each service component, including:

- The IMAP and POP logs created by the Dovecot service for local delivery events, located at `/var/log/mailaccess.log`
- The SMTP log, created by the Postfix service for Internet delivery and relay events, located at `/var/log/mail.log`
- The Mail Access log, created by the Dovecot service for account login events, located at `/var/log/mail.log`
- The junk mail and virus scanning log, created by the AMaViS service, located at `/var/log/amavis.log`
- The virus log created by the ClamAV service, located at `/var/log/clamav.log`
- The Mailing list service log created by the Mailman service, located at `/var/log/mailman/qrunner`
- The Mailing list error log created by the Mailman service, located at `/var/log/mailman/error`
- The Mailing list delivery log created by the Mailman service, located at `/var/log/mailman/smtp`
- The Mailing list delivery failure log created by the Mailman service, located at `/var/log/mailman/smtp-failure`
- The Mailing list posting log created by the Mailman service, located at `/var/log/mailman/post`
- The Mailing list subscription log created by the Mailman service, located at `/var/log/mailman/subscribe`

Monitoring mail services

Overall mail server health and the status of mail users and of specific messages can be monitored by reviewing currently connected users, mail service queues, and active accounts.

Server Admin also makes it easy to review individual emails that pass in and out of the system by setting up an email address to act as an archive of all incoming and outgoing emails.

Figure 23.17

The Logs page in Server Admin's Mail pane

Local delivery mail service connections

Active local delivery mail service connections for IMAP and POP client users can be reviewed from the Connections page of the Mail pane, shown in Figure 23.18. This listing shows:

- The connected username
- The IP address the user is connected from
- Length of the connection duration
- The type of connection (POP or IMAP)
- Number of concurrent IMAP connections

Figure 23.18

The Connections page in Server Admin's Mail pane

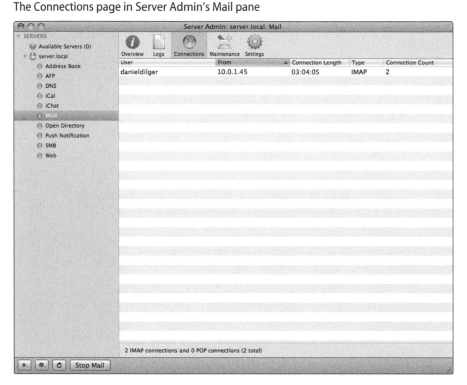

Outgoing Internet mail service queues

The outgoing SMTP mail service queue can be reviewed under the Mail Queue tab of the Mail pane's Maintenance page, shown in Figure 23.19. This listing shows:

- Message ID
- Message sender
- Mail recipients
- Date
- Size

Individual items in the queue can be selected to view a detail of message headers. Click the Retry button to re-attempt delivery or click the Delete button to clear the item from the queue.

Figure 23.19

The Mail Queue pane in Server Admin's Mail pane

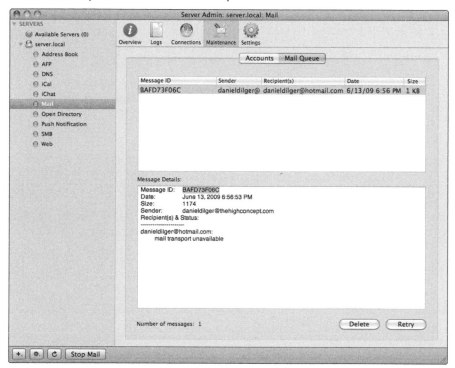

Mail service accounts

Active accounts of users who have logged in to the mail service at least once are listed in the Accounts pane of the Mail pane's Maintenance page, shown in Figure 23.20. This listing shows:

- The account name
- The mail store location of that user's mailbox
- The user's set mailbox quota. This is set from the account's Mail pane of Workgroup Manager. A 0 MB quota means no quota is set.
- The current size of the user's mailbox
- The percentage of the quota reached. If no quota is set, 100% is reported. User warnings at a set threshold as well as the behavior upon reaching 100% of the set quota are configured from the account's Mail tab of Workgroup Manager.

Figure 23.20

The Accounts pane in Server Admin's Mail pane

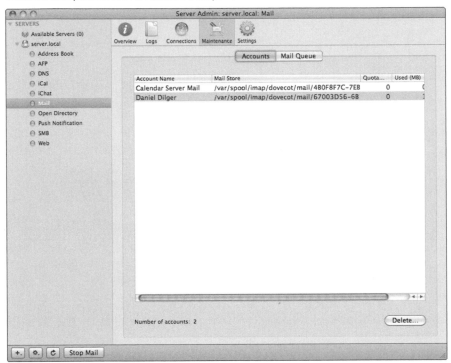

The Delete button can be used to remove individual account mailboxes. It warns that the operation can't be undone.

Archiving mail

You can archive all mail sent to or from accounts on the server into a special mailbox for archiving or review or you can archive mail store messages by simply backing up the mail store. Backups should be performed with the mail service off so the index database remains in sync with mail messages.

To archive messages to a mailbox, follow these steps:

1. **Launch Server Admin and then click Mail.**

2. **Click Settings on the toolbar.**

3. **Click the General tab.**

4. **Click the Copy all mail to check box and then specify the email address for an archive user mailbox.**

5. **Click Save.**

Summary

- Mac OS X Snow Leopard Server pairs two open-source mail packages — Postfix and Dovecot — to supply SMTP Internet mail and local POP and IMAP mail service, respectively. The move to Dovecot is new in Snow Leopard and dramatically improves performance and compatibility with the IMAP specification.

- The mail service uses AMaViS to interface Postfix with SpamAssassin for junk mail filtering and ClamAV for virus detection and quarantine services. All three services are open-source packages integrated to work together.

- The mail service also uses three additional open-source packages: Mailman to support Unix-style mailing lists, SquirrelMail for webmail service, and Sieve for server-side mail filtering to support features such as vacation messages and mailbox sorting.

- The mail service is integrated with Snow Leopard's push notification service for efficient notification of new messages for mobile users and the new Mobile Access service for securing and simplifying access for remote users.

- Mail access is integrated with Open Directory to support secure authentication methods and also provides SSL to secure plain password authentication in order to support a wider array of mail clients.

- Snow Leopard's mail system uses flexible storage options for scaling the service from the local server to multiple mail partitions or high-performance SAN storage.

- Using Xsan, multiple mail servers can cluster to provide automatic failover and distributed server load.

- The mail service can accommodate multiple user aliases and multiple local host aliases and can also support virtual hosting of multiple independent mail servers on the same system servicing multiple domains.

Web Services

Web services have revolutionized how companies build both public-facing and internal information services. The push to deliver the web as an open, interoperable platform has resulted in rapid advancement of technology, from simple information publishing to interactive web applications that support commerce and advanced collaboration tools.

Snow Leopard Server builds a variety of its advanced services on its web services, which in turn are based largely on open-source software. The use of open-source code enables Apple to rapidly incorporate new technologies developed by the community, leveraging advancements made by a variety of different projects all competing to deliver a unique and incrementally superior approach to solving various problems. Apple also develops some of its own projects that are made available as open source to the community, such as its WebDAV-based Calendar Server, which can be obtained for free via the Darwin Calendar Server project for use on any Unix-like operating system.

The web itself was invented at CERN by Tim Berners-Lee by using NeXTSTEP, the precursor to Mac OS X. Apple's pioneering but proprietary HyperCard was used as the model for the development of ViolaWWW, a popular web browser for Unix systems. The concept of the web as a free and open computing platform was developed further by the NCSA (National Center for Supercomputing Applications), funded by the U.S. government. This resulted in the free Mosaic browser and the HTTPd (HyperText Transfer Protocol daemon) web server.

HTTPd was improved in a series of patches submitted by users that resulted in it getting the name Apache server as a clever pun. Apache continues to be an extremely popular web server, as is the web server software used in Mac OS X Server. This chapter describes how the web services work, what's involved in their planning, how they're configured, and how to maintain and monitor them.

Introduction to Web Services

Snow Leopard Server makes it easy to both serve a central directory of web documents and provide home folder web services for local users. Web services also provide the foundation for wiki services, blogs, the web calendar, and webmail.

Apache web services

Apple's use of the popular, open-source Apache web server makes it easy for administrators to incorporate code modifications and install modules that extend the software's functionality. Additionally, many resources are available to help fine-tune and customize Apache's configuration files.

Snow Leopard Server uses Apache 2.0 by default. Automatic migration from the Apache 1.3 version that shipped in earlier versions of Mac OS X Server has been available since Leopard Server, but there are some security factors you should consider before upgrading to Apache 2.0 for users with advanced web server configurations.

WebDAV

WebDAV is a key feature of the Mac OS X Server web services. It forms the basis of a variety of advanced services in Snow Leopard Server, including Address Book Server and Calendar Server, and also offers a secure method for uploading files as an alternative to FTP.

Mac OS X desktop users can connect to WebDAV shares via the Finder and access them as mounted server volumes, making it easy to upload and modify web content. WebDAV uses realms, each of which has its own defined access privileges for users. In order for Apache to serve these files to web clients and accept changes and uploads, the www group account that the Apache process is a member of must have read and write access to the files being served.

CGI scripting

Common Gateway Interface (CGI) scripting enables users to invoke an application process that the web server will spawn, provide information typed by the user, and then receive a return result that's provided to the client. CGI scripts make it easy to add functionality to a website by using a scripting language such as Perl or Python. After scripts are copied to the default location at `/Library/WebServer/CGI-Executable`, CGI scripting must be enabled for the website.

Users can then be directed to a URL that invokes an available script that manages a given task, such as `www.example.com/webmail.cgi`. CGI scripting was designed as a lowest common denominator for a variety of web servers, so it's not the highest-performance way to deliver application features to a website.

Custom Apache modules can enable additional software routines to be run within the web server itself, instead of as an external process, and are therefore more efficient. However, there are many CGI scripts available that provide useful features in scenarios where performance isn't the primary consideration.

Using SSI

Server Side Includes (SSI) is a feature that enables the server to paste a scripted result or a block of static information into every page across a site. This can include calculated information, such as a date stamp, or be used to add identical headers or footers to a website's component pages, enabling an administrator to edit the shared content centrally and roll out the changes across the site automatically instead of redesigning each page individually. If multiple websites are defined, SSI as a feature can be selectively enabled on a specific website.

SSL encryption

SSL is a standard originally created by Netscape for allowing web servers to secure a confidential connection with a user, encrypt transmissions, and authenticate as a trusted entity.

Netscape's SSL 3.0 formed the basis of the IETF TLS specification, which has since technically replaced SSL.

However, TLS is still commonly referred to as SSL, particularly by Apple within its Server Admin interface. For this reason, I consistently refer to SSL/TLS as SSL to avoid confusion.

SSL works by using public-key cryptography. The server retains a private key and publishes a public key to users. Information encrypted by the public key can be decrypted only by using the private key.

This enables users who trust the public-key certificate (which is often itself signed by a trusted third-party Certificate Authority) to generate a random number, encrypt it with the server's public key, and then send the result to the server. Only the server can decrypt this information via its secret public key.

This exchange enables the server and client to create session keys for further encrypted communications. No third parties can intercept and decrypt the initial exchange of the encrypted random number, so the keys generated on both ends enable the client and server to continue confidential, encrypted communications.

This results in a security upgrade from HTTP to HTTPS, allowing the client to provide private information, such as login information, and receive private information in response, such as banking details.

To support SSL, the server must generate its own self-signed certificate identity (which clients have to assume trust in) or obtain a signed version of that identity endorsed by a Certificate Authority, a step that enables clients to automatically trust the server's public-key certificate as reputable if it matches the URL it was received from by the client. SSL must also be activated on the web server.

Webmail, wikis, blogs, and RSS

Integrated into Snow Leopard Server's general-purpose Apache web services are a variety of specialized web services, including webmail, collaborative wikis, blogs, and RSS features.

These features provide easy-to-use applications of web technologies that enable network users to authenticate with Open Directory, post blog entries, edit wiki pages, and generate Atom XML and RSS feeds of updates. Webmail enables users to access their email through a browser.

CROSS-REF
For more on webmail, wikis, blogs, and web calendar services, see Chapter 25.

Planning Web Services

If you're migrating existing web services to Snow Leopard Server, your plans should accommodate transitioning to Apache 2.2. If you're initiating new web services, the default installation of Snow Leopard Server begins with Apache 2.2, as it did with Leopard Server.

To set up basic web services, you need:

- A registered domain name for your web server and a properly configured DNS
- A web folder, which by default starts at `/Library/WebServer/Documents`
- HTML content, starting with a default web page visitors will see

Website configuration

From the Sites page of Server Admin's Web pane, you define your site and configure it with:

- An IP address and port number (port 80 by default)
- Your web folder, default index files, and error page
- An administrative email contact
- Site options, including support for WebDAV, CGI, SSI, and SSL
- Support for realms with user access permissions
- Access and error logging details, including a format string suited to web analytics
- Website and URL aliases and redirects
- Reverse proxy settings, used for load-balancing access to a pool of web servers, uses a Sticky Session identifier to enable persistence for web applications serving a client session that needs to be routed back to the same server.
- Optional support for wikis, blogs, web calendars, and webmail services

Web service configuration

The Settings page of Server Admin's Web pane is used to define general settings that apply to all sites running on the server. The General pane presents configuration settings that pertain to:

- The maximum number of simultaneous HTTP connections Apache can service concurrently (additional users receive a message saying that the server is busy)
- A connection timeout period for users after their last page request

- The number of spare servers Apache spawns to handle new website requests
- Options to allow persistent connections
- A check box to enable Tomcat, a Java Servlet container for running server-side Java applications based on the JavaServer Pages specification

The MIME Types pane is used to associate documents with a given suffix with a specific type of file, enabling the server to present it to the user appropriately.

MIME (Multipurpose Internet Mail Extensions) originated as a standard for enabling email messages to include document attachments or other message sections to be interpreted in special ways, such as encrypted data.

For web servers, MIME types are used to identify specialized information so the client's web browser can interpret it in a useful way, such as rendering PDF data graphically rather than just presenting the data as encoded text within the browser. A variety of common MIME types are already defined, but additional custom types can be entered as needed. Content handlers similarly associate file suffixes with a particular server behavior, such as associating .cgi files as CGI scripts to be executed rather than simple documents to be served to the user.

The Proxy pane is used to enable a forward proxy, with optional access control limited to a specific domain. A forward proxy is used to provide your clients with cached access to other web servers, accelerating requests for the same data. It can also be used to block access to sites specified on this tab. It's commonly used to funnel all inbound web traffic through a specific server, with all other access blocked by the firewall, enforcing the blocked sites and mandating the caching.

A reverse proxy, in contrast, is used for load-balancing access to a pool of web servers or for relaying internal web servers under a single namespace with optional SSL support, typically to service public users entering the firewall. This is the opposite of a forward proxy, which typically serves internal users, directing their outbound requests through the firewall via the proxy server. A forward proxy also requires clients to be specifically configured to use it, whereas a reverse proxy doesn't require any special configuration on the client side.

The Modules pane is used to enable or add new Apache modules to the web service to activate web technologies on the server as needed.

The Wiki pane specifies a data store for all wikis active on the server, which is by default located at /Library/Collaboration. A maximum attachment size can be specified to limit the size of files that wiki users can upload.

Specific users or groups can be defined as wiki creators; otherwise, every user will have default permissions to create wikis. A pop-up menu enables the administrator to choose the default wiki theme.

An SMTP relay for delivering wiki welcome messages can be configured as well as external servers for providing calendar services and accessing server-side rules for email, if those services are operating on a different server than the wiki.

Apache modules

Server Admin makes installing, enabling, or disabling Apache modules easy, but administrators should have a clear, functional plan prior to making changes to the installed modules and be fully aware of the implications when making changes.

Some modules depend on others, whereas others are mutually exclusive. For example, `auth_digest_module` and `digest_module` can't be both enabled at once, whereas `dav_module` and `dav_fs_module` must both be either enabled or disabled together.

Modules are also specific to the version of Apache they're designed to be used with, so modules for Apache 1.3 can't be used in Apache 2.2.

Mac-specific modules

Apple provides a series of Apache modules designed to support Mac OS X features. These include the following:

- `mod_macbinary_apple`, supplied only for Apache 1.3, is used to encode files with resource forks (or other Mac-specific features, such as type and creator codes) in the MacBinary format for direct downloads from your website.

- `mod_auth_apple` enables the server to authenticate users against file system service domains in the server's Open Directory search policy.

- `mod_hfs_apple` enables case-insensitive HFS+ volumes to require case to be typed as it appears for files on the web server.

- `mod_digest_apple` enables digest authentication for a WebDAV realm by using Open Directory rather than static `htdigest` files. It doesn't send passwords in cleartext.

- `mod_auth_digest_apple` is a newer version of `mod_digest_apple` that requires the Open Directory master to at least use Leopard Server.

- `mod_spnego` supports Kerberos authentication for Open Directory accounts by using the SPNEGO (Simple and Protected GSSAPI Negotiation Mechanism) protocol.

- `mod_encoding`, along with module `mod_dav`, allows WebDAV file names to use Japanese characters.

- `mod_bonjour` lets administrators manage how sites register with multicast DNS.

Web application modules

Apple also bundles a variety of Apache modules designed to support popular web application environments in Mac OS X Server. These include the following:

- Tomcat is the official reference implementation of Sun's Java Servlets (server-side Java applications) and JavaServer Pages specifications on Apache. Tomcat must also be enabled from the General tab of the Settings page in the Web pane of Server Admin.

- `libphp5` enables PHP, a server-side, C-like scripting language that embeds PHP code into HTML pages to tie dynamic logic into the pages being served instead of dynamically generating HTML by using an external web application. Mac OS X Server's webmail is based on PHP.

- `mod_perl` and `mod_python` integrate the Perl and Python interpreters into the web server, allowing existing Perl or Python CGI scripts to run directly without modification, making them faster and able to consume fewer system resources.

SSL security

SSL encryption is also implemented in Apache as a module. It supports SSLv2, SSLv3, and TLS 1.0. Using SSL requires a certificate identity, which includes a private key maintained by the server and a public key distributed to client users.

This key combination enables untrusted clients to trust the server and create a securely confidential and encrypted connection with it to safeguard authentication credentials passed to the server and subsequent information exchange.

The SSL session operates above TCP/IP and below HTTP, securely encrypting all information before it's sent. Once established, the client's browser indicates the session is using SSL by presenting a lock icon and designating the URL protocol as HTTPS.

Enabling SSL features requires generating a self-signed certificate identity by using Certificate Assistant and optionally submitting a CSR (Certificate Signing Request) to have the certificate identity signed by a trusted third party, a step that enables clients to automatically trust the public-key certificate they receive from the server as legitimate to the URL they receive it from.

WebDAV realms

Once WebDAV support is enabled, a site can be configured with realms that define user access permissions. Because WebDAV is a superset of HTTP, standard browsers can read from WebDAV shares as long as the user is authorized to access the files.

However, most browsers can't directly write to WebDAV shares. The Mac OS X Finder, along with other WebDAV client software, can be used to upload and modify files as long as the user has authorized access.

In the Realms tab of the Sites page in Server Admin's Web pane, a new realm can be defined by specifying:

- A realm name, presented to users when they log in to the WebDAV share

- An authentication mechanism, which can be basic (which sends passwords in cleartext), digest (which performs an encrypted hash of passwords), or Kerberos (the most secure option using certificates but requires the server be joined to a Kerberos domain)

- A folder being shared by the web service. A single folder can only be managed by a single realm.

Once a realm is created, users and groups can be assigned privileges to the realm's files:

- **Browse only.** Permits regular web browsing only
- **Browse and Read WebDAV.** Permits browsing the website and reading website files by using WebDAV
- **Browse and Read/Write WebDAV.** Permits browsing the website and reading or writing website files by using WebDAV
- **None.** Prevents any access to the files

Virtual hosting and multihoming

The Mac OS X Server web service can host multiple different websites under the same IP address but different DNS names, a feature known as *virtual hosting*, or the same site under different IP addresses, a feature designed to improve client access reliability and performance and referred to as *multihoming*.

Virtual hosts

Multiple web hosts can be configured within Server Admin's Web pane by using the Sites page, with each configured to respond to requests at a specific IP address and port number or a specific DNS name. Each is considered a virtual host.

Website aliases

If you want the same site to appear under various aliases instead of setting up multiple sites, you can add multiple aliases to the same site definition. Under the Aliases tab of the Sites page of Server Admin's Web pane, you can specify web server aliases that the site will be published as.

For example, `www.example.com` could also be served as `investor.example.com` by adding it as an alias. This also requires that your DNS be configured to direct both names to the same IP address so clients can reach the server.

Multihoming

A website may also be configured to respond to requests from multiple IP addresses for improved performance or reliability. For example, a web server might be configured with two separate IP addresses supplied by different ISPs, enabling the server to remain available even if one provider's uplink were to fail.

This can be set up by configuring multiple IP addresses in Apache or simply by using the default wildcard configuration for the web service's IP address, which enables Apache to respond to all requests made from any IP addresses configured on the server.

Web Services Setup and Configuration

Setting up web services requires configuring server-specific features and settings for each site being served as well as enabling and configuring any special features, such as CGI scripting or SSL security.

To enable the web service configuration in Server Admin, follow these steps:

1. Launch Server Admin and then connect to the desired server.

2. Select a server listing and then click Settings on the toolbar.

3. Click the Services tab.

4. Click the check box for Web.

5. **Click Save.** Web should now appear in the list of configurable services for the selected server, as shown in Figure 24.1.

Figure 24.1

Enabling Server Admin's Web pane

Configuring the web service

Unless you have special needs, the default settings of the web service, configured in the Settings page of Server Admin's Web pane, may be adequate.

General settings

To set the general web service configuration in Server Admin, follow these steps:

1. **Launch Server Admin and then connect to the desired server.**

2. **Click Web and then click Settings on the toolbar.**

3. **Click the General tab, shown in Figure 24.2.**

Figure 24.2

The General pane of the Settings page in Server Admin's Web pane

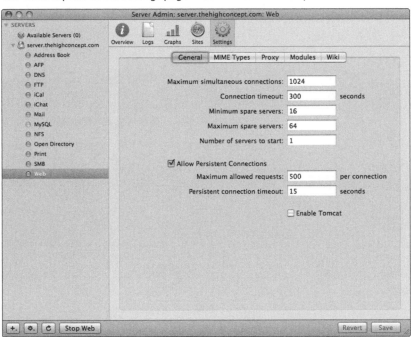

4. **Type the maximum simultaneous connections the server will handle before reporting a busy message.** The default is 1024.

5. **Type a connection timeout period in seconds to specify how quickly the connection is dropped following the user's last page request.** The default is 300.

6. Type the number of servers to start and the minimum and maximum spare servers to maintain. Servers at start are created when the web service starts up, and additional spare servers are launched each second until the minimum is reached. If idle spare servers exceed the maximum, the server stops spawning new ones.

7. Click the Allow Persistent Connections check box and then configure the persistent connection settings if web application sessions should be maintained to allow a user to continue to be serviced by the same server.

8. Click the Enable Tomcat check box to serve Java servlets and JSP.

9. Click Save.

MIME type settings

To configure MIME type settings, follow these steps:

1. Launch Server Admin and then connect to the desired server.

2. Click Web and then click Settings on the toolbar.

3. Click the MIME Types tab, shown in Figure 24.3.

Figure 24.3

The MIME Types pane of the Settings page in Server Admin's Web pane

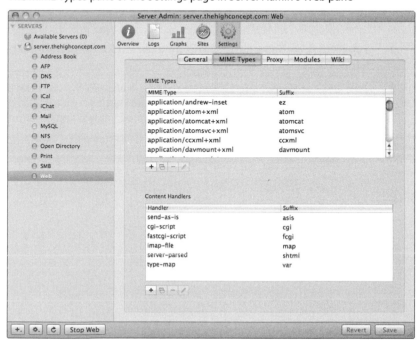

4. **Add a MIME type association by clicking the Add (+) button.** A sheet drops down.

5. **Type a MIME type definition and any file type suffix you want to associate with it.**

6. **Click OK.** You can also edit or duplicate an existing MIME type definition by selecting the item and then using the duplicate button marked with a double window icon or edit the entry by using the Edit button marked with a pencil icon.

7. **Edit content handlers the same way.** Content handlers you specify, such as PHP or CGI, must be activated in order for the server to use them. CGI is activated for a site by using the Options tab of the Sites page of the Web pane.

8. **Click Save.**

Forward Proxy settings

To configure forward proxy settings, follow these steps:

1. **Launch Server Admin and then connect to the desired server.**

2. **Click Web and then click Settings on the toolbar.**

3. **Click the Proxy tab, shown in Figure 24.4.**

4. **Click the Enable Forward Proxy check box.** To limit access to this proxy to a specific domain, click the Control Access To Proxy check box and then specify a domain.

5. **Optionally, specify a different cache folder location.** Content cached by the proxy is stored here. The owner and group of the selected folder must be www.

6. **Type a disk cache target size and time period for emptying the cache.** Once the target size is reached, the oldest cache files are deleted.

7. **To block caching of and access to specific websites through the proxy, click the Add (+) button and then type their domain names.** You can also drag in a listing of sites to block by using a CSV (comma separated values) text file supplying the URLs you want to block.

8. **Click Save.**

Figure 24.4

The Proxy pane of the Settings page in Server Admin's Web pane

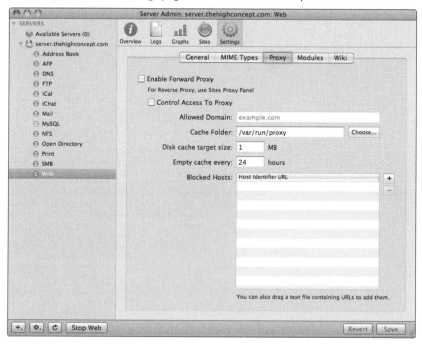

Apache Module settings

To configure Apache modules, follow these steps:

1. **Launch Server Admin and then connect to the desired server.**

2. **Click Web and then click Settings on the toolbar.**

3. **Click the Modules tab, shown in Figure 24.5.**

4. **Enable modules as desired by clicking their check boxes.** Make sure the module you enable is compatible with other installed modules and the version of Apache you're running. If you disable a module, make sure other modules don't depend on it.

5. **Add a new module by clicking the Add (+) button, and in the sheet that drops down, specify a module name and then select the path of the module file.** Modules are typically installed within the `/usr/libexec/` directory.

6. **Click OK and then click Save.** Test that the module changes are working as expected.

Figure 24.5

The Modules pane of the Settings page in Server Admin's Web pane

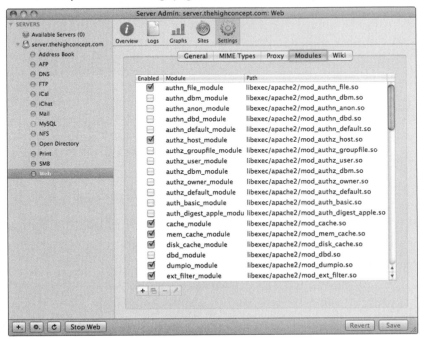

Wiki settings

To configure wiki settings, follow these steps:

1. **Launch Server Admin and then connect to the desired server.**

2. **Click Web and then click Settings on the toolbar.**

3. **Click the Wiki tab, shown in Figure 24.6.**

4. **Specify a data store for wiki information and attachments.** The default location is `/Library/Collaboration/`.

5. **Specify a maximum attachment size for files uploaded by wiki users.** This includes documents users submit to the wiki, such as graphics or podcasts.

6. **Select a default theme for wikis.** Users can change the theme later, as desired.

Figure 24.6

The Wiki pane of the Settings page in Server Admin's Web pane

7. **Add users or groups allowed to create wikis.** By default, all users have wiki creation permissions.

8. **Click the Configure button to customize the SMTP relay details.** From the sheet that drops down, specify a sender email address, SMTP relay DNS name and port number, and a username and password to use when sending wiki welcome messages. Click Done when finished.

9. **Click the Configure button to define external web services.** From the sheet that drops down, specify a calendar server and/or email server by DNS name, optionally specifying an SSL connection. This connects web calendars to the wiki pages and enables webmail users to set server-side mail rules. Click Done when finished.

10. **Click Save.**

Configuring websites

By default, the web service enables a generic website configured to respond to any HTTP requests made to port 80 of any of the IP addresses configured on the server. These settings are customized by using the Sites page of the Web pane in Server Admin. The default site is located at the web root of /Library/WebServer/Documents and includes a basic index page with a welcome screen that links to blogs, wikis, and My Page, a central collaboration page to which users can log in to see recent content updates for the wikis and blogs they follow on the server. Serving basic web pages is as simple as copying HTML files to the defined web root. To configure general site settings, follow these steps:

1. **Launch Server Admin and then connect to the desired server.**

2. **Click Web and then click Sites on the toolbar.**

3. **Click the General tab, shown in Figure 24.7.**

Figure 24.7

The Sites page in Server Admin's Web pane

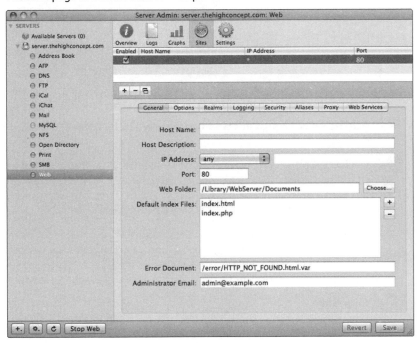

4. **Select an existing site or create a new site definition by clicking the Add (+) button.** An existing site configuration can also be duplicated by using the button with a double window icon. The list of configured sites can be selectively enabled by using the check box to display the configured DNS hostname, IP address, and port number for each site.

5. **Type a fully qualified domain name for the selected site's hostname, along with a host description.** If you're going to serve only one host, you can leave the host blank so the web server responds to requests directed to any DNS name that resolves to that server.

6. **Type an IP address and port number for the selected site.** The default HTTP web port is 80, whereas the default HTTPS port for SSL websites is 443.

7. **Choose a web folder for the selected site's documents.** The default location is at `/Library/WebServer/Documents/`. Multiple websites can be defined within this folder. Users on the system are also given a website located within their home folder, which is published as the URL `http://server.example.com/~username/`.

8. **Type a default index file name and error file name for the server to use for this site.** The default index file is served when a user sends a general web request to the site's domain name without specifying a file. This index file is presented instead of a folder listing of the documents in the given directory of the web root. If no index file is available, the server presents a folder listing instead if folder listings are enabled in the Options tab of the Sites page. Otherwise, the user receives an error.

9. **Optionally, specify an administrator email that's published with error reports so users can report problems.**

10. **Click Save.**

To configure site options, follow these steps:

1. **Launch Server Admin and then connect to the desired server.**

2. **Click Web and then click Sites on the toolbar.**

3. **Click the Options tab, shown in Figure 24.8.**

4. **Enable options presented by the five check boxes:**

- **Folder Listing.** Enables the server to present a basic catalog of the files within a directory if no index page exists. If you don't want to reveal the hosted documents within the web root of the selected site, don't click this check box.

- **WebDAV.** Enables read and write access to the selected site from WebDAV client software, including the Mac OS X Finder and various web design tools that use WebDAV to upload and modify files. Access permissions for WebDAV are configured on the Realms tab of the Sites page.

- **CGI Execution.** Enables the selected site to run installed CGI scripts within `/Library/WebServer/CGI-Executable/` when requested by clients by using a URL specifying a given script, such as `www.example.com/cgi-bin/scriptname`.

- **Server Side Includes (SSI).** Enables documents within the specified site to invoke SSI commands for incorporating dynamic content as they're served. This can include basic commands, such as expanding a code to insert the current date and time in the web page or including an external HTML document within the current page as its header or footer.

- **Allow All Overrides.** Directs the web service to look for and use `.htaccess` files (for managing file access on a per-directory basis) within each folder of the selected site on each client request for a document.

5. Click Save.

Figure 24.8

The Options pane of the Sites page in Server Admin's Web pane

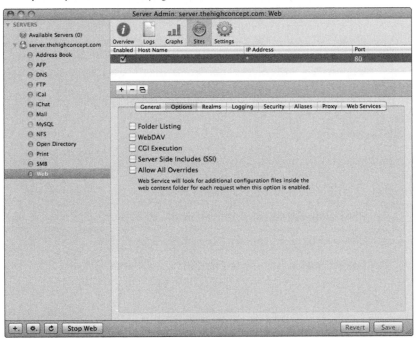

To configure a site's WebDAV realm setting, follow these steps:

1. **Launch Server Admin and then connect to the desired server.**

2. **Click Web and then click Sites on the toolbar.**

3. **Click the Options tab.**

4. **Click the WebDAV check box.**

5. **Click the Realms tab, shown in Figure 24.9.**

6. **Define a new WebDAV realm by clicking the Add (+) button.** An existing realm configuration can also be duplicated by using the button with a double window icon or edited by using the button with a pencil icon. A sheet appears asking for:

   ● A realm name, which is presented to users when they log in to the WebDAV share

   ● An authentication mechanism, either basic (which sends passwords in cleartext), digest (which performs an encrypted hash of passwords), or Kerberos (the most secure option using certificates but requires the server be joined to a Kerberos domain)

   ● A folder being shared by the web service. A single folder can only be managed by a single realm. If a second realm is created for the same folder, the original realm definition is overwritten.

7. **Click OK to complete the realm definition for the specified folder.**

8. **Assign users and groups privileges for a selected realm by using the Add (+) button.** For each user or group, select the following permission type by using the pop-up control in the Permissions column:

   ● **Browse only.** Permits regular web browsing only

   ● **Browse and Read WebDAV.** Permits browsing the website and reading website files by using WebDAV

   ● **Browse and Read/Write WebDAV.** Permits browsing the website and reading or writing website files by using WebDAV

   ● **None.** Prevents any access to the files

9. **Click Save.** The assigned permissions are granted based on the most permission allowed, so if the default Everyone user is given read and write WebDAV access but a user is assigned browse-only access, the user's more restrictive permission record is discarded.

Figure 24.9

The Realms pane of the Sites page in Server Admin's Web pane

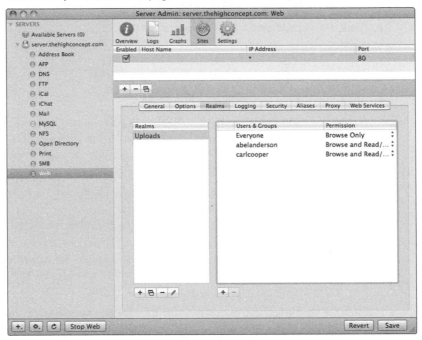

To configure a site's logging settings, follow these steps:

1. **Launch Server Admin and then connect to the desired server.**

2. **Click Web and then click Sites on the toolbar.**

3. **Click the Logging tab, shown in Figure 24.10.**

4. **Enable and configure Access Logs, optionally setting the logs to archive every set number of days.** The log file location can be customized; the default location for the access log is `/var/log/apache2/access_log`. The access log format can also be customized to report specific information suited to the web analytics system you plan to use. The default format is Common Log Format, which is defined by the string `%h %l %u %t "%r" %>s %b`. This supplies:

- `%h`, the remote user host making a request
- `%l`, the remote user logname
- `%u`, the remote username

- %t, the time of the request
- "%r", the first line of the request (the file being requested)
- %>s, the status of the last request (if successful or not)
- %b, the size of the request in bytes

If you're planning to perform useful web log analytics, you should change the format string to the Combined Log Format string of %h %l %u %t \"%r\" %>s %b \"%{Referer}i\" \"%{User-agent}i\". This instructs the web service to log two extra bits of information that are important in analyzing where visitors are coming from and what browser they're using:

- \"%{Referer}i\" reports the referring server that linked to your site.
- \"%{User-agent}i\" supplies information about the user's client browser. For example, Safari 4 running on an Intel Mac running Leopard 10.5.7 reports this user-agent: Mozilla/5.0 (Macintosh; U; Intel Mac OS X 10_5_7; en-us) AppleWebKit/528.18.1 (KHTML, like Gecko) Version/4.0 Safari/528.17.

Figure 24.10

The Logging pane of the Sites page in Server Admin's Web pane

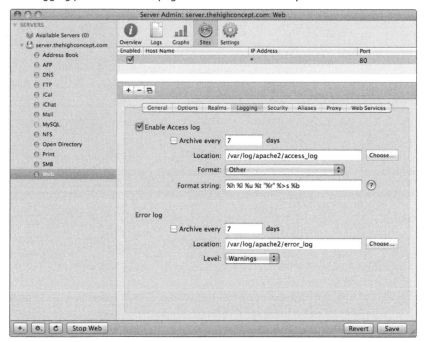

5. **Enable error log archiving, location, and logging level.** The more information logged, the more overhead the web service requires. The default location of the error log is `/var/log/apache2/error_log`.

6. **Click Save.**

To configure a site's SSL settings, follow these steps:

1. **Launch Server Admin and then connect to the desired server.**

2. **Click Web and then click Sites on the toolbar.**

3. **Click the Security tab, shown in Figure 24.11.**

Figure 24.11

The Security pane of the Sites page in Server Admin's Web pane

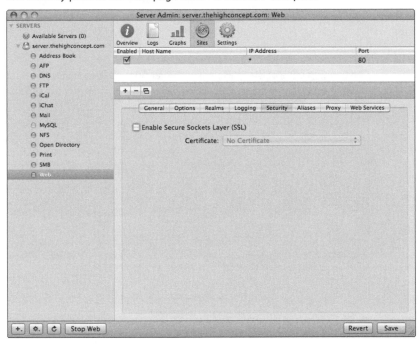

4. **Enable SSL for the selected site by using the check box, providing a certificate identity to be used for SSL from the pop-up menu.** Select an installed certificate or use the Manage Certificates option to generate a new self-signed certificate identity. Enabling SSL support for the site configures it to use port 443 and results in documents being served by using the HTTPS protocol.

5. **Click Save.** The web service prompts you to approve a restart.

CROSS-REF

For more on using and creating certificates in Server Admin, see Chapter 9.

To configure a site's aliases, follow these steps:

1. **Launch Server Admin and then connect to the desired server.**

2. **Click Web and then click Sites on the toolbar.**

3. **Click the Aliases tab, shown in Figure 24.12.**

4. **To enable virtual hosts by name, replace the wildcard setting under Web Server Aliases with the specific DNS hostnames you want the selected site to respond to by using the Add (+) button to add multiple fully qualified domain names.** An existing alias can also be duplicated by using the button with a double window icon or edited by using the button with a pencil icon. The domain names used as aliases of the selected site, such as `www.example.com` and `server.example.com`, must also be configured to point to the server within DNS in order for visitors to use the alternate names to reach the server.

Figure 24.12

The Aliases pane of the Sites page in Server Admin's Web pane

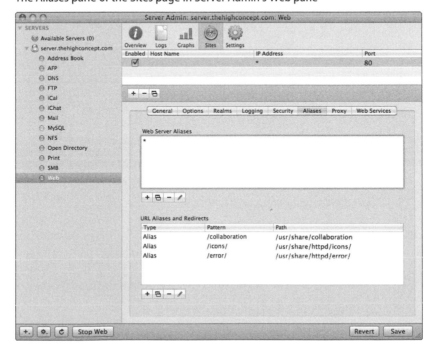

5. **Enable URL aliases and redirects within the lower area to point user requests for a specific URL directory to a different location.** By default, the following redirects are already configured:

- `/collaboration` is redirected to `/usr/share/collaboration` to obtain the CSS (Cascading Style Sheets) used by wiki and blog pages and their Spotlight search.

- `/icons/` is redirected to `/usr/share/httpd/icons` to access the standard collection of icons included with Apache.

- `/error/` is redirected to `/usr/share/httpd/error` to access Apache's standard collection of error pages.

Additional redirects can be defined by clicking the Add (+) button, which drops down a sheet asking for a type, which can be selected from the pop-up menu to be any of the following:

- An Alias to another folder

- An AliasMatch by using a wildcard character

- A Redirect to another server

- A MatchRedirect by using a wildcard character to redirect specific requests matching a specific definition

The selected type then needs a pattern and path, where the pattern supplies either the simple URL path to be substituted or a wildcard regular expression to be matched, and the path supplies the destination the user is redirected to in order to obtain the requested resource. For example:

- An alias linking the pattern `/images` to the path `/Library/WebServer/Documents/Images` could be used to maintain a central repository of all the various sites' images on the server within the same Images location.

- A redirect linking the pattern `/store` to path `https://store.example.com` could be used to redirect users clicking a store link to a separate, SSL-enabled site for secure access.

- A match redirect rule linking the pattern `(.*)\.gif$` to the path `http://www.example.com$1.jpg` would result in requests for a GIF with a specific name to be substituted by a JPEG of the same name, located on a different server.

When finished defining each URL alias or redirect, click Done.

6. **Click Save.**

To configure a site's reverse proxy settings, follow these steps:

1. **Launch Server Admin and then connect to the desired server.**

2. **Click Web and then click Sites on the toolbar.**

3. Click the Proxy tab, shown in Figure 24.13.

Figure 24.13

The Proxy pane of the Sites page in Server Admin's Web pane

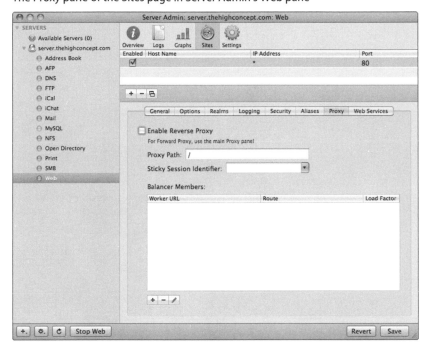

4. Click the Enable Reverse Proxy check box for the selected site.

5. Type a proxy path.

6. Type a sticky session identifier, which is used to attach a site visitor to the server that initiated his or her session. This allows visitors to a site supported by multiple web servers behind the scenes to remain connected to the same server instead of being passed to another server in the pool that doesn't know about their existing session.

7. Add balancer members by clicking the Add (+) button. A sheet drops down asking for the following:

- A server URL for the balancer, which is used to share website traffic across a pool of member servers by binding and routing a set load to each member. This improves performance and prevents a single server from being overwhelmed by excessive web traffic.

- A route, the value appended to the sticky session ID to keep track of a specific server
- A load factor, which is a number between 1 and 100 used to define how much load the balancer member server handles

8. **Click Done to add each balancer member.**

9. **Click Save.**

To configure a site's web collaboration services, follow these steps:

1. **Launch Server Admin and then connect to the desired server.**

2. **Click Web and then click Sites on the toolbar.**

3. **Click the Web Services tab, shown in Figure 24.14.**

Figure 24.14

The Web Services pane of the Sites page in Server Admin's Web pane

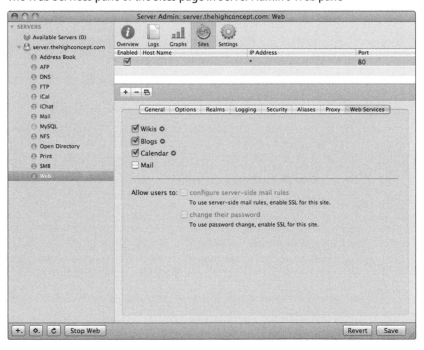

4. **Enable collaboration services for the selected site by clicking these check boxes:**
   - **Wikis.** Enables support for user-edited wiki websites
   - **Blogs.** Enables support for user-created blog journals
   - **Calendar.** Enables web access to Calendar Server data
   - **Mail.** Enables web access to mail server data

5. **Optionally, enable users to configure server-side mail rules, a feature that requires SSL support to be enabled on the site.**

6. **Optionally, enable users to change their passwords, a feature that requires SSL support to be enabled on the site.**

7. **Click Save.**

CROSS-REF
For more on wikis, blogs, and webmail, see Chapter 25.

Managing and Monitoring Web Services

The Overview page of Server Admin's Web pane presents a status report of when the service was started, the version of Apache being used, the web requests being served per second, and the current network data throughput.

Monitoring web services logs

The Logs page of the Web pane, shown in Figure 24.15, presents a listing of the events for each defined website, recorded in:

- The Apache Access Log, which records each user request, located by default at `/var/log/apache2/access_log`
- The Apache Error Log, which notes configuration and serving problems, located at `/var/log/apache2/error_log`
- The Error Log for the wikid process, located at `/Library/Logs/wikid/error.log`
- The Access Log for the wikid process, located at `/Library/Logs/wikid/access.log`

Figure 24.15

The Logs page in Server Admin's Web pane

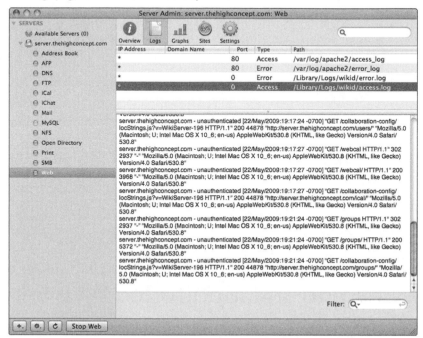

Additional sites defined for the web service each maintain their own access and error logs, listing them separately in the Logs page. Administrators may need to configure the logging format string within the Logging pane of the Sites page for each site in order to record enough useful logging information to provide informative web analytics reports.

Working with web applications

Snow Leopard Server provides a variety of different web application development and deployment environments for building dynamic sites. Users can select from the default options Apple configures, use a combination of tools, or install support for their own web development tools when the default versions aren't sufficient.

Apache Axis

Apache Extensible Interaction System (Axis) is an XML-based web service framework that acts as a Java and C++ implementation of Simple Object Access Protocol (SOAP). It's used to add web services interfaces to web applications.

Apache Axis can be used to write web applications based on the Axis libraries, which are then commonly deployed by using Tomcat. The Axis 1.1 bundled with Mac OS X Server isn't typically used as an application server itself, although users can install support for Axis2, which is designed to act as a stand-alone server.

Tomcat Java servlets and JSP

Apache Tomcat is a servlet container that implements Sun's Java Servlet and JavaServer Pages (JSP) specifications, providing a 100-percent pure Java web server environment for Java code to run.

Java servlets are applications written in Java that run on the web server, as opposed to client-side Java, which is designed to run within a user's browser. JSP is designed to embed Java servlets into web pages.

The Tomcat management console and status service are turned off by default. Consult the online documentation at `http://tomcat.apache.org/tomcat-6.0-doc/index.html` for details on how to enable, secure, and deploy these services.

MySQL

MySQL is an open-source relational database management solution (RDBMS) commonly used to provide a data store for web applications by using PHP or similar scripting languages to build dynamic websites.

Mac OS X Server bundles MySQL and integrates a simple management interface into Server Admin.

To enable MySQL service configuration in Server Admin, follow these steps:

1. **Launch Server Admin and then connect to the desired server.**

2. **Select a server listing and then click Settings on the toolbar.**

3. **Click the Services tab.**

4. **Click the check box for MySQL.**

5. **Click Save.** MySQL should now appear in the list of configurable services for the selected server, as shown in Figure 24.16.

Figure 24.16

Enabling the MySQL pane in Server Admin

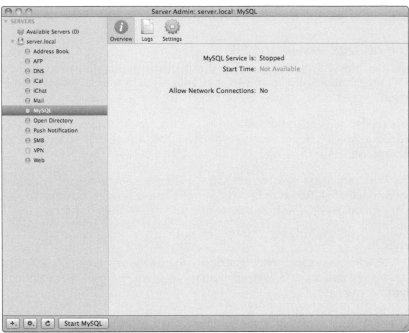

The Logs page of the MySQL pane presents a listing of the events recorded in:

- The MySQL Admin Log, located at `/Library/Logs/MySQL.log`
- The MySQL Service Log, located at `/var/log/mysql_service.log`

The Settings page of the MySQL pane, shown in Figure 24.17, provides a database location, located by default at `/var/mysql`, an option to change the MySQL root password, and a check box to enable network connections to the database.

Ruby on Rails

Ruby on Rails is a popular web application framework that uses the Ruby programming language. It's notable for enabling rapid web application development, its flexible scalability, its support for the Model-View-Controller (MVC) development architecture for efficient organization of code, and because it makes extensive use of Ajax technologies via the Prototype and Script.aculo.us libraries. Rails development has replaced a lightweight implementation of SOAP with an approach referred to as REST (REpresentational State Transfer), a set of network architecture principles that outline how resources are defined and addressed.

Figure 24.17

The Settings page in the MySQL pane in Server Admin

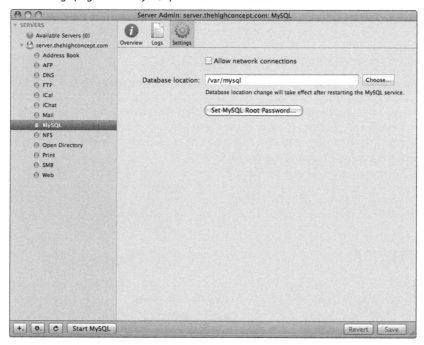

Apple began bundling Ruby on Rails with Mac OS X Leopard. It included several useful component packages preinstalled, including the Mongrel web server.

Apple enhanced Mongrel with support for persistent launching across reboots by using `launchd` as well as Bonjour service advertising, which enables Server Admin to discover instances of Mongrel running and to add these as selectable options within the Balancer Members configuration of the Proxy tab with the Sites page of Server Admin's Web pane.

WebObjects

Acquired alongside NeXTSTEP, the basis for Mac OS X, Apple also inherited WebObjects as a web application server. Apple integrated WebObjects into Mac OS X Server with an unlimited deployment license beginning with Tiger Server.

WebObjects is used to develop web services and Java server applications that can connect to a variety of databases to generate dynamic HTML content, and Apple itself makes wide use of WebObjects in its online retail stores, iTunes, MobileMe, and the iPhone App Store.

However, WebObjects deployment is now missing in Snow Leopard Server. Most WebObjects users take advantage of its ability to run on any server supporting Java, meaning WebObjects can still be deployed on Snow Leopard Server; it just lacks any special service configuration pane within Server Admin.

Monitoring web services performance

The Logs page of the Web pane presents a raw listing of the requests events for each defined website. Enhanced monitoring of this information can be performed by using a web logs analytics program, which parses the logs to create detailed reports on who is visiting your site, from where they're visiting, what errors are occurring and why, what client browsers they're using, how long it takes to serve requests, how much overall workload the server is performing, and how efficiently it's doing it, among many other things.

The Graphs page of the Web pane presents a very simple timeline showing user requests and throughput over a set period of hours or days.

Summary

- Mac OS X Server uses Apache to supply a flexible, modular web server capable of hosting multiple sites or hosting dynamic web applications.

- The web service incorporates support for WebDAV to enable clients to mount shares in the Finder or connect from web development tools for secure uploads as an alternative to using FTP.

- Other common services supported by Apache are easy to configure within Server Admin, including support for CGI scripts, SSI commands, SSL security, and many other features implemented by using Apache modules.

- Apache provides forward proxy services for filtering and caching web access for users sitting inside an organization's firewall as well as a reverse proxy for enabling outside users to access internal resources relayed through the same server for load-balancing or security-related purposes.

- Apple supports a variety of open-source web development tools, from Apache Tomcat for Java servlet deployment to PHP and MySQL to Ruby on Rails.

Web Collaboration Services

A pple has progressively expanded its collaboration services — built on Mac OS X Server's open, standards-based foundation of web services supplied by Apache — to provide users easy access to information-sharing services via a simple web browser.

Web-based collaboration services in Mac OS X Server started with a simple webmail service that used off-the-shelf software to enable users to access their email accounts via a basic web interface.

Apple later added basic blogging support to Tiger Server based on Blosjom, which enabled administrators to set up simple weblogs for users to make publishing regular information on the web easy.

In Leopard Server, web-based collaboration tools took off with the advent of a new wiki feature that enabled organizations to set up a website users could log in to to update, edit, and expand on.

Unlike traditional wiki software, such as the PHP-based MediaWiki software that powers Wikipedia, Apple's wiki services in Mac OS X Server don't drop users into a special markup, code-editing mode that requires using simplified HTML-like syntax.

Instead, wiki editors working with sites hosted by Mac OS X Server can simply click an Edit button appearing on the wiki's web page, authenticate with their account information, and then select elements of the page to edit directly within a graphical interface.

Users can also upload files into the wiki and make these available for others in their workgroup to download. Wiki services are also integrated into blogs for posting regularly updated entries and granting calendar access for scheduling events in personal or group calendars.

Both wiki and blog pages can generate RSS (Really Simple Syndication) feeds that make it easy for others to see when changes have been made or to aggregate updates into a centralized news update page.

This chapter describes how Apple's web collaboration services work, what's involved in planning the services, how they're configured, and how to maintain and monitor wikis, blogs, webmail, and web calendars.

In This Chapter

Introduction to web collaboration services

Planning web collaboration services

Web collaboration services setup and configuration

Managing and monitoring web collaboration services

Introduction to Web Collaboration Services

Publishing information by using web standards makes it easy for users to access information from anywhere by using any modern web browser on virtually any desktop platform or the greatly improved mobile web experience provided by the WebKit-based browsers now available on the iPhone and iPod touch and other mobile devices, including Google's Android, RIM's latest BlackBerry devices, and Palm's new WebOS.

In addition to not needing any special client software, web-based publishing can also provide a simple server-side solution to collaborative group editing, file distribution, cross-linking of information, label tagging, and syndication feeds that enable users to aggregate information from various sources — all without the complex and expensive custom development typically required to deliver these features.

With Snow Leopard Server, Apple makes some unique contributions to web-based collaboration services that unsurprisingly feature ease of use and an attractive design. These elements combine to make the various components of Snow Leopard Server's web-based collaboration services practical, powerful, and professional-looking.

Wikis

A *wiki* is a website powered by software that enables end users to submit additions and changes to the site's content. Inspired by Apple's HyperCard, Ward Cunningham developed the first wiki software to enable users to quickly link together pages of information without needing to know how to author websites in raw HTML, install additional software on the client side, or focus on the presentation of their content.

Because the job of wiki software is to make information publishing quick and simple, Cunningham named his project after the Wiki Wiki Shuttle buses in the Honolulu International Airport. Wiki comes from the Hawaiian word for quick.

Text-based wikis

To simplify and quicken the task of updating web pages, typical wiki software presents a markup editing field where editors select a portion of the page to update and are then presented with basic formatting tools to style text and link in other pages of information.

For example, the MediaWiki software behind Wikipedia uses double brackets to link a word to other articles on the site and other specialized markup for typing an external citation or inserting uploaded images into an article.

Graphic buttons can be used to generate markup code for styling purposes, such as to make text bold or to create different levels of subheadings, or users can learn the markup code they can manually type. Figure 25.1 shows what a typical Wikipedia article's markup looks like.

Figure 25.1

Wikipedia's text-centric wiki editing

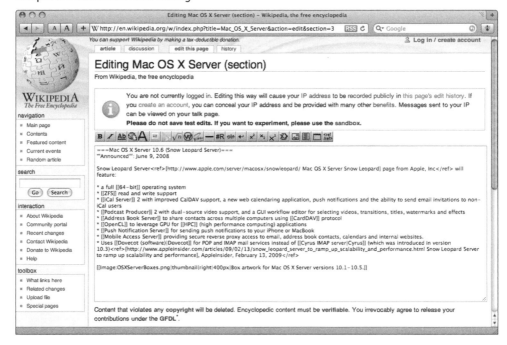

Mac OS X Server's graphical wiki services

Building on the concept of the wiki as a quick way to publish information that other users can expand on, correct, or link to other articles, Apple developed its own wiki software in Mac OS X Leopard Server, written in Python and employing the Twisted framework.

The most obvious enhancement is its fully graphical content editing. Instead of forcing users to learn a special markup language, Apple's wiki software presents a WYSIWYG (what you see is what you get) editor that handles subheadings, bulleted or numbered lists, hyperlinks, rich-text styling, tables, inline graphics, videos or audio files, and file attachments.

Users can even drag and drop files into a browser to create an attachment. Wiki uploads also support automatic zip archiving of a group of files for easy downloading.

As shown in Figure 25.2, the content appears in the editing view the same as it appears on the page instead of as markup code the user has to blindly edit until the saved result matches the intended formatting.

Figure 25.2

Mac OS X Server's graphical wiki editor

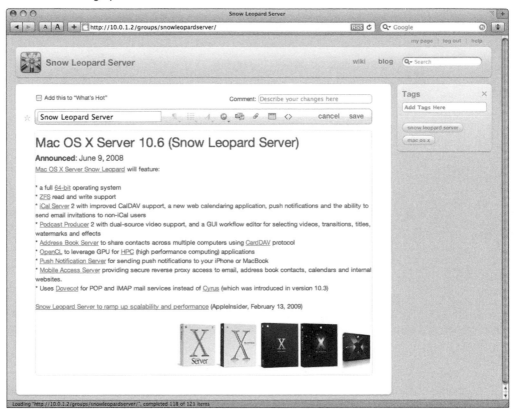

Users can also add tags to articles to associate entries by subject, mark content as hot, and type a comment describing new changes made. The wiki maintains a change history, which enables users to revert to a previous version of an article.

Once saved, the wiki entry appears just as it was typed, automatically generating an entry in the site's Recent Changes RSS feed. Saved pages present a simple editing control with an Add (+) button and an Edit button marked with a pencil icon, as shown in Figure 25.3.

Figure 25.3

Mac OS X Server's wiki content presentation

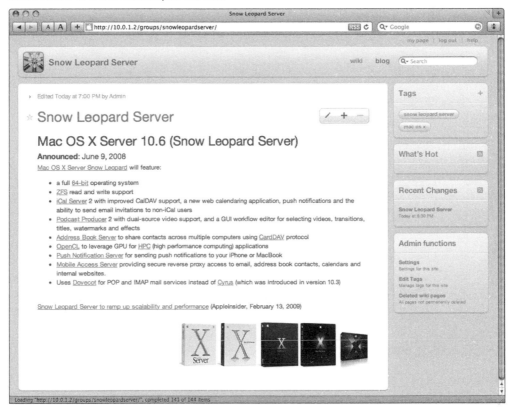

The wiki owner and administrators can assign users privileges to edit or simply view wiki pages.

For users who want to add specialized elements to a wiki entry, the editor also presents raw HTML generated by the graphical editor, as shown in Figure 25.4.

Wiki themes

The overall appearance of individual wikis is managed by CSS and templates built in XSL (Extensible Stylesheet Language). Apple includes a library of themes and recommends that users who want to develop their own custom theme begin by duplicating and modifying the Wireframe theme located at `/Library/Application/Support/Apple/WikiServer/Themes/wireframe.wikitheme/`.

Figure 25.4

Mac OS X Server's raw HTML editor

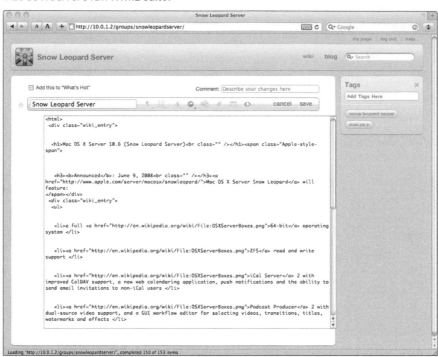

The XML DTD (Document Type Definition) `plist` file within the theme can be modified to change the basic layout of elements on the page, whereas styling features such as text size and colors can be changed within its CSS files. More complex themes can incorporate dynamic elements by using JavaScript or custom theme elements built in XSL.

Wiki file structure

The wiki service in Snow Leopard Server is saved by default within the directory at `/Library/ Collaboration`. This location may be changed within the Web Services pane of the Sites page in Server Admin's Web pane, which is also where the wiki service itself is enabled.

Within this directory, all wikis created on the server are saved within a Groups folder inside a subfolder based on the name of the wiki, such as `/Library/Collaboration/Groups/ wikiname/`.

The component files of a wiki entry (named "article" here) are contained within the folder `/ Library/Collaboration/Groups/wikiname/wiki/article.page/`.

The HTML content of the wiki entry is saved at `/Library/Collaboration/Groups/wikiname/wiki/article.page/page.html`.

Metadata related to the same wiki entry is saved at `/Library/Collaboration/Groups/wikiname/wiki/article.page/page.plist`.

A version history database for the entry is saved at `/Library/Collaboration/Groups/wikiname/wiki/article.page/revisions.db`.

Image files associated with the entry are saved within `/Library/Collaboration/Groups/wikiname/wiki/article.page/images/`.

Any file attachments related to the entry are saved to `/Library/Collaboration/Groups/wikiname/wiki/article.page/attachments/`.

Blogs

Derived from weblog, a *blog*, like a wiki, similarly uses special server-side software to make publishing information on the web easy for users who are focused primarily on delivering regular new content rather than crafting original presentation for a series of web pages.

Unlike a typical group-edited wiki, however, blogs are commonly centered on an author and present regular new content updates in sequence, as opposed to constantly updating and revising the same information in a subject-oriented article format.

Blogs typically publish a syndicated feed of updates, making it easy for readers to watch for new content. By adding audio or video attachments to the feed, a blog becomes a podcast that enables users to download media files for direct or offline playback on a mobile device.

Apple's blogging software in Snow Leopard Server is tightly integrated into its wiki solution, with both sharing the same graphical editing features, tagging, RSS feed generation, and support for inline media files and file attachments, as shown in Figure 25.5.

Once saved, a blog entry also presents a field to allow readers to post comments as well as a navigation element that takes users between the main blog listing and individual entries or between entries, as shown in Figure 25.6.

Snow Leopard Server blogs may be assigned to a group for collaborative posting or set up for individual users. Adding new entries and editing blog posts are identical to editing wiki pages and adding new articles, with the same Add, Delete, and Edit buttons.

Blogging as a service is enabled from the Web Services pane of the Sites page of Server Admin's Web pane.

Figure 25.5

Mac OS X Server's blog entry interface

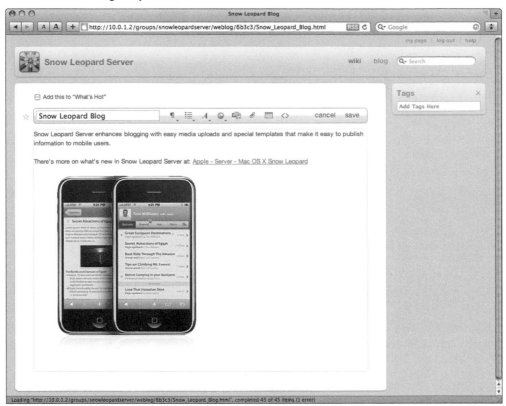

Web-based email

Webmail in Mac OS X Server is delivered by SquirrelMail, an open-source PHP package. Using webmail requires a functional IMAP mail service because webmail itself is just an interface to the mail server. The webmail service is enabled in the Web Services pane of the Sites page of Server Admin's Web pane.

By default, Snow Leopard Server expects to use the local mail server, but webmail can be configured to access IMAP mailboxes served by a mail service running on a separate server.

Figure 25.6

Blog entry comments and navigation

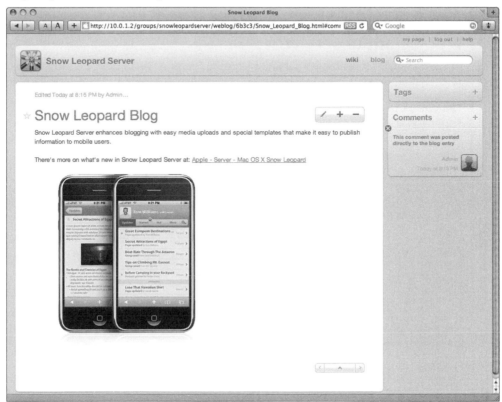

The webmail configuration is stored within /etc/squirrelmail/config/config.php, which can be edited either manually or by using a Perl configuration script by typing the command sudo /etc/squirrelmail/config/conf.pl.

Either way, various elements of the webmail service can be configured, including:

- The service's organization name
- Site logo presented at login
- Mail server settings
- Location of special IMAP folders, such as sent items, drafts, or trash
- Plug-ins and language-encoding features
- Themes and appearance settings

Webmail is linked from the wiki and blog pages but directs to the separate site located at `www.example.com/webmail/src/login.php`. The service must be manually customized to appear cohesive with other web collaboration services.

Web calendar service

Unlike webmail, the web calendar Snow Leopard Server serves is built by using the same Twisted framework as the wikis and blogs so it appears cohesive and works similarly.

With the web calendar service enabled within the Web Services pane of the Sites page of Server Admin's Web pane, a calendar link appears next to the wikis, blogs, and mail navigation links in the web collaboration pages. Once a user is logged in, the web calendar interface is accessible at `www.example.com/ical`, as shown in Figure 25.7.

Figure 25.7

The web calendar interface

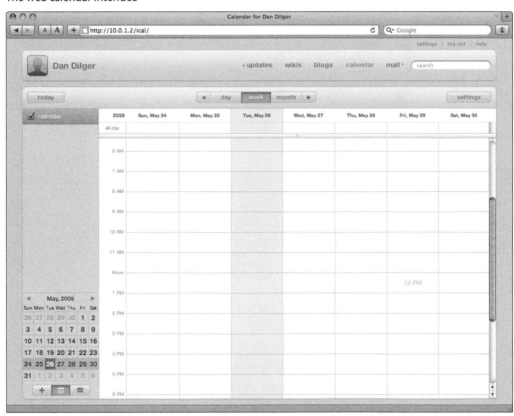

Editing calendar events is similar to the desktop iCal client in Mac OS X: Simply drag to define a new event in the daily, weekly, or monthly view, and a detail dialog box pops up to type the event's details, as shown in Figure 25.8.

Figure 25.8

Editing events on the web calendar

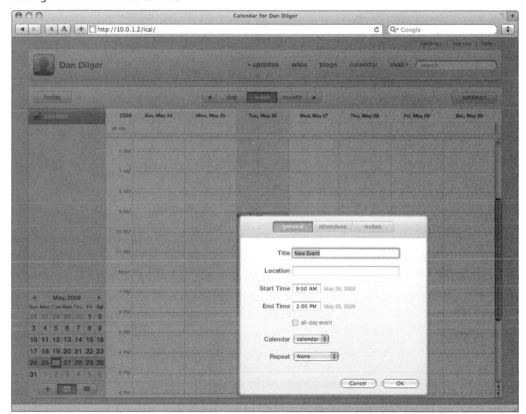

Planning Web Collaboration Services

Web collaboration services in Snow Leopard Server are easy to expand on as needed from right within the online wiki interface. That makes it easy to scale services to fit your needs.

Initial setup of wikis, blogs, webmail, and web calendar services involves some initial planning to take care of a few prerequisite steps. You need to have the following in place:

- Properly configured web services with a registered domain name for your web server and properly configured DNS

- A configured website for collaboration services, which is managed within the Web pane of Server Admin. Depending on your security needs, this may require a certificate identity for enabling SSL support on the site.

- Defined user accounts for which you've assigned privileges for creating new wikis and blogs, which are configured on the Wiki pane of the Settings page of Server Admin's Web pane. By default, all users can create new wikis.

- Group accounts set up for collaborative wikis, shared calendars, and group blogs. Groups are managed within Workgroup Manager. Access to wikis is managed from the web interface.

- Configured and functioning email and calendar services, both of which are configured within Server Admin. External services running on a separate server can be configured on the Wiki pane of the Settings page of Server Admin's Web pane.

CROSS-REF
For more on Server Admin, see Chapter 9. For more on Workgroup Manager, see Chapter 10.

Other web collaboration plans you need to address include ensuring you have enough disk space to accommodate your users' needs. Although the HTML and metadata content of wikis and blogs is likely to be negligible, you need to prepare for and then monitor how users work with file attachments and potentially large media files.

From the Wiki pane of the Settings page of Server Admin's Web pane, shown in Figure 25.9, you can set a limit on the size of attachments users may upload into their wikis or blogs. The default is set to 50 megabytes.

However, even with limits in place, regular uploads, such as podcasts, may begin to require significant disk storage. Given that the default location of collaborative content is on the server's boot drive, you may need to plan to move the data store to a drive with sufficient storage to meet your organization's needs.

Figure 25.9

The Wiki pane of the Web pane's Settings page

Web Collaboration Services Setup and Configuration

To configure the web collaboration services from Server Admin, first enable the web service within the desired server's listing of configured services and then do the following:

- Configure web services.
- Create a website for collaboration services.
- Enable and configure specific collaboration services.
- Configure web permissions.
- Turn on the web service.
- Advertise client access.

Enabling web services

Setting up web collaboration services requires activating the web service, configuring the settings for the site being served, and enabling any special web server features, such as SSL security. Additional configuration is done within the web collaboration site itself.

To enable web service configuration in Server Admin, follow these steps:

1. **Launch Server Admin and then connect to the desired server.**

2. **Select a server listing and then click Settings on the toolbar.**

3. **Click the Services tab.**

4. **Click the check box for Web.**

5. **Click Save.** Web should now appear in the list of configurable services for the selected server, as shown in Figure 25.10.

Figure 25.10

Enabling the Web pane in Server Admin

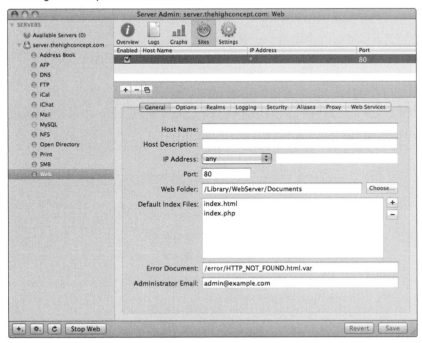

CROSS-REF
For more on configuring web services and enabling SSL, see Chapter 24.

Enabling web collaboration features for a site

Once the web service is configured, additional web-based collaboration features can be turned on, including Apple's unique wiki, blogs, and web calendar as well as the bundled webmail service.

To enable a site's web collaboration services, follow these steps:

1. Launch Server Admin and then connect to the desired server.

2. Click Web and then click Sites on the toolbar.

3. Click the Web Services tab, shown in Figure 25.11.

Figure 25.11

The Web Services pane of the Sites page in Server Admin's Web pane

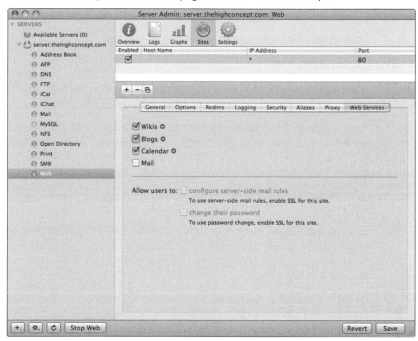

4. **Enable collaboration services for the selected site by using the check boxes for:**
   - **Wikis.** Enables support for user-edited wiki websites
   - **Blogs.** Enables support for user-created blog journals
   - **Calendar.** Enables web access to Calendar Server data
   - **Mail.** Enables web access to mail server data

5. **Optionally, enable users to configure server-side mail rules, a feature that requires SSL support to be enabled on the site.**

6. **Optionally, enable users to change their passwords, a feature that requires SSL support to be enabled on the site.**

7. **Click Save.**

Configuring collaboration features in the web service

Web collaboration services are configured within Server Admin under the Web Services tab of the Sites page of the Web pane. However, much of the actual configuration of web collaboration services is performed within the wiki website itself. To configure wiki settings, follow these steps:

1. **Launch Server Admin and then connect to the desired server.**

2. **Click Web and then click Settings on the toolbar.**

3. **Click the Wiki tab.**

4. **Specify a data store for wiki information and attachments.** The default location is at `/Library/Collaboration/`.

5. **Type a maximum attachment size for files uploaded by wiki users.** This includes documents users submit to the wiki, such as graphics or podcasts.

6. **Choose a default theme for wikis.** Users can change the theme later.

7. **Add users or groups allowed to create wikis.** By default, all users have wiki creation permissions.

8. **Use the Configure button to customize the SMTP relay details.** From the sheet that drops down, specify a sender email address, SMTP relay DNS name and port number, and a username and password to use when sending wiki welcome messages. Click Done when finished.

9. **Use the Configure button to define external web services.** From the sheet that drops down, specify a calendar server and/or email server by DNS name, optionally specifying an SSL connection. This connects web calendars to the wiki pages and enables webmail users to set server-side mail rules. Click Done when finished.

10. **Click Save.**

Configuring collaboration services on the web

Once enabled, web collaboration services are accessed from the configured website on the server. The default web page presented by Mac OS X Server, shown in Figure 25.12, links to:

- **My Page.** A central listing of content updates aggregated from other users' wikis and blogs and group wikis and blogs
- **Wikis.** A listing of all shared wikis, including a link to create a new wiki
- **Blogs.** A listing of all shared blogs, including a link to create a new blog

Figure 25.12

The default web page that links to web collaboration services

My Page

To access My Page, users must first log in to the site. If you make your collaboration website publicly accessible, you should enable SSL security on the site; otherwise, your users are sending their passwords in the clear. Once logged in, My Page presents all the shared wikis and blogs on the site. The Show control enables this listing to show:

- **All items.** Displays a list of every user and group wiki and blog
- **My pages.** Displays just the wikis and blogs created by the logged-in user
- **Starred pages.** Displays only items the user has previously selected by starring the wiki or blog
- **Hot pages.** Contain content marked by the creator as hot

Within the My Page listing, you can customize the content being presented by:

- Performing a content search
- Selecting either All or Unread content from the column header. You can also mark all content as read.
- Clicking an item's follow dot to highlight it in blue, which tracks that wiki's or blog's RSS feed to indicate when new updates or comments are made.

When new content is being followed, a blue dot is indicated next to the item and in the Updates navigation link as well as in the Show control next to any categories containing followed items.

New updates or comments are also indicated by a button control for any wikis or blogs being followed. Clicking the button opens a detail view of the updates and comments, shown in Figure 25.13.

Wikis

Selecting wikis from the main page or from the wikis link in the navigation bar presents a listing of group and user wikis viewable by the current user. The list can be filtered by using the search field, and multiple pages of wikis can be navigated by using the page controls at the bottom of the listing. Buttons presented allow you to watch for or hide the updates count for new content related to the wiki.

Figure 25.13

My Page with the new updates button activated for a followed blog

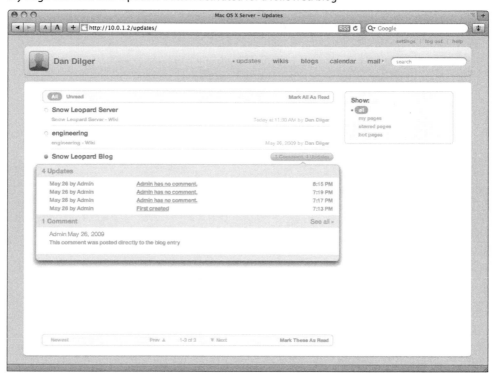

CAUTION

When a wiki owner or administrator mouses over the names of wikis in the listing, an X icon appears. This button can be used to delete the entire wiki. If clicked, a confirmation dialog box appears to explain that taking this action permanently deletes the wiki and all pages it contains and that you can't undo this action.

To create a new wiki, follow these steps:

1. Browse to the wiki page of the server at www.example.com/groups, **as shown in Figure 25.14.**

Figure 25.14

Wiki listings

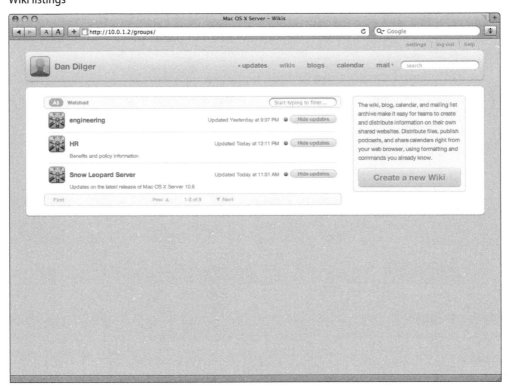

2. **Click the Create a new Wiki button.** The pop-up control in Figure 25.15 appears, allowing you to configure the new wiki settings.

Figure 25.15

Creating a new wiki

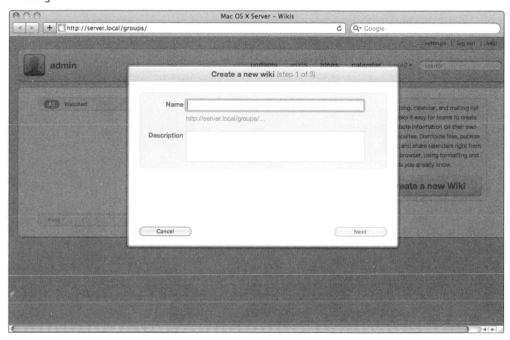

3. Type a wiki name and description — which are presented in listings — as shown in Figure 25.16 and then click Next.

Figure 25.16

Naming and describing the wiki

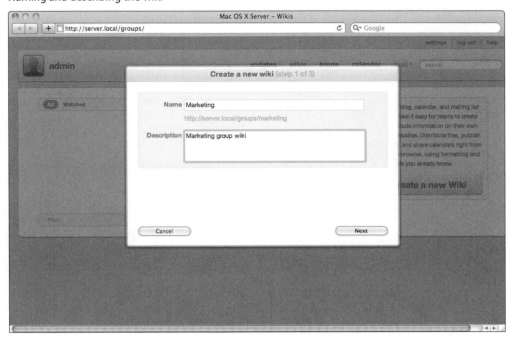

4. Choose a theme for the new wiki, as shown in Figure 25.17, and then click Next.

Figure 25.17

Choosing a theme for the wiki

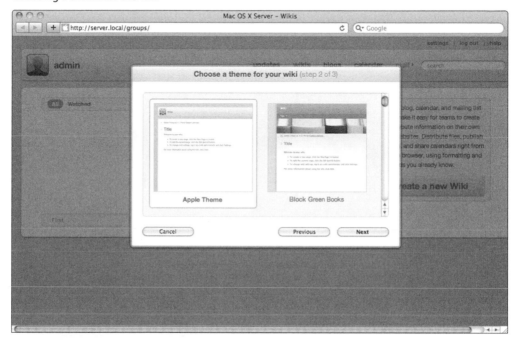

5. **Type wiki access rules, as shown in Figure 25.18.** If the wiki is intended to be public and to be read and edited by anyone, you can optionally choose to require users to log in to read or to write changes.

If the wiki is private, you can add users from Open Directory and then assign them read-only or read-and-write access. This step also sends a welcome message to the users assigned privileges on the wiki if the check box to do so is enabled.

Figure 25.18

Setting wiki access

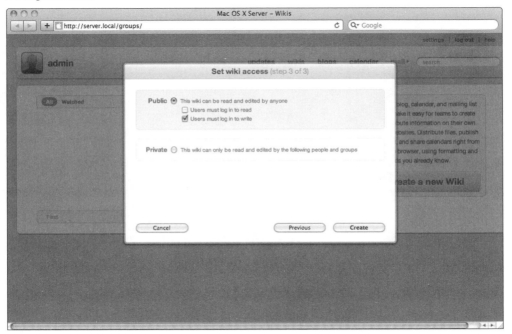

6. **Click Create.** The wiki is created, and as shown in Figure 25.19, a button is presented to close the configuration assistant pop-up and open the new wiki.

Figure 25.19

Click this button to go to the wiki.

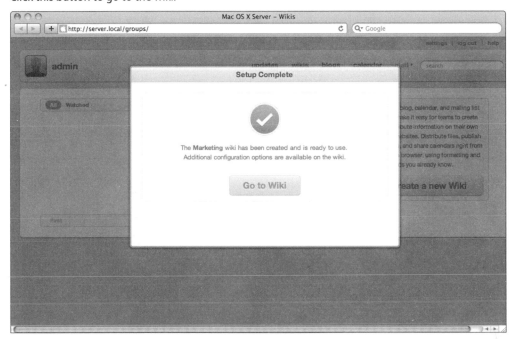

To configure the settings of an existing wiki, follow these steps:

1. **Browse to the selected wiki page at** `www.example.com/groups/wiki-name`.

2. **Click Settings in the Admin functions box.** You need to be an administrator or the group's owner. Group ownership is set within Workgroup Manager.

3. **The Settings page presents a series of tabs:**

   - **General.** Sets an icon graphic for the wiki and presents settings to change its name, description, and theme and to set an email contact

   - **Services.** Offers to activate a calendar, mailing list, and blog for the wiki, with the option to turn blog items containing attached media into a podcast that can be published to iTunes. An iTunes category can be specified to make finding the podcast easier for users.

   - **Permissions.** Sets the wiki as public or private; enables private wikis to define users with read-only or full editing access; defines administrators for the wiki; sets comments as open to anyone, restricts them to authenticated users, or disables them; and sets comment moderation to off or to only anonymous comments, or activates a waiting period for all comments.

   - **Sidebar.** Sets a custom title and enables the creation of search tags for filtering patching pages by a subject tag

   - **Advanced.** Enables the wiki to appear to all virtual hostnames configured on the site or to be restricted to specific hostnames

4. **Save the settings for each page as changes are made.** Return to the wiki listings by using the navigation link at the top of the page.

Blogs

Selecting blogs from the main page or from the blogs link in the navigation bar presents a listing of group and user blogs viewable by the current user.

The list can be filtered by using the search field, and multiple pages of blogs can be navigated by using the page controls at the bottom of the listing. Buttons presented allow you to watch for or hide the updates count for new content related to the blog.

To create a new user blog, follow these steps:

1. **Browse to the blogs page of the server at** `www.example.com/users`**, as shown in Figure 25.20.**

2. **Click the Create my Blog button.** A pop-up control appears for configuring the new wiki settings.

3. **Type the user's name as the blog name.** Don't give the blog a random name here; otherwise, the system will complain that the given user doesn't have permission to create a blog.

4. **Click Create.** The new blog is now ready for use and can be named in configuration settings.

Figure 25.20

Blog listings

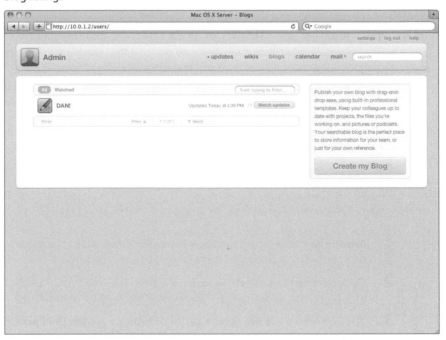

To create a new group blog, follow these steps:

1. **Browse to the selected group wiki at** `www.example.com/groups/wiki-name` **that you want to connect to a blog.**

2. **Click Settings in the Admin functions box.** You need to be an administrator or the group's owner. Group ownership is set within Workgroup Manager.

3. **Click the Services tab and then enable a group blog by clicking the check box.** Access permissions to edit or view the blog match the group wiki permissions, which are set by using the Permissions tab.

4. **Save the settings.** Group members now have a common blog associated with their group wiki, which they can use to post entries. The blog is at `www.example.com/groups/wiki-name/blog`.

To configure the settings of an existing personal blog, follow these steps:

1. **Browse to the selected personal blog page at** `www.example.com/users/user-name`**.**

2. **Click Settings in the Admin functions box.**

3. **The Settings page presents a series of tabs:**

- **Account.** Sets an icon graphic for the blog and the user's My Page and presents an option to set an email contact

- **Blog.** Sets a blog name and theme. It also supplies the option to turn blog items containing attached media into a podcast that can be published to iTunes. An iTunes category can be specified to make finding the podcast easier for users.

- **Blog Access.** Sets the blog as public or private. Public blogs can be set so that users must log in to be able to read it. Private blogs can define users with read-only or full editing access. Comments can be set as open to anyone, restricted to authenticated users, or disabled. Comment moderation can be set to off, to only anonymous comments, or to hold all comments for review.

4. **Save the settings for each page as changes are made.** Return to the blogs listings by using the navigation link at the top of the page.

To configure the settings of an existing group blog, follow these steps:

1. **Browse to the selected group wiki page connected to the blog at** `http://www.example.com/groups/wiki-name`.

2. **Click Settings in the Admin functions box.** You need to be an administrator or the group's owner. Group ownership is set within Workgroup Manager.

3. **The Settings page presents a series of tabs, as shown in Figure 25.21:**

- **General.** Sets an icon graphic and presents settings to change its name, description, and theme and to set an email contact

- **Services.** Offers to activate a calendar, mailing list, and blog for the wiki, with the option to turn blog items containing attached media into a podcast that can be published to iTunes. An iTunes category can be specified to make finding the podcast easier for users.

- **Permissions.** Sets the blog's wiki as public or private; enables private wikis to define users with read-only or full editing access; defines administrators for the wiki; sets comments as open to anyone, restricted to authenticated users, or disabled; and sets comment moderation to off or to only anonymous comments or activates a waiting period for all comments.

- **Sidebar.** Sets a custom title and enables the creation of search tags for filtering patching pages by a subject tag

- **Advanced.** Enables the blog's wiki to appear to all virtual hostnames configured on the site or be restricted to specific hostnames

4. **Save the settings for each page as changes are made.** Return to the blog or wiki listings by using the navigation link at the top of the page.

Figure 25.21

Wiki settings

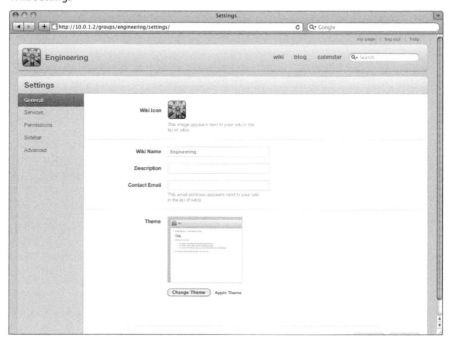

Web calendar

Using the web calendar in Mac OS X Server's collaboration services requires first setting up the iCal service, enabling the web service and support for wikis and blogs, and then enabling web calendars as a collaboration feature.

To enable a site's web calendar service, follow these steps:

1. **Launch Server Admin and then connect to the desired server.**

2. **Click Web and then click Sites on the toolbar.**

3. **Click the Web Services tab.**

4. **Click the Calendar check box.**

5. **Click Save.**

Unlike wikis and blogs, which are largely configured within the web interface, the web calendar simply acts as a web client for iCal Server. However, unlike the webmail client, the calendar offers the same animated, responsive interface as wikis and blogs because it's similarly written using the same Twisted framework.

Using the web calendar is as simple as logging in to the wiki site and then clicking Calendar in the navigation bar. A simple Settings button allows users to specify their time zone, set their availability as weekdays or custom, and start the week on a given day.

Multiple calendars can be created by using the Add (+) button in the lower left.

Clicking a calendar's information button, which appears when you mouse over the calendar name, offers options to:

- Change the calendar's name
- Choose a calendar color
- Subscribe to the calendar in iCal. This imports events to the desktop client but doesn't enable iCal to edit events. You can also manually subscribe to a web calendar via `www.example.com:8008/calendars/groups/group-name/calendar/`.

Webmail

Using the webmail client in Mac OS X Server's collaboration services requires first setting up mail service, enabling the web service and support for wikis and blogs, and then activating webmail as a feature on the site.

To enable a site's webmail service, follow these steps:

1. **Launch Server Admin and then connect to the desired server.**

2. **Click Web and then click Sites on the toolbar.**

3. **Click the Web Services tab.**

4. **Click the Mail check box.**

5. **Optionally, enable users to configure server-side mail rules, a feature that requires SSL support to be enabled on the site.**

6. **Optionally, enable users to change their passwords, a feature that requires SSL support to be enabled on the site.**

7. **Click Save.**

Like the web calendar, webmail simply acts as a web client for the mail service. However, unlike the web calendar client, webmail uses a basic interface that doesn't match the richness of the wikis, blogs, and web calendar.

Webmail, shown in Figure 25.22, offers a simple and dated-looking interface that appears to have changed little in the last decade.

Figure 25.22

Webmail

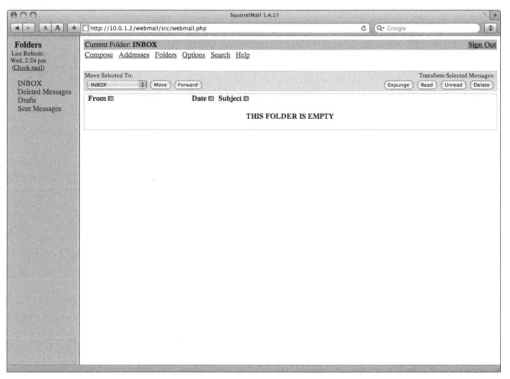

Access control for users and groups

Steps for managing access control for users and groups within web collaboration services depend on the service being managed.

To configure wiki users, follow these steps:

1. Launch Server Admin and then connect to the desired server.

2. Click Web and then click Settings on the toolbar.

3. Click the Wiki tab.

4. Add users or groups allowed to create wikis by clicking the Add (+) button and then dragging in users and groups from the pane that appears. By default, all users have wiki creation permissions.

5. Click Save.

To configure blog users, follow these steps:

1. From Server Admin, select the server name of the collaboration server.

2. Click the Settings page and then click the Access tab.

3. From the Services pane within Access, choose the Blog service in the left column.

4. Click the Allow only users and groups below radio button above the right column.

5. Click the Add (+) button. A Users & Groups sheet opens.

6. Drag users or groups to the access list on the right to define who has blog access. By default, all users have access to create blogs.

7. Click Save. Access to creating blogs is now limited to the selected users.

To configure web calendar users, follow these steps:

1. From Server Admin, select the server name of the calendar server.

2. Click the Settings page and then click the Access tab.

3. From the Services pane within Access, choose the iCal service in the left column.

4. Click the Allow only users and groups below radio button above the right column.

5. Click the Add (+) button. A Users & Groups sheet opens.

6. Drag users or groups to the access list on the right to define who has calendar access.

7. Click Save.

To configure webmail users, follow these steps:

1. From Server Admin, select the server name of the mail server.

2. Click the Settings page and then click the Access tab.

3. From the Services tab within Access, choose the mail service from the left column.

4. Click the Allow only users and groups below radio button above the right column.

5. Click the Add (+) button. A Users & Groups sheet opens.

6. Drag users or groups to the access list on the right to define who has mail service access.

7. Click Save.

Security

Security for web collaboration services can be enhanced in three ways:

- Limiting access to your website by using firewall rules
- Limiting read and write access to wikis and blogs to specific users and groups
- Implementing SSL security on your collaboration website to enable encrypted authentication

Managing and Monitoring Web Collaboration Services

Ongoing management of wiki and blog collaboration services, apart from basic service configuration and user creation, is performed within the online wiki interface rather than within Server Admin.

Managing wiki and blog pages

Once you have wikis and blogs created and configured, users with access privileges can review and contribute.

To add new content to a wiki or blog, follow these steps:

1. **Browse to the selected wiki page at** `www.example.com/groups/wiki-name` **or to a blog page at** `www.example.com/users/blog-name`**.**

2. **Click the Add (+) button.** You're prompted to type a name for the new wiki page or blog entry.

3. **A new content editor opens.** From this page, you can:

- Rename the page or entry.
- Apply paragraph styles to text.
- Create bulleted lists, numbered lists, and indented text sections.
- Apply character styles and highlighting to text.
- Insert a hyperlink.
- Insert media, such as images, audio, or QuickTime movies.
- Attach files to the article or entry.
- Insert tables.
- View the raw HTML for the page.
- Provide a comment describing the changes you're making.

- Mark the content to appear under the What's Hot RSS feed.
- Enable the star to follow future wiki or blog changes on your My Page.
- Add tags to the wiki article or blog entry.
- Save the page.

4. **Once saved, the wiki or blog changes are advertised to any watchers.** Users can:

- Click the Edit button marked with a pencil to edit the entry.
- Add new tags to the wiki article or blog entry.
- Add new comments to the wiki article or blog entry.
- Click the revisions entry to see who has made wiki changes, when, and why.
- Save the page.

To use hyperlinks within a wiki or blog entry, follow these steps:

1. **Browse to the selected wiki page at** `www.example.com/groups/wiki-name` **or to a blog page at** `www.example.com/users/blog-name`.

2. **Click the Edit button marked with a pencil icon.**

3. **To add a hyperlink to a new page, select the text you want to link to the new page and then choose New Page from the hyperlink icon in the editing toolbar.** This presents a pop-up menu asking for the name of the new page (which is by default the same as the text you selected).

4. **To add a hyperlink to a page by using search (which suggests other pages dynamically), select your text and then choose Search from the hyperlink menu.** A listing of related pages appears, and you can supply search words to locate the desired page.

5. **To add a hyperlink to a URL, select your text and then choose Enter URL from the hyperlink menu.**

6. **Remove a hyperlink by selecting it and choosing Unlink from the hyperlink menu.**

7. **The hyperlink menu also suggests other wiki or blog pages that you may want to link to the selected text.**

To review revisions to a wiki entry, follow these steps:

1. **Browse to the selected wiki page at** `www.example.com/groups/wiki-name`.

2. **Select the wiki page you want to review for changes.**

3. **Click the disclosure triangle next to the line starting with Edited and supply the date and editor of the most recent change.** It expands to show a series of edits.

4. Click each updated entry in the list to review changes.

5. Click Compare to highlight content changed in the selected revision, as shown in Figure 25.23.

Figure 25.23

Wiki document history version comparison

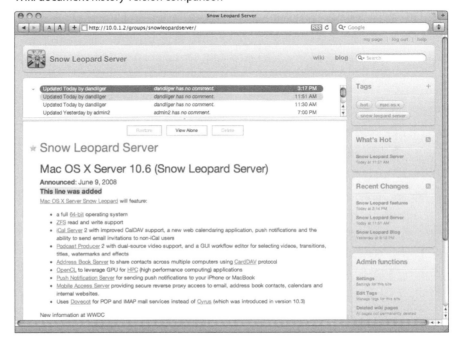

6. Click View Alone to remove the highlighted changes.

7. Click Restore to return the wiki entry to an earlier revision.

8. Click Delete to remove an earlier revision entry from the database.

9. Click the triangle by the latest revision to hide the document history details.

To follow or subscribe to an RSS feed of wiki or blog updates, follow these steps:

1. Browse to the selected wiki page at `www.example.com/groups/wiki-name` or to a blog page at `www.example.com/users/blog-name`.

2. Select a wiki page, and in the sidebar, click RSS icons for:
   - What's Hot, a feed of new content marked as hot by its creator
   - Recent Changes, a feed of changes across the server

3. Alternatively, you can follow changes to a specific wiki or blog by marking items within the Updates page, which highlights any new updates or comments attached to those items. Click the blank circle in front of the wiki or blog name, and it highlights to indicate you're following the item's changes.

Managing wiki and blog comments and tags

Tags are used to group, identify, categorize, and quickly find related wiki and blog pages. Use tags as an easy-to-use organizational system to link content by its department or project, by subject, or by any other criteria that makes sense.

Anyone who can edit wiki or blog content can add or remove tags and search for tagged items to quickly find related content.

To add or edit tags on a wiki or blog entry, follow these steps:

1. Browse to the selected wiki or blog page you want to tag.

2. Click the Add (+) button in the Tag box, shown in Figure 25.24.

Figure 25.24

Adding a tag to a wiki or blog

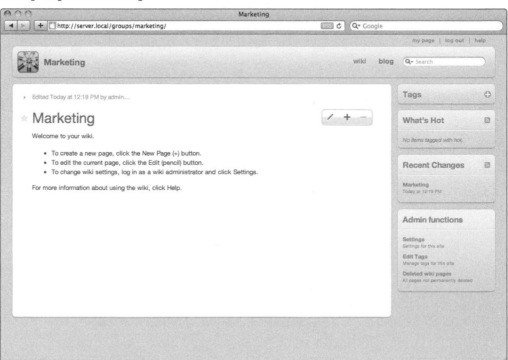

3. **Type a tag and then press Return, as shown in Figures 25.25 and 25.26.** Type additional tags as desired. Each tag typed appears in the Tag box.

4. **To remove a tag, edit the page by using the button marked with a pencil icon, mouse over the selected tag, and then click the Close button that appears.** A confirmation dialog box appears warning you that the tag will be permanently removed. Alternatively, simply drag the tag out of the Tag box and it disappears.

5. **To discover related content with the same tag, click the tag buttons in the Tag box.** A search result shows similarly tagged blog entries and wiki articles.

6. **Click Save.** Now when you add a new blog entry, you're prompted to enable the check box to add podcast media to this entry. A Subscribe in iTunes link is also added to the page. This adds the podcast directly from the server to a user's copy of iTunes; it doesn't publicly list the podcast in the iTunes Store.

Figure 25.25

Typing a tag name

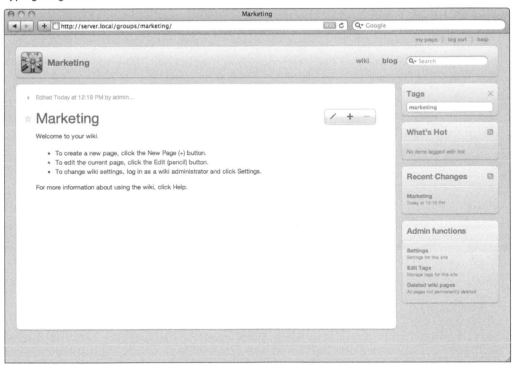

Figure 25.26

How the tag appears on the wiki or blog

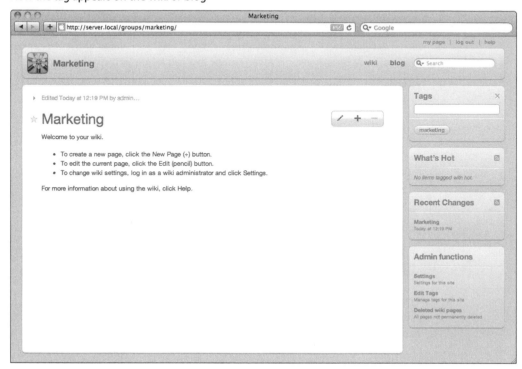

To add, remove, or moderate comments on a blog entry, follow these steps:

1. **Browse to the selected blog page you want to comment on.**

2. **Click the Add (+) button in the Comments box.**

3. **Type a comment and then press Return, as shown in Figure 25.27.** Your comment appears with your name, icon, and a time and date stamp, as shown in Figure 25.28.

Figure 25.27

Adding a comment to a wiki or blog

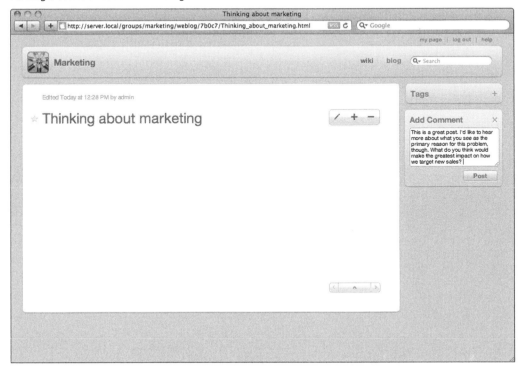

4. **To remove a comment on your blog, mouse over the selected comment and then click the Close button that appears.** A confirmation dialog box appears warning you that the tag will be permanently removed.

5. **If comment moderation is enabled, approve or delete waiting comments by selecting Moderate comments from the Admin functions box.**

Figure 25.28

How the comment appears on the wiki or blog

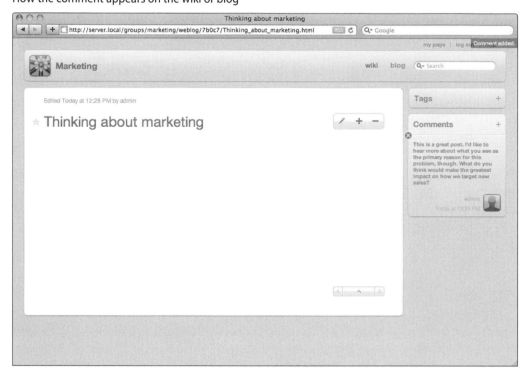

Enabling blog podcasts in group and personal blogs

If a blog is designated as podcast-enabled, any blog entries with attached media files are made available through a podcast-enabled RSS feed.

To add podcast media to a group blog, follow these steps:

1. **Browse to the selected blog's group wiki page at** www.example.com/groups/ wiki-name.

2. **Click Settings in the Admin functions box.** You need to be an administrator or the group's owner. Group ownership is set within Workgroup Manager.

3. **From the Settings page, click the Services tab.**

4. **Click the check box to turn blog items containing attached media into a podcast that can be published through iTunes.** An iTunes category can be specified to make finding the podcast easier for users.

5. **Click Save.** Now when you add a new blog entry, you're prompted to enable the check box to add podcast media to this entry. A Subscribe in iTunes link is also added to the page. This adds the podcast directly from the server to a user's copy of iTunes; it doesn't publicly list the podcast in the iTunes Store.

To add podcast media to a personal blog, follow these steps:

1. **Browse to the selected personal blog page at** `www.example.com/users/user-name.`

2. **Click Settings in the Admin functions box.**

3. **From the Settings page, click the Blog tab.**

4. **Click the check box to turn blog items containing attached media into a podcast that can be published through iTunes.** An iTunes category can be specified to make finding the podcast easier for users.

5. **Click Save.** Now when you add a new blog entry, you're prompted to enable the check box to add podcast media to this entry. A Subscribe in iTunes link is also added to the page. This adds the podcast directly from the server to a user's copy of iTunes; it doesn't publicly list the podcast in the iTunes Store.

Using search

The search box in wikis and blogs not only presents simple search results across the site but also suggests recent tags to use for subject searching or presents a listing of all tags or recent changes.

Search results are initially presented for the currently selected blog or wiki, but a link to search all wikis and blogs presents wider search results. Search results can be organized by date, title, or author.

Mobile web collaboration

When accessed from the iPhone or iPod touch, pages of recent updates, wikis, and blogs are all presented in a custom interface tailored to the device, as shown in Figure 25.29.

Users can log in and review their followed wikis and blogs, search for content, and add tags and comments. The only feature missing is editing and adding new wiki articles and blog entries.

This mobile theme is enabled by default and requires no special configuration.

Figure 25.29

The iPhone theme for keeping current on wiki and blog content

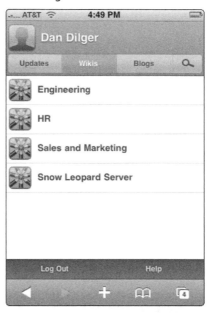

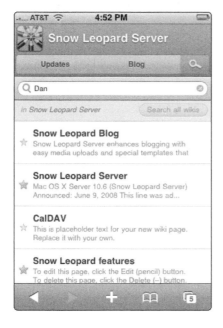

Monitoring web collaboration logs

Wiki error and access logs are available from the Logs page of the Web Services pane in Server Admin, shown in Figure 25.30, which presents a listing of the events for each defined website, recorded in:

- The Access Log for the `wikid` process, located at `/Library/Logs/wikid/access.log`
- The Error Log for the `wikid` process, located at `/Library/Logs/wikid/error.log`

Figure 25.30

The Logs page in Server Admin's Web pane

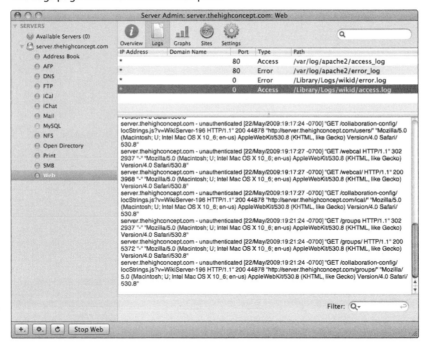

Summary

- Mac OS X Server provides a rich wiki, blog, and web calendar interface for group collaboration and independent content publishing. Apple also includes an old webmail stand-in to provide basic web access to your mailbox.
- Web collaboration features are dependent on the web service as well as iCal Server and mail service.

- Web collaboration features are enabled and configured within the Web Services pane of Server Admin, but many wiki and blog settings are performed entirely within the web interface.

- Snow Leopard Server's wikis and blogs are designed to be easy to edit without needing to know any markup code. It's also easy to add media files, such as graphics, audio files, and videos, all of which appear inline in content, as well as attaching other documents for easy download.

- New content in wikis and blogs is easy to track with following features that highlight new updates and comments, tagging features that link together content by subject or project or author, and RSS feeds of recent changes and content marked as hot.

- The web calendar enables groups to share access to scheduled events and also maintains personal calendars for users.

- An iPhone interface to blogs and wikis enables reviewing new content and adding comments and tags from an iPhone or iPod touch.

iCal Server

M ac OS X Server's iCal Server debuted in Leopard Server as a centralized solution for scheduling meetings and coordinating events. In Snow Leopard, iCal Server 2 gains group and shared calendars, push notification of event updates, and the ability to coordinate meeting requests with external users.

Apple's iCal Server software is largely built in Python by using the Twisted framework, just like the wiki and blog web collaboration services in Mac OS X Server. It's also noteworthy for being offered as an Apache License 2.0 open-source project under the name Darwin Calendar Server.

Mac OS X Server's iCal Server is also notable for being the first commercial calendar server implementing the CalDAV standard for interoperable event scheduling between vendors.

The CalDAV specification builds calendaring extensions into the WebDAV protocol, enabling shared calendaring to be performed by a specialized web server.

Apple is part of CalConnect, the calendaring and scheduling consortium working to promote the IETF's development of CalDAV. CalConnect is composed of a series of companies and universities seeking interoperable, standards-based calendaring and a variety of calendar product vendors, including Google, IBM, Kerio, MeetingMaker, Microsoft, the Mozilla Foundation, Novell, Oracle, Sun, Symbian, and Yahoo.

With CalDAV support in the iCal client on the Mac desktop, in iPhone 3.0 software for mobile devices, and in Mac OS X Server's iCal Server, Apple delivers a full calendaring platform that's also designed to work on alternative platforms with the Darwin Calendar Server and to interoperate with other software designed to implement the CalDAV standard, including existing calendar products from Mozilla and the OSAF (the Open Source Application Foundation, founded by Mitch Kapor), online calendaring services from Google and Yahoo, and third-party plug-in support for Microsoft's Outlook client.

This chapter describes how Apple's iCal Server works, what's involved in planning calendar services, how they're configured, and how to maintain and monitor the services.

Introduction to iCal Server

Snow Leopard Server's use of the open, interoperable CalDAV specification as the basis for its calendaring services enables it to fit into the plans of large organizations interested in deploying solutions that aren't tied to a single vendor.

Previously, companies looking for a shared calendaring product had to invest in a proprietary package, such as IBM's Lotus Notes, Microsoft's Exchange Server, Novell's GroupWise, or PeopleCube's MeetingMaker, the product Apple itself had been using for its internal scheduling services. Having your corporate data locked up in a proprietary system can make moving to a new calendaring solution prohibitively expensive or impractical.

The premise of CalDAV is to open up interoperability so vendors can compete to deliver better solutions. As a relatively new entry into the calendaring market, Apple applied open standards to create a better product that promises future interoperability with other products, not just on the server side but also in terms of desktop and mobile clients as well as interoperability with CalDAV-compliant cloud calendaring services, such as those from Google and Yahoo.

By making iCal Server an open-source project, Apple hopes to increase adoption of CalDAV compliance, enabling Linux distributions to add calendaring services without having to implement the standard from scratch.

Additionally, iCal Server users can contribute toward community development of the software and have some assurance that an investment in a CalDAV-compliant calendaring server isn't wholly dependent on Apple's own internal development efforts.

The web-based architecture of iCal Server

Because CalDAV is based on WebDAV, iCal Server acts as a specialized web server for accessing, publishing, and presenting event data. This makes it easy to scale the service by using hardware load balancers designed to work with web servers.

The iCal service process can also be configured to operate as a master to coordinate multiple delegate slave processes or to act as a combined master/slave process that can spawn multiple slaves, each of which can run on separate processor cores to handle replying to incoming client requests in parallel.

The file-centric architecture iCal Server uses to store event data allows for flexible storage options, is easier to back up and recover, and is less prone to unrecoverable corruption problems when compared to calendaring and messaging servers that store events in a huge database, as Microsoft's Exchange Server does.

Instead of maintaining a massive, centralized database, iCal Server uses flat files to store event data within the default location of `/Library/CalendarServer/Documents/`.

Access to calendar data is managed by standard POSIX file system permissions and ACLs, which enable fine-grained access control. Backing up these files requires only basic support for retaining file system extended attributes, not a complex backup plug-in designed to interface with a proprietary backup API, as other calendaring systems require.

For performance, the system uses individual SQLite databases to provide fast access to calendar events, to-do tasks, and the user free/busy data stored in standard `.ics` files. These databases can be deleted, and they can be re-created as needed, apart from one database that maintains delegate relationships.

A standards-based architecture

The iCal service in Mac OS X Server builds on a variety of documented, standard protocols and document formats, each of which is codified in IETF RFC documents. This results in a known, familiar architecture built on proven technologies:

- **HTTP (RFC 2616).** This serves as the distribution protocol for transferring events as resources between iCal Server and calendar clients.
- **WebDAV (RFC 2518).** This is iCal Server's protocol for reading and writing calendar event files on the server.
- **CalDAV (RFC 4791).** This is an extension of WebDAV designed to handle calendaring-specific features, such as searching for free/busy information and managing invitations.
- **iCalendar (RFC 2445).** This is the standard text format for describing events and to-do items. Individual events are saved in `.ics` files, and collections of these files are interpreted as a calendar.
- **iTIP (iCalendar Transport-Independent Interoperability Protocol, RFC 2446).** This is a standard mechanism for making and responding to event invitations to enable compatibility with other calendar systems.

Additionally, Apple integrates iCal Server with Mac OS X Server's Open Directory and Kerberos for authentication. This enables iCal Server to fit into larger organizations that use directory systems that Open Directory can integrate into, such as Active Directory or other LDAP systems.

A unique approach to calendaring

The design of iCal Server, the Mac OS X iCal desktop client, and the wiki collaboration web calendar client further a strategy that rethinks certain elements of calendaring.

One of the novel features of iCal is its use of multiple, overlapping calendars. Instead of each user having a single calendar, the application debuted with support for multiple calendars containing related events, such as different projects, a personal calendar, or multiple calendar subscriptions containing a list of scheduled events or holidays.

Each calendar could be selectively displayed in a composite of color-coded, translucent overlays, enabling users to view multiple calendars together.

Publishing and subscribing to shared calendars by using iCalendar files shared from a WebDAV server was also new and paved the way for iCal Server to share and fully synchronize bidirectional changes to the same event collections among networked users, adding the additional sophistication of CalDAV and iTIP to support meeting invitations and free/busy scheduling.

Snow Leopard Server's calendars support events involving location and resource assignments, attendee invitations, and shared file attachments. Attendees are sent an invitation they can accept or decline, and their availability and acceptance status are tracked and updated within the event. Meeting changes are updated to all attendees.

Location and resource calendaring features

Along with iCal Server, Leopard Server added a Directory application (now called iCal Server Utility in Snow Leopard Server) for creating and managing two special calendar types associated with directory accounts that are neither users nor groups:

- **Locations.** These are rooms or other landmarks not associated with a specific person that are used to book conference rooms or other places associated with meetings. Locations can be configured to auto-accept meeting request invitations, enabling users to browse up-to-date availability information and directly book a location for their meetings.
- **Resources.** These are shared equipment, such as an automobile, conference phone, copier, digital camera, notebook, printer, projector or projection screen, scanner, or video camera. By defining resources in the company directory and enabling them to auto-accept meeting request invitations, users can look up what resources are available and schedule their use.

Using iCal Server Utility, administrators can create new locations and then configure them to include:

- A unique name and custom graphic icon
- A primary contact or owner
- An address and phone number
- A note field
- An assigned calendar delegate
- A map to the location or resource. Maps are images managed separately within iCal Server Utility by an administrator. Maps added to the company directory can be more accurate or detailed than a generated Google map. After being defined, a map can be associated with a location or resource record and subsequently viewed by users. A pushpin can be used to designate a specific location on a map.

A resource is additionally assigned a type (such as projector or scanner) and description, and locations are assigned a building name, floor, and capacity. Meeting requests created in iCal or the web calendar interface specify a single location and can invite any number of resources, along with individual attendees.

The availability of a location or resource can be determined in iCal by browsing available meeting times within an event's detail record or from the web calendar interface by viewing the event detail's Attendee pane.

Working with locations and resources is detailed later in this chapter.

Secure Mobile Access and push notifications

Apple is also enhancing Snow Leopard Server's iCal Server 2 with support for:

- **Mobile Access.** This secures access to the calendar server for mobile devices by using SSL rather than requiring users to set up a VPN session.
- **Push Notification Server.** This provides a built-in way to efficiently update clients of event changes in their calendars by using XMPP Publish and Subscribe technology.

CROSS-REF

For more on Mobile Access, see Chapter 32. For more on push notifications, see Chapter 33.

Planning Calendar Services

Initial setup of calendar services involves some initial planning to take care of a few prerequisite steps. You need:

- A registered domain name for your server and a properly configured DNS that enables reverse lookup of the server
- A firewall configuration that allows clients to access the calendar server over the designated TCP port. By default, this is 8008, or 8443 for SSL connections. Mobile Access may be used to enable secure remote access to iCal Server.
- User accounts for calendar users stored in Open Directory or an Active Directory system configured to integrate with the server or another LDAP directory with schema to support the iCal service
- Configured and functioning email and calendar services, both of which are configured within Server Admin. External services running on a separate server can be configured on the Wiki pane of the Settings page of the Web Services pane.

Other calendar server plans you need to address include ensuring you have enough disk space to accommodate your users' needs. Although the iCalendar and SQLite files are small, you need to prepare for and then monitor how users will work with file attachments that are attached to calendar items.

From the General pane of the Settings page of the iCal pane, shown in Figure 26.1, you can set a limit on the size of attachments users may upload into their calendar items. The default is set to

1 MB. You can also set a user quota, set by default to 100 MB, and then change the calendar data store to a different location from the default location of `/Library/CalendarServer/Documents/`.

Figure 26.1

The General pane of the iCal pane's Settings page

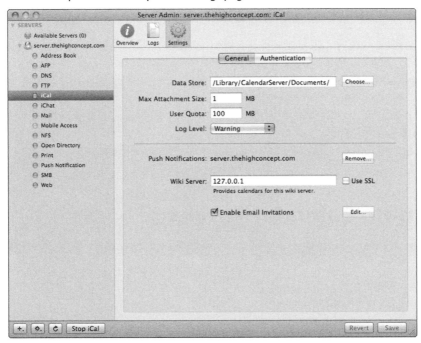

Given that the default location of calendar data is on the server's boot drive, you may need to plan to move the data store to a drive with sufficient storage to meet your organization's needs.

iCal Service Setup and Configuration

Setting up calendar services requires activating the iCal service, configuring service settings, and then configuring client systems to work with the service. To use group calendars, you also need to enable the web service and enable wiki and web calendar services.

CROSS-REF
For more on configuring the web service, see Chapter 24. For more on web collaboration, including wikis and web calendars, see Chapter 25.

To enable iCal service configuration in Server Admin, follow these steps:

1. **Launch Server Admin and then connect to the desired server.**

2. **Select the server listing and then click Settings on the toolbar.**

3. **Click the Services tab.**

4. **Click the check box for iCal.**

5. **Click Save.** iCal should now appear in the list of configurable services for the selected server, as shown in Figure 26.2.

Figure 26.2

Enabling the iCal pane in Server Admin

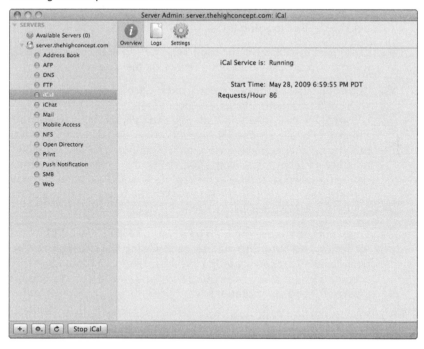

Configuring iCal service settings

To configure iCal services, follow these steps:

1. Launch Server Admin and then connect to the desired server.

2. Select the iCal service and then click Settings on the toolbar.

3. Click the General tab.

4. Set the data store location, which will contain all users' and groups' calendar data and event file attachments. The default location is `/Library/ CalendarServer/Documents/`. To specify a different location on another server, you need to use its local file system mount point instead of providing a network URL.

5. Set the maximum attachment size, which describes the upper limit for all the files attached to a single event.

6. Set the user quota level, which limits the total size of all the file attachments a single user can add to events in his or her calendar. This quota applies to all users. There's no limit on the number of files that can be attached to events, as long as the quota or maximum attachment size isn't exceeded.

7. Set the desired logging level.

8. Configure the Push Notification Server. Push notification is activated by default by using the local push notification service on the local server.

9. Configure the wiki server to be used for group calendars that integrate into other web collaboration services. The default setting is `127.0.0.1`, the loopback address of the server itself, meaning both wiki and calendar services are running on the same server. Optionally, enable SSL encryption by using the check box if the wiki service is running on an SSL-enabled website. To configure wiki and calendar services running on different servers, specify the DNS name of the remote wiki service here and then define the calendar service in the remote server's Wiki pane of the Web Services pane's Settings page by clicking the External Web Services: Configure button and then typing the DNS name of the calendar server.

10. Email invitations are enabled by default, so click the Edit button to configure the incoming and outgoing mail server by using the sheet shown in Figure 26.3. The default values are configured to use the mail service running on the local server. The account `com.apple.calendarserver@www.example.com` is automatically created to send out invitations.

11. Click Done and then click Save.

Figure 26.3

The default email invitations configuration

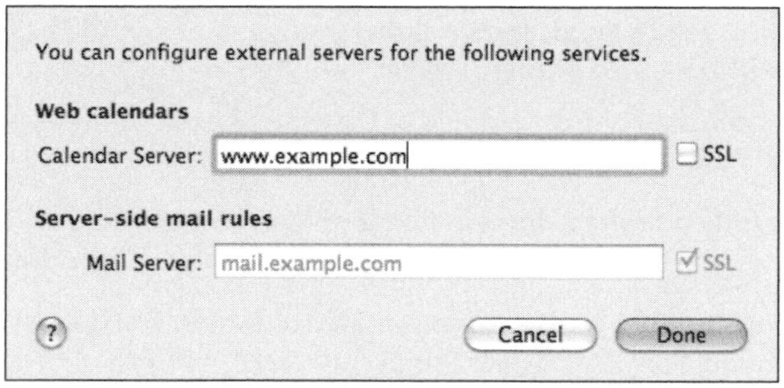

> You can configure external servers for the following services.
>
> **Web calendars**
>
> Calendar Server: `www.example.com` ☐ SSL
>
> **Server-side mail rules**
>
> Mail Server: `mail.example.com` ☑ SSL
>
> ⑦   (Cancel) (Done)

To configure iCal service authentication, follow these steps:

1. **Launch Server Admin and then connect to the desired server.**

2. **Click iCal and then click Settings on the toolbar.**

3. **Click the Authentication tab, shown in Figure 26.4.**

Figure 26.4

The Authentication pane of the iCal pane's Settings page

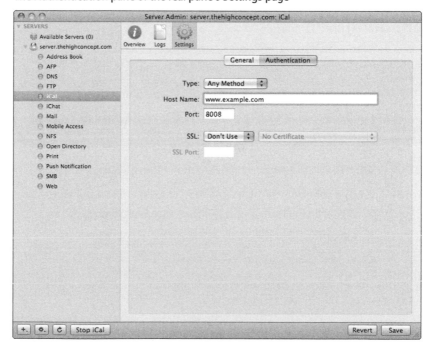

4. **Choose the authentication type from the pop-up menu.** The options are:
   - **Kerberos.** Provides strong encryption requiring Kerberos v5 support on the server
   - **Digest (RFC 2617).** Sends secure login names and encrypted passwords without requiring a configured Kerberos realm
   - **Any Method.** Uses either Kerberos or Digest authentication depending on which the client chooses

5. **Specify the fully qualified domain name of the calendar server.** This must resolve correctly when the server performs a reverse lookup of its IP address.

6. **Specify a port number to use when talking to clients.** The default is 8008. Make sure that any firewalls allow traffic over this port to clients who need to access the server.

7. **Specify an SSL port number and certificate identity.** The default port is 8443. SSL can be set to:
   - Use
   - Don't Use
   - Redirect

8. **Alternatively, configure the Mobile Access service to enable secure remote access to external users by using SSL and then supply that service with the calendar server's internal port number.**

9. **Click Save.**

Enabling web calendars

If you've already configured web collaboration services, you can enable web calendars for individual users as well as group calendars associated with a group wiki.

To enable web calendars for a website, follow these steps:

1. **Launch Server Admin and then connect to the desired server.**

2. **Select the web service and then click Sites on the toolbar.**

3. **Click the Web Services tab, shown in Figure 26.5.**

4. **Enable collaboration services for the selected site by using the check boxes for:**
   - **Wikis.** To enable support for user-edited wiki websites
   - **Calendar.** To enable web access to iCal Server data

5. **Click Save.** User and group web calendars are now enabled.

Access user web calendars for any user accounts with the iCal service at `http://www.example.com/ical/`.

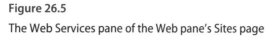

Figure 26.5

The Web Services pane of the Web pane's Sites page

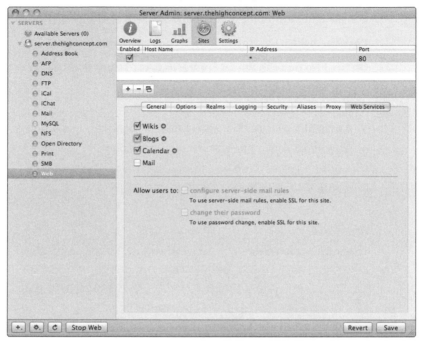

Group calendars are created and enabled within the administrative settings configuration of a group wiki. Once enabled, the group's web calendar is subsequently available at `http://www.example.com/groups/`*group-name*`/calendar/`.

Creating location and resource calendars

Location and resource calendars are created and configured within Snow Leopard Server's iCal Server Utility (formerly called Directory.app in Leopard Server), a component of Apple's Server administration tools.

You can reserve locations and equipment by including the corresponding special calendars in a meeting invitation's attendee list. Both can be configured to auto-accept meeting requests, enabling up-to-date availability reporting as users book them.

Once defined, users can create meeting invitations that specify a single location and multiple resources, along with other individual attendees. If configured to auto-accept meeting invitations, any request to book a location or resource automatically schedules the event in the calendar associated with those items, and those reservations are visible to other users browsing the location's or resource's availability.

To create a location in iCal Server Utility, follow these steps:

1. **Launch iCal Server Utility.** You must have administrative privileges on the directory domain and have your system bound to the directory as a Network Account Server.

2. **Click the Add (+) button and then choose New Location.**

3. **On the Info pane shown in Figure 26.6, configure the location's details to include:**
   - A unique name and an optional graphic icon
   - A primary contact for the location
   - A map to the location. Maps are created separately in iCal Server Utility.
   - An address and phone number for the location
   - A building name, floor, and seating capacity for the location
   - A note field of additional details

Figure 26.6

Creating a location record in iCal Server Utility

4. **Click Save.** The location record is saved in the directory, and a new calendar is created to schedule events that users associate with it. The location name auto-resolves for users scheduling it as the location for a new event.

To create a resource in iCal Server Utility, follow these steps:

1. Launch iCal Server Utility. You must have administrative privileges on the directory domain and have your system bound to the directory as a Network Account Server.

2. Click the Add (+) button and then choose New Resource.

3. On the Info pane shown in Figure 26.7, configure the resource's details to include:

- A unique name and an optional graphic icon
- A resource type and description field. Types can include automobile, conference phone, copier, digital camera, notebook, printer, projector or projection screen, scanner, or video camera.
- An owner for the resource
- A map to the resource. Maps are created separately in iCal Server Utility.
- An address for the resource
- A note field of additional details

Figure 26.7

Creating a resource record in iCal Server Utility

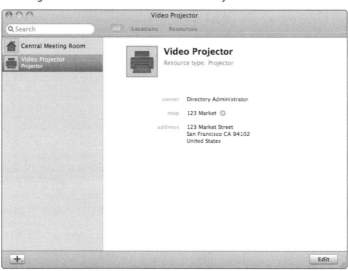

4. Click Save. The resource record is saved in the directory, and a new calendar is created to schedule events that users associate with it. The resource name auto-resolves for users scheduling it as an attendee in a new event.

Assigning maps to location and resource records

Custom maps can be created in iCal Server Utility to help users find the location of conference rooms or equipment within a campus or floor plan.

To create a map in iCal Server Utility, follow these steps:

1. Launch iCal Server Utility. You must have administrative privileges on the directory domain and have your system bound to the directory as a Network Account Server.

2. Choose File ⇨ Edit Maps. The Edit Maps window, shown in Figure 26.8, opens.

Figure 26.8

Creating a map in iCal Server Utility

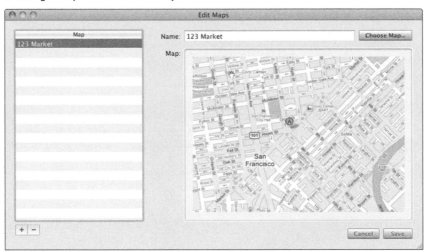

3. Click the Add (+) button to define a new map using a unique name.

4. Click the Choose Map button and then choose any image file. This can be a Google map screenshot or custom artwork representing a campus or building floor plan.

5. Click Save. The map record is saved in the directory and can be attached to location or resource records.

To assign and configure a map for a location or resource, follow these steps:

1. Launch iCal Server Utility. You must have administrative privileges on the directory domain and have your system bound to the directory as a Network Account Server.

2. Choose a location or resource record, click the Edit button, and then assign the record a defined map from the pop-up menu.

3. Click the Detail button to open the Map editor, shown in Figure 26.9.

Figure 26.9

Configuring a map in iCal Server Utility

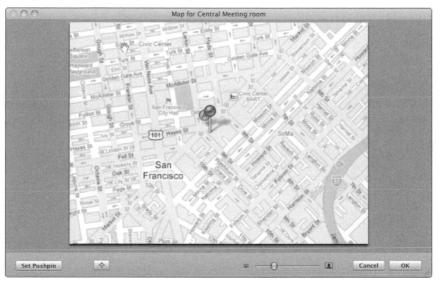

4. Click the Set Pushpin button to mark a specific location on the map and then use the Zoom control to arrange the graphic placement of the map as desired.

5. Click OK. When a user clicks on the map link within a location or resource record, the associated map is shown with the pushpin location defined by the administrator. The user can zoom in and out as desired.

Using iCal Server calendars within iCal

Once iCal Server is configured to begin serving calendars, you can configure desktop clients running iCal or an equivalent CalDAV calendar client to either:

- Subscribe to a read-only view of a user or group calendar maintained by the iCal service
- Synchronize edits to a server calendar in both directions by setting up a calendar server account

To subscribe to a calendar hosted by iCal Server, follow these steps:

1. **Navigate to a user's web calendar at** `www.example.com/ical/` **or select the group calendar associated with a wiki at** `www.example.com/groups/` `wikiname/calendar/.`

2. **Click the Information button, which appears when you mouse over the calendar name.** The Calendar Settings dialog box, shown in Figure 26.10, opens.

Figure 26.10

Subscribing to a server calendar from the web interface

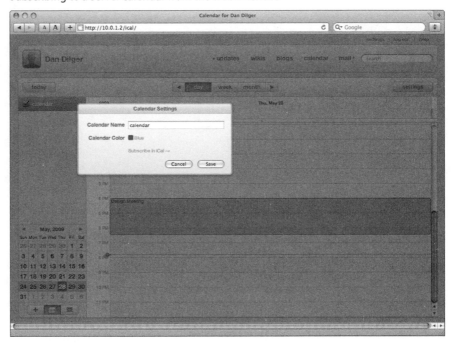

3. **Click the Subscribe in iCal link.** The hyperlink launches iCal, and the calendar is subscribed as read-only. The hyperlink for a user calendar follows this format: `webcal://www.example.com:8008/calendars/__uids__/659F1BE8-` `F6C2-4847-BCAC-0C11D0D33D6F/calendar.` The hyperlink for a group calendar associated with a wiki follows this format: `webcal://www.example.com:` `8008/calendars/__uids__/wiki-wikiname/calendar.`

4. **Authenticate to the server by using your network account.** The selected server calendar appears in iCal under Subscriptions, and it's read-only.

To configure a subscribed calendar hosted by iCal Server, follow these steps:

1. Launch iCal.

2. Right-click on the subscribed calendar name and then choose Get Info from the pop-up menu. The sheet shown in Figure 26.11 appears.

Figure 26.11

The iCal info sheet for a subscribed calendar

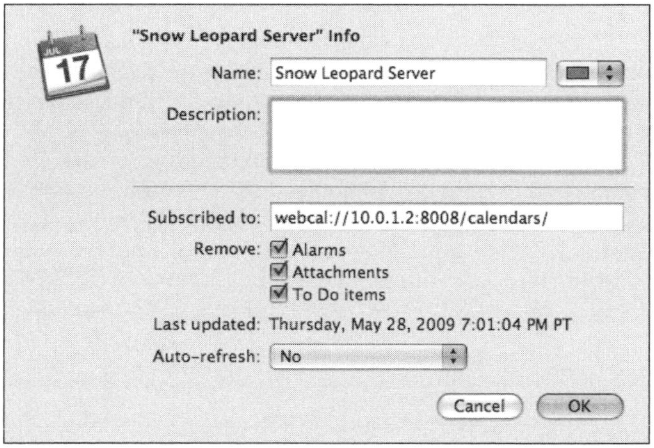

3. Set the desired auto-refresh period. The default is no refresh; options include every 5 minutes, every 15 minutes, or every hour, day, or week.

4. Optionally, choose a unique color and name for the subscribed calendar display.

5. Click OK.

To configure iCal to synchronize with a calendar hosted by iCal Server, follow these steps:

1. Launch iCal, open Preferences, and then click Accounts.

2. Click the Add (+) button to display the server configuration assistant sheet.

3. Using Mac OS X Snow Leopard, set the account type to Automatic and then type your email and password or choose CalDAV as the account type, as shown in Figure 26.12, and then provide:

- The username and password for the network account on the server
- The address of the calendar server

If the client computer is connected to the Open Directory domain as a Network Account Server in the Accounts pane of System Preferences, the CalDAV account setup assistant automatically configures the iCal Server account. Mac OS X Leopard iCal 3.0 users must provide:

- A Description name for your server calendar
- The username and password for the network account on the server

The user must log in to web collaboration services, open his or her calendar, click the information icon next to his or her calendar name, and then copy the URL link provided to Subscribe in iCal. The subscription link provided follows this format: `webcal://www.example.com:8008/calendars/__uids__/659F1BE8-F6C2-4847-BCAC-0C11D0D33D6F/calendar`. If you simply click this link, the calendar is subscribed as read-only in iCal after the user authenticates with his or her account and password. To fully synchronize with the server calendar, the user must take the UID number from the webcal hyperlink above and use it in an HTTP- or HTTPS-formatted account URL. If SSL isn't enabled on the iCal Server and with the default port assignment configured in Server Admin, it follows this format: `http://www.example.com:8008/principals/__uids__/659F1BE8-F6C2-4847-BCAC-0C11D0D33D6F/`. With SSL enabled by using the default port assignment, it uses this format: `https://www.example.com:8443/principals/__uids__/659F1BE8-F6C2-4847-BCAC-0C11D0D33D6F/`

Figure 26.12

iCal Server account setup in iCal

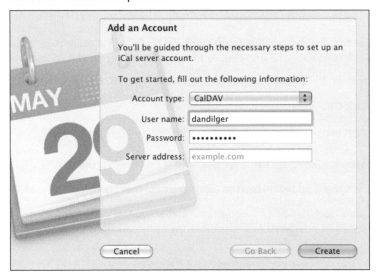

4. **Click Add to set up the iCal Server account in the iCal client.** The iCal Server config-uration is listed in the Accounts pane of iCal Preferences. The selected CalDAV account's server calendars now appear in iCal's list of calendars under the description assigned to them, as distinguished from local or MobileMe calendars, Delegate calen-dars, or any `.ics` Subscriptions. Events in synchronized iCal Server calendars can be freely edited, and any changes are reflected in the web calendar and on other CalDAV clients, such as the Calendar app in iPhone 3.0. Changes made elsewhere are also pushed to iCal.

To configure settings for a calendar synchronized with iCal Server, follow these steps:

1. **Launch iCal, open Preferences, and then click Accounts.**

2. **Configure Availability from the Account Information pane, shown in Figure 26.13.** The default setting is weekdays from 8 a.m. to 6 p.m. Use the Custom radio but-ton to set up an availability schedule of specific hours for given days of the week.

Figure 26.13

Configuring server account settings in iCal

3. **Set a refresh period.** The default is Push, which updates events by using the push notification service. Other options include manually, every minute, or every 5, 15, or 30 minutes.

To create additional server calendars synchronized with iCal Server, follow these steps:

1. Launch iCal.

2. Select your server calendar from the list.

3. Add a new calendar by using the Add (+) button. Name the calendar. Your new server-side calendar is also visible within the web calendar view. Additional calendars may also be created from the web interface. Each can be selectively viewed from iCal, the web interface, or another WebDAV client.

To send a meeting invitation by using iCal Server, follow these steps:

1. Launch iCal or open the web calendar interface.

2. Create a new event, open the event detail, shown in iCal in Figure 26.14, and then assign the new event:

- A location, which should auto-resolve from the directory

- Names of attendees you want to invite. Directory users auto-resolve. External users may also be invited by their email addresses.

- Resources you want to reserve, which are invited as attendees. These should similarly auto-resolve from the directory.

- Any files you want to make available to all invited attendees.

Figure 26.14

iCal event details for a meeting invitation

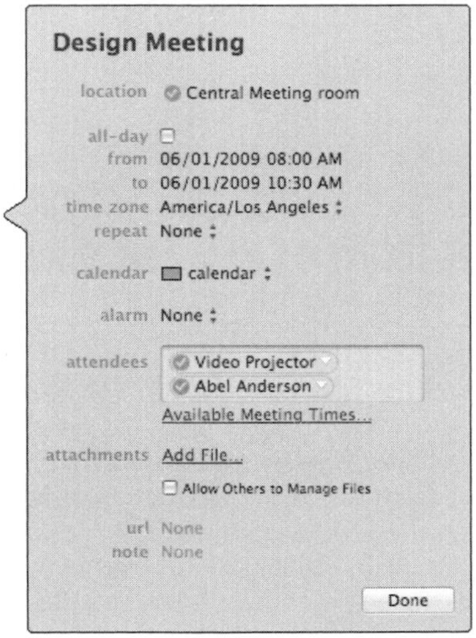

3. **Click the Available Meeting Times link to view free/busy information for the selected location, attendees, and any resources.** A display of availability information as it appears in iCal is shown in Figure 26.15, and a similar display of availability within the web calendar is shown in Figure 26.16.

Figure 26.15

iCal availability information for invited attendees, the location, and resources

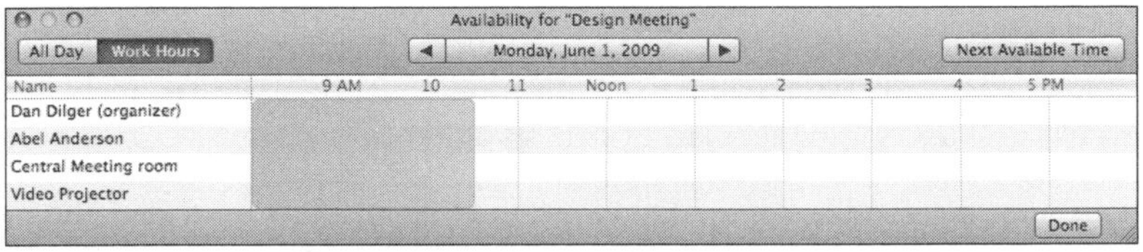

Figure 26.16

Web availability information for invited attendees, the location, and resources

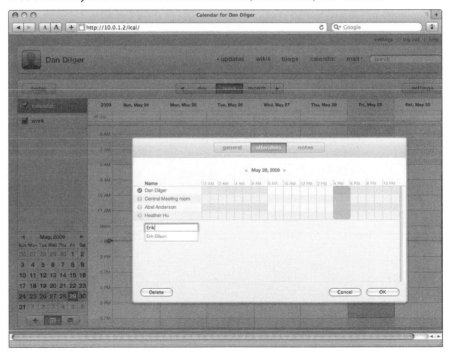

4. **Click Done.** Invitations are sent to all listed attendees, who can then respond as accepting, declining, or tentatively accepting (with maybe). Associated locations and resources configured to auto-accept invitations will book the event in their calendars. Updates made to the event are sent to invited users, and responses from invited users are reflected within the event details.

Access control for users and groups

User privileges to create calendars can be configured in Server Admin by using an SACL. Once a user is granted iCal service access and has created an account, that user has full access to modify events within the calendar and to create additional calendars. He or she may then delegate access to other users to either view or edit his or her calendars.

Similarly, group calendars are enabled from the wiki interface, and all delegation and access control is also done with the web client interface. There's no calendar delegation control within Server Admin.

To limit access to the iCal service in Server Admin, follow these steps:

1. **From Server Admin, select the server name of the calendar server.**

2. **Click Settings and then click the Access tab, shown in Figure 26.17.**

Figure 26.17

Configuring access to the iCal service in Server Admin

3. **From the Services pane, select the iCal service from the left column.**

4. **Click the Allow only users and groups below radio button above the right column.**

5. **Click the Add (+) button.** The Users & Groups sheet opens.

6. **Drag users or groups to the access list on the right to define users who can have calendar access.**

7. **Click Save.**

To delegate access to your server calendar from iCal, follow these steps:

1. **Launch iCal, open Preferences, and then click Accounts.**

2. **Click the Delegation tab, shown in Figure 26.18.**

Figure 26.18

Reviewing your delegate access to other server calendars in iCal

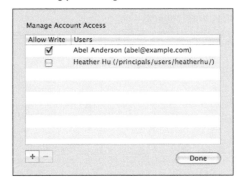

3. **Click the Edit button.** The sheet shown in Figure 26.19 drops down.

4. **To create a new delegate, click the Add (+) button and then type the username of the user to whom you want to delegate maintenance of your account's personal calendars on the server.**

5. **Click the check box for Allow Write to enable full editing access to your calendars by the selected delegate user.** The default privilege is read-only access.

6. **Click Done.** The selected user is now able to access all your server calendars. You can't selectively delegate access only to specific calendars associated with an account.

To view your delegate access to server calendars from iCal, follow these steps:

1. **Launch iCal, open Preferences, and then click Accounts.**

2. **Click the Delegation tab.**

3. **Review the Accounts I can access section.** Users who have delegated access of their calendars to you are listed, along with the level of privileges, either read-only or read and write.

4. **To view delegated calendars in iCal, click the Show check box for any of the users who have delegated you access.** Their server calendars appear in the calendar listing under Delegates in iCal.

5. **To selectively enable viewing of specific delegated calendars, click the check box next to the user and any desired calendars associated with that user's iCal Server account.**

Figure 26.19

Configuring delegate access to your calendar in iCal

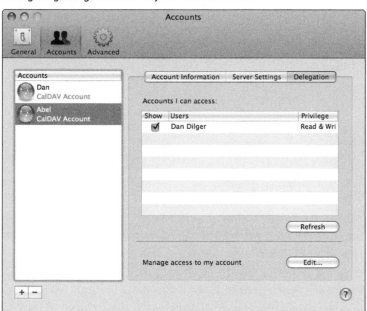

Calendar service security

Security for calendaring services can be enhanced in three ways:

- Limiting outside access to your calendar server by using firewall rules
- Limiting access to the iCal service to specific users and groups
- Implementing SSL security on your calendar server and web collaboration website to enable encrypted authentication and secure transport

To enable SSL security for the iCal service, follow these steps:

1. **Launch Server Admin and then connect to the desired server.**

2. **Select the iCal service and then click Settings on the toolbar.**

3. **Click the Authentication tab.**

4. **Choose the authentication type from the pop-up menu.** The options are:

- **Kerberos.** Strong encryption requiring Kerberos v5 support on the server
- **Digest (RFC 2617).** Sends secure login names and encrypted passwords without requiring a configured Kerberos realm
- **Any Method.** Uses either Kerberos or Digest authentication depending on which the client chooses

5. **Type an SSL port number and certificate identity for iCal Server.** Alternatively, configure the Mobile Access service to enable secure remote access to external users using SSL and then supply that service with the calendar server's internal port number.

6. **Click Save.**

Managing and Monitoring iCal Server

iCal Server only presents a limited user interface in Server Admin, so ongoing maintenance is mostly limited to monitoring its logs for error conditions or troubleshooting.

Monitoring iCal service logs

iCal Server error and access logs are available from the Logs page of the iCal pane, shown in Figure 26.20, which presents a listing of the events related to both web calendar users and mobile and desktop client access:

- The Calendar Server Log, located at `/var/log/caldavd/access.log`
- The Calendar Server Error Log, located at `/var/log/caldavd/error.log`

Figure 26.20

The Logs page of the iCal pane

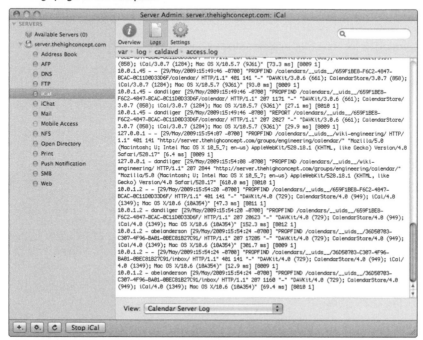

Monitoring push notification logs

Push Notification Server logs are available from the Logs page of the Push Notification pane, shown in Figure 26.21, which presents a listing of the events related to the Push Notification Server and the XMPP Server used to deliver notifications:

- The Push Notification Server Error Log, located at `/var/log/idavoll/error.log`
- The XMPP Server Log, located at `/var/log/system.log`

Figure 26.21

The Logs page of the Push Notification pane

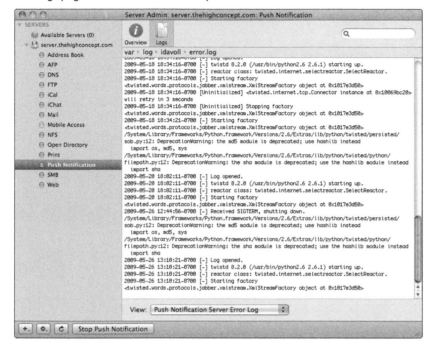

Summary

- iCal Server 2 in Snow Leopard Server provides individual and group calendars that can be accessed from the web calendar interface, the desktop iCal, and other desktop clients and mobile devices that support CalDAV, an open, interoperable specification for collaborative calendaring.

- Web calendar features depend on the web service as well as web collaboration services and wiki settings.

- iCal Server is enabled and configured within the iCal pane of Server Admin, but many calendar creation and delegation features are performed entirely within the calendar client interface.

- Calendar users can delegate access to another user to enable the delegate to view or edit all the calendars associated with their accounts.

- Snow Leopard Server's calendars support events involving location and resource assignments, attendee invitations, and shared file attachments. Users are sent an invitation they can accept or decline, and their availability and acceptance status are tracked and updated within the event. Meeting changes are updated to all attendees.

- Calendars hosted by the iCal service can be subscribed to as read-only by clients supporting iCalendar subscriptions or synchronized bi-directionally to CalDAV clients, such as Mac OS X's iCal, the iPhone 3.0 Calendar, or third-party calendar clients that support the CalDAV specification.

iChat Services

M ac OS X Server's iChat Server debuted in Tiger Server as a standards-based instant messaging solution for workgroups.

Although Apple's original iChat client was designed primarily to be interoperable with AOL's proprietary Instant Messenger service and only offered limited support for open instant messaging over the local network by using Bonjour, iChat Server and the latest iChat client for the Mac OS X desktop have embraced Jabber, which uses the open, interoperable XMPP.

The use of XMPP has enabled Apple's Jabber-savvy iChat client to work with Google Talk and other chat services built by using XMPP as well as making iChat Server compatible with a variety of alternative chat clients supporting the protocol.

In contrast, the proprietary instant messaging protocols used by AIM, Yahoo IM, and Microsoft's Windows Live Messenger all require some type of an external gateway to interact with each other, just like the old days of email, where CompuServe, The Source, and GEnie each provided mail messaging services to their own users, but they were incompatible with each other.

Back then, mail services first opened Internet gateways and then began providing standard Internet email services. Jabber's XMPP was designed to do the same for instant messaging today, enabling organizations to set up Jabber IM servers that can federate with each other's XMPP messaging servers to distribute users' instant messages across domains.

In addition to being able to send instant messages, XMPP also addresses the key enabling technology behind IM: presence information, which shows when users are online and available to receive an instant message, commonly presented as a buddy list.

iChat supports AOL's proprietary OSCAR presence information, automatic local network presence discovery by using Bonjour, and the presence information relayed by Jabber XMPP servers.

iChat client software also uses this presence information for Jabber text chats as well as for setting up multi-user audio and video conferencing sessions, instant document transfers, and screen-sharing sessions.

In This Chapter

Introduction
to iChat Server

Planning iChat services

iChat Server setup
and configuration

Managing and
monitoring iChat services

However, audio and video transmissions are sent via SIP (Session Initiation Protocol) rather than Jabber, and iChat Server similarly doesn't play a role in performing screen sharing between iChat clients.

iChat Server enables iChat users and other XMPP clients to authenticate against Open Directory and optionally Kerberos for instant messaging chats between local users; browse presence information; and relay messages to users connected to other instant messaging servers via support for server-to-server federation with other Jabber servers.

This chapter describes how Apple's iChat Server works, what's involved in planning instant messaging, how it's configured, and how to maintain and monitor the service.

Introduction to iChat Server

Snow Leopard Server's use of the open, interoperable XMPP specification as the basis for its instant messaging services enables it to fit into the plans of large organizations interested in deploying solutions that aren't tied to a single technology provider.

Previously, companies looking for an instant messaging service product would need to either use an outside, consumer-oriented service — few of which provide much in the way of security — or invest in a proprietary package that offered local instant messaging features.

The premise of Jabber's XMPP is to open up interoperability so individual vendors can compete to deliver better solutions and still cooperate to allow those offerings to work together.

Additionally, iChat Server's use of the increasingly popular XMPP standard means that users can have some assurance that an investment in Apple's instant messaging services isn't wholly dependent on the company's own internal development efforts but that outside development can and will be incorporated into Apple's Mac OS X Server offerings.

A standards-based architecture

The iChat service in Mac OS X Server builds on a variety of documented, standard protocols and document formats, each of which is codified in IETF RFC documents or by the XMPP Standards Foundation as XEPs (XMPP Extension Protocols). This results in a known, familiar architecture built on proven technologies:

- XMPP (RFC 3920) serves as the distribution protocol for transferring and routing small messages as XML data for real-time chat and to deliver presence discovery between iChat Server and iChat clients. Jabber is the brand name applied to an implementation of the standard.
- MultiUser Chat (XEP-0045) is the protocol used to enable multi-user text chats, implemented by the Jabber MU module.
- PubSub (XEP-0060) is the protocol used by the push notification service for publishing changes in iCal Server and the mail service to mobile clients.

- SOCKS5 Bytestreams (XEP-0065) is the protocol used to send direct binary file transfers between chat clients, either directly or through the Jabber Proxy65 module.
- TLS (RFC 5246) serves as the cryptographic protocol for providing security and data integrity between the iChat Server and clients and between federated XMPP servers.

Additionally, Apple integrates iChat Server with Mac OS X Server's Open Directory and Kerberos for authentication. This enables iChat Server to fit into larger organizations that use directory systems that Open Directory can integrate into, such as Active Directory or other LDAP systems.

iChat Server's instant messaging features

Snow Leopard Server's iChat Server provides easy access to a variety of instant messaging features, including:

- Presence information for populating and updating buddy lists, including an auto-buddy feature for adding newly created users to existing users' buddy lists
- C2S (client to server) chats between local users
- Direct file exchange between users or relayed through the iChat Server file transfer proxy to enable sending files through firewalls
- S2S (server-to-server) federations between XMPP IM servers
- Encrypted chats and federation traffic by using TLS/SSL
- Archiving of user chats
- MU (multi-user) chat rooms that enable groups of users to participate in server-hosted discussion chats

Federating instant messaging servers

iChat Server can be configured to federate with other iChat Servers or other XMPP-compliant servers or services, including Google Talk, by using the server-to-server (S2S) federation features of XMPP. This enables users with accounts on the local iChat Server to exchange text messages or files with users with Jabber accounts on another domain.

To set up federations with other XMPP services on outside domains, servers must be configured to establish mutual connections with each other, negotiating the level of communication security desired for communications between the servers.

iChat Server can be set up to require that all sessions with federated instant messaging servers use SSL encryption and block any sessions with servers that don't support encryption. To establish encrypted sessions, both servers must supply public-key certificates, either self-signed or signed by a recognized Certificate Authority.

CROSS-REF
For more on working with certificate identities in Server Admin, see Chapter 9.

iChat Server and push notifications

Snow Leopard Server's iChat Server also acts as the engine that drives the Push Notification Server, which is used to efficiently update clients and, in particular, mobile devices about event changes in their calendars and address books by using XMPP Publish and Subscribe technology.

For the push notification service to work, iChat Server must be configured and running, and the Notification User must be granted access to the iChat service in Server Admin.

CROSS-REF
For more on push notification, see Chapter 33.

Planning iChat Services

Initial setup of iChat services involves some initial planning to take care of a few prerequisite steps. You need:

- A registered domain name for your server and a properly configured DNS that enables reverse lookup of the server
- A firewall configuration that allows clients to access iChat Server over the designated ports used for instant messaging:
  - TCP/UPD 5190 iChat XMPP text instant messaging and file transfers
  - TCP 5220, 5222 iChat Server without SSL (now commonly used with TLS)
  - TCP 5223 iChat Server with SSL
  - TCP 5269 iChat Server server-to-server federation
  - UDP 5297, 5298, 5353, 5678 iChat Bonjour local discovery
  - TCP 5298 iChat Bonjour local discovery
  - TCP 7777 iChat Server file transfer proxy

  iChat also uses a variety of additional ports for its video-conferencing features:
  - UDP 16384-16403 RTP and RTCP (Real-time Transport Protocol and RTP Control Protocol) for packet delivery of audio/video-conferencing content and to monitor data transmission statistics and quality of service, respectively
  - UDP 5060 SIP (Session Initiation Protocol) for signaling and controlling audio/video-conferencing content
- User accounts for instant messenger clients stored in Open Directory or an Active Directory system configured to integrate with the server

Other instant messaging server plans you need to address include ensuring you have enough disk space to accommodate chat archives, if they're enabled. Archived messages are saved to `/var/jabberd/message_archives` and can be archived every set number of days to save space.

Because the default location for saving chat messages is on the server's boot drive, you may need to plan to relocate archives to provide sufficient storage to meet your organization's needs.

iChat Service Setup and Configuration

To configure instant messaging services from Server Admin, first enable the iChat service within the desired server's listing of configured services and then do the following:

- Configure the service.
- Configure iChat clients.
- Configure client access to the service.
- Turn the service on.

Enabling iChat services

Setting up instant messaging services requires activating the iChat service, configuring service settings, and then configuring client systems to work with the service.

To enable iChat service configuration in Server Admin, follow these steps:

1. **Launch Server Admin and then connect to the desired server.**
2. **Select the server listing and then click Settings on the toolbar.**
3. **Click the Services tab.**
4. **Click the check box for iChat.**
5. **Click Save.** iChat should now appear in the list of configurable services for the selected server, as shown in Figure 27.1.

Configuring iChat service settings

The iChat service needs to be configured to support domain names on the server, requires settings for authentication and SSL security and federation with other servers, and can be set up to log events as desired.

Figure 27.1

Enabling the iChat pane in Server Admin

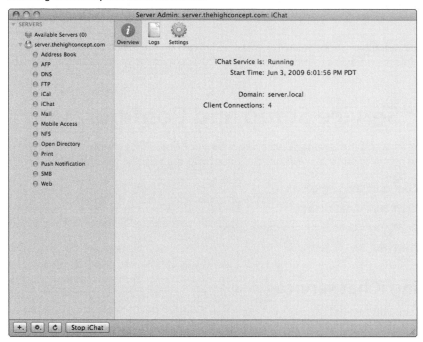

To configure iChat services, follow these steps:

1. **Launch Server Admin and then connect to the desired server.**

2. **Select the iChat service and then click Settings on the toolbar.**

3. **Click the General tab, shown in Figure 27.2.**

4. **Define host domains by adding them to the list.** iChat Server can host multiple domain names, with each virtual host supported as a Jabber realm. To log in to and interact with the server, users supply a Jabber ID, which pairs their username and realm similarly to an email address, in the format user@realm.

5. **Set the authentication method for users.** Options include:

   ● **Standard.** Allows only password authentication

   ● **Kerberos.** Allows authentication only by using an Open Directory master enabled to support Kerberos or another Kerberos realm; this must match the name of the Jabber realm being served

   ● **Any Method.** Accepts both password and Kerberos authentication

Figure 27.2

Configuring the iChat service in Server Admin

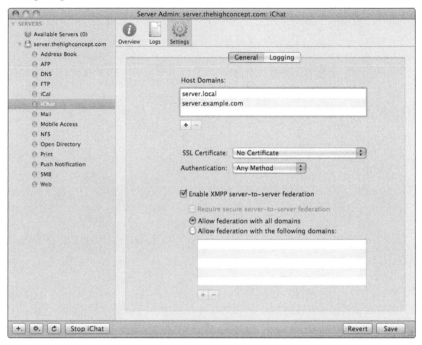

6. **Choose an SSL certificate to be used from the pop-up menu for server-to-server and server-to-client encryption.**

7. **Click the check box to enable XMPP server-to-server federation.**

8. **Optionally, click the check box to require federation to use SSL security.** Any XMPP servers that don't support SSL security can't connect to your server.

9. **Select server-to-server federation to allow local users to chat either with users on any other domains or with users only on the explicit list of domains provided.** Any XMPP servers from domains not on this list can't connect to your server.

10. **Click Save.**

To configure iChat service message logging, follow these steps:

1. **Launch Server Admin and then connect to the desired server.**

2. **Select the iChat service and then click Settings on the toolbar.**

3. **Click the Logging tab, shown in Figure 27.3.**

Figure 27.3

The Logging pane of the Settings page of Server Admin's iChat pane

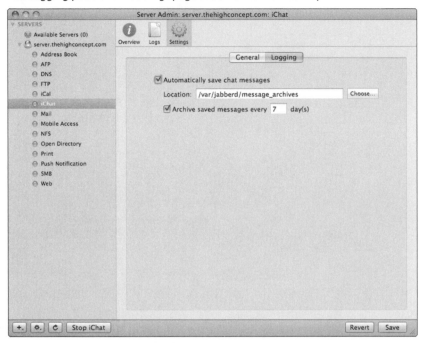

4. **Click the check box to enable chat message logging.**

5. **Specify a file system location for saving message transcripts.** The default location is `/var/jabberd/message_archives`. Click the Choose button to change this.

6. **Click the check box to enable archiving saved messages every set number of days.**

7. **Click Save.**

Configuring iChat Server from iChat

Once iChat Server is up and running, you can configure desktop clients running iChat or an equivalent XMPP chat client to connect to the server using their Jabber ID.

To connect to iChat Server from iChat, follow these steps:

1. **Open iChat and then choose Preferences.**

2. **Click Accounts on the toolbar.**

3. **Click the Add (+) button.** From the account setup sheet that drops down, shown in Figure 27.4, do the following:

- Choose Jabber as the Account Type from the pop-up menu.
- Type a full Jabber ID as the Account Name. This is formatted as username@realm.
- Type the account's password.
- Optionally, type a server name and port used by the iChat Server and then select the use of SSL and Kerberos. These settings aren't necessary if the server being configured is on the local network.

Figure 27.4

Creating an iChat Server account in iChat

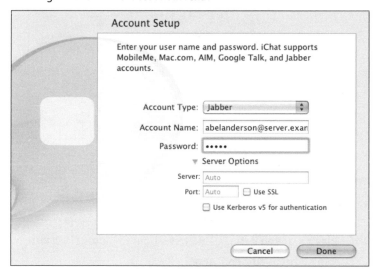

4. **Click Done.** The selected server is configured as a Jabber account in iChat. A buddy list opens and a presence status can be configured.

To configure the iChat Server account in iChat, follow these steps:

1. **Open iChat and then choose Preferences.**

2. **Click Accounts on the toolbar.**

3. **Select the Jabber account linked to iChat Server.** Under the Account Information tab, shown in Figure 27.5, you can:

- Enable the account as active.
- Set the account to log in automatically when iChat is opened.
- Provide a custom description for the account list.

Figure 27.5

Configuring an iChat Server account in iChat

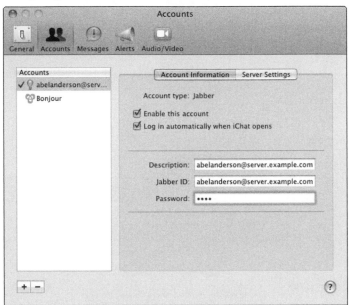

4. **Under the Server Settings tab, you can:**
   - Modify the server name and port.
   - Set the account to use SSL encryption.
   - Display a warning if the password is about to be sent in cleartext.
   - Enable Kerberos authentication.
   - Set a location for the client, which is by default set to the client computer name.

5. **Click Done.**

Populating iChat buddy lists from iChat Server

After setting up accounts to use iChat Server, iChat users previously needed to manually add other users in the organization to their buddy lists unless the Auto Buddy List feature was enabled, a feature that adds other directory users to their buddy lists and updates this as accounts are created or removed from the directory.

In Snow Leopard Server, Auto Buddy is enabled by default.

To obtain details of the current Auto Buddy iChat service configuration, follow these steps:

1. **Open Terminal.**

2. **Type** sudo serveradmin settings jabber**.**

3. **Type an administrative password.**

4. **A listing of detailed service configuration settings is returned, including the settings presented in the Server Admin graphical interface as well as those that aren't, including the status of the Auto Buddy feature indicated in the line** `jabber:enableAutoBuddy = yes`**.**

Creating multi-user chat conferences

iChat Server is configured to automatically host multi-user chats, commonly referred to as conference rooms or chat rooms. From iChat, users only need to specify a chat room name. The server automatically confirms the room and allows the user to invite additional users.

Each invited user is sent a request to join the room. Conferences are handled through a sub-domain based on the primary Jabber realm of the iChat Server, so a server named `server.example.com` also needs a secondary DNS entry pointing to it named `conference.server.example.com` in order to support conference rooms.

If you don't have the capacity to create your own DNS subdomain, you should be able to use local link addressing, such as `server.local`, for your primary Jabber realm. However, using a local link address restricts the use of multi-user conferences to users within the local subnet.

To create a multi-user chat room in iChat, follow these steps:

1. **Open iChat.**

2. **From the File menu, choose Go to Chat Room.**

3. **Choose your Jabber account from the pop-up menu, type a Room Name, and then click Go.** A new chat window opens, and it reports an automatic confirmation for the room:

   ```
   This room is locked from entry until configuration is
       confirmed.
   Configuration confirmed: This room is now unlocked.
   ```

4. **Drag users from your buddy list to the chat room's drawer to invite them.**

5. **Invited users receive an invitation message in iChat.** If the inviting user is `dandilger` and the chat room is named `artgroup`, the invite states:

```
Invitation
You have been invited to the artgroup@conference.server.
    example.com room by artgroup@conference.server.example.
    com/dandilger
Reason: Please join me in this chat.
```

6. **Users can accept the invite and participate in the group chat.** The room continues in existence as participants enter and leave until the last user exits. If a user attempts to create a new room using the name of a room already in use, they simply join the existing group chat.

Access control for users and groups

Access to the iCal service can be configured in Server Admin by using a SACL. In addition to the users and groups granted chat access from the iChat service, a Notification User must also be allowed access to enable the push notification service to work.

To limit access to the iChat service in Server Admin, follow these steps:

1. **From Server Admin, select the server name of the calendar server.**

2. **Click Settings on the toolbar and then click the Access tab, shown in Figure 27.6.**

3. **Under the Services tab within Access, select the iChat service from the left column.**

4. **Click the Allow only users and groups below radio button above the right column.**

5. **Click the Add (+) button.** The Users & Groups sheet opens.

6. **Drag users or groups to the access list on the right to define users who can have instant messenger access.**

7. **Click Save.**

iChat Server security

Security for instant messaging services can be enhanced in a variety of ways:

- Limiting outside access to your iChat Server using firewall rules
- Limiting access to the iChat service to specific users and groups
- Implementing SSL security for client connections to enable encrypted authentication and secure transport for client-to-server chats
- Implementing and requiring SSL security for federated server connections to ensure encrypted authentication and secure transport for server-to-server communications

Figure 27.6

Configuring access to the iChat service in Server Admin

To enable SSL security for the iChat service, follow these steps:

1. **Launch Server Admin and then connect to the desired server.**

2. **Select the iChat service and then click Settings on the toolbar.**

3. **Click the General tab.**

4. **Select an SSL certificate to be used from the pop-up menu for server-to-server and server-to-client encryption.**

5. **Click the check box to enable XMPP server-to-server federation.**

6. **Optionally, click the check box to require federation to use SSL security.** Any XMPP servers that don't support SSL security can't connect to your server.

7. **Select server-to-server federation to work with any domains or with only the explicit list of domains provided.** Any XMPP servers from domains not in this list can't connect to your server.

8. **Click Save.**

Managing and Monitoring iChat Server

The Overview page of the iChat pane in Server Admin shows when the service was last started, the primary domain name being used as the Jabber realm, and the number of client connections, which includes the Push Notification Server's connection.

Monitoring iChat service logs

iChat Server error and access logs are available from the Logs page of the iChat pane in Server Admin, shown in Figure 27.7:

- The iChat Service Log, located at `/var/jabberd/log/access.log`
- The File Proxy Log, which tracks file transfers handled by the server, located at `/var/jabberd/log/proxy65.log`
- The Multiuser Conference Log, located at `/var/jabberd/log/mu-conference.log`

Figure 27.7

The Logs page in the iChat pane in Server Admin

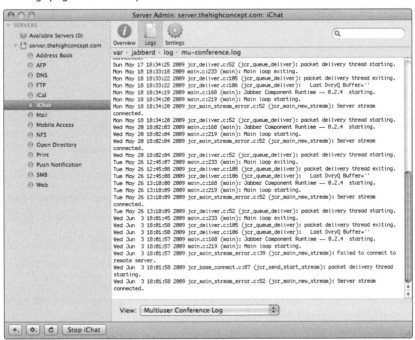

Monitoring push notification logs

Push Notification Server logs are available from the Logs page of the push notification pane in Server Admin, shown in Figure 27.8, which presents a listing of the events related to the Push Notification Server and the XMPP Server used to deliver notifications:

- The Push Notification Server Error Log, located at `/var/log/idavoll/error.log`
- The XMPP Server Log, located at `/var/log/system.log`

Figure 27.8

The Logs page in the Push Notification Server pane in Server Admin

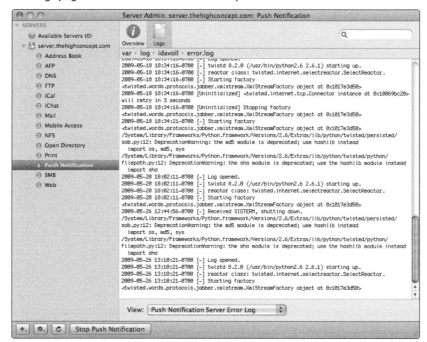

Summary

- iChat Server in Snow Leopard Server provides individual and group chat, handles file transfers through a proxy to enable users to send files through firewalls, and manages presence information reported by clients so other clients can see who's available.
- iCal Server provides standards-based messaging services designed to be interoperable with other XMPP Jabber clients and services.

- XMPP chats and presence information can be relayed across domains by using federation with other XMPP servers. iChat Server can federate with any domains or with a specifically outlined number of domains, optionally requiring SSL encryption to secure communications.

- The iChat service is also used to deliver push notification service messages to devices listening for mail and calendar updates by using its support for PubSub.

Address Book Server

A ddress Book Server is new to Snow Leopard Server. It serves as a centralized solution for sharing and synchronizing contacts — patterned after the calendar features of iCal Server — and provides a gateway to directory services to allow users to query for contact information by using mail, Address Book, or other client software.

Apple's Address Book Server software is largely built in Python by using the Twisted framework, just like iCal Server and the wiki and blog web collaboration services in Mac OS X Server are.

Mac OS X Server's Address Book Server is notable for being the first commercial calendar server implementing the CardDAV standard for interoperable contact publishing.

The CardDAV specification builds contact extensions into the WebDAV protocol, enabling a specialized web server to perform contact sharing.

With CardDAV support in the Address Book client on the Mac desktop, in iPhone 3.0 software for mobile devices, and in Mac OS X Server's Address Book Server, Apple delivers a consistent, open mechanism for contact sharing that's efficient and delivers security enhancements over sharing contact data by mixing it into the LDAP directory.

Although contact information can be copied into an LDAP directory for shared access, this imposes limits as to what data can be shared because either the LDAP schema must be modified to support the widest potential range of contact information users might want to maintain or complex client configuration is required to map data fields between the client and the directory on the server. Because clients can use different directory mappings, it's also easy for fields to be interpreted differently.

Using LDAP also requires giving users write access to portions of the directory. Because the directory maintains sensitive information, even a small mistake in access control configuration can result in the potential of a significant security breach.

CardDAV pairs the well-known, popular vCard format with the similarly well-documented WebDAV protocol to deliver a system that's easy to support even on limited mobile clients.

This chapter describes how Apple's Address Book Server works, what's involved in planning calendar services, how to configure the server, and how to maintain and monitor the services.

28 ▶ In This Chapter

Introduction to Address Book Server

Planning for Address Book services

Address Book Server setup and configuration

Managing and monitoring Address Book Server

Introduction to Address Book Server

Snow Leopard Server's use of the open, interoperable CardDAV specification as the basis for its contact-sharing services enhances its value to large organizations interested in deploying solutions that aren't tied to a single vendor. The premise of CardDAV is to open up interoperability so vendors can compete to deliver better solutions.

The web-based architecture of Address Book Server

Because CardDAV is based on WebDAV, Address Book Server acts as a specialized web server for accessing, publishing, and presenting contact data. This makes it easy to scale the service by using hardware load balancers designed to work with web servers.

The file-centric architecture that Address Book Server uses to store contact data allows for flexible storage options, is easier to back up and recover, and is less prone to unrecoverable corruption problems when compared to calendaring and messaging servers that store events in a huge database like Microsoft's Exchange Server does.

Instead of maintaining a massive, centralized database, Address Book Server uses flat files to store contact data in conventional vCard files within this default location: `/Library/AddressBookServer/Documents/`.

Access to contact data is managed by standard POSIX file system permissions and ACLs, which enable fine-grained access control. Backing up these files requires only basic support for retaining file system extended attributes, not a complex backup plug-in designed to interface with a proprietary backup API, as other contact management and messaging systems require.

For performance, the system uses individual SQLite databases to provide fast access to contact data stored in standard `.vcf` files. These databases can be deleted and are re-created as needed.

A standards-based architecture

The Address Book service in Mac OS X Server builds on a variety of documented, standard protocols and document formats, each of which are codified in IETF RFC documents. This results in a known, familiar architecture built on proven technologies:

- **HTTP (RFC 2616).** Serves as the distribution protocol for transferring events as resources between Address Book Server and contact clients
- **WebDAV (RFC 2518).** Address Book Server's protocol for reading and writing vCard contact files on the server
- **CardDAV (currently an IETF draft).** An extension of WebDAV designed to handle contact-specific features, such as server-side searching
- **vCard (RFC 2426).** The standard text format for describing contact items. Individual contacts are saved in `.vcf` files, and collections of these files are interpreted as address books.

Additionally, Apple integrates Address Book Server with Mac OS X Server's Open Directory and Kerberos for authentication and contact information. This enables Address Book Server to fit into larger organizations that use directory systems that Open Directory can integrate into, such as Active Directory or other LDAP systems.

Thanks to Address Book Server's gateway feature, network users can look up contact information for anyone listed in any of the directory services that the Address Book Server is bound to by using any client application that supports the standard Address Book API in Mac OS X. Querying directory service contact information does require Mac OS X 10.6 Snow Leopard versions of applications:

- Address Book 5.0 for querying directory service contacts
- Mail 4.0 for automatic lookup for email addresses
- iChat 5.0 for finding available users and groups

Other client applications that support the CardDAV protocol and the Address Book API should also work with Address Book Server.

Apple is also integrating Snow Leopard Server's Address Book Server with support for Mobile Access, which secures access to the contact server for mobile devices by using SSL rather than requiring users to set up a VPN session.

CROSS-REF

For more on Mobile Access, see Chapter 32.

Following the pattern of iCal with Address Book

Apple released its central Address Book in Mac OS X prior to the release of iCal, but both were based on emerging standards for data exchange:

- Address Book uses vCards to represent contact data
- iCal uses iCalendar files to represent event data

Both applications support the practice of publishing these standard data files to a central WebDAV server to enable other users to subscribe to them as an information feed in order to receive contact or calendar event updates.

Just as iCal Server extends this support to enable users to fully synchronize bi-directional changes to the event calendars among networked users, Snow Leopard Server similarly enables network users to publish personal and group address books of contacts to Address Book Server for access from multiple computers, including remote system and mobile devices.

Additionally, Apple is publishing Snow Leopard's Address Book Server code as an open-source project in parallel to the Darwin Calendar Server to help foster adoption of the new standard for contact management.

Planning for Address Book Services

Initial setup of calendar services involves some initial planning to take care of a few prerequisite steps. You need:

- A registered domain name for your server and a properly configured DNS that enables reverse lookup of the server
- A firewall configuration that allows clients to access the calendar server over the designated TCP port. By default, this is 8800 or 8443 for SSL connections. Mobile Access may be used to enable secure remote access to Address Book Server.
- User accounts for Address Book Server clients stored in Open Directory or an Active Directory system configured to integrate with the server or another LDAP directory with schema to support the Address Book service

Other Address Book Server issues you need to address include ensuring you have enough disk space to accommodate your users' needs. The stored vCard and SQLite files are small and don't need to use the general-purpose file attachments to calendar items in iCal Server. The size of graphic icons used in Address Book contact entries is also small.

Under the General tab of the Settings page of Server Admin's Address Book pane, shown in Figure 28.1, you can set a user quota on the size of individual users' address books, set by default to 100 MB, and change the address book data store to a different location from the default of `/Library/AddressBookServer/Documents/`.

Given that the default location of address book data is on the server's boot drive, you may need to plan to move the data store to a drive with sufficient storage to meet your organization's needs.

Address Book Server Setup and Configuration

To configure contact sharing services from Server Admin, first enable the Address Book service within the desired server's listing of configured services and then do the following:

- Configure the service.
- Configure Address Book clients.
- Configure client access to the service.
- Turn the service on.

Figure 28.1

The General pane of the Address Book pane

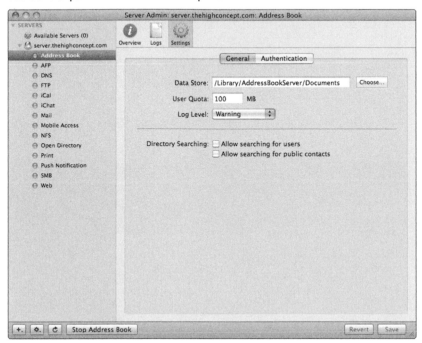

Enabling Address Book services

Setting up contact services requires activating the Address Book service, configuring service settings, and then configuring client systems to work with the service.

To enable Address Book service configuration in Server Admin, follow these steps:

1. **Launch Server Admin and then connect to the desired server.**

2. **Select the server listing and then click Settings on the toolbar.**

3. **Click the Services tab.**

4. **Click the check box for Address Book.**

5. **Click Save.** Address Book should now appear in the list of configurable services for the selected server, as shown in Figure 28.2.

Figure 28.2

Enabling the Address Book pane

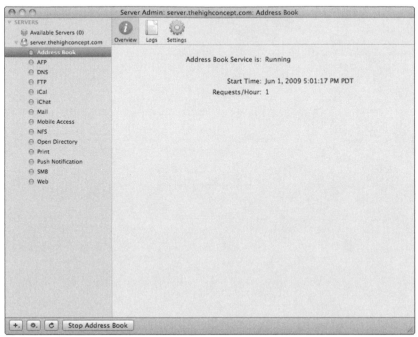

Configuring Address Book service settings

The Address Book service needs to be configured to specify the location of the server's data store, requires settings for authentication and SSL security, and can be set up to log events as desired.

If you're currently using shared contacts in Leopard Server, these can be imported in the new Address Book Server by using a supplied command-line tool.

To configure Address Book services, follow these steps:

1. **Launch Server Admin and then connect to the desired server.**

2. **Click Address Book and then click Settings on the toolbar.**

3. **Click the General tab.**

4. **Set the data store location that will contain all users' and groups' contact data.**
The default location is `/Library/AddressBookServer/Documents/`. To specify a different location on another server, you need to use its local file system mount point instead of providing a network URL.

5. **Set the user quota level, which limits the total size of all the address book records a user can store on the server.** This quota applies to all users. There's no limit on the number of individual contacts a user can maintain as long as the quota isn't exceeded.

6. **Set the desired logging level.**

7. **Configure directory search for users and for public contacts by clicking these check boxes:**

- **Allow searching for users.** Activates the directory service gateway that enables users to query for users' contact information across any of the directory servers the Address Book Server is bound to

- **Allow searching for public contacts.** Allows access to public users from Directory. app in Mac OS X Leopard Server 10.5

8. **Click Save.**

To configure Address Book service authentication, follow these steps:

1. **Launch Server Admin and then connect to the desired server.**

2. **Click Address Book and then click Settings on the toolbar.**

3. **Click the Authentication tab, shown in Figure 28.3.**

Figure 28.3

The Authentication pane of the Settings page of the Address Book pane

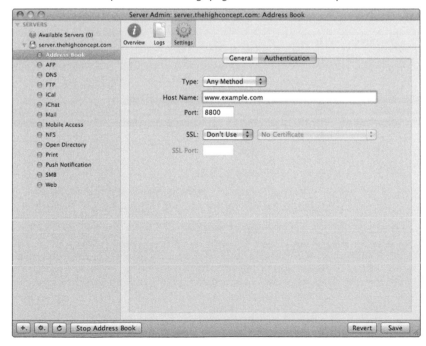

4. **Choose the authentication type from the pop-up menu.** The options are:

    - **Kerberos.** Uses strong encryption requiring Kerberos v5 support on the server

    - **Digest (RFC 2617).** Sends secure login names and encrypted passwords without requiring a configured Kerberos realm

    - **Any.** Uses either Kerberos or Digest authentication depending on which the client chooses

5. **Type the fully qualified domain name of the Address Book Server.** This must resolve correctly when the server performs a reverse lookup of its IP address.

6. **Type a port number to use when talking to clients.** The default is 8800. Make sure that any firewalls allow traffic over this port to clients who need to access the server.

7. **Type an SSL port number and certificate identity if you're enabling SSL.** SSL can be set to:

    - Use

    - Don't Use

    - Redirect

8. **Alternatively, configure the Mobile Access service to enable secure remote access to external users by using SSL and then supply that service with the calendar server's internal port number.**

 CROSS-REF
For more on configuring the Mobile Access service, see Chapter 32.

9. **Click Save.**

To import Directory contacts from Leopard Server to Address Book Server, follow these steps:

1. **Upgrade the server to Snow Leopard Server.**

2. **Launch Terminal and then run this command:**

```
ContactsMigrator -s /LDAPv3/www.example.com -d http://www.
    example.com:8800/addressbooks/groups/mygroup/addressbook/
    -u username -p password
```

    Where `www.example.com` is the fully qualified domain name of your server, and `username` and `password` are your local administrator credentials.

Using server contacts within Address Book

Once Address Book Server is configured to begin serving contacts, you can configure desktop clients running Address Book or an equivalent CardDAV contact client to synchronize contacts to the Address Book Server account.

To configure Address Book with a server account, follow these steps:

1. **Launch Address Book 5.0, which is the version that ships with Mac OS X Snow Leopard.**

2. **Open Preferences and then click the Accounts icon on the toolbar to display the Accounts pane.**

3. **Configure your server account by clicking the Add (+) button to open the server configuration assistant sheet, shown in Figure 28.4.**

Figure 28.4

Address Book Server account setup

4. **Set the account type to Mac OS X Server by using the pop-up menu and typing the following:**
   - The username and password for the network account on the server
   - The address of the calendar server

5. **Click Create.** If the client computer is connected to the Open Directory domain as a Network Account Server in the Accounts pane of System Preferences, the account setup assistant configures the Address Book Server account automatically.

The selected account's Address Book Server contacts now appear in Address Book's list of contacts under the listing username@Address Book Server-name, as distinguished from the local contacts listed as On My Mac and the listing for searching Directory Services. Events in Address

Book Server calendars can be freely edited, and any changes are updated to the server and visible to other CardDAV clients, such as the Contacts app in iPhone 3.0. Changes made elsewhere are also pushed to Address Book.

To configure settings for Address Book Server contacts, follow these steps:

1. **Launch Address Book 5.0.**

2. **Open Preferences and then click Accounts on the toolbar to display the Accounts pane, shown in Figure 28.5.**

Figure 28.5

Configuring server account settings in Address Book

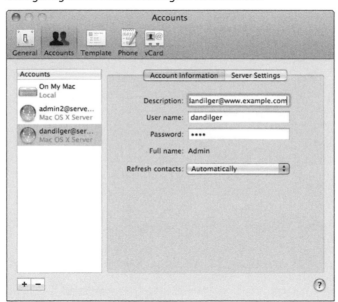

3. **Choose the server account from the accounts list.**

4. **Set a refresh period.** The default is automatically, which updates contacts at regular intervals and should eventually support push notification from Address Book Server. Other options include every minute, every 5, 15, or 30 minutes, or every hour.

5. **Click the Server Settings tab, shown in Figure 28.6.** This presents the Address Book Server name and path to the user's contact files on the server, which follows this format:

```
/principals/__uids__/ECA375B9-57C8-4D99-AFFD-20DDCC61DF10
```

Figure 28.6

Configuring server settings in Address Book

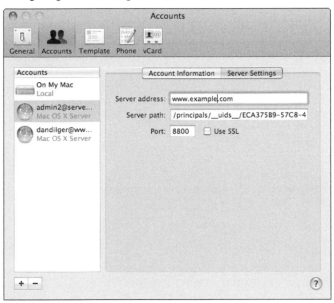

6. If the server employs SSL, click the Use SSL check box and then type the server's SSL port number.

Access control for users and groups

User privileges to create server address books can be configured in Server Admin by using a SACL. Once a user is granted Address Book service access and creates an account, that user has full access to modify contacts within the address book.

To limit access to the Address Book service in Server Admin, follow these steps:

1. From Server Admin, select the server name of the contact server.

2. Click the Settings page and then click the Access tab, shown in Figure 28.7.

3. From the Services pane within the Access tab, select the Address Book service from the left column.

4. Click the Allow only users and groups below radio button above the right column.

5. Click the Add (+) button. The Users & Groups sheet opens.

Figure 28.7

Configuring access to the Address Book service

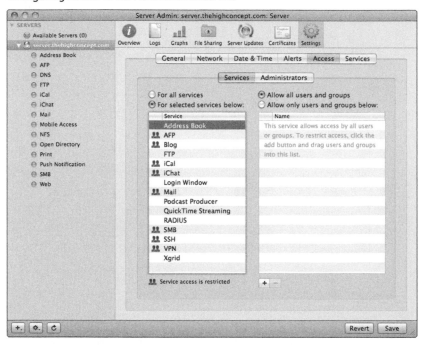

6. **Drag users or groups to the access list on the right to define users who can have Address Book Server access.**

7. **Click Save.**

Address Book service security

Security for Address Book services can be enhanced in three ways:

- Limiting outside access to your Address Book Server by using firewall rules
- Limiting access to the Address Book service to specific users and groups
- Implementing SSL security on your Address Book Server to enable encrypted authentication and secure transport

To enable SSL security for the Address Book service, follow these steps:

1. **Launch Server Admin and then connect to the desired server.**

2. **Click Address Book and then click Settings on the toolbar.**

3. **Click the Authentication tab.**

4. **Choose the authentication type from the pop-up menu.** The options are:

   - **Kerberos.** Uses strong encryption requiring Kerberos v5 support on the server
   - **Digest (RFC 2617).** Sends secure login names and encrypted passwords without requiring a configured Kerberos realm
   - **Any Method.** Uses either Kerberos or Digest authentication depending on which the client chooses

5. **Type an SSL port number and certificate identity for Address Book Server.**

6. **Alternatively, configure the Mobile Access service to enable secure remote access to external users by using SSL and then supply that service with the calendar server's internal port number.**

CROSS-REF

For more on configuring the Mobile Access service, see Chapter 32.

7. **Click Save.**

Managing and Monitoring Address Book Server

The Overview page of the Address Book Server pane in Server Admin simply shows when the service was last started. Like iCal Server, Address Book Server will likely also enable push notification support. Apart from the limited details on the Overview page, Server Admin also exposes service logs for troubleshooting.

Address Book Server error and access logs are available from the Logs page of the Address Book pane, shown in Figure 28.8, which presents a listing of the events related to both mobile and desktop client access:

- The Address Book Server Log, located at `/var/log/carddavd/access.log`
- The Address Book Server Error Log, located at `/var/log/carddavd/error.log`

Figure 28.8

The Logs page of the Address Book pane

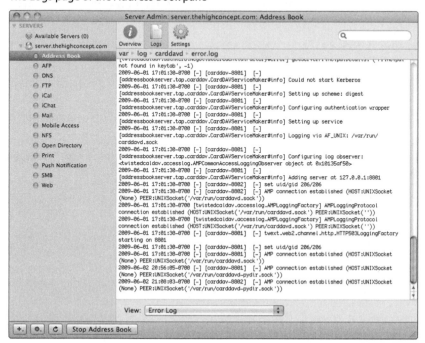

Summary

- Address Book Server 2 in Snow Leopard Server provides individual and group contacts that can be accessed from the desktop Address Book client in Mac OS X and other desktop clients and mobile devices that support CardDAV, which is an open, interoperable specification for server contacts.

- Address Book Server is enabled and configured within the Address Book pane of Server Admin, but contact management features are performed entirely within the Address Book client interface.

QuickTime Streaming Server

Mac OS X Snow Leopard Server carries forward QuickTime Streaming Server, Apple's streaming server technology for delivering live and on-demand media streaming.

With streaming, rather than delivering media files to your audience, QuickTime Streaming Server is used to send a media stream via Real-Time Streaming Protocol (RTSP) and Real-time Transport Protocol (RTP).

QuickTime Streaming Server is used to broadcast AAC (Advanced Audio Codec) or MP3 audio and MPEG-4 video, including the standard H.264 video codec and 3GPP (3rd Generation Partnership Project) content targeted at simpler mobile phones.

QuickTime Streaming Server can deliver streams of:

- Broadcasts of live events
- Media files on demand
- Playlists of pre-recorded content

When initially released alongside QuickTime 4 in 1999, QuickTime Streaming Server was attempting to catch up in the new gold rush then centered around the streaming broadcast of Internet audio and video.

Apple had pioneered video playback and editing on the desktop with QuickTime, but the emergence of the commercial Internet in the mid-1990s put a lot of momentum behind rivals with streaming technology Apple lacked in QuickTime, led by RealNetworks, with a determined effort by Microsoft to take over the market with Net Show.

Apple worked to catch up by adding streaming features to QuickTime 4 and launching QuickTime Streaming Server in 1999 and then adding QuickTime Broadcaster to QuickTime 6 in 2002.

Since then, the imagined market for streaming media has largely failed to materialize as originally envisioned. There are still a number of practical purposes for QuickTime Streaming Server; Apple regularly uses its own technology to stream some of its media events.

However, with the emergence of podcasting, which distributes content as standard media files via direct demand or RSS automated feeds, much of the growth that was expected to be

In This Chapter

Introduction to QuickTime Streaming Server

Planning streaming media services

QuickTime Streaming Server setup and configuration

Managing and monitoring QuickTime Streaming Server

distributed via Internet streaming is now being supplied through the distribution of standard media files.

Apple has capitalized on this shift with Podcast Producer, diverting much of its development and attention away from QuickTime Streaming Server, a product that now gets scarce mention on Apple's website.

CROSS-REF
For more on Podcast Producer, see Chapter 30.

Apple is also shifting its streaming efforts from the RTSP technology used by QuickTime Streaming Server to the new HTTP Live Streaming protocol that debuted with iPhone 3.0. Snow Leopard's QuickTime X also supports the new streaming technology, which doesn't require a dedicated streaming server but can use a standard web server.

Depending on your circumstances, QuickTime Streaming Server may still serve as a solution to problems that Podcast Producer doesn't, such as broadcasting live events or simulating an Internet radio or TV station with constant streaming playback of scheduled content.

This chapter describes how QuickTime Streaming Server works, what's involved in planning media streaming services, how they're configured, and how to maintain and monitor the QuickTime Streaming Server service.

Introduction to QuickTime Streaming Server

QuickTime Streaming Server is a standards-based streaming server that's older than the desktop version of Mac OS X; the software was first delivered with the original Mac OS X Server 1.0 release in 1999.

A media streaming server is used to deliver a real-time presentation of audio or video content to an audience over the Internet by using RTP and RTSP, comparable to HTTP that web servers use to deliver content that doesn't require real-time delivery.

Video streaming versus progressive download

QuickTime was originally conceived to produce and deliver static media files, often delivered via CD-ROM. As the web began to take off, the idea of distributing these relatively large files over slow dial-up connections shifted interest toward streaming, where buffered streams of content could deliver information in real time instead of requiring a substantial initial download.

Progressive download

Apple's first response was called Fast Start. It was billed as a sort of streaming, but it really just involved delivering enough content at the beginning to enable users to begin watching the video before it was fully downloaded.

This is faster than real-time delivery because it relies on the ability to deliver media faster than it can be played back. If the user's playback catches up to the download pace, playback stops until more content can be delivered.

Because the initial part of the movie has been downloaded as a file, the user can rewind and then interactively replay the movie at any point within the downloaded portion without disturbing the progressive download of the rest of the movie.

Progressive download is analogous to movie playback from a DVD; it takes some time to obtain the disc, but once you have it, you can play it back repeatedly anyway you like — and in high quality.

Apple uses progressive downloads to serve movie trailers, iTunes movies and media, and iTunes U and other podcast content.

Multiple reference versions of a movie can be hosted for progressive download to different devices, such as standard or high-definition versions for playback on Apple TV or a desktop computer, or separate mobile versions for delivery to iPhones with different access to bandwidth, whether Wi-Fi, 3G, or EDGE.

Progressive downloads use standard HTTP for delivery and can therefore be served from a normal web server.

Real-time streaming

In real-time streaming, the user watches a stream as it's delivered, with only minimal buffering to prevent playback interruption. If the stream is delayed long enough, playback stops. However, the user can't replay previous content because the client doesn't save the stream.

Backtracking to the beginning isn't possible, and the beginning of a live broadcast can't be downloaded again. If streaming content on demand, some access to locally cached portions of the stream can be scrubbed through by the user, but picking a new point to begin streaming requires negotiating the delivery of a different part of the stream, interrupting the stream delivery already in progress.

Streaming media is analogous to watching a movie broadcast on TV; it takes no time to obtain the signal, but you have to watch it as it plays, and you can't watch it again after it's finished. Viewing quality also depends on the quality of the signal's encoding and how good your reception is.

Apple uses streaming to deliver live events, such as public access to its quarterly earning-results conference calls.

Live broadcast streaming

QuickTime Streaming Server can be used to stream static QuickTime content from local storage or it can deliver live streams from a video camera with the help of broadcasting software that encodes the video for streaming.

With a live or simulated live broadcast, all the users who receive the stream see the playback occurring at the same moment in time.

When performing live streaming of a broadcast, the server is said to *reflect* the broadcast to the listening clients.

QuickTime Broadcaster

Apple supplies QuickTime Broadcaster to support the capture and encoding of live video. The software can be used to send a single stream to a recipient, called *unicasting*.

Multicast transmission

If you have a local network that supports multicast transmissions, QuickTime Broadcaster can be used to deliver a single stream to multiple users via multicast. This enables anyone on the network to receive the same stream, similar to how anyone can tune into an over-the-air television broadcast.

You can't support multicast transmission across the Internet because ISPs block multicast traffic. However, sites with access to an Internet2 Network or a private network link supporting multicast transmissions may be able to use multicast delivery of the single stream from QuickTime Broadcaster to reach their intended users.

Pairing QuickTime Streaming Server

To stream to multiple users across the Internet, QuickTime Broadcaster is paired with QuickTime Streaming Server to replicate the stream for reflection to multiple streaming clients to allow them to receive the broadcast.

QuickTime Broadcaster can also use multicast transmission. For example, the application could be used to deliver a single stream across the Internet to a QuickTime Streaming Server that could subsequently multicast the stream to a number of users at that site. If multicast transmission isn't possible, QuickTime Streaming Server delivers multiple unicast streams to clients in parallel. This puts more load on the network because each stream requires its own bandwidth.

Load balancing and relays

If you're serving broadcasts to a limited number of clients, you may be able to run QuickTime Broadcaster and QuickTime Streaming Server on the same machine. The number of users you can support depends on your client and the capacity of the server.

Apple rates a typical Mac Pro running both QuickTime Broadcaster and QuickTime Streaming Server as capable of serving about 200 DSL 1.5 Mbps users or 400 dial-up users, which may be appropriate for the broadcast of a class or meeting within a company.

To serve more users, you can configure QuickTime Broadcaster and QuickTime Streaming Server to run on separate machines.

You can also configure multiple QuickTime Streaming Servers to act as relays, receiving a stream and then reflecting the content to local clients to balance the load and improve the streaming experience for all your viewers.

Audio and video compression

QuickTime Broadcaster allows you to optimize your broadcast by configuring audio and video compression settings for the codecs you use, supplying presets to provide a recommended starting point.

It makes sense to select your audio settings first because users will forgive compressed video glitches more than audio that drops out or is too difficult to understand.

Presets provide suggested settings for different kinds of content. For example, the default setting for audio is 16-bit 8 kHz mono, with the MPEG-4 AAC Low Complexity encoder set to best quality.

For video, presets provide options tuned to the bandwidth available to your viewers:

- Clients on a local network should be able to support a 1372 Kbps video data rate supplied by using the H.264 codec, with a 480 × 360 resolution at 30 frames per second.
- Dial-up users require something closer to 30 Kbps, which can be provided by using the same H.264 codec, with a 160 × 120 resolution and limited to 6 frames per second.

Transmission and the Session Description Protocol

A streaming client, such as QuickTime Player, requires initial configuration information about the streaming session. This is delivered in a Session Description Protocol (SDP) file. The client's player opens the SDP file to begin a streaming video session.

Using QuickTime Broadcaster, you select one of three transmission types, which creates an SDP file for you after you supply the required information on how you're serving the stream:

- **Automatic Unicast (Announce).** Automatically creates an SDP file with the name you supply on the QuickTime Streaming Server you specify by DNS name or IP address. Unless you're using QuickTime Broadcaster and QuickTime Streaming Server on the same server, QuickTime Broadcaster asks for a broadcaster account's username and password to allow the SDP file to be created on the streaming server.
- **Manual Unicast.** Creates an SDP file with a target IP address for the single client system you're broadcasting to, which may be either a single QuickTime Player or manually copied to QuickTime Streaming Server to enable the stream to be subsequently reflected to other clients. You can also supply custom port settings for audio and video.
- **Multicast.** Creates an SDP file with a multicast IP address for client systems you're broadcasting to. It can generate multicast IP addresses for you for audio and video or you can supply your own. You can also supply custom port settings for audio and video as well as a Time-to-Live (TTL) number, which limits the number of routers the stream can be passed through before it stops being transmitted to new subnets.

After manually creating an SDP file, you distribute it to users to open in a streaming client, such as QuickTime Player.

Streaming video on demand

QuickTime Streaming Server can also be used to serve content on demand, such as from a library of movies or archived presentations.

Video streamed by QuickTime Streaming Server needs to be pre-processed to supply a hinting track, which tells the streaming server how to package the data to be sent over the network. The hinting process optimizes the number of streams the server can support by offloading the computationally intensive process to a preliminary processing step.

Because this static content is already prepared for streaming, there's no need to involve the use of broadcasting software. However, QuickTime Broadcaster can capture an archive of the live content being delivered and can hint this movie for subsequent re-streaming.

Video streaming with RTSP and RTP

Because streaming requires real-time delivery, it uses special delivery protocols and therefore needs to be served from a specialized media streaming server. QuickTime Streaming Server uses:

- **Real-time Transport Protocol (RTP).** An IETF standard for delivering audio and video data that prioritizes timely delivery over reliability because media applications can tolerate missing information better than late information. Missing packets can be skipped over by simply degrading playback, but content that's held up waiting for lost packets to be re-sent ends up stopping playback entirely. For this reason, RTP uses the User Datagram Protocol (UDP) for transport, as opposed to the Transmission Control Protocol (TCP), which imposes overhead related to establishing the connection and performing error control. RTP uses UDP ports 6970–9999 but can also be limited to 6970–6999.

- **Real-Time Streaming Protocol (RTSP).** An IETF network control protocol for initiating and controlling playback of audio and video streams, enables clients to request an SDP file, set up stream transports, begin playback, and tear down the session. RTSP uses TCP as its transport protocol because playback control messages prioritize reliable delivery over timely delivery; specifically, it uses TCP port 554. It can also be configured to use TCP 7070, the same port used by Real Server for streaming. RTSP is similar to HTTP but is *stateful*, meaning that it maintains an interactive session throughout the stream. Web servers are *stateless*, where each request for a document is serviced as an independent transaction unrelated to previous requests.

- **Shoutcast.** An open-network protocol serving MP3 and AAC audio streams over HTTP, is principally used for Internet radio stations. Shoutcast uses TCP ports 8000 and 8001. Apple describes this feature as Icecast-compatible MP3 streaming.

The main problem with using RTP and RTSP for media streaming is that many firewalls block both UDP traffic and many of the other ports used by the protocols. A decade ago, it appeared that the problem would be solved, as firewall administrators opened up ports to support video streaming, but that largely didn't happen.

As a workaround, you can configure QuickTime Streaming Server to serve media streams over TCP port 80, which encapsulates all RTSP and RTP traffic inside TCP packets and then delivers them by using a port that most firewalls leave open to allow regular web traffic.

This requires more work by the server and also decreases the performance of the network but may be required to reach your clients over the Internet.

If your QuickTime Streaming Server is running on a server also configured to serve web pages, you can't operate both services on the same port. You either need to use unique IP addresses for each service or run them on separate servers.

Planning Streaming Media Services

Initial setup of QuickTime Streaming Server involves some planning related to the hardware and software requirements of your server and client users; security considerations; and preparing your content for streaming.

Hardware and software requirements

To view streaming video in QuickTime Player, a client must be running at least QuickTime 4, which is now nearly ten years old. Other software capable of working with RTP/RTSP streaming video should also work, as long as it supports the video codecs you use to publish your content.

Because the technology was developed to support dial-up clients, broadband clients should have no problem receiving streaming video you publish if you can keep up with the demand.

The minimum requirements for QuickTime Streaming Server are pretty low because the system was designed to work on PowerMac G3 systems. However, to keep up with the demands by lots of concurrent client connections, you need fast network connectivity and access to enough fast storage.

Successful deployment of streaming media services requires some advanced planning, including:

- A consideration of your intended viewers' bandwidth and client software
- For live broadcast, an assessment of appropriate recording equipment
- Whether you need to manage access to your media files
- How much and what kind of storage you need
- How much network bandwidth you need to serve your intended audience
- What server hardware is needed to support the level of service expected

Security

Because QuickTime Streaming Server can be configured to explicitly serve streams only to specific clients, there's some innate security built in from the start. You can also configure the service to use Open Directory authentication to limit access to the service to specific users.

You can configure access limitations in the SACL for the QuickTime Streaming service in Server Admin.

You can also use folder-level access security, which uses `qtaccess` files placed in each media directory. These work like Apache's `htaccess` files to limit access to client users requesting access to content on the server. These files specify access by using either Digest or Basic authentication via an independent set of accounts you must manage manually.

Preparing content

To stream existing QuickTime content efficiently, you need to make sure you're using a codec optimized for streaming playback, such as H.264, with a bit rate appropriate for streaming.

The movie also needs a hinting track, which can be supplied by QuickTime Player Pro 7. Snow Leopard's QuickTime Player X doesn't offer a hinting command.

Command-line tools for performing hinting include the free GPAC suite, which contains a program called MP4box. Visit `http://gpac.sourceforge.net` for more on GPAC.

Save the movie to your Movies folder within the Media directory, which by default is located at `/Library/QuickTimeStreaming/Movie`. Apple provides a number of test movies within this folder.

From QuickTime Player, open the URL `rtsp://example.com/sample_300kbit.mov` to test playback from your server, replacing example.com with your server's domain name.

While Safari and Firefox can correctly interpret `rtsp` URLs and open a configured helper application, other browsers might not know what to do with them. This means you may not be able to rely on simply linking an RTSP URL to your web page to make media streams available.

QuickTime Streaming Server Setup and Configuration

The original configuration interface for QuickTime Streaming Server was supplied as a web-based tool. It's no longer enabled by default, but you can manually activate that web service configuration from Server Admin under the Access tab of the Settings page.

To configure the QuickTime Streaming service from Server Admin, first enable the service within the desired server's listing of configured services and then do the following:

- Configure general server settings.
- Set security and access settings.
- Set IP bindings and relay settings.
- Prepare media for streaming.
- Configure QuickTime Broadcaster.

To enable QuickTime Streaming service configuration in Server Admin, follow these steps:

1. **Launch Server Admin and then connect to the desired server.**

2. **Select the server listing and then click Settings on the toolbar.**

3. **Click the Services tab.**

4. **Click the check box for QuickTime Streaming.**

5. **Click Save.** QuickTime Streaming should now appear in the list of configurable services for the selected server, as shown in Figure 29.1.

Figure 29.1

The QuickTime Streaming pane in Server Admin

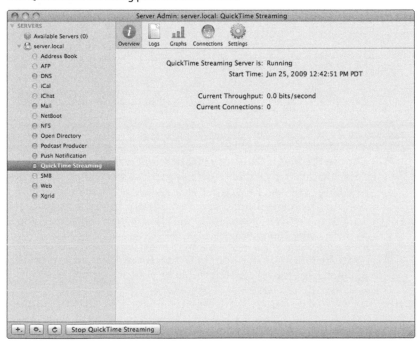

To configure general QuickTime Streaming Server services, follow these steps:

1. **Launch Server Admin and then connect to the desired server.**

2. **Click QuickTime Streaming and then click Settings on the toolbar.**

3. **Click the General tab, shown in Figure 29.2.**

Figure 29.2

The General pane of the QuickTime Streaming pane

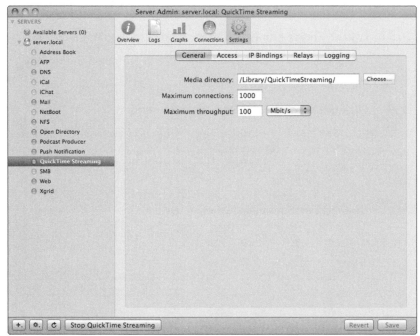

4. **Choose the Media Directory location that will contain your streaming media.** The default location is `/Library/QuickTimeStreaming/`. This works like the web root of the web service; you can also activate home folder streaming that enables users to stream media from their home folders from the Access pane, as noted shortly. To specify a different location for the primary Media Directory, you need to set that folder's ownership to the qtss user.

5. **Type the maximum number of connections.** The default is 1000. If this is exceeded, additional users who attempt to initiate a stream receive error 453, meaning the server is busy or there's not enough bandwidth.

6. **Type the maximum throughput, in Mbit/s.** The default is 100. If this is exceeded, additional users who attempt to initiate a stream receive error 453.

7. **Click Save.**

To configure Access settings, follow these steps:

1. **Launch Server Admin and then connect to the desired server.**

2. **Click QuickTime Streaming and then click Settings on the toolbar.**

3. **Click the Access tab, shown in Figure 29.3.**

Figure 29.3

The Access pane of Server Admin's QuickTime Streaming pane

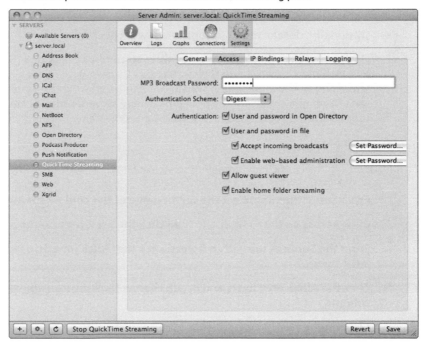

4. **Type the MP3 Broadcast Password.** This is used to authenticate Shoutcast radio broadcast to another server.

5. **Set authentication settings:**
   - **Click the User and password in Open Directory check box.** Configure access in the SACL for QuickTime Streaming, as noted shortly.
   - **Click the User and password in file check box.** This uses `qtaccess` files that work like Apache's `htaccess` files to limit access to client users, as described shortly. Also, choose an authentication scheme from the pop-up menu. Choose either Digest or Basic, which sends cleartext passwords.

6. **Click the Accept incoming broadcasts check box and then set a password by clicking the button.** This creates a broadcast user account that QuickTime Broadcaster can use to automatically copy an SDP to the server.

7. **Optionally, click the Enable web-based administration check box and then set a password by clicking the button.** This enables basic service configuration from the web on port 1220 by using Apple's original and quite dated configuration pages: `http://localhost:1220`.

8. **Optionally, deselect the Allow guest viewer check box.**

9. **Optionally, click the Enable home folder streaming check box.** This enables users to save hinted movie files to their `~/Sites/Streaming` folder, and QuickTime Streaming Server makes them available at a URL following the pattern of `rtsp://server.example.com/~user/movie.mp4`, where server.example.com is your server, user is the name of the user, and movie.mp4 is the name of your media file.

10. **Click Save.**

To limit access to the QuickTime Streaming service in Server Admin, follow these steps:

1. **From Server Admin, select the server name of the contact server.**

2. **Click Access on the toolbar and then click the Services tab, shown in Figure 29.4.**

3. **From the Services tab within Access, click the QuickTime Streaming service in the left column.**

4. **Click the Allow only users and groups below radio button above the right column.**

5. **Click the Add (+) button.** The Users & Groups sheet opens.

6. **Drag users or groups to the access list on the right to define users who can have QuickTime Streaming Server access.**

7. **Click Save.**

Figure 29.4

Configuring access to the QuickTime Streaming service

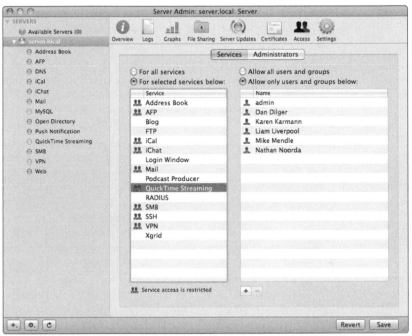

To limit folder access to media by using `qtaccess` files, follow these steps:

1. **Create user accounts with passwords by using the** qtpasswd **command-line utility.** Simply type **qtpasswd** and a username and then type the desired password. To change a password, repeat the same step again.

2. **Protect a specific folder by creating a** `qtaccess` **file and placing it in the media directory you want to protect.** Like an `htaccess` file in Apache, a `qtaccess` file designates specific users who may access files within the directory, forcing a login. Contents of the plaintext file look like Listing 29.1, with some elements optional.

LISTING 29.1

```
AuthName <message>
AuthUserFile <user filename>
AuthGroupFile <group filename>
require user <username1> <username2>
require group <groupname1> <groupname2>
require valid-user
require any-user
```

In creating the file:

- <message> is some optional text within quotation marks that your visitors see when the login window appears.

- <user filename> is the path and file name of the user file. The default is /Library/QuickTimeStreaming/Config/qtusers.

- <group filename> is the path and file name of the group file. The default is /Library/QuickTimeStreaming/Config/qtgroups. Managing a group file is optional, but if you have lots of users to manage, it may be easier to create groups and then use group names to manage access rather than individual qtaccess users.

- <username> is the user authorized to log in and view the media files. The user's name must be in the user file specified.

- <groupname> is a group of authorized users; it must be listed in the group file you specified.

If you add the line require valid-user, it allows access to any user in your user file after prompting visitors for a username and password; require any-user allows any user to view media without providing a username or password.

Using AuthScheme basic or AuthScheme digest overrides the global authentication setting on a per-folder basis.

3. **To disable authentication, rename or remove the** qtaccess **file from the folder.**

IP bindings set what IP addresses the QuickTime Streaming service listens to for all the addresses configured for the server.

To configure IP bindings settings, follow these steps:

1. **Launch Server Admin and then connect to the desired server.**

2. **Click QuickTime Streaming and then click Settings on the toolbar.**

3. **Click the IP Bindings tab, shown in Figure 29.5.**

4. **Click the Enabled streaming on selected addresses only radio button.** Click the check boxes to bind QuickTime Streaming Server to the desired IP addresses. If the server is configured to stream media on port 80, it can't be configured to bind to addresses also in use by the web service.

Figure 29.5

The IP Bindings pane of the QuickTime Streaming pane

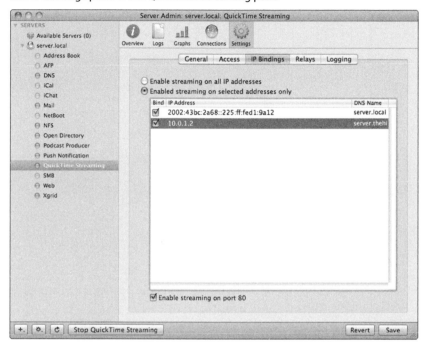

5. **Optionally, click the Enable streaming on port 80 check box.** This enables encapsulation of RTP and RTSP streams within TCP over port 80 to allow streams to get through firewalls easier but incurs processing overhead and requires more available network bandwidth to serve the same number of users.

6. **Click Save.**

Relays accept a media stream from one QuickTime Streaming Server and then relay it to another QuickTime Streaming Server.

To configure relay settings, follow these steps:

1. **Launch Server Admin and then connect to the desired server.**

2. **Click QuickTime Streaming and then click Settings on the toolbar.**

3. **Click the Relays tab, shown in Figure 29.6.**

Figure 29.6

The Relays pane of the QuickTime Streaming pane

4. **Click the Add (+) button below the left-hand list to set up a relay source.** A sheet drops down.

5. **Type a Relay Name.**

6. **Type a Relay Type to define the source of the relay and then use the pop-up control to select from the three options:**

   ● **Request Incoming Stream.** Tells the streaming server to send a request to the source computer for the incoming stream before it gets relayed. Use this type to relay a reflected live broadcast from another server or to request a stored file and turn it into an outgoing live stream. Request Incoming Stream is typically used with unannounced UDP streams from QuickTime Broadcaster or other streaming encoders. Provide the source system's IP address, the path to the stream, and the username and password of the source's broadcaster account if the source requires authentication.

- **Unannounced UDP.** Tells the server to relay streams on specific IP address and port numbers. Provide the source system's IP address and UDP ports used and set a multicast time to live. The default is 16.
- **Announced UDP.** Tells the server to wait for the incoming stream and then relay it. This requires using the RTSP announce protocol. Announced UDP is used with Automatic (Announced) broadcasts from QuickTime Broadcaster or other streaming encoders that support the RTSP announce protocol.

7. **Click the Add (+) button below the right-hand list to set up a relay destination for a defined relay source.** A sheet drops down.

8. **Type a destination IP address.**

9. **Type a Destination Type for the relay and then use the pop-up control to select from the two options:**

- **Unannounced UDP.** Tells the server to relay the stream to the destination IP address by using the base UDP port number. This requires generating an SDP file manually.
- **Announced UDP.** Tells the server to relay and announce the stream to the destination IP address. The SDP file is generated at the destination by using the mount point and username and password you provide.

10. **Click Save.**

To prepare QuickTime content for streaming, follow these steps:

1. **Make sure your content uses a codec optimized for streaming playback, such as H.264, with a bit rate appropriate for streaming.**

2. **Open QuickTime Player 7.** You can't use Snow Leopard's QuickTime Player X.

3. **Open a media file.**

4. **Choose Export from the File menu.**

5. **Choose Movie to Hinted Movie from the Export pop-up menu, as shown in Figure 29.7.**

6. **Click the Options button.** You can click the Optimize hints for server check box. This creates larger files but allows for more efficient streaming. There are additional settings available for the audio and video track behind the Track Hinter Settings buttons.

7. **Click OK to exit the options settings.**

8. **Click Save.**

Figure 29.7

Creating a hinted movie in QuickTime Player 7

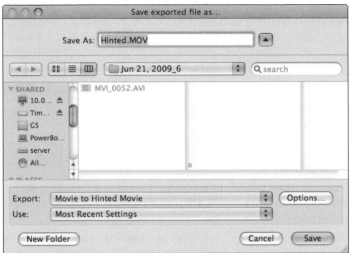

To use QuickTime Broadcaster to serve live video, follow these steps:

1. **Connect a camera or other video input device to your broadcast system.**

2. **Open QuickTime Broadcaster and then click Show details.**

3. **Configure audio and video settings from the Audio and Video tabs.**

4. **Click the Network tab, shown in Figure 29.8, and from the Transmission pop-up menu choose either:**

- **Manual Unicast.** To send a stream to a single client. Type the IP address of the target client system computer and then go to the File menu and choose Export SDP to create a file you send to your client user to initiate the broadcast.

- **Automatic Unicast (Announce).** To create an SDP file with the name you supply on the QuickTime Streaming Server you specify by DNS name or IP address. Unless you're using QuickTime Broadcaster and QuickTime Streaming Server on the same server, QuickTime Broadcaster asks for a broadcaster account's username and password to allow the SDP file to be created on the streaming server.

5. **Click the Broadcast button to begin streaming.**

Figure 29.8

Configuring QuickTime Broadcaster

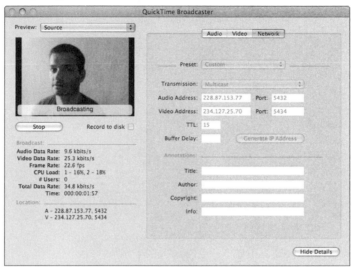

Managing and Monitoring QuickTime Streaming Server

From Server Admin, you can monitor the status of QuickTime Streaming Server by reviewing the logs, graphs, and the list of current client connections, observing the load and bandwidth being consumed by streaming media users.

Monitoring QuickTime Streaming Server logs

Error and access logs for QuickTime Streaming Server are available from the Logs page of the QuickTime Streaming Server pane in Server Admin, shown in Figure 29.9.

Access logs are maintained in a standard web server format that can be analyzed by logging tools:

- The QuickTime Streaming Server Access Log, located at `/Library/QuickTimeStreaming/Logs/StreamingServer.log`
- The QuickTime Streaming Server Error Log, located at `/Library/QuickTimeStreaming/Logs/Error.log`

Figure 29.9

The Logs page of the QuickTime Streaming pane

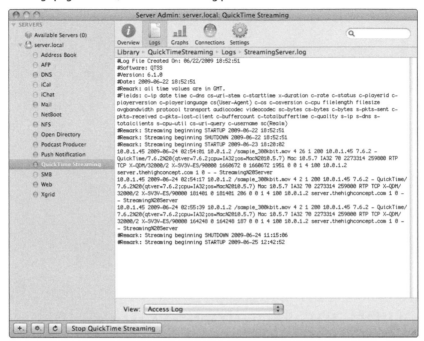

To enable logs and set logging archives, follow these steps:

1. Launch Server Admin and then connect to the desired server.

2. Click QuickTime Streaming and then click Settings on the toolbar.

3. Click the Logging tab, shown in Figure 29.10.

4. Click the Enable Error log and Enable Access log check boxes and then set an archive interval.

5. Click Save.

Figure 29.10

The Logging pane of the QuickTime Streaming pane

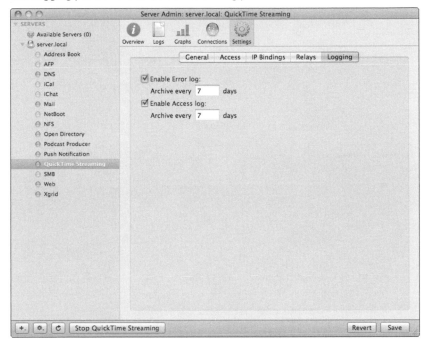

Monitoring QuickTime Streaming Server clients

Active client connections can be reviewed from the Connections page of the QuickTime Streaming pane, shown in Figure 29.11. This listing shows:

- The type of connection
- The IP address the user is connected from
- The bit rate of the connection
- The number of bytes sent
- The percentage of packet loss occurring
- The length of the connection duration
- The path of the media in use

Figure 29.11

The Connections page of the QuickTime Streaming pane

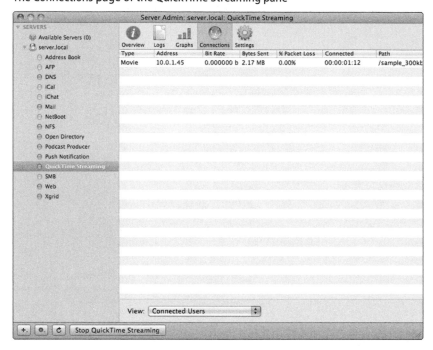

Using the View pop-up menu, the Connections page can also be used to review active relays, including:

- The relay name
- The IP address of the relay source
- The IP address of the destination
- The bit rate of the connection
- The number of bytes sent

The average client connections and network throughput of the server can be reviewed from the Graphs page of the QuickTime Streaming pane, shown in Figure 29.12.

The listing can be set to activity over the past hour, over the last 2, 4, 6, 12, or 24 hours, or over the past 2, 3, 5, or 7 days.

Figure 29.12

The Graphs page of the QuickTime Streaming pane

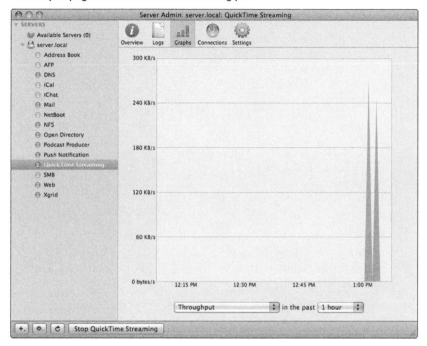

Summary

- Mac OS X Server supports royalty-free streaming media services via the QuickTime Streaming Server of static video playlists, live video feeds, or MP3 or AAC audio.

- Progressive downloads use HTTP to send files; QuickTime Streaming Server uses RTP and RTSP to send real-time streams of media files instead.

- Streams can be sent directly to clients by unicast transmission or one to many by using multicast, although the Internet doesn't support multicast transmissions.

- Streaming settings are delivered to clients via SDP files that are used to initiate a streaming session.

- QuickTime Broadcaster is used to encode live video and delivers a single stream; QuickTime Streaming Server can be used to reflect that live broadcast stream to multiple users.

Podcast Producer

Mac OS X Snow Leopard Server's Podcast Producer 2 enhances the video encoding, publishing, and distribution product that debuted in Leopard Server with a simplified setup, easy-to-use workflows, and a new Podcast Library for archiving content.

Podcasting has taken off in a big way ever since the large storage capacity offered by the iPod was matched with an efficient, easy way to obtain new content by using RSS feeds.

Apple added podcasting support to iTunes to make it easy to find and subscribe to feeds created by publishers to make their content accessible. The company then encouraged universities to publish their content in iTunes U, offering a simple way to publish content with authenticated access.

The company also delivers consumer video capture and editing tools and software for crafting podcast feeds for publishing directly to iTunes, along with professional and prosumer video-editing tools in Final Cut Studio and Final Cut Express.

Podcast Producer fills in the middle step for organizations and companies, allowing the automated capture of presentations that are submitted to a central server for processing to add titles and branding and then encode them for various devices.

In addition to creating podcasts aimed at mobile users, Podcast Producer can also be used to target high-quality video content for desktop computers and appliances, such as Apple TV.

Podcast Producer can also pair up with QuickTime Streaming Server to deliver real-time media streaming of produced content to a wide audience.

CROSS-REF
For more on QuickTime Streaming Server, see Chapter 29.

This chapter describes how Podcast Producer works, what's involved in planning podcast production, how it's configured, and how to maintain and monitor production workflows.

In This Chapter

Introduction to Podcast Producer

Planning podcast production

Podcast Producer setup and configuration

Managing and monitoring Podcast Producer

Introduction to Podcast Producer

Podcast Producer automates the process of obtaining media content, processing it according to workflows using distributed Xgrid clusters, and then advertising its availability to users for download to their devices.

Podcast Capture

The first link in the chain begins with user capture. Podcast Capture is a client application that logs in to the server by using Open Directory authentication and allows the upload of audio or video by using any capture sources QuickTime recognizes. A web-based version of Podcast Capture can also be used.

To perform a capture and upload it to the server, the user initiates the recording of:

- Audio from a microphone
- Video from an attached or built-it USB or FireWire camera
- Video from a screen capture

The capture user then issues a command to publish and specifies a workflow defined on the server. The captured content is then uploaded to the server. Alternatively, the user can also upload previously captured QuickTime movies to the server.

In Podcast Producer 2, dual capture can be used to combine two Podcast Capture feeds into a picture-in-picture presentation, such as pairing a speaker with his or her presentation documents.

An automated capture system can also be configured so captures can be initiated and managed centrally at the server.

The Podcast Capture application is a graphical front end for the `/usr/bin/podcast` command, which can be used alone to automate content uploads to the server. The podcast tool communicates with the server via secure SSL.

Podcast Producer Server

The central control of Podcast Producer is at the server, where you can use:

- Server Admin to set up a shared file system on an Xsan SAN or as an NFS export, which is used for:
  - Uploading QuickTime movies via Podcast Producer agents for processing by the Podcast Producer server
  - Keeping a cached copy of workflows. The Xgrid controller uses the workflows stored in the shared file system to process QuickTime movies.
  - Storing the podcasts generated by Xgrid agents

- Server Admin to configure the Xgrid service and controller to be used for processing QuickTime movies
- Server Admin to control and monitor access to cameras via the Podcast Producer agent `pcastagentd` process, which uses an Advanced Encryption Standard (AES) secured tunnel to allow the server to securely control the agent
- Server Admin to control and monitor access to workflows, which are Xgrid jobs
- Podcast Composer to customize workflow properties

Podcast Composer workflows

New to Snow Leopard, the Podcast Composer application is designed to create simple work-flows to automate the completion and publishing of podcasts.

It offers an intuitive interface that groups the process of building a workflow into seven stages and guides you through the steps required to create a workflow:

- Information identifying the workflow
- Import for defining one of the following content sources:
  - A single source
  - Dual source
  - Montage created by QuickLook
- Edit for adding:
  - An introduction video
  - Titles
  - Watermark branding
  - An introduction overlay
  - An exit movie sequence
- Export for selecting an output format targeted to a specific device, such as:
  - iPod/iPhone video
  - Apple TV video
  - Mobile video
  - Audio output
- Publish for specifying a publishing destination, which may include:
  - Podcast Library
  - Local wiki site
  - Final Cut Server
  - A folder
  - Another workflow

- Notify for announcing the new content, which may include:
  - Email message to the administrator, submitter, or other users
  - iChat message to the administrator, submitter, or other users
  - Publishing a feed update to the iTunes Podcast Directory
  - Publishing a feed update to iTunes U
  - Pinging an external service URL
- Summary, which checks your workflow for any problems, saves it, and then allows you to deploy it on the server

The Podcast Producer server also provides some sample workflows to define common encoding and publishing tasks for encoding and publishing QuickTime movies as podcasts.

You can modify these workflows or create your own. The sample workflows define a set of default properties that you can configure in Server Admin. New properties can also be defined in your own custom workflows by using the Podcast Producer server to configure their values.

Workflows are text files that describe Xgrid jobs, and they can be custom-edited manually as needed to fit your circumstances. Workflows can incorporate command-line tools such as Unix shell scripts or invoke QuickTime APIs to do anything QuickTime can do, including Quartz composition effects.

For example, the included `qc2movie` tool exports a Quartz Composer composition into a QuickTime movie by adding a track containing the composition.

Xgrid

Podcast Producer configures an Xgrid controller for distributing the processing of QuickTime movies on one or more Xgrid agents.

Using Xgrid agents spreads the intensive work of processing QuickTime movies across machines that are otherwise sitting idle, allowing you to scale the throughput of your Podcast Producer system simply by increasing the number of Xgrid agents available.

The Podcast Producer server uses Blocks Extensible Exchange Protocol (BEEP) and Kerberos authentication to securely communicate with the Xgrid controller by using the `xgrid` command-line tool. The Podcast Producer server and Xgrid controller must belong to the same Kerberos realm. The server then uses Kerberos tickets to authenticate when it submits jobs to the Xgrid controller.

The Xgrid agent also authenticates to the Xgrid controller by using BEEP and Kerberos but communicates back to the server by using SSL. The Xgrid agent may call the Podcast Producer server to obtain property values and responses to challenges.

For example, an Xgrid agent may attempt to post to a blog that requires authentication; the agent sends the challenge to the Podcast Producer server and then receives a response it can pass to the blog in order to be granted access.

CROSS-REF
For more on Xgrid, see Chapter 18.

Planning Podcast Production

Initial setup of Podcast Producer involves some planning related to the hardware and software requirements of your server, client users, and helper agents that participate in preparing content and the software prerequisites that need to be in place prior to starting the Podcast Producer service.

Hardware requirements

Podcast Producer uses remote capture agents to obtain video, and it leverages the distributed processing technology of Xgrid to accelerate the rendering of media workflows built using that captured video.

Podcast Producer agent

To capture video, an agent must be running at least Mac OS X Leopard and needs 20 GB of free storage space and at least 100 Mbps Ethernet networking. You also need the appropriate capture hardware for audio or video.

Gigabit Ethernet provides for much faster video uploads. Consider configuring upload bandwidth at the switch level to prevent the network from being overwhelmed.

Podcast Producer server

The minimum requirement for a Podcast Producer 2 server is simply a Snow Leopard Server with network access. To work with multiple capture and Xgrid agents, you need fast network connectivity and access to enough fast storage.

Only very small deployments can expect to use the local server's storage for podcasts. You should plan on using RAID arrays and Xsan to provide high-availability, scalable, high-performance storage for your Podcast Producer server.

Podcast Producer Xgrid agent

Xgrid agents handling the distributed processing of Podcast Producer workflows need a graphics card capable of supporting Quartz Extreme.

The number of compute node agents you need depends on your workload:

- The number of capture systems and manual submissions you'll be managing
- The submission schedule for capture systems and manual submissions
- The type and complexity of workflows being used, which determines the time needed to complete the processing and publishing of podcasts and how many of these tasks can be performed in parallel

The more Xgrid nodes you use in your Podcast Producer deployment, the more network bandwidth you need. An Xsan shared file system provides the necessary bandwidth required to process the data between nodes.

Software requirements

In addition to simply running Snow Leopard Server, Podcast Producer also requires a series of other services to be configured to support it:

- **DNS.** For name resolution
- **Mail.** SMTP service for notifications
- **Open Directory.** For authentication, with a configured Kerberos realm
- **QuickTime Streaming Server.** If you want to support media streaming of the content you produce
- **Xsan cluster file system or NFS export.** For the Podcast Library
- **Web services.** For access to web capture and the Podcast Library
- **Xgrid.** For distributed processing of workflows

Podcast Producer Setup and Configuration

To configure Podcast Producer from Server Admin, first enable the service within the desired server's listing of configured services and then do the following:

- Run the Setup Assistant.
- Review general server settings.
- Configure workflow properties.
- Set service access settings.
- Configure capture agents.
- Configure workflows.

To enable Podcast Producer configuration in Server Admin, follow these steps:

1. **Launch Server Admin and then connect to the desired server.**
2. **Select the server listing and then click Settings on the toolbar.**
3. **Click the Services tab.**
4. **Click the check box for Podcast Producer.**
5. **Click Save.** Podcast Producer should now appear in the list of configurable services for the selected server, as shown in Figure 30.1.

Figure 30.1

The Podcast Producer pane in Server Admin

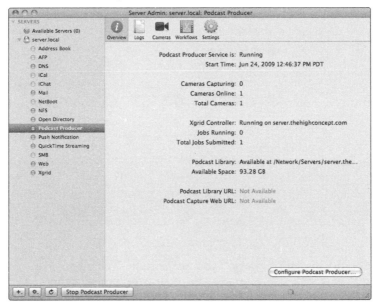

Configuring the Podcast Producer service

The required services needed in order to run Podcast Producer can be set up automatically by using the Setup Assistant launched from the Podcast Producer pane in Server Admin.

To configure initial Podcast Producer services by using the assistant, follow these steps:

1. **Launch Server Admin and then connect to the desired server.**

2. **Click Podcast Producer.**

3. **Click the Overview tab and then click Configure Podcast Producer.** The Setup Assistant, shown in Figure 30.2, opens.

4. **Choose one of the following configuration setup types:**

- **Express setup.** This automatically starts up and configures all the required services for you.

- **Standard setup.** This walks you through the steps to configure the required services.

Figure 30.2

The Podcast Producer Setup Assistant

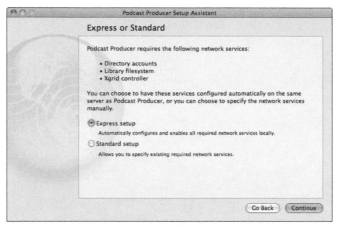

5. **Set up directory services.** If your server is already configured as an Open Directory master with Kerberos support, you can use the local directory service. Otherwise, select a directory server supporting Kerberos authentication that you can use.

6. **Create a workflow execution user.** The assistant performs this step for you, as shown in Figure 30.3.

Figure 30.3

The Podcast Producer workflow user configuration

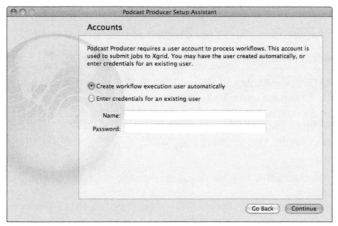

7. **Create a Podcast Library to store configuration information, recordings, and completed podcasts.** The default location is `/Library/PodcastProducer/Shared`, but the recommended location for storing the Podcast Library is on an Xsan volume. If you don't have an Xsan file system, you can enable an auto-mounted NFS share to use for the Podcast Library instead, as shown in Figure 30.4.

Figure 30.4

The Podcast Producer Library configuration

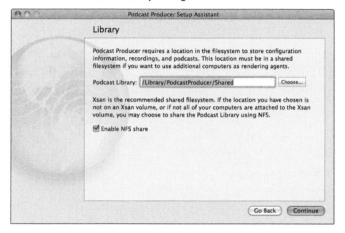

8. **Select an existing Xgrid controller; if no controller is selected, the Setup Assistant will offer to set up a local Xgrid controller and agent for you, as shown in Figure 30.5.**

9. **Confirm the settings overview presented and then click Continue.**

10. **Authenticate as a directory administrator.**

11. **From the Summary page, click Done to complete the assistant.** Links to the Podcast Capture Web app, the RSS feeds of the Podcast Library, and Podcast Composer are presented, as shown in Figure 30.6.

Figure 30.5

The Podcast Producer Xgrid configuration

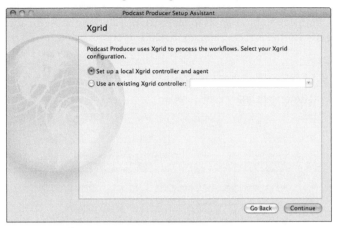

Figure 30.6

The Setup Assistant Summary

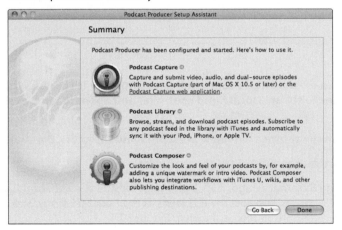

Because the Setup Assistant establishes your entire configuration for you, you probably only need to review the settings in Server Admin.

To configure general Podcast Producer services, follow these steps:

1. Launch Server Admin and then connect to the desired server.

2. Click Podcast Producer and then click Settings on the toolbar.

3. Click the General tab, shown in Figure 30.7.

Figure 30.7

The General pane of the Podcast Producer pane

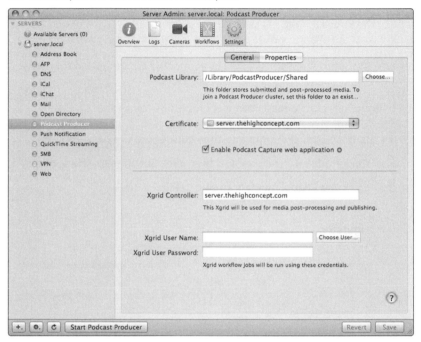

4. **Choose the Podcast Library's location, which stores your submitted captures and post-processing podcasts.** The default location is presented in full server mount notation — `/Network/Servers/server.example.com/Library/PodcastProducer/Shared/` — if the server is configured to use a local Podcast Library shared via NFS. The recommended configuration uses an Xsan shared file system on a SAN.

5. **Choose an SSL certificate used to secure authentication with agents.**

6. **Click the Enable Podcast Capture web application check box.**

7. **Choose an Xgrid controller to manage the distribution of post-processing and publishing tasks.** The controller's Xgrid agents must be bound to the same Open Directory server used by Podcast Producer. Xgrid agents must also be Kerberized in the same realm used by the Podcast Producer server. They also require access to the shared file system.

8. Type the Xgrid username and password for authenticating Xgrid workflow jobs.

9. Click Save.

Podcast Producer properties

A series of default and custom properties are defined under the Properties tab of the Settings page of the Podcast Producer pane. These properties are sent to Xgrid agents as workflows require. You can change values to customize workflow operations.

Because the Setup Assistant establishes your entire configuration for you, you probably only need to review the settings presented here initially.

To configure general Podcast Producer properties, follow these steps:

1. Launch Server Admin and then connect to the desired server.

2. Click Podcast Producer and then click Settings on the toolbar.

3. Click the Properties tab, shown in Figure 30.8.

Figure 30.8

The Properties pane of the Podcast Producer pane

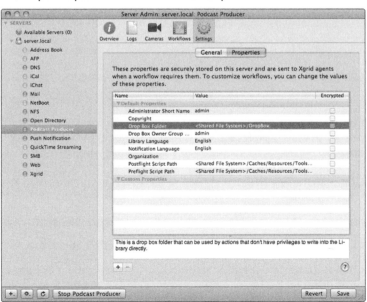

4. **Review the default properties configured by the Setup Assistant.** This includes values for:

   - **Administrator Short Name.** In Leopard Server, this was typically `pcastadmin` but can be the name of the user that ran the Setup Assistant. This is the address Podcast Producer uses to email its automatic notifications.

   - **Copyright.** Set to a blank value; you can add your own text to type a copyright string into your workflows.

   - **Drop Box Folder.** This is set to `/DropBox` within the defined shared file system of the Podcast Library.

   - **Drop Box Owner Group.** This is set to the group of the user that ran the Setup Assistant.

   - **Library Language.** This is set to your default language; used for content displayed in the Podcast Library web interface.

   - **Notification Language.** This is set to your default language; used for email and blog announcements.

   - **Organization.** This is set to a blank value; you can add your own text to type an organization string into your workflows.

   - **Postflight Script Path.** This is set up within the defined shared file system of the Podcast Library at `/Caches/Resources/Tools/postflight_script`. This script is run at the end of each workflow.

   - **Preflight Script Path.** This is set up within the defined shared file system of the Podcast Library at `/Caches/Resources/Tools/preflight_script`. This script is run at the beginning of each workflow.

5. **Optionally, you can add custom properties.** This can include values for:

   - **An Approval Email List.** A list to send workflow approval request mail

   - **An Audience Email List.** A list for new podcast announcements from Podcast Producer

   - **An Audience SMS List.** A list of SMS recipients of new podcast announcements from Podcast Producer

   - **An Exit Video Path.** The path to a QuickTime movie in the shared file system to add to the end of podcasts

   - **An Intro Transition Duration.** The transition duration in seconds between the introduction video and the main content

   - **An Introduction Video Path.** The path to a QuickTime movie in the shared file system to add at the beginning of a podcast

   - **The iTunes U Posting Credentials.** For a user that can post content to an institution's iTunes U site

   - **The iTunes U Shared Secret.** For authentication

- **The iTunes U Site URL.** For the iTunes site to post podcasts
- **The iTunes U Tab ID.** For the table view of the iTunes site where podcasts are posted
- **The QTSS URL.** For the QuickTime Streaming Server used to stream new podcasts
- **QuickTime Streaming Media Root.** The media folder on the shared file system where podcast streams are stored
- **A Quartz Composer Filter.** Used by workflows for applying filtering compositions to podcasts
- **A Quartz Composer Introduction or Exit Transition.** Used by workflows that apply transition compositions between the introduction or exit video and the main content
- **An SMTP Server.** The hostname of the SMTP mail server used by workflows to send mail notifications
- **A Watermark Image.** The path to an image on the shared file system used by workflows that apply watermarks to podcasts
- **A Web Document Root.** The web server root folder on the shared file system where new podcast streams are published
- **A Web URL.** The base URL of the web server where podcasts are published

6. **Click Save.**

To limit access to the Podcast Producer service in Server Admin, follow these steps:

1. **From Server Admin, select the server name of the contact server.**

2. **Click Access on the toolbar and then click the Services tab, shown in Figure 30.9.**

3. **Under the Services tab within Access, select the Podcast Producer service from the left column.**

4. **Click the Allow only users and groups below radio button above the right column.**

5. **Click the Add (+) button.** The Users & Groups sheet opens.

6. **Drag users or groups to the access list on the right to define users who can have Podcast Producer access.**

7. **Click Save.**

Figure 30.9

Configuring access to the Podcast Producer service

Configuring Podcast Producer capture agents

After configuring the Podcast Producer service, you can bind Macs you want to use for remote audio and video recording to the Podcast Producer service via the client Podcast Capture application.

To bind a system to Podcast Producer via Podcast Capture, follow these steps:

1. Launch Podcast Capture from the `/Applications/Utilities` **folder of the client.**

2. Authenticate as a network directory user.

3. Click the Audio/Video icon in the Podcast Producer Preferences toolbar, shown in Figure 30.10.

Figure 30.10

Sharing a Podcast Producer client with the Podcast Producer server

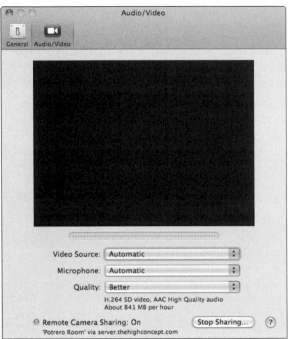

4. **Choose Video and Microphone sources from the pop-up menus of available cameras and mikes installed on the system and then choose a codec preset from the Quality pop-up menu.** The default is H.264 SD video and AAC High Quality audio, with a bit rate of about 841 MB per hour.

5. **Click the Start Sharing button and then authenticate as a local user.**

6. **Type a descriptive camera name on the sheet that drops down.** This identifies the recording system to the remote administrator on the Podcast Producer server.

7. **Click Bind and then authenticate as a Podcast Producer server administrator.**

To review camera configuration in Podcast Producer, follow these steps:

1. **Launch Server Admin and then connect to the desired server.**

2. **Click Podcast Producer.**

3. **Click Cameras on the toolbar, shown in Figure 30.11.**

Figure 30.11

Configuring cameras in the Podcast Producer pane

4. **Review the Capture Agents bound to the server.** Each shows the:
- Camera name assigned during binding
- When the camera was last used
- The current user
- The current status

5. **Click Remove Camera to unbind a Capture Agent's camera.**

6. **To restrict access to a camera, click the camera and then click the Allow access to** *camera name* **for the following users and groups radio button.** Use the Add (+) button to add users and groups. You can also change permissions for a selection of cameras.

7. **Use the search field to filter viewing of a specific set of cameras by name or use the pop-up menu to search for cameras in use by a specific user or with a specific status.**

8. **Click Save.**

To submit content to the server from Podcast Capture, launch Podcast Capture and then log in to the desired server. A podcast type selection window, shown in Figure 30.12, opens.

Figure 30.12

Recording using Podcast Capture

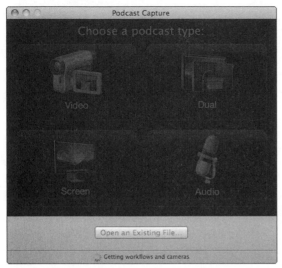

You can then follow the steps for the tasks you want to take:

To capture video with audio:

1. **Click the Video button.** A video preview opens.

2. **Use the pop-up menu to select the video input camera and its audio input.**

3. **Click Record and then click Pause when finished.**

4. **Click Publish to upload the capture.**

5. **Choose a workflow from the pop-up menu listing of workflows on the server.**

6. **Type a title and description.**

7. **Click Done.** The podcast begins uploading, and you can then begin a new podcast.

To capture audio only:

1. **Click the Audio button.** A recorder preview opens.

2. **Use the pop-up menu to select the desired audio input.**

3. **Click Record and then click Pause when finished.**

4. **Click Publish to upload the capture.**

5. **Choose a workflow from the pop-up menu listing of workflows on the server.**

6. **Type a title and description.**

7. **Click Done.** The podcast begins uploading, and you can then begin a new podcast.

To capture the screen:

1. **Click the Screen button.** A preview opens.

2. **Use the pop-up menu to select the desired audio input.**

3. **Click Record and then click Pause when finished.** You can also press F2 to start or stop recording.

4. **Click Publish to upload the capture.**

5. **Choose a workflow from the pop-up menu listing of workflows on the server.**

6. **Type a title and description.**

7. **Click Done.** The podcast begins uploading, and you can then begin a new podcast.

To publish an existing file:

1. **Click the Open an Existing File button.** A file dialog box opens.

2. **Choose the media file to upload.**

3. **Choose a workflow from the pop-up menu listing of workflows on the server.**

4. **Type a title and description.**

5. **Click Done.** The podcast begins uploading, and you can then begin a new podcast.

Configuring Podcast Producer workflows

Podcast Producer defines workflows as recipes that take captured video, perform editing and effects on them, and then create output files targeted to specific devices. Once created, these workflows are maintained by the server so remote users submitting captured video can select the appropriate workflow from those listed as available on the server. The server then accepts the captured video and begins the tasks outlined in the workflow.

To review workflow configuration in Podcast Producer, follow these steps:

1. **Launch Server Admin and then connect to the desired server.**

2. **Click Podcast Producer.**

3. **Click Workflows on the toolbar, shown in Figure 30.13.**

Figure 30.13

Configuring workflows in the Podcast Producer pane

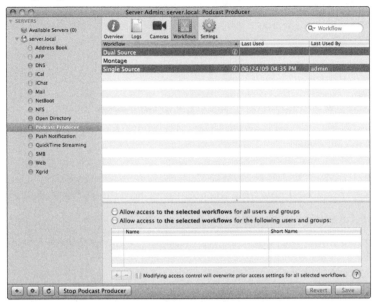

4. **Review the workflows configured on the server.** Each shows the:

   • **Workflow name.** Click the workflow, and an information icon appears. When you click it or, alternatively, double-click the workflow name, it presents an inspector with more detail, including the name of the file, assigned description, and notes related to it.

   • **When the workflow was last used**

   • **Most recent user**

5. **To restrict access to a workflow, click the workflow and then click the Allow access to** *workflow name* **for the following users and groups radio button.** Click the Add (+) button to add users and groups. You can also change permissions for a selection of workflows together.

6. **Use the search field to filter viewing of a specific set of workflows by name or use the pop-up menu to search for workflows last used by a specific user or by using the workflow's file name.**

7. **Click Save.**

A workflow is a *bundle* that stores all the files related to it in a self-contained package that appears to be a file but is actually a directory. Contents of a bundle can be viewed in the Finder by right-clicking and then choosing Show Package Contents.

Workflows are stored by default at /System/Library/PodcastProducer/Workflows, but user-created workflows should be saved to the local library directory at /Library/PodcastProducer/Workflows to avoid inadvertent overwriting by a system software update.

If the same workflow is copied into both directories, the local copy is used rather than the system version.

A workflow bundle contains the following files:

```
/Contents/Info.plist
/Contents/version.plist
/Contents/Resources/accounts.plist
/Contents/Resources/configuration.plist
/Contents/Resources/sources.plist
/Contents/Resources/template.plist
/Contents/Resources/Compositions/<any Quartz Compositions>
/Contents/Resources/Images/<any graphics>
/Contents/Resources/Movies/<any video>
/Contents/Resources/Presets/<any output presets>
/Contents/Resources/Templates/<any mail or blog templates>
/Contents/Resources/Tools/<any scripts>
```

Workflow templates provide instructions for the Xgrid agent to execute. They consist of a variety of job specifications outlined in a property list file, including a series of tasks that each represents a command script that can contain property keys and cite dependencies.

Property keys represent default and custom properties as defined in Server Admin. Podcast Producer substitutes the property key placeholders in the workflow with values you supply.

Dependencies allow the Xgrid controller to determine which tasks it can schedule in parallel. If a task is dependent on another task that hasn't completed, it can't be run. Multiple encoding tasks of the same output can be run in parallel if enough Xgrid agents are available to run the tasks concurrently.

Managing and Monitoring Podcast Producer

From Server Admin, you can monitor the status of Podcast Producer by reviewing the workflow status of agents, controllers, and jobs within Xgrid Admin, and you can review system logs to assist in troubleshooting problems.

Monitoring workflow job status in Xgrid Admin

Because Podcast Producer is designed to submit workflows to Xgrid for distributed computation as jobs, you can monitor the status of its jobs by using Xgrid Admin.

To review a workflow's Xgrid job status, follow these steps:

1. **Launch Xgrid Admin.**

2. **Type the name of the controller you want to monitor and then authenticate with it.**

3. **Click the server icon of the Controller or Grid you want to monitor jobs on from the source list.**

4. **Click Jobs, shown in Figure 30.14.** This page presents a status report that shows all current jobs and also shows the following for each one:

   - Job name
   - Current status of the job
   - Date it was submitted
   - Current progress
   - CPU power it's currently consuming
   - Number of tasks involved

   Selecting a job listing presents additional detail in the pane below it:

   - The job's identifier number
   - Time stamp showing when it was started
   - Time stamp showing when it was stopped

   Individual job listings are also marked with colored indicators to make their current status more obvious:

   - Clear means the job is pending.
   - Gray means the job is submitting.
   - Green means the job is running.
   - Red means the job has failed or cancelled.
   - Blue means the job is complete.

   Controls below the job listing allow you to remove, stop, or pause jobs from the selected grid or controller. You can't move jobs between grids or controllers.

CROSS-REF

For more on working with Xgrid, see Chapter 18.

Figure 30.14

The Jobs page in Xgrid Admin

Monitoring Podcast Producer logs

Error and access logs for Podcast Producer are available from the Logs page of the Podcast Producer pane, shown in Figure 30.15:

- The Podcast Producer Server Log records Podcast Producer server activity of the `pcastserverd` process. It's located at `/Library/Logs/pcastserverd/pcastserverd_out.log`.

- The Podcast Producer Server Error Log records error messages generated by the Podcast Producer server. It's located at `/Library/Logs/pcastserverd/pcastserverd_error.log`.

- The Podcast Producer Server Startup Log records startup messages generated by the Podcast Producer server. It's located at `/Library/Logs/pcastserverd/startup.log`.

- The Podcast Producer HTTP Access Log records all requests processed by the `httpd` Apache server instance used by Podcast Producer. It's located at `/Library/Logs/pcastserverd/apache_access.log`.

- The Podcast Producer HTTP Error Log records HTTP error messages. It's located at `/Library/Logs/pcastserverd/apache_error.log`.

- The Podcast Producer Application Log records external HTTP requests to the Podcast Producer. It's located at `/Library/Logs/pcastserverd/application.log`.

Figure 30.15

The Logs page of the Podcast Producer pane

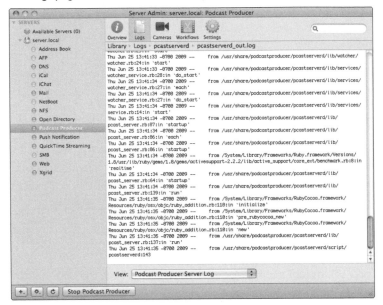

Summary

- Mac OS X Server's Podcast Producer enables organizations to set up a powerful work-flow for accepting podcasts captured by clients, performing editing, titling, and other branding, and then creating output videos in a variety of formats targeted to different devices.

- Podcast Capture allows clients to record video, audio, or screen captures, or to submit pre-recorded content to the server by using a specified workflow.

- The Podcast Producer service authenticates clients by using Open Directory and then accepts uploads and applies workflow processing by spinning the job off to the Xgrid controller, which splits the job into tasks that are assigned to Xgrid agents.

- Podcast Producer can automatically submit podcasts to iTunes and iTunes U, publish them for local retrieval in the Podcast Library, or make them available on a file share. It can also produce streams for royalty-free streaming media services via QuickTime Streaming Server.

Print Services

S now Leopard Server's print services allow organizations to centralize management of print jobs, including imposing print quotas for users.

Using print services requires an advanced configuration server; standard and workgroup configuration servers are limited to simple printer sharing, which works identically to the shared printers created by Mac OS X desktop users.

The advantages of setting up full print services include:

- The ability to set page quotas for specific users
- The ability to set page quotas for specific printer queues
- Centralized management of printer jobs and errors
- Reduced print job delays for network clients
- The ability to maintain logs of print use

Print services in Mac OS X Server rely on CUPS (Common Unix Printing System), an open-source project Apple adopted for use in Mac OS X Jaguar in 2002 and subsequently acquired in 2007.

CUPS remains the default printing system for most Linux distributions, and Apple continues to work with the open-source community to develop and enhance the software.

The modular CUPS package was originally designed to bridge the compatibility divide between AT&T's System V and Berkeley's BSD flavors of Unix (including Linux) to offer a unified interface and give printer makers a standard way to deliver custom printer drivers to users of Unix-like operating systems.

CUPS began using the LPR/LPD (Line Printer Remote/Line Printer Daemon) protocol from BSD but has since moved toward the more modern IPP (Internet Printing Protocol) developed by Novell and Xerox. IPP, which is based on HTTP, supports features such as access control, authentication, and job encryption. In Mac OS X, Apple has also integrated support for legacy AppleTalk printing (now deprecated), LPR, and SMB Windows print sharing via Samba.

This chapter describes how the print services work, what's involved in planning print services, how print queues are configured, and how to maintain and monitor them.

In This Chapter

Introduction
to print services

Planning print services

Print services setup
and configuration

Managing
and monitoring
print services

Introduction to Print Services

Without configuring managed print services, users will typically print directly to network printers by using the printer's integrated support for AppleTalk, IPP, LPR, or some other proprietary protocol, such as HP's JetDirect.

This requires users to wait for the job to complete because their computer stays occupied spooling the print job to the printer. Any errors the printer encounters, such as an out-of-paper warning, are reported to the user to solve. There's also no easy way to keep track of or manage the jobs a printer is performing or a user is submitting beyond the simple page count recorded by the printer.

CUPS

With a print service running on the server, print queues can be established for each printer. Users then submit their print jobs to the server queue instead of directly to the printer. This enables end users to move on to other tasks or even put their systems to sleep while the server queue manages print jobs for them.

Because all print jobs pass through the CUPS software on the server, an administrator can subsequently:

- Manage which users have access privileges to which printer queues
- Set quota limitations per user and per printer
- Log print jobs centrally
- Manage printer errors and consumable warnings
- Set priority for print jobs

Snow Leopard Server uses the latest CUPS 1.4 software, which adds:

- A revised web interface available at `http://localhost:631`
- Support for Bonjour (DNS-SD) printer discovery and resolution
- SNMP support for centralized monitoring of printer supplies and status
- IPP 2.0 support
- Print job scheduler sandboxing for enhanced job isolation and security

Print queues

Each print queue typically serves a single printer, although a print pool can be defined to create a single queue that prints to the first available printer in a defined selection of printers.

Queues are defined in the Print services pane of Server Admin. Network printers supporting LPR or IPP or directly attached USB printers can be assigned a queue with:

- A set display name
- Optional quota support (configured within Workgroup Manager)
- Options for sharing the device via any of the supported printing protocols
- Support for Bonjour printer discovery
- A listing in the directory domain

Printing protocols

The CUPS technology Mac OS X uses for its printing architecture is helping to streamline printing by mainstreaming IPP as the way to print; Linux also uses CUPS. Other printing protocols are still supported for legacy purposes, but the need to use these other protocols is waning.

AppleTalk

Previously supported in Leopard Server, AppleTalk is now no longer an option for serving printer queues to users. AppleTalk doesn't support authentication, doesn't support monitoring jobs from the Print & Fax pane of System Preferences, and doesn't support native drivers, making it less than suitable as a modern printer queue protocol.

The main feature of AppleTalk is its simple printer-discovery browsing, but Bonjour now enables other protocols to advertise their availability over standard TCP/IP. Snow Leopard no longer supports AppleTalk as a network protocol.

LPR

Macs and Unix systems both support LPR printing, and third-party tools add support for Windows clients. LPR clients create and deliver a PostScript job to the server queue, which can then either deliver it to a PostScript printer or rasterize it to a PDF for use with an inkjet printer by using the CUPS `ps2pdf` utility.

A PPD (PostScript Printer Description) file is used by CUPS to define the printer's capabilities and features as the job enters its filtering stage between being received by the server queue and being output to the printer. CUPS also uses PPD-style files (called CUPS-PPDs) for non-PostScript devices to similarly describe their available features and capabilities.

However, LPR itself doesn't support authentication, doesn't support monitoring jobs from the Print & Fax pane of System Preferences, and doesn't support native drivers, making IPP a more attractive alternative for clients that support it.

IPP

Modern Mac, Unix, and Windows clients support IPP, which allows the client system to prepare a printer-specific job by using customized driver software that optimizes the use of features unique to the printer rather than simply adapting PostScript code for generic printer output.

IPP is also unique in its support for Kerberos authentication, and it does support monitoring jobs from the Print & Fax pane of System Preferences.

SMB

To support Windows users, print queues can be shared over SMB. This requires turning on the SMB service in Server Admin because Windows print services are handled by Samba, the same software that handles Windows file sharing.

Samba can support basic authentication but doesn't support native drivers, making IPP a more attractive alternative for Windows clients that support it.

Bonjour printer discovery

Printers shared over IPP are automatically advertised over Bonjour, enabling clients to find them in the Print & Fax pane of System Preferences or on Windows computers with Bonjour support installed. LPR printers can also be advertised over Bonjour by selecting that option in Server Admin on the Queues page of the Print pane.

Windows printers shared over SMB are advertised via WINS to allow Windows clients to find them on the network.

Open Directory printers

Administrators can also add printer records to Open Directory to allow network clients to look up available print queues in the directory. This requires using Workgroup Manager to add a Printers record for the device and define:

- A `PrinterLPRHost` attribute for it containing its IP address or DNS name
- A `PrinterLPRQueue` attribute specifying its queue name (if you're not using the default)
- A `Printer Type` attribute for specifying its "*ModelName" as it appears in its PPD

Planning Print Services

Planning for print services involves collecting information on the protocols your clients require and creating policy for print quotas and access control as needed.

Small networks that lack the centralized needs for managing printers and documenting use may be better served by simple print sharing, which may use either a printer's built-in network server, an appliance printer-sharing device, such as an AirPort base station, or a workstation or server that acts as a basic printer share.

Simple print sharing requires less administration and less setup for new printers and clients, and removes a central point of failure by distributing the task of serving printers. Bonjour, which is bundled on most modern printers, makes it easy for users to discover and set up the printers they need.

However, if authenticated print job security, output monitoring and control, and centralized printer status monitoring are necessary or desirable, the print services in Server Admin can manage those features for your network.

Performance

Optimizing performance and basic network planning related to print services greatly depends on the type of printing users will be doing. Basic document printing requires very little processing on the server because the task of spooling print jobs largely depends on the network, server disk I/O, and the speed of the printer.

The number of printer queues set up on the server is limited only by server resources, but the quantity of jobs the print server must handle concurrently also factors into planning. Large print jobs may involve gigabytes of data, so you may need to run multiple print servers to scale print services to accommodate many users who need to print many large documents at once.

Fortunately, however, printing resources often tend to have spread-out usage patterns, so many organizations find that one server can handle the needs of several printers and many users without having a major impact on other services running on the same server.

Security

If printer authentication is important, you can activate and require Kerberos authentication in Server Admin from the Settings page of the Print pane. This allows users who have logged in to the Kerberos domain to access printer queues by using the same SSO. Client systems must also be configured to join the Kerberos realm, and CUPS must be set up to use Kerberos on their local machines.

It's not possible to limit access to the print queues using SACLs, as is the case with most other services in Server Admin. You can, however, manage which administrators have access to monitor or configure print service settings in Server Admin.

To limit administrative control of print services, follow these steps:

1. **From Server Admin, select the server name of the Print server.**

2. **Click Settings and then click the Access tab.**

3. **From the Administrators pane within Access, click the For selected services below radio button above the left column and then choose a print service from that list.**

4. **Click the Add (+) button under the right-side column of administrators.** The Users & Groups sheet opens.

5. **Drag administrative users or groups to the access list on the right and then use the pop-up menu to define, administer, or monitor access in the Permissions column.**

6. **Click Save.** Print service settings are thus limited to the selected users granted administrator permissions, whereas users with monitor permissions are able to view only the service configuration and update listings.

Print Services Setup and Configuration

Setting up print services requires configuring queues for each printer, defining any special options, and optionally setting up quota support that can be configured per user or group in Workgroup Manager.

To enable print service configuration in Server Admin, follow these steps:

1. **Launch Server Admin and then connect to the desired server.**

2. **Select the server listing and then click Settings on the toolbar.**

3. **Click the Services tab.**

4. **Click the check box for Print.**

5. **Click Save.** Print should now appear in the list of configurable services for the selected server, as shown in Figure 31.1.

Figure 31.1

Enabling the Print pane in Server Admin

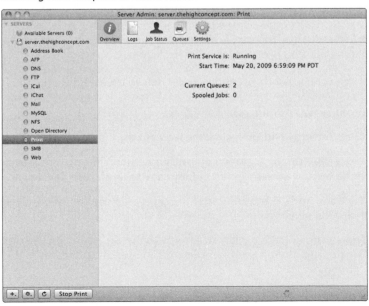

Printer queues

Queues defined by the print server enable centralized management of printing resources, including the enabling of quota limits and defining the protocols the printer will be made available through to clients.

To add a new print queue in print services, follow these steps:

1. **From Server Admin, select the print service of the selected server.**

2. **Click the toolbar button to reach the Queues page, shown in Figure 31.2.** Any directly connected USB printers appear in the list. Any network printers you want to create queues for need to be added.

Figure 31.2

Queues in the Print pane in Server Admin

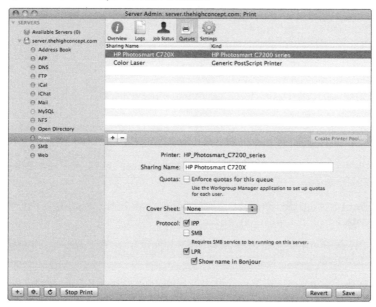

3. **Click the Add (+) button.** For an LPR or IPP printer, choose LPR and type its address. If you're not using the default queue on the server, deselect the check box and provide a custom queue name.

4. Set queue options for defined printers. For either directly attached USB printers or network-connected printers, select the printer you want to share with a queue. The lower pane provides options to type:

- A sharing name, which is the label network users see in their browse list. For some Unix and Windows clients, this may need to avoid spaces and special characters and be limited to a total of 12 characters.

- A quota-enabling check box. Quota restrictions are configured within Workgroup Manager.

- An option to use a coversheet, which is added to every print job.

- Options to share the printer by using IPP, SMB (which requires the SMB service to be on), or LPR. A separate check box enables Bonjour advertising for LPR printers.

5. Click Save. The print queue is now made available and advertised to network users.

Advertising print services

Many printers support automatic discovery via Bonjour, but this typically only works on the local subnet. To make available printers visible to users across the organization, they can be added to the directory as printer records, which will then be available to users via directory browsing.

To add a print queue to Open Directory, follow these steps:

1. From Workgroup Admin, select the desired directory domain and then authenticate.

2. Click the Show All Records tab and inspector check box in Workgroup Admin Preferences.

3. Once active, this shows the All Records tab in the accounts list, which is marked with a bull's-eye target icon.

4. Click the All Records tab, choose Printers from the pop-up menu, and then click New Record.

5. In the new record's RecordName field, type the printer's display name.

6. Click New Attribute.

7. In the sheet that appears, click the Attribute Name pop-up menu and choose PrinterLPRHost, type the queue's IP address or DNS name in the text field, and then click OK.

8. Click New Attribute.

9. In the sheet that appears, click the Attribute Name pop-up menu and choose PrinterLPRQueue, type its queue name (if you're not using the default) in the text field, and then click OK.

10. Click New Attribute.

11. In the sheet that appears, click the Attribute Name pop-up menu and choose Printer Type, type its "*ModelName" as it appears in its PPD, and then click OK.

12. Click Save. The print queue now appears in directory listings for network users.

Printer pools

A print pool is a queue associated with multiple printers. This allows users to send jobs to a central queue, which results in printing a job on the first available printer. It only makes sense to assign printers to a poll if they all have the same matching features. To add a new print pool queue in print services, follow these steps:

1. From Server Admin, select the print service of the selected server.

2. Click the toolbar button to reach the Queues page.

3. Select two or more printers in the list. The printers should be the same make and model.

4. Click Create Printer Pool, type a name for the pool, and then select the same options as a standard print queue.

5. Click Save. The print pool queue can now accept jobs and output them to the first available printer in the pool.

Printer quotas

Enable quota support for a printer queue when setting up the queue in Server Admin. Use the Print pane in Workgroup Manager to configure a directory user's print quota, either across all printers or per queue, specifying settings limiting the user to a set number of pages within a set number of days for each printer as desired.

CROSS-REF
For more on configuring print queues in Workgroup Manager, see Chapter 10.

Managing and Monitoring Print Services

The Overview page of the Print pane in Server Admin presents a status report of when the service was started, the current number of configured printer queues, and the currently spooled jobs waiting to print.

Monitoring printer logs

The Logs page of the Print pane, shown in Figure 31.3, presents a list of the events recorded in:

- The Print Service Log, which tracks configuration changes, located at `/Library/Logs/PrintService/PrintService_admin.log`
- The Error Log for the CUPS process, located at `/var/log/cups/error_log`
- The Access Log for the CUPS process, located at `/var/log/cups/access_log`
- The Page Log, which records users and the jobs they submit, located at `/var/log/cups/page_log`

Figure 31.3

The Logs page of the Print pane in Server Admin

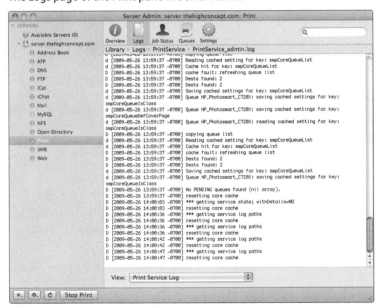

From the Settings page, shown in Figure 31.4, a maximum log size can be set with an option to archive the server's logs. A logging level pop-up menu sets the desired level of events recorded, from none to only emergency events to very general information to detailed debugging data.

After configuring logging settings, click Save. CUPS and Server Admin then adjust the level of details presented on the Logs page.

Figure 31.4

The Settings page of the Print pane

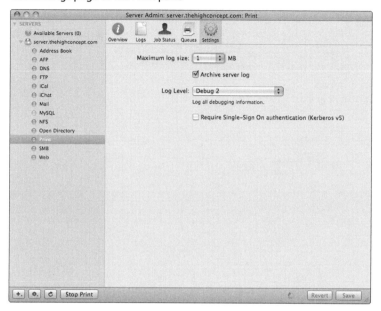

Managing print jobs

The Job Status page of the Print pane, shown in Figure 31.5, shows each of the queues, how many pending jobs each has, the printer's status, the protocols that queue is serving, and the kind of printer it is. Two buttons enable an administrator to pause or resume a selected print queue.

A job detail for the selected print queue is listed in the lower half of the pane, with a detail of that queue's jobs by ID and the submitting user as well as the job name, its status, and its size. Three buttons enable an administrator to pause, resume, or remove a selected print job from a queue.

Figure 31.5

The Job Status page of the Print pane

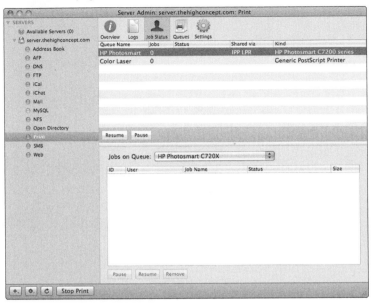

Summary

- Mac OS X Server can provide authenticated, centralized print services that manage access and set quotas for printing resources.

- Apart from using the print services configured within Server Admin, Mac OS X Server can also share directly connected printers as basic shared printers, just like a desktop system or network appliance.

- Mac OS X Server uses CUPS for its printing architecture. Other features of CUPS are available from its web-based interface at `http://localhost:631`.

- Snow Leopard no longer supports AppleTalk as a network protocol for print sharing. Most modern clients should support IPP, which, along with Bonjour, delivers the features of AppleTalk, including advanced security options and support for using advanced client driver software to send jobs to print queue printers.

Mobile Access Server

M obile Access is a new feature of Snow Leopard Server designed to enable companies to expose email and web-based services, including access to CalDAV iCal Server and CardDAV Address Book Server, to outside mobile users securely and with minimal client configuration.

Granting remote access to corporate email and messaging services has typically required a VPN connection, which creates a secure tunnel across the Internet and through a firewall to allow authenticated outside users to check email, work with their calendars, and access other corporate information services.

The downside to requiring VPN access is that users have to deal with increased complexity and are forced to manually establish a secure connection every time they want to access internal resources.

The problem is even worse for mobile device users, who are regularly transitioning between Wi-Fi and mobile networks that may not support certain VPN configurations.

In contrast to setting up a general-purpose VPN connection, Mobile Access enables email and web services to use standard TLS encryption to access internal servers with the same level of security that banks use to secure their online transactions.

This results in mobile devices being able to access private data without making any security compromises in the name of convenience.

This mechanism also enables all other public Internet traffic on the device to work normally without the added overhead imposed by a VPN tunnel.

This chapter describes how Apple's Mobile Access works, what's involved in planning Mobile Access services, how Mobile Access is figured, and how to maintain and monitor the services.

Introduction to Mobile Access

Snow Leopard Server's use of the open, interoperable CalDAV and CardDAV specifications as the basis for its calendaring- and contact-sharing services makes access to these services identical to access to any other websites; both servers are implemented as specialized HTTP WebDAV servers. Snow Leopard's web collaboration servers, including wikis and blogs, also use the same standard HTTP WebDAV architecture. This makes it easier to secure access to all these services as well as to secure access to both static internal websites and to other custom dynamic web applications under the same umbrella.

Standard methods for securing access to web-based services are also commonly used to secure access to incoming IMAP and outgoing SMTP email servers. In Snow Leopard Server, Apple has consolidated an interface for configuring all these services in one place, even if they're running on different servers within the company.

A standards-based architecture

Mobile Access builds on a variety of documented, standard protocols, each of which is codified in IETF RFC documents. This results in a known, familiar architecture built on proven technologies:

- **TLS (RFC 5246).** Serves as the cryptographic protocol for providing security and data integrity between the Mobile Access Server and remote mobile clients
- **HTTP (RFC 2616).** Serves as the distribution protocol for transferring web page, calendar, and contact resources between the server and contact clients
- **WebDAV (RFC 2518).** The protocol used for reading and writing Address Book Server contact files, iCal Server calendars, and wiki collaboration resources on the server
- **IMAP (RFC 3501).** Provides client access to an email mailbox on the server
- **SMTP (RFC 5321).** Enables clients to relay outgoing mail to the server

Mobile Access acts as a reverse proxy to serve internal services to external clients from a single domain name and potentially by using a single SSL certificate, allowing all the internal services to run on the same server or on multiple internal servers.

Simplicity for mobile clients

Mobile Access enables mobile devices to be configured to securely access email and web-based collaborative messaging services with minimal configuration by using standard security measures already widely deployed.

Most mobile devices already support SSL-enabled IMAP and SMTP, and web-enabled devices similarly have universal support for SSL encryption.

Apple's iPhone and iPod touch are clearly the target devices envisioned for use with Mobile Access, but because the service is based on standards, any device that supports remote access to Snow Leopard services should have no configuration problems.

Applying SSL security to all externally available services from the same Mobile Access server allows using the same domain name and, therefore, the same certificate authority to secure all those services, streamlining the process of either obtaining Certificate Authority–signed identities or distributing a single self-signed root certificate to your mobile users.

Planning for Mobile Access Services

The initial setup of Mobile Access services involves some planning to take care of a few prerequisite steps. You need:

- A registered domain name for your Mobile Access server and a properly configured DNS that enables reverse lookup of the server and proper remote access
- A certificate identity for SSL security
- A firewall configuration that allows clients to access the services by using the designated TCP ports. By default, this includes these ports:
  - 993 for IMAP
  - 587 for SMTP
  - 443 for standard SSL websites
  - 8443 for Address Book Server and iCal Server
- Accounts for remote access users stored in Open Directory or an Active Directory system for authentication
- Properly configured services, including mail, web, Address Book, and iCal Servers

You also need to know the location and configuration of any mail, web, Address Book, and iCal Servers within your organization that you plan to export via Mobile Access and whether these use SSL internally. Mobile Access can relay SSL-secured access to internal servers — whether they're internally using SSL or not.

Mobile Access Server Setup and Configuration

To configure Mobile Access services from Server Admin, first enable the service within the desired server's listing of configured services and then do the following:

- Configure each related service to use Mobile Access.
- Configure user access to the service.
- Turn on the service.
- Configure clients to access services through the proxy.

Enabling Mobile Access services

Setting up Mobile Access services requires activating the Mobile Access service, configuring service settings, and then configuring client systems to work with the service.

To enable Mobile Access service configuration in Server Admin, follow these steps:

1. **Launch Server Admin and then connect to the desired server.**

2. **Select the server listing and then click Settings on the toolbar.**

3. **Click the Services tab.**

4. **Click the check box for Mobile Access.**

5. **Click Save.** Mobile Access should now appear in the list of configurable services for the selected server, as shown in Figure 32.1.

Figure 32.1

Enabling the Mobile Access service in Server Admin

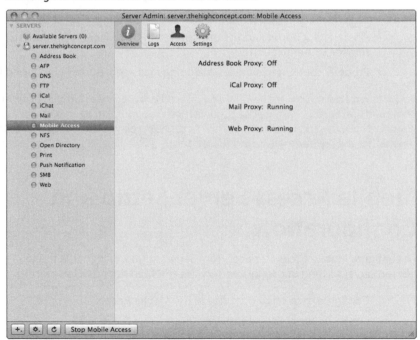

Configuring Mobile Access service settings

Mobile Access can be set up to provide secured proxy access to the local Address Book Server, iCal Server, mail, and web services or to services running on another server.

To configure Mobile Access services, follow these steps:

1. **Launch Server Admin and then connect to the desired server.**

2. **Click Mobile Access.**

3. **Click Settings on the toolbar, shown in Figure 32.2.**

Figure 32.2

Configuring Mobile Access services

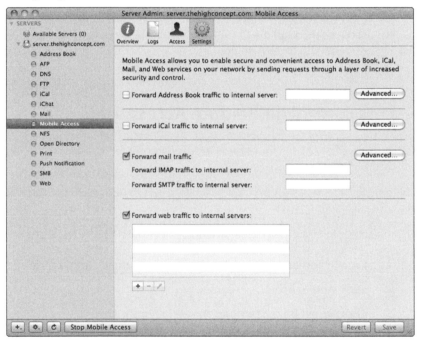

4. **Click the Forward Address Book traffic to internal server check box to proxy private Address Book services through the Mobile Access server by using SSL.** A single internal Address Book Server can be configured.

5. **Click the Forward iCal traffic to internal server check box to use SSL in proxying private iCal services through the Mobile Access server.** A single internal iCal Server can be configured.

6. **Click the Forward mail traffic check box to use SSL to proxy IMAP and SMTP mail services through the Mobile Access server.** The internal IMAP and SMTP servers can be different servers or the same server.

7. Configure proxy access to Address Book, iCal, and incoming and outgoing mail servers by typing the internal address of each server.

8. Click the Advanced button for Address Book, iCal, or the mail service to set the connection type and port number used for:

- Internal connections from Mobile Access to local servers. This may be set to use either an SSL or a non-SSL port to access the internal site.

- External connections from Mobile Access to remote mobile users. An SSL certificate identity must be specified, and a nonstandard SSL port can be configured for use in addition to the typical SSL ports that appear as default values.

9. Click the Forward web traffic to internal servers check box to proxy private web services through the Mobile Access server by using SSL. Any number of internal websites can be configured.

10. Click Save.

Access control for Remote Access users

User access to proxy services in Remote Access is unique in that it's managed within the Mobile Access pane and not from the general Access pane of the Settings page in Server Admin, as is the case with most other services.

This enables Mobile Access to allow selective access to Address Book, iCal, mail, and web services for each defined user.

To limit access to Mobile Access services in Server Admin, follow these steps:

1. Launch Server Admin and then connect to the desired server.

2. Click Mobile Access.

3. Click Access on the toolbar, shown in Figure 32.3.

4. Click the Allow access to the selected proxies for these users and groups radio button.

5. Click the Add (+) button. The Users & Groups sheet opens.

6. Drag users or groups to the access list.

7. Click the check boxes for each proxy service you want to make available to the selected users.

8. Click Save.

Figure 32.3

Configuring access to the Mobile Access service

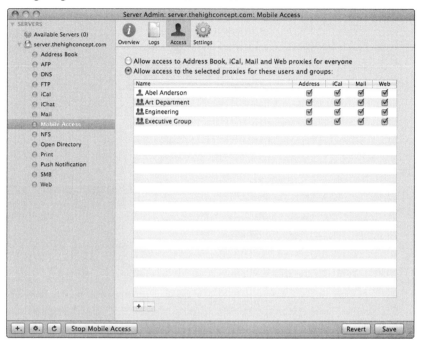

Mobile Access service security

Security for services can be enhanced in three ways with Mobile Access:

- Limiting outside access to your internal servers by using firewall rules
- Limiting access to the Mobile Access service to specific users and groups
- Implementing centralized SSL security with the Mobile Access Server to enable encrypted authentication and secure transport to internal services

Managing and Monitoring Mobile Access Server

The Logs page of the Mobile Access pane in Server Admin, shown in Figure 32.4, presents a listing of the events related to client access and errors:

- The Address Book Access Log, located at `/var/securityproxy/addressbook_access.log`
- The Calendar Access Log, located at `/var/log/securityproxy/calendar_access.log`
- The Mail Access Log, located at `/var/log/securityproxy/mail_access.log`
- The Mail Error Log, located at `/var/log/securityproxy/mail_error.log`
- The Web Access Log, located at `/var/log/securityproxy/web_access.log`
- The Web Error Log, located at `/var/log/securityproxy/web_error.log`

Figure 32.4

The Logs page of the Mobile Access pane

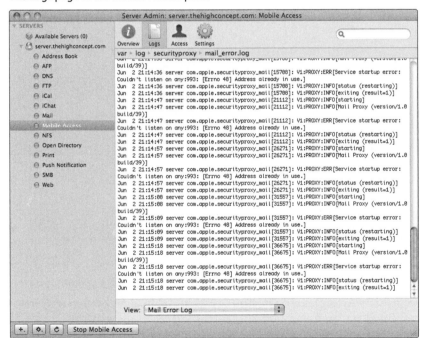

Summary

- Mobile Access in Snow Leopard Server provides a secure proxy for exposing internal services to mobile users from a single interface and by using a single domain name.
- Enabling Mobile Access streamlines the availability of secured mail and web-based collaboration and messaging services to remote users of mobile devices, such as the iPhone and iPod touch.

Push Notification Server

Push notification is a new feature of Snow Leopard Server designed to provide efficient, rapid notifications to clients when new information is available for access.

Although potentially useful for a variety of purposes, push notification in Snow Leopard is primarily provided to deliver push messaging features to the mail and iCal services.

Push notification is particularly useful to mobile devices — which seek to balance rapid access to new information, such as incoming emails or calendar changes — because of their limited battery size, a factor that puts a damper on how often they can ask for new data.

If the client device checks for new messages only every 15 minutes, it's occasionally 15 minutes late in discovering an urgent new message. If it polls more frequently than that, it wastes a lot of battery power because most of the time, the client connects to the network to ask for new data and finds nothing new.

The solution to this engineering challenge is push messaging, which lets a mobile device coast in low-power mode until new information is available on the server. The server then initiates a notification to the client, letting the client obtain the new information promptly and efficiently.

With push messaging, mobile devices spend the resources to connect to the network and download new data only when something is actually available, which can be far more efficient than regularly polling the server for new information. Providing push messaging requires the server to support a mechanism for pushing a notification of new events, and the client device also needs to support this push system.

This chapter describes how Apple's push notification works, what's involved in planning push notification services, how they're configured, and how to maintain and monitor the services.

Introduction to Push Notification Server

Push messaging on some devices, such as Microsoft's Direct Push for Windows Mobile phones, works by issuing a long-lived HTTPS request for new changes to a Client Access server, typically every 15 minutes. If the server discovers that new data for the client has arrived, it responds to the request, and the client phone can obtain the updates.

However, this type of push messaging requires the phone to essentially sit on hold with a constantly open HTTPS connection that waits for the server to respond. It also requires the mobile network and any firewalls to support long-lived HTTPS requests.

The push notification services in Mac OS X Server use Idavoll, an implementation of the XMPP PubSub (publish and subscribe) service, written in Python by using the Twisted framework.

XMPP is the instant messaging protocol behind Jabber and iChat Server. PubSub is part of that protocol, designed to publish feeds of information updates to subscribers, similar to how the Twitter system works to send updated tweets to a variety of subscribers.

Instead of the client maintaining HTTPS requests over 15-minute intervals, PubSub is designed to publish server-initiated messages to subscribed clients, enabling the client to essentially doze off while waiting for the phone to ring. This results in a more battery-efficient and flexible push mechanism.

Snow Leopard Server's use of the open, interoperable XMPP PubSub specification as the basis for its push notification services leverages the company's parallel efforts to provide push notification services for third-party developers in iPhone 3.0 as well as the company's MobileMe push messaging services.

This means that the iPhone and iPod touch have a single incoming notification system for:

- Third-party applications
- Mac OS X Server messaging services, such as email and calendars
- MobileMe push messaging services

Push notification builds on documented, standard protocols managed by the XMPP Standards Foundation as XEPs (XMPP Extension Protocols). This results in a known, familiar architecture built on proven technologies:

- XMPP serves as the instant messaging protocol for delivering notifications to clients.
- PubSub (XEP-0060) is the protocol used in publishing changes to iCal Server and the mail service to mobile clients.

Services on Mac OS X Server that support using push notification services are configured within their own interfaces. The Push Notification pane in Server Admin provides only a detail of the services running and a log of push events.

Planning Push Notification Services

The initial setup of push notification services involves some planning to take care of a few prerequisite steps. You need:

- A registered domain name for your Push Notification Server and a properly configured DNS that enables reverse lookup of the server and proper remote access
- A firewall configuration that allows clients to access the services by using the designated TCP ports
- Accounts for push users stored in Open Directory or an Active Directory system for authentication
- Properly configured services supporting push, including mail and iCal Server

Planning for `push notification` services is pretty minimal because the service is so deeply integrated as a core service that it's essentially turned on or off.

Disk and network resources that push notification services use are minimal, although the processing load associated with servicing lots of mobile devices needs to be monitored.

Push Notification Setup and Configuration

Setting up push notification services requires activating the Push Notification pane, configuring service settings, and then configuring client systems to work with the service.

To enable push notification services configuration in Server Admin, follow these steps:

1. **Launch Server Admin and then connect to the desired server.**

2. **Select the server listing and then click Settings on the toolbar.**

3. **Click the Services tab.**

4. **Click the check box for Push Notification.**

5. **Click Save.** Push Notification should now appear in the list of configurable services for the selected server, as shown in Figure 33.1.

Figure 33.1

Enabling the Push Notification pane

To configure push notification services for mail services, follow these steps:

1. **Launch Server Admin and then connect to the desired server.**

2. **Click Push Notification.** Make sure the service is on.

3. **Click Mail and then click the Settings on the toolbar.**

4. **Under the General tab, shown in Figure 33.2, click the Add button next to the Push Notification Server listing.** A sheet drops down.

5. **In this sheet, type the following:**

- A DNS name for the Push Notification Server. This may be the local server.
- An administrative username and password to log in to the server

6. **Click Connect.** The Push Notification Server should now be listed in the mail configuration.

7. **Click Save.**

Figure 33.2

Enabling push notification for mail services

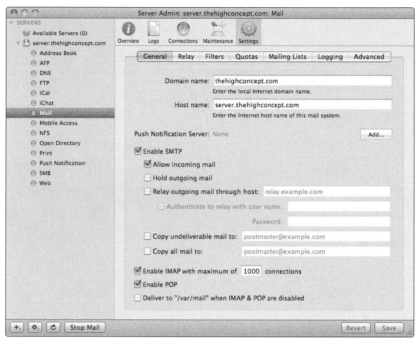

To configure push notification services for iCal Server, follow these steps:

1. **Launch Server Admin and then connect to the desired server.**

2. **Click Push Notification.** Make sure the service is on.

3. **Click iCal and then click Settings on the toolbar.**

4. **In the General pane, shown in Figure 33.3, click the Add button next to the Push Notification Server listing.** A sheet drops down.

5. **In this sheet, type the following:**

- A DNS name for the Push Notification Server. This may be the local server.
- An administrative username and password to log in to the server

6. **Click Connect.** The Push Notification Server should now be listed in the iCal Server configuration.

7. **Click Save.**

Figure 33.3

Enabling push notification for iCal Server

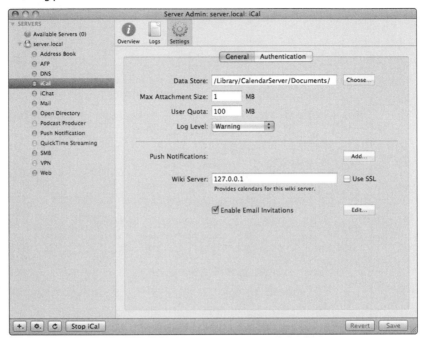

To review the configured push notification services, follow these steps:

1. **Launch Server Admin and then connect to the desired server.**

2. **Click Push Notification.**

3. **Click Overview on the toolbar to display the Overview page, shown in Figure 33.4.**

4. **Mail and iCal services running on any servers configured to use this push notification service are listed.**

5. **Configure another local or remote service to use push notification from that service's settings pane within Server Admin.**

Figure 33.4

The Overview page for push notification

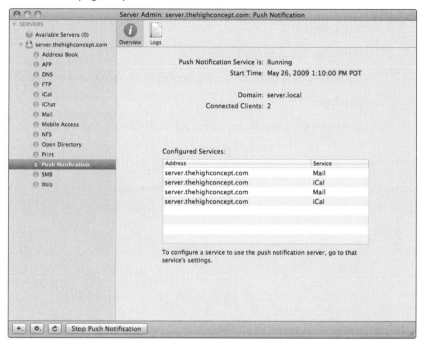

Access control for push notification users

User access control to push notification services is unique in that it's managed at the mail or iCal service level and not from the general Access pane of the Settings page in Server Admin, as is the case with most other services. Because push notification services use XMPP, a Notification User is given access to the iChat service from the general Access tab of the Settings page in Server Admin. This must be enabled for push messaging to work.

To limit access to mail or iCal services in Server Admin, follow these steps:

1. Launch Server Admin and then connect to the desired server.

2. Select the server name and then click Settings.

3. Click the Access tab and then click the Services tab.

4. Under the list of services, click Mail.

5. **Click the Add (+) button.** The Users & Groups sheet opens.

6. **Drag users or groups to the access list to enable mail service.**

7. **Click Save.**

8. **Under the list of services, click iCal.**

9. **Drag users or groups to the access list to enable the iCal service.**

10. **Click Save.**

11. **Under the list of services, select iChat, shown in Figure 33.5.**

Figure 33.5

The Notification User in iChat's SACL in Server Admin

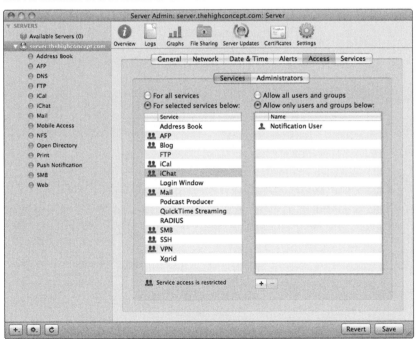

12. **Drag users or groups to the access list to enable the iChat service.** The Notification User must be included in this listing.

13. **Click Save.**

Push notification services security

Security for services can be enhanced in two ways with push notification:

- Limiting outside access to your internal servers by using firewall rules
- Limiting access to mail, iCal, and iChat services to specific users and groups

Managing and Monitoring Push Notification Server

The Logs page of the Push Notification pane in Server Admin, shown in Figure 33.6, presents a listing of the events related to client access and errors:

- The Push Notification Server Error Log, located at `/var/log/idavoll/error.log`
- The XMPP Server Log, located at `/var/log/system.log`

Figure 33.6

The Logs page of the Push Notification pane

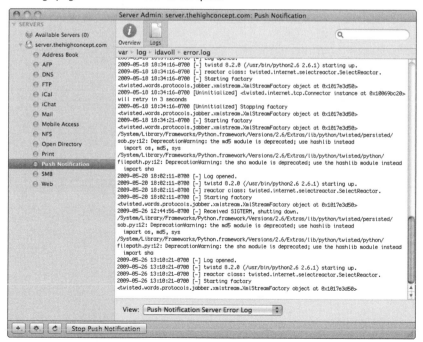

Summary

- Push notification in Snow Leopard Server enables mobile clients to obtain updates efficiently by alerting them only when new messages or calendar updates are available.

- Enabling push notification mail and iCal services to remote users of mobile devices, such as the iPhone and iPod touch, is handled within the configuration panes for mail and iCal Server. Operation of the Push Notification Server is largely automatic.

Managing Network Client Computers

Managing Client Systems with NetBoot

NetBoot is a feature provided with Mac OS X Server that enables administrators to create and manage disk images that client machines on the network can boot from directly, simplifying the process of rolling out security patches, system updates, and application upgrades.

Instead of managing software on each machine individually, a single disk image can be modified in one place and subsequently used to boot up a variety of machines on the network.

Multiple NetBoot disk images can be defined for different tasks or types of users, allowing systems to be completely reconfigured, even several times a day.

For example, NetBoot can be used to periodically boot systems by using different images so machines in the same lab could be used for different classes, with each set up with a unique set of applications or even different operating system versions.

It's even possible to use NetBoot to start up systems by using a network disk image without needing a local disk at all, achieving the premise envisioned for the low-maintenance, thin client network computer.

Mac OS X Server supplies the following tools for working with disk images that the NetBoot service uses:

- System Image Utility to create NetBoot disk images
- Server Admin to configure the NetBoot service
- PackageMaker, a component of the Xcode developer tools, to create install files for adding new software to existing disk images

This chapter introduces how NetBoot works, the plans you need to implement NetBoot on your network, how to set up disk images for network booting, and the tools Snow Leopard Server provides for managing NetBoot.

Introduction to NetBoot

The NetBoot feature of Mac systems based on a PowerPC G3 or a newer processor is enabled by the sophisticated firmware used to start the system:

- OpenFirmware, used by PowerPC Macs
- EFI (Extensible Firmware Interface), used by Intel Macs

A Mac can be configured to search for a network volume to boot from either by:

- Selecting Network Startup from the Startup Disk pane in System Preferences
- Setting NVRAM boot-args by using the `nvram` command
- Holding down the Option key at boot and then selecting a network boot device
- Holding down the N key at boot

With any of these methods, the system starts with its normal power-on self-test (POST) and a chime sound and then attempts to find a NetBoot server that can supply it with an initial boot configuration.

Obtaining initial NetBoot configuration

A specialized DHCP service, which the `bootpd` process provides by using an Apple-developed extension called BSDP (Boot Service Discovery Protocol), enables obtaining the initial NetBoot configuration. Once the Mac begins talking to the DHCP service on the NetBoot server, it displays a blinking world globe icon.

The Mac responds to the server by supplying its MAC hardware address, processor architecture type, and system identifier model. This allows the NetBoot server to identify the appropriate bootable disk image for it.

A network bootable image `.nbi` folder created by System Image Utility contains a regular Mac-bootable system disk image `.dmg` file and also contains:

- `booter`, a copy of the BootX startup file from Mac OS X that the Mac's firmware uses to load the kernel and begin the startup process
- `mach.macosx`, the Mac kernel used to boot the system software disk image
- `mach.macosx.mkext`, the kernel extension (driver) cache used by the kernel at startup
- `NBImageInfo.plist`, a property list file containing the NetBoot image's configuration, including values for:
  - **Architectures.** An array of strings of the CPU architectures the image supports
  - **Backward Compatible.** Whether the image works with previous systems

- **BootFile.** The name of the boot file: `booter`
- **Description.** Text describing the image
- **Enabled and Disabled System Identifiers.** Specific Mac system types the image is set to work with or not
- **Index.** A value numbered between 1 and 4095 to indicate a local image unique to the server or between 4096 and 65535 to specify that an identical copy is also available on other NetBoot servers for load balancing
- **IsDefault.** True specifies this image file as the default boot image on the subnet.
- **IsEnabled.** Sets whether the image is available to NetBoot clients
- **IsInstall.** True indicates a Network Install image; false indicates it's a NetBoot image.
- **Language String.** Specifies the language to be used while starting from the image
- **Name.** The name of the image as it appears in the Mac OS X System Preferences pane within System Startup
- **OS Version.** Specifies the version of Mac OS X used
- **RootPath.** Specifies the relative path to the disk image on the server or the path to an image on another server
- **SupportsDiskless.** True sets up support on the NetBoot server for hosting the shadow files required by diskless clients.
- **Type.** The hosting protocol, either NFS or HTTP

The NetBoot server hosts the NetBoot disk image folder on the network via an HTTP or an NFS export. The default location for the NetBoot disk image folder in the first designated volume is `/Library/NetBoot/NetBootSP0/image-name.nbi`, with the `0` incremented for each new NetBoot volume that's defined, resulting in successively numbered share points: `NetBootSP1`, `NetBootSP2`, and so on.

The same initial directory is also soft-linked to `/private/tftpboot/NetBoot/NetBootSP0` and made available as a TFTP file share. TFTP (Trivial File Transfer Protocol) is an ultra-light version of the FTP protocol that embedded devices commonly use.

Downloading Mac OS X startup files

The NetBoot server provides a URL to the `booter` file of the appropriate NetBoot disk image to the client machine, which begins downloading the `booter` file, the kernel, and its kernel extension cache from the network disk image folder by using TFTP. At this point, the Mac is still running from firmware; TFTP enables it to load the Mac OS X kernel and begin the normal boot process.

Since the move to Intel Macs, NetBoot servers have needed to provide two sets of boot files: one for PowerPC and one for Intel machines. There was also a PowerPC version in the previous location at the root of the disk image folder for backward-compatibility.

This results in a file structure within `/Library/NetBoot/NetBootSP0/image-name.nbi`, which looks like this:

```
booter
mach.macosx
mach.macosx.mkext
NBImageInfo.plist
Image-name.dmg
ppc/booter
ppc/mach.macosx
ppc/mach.macosx.mkext
i386/booter
i386/mach.macosx
i386/mach.macosx.mkext
```

With the move to a 64-bit kernel in Snow Leopard, the server provides two sets of Intel boot files: one for 32-bit Intel and one for 64-bit Intel booting. This results in a file structure within `/Library/NetBoot/NetBootSP0/image-name.nbi`, which looks like this:

```
mach.macosx.mkext
NBImageInfo.plist
Image-name.dmg
i386/booter
i386/mach.macosx
i386/mach.macosx.mkext
i386/x86_64/mach.macosx
i386/x86_64/mach.macosx.mkext
```

During the TFTP file download, an Apple logo is drawn on the client's screen and a spinning world globe icon is shown. `Booter` then launches the kernel, which is sophisticated enough to mount the disk image via NFS or HTTP and continues loading Mac OS X. The client's screen displays the standard startup images.

Using shadow files and network shares

While booted over the network, the client machine doesn't interact with the system disk image as a normal Mac OS X startup volume. In order to prevent client users from modifying the NetBoot image, the service directs all client attempts to write to the disk image to independent shadow files maintained for each client instead.

These shadow files allow many clients to boot from the same NetBoot disk image and yet maintain individual sessions. Shadow files are only maintained during the client's session, so any changes the client user makes aren't retained.

In order for NetBoot users to save their documents on the network, they must be given a network home folder or access to other network share points.

Planning NetBoot Deployment

Prior to setting up the service and configuring disk images for NetBoot, you need to collect some information and make sure your client systems, your network, and your server all meet the minimum requirements.

Client systems:

- Must meet the basic requirements for Mac OS X Snow Leopard
- Must be updated to use the latest firmware available
- Must use built-in Ethernet; there's no support for using multiple Ethernet ports or NetBoot over wireless networking. Apple discourages even attempting to try to use wireless networking.

The network:

- Must supply wired Ethernet; there's no support for NetBoot over wireless networking.
- Must support at least 100 Mb Fast Ethernet. Using a hub, you can only support fewer than 10 users. With a Fast Ethernet switch, you can support up to about 50 users. With Gigabit Ethernet, you can support additional users, particularly when using server-side link aggregation or multiple network interfaces servicing different subnets.
- Must allow traffic over the required ports used by DHCP (UDP ports 67 and 68), NFS (TCP and UDP on port 2049), HTTP (TCP port 80), TFTP (TCP and UDP on port 69), and AFP (TCP port 548)

The server:

- Needs to support Gigabit Ethernet and, ideally, use link aggregation to support more concurrent client connections
- Must be site-licensed to serve software in images. Apple provides site licensing for NetBoot, Mac OS X, and Mac OS X Server.

- Must supply adequate storage to support NetBoot disk images, the total size of which depends on the size and configuration of the system image and the number of images stored. Images may be stored across volumes or stored on and served by multiple servers for performance.

- Must supply adequate storage for the shadow files for any users working from diskless client systems

NetBoot Setup and Configuration

Setting up NetBoot services requires enabling the NetBoot service in Server Admin and then do the following:

- Configuring basic NetBoot services, such as the network interfaces that will be used to serve and the volumes that will store your NetBoot disk images and shadow files for client data

- Creating NetBoot images by using System Image Utility

- Enabling your created disk images and configuring the default NetBoot image for clients to use

- Optionally configuring NetBoot and DHCP filtering to allow NetBoot only by specific machines by MAC address or, alternatively, to deny access to specific machines

- Configuring Boot Server Discovery Protocol in DHCP

- Configuring client systems for NetBoot

To enable NetBoot service configuration in Server Admin, follow these steps:

1. **Launch Server Admin and then connect to the desired server.**

2. **Select the server listing and then click Settings on the toolbar.**

3. **Click the Services tab.**

4. **Click the check box for NetBoot.**

5. **Click Save.** NetBoot should now appear in the list of configurable services for the selected server, as shown in Figure 34.1.

Figure 34.1

Enabling the NetBoot pane in Server Admin

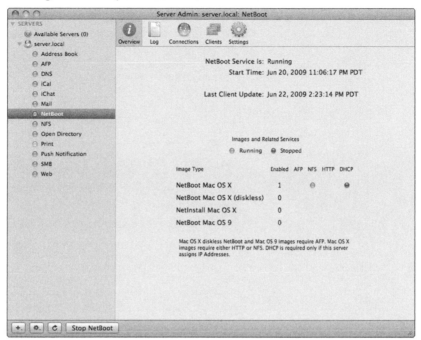

Configuring NetBoot Server

Initial configuration of the NetBoot service is done by using the Settings page of Server Admin's NetBoot pane, shown in Figure 34.2.

To configure basic NetBoot services, follow these steps:

1. Launch Server Admin, click NetBoot, and then click Settings on the toolbar.

2. Click the General tab.

3. Click the check box(es) for the available network port(s) you want to use to serve NetBoot images to clients.

Figure 34.2

Configuring general settings in Server Admin's NetBoot pane

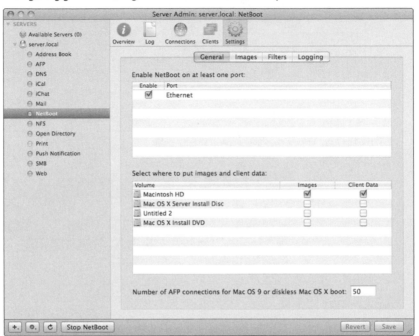

4. **Click the check box(es) for the available volumes you want to use to store NetBoot images.** Enabling a volume creates the directory `/Library/NetBoot/NetBootSP0` and defines it as an NFS share point. Enabling additional volumes creates successively named new share points on each volume: `NetBootSP1`, `NetBootSP2`, and so on. Spreading NetBoot images across volumes allows the service to automatically load-balance users across different volumes. However, there's no performance gain if your volumes are actually partitions on the same drive. You can also serve identical images across different servers; define the image at creation as being served by multiple servers, and it's assigned an index number the system tracks for load balancing. Once you configure a volume for storing image files, don't change the name of the volume or stop file sharing for the NetBoot share point without first deselecting the volume for use in storing image files.

5. **Click the check box(es) for the available volumes you want to use to store NetBoot client data in shadow files.** Enabling a volume for client data creates the directory `/Library/NetBoot/NetBootClients0` and defines it as both an AFP and NFS share point. Enabling additional volumes creates successively named new share points on each volume: `NetBootClients1`, `NetBootClients2`, and so on. Spreading shadow files across volumes allows the service to automatically load-balance users across different volumes. However, there's no performance gain if your volumes are actually partitions on the same drive. If you don't enable shadow files on the server, clients will save shadow files locally on their system, requiring a local disk. Once you configure a volume for shadow files, don't change the name of the volume or stop file sharing for the NetBoot share point without first deselecting the volume for use in storing shadow files.

6. **Set a maximum number of AFP connections for NetBooting Mac OS 9 or diskless booting.**

7. **Click Save.**

Creating NetBoot images by using System Image Utility

Using System Image Utility — installed within `/Applications/Server` on the server and available as part of the server admin tools on the installer DVD — you can create Mac OS X NetBoot images that can then be used to boot client systems over the network.

You can also build an Automator workflow to create a NetBoot image that allows advanced customization of your images.

To create a NetBoot image, follow these steps:

1. **Launch System Image Utility.** You must be a local administrator to create new NetBoot images.

2. **From the main page, shown in Figure 34.3, select an image source from the Sources list.** If no sources are available, insert a Mac OS X Install DVD or mount a valid boot volume, such as a configured computer operating in FireWire target mode. You can't create a NetBoot image from the boot volume of the computer you're currently working on. Your source volume must be Mac OS X Snow Leopard 10.6 or later to create a new boot image.

3. **Click the NetBoot Image radio button and then click Continue.**

4. **Configure the image settings:**

- **Image Name.** Type a name to identify the image in the Startup Disk preferences pane on client computers.

- **Description.** Optionally, type information describing the image. Clients won't see the description.

- **Click the check box if the image is served from more than one server to generate an index ID for NetBoot server load balancing.** The index number is recorded in the `NBImageInfo.plist` file, with a number below 4096 indicating an image unique to the server and higher numbers used to designate duplicate, identical images stored on multiple servers for load balancing.

- **If your source volume is an installation DVD, type a username, short name, and password to create a local administrator account.**

Figure 34.3

Creating a new NetBoot image

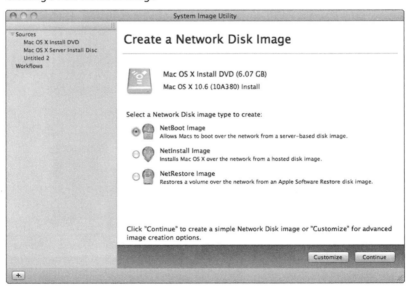

5. **Click Create.**

6. **Choose a location to save the image.**

7. **Click Save and then authenticate as a local administrator.** After System Image Utility creates the image, copy it to the `/Library/NetBoot/NetBootSP0` share point on the server for use by the NetBoot service, replacing `0` with the appropriate number.

Creating a NetBoot image workflow

System Image Utility lets you build workflows to create customized NetBoot images by using Automator Actions to perform a series of tasks, such as customizing a software package or adding a user account.

Each Automator Action is designed to perform a single task combined with other actions in a workflow to provide modular, programmatic customization of your NetBoot image.

Provided Automator Actions for creating a NetBoot image include:

- **Add User Account.** Enables you to set up additional local users for the image, including configuring as a local admin
- Apply System Configuration Settings:
  - Can configure LDAP bindings for the system
  - Can obtain a computer name and local hostname settings from a specified file or generate a unique computer name starting with the label you provide and appending a unique number
  - Can transfer the computer preferences of the original computer used to create the image by choosing Change ByHost preferences to match client after install
- **Create Image.** Adds the NetBoot creation step to the workflow and optionally allows specifying an image index
- **Define Image Source.** Specifies the source for the disk image creation. This is the starting point of every NetBoot workflow.
- **Filter Clients by MAC Address.** Allows the NetBoot image to work only with systems with the MAC hardware addresses specified or, alternatively, denies it the ability to work on the MAC hardware addresses specified

To create a NetBoot image by using a workflow, follow these steps:

1. **Launch System Image Utility.** You must be a local administrator to create new NetBoot images.

2. **Click Customize on the main page.**

3. **A simple workflow is presented, as shown in Figure 34.4, allowing you to:**
   - **Define Image Source.** Specifies the source for the disk image creation. This is the starting point of every NetBoot workflow.
   - **Create Image.** Adds the NetBoot creation step to the workflow for setting the same configurations as when you perform a normal NetBoot image.

4. **From the Automator Library inspector that appears, as shown in Figure 34.5, you can customize the workflow by dragging Automator Actions into the workflow to add additional configuration options.**

Figure 34.4

Creating a new NetBoot image by using a workflow

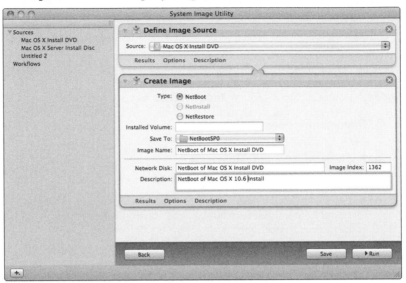

Figure 34.5

The Automator Library

5. **Configure the options of the assembled workflow, as shown in Figure 34.6.** Your workflow ends with the Create Image action.

Figure 34.6

A configured workflow for creating a NetBoot image

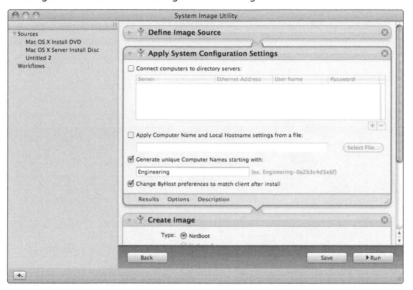

6. **Click Save to save your workflow.** Type a name, choose a location, and then click Save.

To run a saved NetBoot workflow to create an image, follow these steps:

1. **Launch System Image Utility.** You must be a local administrator to create new NetBoot images.

2. **Choose your workflow from the Sources list.**

3. **To add a workflow not in the list, click the Add (+) button, choose Add Workflow from the pop-up menu, and then choose your saved workflow file.**

4. **Click Run to use the workflow and then authenticate as a local administrator if prompted.** After the image is created, copy it to the `/Library/NetBoot/` `NetBootSP0` share point on the server for use by the NetBoot service, alternatively replacing `0` with the appropriate number of the share point you want to serve it from.

Enabling NetBoot images

After using System Image Utility to create a NetBoot image, copy the image's `.nbi` folder into `/Library/NetBoot/NetBootSP0` on the server for the NetBoot service to use, replacing 0 with the appropriate number. You can then enable the image in Server Admin.

To configure basic NetBoot services, follow these steps:

1. **Launch Server Admin, click NetBoot, and then click Settings on the toolbar.**

2. **Click the Images tab, shown in Figure 34.7.**

Figure 34.7

The Images pane in Server Admin's NetBoot pane

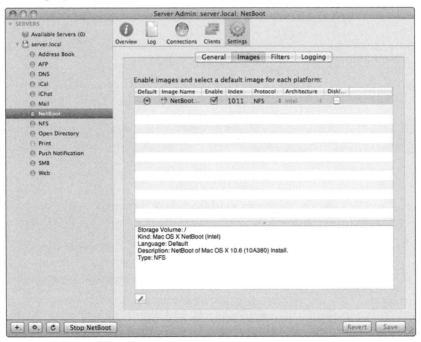

3. **Click check box(es) for the image(s) you want to serve to clients.** For each, select the protocol used to serve the image, either NFS or HTTP. If you select HTTP, the name of your image can't include spaces. You also need to start the web service.

4. **Click the check box for the NetBoot image you want to use as the default.** The default image is used when clients force a NetBoot by holding the N key while starting up. Otherwise, available images are presented for the user to select during an Option-key boot or from the Startup Disk pane in System Preferences. If you use diskless clients, you must specify their image as the default. If you're serving images for multiple architectures, select a default image for each.

5. **Optionally, restrict use of an image to specific models or to specific machines by MAC hardware address by clicking the Edit button marked with a pencil icon.**

6. **From the sheet that drops down, click either or both radio buttons:**
   - **Allow only computers below.** Enables the specific models you want to be able to boot from the image
   - **Allow only clients listed below.** Specifies the MAC addresses you want to be able to NetBoot from the image. Alternatively, choose Deny only clients listed below to specify the MAC addresses you don't want to be able to NetBoot from the image.

7. **Click OK.**

8. **Click Save.**

Filtering NetBoot clients

You can restrict specific client machines by MAC hardware address from using your NetBoot server or, alternatively, allow only specific systems. You can also apply filter settings on a per-image basis as described previously.

To filter access to NetBoot services, follow these steps:

1. **Launch Server Admin, click NetBoot, and then click Settings on the toolbar.**

2. **Click the Filters tab, shown in Figure 34.8.**

3. **Enable or disable NetBoot/DHCP filtering by clicking the appropriate check box:**
   - **Allow only clients listed below.** Specifies the MAC addresses of systems you want to be able to use NetBoot
   - **Deny only clients listed below.** Specifies the MAC addresses you don't want to be able to use NetBoot

4. **Look up a machine's MAC address by typing its DNS name or IP address in the Host Name field and then click Search.**

5. **Click Choose to import values from a file that lists a series of MAC addresses and then click Extract.**

6. **Click Save.**

Figure 34.8

The Filters pane of the NetBoot pane

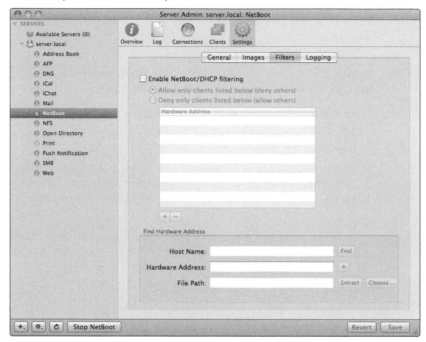

Boot Server Discovery Protocol and DHCP

Client discovery of available NetBoot servers relies on the client broadcasting for a server that responds to the Boot Service Discovery Protocol (BSDP). Routers are typically configured to block broadcast traffic from being routed to other subnets.

To provide NetBoot service across subnets, you have to configure your routers to pass BSDP traffic to the NetBoot server. This should be possible if your router supports DHCP helper or DHCP relay agent features.

It's possible to configure a third-party DHCP server to perform BSDP, but it makes more sense to enable NetBoot servers to act as their own DHCP service and then configure NetBoot filtering to allow DHCP services only for systems configured to NetBoot.

NetBoot actually uses BootP, a subset of the DHCP protocol. Any BootP devices that try to obtain an IP address from the NetBoot server fail because NetBoot server doesn't assign IP addresses unless the server is also configured to act as a full DHCP server.

You can prevent the NetBoot BootP server from responding to requests for IP addresses by using the `dscl` command to open the local folder on the NetBoot server and then add a key named `bootp_enabled` with no value to the `/config/dhcp/` folder:

```
dscl . -create /Config/dhcp bootp_enabled ""
```

Another potential problem for NetBoot relates to Initial Connectivity Delay, a short router-imposed delay to network connectivity that occurs when a managed switch is configured to automatically detect problems with network devices.

Protocols such as PortFast or Spanning Tree Protocol are intended to prevent problems such as network looping by probing the attached network interface when a connection is first detected on a port. This can result in a 15–30 second delay before the port starts working.

Initial Connectivity Delay isn't necessary on ports connected to known host systems, and if active, it can prevent NetBoot from working because the client needs immediate network access to find and begin its connection with the NetBoot server.

Disabling these managed switch protocols for the ports used by NetBooting client systems can resolve the problem.

Configuring client systems for NetBoot

A Mac can be configured to search for a network volume to boot from either by:

- Selecting Network Startup from the Startup Disk pane in System Preferences
- Setting NVRAM boot-args by using the `nvram` command
- Holding down the Option key at boot and then selecting a network boot device
- Holding down the N key at boot

If you're using diskless systems, which you may want to do to prevent users from copying files locally or from booting a locally installed system, users must initially start up by using the N key, and they can then set the desired NetBoot volume from Startup Disk, which saves the option in NVRAM for subsequent booting.

You can also configure how a system booted from a particular NetBoot image uses shadow files by editing the configuration of the image's `/etc/hostconfig`.

To configure NetBoot shadow file behavior for an image, follow these steps:

1. **Prior to creating your NetBoot image, type** `sudo pico /etc/hostconfig` **to edit the value for** NETBOOT_SHADOW **by adding one of the following lines:**

- `NETBOOT_SHADOW=-NETWORK` to attempt to use a network share point for shadow files and using the local disk if a `NetBootClients` share can't be found
- `NETBOOT_SHADOW=-NETWORK_ONLY` to attempt to use a network share point for shadow files failing to boot if a `NetBootClients` share can't be found

- `NETBOOT_SHADOW=-LOCAL` to attempt to use the local disk for shadow files and use a network share point if a local disk isn't available
- `NETBOOT_SHADOW=-LOCAL_ONLY` to attempt to use the local disk for shadow files and fail to boot if a local disk isn't available

2. **Save, exit, and then create a NetBoot image by using the configured system.**

Managing and Monitoring NetBoot

The Overview page of Server Admin's NetBoot pane presents a status report including:

- If the service is currently active
- When the service was started
- The last client update
- The number of enabled Mac OS X NetBoot images
- The number of enabled Mac OS X images configured for diskless booting
- The number of enabled Mac OS 9 NetBoot images
- The protocols enabled for Mac OS X NetBoot: AFP, NFS, HTTP, and DHCP
- The protocols enabled for Mac OS X images configured for diskless booting
- The protocols enabled for Mac OS 9 NetBoot images

Monitoring NetBoot Logs

The Logs page of the NetBoot pane presents logs reported in `var/log/system.log`.

The logging level of the service can be configured under the Logging tab of the NetBoot pane's Settings page — from all events to errors only.

Monitoring NetBoot clients

The Connections page of the NetBoot pane, shown in Figure 34.9, lists currently connected NetBoot clients that have booted from an image on the server. It presents a hostname, an IP address, and a status.

Figure 34.9

The Connections page in Server Admin's NetBoot pane

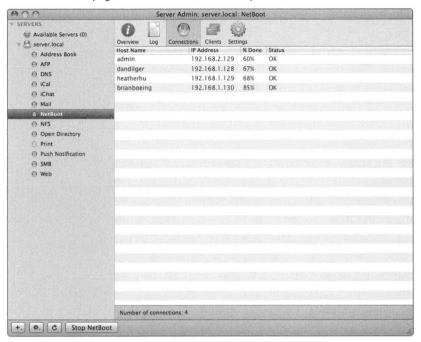

The Clients page of the NetBoot pane, shown in Figure 34.10, lists all the NetBoot clients that have ever booted from an image on the server. It presents a hostname, an IP address, and a hardware address.

Selecting a client presents more detail, including the system type, client name, image name, and index as well as the last time the client booted from the image.

Hosting NetBoot images on multiple servers

You can distribute the load of serving NetBoot images by setting up multiple NetBoot servers on your network. Copy the same image to a share point on each server after assigning the copies the same image index ID in the range between 4096 and 65535.

This advertises the images to client systems as being the same image. When users select the image, they boot from it by using a round-robin selection of one of the available servers.

It's also possible to serve the same image from different share point volumes of the same server by using the same index ID number to distribute load between disks.

Figure 34.10

The Clients page in the Server Admin's NetBoot pane

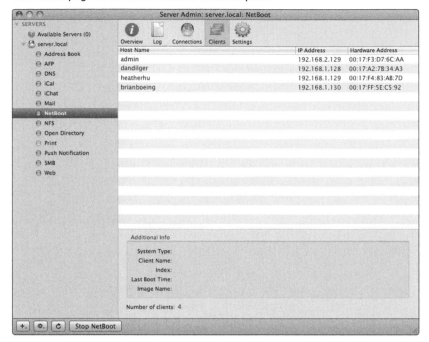

Summary

- Mac OS X Snow Leopard Server provides the NetBoot service to allow clients to boot directly from a disk image served over the network, enabling centralized management of client systems.

- Client machines can all use the same image for booting and save independent client data to shadow files to keep the served disk image from being altered. By default, the client uses shadow files served on the network but can use the local disk if there are no share points available for use.

- System Image Utility is used to create network bootable disk images from an installer DVD or from an existing system.

- Support for Automator Actions enables System Image Utility to build workflows for customizing image creation with special configurations.

- Both the NetBoot service and individual NetBoot images can be configured to filter access to clients based on the MAC hardware address of the client system or the system identifier of the Mac model.

Managing Client Systems with NetInstall and NetRestore

N etInstall and NetRestore are features provided with Mac OS X Server that enable administrators to create and manage disk images that client machines on the network can boot from to update or re-image their local disk, simplifying the process of rolling out security patches, system updates, and application upgrades.

Instead of managing software on each machine individually, NetInstall and NetRestore allow disk images to be managed in one place — on the NetBoot server — and subsequently used to boot and update or image a variety of machines on the network.

NetInstall and NetRestore are closely related to NetBoot and even use the same delivery system and network configuration service. The difference is that whereas NetBoot is designed to replace the local boot hard drive with a network substitute image, NetInstall and NetRestore are designed to act like a network substitute for a local DVD drive for installing or updating software.

NetRestore is a new feature in Snow Leopard Server and is based on Apple Software Restore, a tool used to completely re-image a client computer's disk.

Multiple NetInstall and NetRestore disk images can be defined for different tasks or types of systems by using Automator Actions, allowing you to roll out software or reconfigure machines according to customized workflows you create.

For example, NetInstall can be used to set up unattended installations, and NetRestore can be used to periodically image systems by using different boot images so machines in the same lab could be used for different classes, with each set up with a unique set of applications or even different operating system versions.

NetBoot does something similar but without using a local disk. Which approach you choose depends on your circumstances and the effect you're hoping to achieve. Of course, the time and network resources involved in reinstalling software on a client computer's local hard drive or reimaging it over the network will also need to figure into planning stages of how you implement NetInstall and NetRestore.

This chapter introduces how NetInstall and NetRestore work, the plans you need to make to implement them on your network, how to set up disk images for network access, and the tools Snow Leopard Server provides for managing the NetBoot service they use.

Introduction to NetInstall

NetInstall works similarly to NetBoot, but instead of serving as the client machine's replacement hard drive, a NetInstall image only boots up the client computer long enough to install the software on the image.

The client user then restarts from his or her own local hard drive. So, again, whereas a NetBoot image substitutes a client computer's boot hard drive, a NetInstall image replaces the use of an installation DVD.

As with a bootable DVD, NetInstall makes it easy to reinstall a machine's operating system and update its applications stored on the local hard drive. By using the same network service as NetBoot, NetInstall centralizes client system administration and avoids any need to manually run around inserting an install disc into each client system.

The process of creating images for use with NetInstall is also similar to NetBoot, using the same System Image Utility. Support for Automator workflows enables you to customize images that can be used to:

- Filter images to work only with specific systems
- Reconfigure the client system's boot disk partitions
- Automate software installation by using predefined installation settings

This provides a powerful tool for client management — one that can result in client data loss if applied incorrectly because network images can be designed to wipe or repartition the client's drive.

You should be sure that access to NetInstall images is managed carefully and that users understand how they work. Prior to performing automated network installations, you should instruct users to back up any local data.

In addition to working as a full disk installer, you can also use NetInstall to apply a series of packages you can create by using PackageMaker, a component of the Xcode developer tools used to create install files for adding new software to existing disk images.

CROSS-REF
For more on deploying NetInstall by using the NetBoot service, obtaining the initial NetBoot configuration, and downloading Mac OS X startup files, see Chapter 34.

While booted over the network, client machines don't interact with the network disk image as a normal Mac OS X startup volume. In order to prevent client users from modifying a NetBoot image, the service directs all client attempts to write to the disk image to independent shadow files maintained for each client instead.

When performing a NetInstall, however, the system doesn't use shadow files, so there's no option to designate a NetInstall image as being diskless. Instead, NetInstall sets up a local RAM disk, as needed, for writable storage during the install session.

Introduction to NetRestore

NetRestore is a new component of the NetBoot and NetInstall features added in Snow Leopard. It's used to clone a client machine from an existing image. It can also use multicasting to clone multiple client machines at once.

In comparison to NetBoot acting as a network boot disk replacement and NetInstall serving as a network DVD drive, NetRestore is a little like a network substitute for a directly attached FireWire hard drive used for disk imaging. If you're familiar with tools for Windows deployment, NetRestore is similar to Symantec Ghost and Microsoft's Windows Automated Installation Kit.

NetRestore is based on Apple Software Restore, a command-line tool used to completely re-image a client computer's disk. Apple originally developed the software for internal use to wipe machines back to factory settings. In the days of the Classic Mac OS, it also provided the tool to large organizations to help manage their systems.

With the release of Mac OS X, Apple continued to ship a Classic Mac OS version of the Apple Software Restore tool for imaging the new operating system. With the release of 10.2, Apple ported the software to a Unix command-line tool called `asr`.

The new tool enabled a variety of new features in addition to copying drive images locally:

- **It can restore images from an HTTP or HTTPS server.**
- **It can act as a multicast server to send data addressed to multiple computers at once for concurrent imaging (one to many).** Previously, it could only do unicast transmissions to a single host on the network (one to one). Multicast transmissions specify a source URL by using the protocol `asr://`.
- **It can restore files to a disk image rather than to a disk.**

Depending on its circumstances and configuration, `asr` can perform two types of imaging:

- **Block copy efficiently sends a clone of the source image to the target.** This requires that the source be an unmounted volume or disk image or a volume mounted as read-only and that the source and target file formats match. A source image based on an HFSX (HFS+ case-sensitive) disk can't be restored to a regular case-insensitive

HFS+ drive because of the possibility of file name collision. In other words, HFSX can support file.txt and FILE.txt in the same directory, whereas HFS can't. Multicast deployment of NetRestore images requires the capacity to do a block copy.

● **File copy performs a file-by-file copy.** This takes much longer because the system has to rewrite each file on the new file system.

A third-party tool named NetRestore, maintained by Mike Bombich, has provided a graphical interface for asr since it was released with Mac OS X Jaguar. Bombich ended support for that tool last year.

That version of NetRestore supported customized deployment features, including the ability to set the computer name and automatically run post-deployment scripts. Bombich also maintained NetRestore Helper, a tool for booting Macs by using a NetInstall image to run NetRestore without needing to boot from a local hard drive or CD/DVD.

Apple's new NetRestore feature bundled in Mac OS X Snow Leopard Server uses the same type of Automator Action workflows used to create NetInstall and NetBoot images, allowing for a variety of deployment customizations as well as integration with NetInstall for automated deployment of images.

CROSS-REF
For more on planning, deploying, setting up, and configuring NetInstall and NetRestore, see similar requirements for NetBoot in Chapter 34.

Creating NetInstall images with System Image Utility

Using System Image Utility — installed within /Applications/Server on the server available as part of the server admin tools on the installer DVD — you can create Mac OS X NetInstall images that can then be used to install software on client systems over the network.

You can also build an Automator workflow to create NetInstall images that allow advanced customization.

To create a NetInstall image, follow these steps:

1. **Launch System Image Utility.** You must be a local administrator to create new NetInstall images.

2. **From the main page, shown in Figure 35.1, select an image source from the Sources list.** If no sources are available, insert a Mac OS X DVD or mount a valid installer boot volume, such as a FireWire drive. You can't create a NetInstall image from the boot volume of the computer you're currently working on. Your source volume must be Mac OS X Snow Leopard 10.6 or later. While NetBoot images created with Mac OS X Server v10.4 and v10.5 can be reused, Snow Leopard Server 10.6 only supports creating disk images for machines that can run Snow Leopard.

Figure 35.1

Creating a new NetInstall image

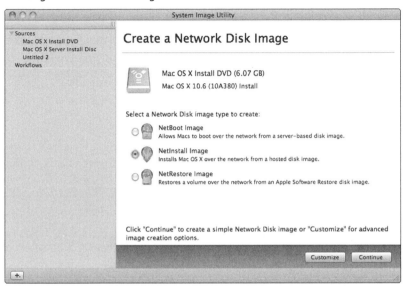

3. **Click the NetInstall Image radio button and then click Continue.**

4. **Configure the image settings:**

   - **Image Name.** Type a name to identify the image in the Startup Disk preferences pane on client computers.

   - **Description.** Optionally, type information describing the image. Clients won't see the description.

   - **Click the check box if the image is served from more than one server to generate an index ID for NetBoot server load balancing.** The index number is recorded in the NBImageInfo.plist file, with a number below 4096 indicating an image unique to the server and higher numbers used to designate duplicate, identical images stored on multiple servers for load balancing.

5. **Click Create.**

6. **Choose a location to save the image.**

7. **Click Save and then authenticate as a local administrator.** After System Image Utility creates the image, copy it to the /Library/NetBoot/NetBootSP0 share point on the server for use by the NetBoot service, replacing 0 with the appropriate number.

Creating a NetInstall image workflow

System Image Utility lets you build workflows to create customized NetInstall images by using Automator Actions to perform a series of tasks, such as automating the installer process or partitioning the drive.

Each Automator Action is designed to perform a single task combined with other actions in a workflow to provide modular, programmatic customization of your NetInstall image.

Provided Automator Actions for creating a NetInstall image include:

- **Define Image Source.** Specifies the source for the disk image creation. This is the starting point of every NetInstall workflow.
- **Partition Disk.** Allows the installation to begin by reconfiguring the partition map of the local drive. This destroys any data on the drive.
- **Enable Automated Installation.** This specifies the target volume for the installation, offers an option to erase prior to installing, and selects a main language.
- **Customize Package Selection.** Allows you to choose the visible and default options presented by the installer. For example, for the Mac OS X Snow Leopard installer, this includes:
  - Essential System Software
  - Printer Support
  - Additional Fonts
  - Language Translations
  - X11
  - Rosetta
- **Add Packages and Post-Install Scripts.** This adds packages created by PackageMaker to the NetInstall image.
- Apply System Configuration Settings:
  - Can configure LDAP bindings for the system
  - Can obtain a computer name and local hostname settings from a specified file or generate a unique computer name starting with the label you provide and appending a unique number
  - Can transfer the computer preferences of the original computer used to create the image by choosing Change ByHost preferences to match client after install
- **Filter Clients by MAC Address.** This allows the NetInstall image to work only with systems with the MAC hardware addresses specified or, alternatively, denies it the ability to work on the MAC hardware addresses specified.
- **Filter Computer Models.** This allows the NetInstall image to work only with the Mac models specified or, alternatively, denies it the ability to work on the Mac models specified.
- **Create Image.** This adds the NetInstall creation step to the workflow and optionally allows specifying an image index.

To create a NetInstall image by using a workflow, follow these steps:

1. **Launch System Image Utility.** You must be a local administrator to create new NetInstall images.

2. **Click Customize on the main page.**

3. **A simple workflow is presented, as shown in Figure 35.2, allowing you to:**
   - **Define Image Source.** Specifies the source for the disk image creation. This is the starting point of every NetInstall workflow.
   - **Create Image.** This adds the NetInstall creation step to the workflow for setting the same configurations as when you perform a normal NetInstall image.

Figure 35.2

Creating a new NetInstall image by using a workflow

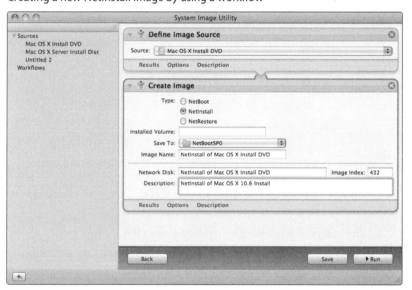

4. **From the Automator Library inspector that appears, as shown in Figure 35.3, you can customize the workflow by dragging Actions into the workflow to add additional configuration options.**

5. **Configure the options of the assembled workflow, as shown in Figure 35.4.** Your workflow ends with the Create Image action.

6. **Click Save to save your workflow.** Type a name, choose a location, and then click Save.

Figure 35.3

The Automator Library

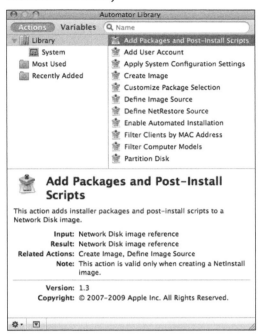

To run a saved NetInstall workflow to create an image, follow these steps:

1. Launch System Image Utility. You must be a local administrator to create new NetBoot images.

2. Choose your workflow from the Sources list.

3. To add a workflow not in the list, click the Add (+) button, choose Add Workflow from the pop-up menu, and then choose your saved workflow file.

4. Click Run to use the workflow and then authenticate as a local administrator if prompted. After the image is created, copy it to the `/Library/NetBoot/ NetBootSP0` share point on the server for use by the NetBoot service, alternatively replacing `0` with the appropriate number of the share point you want to serve it from.

Figure 35.4

A configured workflow for creating a NetInstall image

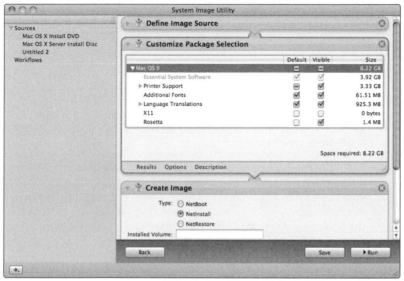

Updating NetInstall images with packages

To add application software or other files during image creation instead of installing the applications or files on the image source volume before you create the image, you need to bundle them together into a special file called a package.

A *package* is a file with a `.pkg` extension that contains a collection of compressed installer files and related information used to install software in Mac OS X. To view the contents of a package within the Finder, Control+click the package and then choose Show Package Contents from the pop-up menu.

To create new packages, you can use the PackageMaker tool included with Apple's Xcode development tools. Xcode can be installed from the Mac OS X Server Installer DVD within Other Installs.

In addition to the graphical PackageMaker app, you can also use the command-line `package-maker` tool installed at `/Developer/usr/bin/packagemaker`. Use of the tool is documented on its man page.

After creating packages, you can add them to your NetInstall image by using the Add Packages and Post-Install Scripts Automator Action within a System Image Utility workflow. Post-install scripts provide the ability to customize each computer you deploy by using NetInstall.

Creating NetRestore images with System Image Utility

Using System Image Utility, installed within /Applications/Server on the server available as part of the server admin tools on the installer DVD, you can create Mac OS X NetRestore images that can then be used to image client systems over the network.

You can also build an Automator workflow to create NetRestore images that allow advanced customization.

To create a NetRestore image, follow these steps:

1. **Launch System Image Utility.** You must be a local administrator to create new NetRestore images.

2. **From the main page, shown in Figure 35.5, select an image source from the Sources list.** If no sources are available, insert a Mac OS X Install DVD, mount a valid volume, such as a FireWire drive, or attach a configured system you want to image via FireWire target mode. You can't create a NetRestore image from the boot volume of the computer you're currently working on. Your source volume must be Mac OS X Snow Leopard 10.6 or later.

Figure 35.5

Creating a new NetRestore image

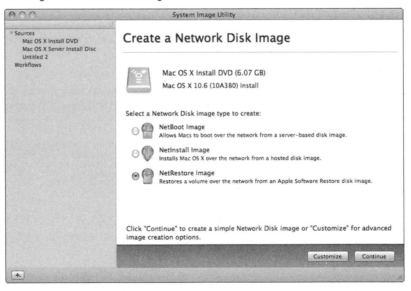

3. **Click the NetRestore Image radio button and then click Continue.**

4. **Configure the image settings:**

   * **Network Disk.** Type a name to identify the image.

   * **Description.** Optionally, type information describing the image. Clients won't see the description.

   * **Click the check box if the image is served from more than one server to generate an index ID for NetBoot server load balancing.** The index number is recorded in the `NBImageInfo.plist` file, with a number below 4096 indicating an image unique to the server and higher numbers used to designate duplicate, identical images stored on multiple servers for load balancing.

5. **Click Create.**

6. **Choose a location to save the image.**

7. **Click Save and then authenticate as a local administrator.** After System Image Utility creates the image, copy it to the `/Library/NetBoot/NetBootSP0` share point on the server for use by the NetBoot service, replacing `0` with the appropriate number. Alternatively, you can host the NetRestore image by using `asr` to perform multicast deployment.

Creating a NetRestore image workflow

System Image Utility lets you build workflows to create customized NetRestore images by using Automator Actions to perform a series of tasks, such as customizing a system configuration or adding a local user account.

Each Automator Action is designed to perform a single task combined with other actions into a workflow to provide modular, programmatic customization of your NetRestore image.

Provided Automator Actions for creating a NetRestore image include:

* **Define Image Source.** Specifies the source for the disk image creation. This is one starting point for a NetRestore workflow.

* **Define NetRestore Source.** Specifies a URI source for the disk image creation. The window can display a list of available ASR multicast streams or other NetRestore sources advertised by using Bonjour as a starting point for a NetRestore workflow.

* **Partition Disk.** Allows the installation to begin by reconfiguring the partition map of the local drive. This destroys any data on the drive.

* **Add Packages and Post-Install Scripts.** This adds packages created by PackageMaker to the NetRestore image.

* Apply System Configuration Settings:

   * Can configure LDAP bindings for the system

   * Can obtain a computer name and local hostname settings from a specified file or generate a unique computer name starting with the label you provide and appending a unique number

- Can transfer the computer preferences of the original computer used to create the image by choosing Change ByHost preferences to match client after install

- **Filter Clients by MAC Address.** This allows the NetRestore image to work only with systems with the MAC hardware addresses specified or, alternatively, denies it the ability to work on the MAC hardware addresses specified.

- **Filter Computer Models.** This allows the NetRestore image to work only with the Mac models specified or, alternatively, denies it the ability to work on the Mac models specified.

- **Create Image.** This adds the NetRestore creation step to the workflow and optionally allows specifying an image index.

To create a NetRestore image by using a workflow, follow these steps:

1. **Launch System Image Utility.** You must be a local administrator to create new NetRestore images.

2. **Click Customize on the main page.**

3. **A simple workflow is presented, as shown in Figure 35.6, allowing you to:**

- **Define Image Source.** Specifies the source for the disk image creation. This is the starting point of every NetRestore workflow.

- **Create Image.** Adds the NetRestore creation step to the workflow for setting the same configurations as when you perform a normal NetRestore image

4. **From the Automator Library inspector that appears, you can customize the workflow by dragging Actions into the workflow to add additional configuration options.**

5. **Configure the options of the assembled workflow, as shown in Figure 35.7.** Your workflow ends with the Create Image action.

6. **Click Save to save your workflow.** Type a name, choose a location, and then click Save.

To run a saved NetRestore workflow to create an image, follow these steps:

1. **Launch System Image Utility.** You must be a local administrator to create new NetRestore images.

2. **Choose your workflow from the Sources list.**

3. **To add a workflow not in the list, click the Add (+) button, choose Add Workflow from the pop-up menu, and then choose your saved workflow file.**

4. **Click Run to use the workflow and then authenticate as a local administrator if prompted.** After the image is created, copy it to the `/Library/NetBoot/ NetBootSP0` share point on the server for use by the NetBoot service, alternatively replacing `0` with the appropriate number of the share point you want to serve it from.

Figure 35.6

Creating a new NetRestore image by using a workflow

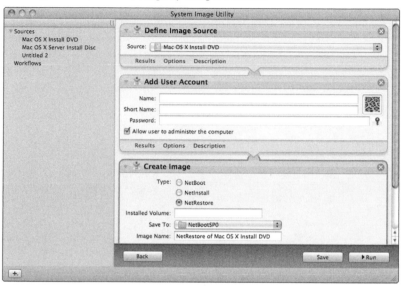

Figure 35.7

Configured workflow for creating a NetRestore image

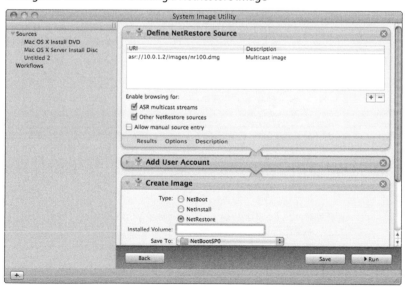

Enabling NetInstall and NetRestore images

After using System Image Utility to create a NetBoot image, copy the image's `.nbi` folder into `/Library/NetBoot/NetBootSP0` on the server for use by the NetBoot service, replacing `0` with the appropriate number. You can then enable the image in Server Admin.

To configure basic NetBoot services, follow these steps:

1. **Launch Server Admin, click NetBoot, and then click Settings on the toolbar.**

2. **Click the Images tab, shown in Figure 35.8.**

Figure 35.8

The Images pane of the NetBoot pane's Settings page

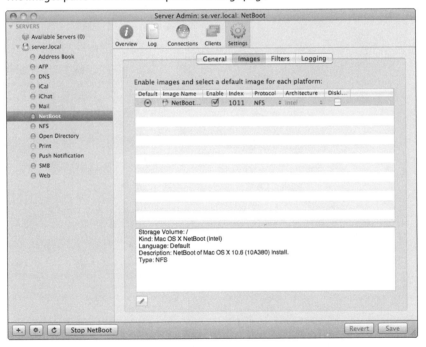

3. **Click the check box(es) for the image(s) you want to serve to clients.** For each, select the protocol used to serve the image, either NFS or HTTP. If you select HTTP, the name of your image can't include spaces. You also need to start the web service.

4. **Click the check box(es) for the NetInstall and NetRestore image(s) you want to use as the default.** The default image is used when clients force a NetBoot by holding down the N key while starting up. Otherwise, available images are presented for the user to select during an Option-key boot or from the Startup Disk pane in System

Preferences. If you're serving images for multiple architectures, select a default image for each.

5. **Optionally, restrict use of an image to specific models or to specific machines by MAC hardware address by clicking the Edit button marked with a pencil icon.**

6. **From the sheet that drops down, click either or both radio buttons:**
   - **Allow only computers below.** This enables the specific models you want to be able to boot from the image.
   - **Allow only clients listed below.** This specifies the MAC addresses you want to be able to NetBoot from the image. Alternatively, choose Deny only clients listed below to specify the MAC addresses you don't want to be able to NetBoot from the image.

7. **Click OK.**

8. **Click Save.**

Filtering NetInstall and NetRestore clients

You can restrict specific client machines by MAC hardware address from using your NetBoot server or, alternatively, allow only specific systems. You can also apply filter settings on a per-image basis as previously described.

You can restrict specific client machines by MAC hardware address from using your NetBoot server or, alternatively, allow only specific systems. You can also apply filter settings on a per-image basis as described previously.

To filter access to NetBoot services, follow these steps:

1. **Launch Server Admin, click NetBoot, and then click Settings on the toolbar.**

2. **Click the Filters tab, shown in Figure 35.9.**

3. **Enable or disable NetBoot/DHCP filtering by clicking the appropriate check box:**
   - **Allow only clients listed below.** This specifies the MAC addresses of systems you want to be able to use NetBoot.
   - **Deny only clients listed below.** This specifies the MAC addresses you don't want to be able to use NetBoot.

4. **Look up a machine's MAC address by typing its DNS name or IP address in the Host Name field and then click Search.**

5. **Click Choose to import values from a file listing a series of MAC addresses and then click Extract.**

6. **Click Save.**

Figure 35.9

The Filters pane of the NetBoot pane

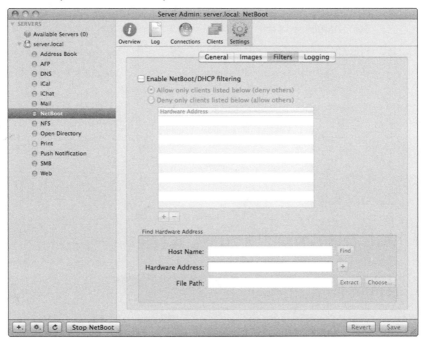

Boot Server Discovery Protocol and DHCP

Client discovery of available NetBoot servers relies on the client broadcasting for a server that responds to the Boot Service Discovery Protocol (BSDP). Routers are typically configured to block broadcast traffic from being routed to other subnets.

To provide NetBoot service across subnets, you have to configure your routers to pass BSDP traffic to the NetBoot server. This should be possible if your router supports DHCP helper or DHCP relay agent features.

NetRestore can perform multicast deployments by using ASR that spans networks if the appropriate multicast addresses are used. Local link multicast addresses only work within the local subnet.

It's possible to configure a third-party DHCP server to perform BSDP, but it makes more sense to enable NetBoot servers to act as their own DHCP service and then configure NetBoot filtering to only allow DHCP services for systems configured to NetBoot.

NetBoot actually uses BootP, a subset of the DHCP protocol. Any BootP devices that try to obtain an IP address from the NetBoot server fail because NetBoot server doesn't assign IP addresses unless the server is also configured to act as a full DHCP server.

You can prevent the NetBoot BootP server from responding to requests for IP addresses by using the `dscl` command to open the local folder on the NetBoot server and then adding a key named `bootp_enabled` with no value to the `/config/dhcp/` folder:

```
dscl . -create /Config/dhcp bootp_enabled ""
```

Another potential problem for NetBoot relates to Initial Connectivity Delay, a short router-imposed delay to network connectivity that occurs when a managed switch is configured to automatically detect problems with network devices.

Protocols such as PortFast or Spanning Tree Protocol are intended to prevent problems such as network looping by probing the attached network interface when a connection is first detected on a port. This can result in a 15–30 second delay before the port starts working.

Initial Connectivity Delay isn't necessary on ports connected to known host systems, and if active, it can prevent NetBoot from working because the client needs immediate network access to find and begin its connection with the NetBoot server.

Disabling these managed switch protocols for the ports used by NetBooting client systems can resolve the problem.

Configuring client systems for NetBoot

A Mac can be configured to search for a network volume to boot from either by:

- Selecting Network Startup from the Startup Disk pane in System Preferences
- Setting NVRAM boot-args by using the `nvram` command
- Holding down the Option key at boot and then selecting a network boot device
- Holding down the N key at boot

Managing and Monitoring NetInstall and NetRestore

The Overview page of Server Admin's NetBoot pane presents a status report that includes:

- Whether the service is currently active
- When the service was started
- The last client update
- The number of enabled Mac OS X NetBoot images
- The number of enabled Mac OS X images configured for diskless booting
- The number of enabled Mac OS 9 NetBoot images
- The protocols enabled for Mac OS X NetBoot: AFP, NFS, HTTP, and DHCP

- The protocols enabled for Mac OS X images configured for diskless booting
- The protocols enabled for Mac OS 9 NetBoot images

Monitoring NetInstall and NetRestore logs

The Logs page of the NetBoot pane presents logs reported in `var/log/system.log`.

The logging level of the service can be configured under the Logging tab of the NetBoot pane's Settings page — from all events to errors only.

Monitoring NetInstall and NetRestore clients

The Connections page of the NetBoot pane, shown in Figure 35.10, lists the currently connected NetInstall and NetRestore clients that have booted from an image on the server. It presents a hostname, an IP address, and a status.

Figure 35.10

The Connections page of the NetBoot pane

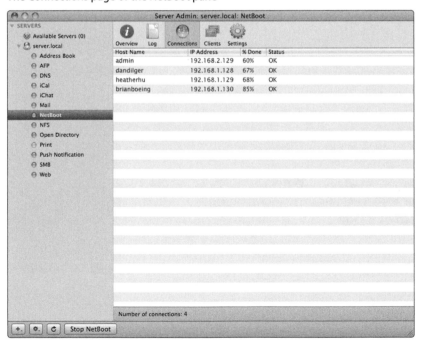

The Clients page of the NetBoot pane, shown in Figure 35.11, lists all the NetInstall and NetRestore clients that have ever booted from an image on the server. It presents a hostname, an IP address, and a hardware address.

Selecting a client presents more detail, including the system type, client name, image name, and index as well as the last time the client booted from the image.

Hosting NetInstall and NetRestore images on multiple servers

You can distribute the load of serving NetInstall and NetRestore images by setting up multiple NetBoot servers on your network. Copy the same image to a share point on each server after assigning the copies the same image index ID in the range between 4096 and 65535.

This advertises the images to client systems as being the same image. When users select the image, they boot from it by using a round-robin selection of one of the available servers.

It's also possible to serve the same image from different share point volumes of the same server by using the same index ID number to distribute load between disks.

Figure 35.11

The Clients page of the NetBoot pane

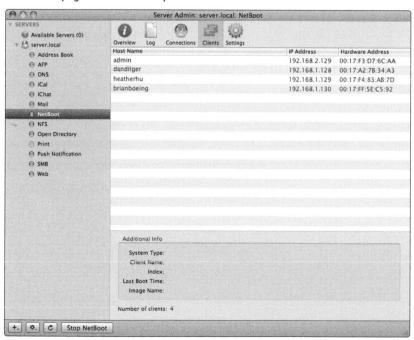

Summary

- Mac OS X Snow Leopard Server provides the NetBoot service to allow clients to perform a NetInstall or NetRestore from an image served over the network, enabling centralized management of client systems.

- System Image Utility is used to create network bootable installation disk images and restorable system images from an installer DVD or from an existing system.

- Support for Automator Actions enables System Image Utility to build workflows for customizing image creation with special configurations.

- Both the NetBoot service and individual NetInstall and NetRestore images can be configured to filter access to clients based on the MAC hardware address of the client system or the system identifier of the Mac model.

Managed Preferences

A central element to managing client computers and users in Mac OS X Server is the principle of managed preferences. Building on the mechanism of application and system preferences in Mac OS X, which store configuration settings in standardized XML files, managed preferences enable administrators to either set or force specific configurations for network users, groups of users or computers, or across groups of computers.

Using managed preferences, an organization can centrally automate the setup of a customized user environment tailored to specific users or to defined computers. Managed preferences can also be used to enforce security policy, preventing users from installing or launching applications and even turning off hardware features, such as Bluetooth or optical disk burning.

Using managed preferences requires network machines to be bound to a directory domain. When the machines start up, they obtain and apply any managed preferences defined for their computer account and any managed computer groups that their computer account belongs to from the directory.

When a user logs in, he or she is presented with a selection of managed groups, known as *workgroups*, which may be used to apply additional managed preferences to the login session. Any managed preferences configured for the user's own individual account are then applied.

This hierarchy of managed preferences results in a simple and straightforward way for administrators to define both a suggested starting point and enforced policies that manage the configuration of computers, workgroups, and users.

This chapter describes how managed preferences work, what's involved in planning for managed preferences, how they're configured within Mac OS X Server's Workgroup Manager interface, and how to maintain and monitor managed preferences.

Introduction to Managed Preferences

Apple's managed preferences in Mac OS X Server are similar in many respects to Microsoft's Group Policy feature in Windows domains and Active Directory, except that rather than using the Windows Registry, Mac OS X clients enforce policy by using preferences files.

Mac OS X preferences

Managed preferences work by configuring optional or mandatory settings to the preference files used by Mac OS X and its bundled and third-party applications. To explain how, first take a look at how Mac OS X uses preference files to store configuration settings.

Unix processes commonly store their configuration settings in basic text files, such as the Apache web server's `httpd.conf`. These are designed to be human readable and editable and are also parsed by the service to obtain its configured settings. Third-party tools may also provide a graphical interface for editing this file. This works fine until the file is edited by a process that either can't understand portions of the configuration file or ignores existing settings when writing it back out.

Mac OS X improves on basic text configuration files by using XML plists to store application and system configuration data. These XML files are simply structured text files, which makes updating and editing them consistent. Apple provides the command-line tool `defaults` for reading and changing preference values, and applications commonly present a graphical interface for setting these values within their Preferences pane.

In some cases, an application or service may support a configuration option that's not exposed in the Preferences pane, leaving `defaults` as the only way to read or set this option. For example, the following line sets the Finder's configuration to show invisible files normally hidden:

```
defaults write com.apple.finder AppleShowAllFiles TRUE
```

Managing preferences

This consistent architecture for setting application preferences is also used by the operating system, enabling automated, secure, and comprehensive control over both built-in features and any type of settings supported by third-party applications that support `defaults`-style XML preferences, as most all modern apps do.

Managed preferences are stored in the domain's LDAP directory in account record attributes named `apple-user-mcxflags`, which identify the account as being managed, and `apple-user-mcxsettings`, which define each preference that's managed. The attributes may be applied to the directory accounts of individual users, groups, or computers or to groups of computers.

A user with defined managed preferences is called a *managed user*. A group with defined managed preferences is called a *workgroup*. A computer with managed preferences is called a *managed computer*.

Managed preferences make sense only for users who don't have local administrative control of their computer; users with local administrative access can opt out of managed preferences at login entirely.

Planning Managed Preferences

Planning the deployment of managed preferences requires setting initial policy that determines how users and machines are managed and then determining how that policy will be implemented through combined layers of managed preferences on users, groups, and machines.

Determining the level of administrative control

Managed preferences may be used to exert varying levels of control over users and computers. When planning the level of control desired, consider how users might be impacted by the restrictions and what level of control is necessary.

For example, it may be preferable to set user environment settings such as the Dock once and then allow users to customize their environment going forward. Forcing unnecessary and arbitrary control over how a user's desktop looks and works with managed preferences may result in preventing the user from being as productive as he or she could be with a more customizable work environment.

Excessive controls forced through managed preferences may also result in unintended consequences that result in additional support calls and lost efficiency, negating one of the main benefits of the feature: reduced administrative efforts and resources.

Managed preferences should be planned in accordance with the number and type of users, what types of computers they're using, how mobile users are, how much administrative privilege individual users have, what access to resources users need, and the type of uses those users and machines have.

CROSS-REF
For more on planning directory-related services, see Chapter 21.

Combining and layering managing preferences

Advanced planning is required to define managed preferences that combine or override properly. Managed preferences can be one of the following:

- **Combined.** Preferences defined on the user, group, computer, and computer group levels are added together. For example, printing, login, applications, System Preferences, and some Dock preferences (related to items that appear in the Dock) combine to create a composite of managed preferences.

- **Overridden.** Incompatible preference settings are trumped in an order of precedence when the same types of settings are defined on more than one level. For example, if one layer of preference sets the Dock on the right side of the screen and another at the bottom, one of the two settings must override the other.

The overriding order of precedence in applying managed preferences that can't be combined follows this series, from most to least dominant:

- User preferences
- Computer preferences
- Computer group preferences
- Group preferences (workgroups)

This order encourages managed preferences to be set broadly by using workgroups and computer groups, with individual user and computer preferences used primarily for setting overriding exceptions to those group-managed preferences. For example, a corporation could set limitations on workgroups and then exclude a specific power user from those limitations by setting an overriding preference for that user.

Setting preferences at the workgroup level makes the most sense when configuring settings that customize the user environment in ways that apply to a functionally related group of individuals.

Managing preferences at the computer group level is most relevant to settings that aren't related to the function of users but rather according to the intended use of those machines.

User and group preferences

With that in mind, the managed preferences for user accounts should typically be reserved for exceptions overriding the preferences related to workgroups or managed computers.

Because workgroup preferences are related to the functional needs of a group, a user who's a member of multiple groups is given the option to select which functional workgroup of managed preferences he or she wants to inherit at login.

Again, an administrative user can bypass the managed preferences entirely. To impose managed preferences on a user, that user can't have administrative privileges on the local machine.

Computer and computer group preferences

Two categories of managed preferences, Energy Saver and Time Machine backups, can be applied only to computer or computer group accounts.

Once again, it makes the most sense to apply managed preferences to groups of computers and then define overriding exceptions to specific computer accounts or to individual user accounts.

Permanence of managed preferences

A preference setting may be configured as being managed:

- **Never.** It's not managed.
- **Once.** The preference is initially set, but the user can change it afterward.
- **Always.** The preference is permanently set.
- **Often (in customized preferences).** The preference is reset at each login.

Preferences for managed computers and workgroups are cached locally on Mac OS X systems; once applied, they remain in place even when the system isn't connected to the network or can't reach the directory domain controller.

User preferences are also cached for mobile account users. When a managed computer isn't connected to the network, only local accounts and network users with mobile accounts can log in. Users with network-only accounts or mobile users who have never previously logged in aren't able to authenticate until the system joins the network again and can contact the directory domain.

Managed Preferences Setup and Configuration

To configure managed preferences for network users, you need to do the following:

- Bind client systems to the network directory server.
- Create accounts for users, groups, computers, and groups of computers.
- Define managed preferences for these accounts in Workgroup Manager.
- Obtain and apply managed preferences as users log in by using their network accounts.. Computers obtaining a directory configuration from DHCP also obtain and apply managed preferences.

Managing preferences in Workgroup Manager

To configure managed preferences in Workgroup Manager, you must bind client computers to the directory domain, create computer accounts, and then define managed preference settings for users, workgroups, or computer accounts or for groups of computers.

To bind a client computer to the directory domain, follow these steps:

1. **Launch System Preferences and then click Network.**
2. **Authenticate with the pane by clicking the lock icon and then choosing Login Options.**

3. **Click the Edit button next to Network Account Server.** A sheet appears.

4. **Click the Add (+) button and then type the DNS name of the directory server.**

5. **Click OK, authenticate, and then click Done.** The local client is now bound to the given directory server and adds it to its local search policy for authentication and contacts.

CROSS-REF

For more on creating computer accounts in Workgroup Manager, see Chapter 10.

Managed preferences for user, group, computer, and computer group accounts are set in Workgroup Manager by using the Preferences icon on the toolbar, which toggles the primary display from account records to Preferences details. The Preferences pane is split between:

● An Overview tab that displays a series of available categories for managed preferences and indicates which have active preferences in place for the selected account, as shown in Figure 36.1. When a category of managed preferences is selected, a detailed preferences editor is displayed. It allows the administrator to set the initial configuration of a preference, such as which applications appear in the Dock, or to force a configuration that the end user can't change, such as disabling Front Row as a feature.

Figure 36.1

The Overview pane in Workgroup Manager

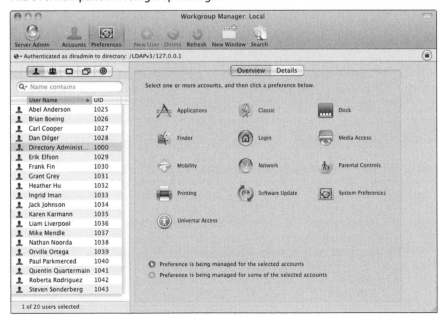

● A Details tab that provides a listing of the managed preferences that have been defined for the selected account, as shown in Figure 36.2.

Figure 36.2

The Details pane in Workgroup Manager

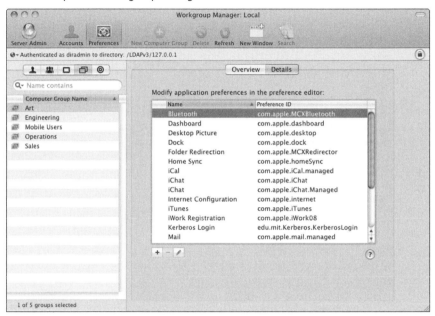

To manage preferences for accounts in Workgroup Manager, follow these steps:

1. **Launch Workgroup Manager and then authenticate with the desired directory domain.**

2. **Select the accounts to be managed.** Multiple accounts can be selected at once from the accounts list, although only one type of account can be selected at once. It's preferable to apply most managed preferences settings to groups and computer groups and manage user and computer records only when creating exceptions to the group management settings.

3. **Click Preferences on the toolbar.** Workgroup Manager displays various categories of preferences that may be managed in the account detail pane.

4. **Choose a category to manage.** From the detail pane that appears, configure the settings as desired and then click Apply Now. Configure other categories as desired. A listing of the manageable preferences available is detailed later in this chapter.

5. **To apply a managed preference to an application that doesn't appear in the graphical interface, click the Details tab and then follow these steps:**

   1. **Select an application or its preference file by clicking the Add (+) button and then choose Once, Often, or Always for managing the preference.** The preference file then appears in the Details tab listing.

   2. **Use the Edit button marked with a pencil icon to open the preference editor.**

   3. **Set values for the attributes within the preference file as desired by using the preference editor and then click Apply Now.**

6. **Test the managed preferences to make sure they behave as expected.**

Manageable preferences in Workgroup Manager

Workgroup Manager presents 15 categories of manageable preferences. Within the application, a managed preference can be applied to a single user, group, or computer or to a computer group or a selection of multiple accounts within the same type. Using Search may help select related accounts in order to apply a managed preference.

The Details tab can be used to import additional preferences options from other applications, which can be similarly configured and applied as a managed preference.

Application preferences

Within the Applications category, there are four tabs of options that can be managed, as shown in Figure 36.3:

- **The Applications tab.** Restricts launch access to an approved list of applications or, alternatively, lists folders containing allowed and disallowed applications. It can only be set to Always or Never. This preference is based on application signatures, so it applies only to clients running Leopard or Snow Leopard. Workgroup Manager signs the approved list of applications. If the signature can't be embedded, such as with applications run from a read-only volume, it uses a detached signature separate from the application. If a signed application is modified, it's no longer approved.

- **The Widgets tab.** Enables specific Dashboard widgets. This preference can only be set to Always or Never and similarly works only under Leopard and Snow Leopard.

- **The Front Row tab.** This allows users to access the feature and makes sense only with Always or Never.

- **The Legacy tab.** Applies to applications on systems prior to Leopard. It restricts application-launching based on bundle IDs rather than application signing, which is a less-secure method of controlling access to applications because users can edit the bundle IDs of their applications to override the managed preference. Three options allow users to run any apps on local volumes, allow approved apps to launch non-approved apps, and allow Unix tools to run, which might be necessary for proper functioning of certain applications.

Figure 36.3

Managing application preferences

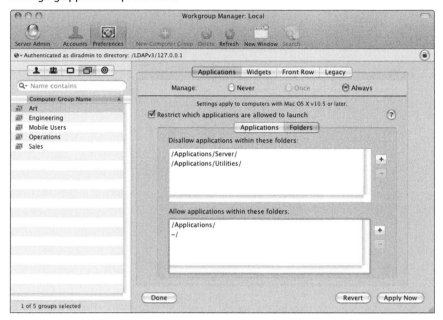

Classic preferences

The Classic category, shown in Figure 36.4, applies to allowing systems prior to Leopard to run Mac OS 9 in the Classic environment. Classic runs only on PowerPC Macs. Managed preferences include specifying the System Folder location to use as well as a variety of options related to startup and the items that appear in the Classic Apple menu.

Dock preferences

The Dock Items tab, shown in Figure 36.5, allows setting the items that appear in the Dock as well as how the Dock itself appears. This setting can be managed Once or Always.

A listing of applications and a separate list of documents and folders can be defined to appear in the Dock and dragged into order of appearance. For workgroups, an option to add the group folder is presented.

Dock items settings can be defined to merge with the user's existing Dock items, and additional check boxes control the display of Applications and Documents folders as well as the user's network home.

Figure 36.4

Managing Classic preferences

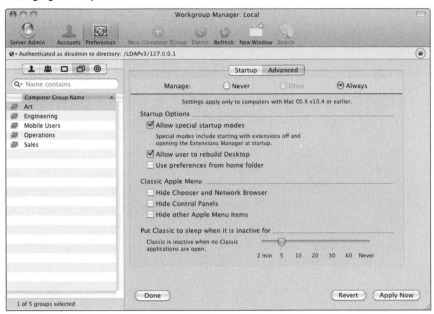

Figure 36.5

The Dock Items pane

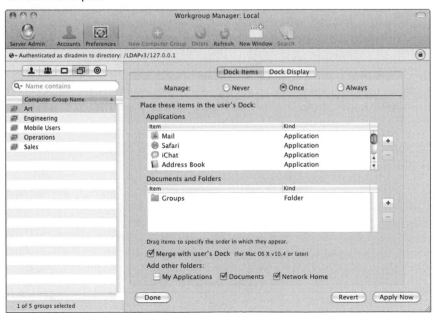

In the Dock Display tab, the Dock size, magnification settings, screen positioning, and minimizing effect can all be set, and options to disable the animated opening of applications and to allow autohiding of the Dock are presented.

Energy Saver preferences

This category, shown in Figure 36.6, sets power management settings for computers or groups of computers, configuring computer and display sleep timers and hard drive sleeping independently for desktop and portable systems running on battery or from a power adapter.

Figure 36.6

Managing Energy Saver preferences

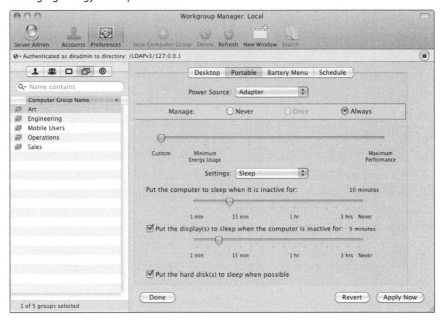

It can also enable a Battery Menu status indicator in the menu bar and set a Schedule to startup and then sleep or power off at a set time every day, on weekdays, on weekends, or on a set day of the week.

The Finder preferences

The Finder category's Preferences tab, shown in Figure 36.7, sets a managed preference Once or Always for using the Simple Finder, for items shown on the desktop, and for preferences such as opening new folders in a new window, displaying items in column view, warning before emptying the trash, and showing file extensions.

Figure 36.7

Managing the Finder preferences

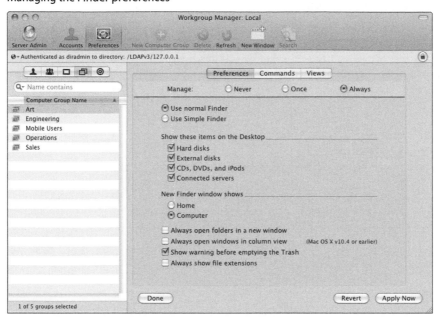

The Commands pane permits turning off the Finder features such as Connect to Server, Go to iDisk, Eject removable media and mountable volumes, disk burning, Go to Folder, and Shutdown and Restart. These features make sense only when set to Always.

The Views tab, shown in Figure 36.8, manages icon size, grid settings, and auto-arrangement on the desktop in the default views of the Finder windows, including showing relative dates and calculating folder sizes, and in the computer view of available volumes. These settings can be made Once or Always.

Figure 36.8

Managing the Finder view preferences

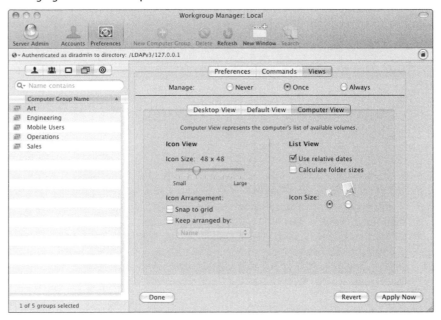

Login preferences

The Login category is available only to computer and computer group accounts and controls a series of settings, including:

- The appearance of the login window, from the Window tab shown in Figure 36.9, including what information about the computer is presented, an optional message section that can be displayed, and the style of the login pane, which can either present only user and password fields or show a list of users to select from. The list can optionally be set to include local accounts, mobile accounts, network users, and computer administrators, and optionally to show an Other option that allows the user to type a different username. The restart and shutdown buttons can also be hidden. The options make sense only when set to Always.

Figure 36.9

Managing Login Window preferences

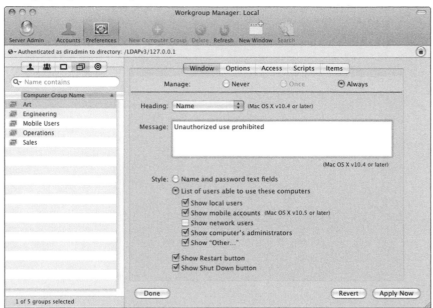

● Login Options, shown in Figure 36.10, include showing a password hint; enabling automatic login, console login, Fast User Switching, or logout after a set number of inactive minutes; preference management disabling by administrative users; setting the computer name to the computer account record name; enabling external accounts and the guest account; and specifying a screen saver and how soon it activates.

● Access, shown in Figure 36.11, allows or denies specific users or groups from logging in, sets whether local non-administrative users may log in, optionally forces local users to pick a workgroup set of managed preferences, allows the user to ignore inherited workgroup settings, can disable the combining of the managed preferences of a user's workgroup memberships, and enables always showing the workgroup selection at login.

Figure 36.10

Managing Login Options preferences

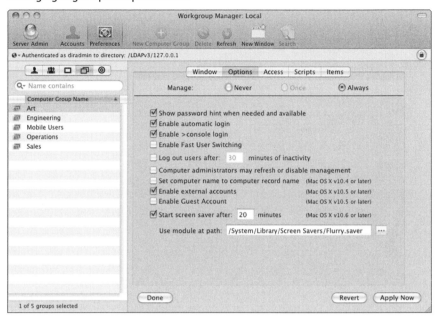

Figure 36.11

Managing Login Access preferences

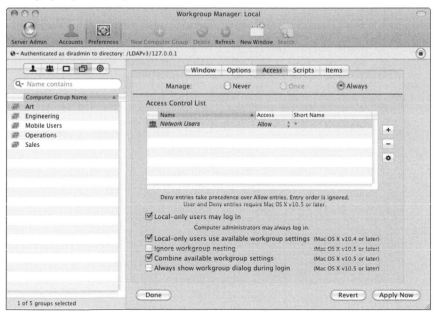

● Scripts, shown in Figure 36.12, enable login and logout scripts to be run and can optionally disable execution of LoginHook and LogoutHook scripts on the client computer.

Figure 36.12

Managing Login Scripts preferences

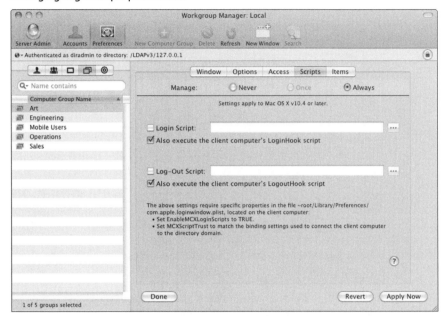

● Items, shown in Figure 36.13, can set a Once or Always preference to the items that open at login. This can include the user's network home share point and group share (if the selected account being managed is a group) and optionally authenticate the mounting by using the user's login name and password. The user can also be prevented from removing or adding any additional login items or from using the Shift key to prevent login items from opening. The login items can also be set to merge with the user's existing defined items.

Figure 36.13

Managing Login Items preferences

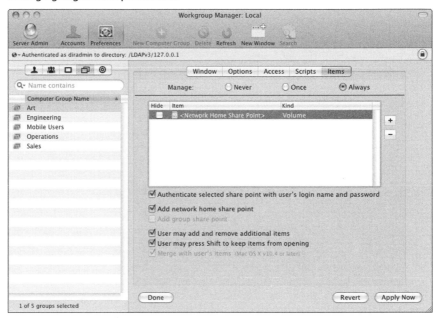

Media Access preferences

This category, shown in Figure 36.14, restricts access to play or record CDs and DVDs unless the user authenticates as a local administrator, and it also offers to force-eject removable media at logout.

It can also force administrative authentication before using internal and external media drives (including floppies, Zip drives, and hard disks), disk images, or DVD-RAM drives or, alternatively, make them read-only.

Mobility preferences

The Mobility category relates to account creation and options for mobile users and sets rules to manage how Portable Home Directories (PHDs) are synced. A PHD copies the user's network home folder locally at first login to allow a mobile user to benefit from the performance of a local home folder while still maintaining a network copy and staying in sync between the two.

Figure 36.14

Managing Media Access preferences

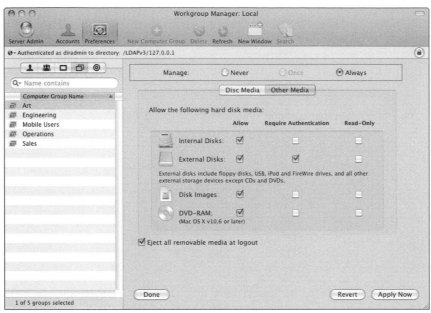

The Account Creation tab, shown in Figure 36.15, can force the creation of a mobile account by using a PHD when the user logs in, optionally requiring confirmation from the user. Setting the preference to require confirmation before creating a mobile account enables the user to optionally log in as a regular network user with no locally cached home folder.

The user's home folder can be set by using his or her network home and default sync settings or based on the local computer's home folder template, which is stored at `/System/Library/ User Template/English.lproj`, or the appropriate template for the language being used.

An Options tab, shown in Figure 36.16, within Account Creation can force home folder encryption by using FileVault, Apple's home folder encryption feature — either by using or requiring the computer master password. FileVault encrypts the user's home folder by using 128-bit AES (Advance Encryption Standard) keys. If the system is stolen, documents and data in the home folder aren't readable without the user's password.

A FileVault *master password* can be used to recover the home directory if the user forgets his or her own password. This is an optional feature. Without a set master password, the user's home folder is unrecoverable if he or she loses the account password; an administrator can't otherwise reset the FileVault password.

Setting a managed preference requiring a master password requires actually setting the master password on the local system; otherwise, the user won't be able to create a mobile account.

Figure 36.15

Managing Mobility Account Creation preferences

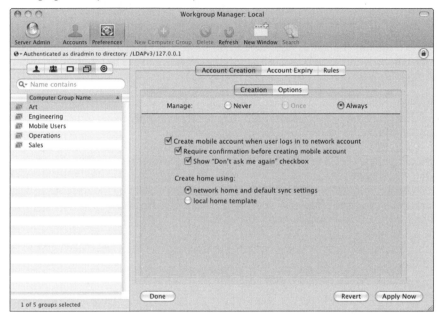

Figure 36.16

Managing Mobility Account Creation option preferences

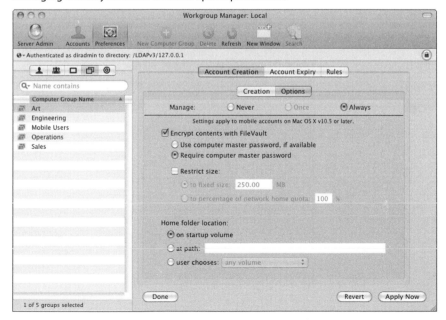

The size of the home folder can be restricted to a set figure or to a percentage of the user's network home quota. The home folder location can be stored locally on the startup volume, at a specified local path, or on a user defined volume, either specifying any volume, any internal volume, or any external volume the user selects.

The second main tab configures Account Expiry, shown in Figure 36.17, allowing forced deletion of mobile accounts after a set number of days after the user's last login. By default, it deletes only the local version after a successful sync.

Expiring old mobile accounts prevents ghost copies of users' home folders from consuming all the local disk space on network computers. Expiry doesn't apply to *external accounts*, where the user's home folder is stored on an external volume.

The third tab, Rules, shown in Figure 36.18, configures Preference Sync either Once or Always, specifying when system-related files, such as the user's `~/Library` directory, are synced, which can be at login, at logout, in the background, or manually by the user. An exclusion list can prevent temp or trash files from being synced. A check box allows the managed settings to be merged with the user's existing settings.

Figure 36.17

Managing Mobility Account Expiry preferences

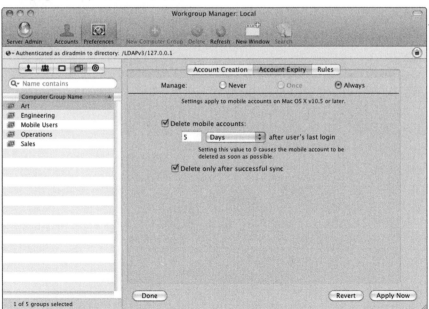

Figure 36.18

Managing Mobility Rules preferences

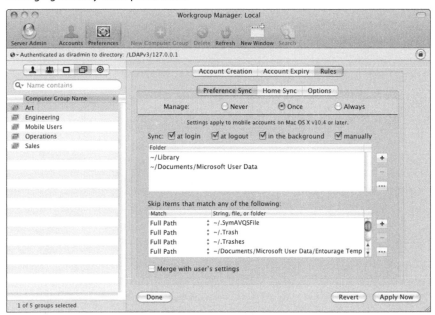

Similar controls are presented to sync folders for Home Sync, and an Options tab sets background sync to occur manually or every set number of minutes, from between 5 minutes and 8 hours. The default setting is every 20 minutes.

A check box can put the mobile account sync status in the menu bar, which indicates when an automatic sync is occurring, enables the user to initiate a manual sync, and shows when the last sync occurred.

CROSS-REF

For more on Portable Home Directories, see Chapter 21.

Network preferences

The Network category enables administrators to set proxy settings for FTP, Web (HTTP), Secure Web (HTTPS), Streaming (RTSP), SOCKS, Gopher, and Automatic Proxy Configuration. A list of hosts and domains that bypass the proxy settings can also be supplied, as shown in Figure 36.19.

Figure 36.19

Managing Network preferences

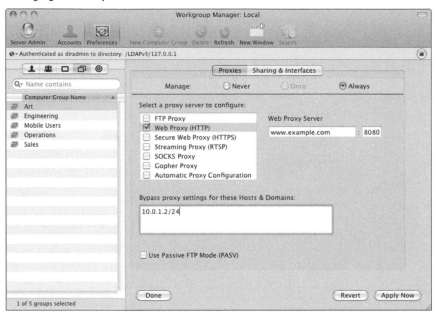

Individual hosts can be specified by fully qualified DNS names or IP addresses; wildcards can be used to include all subdomains on a domain, such as `*.example.com`. Entire subnets can be specified by using CIDR notation, such as `10.0.1.0/24`, which specifies a subnet that ranges from `10.0.1.1` to `10.0.1.254`.

Using the Sharing & Interfaces tab, the pane can also be used to optionally disable Internet Sharing, AirPort wireless networking, and Bluetooth. Disabling Bluetooth applies not only to network sharing but to all Bluetooth features, including support for wireless peripherals, such as mice and keyboards.

Parental Controls preferences

This category supplies two panes of settings that manage Content Filtering and set Time Limits. The first, shown in Figure 36.20, enables administrators to hide profanity in the Dictionary and limit access to websites by either trying to automatically limit access to adult websites or by supplying an approved list of URLs and a blacklist of URLs that are denied access. Settings apply to client systems running Leopard or Snow Leopard.

Figure 36.20

Managing Parental Controls preferences

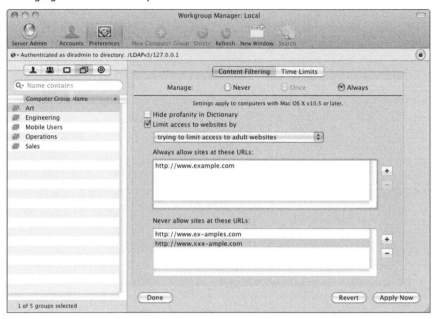

The Time Limits tab can enforce limits that provide a set number of hours of computer access on weekends and weekdays as well as set curfews that prevent computer access outside a set period of time during weekdays and weekends. There's no special support for recognizing holidays according to the configured weekend schedule.

Printing preferences

The Printing category, shown in Figure 36.21, assigns specific printers from those available in the user's printer list. It also offers to allow or deny the user to modify the printer list, connect to printers directly by using USB or FireWire or require administrative user authentication to do this, and to only show managed printers.

The Access pane permits setting the default printer and making specific printers require administrative access prior to use. A separate footer section allows forcing all printed pages to include a footer with the user's name and the date — optionally including the machine's MAC address — in a specified font and size. The footer appears in the specified font on all printed documents in this format:

```
Steve Jobs Wednesday July 1, 2009 1:59:01 PM PT
   0a:1b:2c:3d:4e:5f
```

Figure 36.21

Managing Printing preferences

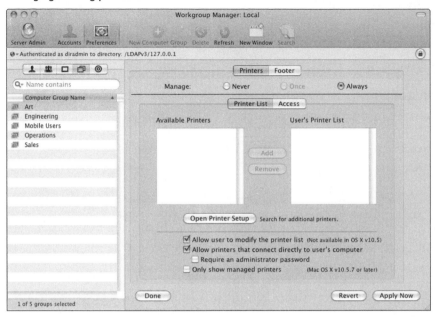

Software Update preferences

The Software Update category sets a server for client computers to access to obtain updates, enabling a local Mac OS X Server system handling Software Update Server. The URL is supplied in this format:

```
http://server.example.com:8088/index.sucatalog
```

CROSS-REF

For more on Software Update Server, see Chapter 37.

System Preferences

The System Preferences category enables the selective hiding of panes within the local system's System Preferences by using a series of check boxes for each pane, as shown in Figure 36.22.

Figure 36.22

Managing System Preferences

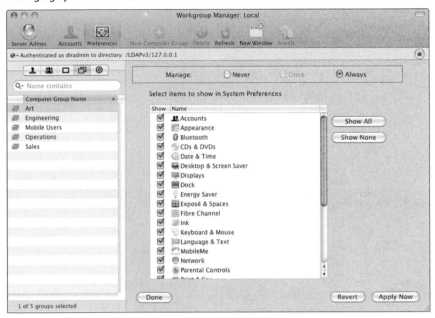

Time Machine preferences

The other category that's supplied only when managing preferences for a computer or group of computers, Time Machine preferences set a URL for a backup destination server share, such as:

```
http://server.example.com/Backups
```

The share point must be designated in Server Admin and be configured to support Time Machine backups. Other settings include specifying Time Machine to back up only the startup volume or all local volumes, an option to skip system files, a default to back up automatically, and a limit setting for total backup storage to a set number of MB, as shown in Figure 36.23.

CROSS-REF
For more on Time Machine Server, see Chapter 38.

Figure 36.23

Managing backup preferences

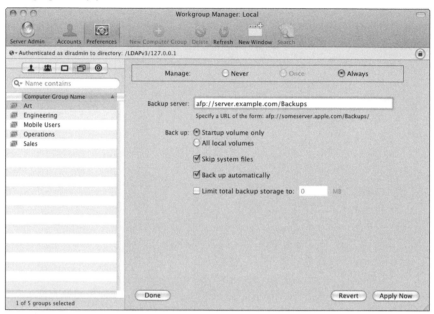

Universal Access preferences

The Universal Access category supplies tabs related to Seeing, Hearing, Keyboard, Mouse, and other Options, as shown in Figure 36.24:

- **Seeing.** The options here are turning on Zoom and setting maximum and minimum zoom, showing a preview rectangle when zoomed out, and smoothing images during zoom. You can also set the display to white on black or grayscale. This pane presents a preview of what the display will look like. These settings can be forced Always or set Once.

- **Hearing.** This offers to flash the screen when an alert sound is played and can be set to Once or Always.

- **Keyboard.** This pane permits enabling Sticky Keys for performing key chords in a sequence and specifying a beep to signal that a modifier key is active and show a display of the pressed keys. It also allows turning on Slow Keys for preventing unintended key repetition, optionally playing a key sound, and setting the acceptance delay for typing. These preferences can be managed Once or Always.

- **Mouse.** You can activate Mouse Keys, which uses the numeric keypad for mouse movement, by setting an initial delay for pointer movement and a maximum speed. These preferences can also be managed Once or Always.

- **Options.** This pane can be used to enable access for assistive devices.

Figure 36.24

Managing Universal Access preferences

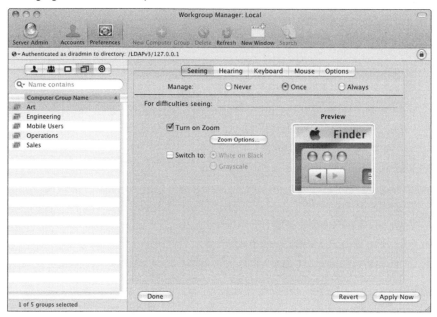

Preferences Editor and the Details tab

For third-party applications and other settings not covered by supplied categories, you can use Workgroup Manager's Preferences Editor to edit and manage customized application-specific preferences.

The Details tab of the Preferences pane in Workgroup Manager allows you to select an application or its preference file, set values for the exposed preference keys, and then set those changes as a managed preference that's applied either:

- **Once.** Allowing the user to change the setting afterward
- **Often.** Allowing the user to change the setting afterward but reapplying the setting at each login
- **Always.** Applying the setting and then not allowing the user to change it

Apple supplies a Core Services bundle that enables administrators to manage a variety of system-related settings from one file at /System/Library/CoreServices/ ManagedClient.app. The bundle can be used to:

- Enable or disable Bluetooth
- Disable Dashboard
- Set a desktop background image

- Customize the Dock appearance
- Customize mobility settings for Home Sync, including how to resolve conflicts
- Configure iCal settings, such as Kerberos and SSL use, and refresh intervals
- Configure iChat settings, such as account name and information, SSL, and Kerberos support
- Set Internet settings, such as the mail server, mail information, default web browser, and default mail application
- Configure iTunes parental controls and enable or disable podcasts or music sharing
- Set iWork registration information
- Set Kerberos name and realm
- Add nonstandard menus to the menu bar
- Change mobile account settings, such as FileVault use, enable sync encryption, set mobile account lifetime, and modify the mobile account creation dialog box
- Type QuickTime registration information
- Enable or disable screen saver passwords
- Change VPN settings, such as VPN server information, username, and authentication type

Safari supplies a couple dozen different manageable preferences, including:

- Set the home page
- Set the default font
- ⌘+click to create new tabs
- AutoFill passwords
- AutoFill credit cards
- Enable Java
- Enable JavaScript
- Ask before submitting insecure forms

Adding Safari using the preference editor results in two entries: The `com.apple.Safari` preference manifest holds most configurable preferences, whereas `com.apple.WebFoundation` includes a configurable preference for the cookie acceptance policy.

Monitoring Managed Preferences

For managed preferences to work properly, a variety of network services must also be in place and operational, including:

- **DHCP.** For assigning IP addresses to clients. This service may be provided by the local server, by the larger organization, or from an appliance device, such as a router. Make sure client computers can obtain a valid IP address on the desired local subnet.

- **DNS.** For hostname lookups. This service may also be provided by the local server, by the larger organization, or from an appliance device, such as a router. Make sure the client can resolve hostnames properly. From the command line, you can use the command `dig server.example.com` to make sure the user can properly resolve the IP address of the directory domain controller.

- **LDAP.** For supplying account and managed preference information. If you're relying on Open Directory for LDAP, you must have local directory domain administrator privileges to make changes to records, including the assignment of managed preferences. If you want to assign managed preferences to users authenticating through a different directory domain, such as Active Directory, you must create a group account on an Open Directory domain, add the external accounts to the group, and then assign the managed permissions to the group. In its default configuration, you can't assign managed permissions to individual users in Active Directory because that directory's schema doesn't support adding managed attributes.

- **NTP.** For proper network time synchronization. This is running on the local server by default. Clients can be set to sync their time with the local server. For managed preferences and directory services to work properly, clients and the server must be synced to the same time.

CROSS-REF

For more on DNS, see Chapter 12. For more on DHCP, see Chapter 13. For more on NTP, see Chapter 19. For more on LDAP and Open Directory, see Chapter 21.

The status of a managed preference is indicated on the Preferences page of Workgroup Manager for the selected accounts. Preferences can be removed from an account by selecting Never as the manage setting for that preference.

Summary

- Managed preferences enable an organization to centrally automate the setup of a customized user environment tailored to specific users or to defined computers and can also be used to enforce security policy.

- Preferences can be managed by user or across a group of users and/or by computer or across a group of computers.

- Layers of managed preferences may either combine together or may override each other depending on how they're configured and the nature of the preference; some preference settings are exclusive, whereas others are additive.

- Managed preferences require properly configured core network services, client computers that are bound to the directory domain, and directory account records for the users, groups, and computers to be managed.

Software Update Server

Apple's Software Update service in Mac OS X enables users to download secure updates from Apple as they're released. However, the size of these updates and their potential impact on organizations that manage large numbers of Macs have resulted in the need for Software Update Server, a locally run service that caches downloaded updates and enables administrators to selectively roll out approved update packages to their users.

Once activated, Software Update Server communicates with Apple's update service to obtain new update listings as they become available and downloads the packages to the server.

The service can be used to download all updates and make them immediately available to users on the local network to prevent each client computer from having to download the same update files directly. That helps to conserve Internet bandwidth.

Administrators might also want to prevent users from installing any updates before they've been tested against the system configurations and software in use locally. Software Update Server can present a listing of available updates and enable administrators to selectively choose which updates users see when they perform an update.

For this to work, users' computers need to be configured to use the local Software Update Server instead of contacting Apple directly. This can be done through a manual command-line configuration on client computers or can be rolled out by using managed preferences.

CROSS-REF
For more on managed preferences, see Chapter 36.

This chapter describes how Software Update Server works, what's involved in planning the service, how the service is configured within Mac OS X Server's interface, and how to maintain and monitor the service.

In This Chapter

Introduction to Software
Update Server

Planning Software
Update services

Software Update Server
setup and configuration

Managing
and monitoring
Software Update Server

Introduction to Software Update Server

Snow Leopard Server's Software Update Server is started from a process unsurprisingly named `softwareupdateserver`. Update retrieval is subsequently handled by a background process named `swupd_syncd`, for Software Update sync daemon.

Updates are served to local clients via `swupd`, which acts as a specialized web server for Software Update packages. The software update configuration is stored at `/etc/swupd/swupd.conf`.

Updates can be performed and configured from the command line, but Server Admin presents a graphical interface for managing the Software Update service. Once started, the service contacts Apple's server and obtains a *catalog*, or listing, of all the available updates.

Software Update packages

The catalog describes the various update packages available, providing a name and description, a version number, a size, and the post date of when the package was first made available.

Individual packages are delivered as `pkm.en` files, which are useable only by Mac OS X Tiger or later. Software Update Server can't manage Software Updates for earlier versions of Mac OS X and doesn't currently support obtaining or delivering Apple Software Updates for Windows computers, including the updates for iTunes, QuickTime, Safari, MobileMe, and other Windows applications for which Apple directly delivers software updates.

Apple signs all the updates delivered through Software Update for security purposes, and Mac clients accept only Apple-signed (and therefore unaltered) update packages. This means that administrators can't use Software Update to distribute their own or other third-party applications or any updates to them nor modify Apple updates they make available to their users.

Serving Software Updates to local users

A Software Update Server can be used to either relay all updates Apple makes available or to selectively enable only those updates the local administrator has approved.

From Server Admin, administrators can select to *copy* (download from Apple) either all the updates that become available or only new updates and then choose to automatically enable all copied updates or selectively approve individual updates. Only enabled updates show up in the Software Update results of users configured to use the local Software Update Server.

Other Software Update settings:

- Enable outdated updates to be automatically deleted
- Limit the bandwidth each user can demand from the Software Update Server

- Customize the location where copied software updates are stored (the default location is `/var/db/swupd/`)
- Serve updates to clients by using a custom port (the default is 8088)

By limiting the bandwidth each user can consume, administrators can prevent software updates from eating up excessive server and network resources.

Apple occasionally revokes updates after publishing them. Revoked updates are automatically removed from the list of updates on the local Software Update Server.

Planning Software Update Services

Getting started with Software Update Server requires evaluating how your users' update downloading patterns might impact your network and making sure your server can accommodate storage needs for all the updates it downloads.

Network capacity considerations

Software Update packages can be fairly large because Apple typically chooses to distribute full updates rather than differential patches. For this reason, administrators should use the fastest networking technology available to support Software Updates and consider how updates are delivered as part of network capacity planning.

If many clients rely on wireless networking, consider setting bandwidth limits for Software Update Server to prevent a few simultaneous updates from consuming the wireless network's capacity. Ideally, your network clients should take advantage of the Gigabit Ethernet ports available on most modern Macs, and your network should support Gigabit Ethernet switches.

Multiple Software Update Servers can be set up to balance the client update load among network segments. Using managed preferences, different groups of computers can be assigned to different Software Update Servers based on their network capacity.

The use of multiple Software Update Servers could be configured to enable wireless notebooks to obtain their updates from a Software Update Server with throttled bandwidth while enabling wired desktops with the Gigabit Ethernet service to download updates from a separate server at full speed.

Software Update Servers all obtain their updates from Apple in parallel, and there's no way for multiple servers to share the same stored pool of update packages.

Server disk capacity considerations

The disk space required to accommodate update packages copied from Apple may grow to a significant figure. Because the updates are stored on the server's startup volume by default, administrators may want to change the download directory to an external volume to prevent updates from consuming all available disk space.

It's also possible to turn off the automatic copying of all available updates and instead choose to only copy items manually as desired. Updates must be copied locally by the server (which may take some time depending on how large they are) prior to enabling them for user downloads via Software Update.

Software Update Setup and Configuration

To configure Software Update services from Server Admin, first enable the service within the desired server's listing of configured services and then do the following:

- Configure the service.
- Initiate a download of available software updates.
- Configure client access, likely via managed preferences.
- Turn the service on.

Service setup in Server Admin

To configure the Software Update service from Server Admin, first enable the service within the desired server's listing of configured services.

To enable Software Update Server configuration in Server Admin, follow these steps:

1. **Launch Server Admin and then connect to the desired server.**
2. **Select the server listing and then click Settings on the toolbar.**
3. **Click the Services tab.**
4. **Click the check box for Software Update, as shown in Figure 37.1.**
5. **Click Save.** Software Update should now appear in the list of configurable services for the selected server.

Once enabled, use the Settings page in the Software Update pane to configure options for the service.

Figure 37.1

Enabling the Software Update pane

To configure Software Update Server settings in Server Admin, follow these steps:

1. **Launch Server Admin and then connect to the desired server.**

2. **Click Software Update and then click Settings on the toolbar.** The Settings page, shown in Figure 37.2, is where you can set the following:

- **Limit user bandwidth to a set figure.** This applies a cap to each user, so a dozen users accessing updates concurrently will consume 12 times the set bandwidth.

- **Store updates in a custom location.** This enables copied updates downloaded from Apple to be stored on a different disk to prevent eating up the system boot volume.

- **Provide updates by using a set port.** Clients need to be configured to use this port to access the Software Update Server.

- **Copy all or new updates from Apple.** This sets all or just new updates to automatically download from Apple's server as they become available. If this isn't checked, updates need to be manually copied from the Updates page.

● **Automatically enable copied updates.** This makes all updates available to local users as soon as they're made available. If this isn't checked, updates need to be manually enabled from the Updates page.

● **Delete outdated software updates.** This removes all updates that have been replaced by a newer version. If this isn't checked, a specific former version of an update can be configured from the Updates page, and users are presented with the former version to download instead of the most recent version available from Apple.

Figure 37.2

The Settings page of the Software Update pane

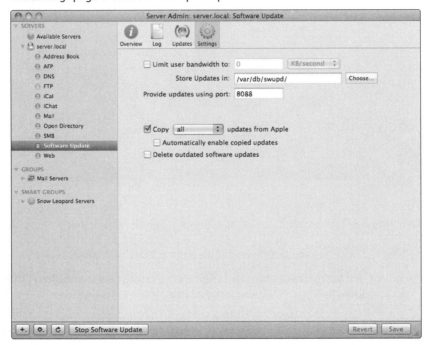

3. **Click Save.** Software Update is now configured and can be turned on by using the Start Software Update button.

Once started, the Software Update Service obtains a catalog listing from Apple's servers. This catalog populates the listing on the Updates page. Depending on how the service has been configured, updates either wait for administrative review or immediately begin to copy locally and are then automatically enabled for users to download.

To manually manage updates in Server Admin, follow these steps:

1. **Launch Server Admin and then connect to the desired server.**

2. **Click Software Update and then click Updates on the toolbar to open the Updates page, as shown in Figure 37.3.**

Figure 37.3

The Updates page of the Software Update pane

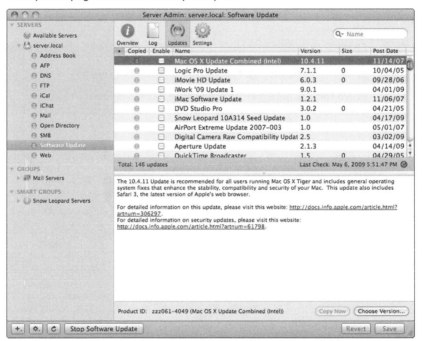

3. **If updates aren't set to copy automatically, click the check boxes for the desired update packages to copy locally and then click the Copy Now button.** The queued updates are marked with a clear ball icon in the Copied column, and when the package download is completed, the ball becomes blue.

4. **If copied updates aren't set to enable automatically, click the Enable check box for the desired update packages.** The update package must first be copied locally before it can be enabled for network users.

5. **If multiple versions of an update package are available and copied locally, click Choose Version to select which version of the update is offered to local network users when they run Software Update.**

6. **To refresh the listing of updates, click the round arrow icon after the Last Check date stamp.** Software Update then syncs with Apple's server and lists any new updates.

Managing access to the Software Update service

It's not possible to limit access to the Software Update Server by using SACLs, as is the case with most services in Server Admin. However, administrative control of the Server Update service can be managed.

To limit administrative control of Software Update Server, follow these steps:

1. **From Server Admin, select the server name of the Software Update Server.**

2. **Click the Settings page and then click the Access tab.**

3. **From the Administrators tab within Access, shown in Figure 37.4, click the For selected services below radio button above the left column and then choose the Software Update service from that list.**

Figure 37.4

Managing access to Software Update administration

4. **Click the Add (+) button under the right-side column of administrators.** The Users & Groups sheet opens.

5. **Drag administrative users or groups to the access list on the right and then use the pop-up menu to define administer or monitor access in the Permission column.**

6. **Click Save.** Modifying Software Update settings are limited to the selected users granted administer permissions, whereas users with monitor permissions are only able to view the service configuration and update listings.

Managing Software Update preferences for clients

Client computers must be configured to use the local Software Update Server. This can be set manually on the local computer by typing defaults write com.apple.SoftwareUpdate CatalogURL *URL* on the command line, `with` *URL* being set to the DNS name of the Software Update Server and path to its catalog, such as `http://server.example.com:8088/index.sucatalog`. Ideally, however, local systems are assigned computer accounts, and a group of all computer accounts (or multiple groups of accounts) can be assigned a managed preference to use the local Software Update Server.

To set a managed preference for the local Software Update Server, follow these steps:

1. **Launch Workgroup Manager.**

2. **Create computer accounts for local systems you want to use the Software Update Server.** Computer accounts require typing an Ethernet ID (MAC address) for each system. A managed preference can also be assigned to the Guest Computer account.

3. **Create a computer group account and then add the desired computers to the group.** Multiple groups can be created to assign different pools of computers to different Software Update Servers.

4. **Manage preferences for the computer group by clicking Preferences on the toolbar.**

5. **Select Software Update from the list of manageable preferences on the Overview tab, as shown in Figure 37.5.**

6. **Select Manage: Always and then type the URL of the Software Update Server.** For example, `http://server.example.com:8088/index.sucatalog`.

7. **Click Apply Now.** Computers should receive the managed preference when users next log in. Managed computers must be bound to the directory domain by using Directory Utility.

CROSS-REF
For more on managed preferences, see Chapter 36.

Figure 37.5

Software Update managed preference configuration in Workgroup Manager

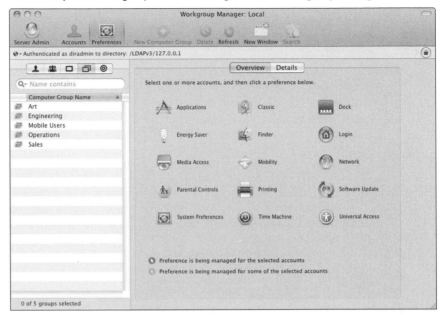

Managing and Monitoring Software Update

After selecting Software Update from the list of services in the Servers list, the Overview page, shown in Figure 37.6, presents a status report, including:

- Whether the service is running and when the service was started
- When the service last checked for updates
- How many update packages have been copied from Apple's update server
- How many updates have been enabled for local users to download
- Whether all or new updates are configured to be copied automatically
- Whether new updates are configured for automatic enabling

The Log page of the Software Update pane, shown in Figure 37.7, presents a listing of the events recorded in three log files:

- The Software Update Service Log at `/var/log/swupd/swupd_syncd_log`, which details the download of packages from Apple's servers
- The Software Update Access Log at `/var/log/swupd/swupd_access_log`, which details the download of packages to local clients

● The Software Update Error Log at `/var/log/swupd/swupd_error_log`, which details the events related to the local download service

Figure 37.6

The Overview page of the Software Update pane

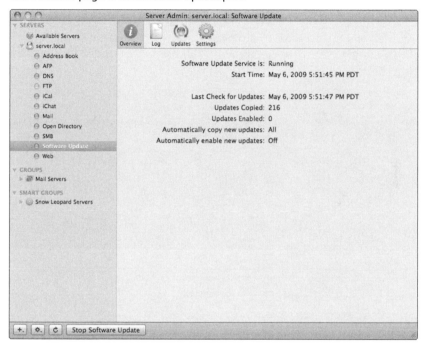

These logs can help in troubleshooting problems with the Software Update Server, indicating if the problem relates to connecting with Apple's servers or if clients are unable to connect to the local server to obtain their updates.

The local Software Update Server must be able to connect to Apple's servers over port 80, including:

● `http://swscan.apple.com`

● `http://swscan.apple.com/content/catalogs/index-1.sucatalog`

● `http://swquery.apple.com/WebObjects/SoftwareUpdateServer`

● `http://swcdn.apple.com`

● `http://swquery.apple.com/WebObjects/SoftwareUpdatesStats`

Additionally, clients must be correctly configured to specify the local Software Update Server, which requires proper DNS entries for the server. Additionally, the clients must be able to access the Software Update Server over the port configured, which is 8088 by default.

The Updates page of the Software Update pane presents a listing of the packages that have been obtained from Apple. A package is only listed and not copied (downloaded locally) unless it's marked with a blue ball in the Copied column. Select a package and then click the Copy Now button to download it to the server.

After copying the package, it must be activated by clicking the Enable check box before local clients using the Software Update Server can see the package in their local listing of available updates.

Figure 37.7

The Log page of the Software Update pane

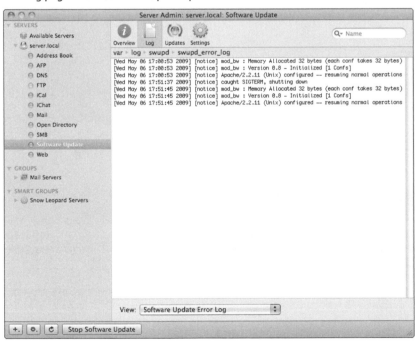

Summary

- Software Update Server allows Mac OS X Tiger or later machines to connect to a local server for software updates, instead of connecting to Apple directly and all downloading the same files repeatedly.

- In addition to conserving bandwidth, Software Update Server can also manage which updates are installed, allowing administrators to selectively enable the updates they've decided to support. Older versions of an update can be enabled instead of the latest available version.

- Client computers on the network can be manually configured to use the local Software Update Server or managed preferences can be used to deploy the configuration across all of an organization's computers.

- Multiple Software Update Servers can be deployed to match the bandwidth throttling of a Software Update Server to the network capacity of specific groups of computers, such as wireless mobile notebooks.

Time Machine Server

Time Machine Server in Mac OS X Snow Leopard Server allows multiple network client machines to use the server as a central destination for their backups, which the server can store on any attached volume.

Time Machine backups are managed on the client side for systems running Mac OS X Leopard or later. The backup feature uses FSEvents, a background process that keeps track of file system events as they happen, to help compile a short list of changed files, enabling Time Machine to only back up incremental changes without requiring a long file system scan to determine which files have changed.

To maintain regular and efficient incremental backups that don't require special software to review the archives as most backup programs do, Time Machine relies on a feature added to the HFS+ file system called *multi-links*, which allows multiple folders to maintain a hard link to the same file on disk. Multi-link files are also called hard links.

Unlike an alias, or *softlink*, a multi-linked file isn't just a file that acts as a pointer to another file; instead, it's one file that exists in multiple directories while only taking up the disk space of a single file (because it's only a single file). One link to the file can be deleted without removing the file from the disk. The file won't be deleted until every last link is removed.

Multi-linked files aren't exposed to regular users but serve only as a key feature to enable Time Machine to create backup folders at regular intervals that appear to contain a full copy of the backup source volume (because they do).

However, each regular new folder of backed-up files actually shares most of the same files as previous backups. Multi-linked files and directories enable these duplications to not require any duplication on disk, resulting in efficient, easy-to-navigate storage of backups.

To back up these multi-linked files to a network file server rather than a locally connected disk, Time Machine uses a sparse disk image, which allows the service to write to a disk image hosting an HFS+ file system that can be saved to a network volume.

Time Machine Server simply supports the features Time Machine needs by using a standard share point. It's turned on with a single button within Server Preferences or may be configured within Server Admin as a share point feature.

This chapter describes how Time Machine Server works, what's involved in planning the service, how the service is configured within Mac OS X Server's interface, and how to maintain and monitor the service.

Introduction to Time Machine Server

Time Machine Server is most basically a file share with support for accommodating client machines' network backups from Mac OS X's Time Machine.

Time Machine versus Time Machine Server

In its standard and workgroup configurations, Snow Leopard Server supports Time Machine backups of the server and acts as a Time Machine Server to store the backups of client computers.

Although in the advanced configuration Server Admin can be used to configure the server to act as a Time Machine Server by setting up a file share with Time Machine support, there's no provision for backing the server up by using Time Machine.

This appears to be related to the fact that an advanced configuration server is complex enough that incremental backups of its configuration wouldn't result in reliable backups, particularly because backups may not adequately capture files that are in use or restore the appropriate file permissions.

This means advanced configuration users need to rely on other backup strategies to maintain backups of the server, ranging from disk duplication to tape backup to a specialized server backup application. However, all configurations of Snow Leopard Server can support acting as a repository for client backups.

Time Machine Server

When Time Machine Server is configured, either during the installation of a standard or workgroup server or manually by using Server Admin on an advanced configuration server, a standard AFP file share is designated that:

- Sets POSIX file permissions to `mode 770` (full read, write, and execute access for both user and group users and no access to other users)
- Sets the POSIX user to `root` and the group to `com.apple.access.backup`
- Enables Bonjour advertisement of the share point as a Time Machine destination

Time Machine Client

Once a share point has been configured to support Time Machine, network clients that want to back up the Time Machine Server can browse the share from the Change Disk sheet available within the Time Machine pane in System Preferences, as shown in Figure 38.1.

Figure 38.1

The Time Machine client backup destination configuration

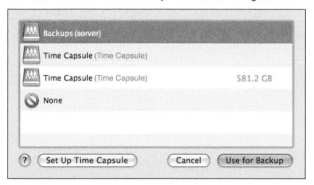

This browse listing is automatically populated via Bonjour. If you plan to back up machines to a Time Machine Server in a different subnet, the routers involved need to support forwarding Bonjour multicast messages between the subnets.

The network account login for connecting the server share is saved to the user's keychain to enable regular backups to mount the share point. If the user's network password changes, Time Machine may complain that the "Backup volume could not be mounted," a problem that can be resolved by updating the keychain's password record for Time Machine by using Keychain Access.

Each client machine's backups are associated with that system's computer name and MAC address, so if client machines are renamed or change their Ethernet network interface, their backups are restarted.

Planning Time Machine Server Services

Operating Time Machine Server involves moving large amounts of data across the network to the server at regular intervals. For this reason, advanced planning is required to ensure that the network can support the traffic required and that the server has adequate disk storage capacity to support the number of users who will use Time Machine to back up their client machines.

Time Machine network capacity planning

Apple positions Time Machine to home users as useable over wireless networking, but outside of the most limited-duty home users, nobody would want to set up several clients to back up data over a wireless network, in part because backups are slow but also because backup traffic quickly consumes the wireless network's capacity, preventing anyone else from working.

Even a single user performing a Time Machine backup can make a significant impact on wireless throughput for other users. This makes fast wired networking an essential part of any plan to deploy Time Machine as a backup strategy. While Apple bills 802.11n wireless networking as suitable for Time Machine, your users will likely find it unworkable. Additionally, if you have more than a few users on your wireless network, a single user's Time Machine backups are likely to overwhelm access to the entire local wireless network.

The network demands of Time Machine backups should be considered in concert with other taxing network operations, including:

- Network home folders
- NetBoot
- Video conferencing
- QuickTime Streaming Server
- Video capture by using Podcast Producer

Time Machine disk capacity planning

The other major capacity planning issue involves where to store the Time Machine backups of client computer users. Whereas the Time Machine client can be configured to back up only to a single destination, Snow Leopard Server can be configured to create any number of Time Machine share points on any available drives.

This enables administrators to configure multiple share points on different volumes and then assign different sets of client computers to the various backup destinations to split the storage demands across several volumes.

Managed client settings can be used to automatically configure computers or groups of computers with a specific Time Machine Server share point for saving their backups and to additionally configure backups to cover the startup volume only or all local backups. Other manageable options allow Time Machine to skip system files, to perform backups automatically, and to limit total backup storage to a set number of MB, as shown in Figure 38.2.

CROSS-REF
For more on managed client configuration, see Chapter 34.

If you're not using managed clients, you can manually configure client machines to exclude system files and other folders that don't need to be backed up in order to save space on the server and to speed up clients' backups.

Figure 38.2

Time Machine managed client configuration in Workgroup Manager

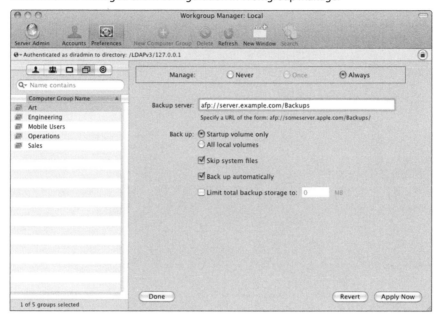

Time Machine Server Setup and Configuration

To configure Time Machine Server to accommodate network users' Time Machine backups on the server, you need to do the following:

- Create an AFP share point.
- Configure the share point's properties to support Time Machine Server.
- Configure clients to use Time Machine Server for their backups.

Server Preferences

Administrators who want to use Time Machine Server to back up client computers by using a standard or workgroup configuration server are initially prompted to optionally select a volume during installation to serve as the destination for client backups.

At any point afterward, this destination volume can also be selected by using the Time Machine pane in Server Preferences. A Time Machine Server share is configured at /Shared Items/ Backups/ on the designated volume.

To enable client backups by using Time Machine Server, open the Time Machine pane of Server Preferences, as shown in Figure 38.3, select a volume, and then turn on the service.

Figure 38.3

The Time Machine pane in Server Preferences

Using Server Preferences, only one Time Machine share point can be created. This means that the selected volume must have enough capacity to accommodate all the machines that will save their Time Machine backups to it. Expect to require twice as much storage for backups as the user has consumed on his or her local drive.

There's also no way to set a limit on how much disk space each user can consume. To create multiple Time Machine destination share points or to enable managed preferences limiting the amount of backup data clients can save, you need to upgrade to the advanced configuration.

CROSS-REF

For more on Server Preferences, see Chapter 7.

Server Admin

To configure a share point for Time Machine Server on an advanced configuration server by using Server Admin, first enable AFP file sharing and then designate a share point. This step may be performed during installation by specifying a volume to use for Time Machine backups. The default settings create a share point at `/Shared Items/Backups/` on the selected volume.

To manually enable client backups by using Server Admin, follow these steps:

1. **Launch Server Admin, select the desired server, and then click File Sharing on the toolbar.**

2. **Click Volumes to view local disks and then click Browse to navigate to the volume and folder you want to share with network users for Time Machine backups.**

3. **With the desired folder selected, click the Share button in the upper right.** The lower half of the window now displays Share Point settings, as shown in Figure 38.4.

Figure 38.4

Share point configuration in Server Admin

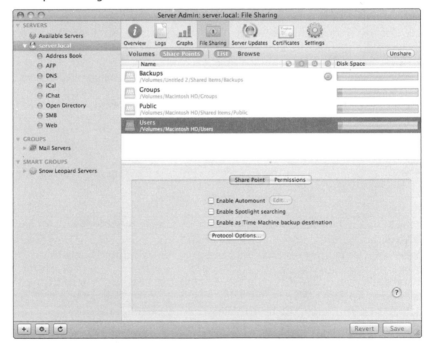

4. **Click the Enable as Time Machine backup destination check box to enable the feature for the new share point.** A Time Machine logo appears on the share point's detail listing, indicating that the service is being advertised via Bonjour and that the share's file permissions have been configured to support Time Machine.

5. **Click Save.** The new share point is now available to network users and shows up in the client browser interface of the Time Machine pane in System Preferences.

Additional share points with Time Machine support can be created on different volumes, and users can be directed to save their backups to an assigned share point or computers can be assigned managed preferences that automatically configure where, what, and how they back up and, optionally, how much disk space their backups can consume.

CROSS-REF
For more on Server Admin, see Chapter 9. For more on managed client configuration, see Chapter 34.

Managing and Monitoring Time Machine Server

Because the Time Machine Server feature is really just a specialized file share, there's no dedicated service pane to monitor in Server Admin, and there aren't any special logs or reporting features. Instead, you can monitor Time Machine backups from the File Sharing page in Server Admin, which presents the share point and the disk space available on its volume.

The performance and network demands of Time Machine can be monitored from the AFP pane in Server Admin by using the Graphs page to monitor throughput.

CROSS-REF
For more on Server Admin, see Chapter 9. For more on the File Sharing service, see Chapter 22.

If the Time Machine volume is located on an external drive, it's important not to remove the drive without properly ejecting it first because any removal of the Time Machine volume terminates backups in progress and could easily result in corrupted backups.

Initial backups can take a long time, so it might make sense to roll out Time Machine sequentially across groups of computers, initiating an overnight backup to the server at a time when network use and server use have the least impact on other users.

Once a full backup has completed, subsequent incremental backups shouldn't take very long. If they do, investigate if there are applications saving data in a format that forces unnecessary backups of large files that may not need to be backed up and consider exempting those files from the backup job.

Files and directories can be excluded from Time Machine backups by adding them to the list presented on the sheet opened by the Options button from the Time Machine pane in System Preferences, as shown in Figure 38.5.

Figure 38.5

Time Machine client exclusion configuration in System Preferences

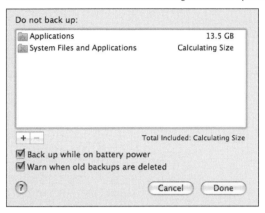

Summary

- Time Machine Server sets up a file share as a backup destination for client users by setting appropriate file permissions and then advertising the share via Bonjour so Time Machine clients can select it.

- Server Preferences can be used to set up a volume for Time Machine backups simply by selecting the volume and then turning on the service.

- To set up multiple Time Machine shares, Server Admin is required. Share points are configured to support Time Machine by simply activating it as a share point feature.

- Once configured, Time Machine performance and use of resources can be monitored in Server Admin under the File Sharing page of the server as well as via the throughput graphs generated by the AFP service.

Glossary

802.1x An IEEE protocol for network access control, used in WEP and supplied by RADIUS authentication

802.11b, 802.11g, and 802.11n IEEE Wireless networking protocols

802.3 An IEEE protocol for Ethernet networking

802.3ad An IEEE protocol for network link aggregation

AAC (advanced audio codec) An ISO MPEG standard for audio compression

access file A text file named `qtaccess` used by QuickTime Streaming Server to authorize access to media by folder, similar to `htaccess` files used by the Apache web server

ACE (access control entry) An entry within an access control list that controls access rights. See *ACL.*

ACL (access control list) A system-maintained listing that either allows or denies access permissions to resources on the system by users and groups

Active Directory Microsoft's proprietary directory and authentication service. It exposes an LDAP interface that Open Directory uses for interoperability.

address A number used to uniquely identify a computer on a network, a block of data on a disk, or a memory location

administrator A user with server or directory domain management privileges. In Mac OS X, also a member of the admin group and wheel group and therefore able to sudo as root.

administrator computer Mac system with the Mac OS X Server Admin tools installed

AFP (Apple Filing Protocol) A file-sharing protocol used to share files and network services. Modern AFP services operate over TCP/IP.

agent In Xgrid, a system in the grid that accepts tasks from the controller. In Podcast Producer, a client system used to capture video feeds.

aggregation Combining disks or network connections into a single logical resource for increased performance

AirPort Apple's brand name for wireless network base stations

AirPort ID The wireless MAC address

alias A file pointing to another file as a softlink. An alias can also refer to a secondary short name that functions as an alternative email address for a user, a Unix command-line substitution, or a DNS entry that points multiple domain names to a single server.

Apache The open-source HTTP web server bundled with Mac OS X Server. The process appears as the HTTP daemon, or `httpd`, when the program is running.

APOP An authentication method. A POP3 mail protocol extension used to ensure that a username and password are encrypted before being used to authenticate to a mail server. APOP is stored as a recoverable password in the Open Directory Password Server.

attribute A named data item containing a specific type of information and belonging to a record or object entry in a directory domain. The actual data that an attribute contains is its value.

authentication The process of validating a user's identity, typically by comparing a submitted name and password against a known value

authorization The process of a service determining the amount of access an authenticated user should be granted to a resource

automatic failover A service replacement that occurs without human intervention

Automount A share point that mounts automatically on a client computer

bandwidth The capacity of a network connection for carrying data, measured in bits or bytes per second

BIND (Berkeley Internet Name Domain) The open-source DNS server bundled with Mac OS X Server. The process appears as the name daemon (named) when the program is running.

binding A connection between a computer and a directory service domain for the purpose of obtaining identification, authorization, and other administrative data

biometrics An authentication method based on unique physiological or behavioral characteristics, such as a fingerprint or signature. Provides an additional factor to authentication.

bit A binary digit, or single piece of information, conveying a value of either 0 or 1

bit rate The speed at which bits are transmitted over a network, expressed in bits per second

block A chunk of data of a given size written to and read from a disk

blog A web log, presenting user-generated entries chronologically

Bonjour A protocol developed by Apple for automatic discovery of computers, devices, and services on IP networks and opened up as an Internet standard. Also referred to by the vendor-neutral names ZeroConf or multicast DNS. Formerly called Rendezvous.

BootP A method of allocating IP addresses to clients on a network prior to DHCP

broadcast The transmission of a message or data to allow any client on the network to read it, in contrast with unicast (sent to a specific computer) or multicast (sent to a select subset of computers)

BSD (Berkeley Software Distribution) A freely licensed distribution of Unix that Mac OS X's core software is based on

byte A basic unit of measure for data, equal to 8 bits. Usually equivalent to a single character.

cache Memory or disk storage that holds frequently accessed data in order to speed up subsequent reads or to buffer write access to a slower medium

canonical name The real name of a server, as opposed to an alias

certificate A file in a specific format that contains the public key half of a public-private keypair, along with identity information, such as name and contact information, and the digital signature of either a Certificate Authority or the key user. Mac OS X Server uses the X.509 certificate.

Certificate Authority An authority that signs and encrypts digital certificates to validate that the public key matches the identity in the certificate

CGI (Common Gateway Interface) A script or program that sends information back and forth between a website and an application to add dynamic features to a website

child A computer that gets configuration information from the shared directory domain of a parent

cleartext Data that lacks encryption

client A computer that requests data or services from another computer or server

cluster A collection of computers interconnected to improve reliability, availability, and performance. Clustered computers run special software to coordinate their activities.

cluster file system A file system for a storage area network (SAN). This is designed to enable multiple systems to concurrently access the same volumes, typically on a RAID appliance, as local storage as opposed to network-attached file systems that provide access to share points from multiple clients — but all through a single server.

codec A tool used for compressing and decompressing data, commonly used for audio and video in QuickTime, Windows Media, and other container formats

command line The shell prompt provided by Terminal

command-line interface (CLI) A method for issuing text commands at a shell prompt

computational cluster A group of workstations or servers grouped together to share processing tasks in order to achieve supercomputer performance

computer account An account record for network hosts maintained in the directory, primarily to apply managed preferences

computer group A collection of computers and computer groups that use the same set of managed preferences. Prior to Mac OS X Leopard, computer lists were used for this purpose.

controller In Xgrid, a system that manages the grid and delivers tasks to agents. In Xsan, short for metadata controller.

crypt password A type of password stored as a hash by using the standard Unix encryption algorithm directly within a user record

CSS (Cascading Style Sheets) A style sheet language used to describe the presentation of a document written in a markup language such as HTML.

CUPS (Common Unix Printing System) The cross-platform printing system used by Mac OS X

daemon A process that runs in the background without exhibiting a graphical interface

DAS (direct-attached storage) An external hard disk drive connected to a computer without using a network interface

data rate The amount of information transmitted per second

decryption The process of recovering encrypted data

default An action taken or configuration used unless the user chooses otherwise

deploy To put configured computer systems into use in a specific environment

DHCP (Dynamic Host Configuration Protocol) A protocol used to dynamically distribute IP addresses and other configurations to client computers at startup

digest A computationally efficient function mapping binary strings of arbitrary length to binary strings of some fixed length

Digest-MD5 authentication An authentication method that encodes passwords sent over the network and stores them in an encrypted form on the password server

digital signature An electronic signature that can be used to verify the identity of the sender of a message

directory domain A specialized database that stores authoritative information about users and network resources for system software and applications

directory services A service that supplies client applications with access to directory domains and other sources of information about users and resources

disc Optical storage media, such as a CD or DVD

disk A rewritable storage device, such as a hard drive, or another form of rewritable storage, such as a RAM disk.

disk image A file used to emulate a disk. Used to distribute software, maintain HFS+ file conventions on foreign file systems, and, with the NetBoot service, start up client computers over the network.

distinguished name A fully qualified name for an object in an LDAP directory. Represented by a sequence of directory entries separated by commas, such as: `cn=user, dc=example, dc=com.`

DNS (Domain Name System) A distributed database that maps IP addresses to domain names

DNS domain name A unique name of a computer as used in the DNS

DNS server Supplies DNS. Also known as a name server.

domain Part of the domain name of a computer on the Internet. It doesn't include the top-level domain designator (for example, `.com`, `.net`, `.us`, `.uk`). The domain name `www.example.com` consists of the subdomain, or hostname, `www`; the domain `example`; and the top-level domain `com`.

DoS attack (denial-of-service attack) An Internet attack that seeks to overwhelm a server with phony requests in order to block legitimate use

dynamic IP address An IP address assigned for a limited lease period or until the client computer no longer needs it

EAP (Extensible Authentication Protocol) An authentication protocol that supports multiple authentication methods

EFI (Extensible Firmware Interface) Firmware that starts up an Intel-based Mac. Performs a `POST`, determines the computer's hardware configuration, finds the boot volume, and starts the system software.

encryption The process of obscuring data to make it unreadable without special knowledge

Ethernet A standard local area networking technology that transmits data in units called packets, usually by using TCP/IP

Ethernet adapter An adapter that connects a device to an Ethernet network

Ethernet ID A hardware MAC address

export In NFS, the term for sharing a folder with clients over a network

external account A Mac OS X mobile account that stores the user's local home folder on an external volume

failover In cluster configurations, the automatic process of a standby system assuming the work of a primary failure

Fast Ethernet The standard for 100 Mbit/s Ethernet

fault tolerance The ability of a system to continue to function despite component failure

file server A computer that serves files to clients

file system A scheme for storing data on storage devices that allows applications to read and write files without having to deal with lower-level details

filter A screening method to control access to a server by an IP address and a subnet mask and sometimes a port number and an access type

firewall A service that scans incoming IP packets and rejects or accepts them based on a set of predefined filters

FireWire A hardware technology for exchanging data with peripheral devices, defined in IEEE Standard 1394

firmware Software stored in read-only memory on a device for initial startup. Firmware allows upgrading a device without changing the actual hardware of the device.

folder A hierarchically organized list of files and/or other folders. Also known as a directory.

forward zone The DNS zone that holds no records of its own but forwards DNS queries to another zone

FTP (File Transfer Protocol) A standard protocol that allows computers to transfer files over a network

gateway A network node that interfaces one network to another. A router is a gateway that links related network segments.

GB (gigabyte) One gigabyte equals 1,073,741,824 bytes.

Gigabit Ethernet The standard for 1 Gbit/s Ethernet, also known as IEEE 802.3z or 1000BASE-T

group A collection of users who are linked via similar access privileges in order to simplify administration

group folder A folder share provided to a group

guest computer A computer that doesn't have a defined computer account

guest user A user who can log in without a username or password

GUID (globally unique identifier) A hexadecimal string that uniquely identifies a user account, group account, or computer list. Also used to provide user and group identity for ACL permissions and to associate particular users with group and nested group memberships. GUIDs are 128-bit values, which makes collision of duplicate GUIDs extremely unlikely.

H.264 An ISO MPEG standard for video compression, equivalent to MPEG-4 Part 10. Also known as MPEG-4 AVC (Advanced Video Coding).

hard link A link between a directory entry and a file stored on disk. When the last hard link to a file is removed, it's considered deleted and no longer visible or accessible without using special recovery software. Deleted files are subject to overwriting.

hinting A process that creates a hinting track for each streamable media track in a QuickTime file. Used by QuickTime Streaming Server to optimize how and when to deliver each frame of media.

home folder A shared folder created for a user's personal use. Mac OS X uses the home folder to store both user preferences and managed preferences.

HTML (Hypertext Markup Language) The standard markup used to deliver web page content

HTTP (Hypertext Transfer Protocol) The client/server protocol for requesting and delivering web pages

IANA (Internet Assigned Numbers Authority) The organization that allocates IP addresses and domain names

iChat The Mac OS X instant messaging application

iChat service The Mac OS X Server service that hosts secure chats by using Open Directory authentication to verify the identity of chatters and SSL to protect the privacy of users while they chat

ICMP (Internet Control Message Protocol) A message control and error-reporting protocol used between host servers and gateways

idle user A user who is connected to a server but hasn't been active for a period of time

IEEE (Institute of Electrical and Electronics Engineers, Inc.) An organization that promotes standards in computing and electrical engineering

IETF (Internet Engineering Task Force) An association of working groups that act with the W3C and ISO to establish standards related to TCP/IP, the Internet protocol suite.

IGMP (Internet Group Management Protocol) An Internet protocol used by hosts and routers to send packets to lists of hosts that want to participate in multicasting. QuickTime Streaming Server uses multicast addressing.

IMAP (Internet Message Access Protocol) A local mail delivery protocol that allows users to store their mail on the mail server instead of downloading it to the local computer

instant messaging Live exchanges of text messages, pictures, audio, or video in real time

Instant On In QuickTime streaming, an advance in Apple's Skip Protection technology designed to reduce buffering times for an instantaneous viewing experience when streaming video on a broadband connection

intranet Network services restricted to members of an organization

IP (Internet Protocol) A method used with Transmission Control Protocol (TCP) to send data between computers over a local network or the Internet. IP delivers data packets and TCP keeps track of data packets.

IP address A unique address used to identify a computer on the Internet

IPP (Internet Printing Protocol) A protocol for printing over the Internet

IPsec A security protocol added to IP to provide data transmission security for L2TP VPN connections. IPsec acts at the network layer, protecting and authenticating IP packets between participating IPsec nodes.

IPv6 (Internet Protocol version 6) The next-generation communication protocol to replace IPv4. IPv6 allows a greater number of network addresses and can reduce routing loads.

ISO (International Standards Organization) An international standards body. ISO standards have the status of international treaties.

ISP (Internet service provider) A company that sells Internet access

Jabber The brand name for XMPP

JavaScript A scripting language used to add interactivity to web pages

JBOD (Just a Bunch Of Disks) An acronym used to refer to a group of physical disks without a RAID configuration

KB (kilobyte) One kilobyte equals 1,024 (2^{10}) bytes.

KDC (Kerberos Key Distribution Center) A trusted server that issues Kerberos tickets

Kerberos A secure, single sign-on (SSO) network authentication system that issues tickets for a specific user, service, and period of time. After a user is authenticated by Kerberos, additional services can be accessed without retyping a password for services that have been configured to accept Kerberos tickets. Mac OS X Server uses Kerberos v5.

Kerberos realm An authentication domain managed by a Kerberos server

kernel The core of an operating system that handles memory management, resource allocation, and other essential low-level services

L2TP (Layer Two Tunneling Protocol) A network transport protocol used for VPN connections based on Cisco's L2F and PPTP. L2TP uses IPsec for packet encryption.

LAN (Local Area Network) A network maintained within a site, as opposed to a Wide Area Network (WAN) used to link distant sites

LAN Manager authentication An authentication method required for older Windows clients to access the Windows services in Mac OS X Server

LDA (local delivery agent) A mail service agent that transfers mail messages from incoming mail storage to the email recipient's inbox

LDAP (Lightweight Directory Access Protocol) A standard client-server protocol for accessing a directory domain

link aggregation Binding multiple physical network links to act as a single logical link to improve capacity and availability of network connections. Linked ports use the same address, as opposed to multi-pathing, where each port uses its own address.

local directory domain A directory of identification, authentication, authorization, and other administrative data that's accessible only on the local computer

local home folder A home folder located on the computer someone is using

logical disk A storage device that appears to a user as a single disk for storing files, even though it might actually consist of more than one physical disk drive

loopback A network interface that refers to the local system. Commonly expressed as 127.0.0.1, but can be any 127.0.0.0/8 address, ranging up to 127.255.255.255.

LPR (Line Printer Remote) A standard protocol for printing over TCP/IP

MAA (mail access agent) A mail service that communicates with a user's email program to download mail message headers to the user's local computer

MAC (Media Access Control) address A hardware address that uniquely identifies each node on a network. For AirPort devices, the MAC address is called the AirPort ID; for Macs, the Ethernet ID.

Mac OS X Apple's desktop and server operating system. Mac OS X combines the ease of use common to the Mac OS with the underlying power of a Unix foundation.

managed client A user, group, or computer with access privileges and preferences under administrative control

managed device A system configured for centralized network management via SNMP. Also called a network element.**managed preferences** System or application preferences under administrative control via settings configured in Workgroup Manager

manual unicast A method for transmitting a live stream to a single QuickTime Player client or to a computer running QTSS. An SDP file is created by QuickTime Broadcaster and manually sent to the viewer or streaming server.

master zone The DNS zone records held by a primary DNS server. A master zone is replicated by zone transfers to slave zones on secondary DNS servers.

MB (megabyte) One megabyte equals 1,048,576 bytes.

MB/s Megabytes per second

Mbit (megabit) One megabit equals 1,048,576 bits.

Mbit/s Megabits per second (sometimes Mbps)

MIME (Multipurpose Internet Mail Extensions) An Internet standard for specifying how a web browser or mail client handles a file with certain characteristics.

Mobile Access A security proxy for mobile users that enables centralized SSL encryption for mail, calendar, contact, and web access.

mobile account An account with both local and network home folders. Mobile accounts cache authentication information and managed preferences. May also be a Portable Home Directory, which supports syncing local and network home folders.

mode A number that describes what access a file's owner, group, and others have to the file

mount To make a remote directory or volume available for access on a local system

MP3 (MPEG-1 audio layer 3) A popular format for compressing music

MPEG Moving Picture Experts Group

MPEG-4 An ISO standard based on the QuickTime container file format that defines multimedia file and compression formats

MS-CHAP (Microsoft Challenge Handshake Authentication Protocol) The standard Windows authentication method for VPN. Microsoft's proprietary version of CHAP.

MTA (mail transfer agent) A mail service that sends outgoing mail, receives incoming mail for local recipients, and forwards incoming mail of nonlocal recipients to other MTAs

MUA (mail user agent) A mail process on a user's local computer

multicast The simultaneous transmission of a message to a specific subset of computers on a network

multicast DNS A protocol developed by Apple for automatic discovery of computers, devices, and services on IP networks. Called Bonjour and previously Rendezvous. It's also referred to as ZeroConf.

multihoming The ability to support multiple network connections

multi-linked file A file or folder in HFS+ that is hard linked by multiple directory records, so that the file or folder appears to be in multiple folders at once while only taking up the disk space of a single file or folder. Deleting a multi-linked file from one folder removes a hard link, but does not delete the file until no additional hard links remain. This feature is used by Time Machine to efficiently store multiple iterations of backups in a way that is easy to browse and recover.

mutual authentication Two-way authentication between two parties. Supported by Kerberos.

MX record (mail exchange record) A DNS entry in a DNS table that specifies and prioritizes the mail servers for the domain

MySQL An open-source relational database management tool frequently used by web servers

name server A server on a network that matches names and IP addresses, such as DNS or WINS

NAS (network-attached storage) Storage made available to a network via a network server operating system

NAT (network address translation) A method of connecting multiple computers to the Internet by using one IP address

nested group A group that's a member of another group

NetBIOS (Network Basic Input/Output System) A program that allowed DOS PCs to communicate

NetBoot server A Mac OS X Server that hosts network disk images for client booting

NetInfo A legacy Apple protocol for accessing a directory domain, originally developed by NeXT

network interface A hardware port for connection to a network, such as Ethernet jacks, AirPort cards, and FireWire ports

NFS (Network File System) A client/server file-sharing protocol developed by Sun

NIC Network interface card

NMS (network management system) A hardware or software solution used to manage devices on a network, such as those that use SNMP

NTP (Network Time Protocol) A network protocol used to synchronize the clocks of computers across a network to a time reference clock

Open Directory Apple's directory services architecture for accessing authoritative information about users and network resources from directory domains that use LDAP, Active Directory, BSD configuration files, or NIS

Open Directory master A server that provides LDAP directory service, Kerberos authentication service, and Open Directory Password Server

Open Directory password A password stored in secure databases on the server and authenticated by using Open Directory Password Server or Kerberos

Open Directory Password Server An authentication service that validates passwords by using a variety of conventional authentication methods required by the different services

open relay A server that receives and automatically forwards mail to another server

open source Cooperative software efforts for the non-proprietary development of software through open peer review by a community

opportunistic locking Also known as oplocks. A feature of the Windows file-sharing service that allows clients to cache open files locally for improved performance. Can't be used when the files are being shared under multiple network file-sharing services.

package install image A file that you can use to install packages

packet A unit of data consisting of header, information, error detection, and trailer records

PAP (Printer Access Protocol) The AppleTalk printing protocol no longer supported in Snow Leopard Server

parent A system that shares its directory domain configuration information with another computer

partition A subdivision of the capacity of a physical or logical disk

password policy A set of rules that regulate the strength and validity of a user's password

Path The location of an item within a file system, represented as a series of folder names separated by slashes (/)

PDC (Primary Domain Controller) In Windows networking, a domain controller that's been designated as the primary authentication server for its domain

PHP A scripting language embedded in HTML to create dynamic web pages

physical disk An actual, mechanical disk. See *logical disk.*

PID (Process ID) A number assigned to a Unix process when it starts

pixel A single dot in a graphic image with a given color and brightness value

PKI (Public Key Infrastructure) A mechanism that allows two parties to a data transaction to authenticate each other and use encryption keys and other information in identity certificates to encrypt and decrypt messages they exchange

plaintext Text that hasn't been encrypted

Podcast Producer Apple's system for building workflows for processing video submitted by clients to produce finished content ready for streaming or publishing in iTunes or via the web

POP (Post Office Protocol) A protocol for retrieving incoming mail. After retrieval, mail is usually automatically deleted from the mail server.

port An IP address number on which applications can selectively listen for incoming traffic. Usually uses either TCP or UDP.

Portable Home Directory Provides a user with both local and network home folders that can be automatically kept in sync

POSIX (Portable Operating System Interface for Unix) A family of open system standards related to Unix

PPD (Postscript Printer Description) file A file that contains information about the capabilities of a particular printer

PPTP (Point-to-Point Tunneling Protocol) The Windows standard VPN protocol. Uses a user-provided password to produce an encryption key.

primary group A user's default group

principal In Kerberos, the name and other identifying information of a client or service that Kerberos can authenticate. A user principal is usually a username and the Kerberos realm. A service principal is usually the service name, the server's fully qualified DNS name, and the Kerberos realm.

private key One of two asymmetric keys used in a PKI security system. The private key isn't distributed and is usually encrypted with a passphrase by the owner. It can digitally sign a message or certificate, claiming authenticity. It can decrypt messages encrypted with the corresponding public key, and it can encrypt messages that can be decrypted only by the private key.

progressive download Movie data pushed via HTTP to the client. Can be viewed by the user during transfer. Not a form of media streaming.

protocol A set of rules that determines how data is sent back and forth between two applications

proxy server A server that sits between a client application, such as a web browser, and a real server. The proxy server intercepts all requests to the real server to see if it can fulfill the requests itself. If not, it forwards the request to the real server.

PTR record (pointer record) A DNS record mapping IP addresses to domain names. Used in reverse lookups.

public key One of two asymmetric keys used in a PKI security system. The public key is distributed to other communicating parties. It can encrypt messages that can be decrypted only by the holder of the corresponding private key, and it can verify the signature on a message originating from a corresponding private key.

Public-key cryptography A method of encrypting data that uses a pair of keys — one public and one private — obtained from a Certificate Authority. One key is used to encrypt messages, and the other is used to decrypt them.

Push Notification Server A network service based on XMPP that provides alerts to clients when new messages or calendar updates are available on the server. Enables mobile clients to check for messages only when new content is actually available.

QuickTime A set of Mac system extensions or a Windows dynamic-link library that supports multimedia playback and editing

QuickTime Player 7 An application that plays, exports, and hints QuickTime movies

QuickTime Player X A simplified version of QuickTime Player designed for efficient playback and basic trim editing. It's new to Snow Leopard.

RADIUS Remote Authentication Dial-In User Service

RADIUS server A computer that provides a centralized database of authentication information for computers on the network, usually for securing Wi-Fi

RAID (redundant array of independent [or inexpensive] disks) A grouping of multiple physical hard disks into a disk array

RAID level A storage allocation scheme used for storing data on a RAID array. Specified by a number, such as RAID 3 or RAID 0+1.

RFC (request for comments) A memorandum published by the IETF to outline how a proposed technology works to foster collaborative, open discourse and peer review. An RFC may eventually be published by the IETF as an Internet standard.

RBL (Real-time Blackhole List) An Internet service that blacklists mail servers known to be or suspected of being open relays for senders of junk mail

Record A DNS address record type that translates domain names to IP (IPv4) addresses

relay In QuickTime Streaming Server, a relay receives an incoming stream and then forwards that stream to one or more streaming servers.

reverse lookup A DNS query made to determine the domain name associated with a given IP address, using PTR records. Mac OS X Server requires correctly configured DNS, including the ability for the system to perform a reverse lookup of its own IP address, in order for many services to work properly.

roaming user profiles The set of personal desktop and preference settings that a user makes, that the Windows domain controller stores on a server, and that Windows applies when the user logs in to the Windows domain from any workstation

root An account on a system that has no protections or restrictions. System administrators use this account to make changes to the system's configuration.

router A computer networking device that forwards data packets to their destinations

RSS (Really Simple Syndication) An XML format that provides a feed for advertising new content

RTP (Real-Time Transport Protocol) An end-to-end network transport protocol for transmitting real-time data over multicast or unicast network services

RTSP (Real-Time Streaming Protocol) An application-level protocol for controlling the real-time delivery of data

SACL (service access control list) Specifies user and group access to specific services. See *ACL*.

Samba Open-source software that provides file, print, authentication, authorization, name resolution, and network service browsing to Windows clients that are using the SMB protocol

SAN (storage area network) A network for transferring data between computer systems and storage elements. Data supplied to client computer systems appears as local block storage rather than file storage.

SASL (simple authentication and security layer) An extensible authentication scheme that allows the Open Directory Password Server to support a variety of network user authentication methods required by the different services of Mac OS X Server

scale To expand a system while continuing to provide functions or services at the same level of performance

schema The attributes and record types or classes that describe the organization of information in a directory domain

SDP (Session Description Protocol) A text file used with QuickTime Streaming Server to provide information about a live streaming broadcast with instructions for receiving the broadcast

search base A distinguished name that identifies where to start searching for information in an LDAP directory's hierarchy of entries

search policy A list of directory domains that a Mac OS X computer searches when it needs configuration information. Also the order in which domains are searched.

shadow files Created by the NetBoot process for each NetBoot client to allow the client to write temporary data

shadow password A password stored in a secure file on the server and authenticated by using a variety of conventional authentication methods required by the different services of Mac OS X Server

share point A folder, volume, or optical disc made accessible over the network. A share point is the point of access at the top level of a group of shared items. Share points can be shared by using AFP, SMB, NFS, or FTP.

shared secret A predefined password that serves as the encryption key seed to negotiate authentication and data transport connections

shell A program that runs other programs. You can use a shell to interact with the computer by typing commands at a shell prompt.

short name An abbreviated name for a user. The short name is used by Mac OS X for home folders, authentication, and email addresses.

SID (security identifier) A unique value that identifies a user, group, or computer account in a Windows NT-compatible domain

slave zone The DNS zone records held by a secondary DNS server. Receives its data by zone transfers from the master zone on the primary DNS server.

SMB (Server Message Block) A protocol that allows client computers to access files and network services. It can be used over TCP/IP, the Internet, and other network protocols but is typically used only over a LAN or VPN because of security issues.

SMTP (Simple Mail Transfer Protocol) A protocol used to send and transfer mail

SNMP (Simple Network Management Protocol) A set of standard protocols used to manage and monitor multiplatform computer network devices

softlink A file that points to another file as an alias. Also called a symbolic link. Unlike a hard link, removing a softlink does not delete the original file it points to.

sparse bundle A type of sparse disk image that uses a bundle of banded chunks rather than a single large file to store the image's data, allowing for more flexible backups under Time Machine.

sparse image A type of disk image that is designed to only take up as much space on disk as the files contained within it. For example, while a conventional disk image of a DVD will consume 4.7 GB, a sparse image of the disc would only be as large as the files contained on it.

Spotlight Apple's search engine for indexing local and server files and metadata

SSL (Secure Sockets Layer) An Internet protocol that allows you to send encrypted, authenticated information across the Internet. More recent versions of SSL are known as TLS (Transport Level Security).

Standalone Server A server that provides services on a network but doesn't get directory services from another server or provide directory services to other computers

Stratum 1 An Internet-wide, authoritative Network Time Protocol (NTP) server that keeps track of the current UTC (Coordinated Universal Time) time. Other stratums obtain time from a lower-numbered stratum server.

streaming Delivery of video or audio data over a network in real time as a stream of packets instead of a single file download

strict locking A feature of Windows services that prevents users of shared files from changing the same file at the same time. With strict locking, the Windows server checks whether a file is locked and enforces file locks instead of relying on the client application to do so.

subdirectory A directory within a directory

subdomain Sometimes called the hostname. Part of the domain name of a computer on the Internet. It does not include the domain or the top-level domain (TLD) designator (for example, .com, .net, .us, .uk). The domain name www.example.com consists of the subdomain www, the domain example, and the top-level domain com.

subnet A subset of a network that requires a router to reach other subnets

subnet mask A number used in IP networking to specify the portion of an IP address that acts as the network number defining its subnet

switch Networking hardware that connects multiple systems with individual channels rather than the shared connectivity of a hub

TB (terabyte) One terabyte equals 1,099,511,627,776 bytes.

TCP (Transmission Control Protocol) A method used with the Internet Protocol (IP) to send data in the form of message units between computers over the Internet. IP handles the actual delivery of the data, and TCP keeps track of the packets for efficient routing through the Internet.

throughput The rate at which a computer can transfer and process data

ticket In Kerberos, a temporary credential that proves a Kerberos client's identity to a service

ticket-granting ticket A special Kerberos ticket that enables a client to obtain tickets for services within the same realm. A client gets a ticket-granting ticket by proving identity — for example, by typing a valid username and password during login.

time server A network server that allows systems to synchronize their clocks to it

Tomcat The official reference implementation for Java Servlet 2.2 and JavaServer Pages 1.1, two complementary technologies developed under the Java Community Process

trusted binding A mutually authenticated connection between a computer and a directory domain

TTL (Time-to-Live) The specified length of time that DNS information is stored in a cache. When a domain name/IP address pair has been cached longer than the TTL value, the entry is deleted from the name server's cache.

tunneling A technology that allows one network protocol to send its data by using the format of another protocol

two-factor authentication A process that authenticates through a combination of two independent factors: something you know (such as a password), something you have (such as a smart card), or something you are (such as a biometric factor). This is more secure than authentication that uses only one factor, typically a password.

UDP (User Datagram Protocol) A communications method that uses the Internet Protocol to send data units called datagrams with minimal overhead. Network applications that have very small data units to exchange may use UDP rather than TCP.

UID (User ID) A number that uniquely identifies a user within a file system. Mac OS X uses the UID to keep track of a user's folder and file ownership.

unicast The transmission of data to a single recipient or client. If a movie is unicast to a user by using RTSP, the user can move freely from point to point in an on-demand movie.

URL (Uniform Resource Locator) The address of a computer, file, or resource that can be accessed on a local network or on the Internet. The URL is composed of the name of the protocol needed to access the resource, a domain name that identifies a specific computer on the Internet, and a hierarchical description of a file location on the computer.

USB (Universal Serial Bus) A standard for communicating between a computer and external peripherals by using an inexpensive direct-connect cable

user profile The set of personal desktop and preference settings that Windows saves for a user and applies each time the user logs in

username The long name for a user. Sometimes referred to as the user's real name.

UTC (Coordinated Universal Time) A standard reference time. UTC is based on an atomic resonance, and clocks that run according to UTC are often called atomic clocks.

virtual domain Another domain that can be used in email addresses for your mail users. Also a list of all the domain names for which your mail server is responsible.

virtual user An alternate email address (short name) for a user. Similar to an alias, but it involves creating another user account.

virtualization The act of combining multiple network devices or services into what appears as a single device or service in order to provide improved performance or increased functionality while also maintaining simplicity

volume A mountable allocation of storage that behaves, from the client's perspective, like a local hard disk, hard disk partition, or network volume.

In Xsan, a volume consists of one or more storage pools. See also *logical disk.*

VPN (virtual private network) A network that uses encryption and other technologies to provide secure communications over a public network, typically the Internet. VPNs are generally cheaper than real private networks using private lines, but they rely on having the same encryption system at both ends. The encryption may be performed by firewall software or by routers.

W3C (World Wide Web Consortium) The primary international standards organization for the World Wide Web. It defines standards for technologies such as CSS, HTML, and XML.

WAN (Wide Area Network) A network maintained across distant sites, as opposed to a LAN within a site

WebDAV (Web-based Distributed Authoring and Versioning) A live authoring environment that allows client users to check out web pages, make changes, and then check the pages back in to the site while the site is running

WebDAV realm A region of a website, usually a folder or directory, defined to provide access for WebDAV users and groups

WEP (Wired Equivalent Privacy) A wireless networking security protocol that has been rendered functionally obsolete, despite remaining in wide use among personal Wi-Fi networks.

wiki A website that allows users to collaboratively edit pages and easily access previous pages by using a web browser

wildcard A range of possible values for any segment of an IP address

Windows domain The Windows computers on a network that share a common directory of user, group, and computer accounts for authentication and authorization. An Open Directory master can provide directory services for a Windows domain.

WINS (Windows Internet Naming Service) A name resolution service used by Windows

WLAN A wireless LAN

workgroup A set of users for whom you define preferences and privileges as a group. Any preferences you define for a group are stored in the group account.

WPA (Wi-Fi Protected Access) A security protocol for wireless networks designed to work with an 802.1X authentication system The most current version is WPA2.

WPA Enterprise Used in Apple documentation to refer to the mode of WPA used in large networks requiring a RADIUS server

WPA Personal A subset of the Wi-Fi Protected Access wireless network security system. Also called WPA-PSK, which uses a single pre-shared key among all the clients rather than a centralized 802.1X authentication server.

X.500 An ISO standard for directory services, related to LDAP

X.509 An ISO standard for identity certificates used in Mac OS X

Xgrid Apple's system for assembling computational grids to allow agents to present jobs to a controller, which breaks it down into tasks for agents to complete

XML An Extensible Markup Language, similar to HTML but more formal and more flexible. HTML expressed in XML is called XHTML.

XMPP (Extensible Messaging and Presence Protocol) An open-source instant messaging protocol used by iChat Server and Push Notification Server

Xsan Apple's SAN cluster file system

Xserve Apple's rack-mounted Mac server hardware

Xserve RAID Apple's now-discontinued RAID appliance designed for SAN storage

zone transfer The method by which zone data is replicated among authoritative DNS servers. Slave DNS servers request zone transfers from their master servers to acquire their data.

Index

M

Everything You Need to Craft
Killer Code for Apple Applications

Whether you are a seasoned developer or just getting into the Apple platform, Wiley's Developer Reference series is perfect for you. Focusing on topics that Apple developers love best, these well-designed books guide you through the most advanced and very latest Apple tools, technologies, and programming techniques. With in-depth coverage and expert guidance from skilled authors who are proven authorities in their fields, the Developer Reference series will quickly become your indispensable Apple development resource.

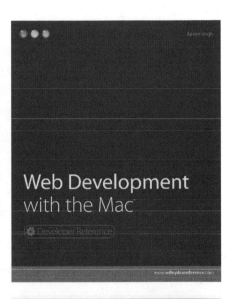

The Developer Reference series is available wherever books are sold.

Take the Book with You, Everywhere

Want tips for developing and working on Apple platforms on your iPhone? Wiley's Developer Reference app puts you in touch with the new Wiley Developer Reference series. Through the app you can purchase any title in the series and then read, highlight, search, and bookmark the text and code you need. To get you started, Wiley's Developer Reference app includes Chapter 21 from *Cocoa Touch for iPhone OS 3*, which offers fantastic tips for developing for the iPhone and iPod touch platforms. If you buy a Wiley Developer Reference book through the app, you'll get all the text of that book including a searchable index and live table of contents linked to each chapter and section of the book.

Here's what you can do

- Jump to the section or chapter you need by tapping a link in the Table of Contents
- Click on a keyword in the Index to go directly to a particular section in the book
- Highlight text as you read so that you can mark what's most important to you
- Copy and paste, or email code samples, out of the book so you can use them where and when needed
- Keep track of additional ideas or end results by selecting passages of text and then creating notes and annotations for them
- Save your place effortlessly with automatic bookmarking, which holds your place if you exit or receive a phone call
- Zoom into paragraphs with a "pinch" gesture

How to purchase

Go to www.wileydevreference.com and follow the link to purchase the app in iTunes.

Wiley's Developer Reference app is just 99¢ and includes Chapter 21, "Using the Game Kit API" from *Cocoa Touch for iPhone OS 3*. When you're ready for a full Developer Reference book, you can purchase any title from the series directly in the app for $19.99.